THE QUALITY OF LIFE IN KOREA

Social Indicators Research Series

Volume 14

This new series aims to provide a public forum for single treatises and collections of papers on social indicators research that are too long to be published in our journal *Social Indicators Research*. Like the journal, the book series deals with statistical assessments of the quality of life from a broad perspective. It welcomes the research on a wide variety of substantive areas, including health, crime, housing, education, family life, leisure activities, transportation, mobility, economics, work, religion and environmental issues. These areas of research will focus on the impact of key issues such as health on the overall quality of life and vice versa. An international review board, consisting of Ruut Veenhoven, Joachim Vogel, Ed Diener, Torbjorn Moum and Wolfgang Glatzer, will ensure the high quality of the series as a whole.

The titles published in this series are listed at the end of this volume.

THE QUALITY OF LIFE IN KOREA

Comparative and Dynamic Perspectives

Edited by

DOH CHULL SHIN
University of Missouri at Columbia, Missouri, USA

CONRAD P. RUTKOWSKI
Institute for Applied Phenomenology, Spring Valley, New York, USA

and

CHONG-MIN PARK
Korea University, Seoul, Korea

Reprinted from *Social Indicators Research*, Volumes 62 and 63 (April 2003)

KLUWER ACADEMIC PUBLISHERS
DORDRECHT / BOSTON / LONDON

A C.I.P. Catalogue record for this book is available from the Library of Congress.

ISBN 1-4020-0947-X

Published by Kluwer Academic Publishers,
P.O. Box 17, 3300 AA Dordrecht, The Netherlands.

Sold and distributed in North, Central and South America
by Kluwer Academic Publishers,
101 Philip Drive, Norwell, MA 02061, U.S.A.

In all other countries, sold and distributed
by Kluwer Academic Publishers,
P.O. Box 322, 3300 AH Dordrecht, The Netherlands.

Printed on acid-free paper

Printed and bound in the Netherlands.

CONTENTS

INTRODUCTION

DOH CHULL SHIN, CONRAD P. RUTKOWSKI and CHONG-MIN PARK

THE QUALITY OF LIFE IN KOREA: COMPARATIVE AND DYNAMIC PERSPECTIVES

In recent years there has been a spurt in research efforts to compare the quality of life across a number of different countries and regions (Estes, 1998; Freedom House, 2001; Prescott-Allen, 2001; Tang, 2000; United Nations Development Programme, 2000; World Bank, 2000). In response to growing public interest and involvement in the globalization of human life, individual scholars and research institutions have attempted to assemble and analyze comparative data on the quality of citizens' lives in various parts of the world (for a comprehensive review of these efforts, see Hagerty et al., 2001). As part of the rising global research movement for human betterment, this special volume of *Social Indicators Research* features the changing quality of life in South Korea (hereinafter Korea), a country known as one of the most politically influential and analytically interesting new democracies (Diamond and Shin, 2000).

KOREA'S PLACE IN A CHANGING WORLD

Throughout the globe, Korea has long been known as one of the four dragon states or economic miracles in Asia (World Bank, 1993). Along with its three neighbors – Hong Kong, Singapore, and Taiwan – Korea transformed one of the world's poorest economies into an economic powerhouse within a single generation (Kim and Hong, 1997). It is now a country with a population of 46 million, and a Gross Domestic Product (hereinafter the GDP) larger than that of ten of the 15 states in the European Union. It is also the only non-Western country that was recently admitted to the Organization for Economic Cooperation and Development (hereinafter the OECD), the exclusive club of industrialized countries.

More recently, Korea has been known for its spectacular rebound from the worst economic crisis since the Korean War of almost

Social Indicators Research **62, 63:** 3–16, 2003.

half a century ago (Haggard, 2000; World Bank, 1998). In the last two months of 1997, Korea became a symbol of the Asian financial crisis that shook financial markets from Hong Kong to Wall Street. With the largest rescue package ever (57 billion dollars) from the International Monetary Fund (hereinafter the IMF), Korea was quickly transformed from an economic powerhouse into a ward of the international financial community. Two years after its humiliating rescue by the IMF, it regained its economic health, and successfully reclaimed its status as an economic powerhouse commanding the world's 11th largest economy. For the past five years, moreover, Korea has carried out a broad range of liberalizing economic reforms in order to transform itself from its age-old crony capitalism, which caused its economic meltdown, into a fully competitive and transparent market economy (D. Kim, 1999). Within all of its major economic organizations, ranging from the business conglomerates known as the *Chaebols*, through commercial banks and labor unions to state enterprises, major restructuring has been taking place.

The Korean political system has been undergoing, for more than a decade, a successful transformation from military rule to a representative democracy (Shin, 1999). By extricating the military from power, Korea has fully restored civilian rule. On every level of government, from the central to provincial and local governments, free and competitive elections are regularly held to choose governors and legislators. These democratically elected governments have consistently maintained and even expanded political rights and civil liberties. Among new democracies in Asia, it is the first country to have peacefully transferred power to an opposition party. It is also the first Asian democracy, in which its government and ruling political parties have tried to reform a recalcitrant news media by means of tax audits and fair trade practices. Within the vast continent of Asia, Korea has become a most vigorous democratic political system.

Ideologically, Korea has been undergoing a period of deep and profound transformation. Since the election of Kim Dae Jung as President in December, 1997, the country has been pursuing better relations with the Communist North (Moon and Steinberg, 1999). In the wake of his "Sunshine Policy" toward the northern half of the Korean peninsula, South Korea's citizens have been freed from the age-old ruling ideology of a right-wing dictatorship featuring opposition to Communism both in principle and in practice. They are no longer forced to subscribe to the government's equating of democracy with anti-Communism. The Korean people are now freely developing new values and ideals for themselves, along with attempting the unification of a divided nation in which they have lived their entire lives.

For more than 30 years, the people in this divided nation have experienced successive waves of deep and rapid transformations. These transformations have affected the cultural, economic, political, and all of the other important aspects of living within their country. Obviously, these changes have secured their country a prominent position in the international community, including membership in the United Nations and the OECD. As an Asian model, one combining prosperity with democracy, the country remains a major player in the global wave of political democratization and economic liberalization still in progress (S. Kim, 2000).

Nonetheless, an increasing number of Koreans question whether their country has truly become a better place within which to live (*Joongang Ilbo*, 2001; Yang et al., 1998). There is no doubt that these changes have brought about a greater degree of material goods and services along with personal freedom for a more comfortable living. These same changes have also brought about a substantial rise in alienation and dehumanization, not to mention a phenomenal rise in public violence and environmental pollution (Park and Kim, 2001; Shin, 1980; Tang, 1998). More than ever before, the country has become vulnerable to massive international movements of capital, as evidenced by the Asian financial crisis five years ago. Solely on the basis of the data that relate to the material aspects of Korean life, it is, therefore, difficult to determine whether the quality of Korean life has been genuinely enhanced during the past three decades of cultural, political, and socio-economic upheavals.

This special volume of *Social Indicator Research* is designed to examine the exact nature of these changes and explicate their human meaning for a comprehensive and dynamic account of the quality of life within Korea. What notable changes have taken place in the various objective conditions under which the Korean people live? Which particular conditions of life have become desirable and undesirable? How do the Korean people feel about their own private and public lives? What particular aspects of their life experiences are positive and which are negative? What kinds of specific life goals and values do the Korean people cherish most for their own existence and that of their country? How do positive and negative life experiences vary across the different segments of the Korean population? How do value priorities vary across the population segments? How have those priorities changed over time? How favorably or unfavorably do the various conditions of Korean life compare with those of other countries? These are the questions that we have explored in the individual articles that immediately follow.

PREMISES

A number of premises underlie the crafting of articles that this volume brought together. The premises are derived from theoretical and empirical research on quality of life. First, it is conceptually assumed that the quality of life is an evaluative property (Allard, 1976; Nussbaum and Sen, 1993; Storrs, 1975). The term "quality" is often used in a non-evaluative, descriptive sense in order to distinguish one particular attribute or character from others. In exploring the quality of Korean life in flux, however, the word "quality" is used as an evaluative term admitting of degrees of desirability or value. Among the various elements of life, only those to which people impute value are included in the parameter of life quality.

Second, it is assumed that human values vary considerably in preference and priority across the different segments of the same population (Cantril, 1965). As they are not only socialized into different life styles, but also command varying kinds and differential amounts of resources, people in different life situations do not always cherish the same things for themselves and their country. Even when they value the same things, they oftentimes assign different priorities to them. The priorities they assign to their values, moreover, shift over time. According to Ronald Inglehart (1977), the great valuation on the acquisition of personal wealth and achievement has been slowly giving way to freedom, equality, and accommodation to nature. In Korea today, "after decades of rushing, there are calls for a more leisurely lifestyle" (*New York Times*, 2001: p. A7).

Third, it is assumed that quality of life is a multi-dimensional phenomenon involving much more than a set of economic conditions and commercial relations. Because human needs, unlike the needs of other forms of life, consist of biological, social, psychological, and growth components, their satisfaction requires more than material and impersonal resources, such as love, recognition, freedom, participation, and fulfillment (Campbell et al., 1976; von Wright, 1972). Viewed in this light, quality of life comprises not only material welfare, but also psychological or subjective well-being. One cannot make a comprehensive and balanced appraisal of life quality, relying solely upon the Gross National Product (hereinafter the GNP) and/or other economic and social indicators, which measure the desirability of life conditions alone.

Fourth, the two dimensions of life quality – objective and subjective – are assumed to be, by and large, distinct entities (Frey and Stutzer, 2002; Lane, 2000; Mullis, 1990). People evaluate their life experiences either positively or negatively, according to their own conception of what is good and right in life. Their evaluations also depend upon how they compare themselves with other people. As a result, there is no extensive relationship between people's sense of well-being and the objective circumstances of their lives. Many affluent people feel as unhappy as their less well-off counterparts. At the same time, many poor people feel as happy as their rich counterparts. Subjective feelings of well-being and ill-being, therefore, cannot be inferred accurately by objective indicators of life conditions. Such subjective feelings can be measured accurately only by asking people directly to what extent they find those conditions pleasant or unpleasant, and/or fulfilling or disappointing.

Finally, it is assumed that the production of more material goods and services do not necessarily enhance one's quality of life (Easterline, 1973, 1995; Inglehart and Klingemann, 2000; Max-Neef, 1995). Only up to a certain point can greater production, of such material resources, have a favorable impact upon people's lives. Beyond that point, however, more production does not necessarily make for a greater quality of life; instead, it can detract from the overall quality of life by causing congestion, pollution, over-regulation, and dehumanization. In evaluating and prescribing the quality of Korean life, life quality is not considered a linear function of material wealth; nor is more production considered an optimal solution to many of the problems facing highly industrialized and urbanized Korean society.

APPROACHES

Much of the research on quality of life is approached from two contrasting perspectives. The most commonly employed approach conceptualizes quality of life mainly in terms of the social and physical conditions in which people live and the attributes of people themselves (Prescott-Allen, 2001). Assuming that such social conditions and personal attributes, such as housing and education, contribute the "general requirements for happiness," this objective approach seeks to assess quality of life by using various objective indicators reported mostly through government agencies. Because these objective indicators usually carry normative connotations, i.e., the more of a measured condition, the better (or vice versa), they are utilized to compare existing community conditions across space and time. The results of such comparisons serve as a basis for determining whether a country is a better place in which to live, or whether said country offers a better quality of life than it did previously.

For example, it is inferred that the quality of life in a country is greater when its people are more educated and informed, live longer, and take advantage of more goods and services. It is also inferred that as the level of education rises, the adequacy and availability of medical care is improved, the amount of substandard housing is reduced, and the purity of the air is improved upon, then the quality of life is thereby enhanced. In this manner, indicators of objectively observable life conditions become equated with direct measures of welfare (United Nations Development Programme, 2000; World Bank, 2000). The quality of life, in this view, lies in the desirable conditions of life that are believed to be necessary for the achievement of a happy or good life.

In contrast, a subjective approach claims that the quality of life is inherently subjective; that is, it is to be found in the eye of the beholder or the one who is experiencing (Campbell, 1981; Campbell et al., 1976). Just as one might perceive that something is good or worthwhile, quality is determined ultimately by the extent to which a person's desires and tastes are satisfied, irrespective of what is available for the person's life. For this reason, substantial increases in material resources and technological advances in the United States, and other developed countries during the final quarter of the last millennium, have failed to bring corresponding changes in feelings of well-being. Hence, to Campbell and many others (Andrews and Withy, 1976; Csikszentmihalyi, 1990; Veenhoven, 1999), the quality of life refers to one's sense of well-being or one's feelings of satisfaction or happiness. The indicators employed are perceptive measures of life experiences and subjective evaluations of life conditions derived from survey research. Seeking to directly tap the quality of life as experienced and perceived by people rather than implying a connection between life conditions and personal well-being, this approach is often called a subjective approach.

As such, there are two contrasting approaches to the study of quality of life. Neither of these two approaches is entirely satisfactory (Environment Protection Agency, 1973). The objective approach could be arbitrary because researchers tend to determine the quality of life independent of the person in question. The subjective approach, on the other hand, tends to be transient, because it focuses solely upon feelings of well-being without any consideration of the personal capacity to sustain such feelings. A third, combined approach would seem preferable, in which objective and subjective indicators are employed, to study both the desirability of life conditions and the nature of life experience (Allard, 1976; Diener and Suh, 1997; Veenhoven, 2000).

The studies reported in this special volume as a whole feature a combined approach to the study of life quality. Substantively, these studies offer a comprehensive account of the quality of Korean life by reckoning the desirability of the objective circumstances in which ordinary Koreans live, as well as their own perceptions and assessments of those circumstances. Methodologically, the studies reveal trends in the objective and subjective dimensions of Korean life by comparing those changes over periods of time. They also determine Korea's place in the world of civilized societies by comparing its life quality ratings with those of other countries. In short, the quality of Korean life is examined from comprehensive, dynamic, and comparative perspectives.

THEMES AND ORGANIZATION

Four main themes have served to organize 22 individual articles into a coherent volume. The transformations – subjective and objective – of Korean life form the organizing theme for the first part of this volume, and its specific domains constitute the guiding theme of the second part. The quality of life that groups of people experience and cherish serves as the theme for the third part. The fourth, final part features the comparisons of the overall quality of Korean life from cross-national and longitudinal perspectives.

Part One of this volume consists of five articles. **Tae-Hwan Kwon** highlights the major features of population changes in the Korean peninsula, and he explores their implications for the building of a nation of well-being. **Doo-Seung Hong** examines social changes in Korean society in terms of shifts in its occupational structure and class stratification, and he notes that Korea has been transformed into a middle class society. **Doh Chull Shin** and **Junhan Lee** look at the democratic transformation of military rule in 1988 and its consequences for civic and political life. **Jiho Jang** examines how adversely the outbreak of the economic crisis in 1997 affected the quality of ordinary citizens' lives, and he agrees with the necessity of the government's special efforts to strengthen the system of social protection. In the last article of Part One, **Aie-Rie Lee** traces changes in Korean culture by analyzing the three waves of the World Value Surveys from 1982 to 1996, and she concludes that contemporary Koreans hold libertarian values and are motivated to engage in political protest. Taken together, the five articles presented in this first part document how the people living in Korea and their living environments have changed over the past four decades.

Part Two consists of ten studies, each of which is devoted to an important component or domain of private and public life. In the first of five articles dealing with private life, **Ok Kyung Yang** examines the changing structure of the decision-making process within Korean families, and she provides evidence of the fact that the Confucian notion of authoritarian and hierarchical family life is no longer widely held in Korean society. **Andrew Eungi Kim** analyzes the impact of religion on life satisfaction, and he shows that individuals with strong religious beliefs and commitment are more satisfied with life than those with little or no participation in religious activities. **Soonman Kwon** examines the health of the Korean people and their health care utilization, and he concludes that the strengthening of primary care will be essential to the further improvement of their health. **Junghyo Kim** and **Junhan Lee** document recent improvements in education and evaluate those changes critically for the formulation of more effective educational policy. **Joung-Woo Lee** shows remarkable improvements in the standard of living with a trend analysis of both income and consumption during the last four decades, and he points out that the heavy concentration of land and wealth hinders the further enhancement of life quality among the Korean people. **Jae-Young Son**, **Yun-Hi Won**, and **Choon-Geol Moon** examine changes in housing conditions in terms of quantity as well as quality, and they found that a significantly greater portion of Korean households are now living in larger and better homes of their own than in the past.

In an attempt to evaluate the quality of public life, **Hee-Jong Joo** investigates crime rates and crime control practices, and he shows that Korean society has recently become a less safe place in which to live. **Meesook Kim** outlines the major components of the Korean welfare system, and she evaluates its adequacy by comparing Korea's social welfare expenditures to those of other OECD countries. **Chong-Min Park** focuses on the quality of local government and democratic citizenship with an analysis of recent public opinion surveys of urban residents, and he concludes that democracy at the local level is still at the electoral stage, not yet fully consolidated. **Dong-Ki Min** reviews and analyzes the government's environmental policy, and he shows that environmental quality has recently improved with increasing financial investments in the environmental sector. **Hun Shik Kim** reviews the changes taken place in the news media in the wake of democratization, and he concludes that the Korean press still faces a variety of restraints. The ten articles presented in the second part of this volume, when considered together, address the question of what specific domains of Korean life fare well and which fare poorly.

Part Three presents five studies that describe and compare the quality of life that particular groups of Koreans experience, and what they feel is of value for their own existence. **Gyung-Jun Yoo** documents that the gender gap in wages has gradually decreased over the past two decades even while discrimination accounts for a greater part of gender wage differentials than in the past. **Meesook Kim** and **Kyung-Ho Cho** compare the quality of life experienced by government employees and private sector employees, and they find that the former, as compared with the latter, express significantly greater levels of dissatisfaction in a large number of life domains. **Eun-Yeong Na** and **John Duckitt** investigate the gender and generational differences in basic values, and they find that such differences exist in three of the four value dimensions surveyed. **Ik Ki Kim** and **Cheong-Seok Kim** look at the patterns of support exchange among generations, and they conclude that the elderly, who both give and receive, are more satisfied with life than those who engage in none or only one of these two activities. **Kyeong-Ho Cha** focuses on feelings of well-being and ill-being among college students, and he finds that certain personality constructs are significantly associated with those feelings.

Whereas the studies reported in the first three parts of this volume are primarily oriented to individual spheres or domains of Korean life or particular groups of the Korean population, the two articles that form Part Four seek to consider the overall quality of Korean life from comparative and dynamic perspectives. **Hyun Song Lee** compares Korea with more developed countries within the OECD in terms of six indices measuring the objective quality of life. In all of the six key life domains, including income, education, and work, Korea is found to trail those countries by more than a decade. **Doh Chull Shin** and **Conrad P. Rutkowski** explore how economic development and other changes taking place in Korea for the past two decades have affected the quality of life experienced by its people. Their analyses of 1981 and 2001 national sample surveys reveal that Korea, as a place to live, has become much less attractive for a majority of its people over the past two decades.

SIGNIFICANCE

The articles assembled in this volume present, individually and jointly, a wealth of data, insights, and perspectives that could advance our understanding of quality of human life on a global scale. By combining rapid economic development and peaceful democratic transition, Korea offers an East Asian model of promoting citizen well-being to the world of democratizing and industrializing countries. To date, little systematic effort has been made to unravel its contours and dynamics, or to evaluate their consequences for academics and policymakers in those countries.

Substantively, this special volume provides the most comprehensive account of the Korean model ever made to date. Unlike prior research on the subject (Cho and Cha, 1998; *Development and Society*, 1998; Korea National Statistical Office, 2001; *Korea Public Administration Journal* 1996; *Social Science and Policy Research*, 1995; Yang et al., 1998), this volume considers not only the objective and subjective dimensions of life quality, but also the key domains of those dimensions. Theoretically, the comparative analyses of those two dimensions, reported on throughout the entire volume, provide a real occasion to expand and refine the current literature on the quality of life, while testing Western notions and theories about human betterment within a non-Western developing country. Strategically, this volume offers comparative assessments of the various efforts the Korean government has made to improve its citizens' lives.

Cross-cultural and cross-regional research on quality of life to date has been confined mostly to advanced industrialized democracies in Europe and America (Diener and Suh, 2000; Radcliff, 2001; Social Science Research Center Berlin, 2000; Veenhoven, 1999). If any generalizations are to be made about human well-being, the scope of our knowledge must be broadened to include non-Western countries in democratization and industrialization.

ACKNOWLEDGMENTS

The preparation of this special volume of *Social Indicators Research* was made possible by a generous research grant from the University of Missouri Research Board (RB 00–105). The financial support of the Research Board is gratefully acknowledged. The editors are thankful to Dr. Junhan Lee and Professor Jeong-Ro Yoon for their generous assistance.

REFERENCES

Allard, E.: 1976, 'Dimensions of welfare in a comparative scandinavia study', Acta Sociologica 19, pp. 227–239.

Andrews, F.M. and S.B. Withey: 1976, Social Indicators of Well-Being (Plenum Press, New York).

Campbell, A.: 1981, The Sense of Well-Being in America (McGraw-Hill, New York).

Campbell, A., P.E. Converse and W.L. Rodgers: 1976, The Quality of American Life (Russell Sage Foundation, New York).

Cantril, H.: 1965, The Patterns of Human Concerns (Rutgers University Press, New Brunswick).

Cho, M.H. and K.H. Cha: 1998, Cross-National Comparative Research on the Quality of Life (in Korean) (Jinmoondang, Seoul).

Csikszentmihalyi, M.: 1990, Flow: The Psychology of Optimal Experience (Harper-Perennial, New York).

Development and Society: 1998, 'Symposium on Quality of Life in South Korea', 27 (December 1998), pp. 1–65.

Diamond, L. and D.C. Shin: 2000, Institutional Reform and Democratic Consolidation in Korea (Hoover Institution Press, Stanford).

Diener, E. and E.M. Suh: 1997, 'Measuring quality of life: Economic, social and subjective indicators', Social Indicators Research 40, pp. 189–216.

Diener, E. and E.M. Suh (eds.): 2000, Culture and Subjective Well-Being (MIT Press, Cambridge, MA).

Easterline, R.: 1973, 'Does money buy happiness', Public Interest 30, pp. 3–10.

Easterline, R.: 1995, 'Will raising the income of all increase the happiness of all?' Journal of Economic Behavior and Organization 27, pp. 35–48.

Environment Protection Agency: 1973, The Quality of Life Concept (Environment Protection Agency: Washington, DC).

Estes, R.J.: 1998, 'Trends in world social development, 1970–95', development prospects for a new century', Journal of Developing Societies 14(1), pp. 1–29.

Freedom House: 2001, Freedom in the World, 2000–2001 (Freedom House, New York).

Frey, B.S. and A. Stutzer: 2002, Happiness and Economics (Princeton University Press, Princeton).

Hagerty, M.R. et al.: 2001, 'Quality of life indexes for national policy: Review and agenda for research', Social Indictors Research 55(1), pp. 1–96.

Haggard, S.: 2000, The Political Economy of the Asian Financial Crisis (Institute for International Economics, Washington, DC).
Inglehart, R.: 1977, Silent Revolution (Princeton University Press, Princeton).
Inglehart, R. and H. Klingemann: 2000, 'Genes, culture, democracy and happiness', in E. Diener and M.E. Suh (eds.), Culture and Subjective Well-Being (MIT Press, Cambridge, MA).
Joonang Ilbo: 2001, 'Upgrade Korea', (December 31), p. 1.
Kim, D.J.: 1999, *Djnomics*: A New Foundation for the Korean Economy (Ministry of Finance and Economy, Seoul).
Kim, K.S. and S.D. Hong: 1997, Accounting for Rapid Economic Growth in Korea, 1963–95 (Korea Development Institute, Seoul).
Kim, S.S. (ed.): 2000, Korea's Globalization (Cambridge University Press, New York).
Korea National Statistical Office: 2001, Social Statistics in Korea (Korea National Statistical Office, Daejun, Korea).
Korea Public Administration Journal: 1996, Symposium on quality of life: Where we are and what needs to be done? (in Korean) (Spring 1996), pp. 1–101.
Lane, R.: 2000, The Loss of Happiness in Market Democracies (Yale University Press, New Haven).
Max-Neef, M.: 1995, 'Economic growth and quality of life: A threshold hypothesis', Ecological Economics 15, pp. 115–118.
Mullis, R.J.: 1990, 'Measures of economic well-being as predictors of psychological well-being', Social Indicators Research 26, pp. 119–135.
Moon, C.I. and D. Steinberg (eds.): 1999, Kim Dao Jung Government and Sunshine Policy Promises and Challenges (Yonsei University Press, Seoul).
Nussbaum, M. and A. Sen (eds.): 1993, The Quality of Life (Oxford University Press, New York).
New York Times: 2001, Korea says it can't wait to slow its fast pace, (December 20), p. A7.
Park, C.M. and S.Y. Kim: 2001, Quality of life in Korea: Global, domain-specific and standards of comparison,' presented at the winter 2001 meeting of the Korean Association of Public Administration held in Seoul, Korea.
Prescott-Allen, R.: 2001, The Wellbeing of Nations (Island Press, Washington, DC).
Radcliff, B.: 2001, 'Politics, markets and life satisfaction: The political economy of human happiness', American Political Science Review 95, pp. 939–252.
Shin, D.C.: 1980, 'Does rapid economic growth improve the human lot? Some empirical evidence', Social Indicators Research 8, pp. 199–221.
Shin, D.C.: 1999, Mass Politics and Culture in Democratizing Korea (Cambridge University Press).
Social Science and Public Policy: 1995, 'Symposium on local governance and quality of life', (in Korean) 2(3), pp. 1–247.
Social Science Research Center Berlin: 2000, Euromodule (Social Science Research Center, Berlin).
Storrs, M.: 1975, 'Quality of life', Social Indicators Research 2(2), pp. 229–248.

Tang, K.: 1998, 'East Asian industrializing countries: Economic growth and quality of life', *Social Indicators Research* 42, pp. 69–96.

Tang, K.: 2000, Social Development in Asia (Kluwer Academic Publishers, Boston).

United Nations Development Programme: 2000, Human Development Report: Human Development and Human Rights (Oxford University Press, New York).

Veenhoven, R.: 1999, 'Qualities of life in individualistic societies', Social Indicators Research 48, pp. 157–186.

Veenhoven, R.: 2000, 'The four qualities of life: Ordering concepts and measure of the good life', Journal of Happiness Studies 1, pp. 1–39.

von Wright, G.: 1972, The Varieties of Goodness (Routledge and Regan Paul, London).

World Bank: 1993, The East Asian Miracle (Oxford University Press, Oxford).

World Bank: 1998, East Asia: the Road to Recovery (Oxford University Press, Oxford.

World Bank: 2000, World Development Indicators 2000 (the World Bank, Washington, DC).

Yang, J.H., I.K. Kim, O.P. Moon and S.J. Lee: 1998, The Quality of Life among Regional Residents in the 21st Century (in Korean) (Jibmoondang, Seoul).

Department of Political Science Doh Chull Shin
University of Missouri
Columbia, MO 65211
USA
E-mail: shind@missouri.edu

Institute for Applied Phenomenology Conrad P. Rutkowski
Spring Valley, NY 10977
USA

Department of Public Administration Chong-Min Park
Korea University
Seoul 136-701, Korea

PART I. THE TRANSFORMATION OF KOREAN LIFE

TAI-HWAN KWON

DEMOGRAPHIC TRENDS AND THEIR SOCIAL IMPLICATIONS

ABSTRACT. This paper examines the major features of demographic transition that Korea experienced during the 20th century in association with changing political, economic, and social conditions. The major demographic changes examined include a population explosion, aging, international migration, urbanization, and changes in the family. The social implications of these changes for the 21st century in Korea are also discussed. The demographic trends of North Korea are sketched in order to provide a lead-in for the population situation on the Korean peninsula as a whole.

INTRODUCTION

Korean society has been subject to a continuous process of transformation during the 20th century. Demographic transition was a major component of this change. It started with a decline in mortality in the early years of the century. Fertility began to vary from its usual level in the early 1960s, and fell to a level below population replacement in the mid 1980s. This whole process of demographic transition took about 60–70 years, including the 20–25 years of fertility transition. The direct outcome of this change was a rapid growth in population. There were about 17.4 million Koreans in 1910 on the entire Korean peninsula, and the population increased to 25.1 million as of 1944. Between 1945–2000, population on the southern half of the peninsula almost tripled, increasing from 16.1 million to 46.1 million (Kwon et al., 1975: p. 7; NSO, 2001b). In the 21st century, the pattern of population growth is expected to change. Population is expected to increase slowly to a maximum of 51 million around 2020, and will enter a stage of negative growth at that point. The population is expected to decrease to about 30 million in 2080, if the current demographic conditions persist.

Population growth usually brings about changes in its composition, which, in turn, is known to have vital implications for society

Social Indicators Research **62, 63:** 19–38, 2003.

as well as its economy. Age structure can be translated into demographic conditions regulating the patterns in the supply of the labor force and economic dependency. From age structure, we can also construct patterns of aging. Korean censuses provide extensive information on family structure and living arrangements, and thus enable us to discuss family related issues in association with demographic changes. These are major areas of concern in this paper. We will first review the trends and issues regarding population growth in the 20th century, and we will then proceed to look into the future.

North Korea will be a troublesome factor in assessing demographic conditions in the coming years in South Korea. The reunification of Korea; a free labor exchange between the two parts; or a large flow of refugees into the South, would drastically alter the demographic pictures of both South and North Korea. So, this paper tries to review briefly the trends in population growth and demographic issues in North Korea. On the basis of all of this, we may be able to get a handle on the overall population situation on the Korean peninsula.

DEMOGRAPHIC TRANSITION IN THE 20TH CENTURY

The Colonial Period (1910–45)

The Korean mortality rate began to decline during the early years of Japanese colonial rule as a response to the introduction of western health measures and its medical system, which began in the late 19th century. The transition of mortality from a high traditional level to a low modern level had progressed without a change in living standard during the colonial period. In other words, the tempo of population growth was accelerated without economic betterment, and accordingly, population pressure on land resources increased.

The life expectancy at birth was 37–38 years during 1925–30, but rose to 43 years in the early part of the 1940s. Most affected were infants and children,[1] and this resulted in a growing proportion of the number of children, as indicated by the change of youth dependency ratio (or the ratio of population at ages 0–14 to population aged 15–64) from 39.7 to 43.2 between 1925 and 1944. The structure of the family had changed little, but a significant difference in the average size of a household began to be noticed between urban and rural areas. For example, family size was 4.7 in cities and 5.3 in villages in 1930 (GGK, 1934: p. T60). Rural to urban migration is considered to have been the major cause of this. Due partly to migration and more to a change in the number of cities and city boundaries, the proportion of population residing in urban areas grew markedly during the entire colonial period. The proportion was 4.8 percent in 1925, but changed to 16.0 percent in 1940, and the number of cities increased from 12 to 20 during this 15-year period.

The Period of Turmoil (1945–60)

The liberation of Korea from Japanese rule in 1945; the division of the country into the American occupied South and the Soviet occupied North; and the Korean War, between 1950–53, disrupted the demographic process completely. During this period of instability and hardship, South Korea experienced a population explosion. The population of the southern half of the Korean peninsula was estimated to be 16136000 at the time of liberation, but it increased to 20167000 in 1949, and 24982000 in 1960, showing a gain of 8.75 million people during 1945–60 (see Table I). Due to a heavy inflow of repatriates from Japan and Manchuria as well as refugees from North Korea, which totaled about 2.5 million, the population of South Korea recorded an unprecedented high growth rate of 6.1 percent during 1945–49. Urban areas experienced a particularly marked growth of population owing to the concentration of incoming migrants in cities all over the country.

The Korean War also caused mass movements of Koreans within and across national boundaries. After the war, migration across national boundaries ceased, and the rate of mortality continued its decline. Population growth subsided during the war years, but a baby boom took place in South Korea during the second half of the 1950s. As a result, South Korea recorded a 2.9 percent annual population growth between 1955–60, the highest rate in the history of Korean demography except for 1945–49, and this occurred without any influx of people from foreign countries, including North Korea. There also was an important change in the age at which one married in this post-liberation era, signaling a departure from traditional marriage. The mean age at first marriage was 21.8 for men

TABLE I

Selected Population Indicators, 1910–1955

	Unit	Whole Korea				South Korea		
		1900	1925	1940	1944	1945	1949	1955
Population	In 000	17082	19020	23547	16136	20167	21502	
Crude birth rate*	%	3.5–4.0	4.2	4.4	4.2		4.2	4.0
Crude death rate*	%	3.3–3.8	3.0	2.3	2.3		2.3	3.3
Natural growth rate*	%	0.2	1.2	2.1	1.9		1.9	0.8
Immigration rate*	%		–0.18	–0.89	–0.22		4.19	0.66
Growth rate*	%	0.2	1.02	1.17	1.80		6.08	1.45
Total fertility rate	Person		6.0	6.2	6.1		6.0	5.6
Life expectancy at birth	Year		37.5	41.5	42.5			49.7
Proportion of urban pop.	%		4.8	16.0			17.1	24.4
Age at marriage: Male			21.1	21.8				24.7
Age at marriage: Female			16.6	17.8				20.5
Youth dependency ratio	%		70.38	76.79	81.60		75.70	74.35
Aged dependency ratio	%		6.90	6.68	7.32		5.89	5.98
Total dependency ratio	%		7.28	83.47	88.92		81.59	80.33
Index of aging	%		9.81	8.69	8.97		7.78	8.05

*The reference period refers to each intercensal period ending in the given year except for 1900.
Source: Kwon et al. (1975).

and 17.8 for women in 1940, but rose to 25.4 and 21.5, respectively, in 1960.

The Period of Fertility Transition (1960–2000)

A change in the fertility rate started in the early 1960s as a societal response to significant population pressure. The major mechanism for this change was the national family planning program, which was adopted in 1962 as an integral part of the first five-year economic development plan. The pace of the reduction in the fertility rate was quite rapid, and it reached a level below that of replacement in about 25 years. This development was accompanied by heavy rural-to-urban migration; rapid urbanization; and the continued extension of life expectancy at birth. As shown in Table II, the proportion of urban population increased from 28.0 to 79.7 percent, between 1960 and 2000, and life expectancy at birth for both sexes increased from 55.3 to 75.5 years during 1960–99. These demographic processes resulted in the slowing of population growth; population reduction in rural villages; and changes in family composition.

The average size of family[2] has declined from 5.7 persons in 1960, to 3.5 in 2000 (see Table II). The proportion of three or more generation families decreased from 29.2 percent in 1960, to 10.0 percent in 2000. In rural villages, extended families frequently dissolved due to migration of the children's family, and as a result the proportion of one-person households and couple-only families greatly increased. According to the population censuses, the proportion of one-person households grew 3.7 times, from 4.2 to 15.5 percent during 1975–2000, and that of couple-only families increased from 5.4 to 14.7 percent during 1970–2000 (NSO, 1998: p. 119, 2001c). These changes were much more salient in rural areas and among the elderly. For example, 10.3 percent of elderly persons aged 65 or higher were reported to be living alone in cities in 1995, whereas the equivalent figure for villages was 18.2 percent (NSO, 1998: p. 127).

Sex selective abortion began to be noticed in the mid 1980s, producing a severe sex imbalance among newly born babies in a new age of low fertility. According to vital registration data, the sex ratio at birth for all parities was normal, 105.3 in 1980, but

TABLE II

Selected Population Indicators, 1960–2000

	Unit	1960	1970	1980	1990	2000
Population (census)	In 000	24989	31466	37436	43411	46136
Crude birth rate	%	4.21	2.99	2.34	1.56	1.34
Crude death rate	%	1.21	0.94	0.67	0.58	0.52
Natural growth rate	%	3.00	2.04	1.67	0.98	0.82
Migration rate	%	–	0.04	0.10	0.05	0.06
Growth rate	%	2.00	2.00	1.57	0.93	0.76
Total fertility rate	Person	6.0	4.5	2.7	1.63	1.47
Life expectancy at birth	Year	55.3	63.2	65.8	71.3	75.5*
Median age of pop.	Year	19.9	19.0	22.2	27.0	32.1
Proportion of urban pop.	%	28.0	41.1	57.3	74.4	79.7
Age at marriage: Male		25.4	27.1	27.3	28.6	30.3
Age at marriage: Female		21.5	23.3	24.1	25.5	27.1
Youth dependency ratio	%	77.3	78.2	54.6	36.9	29.2
Aged dependency ratio	%	5.3	5.7	6.1	7.4	10.2
Total dependency ratio	%	82.6	83.8	60.7	44.3	39.4
Index of aging	%	6.9	7.2	11.2	20.0	35.0
Population at ages 65+	%	2.9	3.1	3.8	5.1	7.3
Ordinary household size	Person	5.6		4.5	3.7	3.1
Relative household size	Person	5.7	5.2	4.8	4.0	3.5
One person household	%	2.3		4.8	9.0	15.5
Persons living alone	%	0.4		1.0	2.4	4.8
Nuclear family	%		71.5	72.9	76.0	82.0
3+ generation family	%	29.2	23.2	18.1	14.0	10.0
Persons living in 3+ G.F.	%		30.4	24.6	19.5	16.6#

*for 1999; # for 1995.

Sources: Kim T-H (1977: pp. 158 & 184); Chang et al. (1996: p. 29); NSO (1996); Kwon & Park (1995: pp. 257–267); NSO (1998: pp. 117–119, 2001b,c).

rose to 109.4 in 1985, and 115.5 in 1994. If we select the fourth births only, the change in sex ratio is more conspicuous; the ratio was reported as 110.2 in 1980 and 237.7 in 1994 (Chang et al., 1995: p. 65). The tendency of sex selective abortion has weakened since the mid 1990s, and the sex ratios for total births and fourth births were reduced to 110.2 and 172.3, respectively, in 2000 (NSO, 2001a).

The change in fertility caused a total reshaping of demographic structure in South Korea. If population is grouped into: youth; labor force population; and the aged, the proportion of the youth (or the population at ages 0–14) has shown marked declines since 1960. The reverse trend is observed for the labor force population and the aged (or population aged 65 and more). But the proportion of the aged remained low until 1995. The meaning of this structural change may be viewed better through dependency ratios. As presented in Table II, the youth dependency ratio, or the relative size of the youth to the labor force population, underwent a drastic reduction in the process of fertility transition. It was 77.3 percent in 1960, but dropped to 36.9 percent in 1990, and further to 29.2 percent in 2000. The aged dependency increased gradually from 5.3 percent in 1960, to 10.2 percent in 2000, and the total dependency was halved in the last 35 years, from 82.6 percent in 1960 to 41.4 percent in 1995. In a word, an economically favorable age structure was an outcome of the fertility transition until the end of the 20th century.

Both fertility transition and decline in mortality are known to cause population aging, and accordingly, the South Korean population, as expected has undergone a process of aging since 1960. As indicated by the index of aging (the ratio of aged population to youth population), and median age of population, the process began to take place in the early 1960s in South Korea. This clearly suggests that fertility decline was the most important factor in the early process of population aging. The index figure was only 6.9 percent in 1960, but increased to 35.0 percent in 2000, and the median age of the population rose from 19.0 to 32.1 during 1970–2000.

The proportion of population aged 65 or more is also used as an indicator of population aging. For example, 7 percent is taken to determine whether a given population is "aged" or not, and 14 percent as a mark of entering the category of a highly aged population. If we judge with these demarcation points, the South Korean population has been facing various problems of population aging since 2000.

TABLE III

Projected Population Indicators, 2000–2050

	Unit	2000	2010	2020	2030	2040	2050
Population	In 000	47008*	49594	50650	50296	48204	44337
Annual growth rate**	%		0.23	0.09	−0.03	−0.13	−0.36
Total fertility rate+	Person	1.47	1.36	1.37	1.39	1.40	1.40
Life expectancy at birth+	Year	75.9	78.8	80.7	81.5	82.3	83.0
No. of net emigrants +	In 1000	21	17	13	11	11	0
Median age of population	Year	31.8	37.4	42.9	47.5	50.9	53.7
Total dependency ratio	%	39.5	38.8	40.9	54.9	71.3	81.6
Youth dependency ratio	%	29.4	23.9	19.6	19.1	19.6	19.0
Aged dependency ratio	%	10.1	14.8	21.3	35.7	51.6	62.5
Index of Aging	%	34.2	62.0	109.0	186.3	263.2	328.4
Population at ages 65+	%	7.2	10.7	15.1	23.1	30.2	34.4

*Adjusted population; **for the previous 10 year period; + assumed for projection.
Sources: NSO (2001d).

DEMOGRAPHIC PROSPECTS IN THE 21ST CENTURY

Population Growth

The National Statistical Office of South Korea (hereinafter the NSO) conducts a population projection for the future after each population census. The most recent projection is the one made for the years 2000–2050 in 2001 based on the 2000 census (NSO, 2001d). The summary results of the projection are presented in Table III.

According to the projection, the population of Korea will grow until it reaches 51 million around 2020. The annual rate of population growth is expected to drop steadily, from 0.77 percent during 1995–2000, to 0.09 percent during 2010–20, and the population will experience absolute declines thereafter. Various assumptions were adopted for the projection. Among them, the most important are those for fertility, and the NSO assumed the total fertility rate (hereinafter the TFR) to be 1.47 for 2000, 1.36 for 2010, and 1.40 for 2040–2050. These assumptions seem to be reasonable considering recent fertility trends in both South Korea and the advanced countries. Reviewing the trends during 1985–97 in South Korea, the TFR varied between 1.56 and 1.77 and showed a continuous decline since 1992 (NSO, 2000a: p. 106). A further reduction to 1.42 was observed in 1999, which may be partly explained as a response to the national monetary crisis that took place in late 1997. A new millennium baby boom was anticipated for the year 2000, but the fertility rise was marginal as indicated by the TFR of 1.48. On the basis of the recent birth registration reports, the NSO predicts that the TFR will drop below 1.4 in 2001, and it sees no sign of change in fertility trends in the foreseeable future.

The age at which women marry is still on the rise. Women's attitudes toward marriage are changing, and the incidence of marriage dissolution through divorce has been increasing rapidly since 1990.[3] It was observed recently in Western societies that those with strong familial orientation consist of those groups with the lowest fertility (Chesnais, 1996). Confucian societies emphasize familial values in every domain of life, and also experience very low fertility or rapid fertility declines presently. In South Korea, the relationship between increasing parental obligations with respect to the future of one's children, and the desire for one- or two-children families can be established easily (Kwon, 1993: pp. 47–52). In a word, there is a high possibility of a further reduction of fertility in South Korea, as postulated by the NSO.

The theory of demographic transition is usually adopted for explaining the population trends of South Korea since 1960 or in the 20th century. According to this theory, the end of transition is the stabilization of population growth, and the transition is thought to complete when fertility reaches a level of population replacement. The theory has little concern for the continuous shrinking of the population, although this is likely to affect all kinds of social arrangements and living conditions in advanced societies. The recent plunge in the level of fertility observed in many low fertility societies is seen as a temporary deviation by most population projections including those of the United Nations.[4] Such an assumption may be justified by the transition theory, but would result in blinding us to the emerging world population crises in the 21st century.

Population Aging

Population aging is expected to continue until the first half of the 21st century, when both population growth and demographic composition are thought to undergo a process of stabilization. According to the projection, the proportion of population aged 65 or higher will increase rapidly, from 7.2 percent in 2000, to 15.1 percent in 2020, to 34.4 percent in 2050. In contrast, the proportion of population aged 0–14 will fall gradually from 21.1 to 10.5 percent. The number of aged in the population will surpass that of the youth population around 2018. The proportion of the labor force in the population, which was 71.7 percent in 2000, will stabilize at around 50–55 percent.

One of the most important features of population aging in South Korea is that its pace is unprecedented. For instance, it took 175 years in France for the proportion of population aged 65 and above to reach 12 percent, starting from 5 percent, 65 years in the United States, and 40 years in Japan. This change will take less than 25 years in South Korea. The pace by itself is enough to suggest the seriousness of problems the elderly in South Korea would face in the coming years. South Korea has already entered the era of aging. Nevertheless, either welfare provisions or policy considerations for the elderly falls mostly into the hands of the family, as the past, despite tremendous changes in longevity and the proportion of the elderly. Elderly only households have increased greatly since 1980, and will increase further. Many of the elderly are poor and ailing, but are not eligible for free medical care and income subsidies. Enlarging employment opportunities for the elderly is often recommended as a viable policy to enhance the quality of their life. The government enacted, however, an opposing measure recently by lowering the age of retirement for teachers and public sector employees. Early exclusion from work would mean the extension of unproductive dependent living in the life cycle of individuals. The more important point is, however, that it implies, for most, exclusion from society and the family. Aging is a continuous process even in developed societies, and the elderly would act as a crucial agent in social change in the future. The recognition of these simple facts is not widely shared in South Korea, even though new serious problems will develop soon while the old ones remain unsolved.

This fast aging would require a change in the responsible agent for elderly care from the family to the state or society. According to the population projection, the aged dependency ratio will double in the next two decades, and increase more than three times in the coming 30 years. This indicates clearly how rapidly the burden of elderly care will grow for an average family. In addition, increasing longevity means an increase in the proportion of elderly in the population, who demand more extensive and intensive care for prolonged periods.

Labor Force Supply and Dependency

The demographic transition of South Korea after 1960, and the expected future demographic processes will result in profound changes in the size and structure of the labor force population. Unlike the last four decades, the proportion of the labor force population will increase to a lesser degree than the total population, and the absolute size of the labor force population will shrink after 2015. Some worry about the prospect of a shortage in the labor supply. Such a concern may be justified in the long run. Even so, the problem can be eased to a large extent by increasing women's participation in the labor force, and by extending the age for leaving the workforce for some time. Though having increased gradually, the women's labor force participation remains low, it being 49.5 percent in 1997, compared to 75.6 percent for men. The aging of the labor force and the lesser entry of young people into it cause concern about the quality of the labor force itself.

Family Related Issues

As discussed above, fertility transition and migration have effected considerable changes in family structure since 1960. Here a question arises whether the trend will continue in a situation of low fertility and very high urban dominance in regional population distribution. Population aging may be interpreted as an important demographic force encouraging the dissolution of extended families and separate living from their children among elderly persons, whose ages range from the high 60s to the low 70s. Urban living is often cited as a determinant of family nucleation. But migration has played a more important role in this process in both rural and urban areas. Another important demographic factor in future family formation will be a serious sex imbalance at birth that was first noticed in the mid 1980s. Strong preference for a son is expected to wane gradually because it is theoretically difficult to persist with low fertility for long.[5] Low fertility is expected to bring about a change in gender preference ultimately, and, therefore, can be regarded as an important agent for social change. Persistent high sex ratios at birth will cause a squeeze in the marriage market. This situation will start to prevail in the early 2010s, and ought to last at least for two decades, thus producing serious changes in the marriage system and family formation behavior.

An immediate impact of boy selective births, combined with low fertility, will be gender differentiation of sibling composition. Selectivity increases steeply with the progression of birth parity, that is, in turn, determined by the sex of the previous birth. For all parities, the chance of terminating family building increases greatly after having a son. This family building behavior would result in the domination of sons in one-child families and daughters in three or more child families. Such a tendency is easily confirmed by the 1995 census. If we select children living with mothers aged between 35 and 44, the children with no or one sibling account for 75 percent. It is also observed that the proportion of boys is much greater in smaller families. For example, 60 percent of one-child families have boys and 62 percent of three or more children families are girl-dominated families. In other words, girls tend to be socialized more in larger families and girl-dominated families, whereas boys would be raised mostly in smaller families or boy only families. This differentiation of family composition would have great implications for the personality formation of children and will continue until the value of son preference disappears.

Fertility transition is known to be associated with women's employment in many ways. Demographic theories usually treat the latter as a determinant of fertility reduction in demographic theories, but the reverse relationship may well be established. In the situation of a shrinking labor force population, women can be view as a reserve force. Also, the lengthy extension of the period free from childcare would lead more women to seek a career and employment outside the home. It is also interesting to note that South Korean parents feel the increasing burdens of their children economically as well as emotionally with fewer children to take care of. South Korean parents assume full responsibilities for their children, not merely for their education, but for their overall success in the world. Families compete with each other to provide better care, better education, and more material support to their children. A growing number of young mothers are currently seeking jobs for this reason.

DEMOGRAPHY OF NORTH KOREA

Data and Projection

The trends and patterns of population in North Korea are very difficult to assemble because of a paucity of data and lack of its reliability. The country reported population totals from time to time until the late 1960s through their national yearbooks. The figures for more recent years are available in their reports to the united Nations, which include the 1986 age composition data as well as the 1993 census results. The population totals between 1949 and 1970 are seen as fairly reliable judging from the changing sex ratios and the population trends discerned from the data. But the quality of data for more recent years is highly suspect. For instance, the sex ratio for the total population was 84.2 in 1986, according to the population figures reported to the United Nations.[6] The total sex ratio can be drawn from two sets of data in the case of the 1993 census. It was reported as 89.2 in the age composition data, but as 94.9 in the population distribution by province data suggesting a relatively higher degree of under-enumeration of men in the age data (CBS, 1995). Eberstadt and Banister (1992) reconstructed the trend and composition of population in the North based on the 1986 data. The United Nations (1999: pp. 160–161) has conducted a series of backward as well as forward population projections for North Korea in connection with its effort to conduct world population projections. The most important assumption involved here is that the levels and patterns of mortality are almost identical between South and North Korea. The validity of this assumption, however, has been strongly challenged (Kwon, 1997). The South Korean government conducted, in 1999, a new population projection for North Korea based on a thorough review of recent socioeconomic conditions

TABLE IV

Population trends of North Korea, 1960–2030

	Unit	(A)		(B)				
		1960	1970	1980	1990	2000	2010	2030
Total population	In 000	10789	14619	17622	19559	22175	23455	25834
Annual growth rate*	%	3.35	3.28	1.66	1.14	0.58	0.46	0.38
Total fertility rate**	Person	6.2	4.3	2.3	2.2	2.0	1.9	1.9
Life expectancy **	Year	61.3	63.2	64.3	66.4	65.2	70.2	75.6
Youth dependency ratio	%			53.01	38.35	37.97	31.12	28.88
Aged dependency ratio	%			4.61	6.65	9.48	12.92	19.14
Total dependency ratio	%			57.61	44.99	47.45	44.05	48.02
Index of Aging	%			8.69	17.33	24.95	41.52	66.26
Population at ages 65+	%			2.9	4.6	6.4	9.0	12.9

*For pervious 5 years; **For the next 5 years for 1960–1990.
Sources: (A) Populations for 1960 and 1970 are from CSB (1992); (B) Those for 1980–2030 are from NSO's projection (1999).

and demographic pictures revealed from the population data for 1986 and 1993. Table IV is prepared from data based on this new projection.

Demographic Path

North Korea has undergone a totally different path of demographic change from that of South Korea. Population growth was minimal in the post liberation period of 1945–49 and negative during 1949–53. As a result, the population was reduced from 9.3 million to 8.5 million between 1945 and 1953. North Korea also experienced a baby boom during 1953–60. Fertility remained high until 1970, and began to decline in the early 1970s. Fertility control policy was pursued for a short time in the 1970s and abandoned in the early 1980s. Recently, fertility is expected to reach a level below replacement due largely to starvation and economic difficulties. The government has revitalized prenatal policies, but fertility is apparently in a downward track according to the stories told by recent defectors from North Korea.[7]

North Korea was better off economically, and had a better health system than South Korea in the 1960s and the early 1970s. This can be interpreted to indicate a lower mortality or a longer life expectancy in the North until the mid 1970s. On the other hand, malnutrition began to prevail in North Korea during the second half of the 1980s, as indicated by a reduction in height of children born since that time.[8] Starvation began to be noticed all over North Korea in 1993 due to a severe shortage of food supplies resulting from a series of famines. The estimate of extra deaths due to starvation during 1995–98 varies greatly from 270000 to 3 million. The Korean government gives the lowest estimate, and the estimate of a Buddhist charity group is the highest (NSO, 1999: p. 2; BC, 1998: p. 29). If we translate the figures into the term of life expectancy, the former means a reduction of four or five years in a five-year period, while the latter means a return to a traditional or pre-modern state.

The South Korean government projection assumed that life expectancy at birth increased marginally during the two decades beginning in the mid-1970s, but was later reduced by four years between 1993 and 1995 in North Korea. In any event, the gap in life expectancy was expected to widen greatly between South and North Korea from the mid-1970s and thereafter. According to the projection, the life expectancies differ little during 1970–75 between South and North Korea, showing around 60 years for men and 66 years for women. But the figures for 1993 became lower in North Korea, by 5.2 years for men and 7.5 years for women, than in South Korea. The difference increased to 11 years for men and 14 years for women in the late 1990s (NSO, 1999: p. 13). The projection assumed a one-year extension of life expectancy at birth every year between 1997 and 2010 and smaller increments thereafter. It may be argued that the assumed level of North Korean mortality for the 1980s and the early 1990s is too high. But if we calculate the life expectancy of women for 1986–93 by using age composition data, even a higher mortality or a less expectation of life is found. This can be interpreted to indicate a high possibility that the actual population size of North Korea would be much smaller than what is presented by the projection.

According to the Korean government projection, the total population of North Korea was 14.9 million in 1970 and 20.2 million in 1990. The population was expected to increase to 22.2 million in 2000, and, subsequently, reach 25.8 million in 2030. These figures correspond to 47–52 percent of the population of South Korea. North Korea is also experiencing population aging, though the degree is slightly behind that of South Korea.

CONCLUDING REMARKS

The 20th century is of particular importance in Korean demography. Demographic transition started in the early years of the century and, was completed in the later years. Rapid population growth was a result of this process. The population on the Korean peninsular increased from 19020000 in 1925 to 25120000 in 1944, and further to 68890000 in 2000. During 1945–2000, population almost tripled in South Korea, and more than doubled in North Korea. Heavy migration of Korean farmers to Japan and Manchuria lessened considerably increasing population pressure prior to the liberation of Korea in 1945.

The post-liberation period of 1945–60 is often characterized as the years of turmoil and instability. South Korea experienced an explosive population growth in this period due to a large influx of repatriates from Japan and Manchuria during 1945–49, refugees from North Korea during 1945–53, and a post-Korean War baby boom between 1953 and 1960. In the North, population growth was very small during 1945–50, and negative during the war years of 1950–53. But there was a post war baby boom in North Korea as well.

The growth of population until 1960 was not accompanied by any betterment of the economy or industrial development, and population pressure felt by individual families increased. Poor farmers were driven from their farms, and left for cities or foreign countries in order to survive. This resulted in the formation of Korean communities overseas and population concentration in cities. Now, Koreans residing in foreign countries on a permanent basis are estimated at about 5 million. In addition, the proportion of the urban population in Korea rose from 5 percent in 1925 to 80 percent in 2000. Fertility began to respond to ever-increasing population pressure in the early 1960s. The pace of fertility reduction was very rapid, and the transition was completed in 20–25 years. But the trend of fertility reduction has not as yet disappeared. South Korean fertility has plunged to the lowest level in the world, and shows no sign of an upturn. The outcome of all of this has been a continuous slowdown in population growth and a rapidly aging population.

Fertility change and the life of South Koreans have interacted rather closely. It is well known that poverty or economic hardship was the major force convincing South Korean couples of the idea of family planning in the 1960s. In addition, various modernization ideas have played a major role in family planning since the mid-1970s. On the other side, the social impacts of fertility decline are easily seen. For example, it caused significant changes in the arrangement of family living, the labor force situation, and the marriage market.

The population of South Korea is expected to decrease after 2020 reversing the trend of the 20the century. Population aging will continue until the median age of population reaches about 55 years, and the proportion of the aged 65 and older is around 35 percent. These simple facts require the total reshaping of social institutions and value systems. South Koreans are uneasy about the future in face of unprecedented changes that are expected in every domain of life both in terms of pace and direction.

North Korea might be a crucial factor in drawing a demographic picture for the future of both South and North Korea. Changes in North-South relations would alter the population situation including labor market conditions in both countries. The reunification of South and North Korea would bring about chaos in every sector of the society. Behaviors related to fertility and family formation, including marriage and mortality conditions, are expected to change greatly, particularly in the North, similar to what East European countries experienced during the 1990s after the collapse of the Soviet Union.

ACKNOWLEDGEMENT

This study was supported by the Grant for Reform of University Education under the BK21 Project of Seoul National University.

NOTES

[1] The risk of deaths before the first birthday was estimated to range between 186 and 241 out of 1000 births for 1920–25, and reduced to 118–151 for 1940–45 (Kwon, 1986: p. 12).
[2] Here, 'family' denotes 'relative household' in the census reports, that is distinguished from 'ordinary household' by excluding one-person household and non-relative household.
[3] According to the marriage tables from vital registration, the total marriage rate for women was 97.7% in 1990 and 88.2% in 1999. If we take the first marriages only, it will be 90.8% and 75.9% respectively. The proportion of first marriages was 92.9% in 1990 and 85.2% in 2000 in the case of women (NSO, 2000b, 2001a).
[4] For example, the United Nations assumed that the TFR will change from 1.48 in 1995 to 1.79 during 2040–50 in Western Europe for medium variant projections which are used most frequently (UN, 1999: p. 50).
[5] The vital statistics show that the sex ratio has decreases continuously since 1994. The ratio was 115.5 in 1994, but changed to 109.2 in 1998. The tempo of normalization is much faster than what was assumed by NSO for the future population projection conducted in 1996 (Chung, 1999).
[6] Regarding the quality of data, see Eberstadt and Binister (1992: pp. 6–12) and Kwon (1990: pp. 440–443).
[7] According to interviews conducted during May 1999 by the author to recent women defectors from North Korea, ten women at ages 31–35 have only one child although most births occurred before 1994. Only one woman had three children, but the last birth was delivered in 1991 in this case. All of them mentioned that one child family ideal prevails in North Korea nowadays and the trend is irreversible.
[8] For overall socioeconomic and health conditions, see Kwon (1997: pp. 110–115). Concerning the height of children, defectors told that the height of soldiers and school children became smaller and smaller, and that children who belonged to the tallest group in North Korea are found to be smallest in South Korea.

REFERENCES

Buddhist Center for Helping North Korean People (BC): 1998, Status of Food Shortage in North Korea (unpublished). (K)

Central Bureau of Statistics (CBS), Democratic People's Republic of Korea: 1992, Health Statistics of the Democratic People's Republic of Korea.

Central Bureau of Statistics (CBS), Democratic People's Republic of Korea: 1995, Tabulation of the Population Census of the Democratic Peoples Republic of Korea (31 December 1993).

Chang, Young-Shik, Nam-Hoon Cho, Hyun-Sang Moon, Yong-Chan Byun and Young-Hee Oh: 1996, New Population Projection: Population Size, and Structural Change, and Policy Tasks (Korea Institute of Health and Social Affairs, Seoul). (K)

Chesnais, Jean-Claude: 1996, 'Fertility, family, and social policy in Western Europe', Population & Development Review, pp. 22–24.

Chung, Hwa-Ok: 1999, 'On constructing current populations', in Population Association of Korea, Summary Proceedings of the Second 1999 Population Association of Korea Congress. (mimeo.) (K)

Eberstadt, Nicholas and Judith Banister: 1992, The Population of North Korea (Institute of East Asian Studies, University of California, Berkeley).

Government General of Korea (GGK): 1934, Census Reports of Korea, 1930. Section of All Korea. Tables of Results (Seoul). (J)

Kim, Tai-Hun: 1997, 'Prospects of population and its social impacts', in Tai-Hwan Kwon, Tai-Hun Kim, Doo-Sub Kim, Kwang-Hee Jun and Ki-Soo Eun (eds.), Understanding the Fertility Transition of Korea (Ilsinsa, Seoul).

Kwon, Tai-Hwan: 1977, Demography of Korea (Seoul National University Press, Seoul).

Kwon, Tai-Hwan: 1986, The Trends and Patterns of Mortality and Health in the Republic of Korea (United Nations, Bangkok).

Kwon, Tai-Hwan: 1990, 'Population development in divided Korea', in Myoung-Kyu Kang and Helmut Wagner (eds.), Korea and Germany: Lessons in Division (Seoul National University Press, Seoul).

Kwon, Tai-Hwan: 1993, 'Exploring socio-cultural explanations of fertility transition in South Korea', in Leete and Alam (eds.), The Revolution in Asian Fertility (Clarendon Oxford Press, Oxford).

Kwon, Tai-Hwan: 1997, 'Evaluating mortality conditions in North Korea', in Marcel P.R. Van den Broecke and Daniel Berze (eds.), Demographic Problems of Countries Changing to a Market Economy: Papers and Proceedings from an ISI-National Statistical Office of Korea Cutting Edge Conference (Editions Voorburg, Voorburg, the Netherland).

Kwon, Tai-Hwan, Hae-Young Lee, Yunshik Chang and Eui-Young Yu: 1975, The Population of Korea (Population & Development Studies Center, Seoul National University, Seoul).

Kwon, Tai-Hwan and Young-Jin Park: 1995, 'Patterns of household and family', in Tai-Hwan Kwon, Tai-Hun Kim and Jin-Ho Choi (eds.), Population and Family in Korea (Ilsinsa, Seoul). (K)

National Statistical Office (NSO), Republic of Korea: 1996, Future Population Projection for Korea. (K)

National Statistical Office (NSO), Republic of Korea: 1997, 1995 Population and Housing Census Report: Volume 1 Whole Country (1).
National Statistical Office (NSO), Republic of Korea: 1998, Social Indicators in Korea, 1998.
National Statistical Office (NSO), Republic of Korea: 1999, Results of Population Projection for North Korea (Unpublished).
National Statistical Office (NSO), Republic of Korea: 2000a, Social Indicators in Korea, 2000.
National Statistical Office (NSO), Republic of Korea: 2000b, Annual Report on Marriages · Divorcees Statistics (Based on Viral Registration), 1999.
National Statistical Office (NSO), Republic of Korea: 2001a, Annual Report on Marriages · Divorcees Statistics (Based on Viral Registration), 2000. (To be published)
National Statistical Office (NSO), Republic of Korea: 2001b, 2000 Population and Housing Census Report: The Summary of Basic Population Characteristics (http:/www.nso.go.kr/eng/release/e_spce00-3-htm#top).
National Statistical Office (NSO), Republic of Korea: 2001c, 2000 Population and Housing Census Report: The Summary of Households and Housing Units (http:/www.nso.go.kr/eng/release/e_spce00-4-htm).
National Statistical Office (NSO), Republic of Korea: 2001d, Future Population Projection for Korea. (To be published) (K)
United Nations: 1999, World Population Prospects: The 1998 Revision, Volume 1: Comprehensive Tables (New York).
Note: K refers works written in Korean and J in Japanese.

Department of Sociology
Seoul National University
Shinlim-Dong, Kwanak-Gu
Seoul, 151–742, Korea
E-mail: thkwon@prome.snu.ac.kr

DOO-SEUNG HONG

SOCIAL CHANGE AND STRATIFICATION

ABSTRACT. Korean society has changed a great deal in the wake of rapid economic development and industrialization that began in the early 1960s. This article examines social change in Korea in terms of shifts in its occupational structure and class stratification. For the past four decades, industrialization has steadily reduced the agricultural labour force and significantly expanded the urban labour force to satisfy the growing manufacturing industry. Many small traditional family businesses have been replaced by highly organized and large-scale modern businesses with salaried workers. At the same time, an increasing number of women have joined the workforce of the diverse modern industrial system. More recently, the demand for high-tech, information-related occupations has been on the rise. These changes in the occupational structure have transformed Korea into a middle class society.

For the past four decades, South Korea (Korea hereinafter) has undergone great social change characterized largely by industrialization. Within a single generation, primitive industrial relations and features vanished, and an advanced industrial structure was established in Korea. As a result, Korea now has quite a different distribution and structure of social classes from the one of four decades ago. This article highlights the main features of social change in Korea by unravelling the dynamics of its occupational structure and class stratification.

OCCUPATIONAL COMPOSITION IN TRANSITION

The spectacular growth of the Korean economy over the past four decades has transformed an agricultural society into a modern industrial one. The rapidly developing economy has also brought about fundamental changes in the occupational configuration as well as the industrial structure in Korea. The most notable changes in the occupational composition can be summarized in the following four main characteristics. First, there has been a drastic decrease in the

Social Indicators Research **62, 63:** 39–50, 2003.

agricultural labour force that is contrasted by a significant increase in the urban labour force. Second, as a result of the expansion of modern industrial organizations and the development of capitalism, there has been a dramatic increase in salaried workers, as opposed to workers who are self-employed or in family business. Third, females more actively participate in the modern industrial system, comprising a significant labour force in their own right, and women's work simultaneously has become diversified. Fourth, due to the recent development of the high-tech and information industry, there has been a remarkable increase in information-related occupations. In the following pages, each characteristic change of Korean occupational composition is examined.

The Decrease of the Primary Industry Sector

Over the past 40 years, the most fundamental change in Korean industry took place in the composition of the three primary industries. Table I illustrates the unmistakable transformation in the composition of persons employed by industry between 1960 and 2000. The number and proportion of workers in the agricultural, forestry, and fishery industries drastically declined, whereas that of the other industrial groups remarkably increased. In 1960, employees of the agricultural, forestry, and fishery industries constituted 79.5 percent of the total economically active population, but this figure was reduced to 8.7 percent four decades later. During the same period, the number of the workers in the sector of social overhead capital (hereinafter the SOC) and other industries increased from 15.1 percent to 70.7 percent of the total economically active population. In addition, the number of employees in the mining and manufacturing industries jumped from 5.4 percent in 1960 to 20.6 percent in 2000. Former agricultural, forestry, and fishery workers were absorbed into the other urban sectors as a result of rapid industrialization.

Another interesting point that Table I suggests is that the SOC and other industries may have attracted many mining and manufacturing workers during the 1990s. The number of the latter has steadily increased between 1960 and 1990, but it dropped by 7.0 percent between 1990 and 2000. The decline in mining and manufacturing workers may have been caused by structural changes in all

TABLE I

Composition of Employed Persons by Industry: 1960–2000 (Unit: %)

Industry	1960	1970	1980	1990	2000*
Agricultural, forestry & fishery	79.5	50.4	34.0	17.9	8.7
Mining & manufacturing	5.4	14.3	22.5	27.6	20.6
SOC & others	15.1	35.3	43.5	54.5	70.7

Source: KNSO, *Social Indicators in Korea.*
Note: *As of December.

TABLE II

Changes in Employment Status: 1960–2000 (Unit: %)

<table>
<tr><th>Employment Status</th><th>1960</th><th>1970</th><th>1980</th><th>1990</th><th>2000</th></tr>
<tr><td>Employer</td><td rowspan="2">47.5</td><td>1.8</td><td>4.0</td><td>5.4</td><td>9.9</td></tr>
<tr><td>Self-employed</td><td>33.0</td><td>31.4</td><td>24.2</td><td>24.8</td></tr>
<tr><td>Unpaid family worker</td><td>30.9</td><td>26.2</td><td>21.1</td><td>10.6</td><td>1.8</td></tr>
<tr><td>Employee</td><td>21.6</td><td>30.0</td><td>43.4</td><td>59.7</td><td>63.5</td></tr>
<tr><td>Total</td><td>100.0</td><td>100.0</td><td>100.0</td><td>100.0</td><td>100.0</td></tr>
</table>

Source: KNSO, *Population and Housing Census.*

of Korean industry in recent years. These statistics clearly suggest that economic activity in Korea shifted from the production of goods to the providing of services over the past four decades.

The Growth of Wage and Salaried Workers

The decrease in agricultural, forestry, and fishery workers ran in parallel with the decrease in the self-employed and unpaid family workers over the last four decades. In Korea, family members used to run the agricultural, forestry, and fishery businesses. Family members also ran many small businesses. Table II illustrates the decrease in such traditional employment types between 1960 and 2000. More than three-quarters (78.4%) were either self-employed (including employer) or unpaid family workers in 1960, but a little over one-third (36.5%) were self-employed or unpaid family workers in 2000. The more dramatic change between the two periods occurred in the group of unpaid family workers. They dropped from 30.9 percent in 1960, to 1.8 percent in 2000. On the other hand, those who were employed by others increased to 63.5 percent in 2000, from 21.6 percent in 1960. The growth of employees, i.e., wage and salaried workers, implies that Korean industry becomes more bureaucratized and institutionalized in recent years. In addition, Korean industrial development altered traditional work relationships as well as expanded the use of modern industrial organizations.

The increase in the number of employees was contributed to, in part, by the increase in clerical and sales workers in Korean industry. They are wage or salaried employees as distinct from those who work on their own. In 1960, employees constituted less than 10 percent of the total number of sales workers, but their share increased to 17.7 percent during the 1980s, and then increased again to 29.6 percent in 2000. In addition, small businesses, which have been traditionally helped by family members, encountered great challenges from large-scale firms with enormous economic power. As the capitalistic competition intensified, small business labour forces were absorbed into the wage or salaried employee groups. Conglomerates increasingly replaced petty traders and self-employed service workers, who played major roles in the previous years in the distribution and service industries.

Moreover, whole-scale urbanization has changed traditional stores into large fancy shopping centers. In the mid-1990s, the emergence of large-scale discount stores, warehouse-type retail businesses, and franchised stores, like those long in existence in the advanced nations of the world, had a huge impact on the distributional industry. As for department stores, the oligopoly of the "big three" companies, Lotte, Hyundai, and Shinsegae, became more conspicuous, and their market share grew to 54.4 percent in 2000 (KOSCA, 2001). These industries have provided a large number of clerical and sales workers.

The Growth of the Female Labour Force

As the composition of industry and employment underwent a significant change, so did the gender ratio within the labour force. The female labour force has recently penetrated into areas that were

TABLE III

Gender Ratio of Workers Aged 20–65 by Occupation in 2000

Occupational group	Ratio
Legislators, senior officials and managers	6
Professionals	62
Technicians and associate professionals	57
Clerks	126
Service workers and shop & market sales workers	192
Skilled agricultural & fishery workers	104
Craft and related trade workers	33
Plant & machine operators and assemblers	18
Elementary occupations	124
All	85

Source: Calculated from raw data of the Economically Active Population Survey (KNSO 2000).
Note: Sex ratio indicates the number of females per 100 male workers.

once exclusively occupied by males. Table III displays gender ratio measured by the number of females per 100 males in the year 2000. The ratio indicates that women are more frequently found than men among clerks, service and sales workers and other unskilled labourers. Among legislators, senior officials, and managers, in striking contrast, the former are outnumbered by the latter by a ratio of 6 to 100.

The feminization of clerical workers has proceeded faster than that of professional, technical, administrative, and managerial workers. In 2000, females constituted 56 percent of clerical workers. Even so, the top positions of this occupational category are occupied normally by males, while those of lower positions are by females. In addition, feminization is also found in the agricultural and fishery sectors, where the gender ratios were no more than 50 during the 1960s, but rose to 104 by 2000. These changes were directly influenced by industrialization and urbanization. When compared with earlier figures, female labour participation also increased in professional positions. The gender ratio had been less than 20 before 1960, but the ratio soared to 62 in the year 2000.

TABLE IV

Percentage of Professional, Technical, and Managerial Workers: 1960–2000

Year	1960	1970	1980	1990	2000
%	3.6	4.8	5.3	8.7	18.7

Source: KNSO, *Population and Housing Census.*

It should be noted that young female workers were hired by many labour-intensive manufacturing concerns during the early stages of industrialization in Korea. Labour-intensive manufacturing concerns depended heavily on cheap female labour. Since the labour-intense industries serve as the backbone for rapid economic growth in the export-oriented Korean economy, female labour participation used to be high among production workers until the 1980s. Since 1990, however, the proportion of female labour participation began to shrink as the labour-intensive industry was replaced by capital-intensive or high-tech industries.

The Advancement of Information Occupations

We now live in a world that can be characterized as the information technology era. As telecommunications and internet technology has enormously advanced since the late 1990s, the demand for workers in related fields has soared to a great extent (Hong et al., 1999). Table IV indicates that the proportion of the major "information occupations" increased between 1960 and 2000. Information occupations often refer to professional, technical, and managerial jobs because they are related to the production and distribution of knowledge and information. Professional work is based on expertise, which is normally achieved by way of professional formal education. Professionals need a high level of knowledge and information, which in turn demands significant compensation (Abbott, 1988; Larson, 1977). Professional, technical, and managerial workers constituted 3.6 percent of the labour force in 1960, but 18.7 percent in 2000. In addition, the proportion of the professional, technical, and managerial workers increased incrementally from 3.6 percent in 1960, to 4.8 percent in 1970, to 5.3 percent in 1980, but then it

TABLE V

Changes in Class Structure: 1960–2000[1] (Unit: %)

Class	1960	1970	1980	1990	2000[2]
Upper-middle	0.9	1.3	1.8	1.9	4.3
New middle	6.6	14.2	17.7	25.5	23.9
Old middle	13.0	14.8	20.8	18.2	24.8
Working	8.9	16.9	22.6	30.6	29.7
Urban lower	6.6	8.0	5.9	6.2	7.6
Farmer	40.0	28.0	23.2	12.7	8.9
Rural lower	24.0	16.7	8.1	4.8	0.8
Total	100.0	100.0	100.0	100.0	100.0

Source: Hong, Kim and Cho (1999: p. 141).
[1]Estimated based on economically active male population.
[2]Estimated based on the Economically Active Population Survey 2000.

sharply swelled to 18.7 percent in the year 2000, from 8.7 percent in 1990.

CLASS STRUCTURE IN TRANSITION

Industrialization and urbanization eventually resulted in the transformation of the class structure in Korea. As Table V shows, Korean class configuration is divided into seven class groups. They are distinguished according to the level of control exercised by individuals over their social resources and economic base (Hong, 1983). Social resources refer to socially valued but scarce resources such as, power, wealth, prestige, and education. On the basis of such socio-economic resources, the Korean class structure is divided into three sectors. Each sector, in turn, is subdivided into several class groups. Specifically, the organizational sector is divided into the upper middle class, the new middle class, and the working class. The entrepreneurial sector is divided into the upper class, the old middle class, and the urban lower class. The agricultural sector is divided into independent farmers and the rural lower class. For empirical applicability, the upper class is combined with the upper-middle class.

The upper-middle class includes doctors, engineers, professionals, and managers who possess profound knowledge and professional skill. The new middle class refers to typical white-collar workers, such as semi-professionals and clerical workers. The old middle class refers to self-employed workers. The working class is equated with blue-collar workers such as production and service workers employed by others. The urban lower class is often called the "marginal class," and it includes street vendors and day labourers. In the agricultural sector, independent farmers constitute the middle stratum of the rural population, but they do not enjoy the same living standard as that of the urban middle class. Finally, poor farmers, farm labourers, and the unemployed constitute the rural lower class.

Table V clearly suggests that class structure in Korea underwent a substantial change between 1960 and 2000. First of all, the distribution of class becomes more bell-shaped in 2000 than that of its rather skewed-shape in 1960, 1970, and 1980. Second, as mentioned above, the proportion of farmers (independent farmers and the rural lower class) has drastically declined from 64.0 percent in 1960, to 9.7 percent in 2000. Third, the population of the working class has increased from 8.9 percent in 1960, to 29.7 percent in 2000. It should be noted that the working class population reached its peak of 30.6 in 1990. Finally, the upper middle population increased from 0.9 percent in 1960, to 4.3 percent in 2000, whereas the rural lower population shrank from 24.0 percent to 0.8 percent during the same period, while the urban lower population remained steady between 6.0–8.0 percent.

The Strong Showing of the Middle Class

During the last four decades, the size of the middle class (the upper-middle class, the new middle class, and the old middle class altogether) increased from 20.5 to 53.0 percent. This method of objective classification suggests a strong showing of the middle class as a whole. The middle class, however, diversified and became heterogeneous in that its subgroups have different demographic and socio-economic characteristics. The overwhelming majority of the upper-middle and new middle class has had at least some college education, and a substantial portion of them graduated from four-

TABLE VI

Self-identified Social Standing: 1991–1999 (Unit: %)

Class	1991	1994	1999
Upper	1.6	1.4	1.1
Middle	61.3	60.4	54.9
Lower	37.1	38.2	44.0

Source: KNSO, *Social Indicators in Korea* (2000: p. 510).

year colleges. Since old middle class people are often recruited from the working class, the educational level of the old middle class is more similar to that of the working class than to the new middle class. As workers get older, they may either move upward into the old middle class or drop down into the urban lower class.

Even by the most conservative method of estimation, there is little doubt that the upper-middle class grew sharply over the past decade. The old middle class of self-employed workers expanded steadily over the past four decades, from 13.0 percent in 1960, through 18.2 percent in 1990, to 24.8 percent in 2000. The new middle class increased to the greatest extent between 1960 (6.6%) and 1990 (25.5%), but then dropped slightly to 23.9 percent in 2000. These changes in class composition obviously indicate that Korean society has moved toward a "middle class society."

Apart from objective indicators measuring the stratification of social classes, there are subjective indicators that tell a bit of a different story. Subjective class identification reveals both how people see themselves in the social hierarchical system, and how they perceive others in terms of class standing. The size of the self-identified middle class becomes enlarged because people, when asked, tend to identify themselves as a member of the middle class. Some empirical studies, therefore, question the adequacy of self-reported subjective class identification. According to the Social Statistics Survey, conducted by the Korea National Statistical Office (2000) in 1991 and 1994, about 60 percent of the respondents answered that they belonged to one of the three middle class subgroups (see Table VI). In fact, this percentage is higher by 15 points than the 45.6 percent that the three objectively determined middle classes – the upper-middle class, the new middle class, and the old middle class – constituted as a whole in 1990 (see Table V). It appears that there was no notable change in Korean subjective class identification in the early 1990s. Almost identical proportions of Koreans reported that they belonged to the middle class in 1991 and 1994.

The class structure in Korea, that was quite stable in the early 1990s, underwent a significant downward shift in the late 1990s. In 1999, for example, the self-identified middle class shrank to 54.9 percent, from 60.4 percent in 1994. During the same period, the self-identified upper class also dropped to 1.1 percent, from 1.4 percent. In sharp contrast, the self-identified lower class swelled to 44.0 percent in 1999, from 38.2 percent in 1994. The downward movement was directly caused by the outbreak in 1997 of the worst economic crisis since the 1960s.

The Myth of Getting Ahead

Industrialization and urbanization are not the only forces that have reshaped Korea's class structure. The desire on the part of Koreans for higher education has also contributed remarkably to a class mobility that resulted in the expansion of the middle class. There is a widespread belief among Koreans that higher social status can be earned as a result of their educational achievement regardless of family background. The expansion of educational opportunities in Korea seems enormous over the past four decades. In 1955, less than one in ten Korean adults (older than 25) received middle (junior high) school education or more. Moreover, only 1.3 percent of Korean adults graduated from college in 1955. In sharp contrast, a majority (64.6%) of Korean adults received high school and higher education in 2000. After graduation, 99.5 percent of middle school students went on to high school, and then 68 percent of high school graduates advanced to college in 2000. As a result, 24.5 percent of Korean adults had some form of college education (Ministry of Education and Human Resources Development, 2001).

The expansion of education opportunity has produced a thick stratum of skilled workers in Korea. In 2000, six out of ten (59%) Korean blue-collar workers received a high school education. On the other hand, the expansion of higher education has had a side effect.

It has not kept pace with demand from the labour market. In other words, the surplus of the college-educated has created a large pool of overqualified workers to fill lesser work positions.

CONCLUDING REMARKS

The transformation of a predominantly agricultural society into an industrialized one was accompanied by a significant change in the economic and social structure. This article has explored the characteristics of recent industrial and occupational changes in Korea, along with the realignment of social classes. Economic development has expedited social and structural mobility in Korea. As a result, the agricultural labour force has dwindled over the past four decades; concomitantly, the urban labour force grew significantly to satisfy the equally thriving manufacturing industry. Many small family businesses were replaced by modernized and organized businesses with salaried workers. Females actively participated in the diverse modern industrial system. More recently, labour's demand for high-tech, information-related occupations increased. In addition to such profound industrial changes, social change brought about a more bell-shaped class distribution in 2000.

ACKNOWLEDGEMENT

This research was supported by a grant for the Reform of University Education under the Brain Korea 21 Project of Seoul National University.

REFERENCES

Abbott, A.: 1988, The System of Professions: An Essay on the Division of Expert Labor (University of Chicago Press, Chicago).
Bank of Korea: 2001, Economic Statistics Yearbook (Bank of Korea, Seoul).
Hong, D.S.: 1983, 'Stratification studies by analysis of occupations', Social Science and Policy Research 5(3), pp. 69–87 (in Korean).
Hong, D.S.: 1992, 'The growth of the middle strata and social change', The State and Civil Society in Korea (Hanul, Seoul) (in Korean).

Hong, D.S.: 1997, 'Social development and changes in occupational structure', in Doo-Seung Hong (ed.), Fifty Years of Korean Society: Social Change and Restructuring (Seoul National University Press, Seoul, pp. 47–78) (in Korean).

Hong, D.S., B.J. Kim and D.K. Cho: 1999, Occupational Structure in Korea (Seoul National University Press, Seoul) (in Korean).

Korea National Statistical Office: 2000, Social Indicators in Korea (KNSO, Daejeon).

Korean Supermarket Cooperative Association: 2001, The Yearbook of Distribution Industry (KOSCA, Seoul).

Larson, M.S.: 1977, The Rise of Professionalism: A Sociological Analysis (University of California Press, Berkeley).

Ministry of Education and Human Resources Development: 2001, Statistical Yearbook of Education (Ministry of Education and Human Resources Development, Seoul).

Park, Y.B.: 1993, 'The trends and characteristics of wage structure in Korea in the 1980s', Korean Labour Review 4, pp. 5–26.

Department of Sociology
College of Social Sciences
Seoul National University
Seoul 151-742
E-mail: dshong@snu.ac.kr

JIHO JANG

ECONOMIC CRISIS AND ITS CONSEQUENCES

ABSTRACT. The financial crisis that began in late 1997, led to a catastrophic downturn of economic and social development in Korea. Rather than dealing with the macroeconomic and financial issues of the crisis, this study analyzes human aspects of the turmoil, that is, the social impact of the economic crisis on Korea. After reviewing indicators of unemployment, poverty, and income distribution in Korea during and after the crisis, this study details the responses and programs that the government undertook to promote employment, to alleviate poverty, and to protect the vulnerable. Since it is expected that the unemployment rate will remain high for a long period even after the economy recovers from the worst of the crisis, this study suggests the necessity of the government's special efforts to strengthen the system of social protection.

1. INTRODUCTION

Since 1997 the Republic of Korea (Korea hereinafter) has experienced an economic shock of unprecedented severity after decades of uninterrupted high growth. Before the economic crisis, many social development indicators of Korea were comparable to those of developed countries. Poverty in Korea declined steeply from 41 percent in 1965 to less than 8 percent in the 1990s (Kim and Leipziger, 1997). Life expectancy increased from 53.9 years in 1960 to 72 years in 1997, and the rate of infant morality decreased from 85 per 1000 to 5 per 1000 for the same period (World Bank, 1999). The adult literacy rate, already high by Third World standards, in 1970 as 88 percent, reached 98 percent in 1994, while the education enrollment rate at all levels, as a percentage of total population between 6 and 23 years of age, rose from 66 percent in 1980 to 82 percent in 1994 (UNDP, 1999). Moreover, according to the United Nation's Human Development Index (HDI), Korea is classified as a high human development country.[1] A trend analysis of the HDI from 1960 to 1997 indicates a continual improvement. The HDI was

Social Indicators Research **62, 63:** 51–70, 2003.

0.398 in 1960, rising to 0.680 in 1975 and 0.761 in 1985. It reached 0.852 in 1997.

However, the financial crisis that began in late 1997 with a foreign currency shortage led to a catastrophic downturn of economic and social development. The crisis and economic restructuring process had major destabilizing consequences, such as shaking confidence in the financial system, disrupting economic activity, forcing many firms into bankruptcy, and producing many other economic problems. Of greater concern than these general negative impacts were those with distributional consequences. Foremost among these was the impact on unemployment and poverty. The effect of the economic crisis on Korea was devastating, particularly for the average citizen who suffered through a period of: the most exacerbating unemployment; frozen wages; a curtailing of non-wage benefits; and an increase in the number of homeless people.

A great deal has been written on the origin and nature of the economic crisis in Korea since its onset (Chang, 1998; Garron, 1998; Haggard, 2000; Pempel, 1999; Radelet and Sachs, 1998; Wade, 2000). However, these studies have dealt with the macroeconomic and financial issues of the crisis, rather than human aspects of the turmoil. Only recently Hoa (2000) brought together a collection of studies on the issue of the social or human dimension of the Asian meltdown. This study is another analysis on the social impact of the economic crisis, specifically on the Korean case. After reviewing indicators of unemployment, poverty, and income distribution in Korea during and after the economic crisis, this study details the responses and programs that the government has undertaken to promote employment, to alleviate poverty, and to protect the vulnerable. The author hopes that this study can be an additional means to help understand pertinent deep-rooted economic issues, and to help develop suitable economic and social policies of national interest. Before examining key social outcomes of the crisis, the next section briefly discusses the current economic situation in Korea, which has continued its recovery from the 1998 recession.

2. ECONOMIC CRISIS AND RECOVERY

Since the financial crisis hit the Korean economy in 1997, the new Kim Dae Jung government has been relatively quick in implementing much-needed reform. It passed a package of financial reform bills accelerating capital market liberalization, restructuring the banking sector and improving prudential supervision of financial transactions through the newly established Financial Supervisory Commission. The government also undertook a series of measures to force big business to: focus their business operations on a small number of core businesses to; diminish debt financing; and enhance the accountability of controlling shareholders and mangers.

As a result, the domestic economy started to show rapid improvement. The GDP growth rate recorded 10.7 percent in 1999 and 8.8 percent in 2000, from –6.7 percent in 1998. Export growth also picked up from –2.8 percent in 1998 to 8.6 in 1999 and 20.1 in 2000, reflecting the increased competitiveness of Korea, following the depreciation of the won (MOFE, 2001). The capital account, which experienced a deficit of $3.2 billion in 1998 as a result of capital outflows, improved to show a surplus of $2 billion in 1999 and $11.7 billion in 2000. As a result of the combined current and capital account surpluses, foreign reserves rose from $74 billion in 1999 to about $96 billion at the end of 2000 (ADB, 2001).

Furthermore, consumer and business sentiment continued to grow stronger. As seen in Table I, a recent survey on household consumption and business activities, which were conducted by the National Statistical Office (NSO) and the Federation of Korean Industries (FKI), resulted in the improvement of economic agents' confidence. For example, Consumer Expectation Index, which represents households' forecast of their consumption six months later, recorded 94.1 in March 2001. Although the index still remains below its base line of 100, meaning that more than half of domestic households answered that they would reduce their consumption in the future, the trend continued upward rising from 92 in February and 89.7 in January. The Business Survey Index also shows an increasing trend to 102.4 in March 2001. This is a signal that more consumers and businesspeople anticipate the economy picking up.

TABLE I

Results of Survey on Household Consumption and Business Activities

	Consumer Expectation Index by the NSO	Business Survey Index by the FKI
July 2000	102.3	91.4
Aug.	102.2	91.1
Sep.	90.9	104.7
Oct.	89.8	91.8
Nov.	82.4	81.0
Dec.	82.2	68.0
Jan. 2001	89.7	62.7
Feb.	92.0	83.0
Mar.	94.1	102.4

Source: National Statistical Office and the Federation of Korean Industries, cited in Ministry of Finance and Economy (2001).
Note: Base value is 100.

From the macroeconomic indicators that show the economy on a recovery path, Korea seems to be pulling itself out of the financial crisis. Even so, the Korean people are still undergoing various hardships. There has been no clear indication, as yet, that Korea is completely out of the woods. The next section assesses the social impact of the economic crisis on employment.

3. UNEMPLOYMENT

The most obvious social effect of the crisis is in the form of increased unemployment, which mounted from total employment, (the unemployment rate was normally below 3.0 percent in the early 1990s) to an historical high unemployment rate of 8.6 percent in February 1999. Table II shows the unemployment rate recorded 6.8 percent in 1998, 6.3 percent in 1999, and 4.1 percent in 2000. It was still higher than the pre-crisis level. According to Kim (2001: p. 5), this was due to the shift in the direction of corporate strategy from one of growth in size to one of higher profitability, in which companies have been reluctant to hire new employees even with the

TABLE II

Unemployment Trend

	Unemployment rate (%)	Number of jobless (10,000)	Participation rate (%)
1996	2.0	42	62.0
1997	2.6	55	62.2
1998	6.8	146	60.7
1999	6.3	135	60.5
2000	4.1	89	60.7
Jan. 2001	4.6	98	—
Feb. 2001	5.0	107	—

Source: Ministry of Finance and Economy (2001).
Note: Percent change over the same month of last year.

economic boom evident since 1999. As a result, the number of the jobless in February 2001 totaled 1070000 increasing by 90000 from the preceding month. The unemployment rate in February 2001 registered 5.0 percent, which was an eleven month high since the rate stood at 4.7 percent in March 2000 (MOFE, 2001).

Furthermore, given the significant decline in the labor force participation rate since 1998, the unemployment problem is actually more pronounced than indicated by official statistics. As seen in Table II, the unemployment problem was moderated by a significant decline in the labor force participation rate from 62 percent to 60 percent. The decrease mainly resulted from the postponement of job searches by younger workers, and a substantial withdrawal from the labor force by discouraged female workers (IMF, 2000: p. 22). In addition, the official rate of unemployment does not include those engaged in compulsory national military service, or those employed in specially created public service projects, such as street cleaning and part-time public sector jobs (Kwon and O'Donnell, 1998: p. 279).

The composition of the ranks of the unemployment by specification of workers is more serious than the overall index indicates. Table III indicates a decline in full-time employment and a corresponding expansion in part-time employment since the crisis began

TABLE III

Employment Trend by Status Workers (Unit: 10000 and %)

	Regular workers		Temporary workers		Daily workers	
	Number	Percentage of the total workplace	Number	Percentage of the total workplace	Number	Percentage of the total workplace
1997	715	54.1	418	31.6	189	14.3
1998	645	53.0	399	32.8	173	14.2
1999	605	48.3	418	33.4	228	18.3
2000	625	47.5	451	34.3	237	18.1

Source: National Statistical Office, cited in Kim (2001: p. 9).

in 1997. The percentage of regular workers in the total number of workers declined by 6.6 percent in 2000 from 1997. Those number fell by 900 thousand for the same period. This is the lowest percentage of workers holding permanent contract in the OECD, followed by Turkey (OECD, 2000). On the contrary, the percentage of temporary workers and daily workers in the total number of workers increased by 2.7 percent and 3.8 percent for the same period, respectively. The average number of temporary workers rose to 330 thousand in 2000 from 1997 and that of daily workers also increased of 480 thousand for the same period (Kim, 2001: p. 8).

The number of employees who work less than 36 hours a week also increased. As seen in Table IV, the average percentage of employees who work less than 36 hours a week in the total number of employees amounted 9.9 percent in 2000, up 2.5 percent from 7.4 percent in 1997. On the other hand, the percentage of employees who work more than 36 hours a week fell to 90.1 percent in 2000 from 92.6 percent in 1997 (Kim, 2001: p. 9).

Unemployment for those in their forties and above has become more serious than that for other age groups. In January 2001 alone, while the unemployment rate for those in the teens, twenties, and thirties decreased, the unemployment rate for those in the forties increased by 16.6 percent and that of those in fifties increased by 17.4 percent (*Hankuk Ilbo* February 20, 2001). The increase of

TABLE IV

Employment Trend by Working Hours (Unit: 10000 and %)

	Less than 36 hours a week		More than 36 hours a week	
	Number	Percentage of the total workplace	Number	Percentage of the total workplace
1997	154	7.4	193	92.6
1998	185	9.4	178	90.6
1999	213	10.6	179	89.4
2000	206	9.9	187	90.1

Source: National Statistical Office, cited in Kim (2001: p. 9).

unemployment in this group, consisting mostly of family heads, amplifies the hardship caused by the crisis.

In addition, there is an underemployment problem. Table V shows that the rate of unemployment increased especially among workers of high school graduates. Before the crisis, the unemployment rate of workers with 12 years of schooling was slightly lower than the unemployment rate of those with a bachelor's degree or higher. In 1996, for example, unemployment rate was 1.1 percent for middle school or below graduates and 2.5 percent for high school graduates, while unemployment rate was 2.6 percent for college or above graduates. However, the unemployment rate of high school graduates was 0.3 to 2.5 percent point higher than that of college or above graduates during the period from 1997 to the end of 2000 (Kim, 2001: p. 9). This reflects the deterioration of occupations, with displaced college students settling for inferior jobs that used to be taken by high school graduates. In other words, the rate of underemployment has been on the rise along with the increase in the rate of unemployment (Lee and Lee, 2000: p. 73).

Such a high level of structural unemployment since 1998 represents a radical departure from past trends. The labor market situation has changed so drastically that it may be difficult to reverse it in the near future. Moreover, the problem of rising unemployment is aggravated for the poor by the lack of a strong social safety net and thus severely affects social cohesion. In the next section, we find

TABLE V

Unemployment Rate by Education Level (Unit: %)

	Middle school or below	High school	College or above	Total
1996	1.1	2.5	2.6	2.0
1997	1.5	3.3	3.0	2.6
1998	5.8	8.2	5.7	6.8
1999	5.2	7.6	5.3	6.3
2000	3.3	4.7	3.9	4.1

Source: National Statistical Office, cited in Kim (2001: p. 10).

that unemployment leads to a corresponding income reduction and increase in poverty as well as income inequality.

4. POVERTY AND INEQUALITY

According to data from the National Statistical Office for 1999, in tandem with rising unemployment, the real income of an urban household during the third quarter of 1998 had plunged to its lowest level in 35 years. Monthly household income of 1.76 million won at the time reflected a drop of 20 percent from the previous year. Table VI shows that the nominal wage that grew by 7.0 percent in 1997 dropped sharply after the crisis due to the deterioration of economic activity and the decline in labor demand. In 1998, the nominal wage rate decreased by 2.5 percent, consumer prices increased at a rate of 7.5 percent, and the real wage decreased by 10.0 percent on a year-to-year basis (Lee and Lee, 2000: p. 57).

Also, deflated income sled to a drastic drop in private household expenditures. Table VII indicates that the average monthly consumption expenditure of urban workers' households decreased 10.7 percent in 1998. In particular, expenditures for foodstuffs, clothing wear, education, culture, and recreation recorded a bigger decline than the average.

The number of homeless increased as well. For example, in September 1998, the number of homeless in Seoul amounted to 2550, which was an abrupt increase from the previous year when

TABLE VI

Changes in Wages and Consumer Price (Unit: %)

	Nominal wage	Consumer price	Real wage
1996	11.9	4.9	7.0
1997	7.0	4.5	2.5
1998	–2.5	7.5	–10.0
1999	—	0.8	—
2000	—	2.3	—

Source: Ministry of Labor, cited in Lee and Lee (2000: p. 76).
Note: Percentage change compared with the same period in the previous year for all industries.

TABLE VII

Changes in Monthly Consumption Expenditures of Urban Workers' Households (Unit: %)

	Total consumption	Foodstuffs	Clothing and footwear	Education culture, and recreation
1996	13.3	11.5	8.4	16.1
1997	4.2	5.0	–6.8	7.7
1998	–10.7	–14.8	–26.0	–12.0

Source: National Statistical Office, cited in Lee and Lee (2000: p. 79).
Note: Percentage change over corresponding period of previous year.

the total number of homeless hovered just around 100 (Lee and Lee, 2000: p. 77). Later, the number of homeless in Seoul was 4700 as of January 1999, falling to a low of 3300 in November 2000, which was still high (*Korea Times* November 16, 2000). Throughout the country, the current number of homeless is put at 6,000.

In addition, Table VIII presents the estimated national poverty rate, which rapidly increased by 16.3 percent in the first quarter of 1998, and peaked at 20.2 percent in the first quarter of 1999 (Bark, 2000).[2] Then, it began to fall down by 14.5 percent in the fourth quarter of 1999. However, this is a dramatic reversal of the trend of rapid poverty-reduction during the pre-crisis period, in which

TABLE VIII

Estimated National Poverty Rate (Unit: %)

		Poverty rate
1996		4.3
1997	1st Quarter	8.8
	2nd Quarter	7.2
	3rd Quarter	6.0
	4th Quarter	7.5
1998	1st Quarter	16.3
	2nd Quarter	17.0
	3rd Quarter	17.8
	4th Quarter	14.9
1999	1st Quarter	20.2
	2nd Quarter	20.0
	3rd Quarter	15.6
	4th Quarter	14.5

Source: Bark (2000).
Note: Poverty rate is based on the real value of the 1994's minimum cost of living.

the poverty rate among urban households was reduced from 20.4 percent in 1975 to 7.4 percent in 1995 (World Bank, 1998).

On the other hand, wages have been rising steadily since the beginning of 1999, reflecting a pick-up in economic activity and a rising demand by workers for increased pay to recover lost ground in 1998. Average wages per full-time worker have increased by about 5.5 percent in the first eight months of 1999 (IMF, 2000: p. 22). Income and household expenditures also increased 4.3 and 12.6 percent in 1999, and 7.3 and 9.1 percent in 2000, respectively, over the corresponding period of the previous year (MOFE, 2001).

Nevertheless, the impact of the crisis on the distribution of income has by no means been inconsequential. While decreasing incomes, skyrocketing prices, and growing household debt in 1998 imposed a harsh life on the majority of the population, high interest rate policy and deregulation of foreign currency benefited a small group of the rich who could continue to live off their bank deposits

TABLE IX

Trend in Nominal Income by quintile (Unit: thousand won)

	1st Quintile	2nd Quintile	3rd Quintile	4th Quintile	5th Quintile
1997	899	1467	1915	2514	3917
1998	757	1327	1768	2365	3754
1999	786	1362	1829	2455	3960
2000	862	1463	1962	2617	4165

Source: National Statistical Office, cited in Kim (2001: p. 11).

(Lee, 1998: p. 223). As a result, income disparity in Korea has been on the rise.

The Gini Coefficient indicates the deterioration of income distribution, continuing to rise from a stable level of 0.28–0.29 before the crisis to 0.317 in 2000 (Kim, 2001: p. 10).[3] In addition, the deteriorated income distributions structure can be plainly seen by the trend in nominal income. As seen in Table IX, the nominal income of the first two quintiles (the first being the lowest income bracket, the fifth being the highest) in 2000 decreased from those of 1997, whereas those of the last three quintiles increased during the same period. Moreover, the income of the fifth quintile in 1999 had already risen over that of 1997, although the income of the first two quintiles hardly surpassed its own figure of 1999 in 2000. Thus, the share of the upper 20 percent of income brackets rose to 40 percent of the total income of all income brackets in 2000 from 37 percent in 1997 (Kim, 2001: p. 11).

Amid the historically high records in unemployment, the gap in income between the rich and poor further widened in a country that had been proud of its heritage of growth with equity. Clearly, the unresolved problems of growing unemployment, depressed incomes for the working population, and a widening income gap remain. The next section analyzes the manner in which the Korean government tackled these issues, focusing on its unemployment insurance plan and other social welfare programs.

5. THE GOVERNMENT'S RESPONSE

The government has put in place various policy measures to address soaring unemployment problems since the outbreak of the crisis. The social safety net provided by the government for labor has included job creation, job retraining and placement, subsides for job keeping, unemployment insurance, and financial aid to subsistence households. For these unemployment countermeasures and support for the low-income class, the government allocated funds amounting to 21.7 trillion won, 10 trillion in 1998 and 11.7 trillion won in 1999 (MOL, 1999: p. 6).

To begin with, a total of 2.5 trillion won per year was spent to provide financial support for an annual average of 3000 thousand unemployed by creating short-term jobs through expansion of public works, such as database construction, forestry management, and repair and maintenance of school and social welfare facilities (MOL, 1999: p. 7). Funding for nearly half a million jobs was provided by local governments and public corporations, with 150 thousand jobs taken up in the late 1998. To facilitate the return of the unemployed into the workforce, the government also introduced a program of loans, of up to 30 million won, to support small and medium-sized business start-ups (IMF, 2000: p. 65).

Second, the government expanded the program of governmental sponsored vocational training, which was first introduced in 1995. The *Basic Vocational Training Act*, which imposed on employers a duty to provide vocational training, was replaced by the new *Workers' Vocational Training Promotion Act* in late 1997. The new program includes re-employment training for those covered by the employment insurance system and employment promotion for those not covered by the insurance system. Training courses were expanded to three courses that last from one month to one year in total; the government pays the full cost of the first course, one-half of the second course, and one-third of the final course (MOL, 1999). In 1998, the number of participants in these programs rose to 260 thousand, almost eight times the enrollment in the previous year, at a budgetary cost of 400 million won (*Chosun Ilbo* 1998 March 2). This level of support continued during 1999 with 280 thousand people enrolled in state-funded vocational training (IMF, 2000: p. 64).

Third, to avoid dismissals, the government provides various temporary wage subsidies to firms that avoid lay-offs. It offers subsidies for up to 8 months for employers who use temporary closures, paid leave, and reduction in working hours to avoid lay-offs. For example, one-half to two-thirds of an employee's wages was paid to those companies that retained workers on paid level, or for firms that sent workers for training (IMF, 2000: p. 65). Moreover, the other wage-related programs for workers became more generous. In July 1998, the Wage Claims Guarantee System was introduced to ensure that workers in bankrupt firms would receive pay for their last 3 months of work (MOL, 1999). The minimum wage system expanded its coverage from firms with more than five workers to all sizes of firms thank to the revised Minimum Wage Act, which took effected in November 2000. Its goal is to cope with the widening gap in income and to strengthen protection of workers in a small-sized workplace (Ko et al., 2000: p. 386).

Fourth, the unemployment insurance system, which was introduced in 1995 as a mandatory program that provided unemployment benefits for displaced workers, expanded its scope from companies with over 30 employees to all workplaces in October 1998. The eligibility requirement of three months' employment for coverage was also shortened to one month. In addition to increasing benefit coverage, the government doubled the minimum duration of benefits to 60 days and extended the maximum duration of benefits from seven to nine months (Lee, 1999).

Accordingly, the increased coverage and the extended duration of the insurance have provided valuable support to the causalities of the restructuring process. In the latter half of 1996, when unemployment insurance benefits were first paid out, the average number of beneficiaries was only 2579 per month. Yet, the figure surged to 75125 in the first half of 1998, recording a 479.9 percent increase over the second half of 1997. In the first half of 1999, when the unemployment rate was a record-high, the number of beneficiaries skyrocketed to 170682 per month (Kim, 2001: p. 25). Indeed, since the beginning of the massive unemployment in 1998, unemployment insurance benefits have played an important role as the foremost social safety net by protecting the livelihood of the jobless. The proportion of regular waged workers covered by the unemployment insurance system doubled from 33 percent to 70 percent (IMF, 2000: pp. 63–64).

Finally, the government has increased its efforts in providing more direct aid for those most needy in society who are left without support due to the incomplete coverage of unemployment benefits. This direct social assistance has been made available through the *Livelihood Protection Program* for those who are unable to work and have low income and few assets, such as the disabled elderly and children. The program includes assistance in paying for living and medical costs of about 1.92 million extremely poor people, who have been designated as targets for public assistance, with a budget of around 2 trillion in 1999 (MOL, 1999). Additionally, the government has adopted a number of other programs of social assistance, such as providing tuition support for children of the unemployed, housing subsidies, assistance in paying for medical insurance premiums, and free food programs for children, the elderly, and the disabled (IMF, 2000: p. 66). For example, in 1999, school expenses for 300 thousand middle and high school students were waived and paid for from public funds amounting to 200 billion won. Simultaneously, lunch money for 150 thousand middle and high school students who could not afford lunch was provided from public funds to 81.6 billion won (MOL, 1999).

Overall, public spending on the social safety net has increased substantially over the past three years. Safety net expenditures have roughly quadrupled compared with the pre-crisis levels, from 0.4 percent of the GDP in 1997 to 1.7 percent in 1999. Thus, social security spending began to eat up a considerable portion of the government's budget. Table X shows that, while the welfare budget had comprised about 4 percent of the general account until 1998, its portion of the general account increased to 4.9 percent and 7.1 percent in 1999 and 2000, respectively. The budget for the Livelihood Program had accounted for below 1 percent of the general account until 1998, but its proportion rose to 1.4 percent and 2.0 percent, in 1999 and 2000 (Kim, 2001: p. 14).

It is undeniable that some positive steps have been taken to reduce the impact of the crisis on workers and the poor. However, the question is how to fund these initiatives. The current restructuring of the financial system places a great deal of pressure on the domestic

TABLE X

Trend in Welfare Budget and General Account (Unit: billion won)

	Livelihood protection (a)	National pension	Welfare budget (b)	General account (c)	a/c (%)	b/c (%)
1996	360.6	16.8	2370.7	58822.8	0.6	4.0
1997	435.7	20.4	2851.2	67578.6	0.6	4.2
1998	574.9	53.7	3112.7	75582.9	0.8	4.1
1999	1135.3	72.9	4161.1	83685.2	1.4	4.9
2000	1727.8*	—	6199.7	86736.4	2.0	7.1

Source: Ministry of Health and Welfare, "The White Paper of Health and Welfare for 1999," "Chronicle of Health and Welfare Statistics for 1999," and "The Budget Plan for 2001," cited in Kim (2001: p. 14).
Note: *Budget for a minimum standard of living by "The Minimum Standard of Living Protection Law".

economy. An IMF estimate suggests that the costs of restructuring the banking system in Korea may run as high as 17.5 percent of the GDP, entailing an annual cost in terms of interest payments of about two percent of the GDP (ADB, 1999: p. 32). In this situation, the government's burden of welfare spending resulted in a sharp increase in its liabilities and fiscal debt. As seen in Table XI, the amount of the central government's liabilities rose to 100.9 trillion won, or 19.5 percent of the GDP in 2000. If the liabilities of the regional governments are included, the total national debt increased by 119.7 trillion won, or 23.1 percent of the GDP (Kim, 2001: p. 12). While the increased tax revenue in 2000 contributed to a fiscal surplus of 5.6 trillion won, or about 1.1 percent of the GDP, the fiscal deficit recorded the increase as 4.2 percent of GDP in 1998 and 2.7 percent in 1999 (Kim, 2001: p. 13).

Furthermore, unemployment countermeasures discussed here do not provide basic income support to all who seek it. Unlike industrialized countries, in which the role of social assistance constitutes a genuine social safety net, the programs in Korea offer relief to only a fraction of those in need. For example, although the unemployment insurance plan has evolved quickly, it still covers a small fraction of the unemployed. It is estimated that only 40 percent of the labor force is covered. The unemployment insurance scheme does not

TABLE XI

Trend in Government Liabilities (Unit: Trillion won, % against the GDP)

	Liabilities of the central government	Liabilities of regional governments	Total national debt
1996	36.8 (8.8)	12.9 (3.1)	49.7(12.0)
1997	50.5 (11.1)	15.1 (3.3)	65.6 (14.4)
1998	71.4 (15.9)	16.2 (3.6)	87.6 (19.5)
1999	90.1 (18.6)	18.0 (3.7)	108.1 (22.3)
2000	100.9 (19.5)	18.8 (3.6)	119.7 (23.1)

Source: Ministry of Finance and Economy, "Current Status of the National Debt and Countermeasures against It," 1999, "Measures to Control the National Debt and Fiscal Deficit," 2000, cited in Kim (2001: p. 12).

cover first-time job seekers and a large number of workers classified as daily workers. Moreover, despite the expanded coverage of the unemployment insurance system, its actual coverage and portion of beneficiaries are still low. The percentage of actual beneficiaries of the unemployment insurance system in the total number of the unemployment was very low, recording 9.6 percent as of June 2000. Also, the system legally covers temporary workers who work more than one month, but, in reality, most small companies cannot afford to pay the insurance premium (Kim, 2001: p. 125). In addition, the system tends to benefit relatively well-off workers, those laid off from the modern sector firms (Park, 1999).

6. CONCLUSION

The sudden outbreak of the Korean economic miracle has imperiled social stability. Millions who labored to forge the miracle have become bewildered victims of the unfolding economic collapse and post-crisis restructuring process. Companies have suffered bankruptcy in increasing numbers over the course of the year. This coupled with massive unemployment with few safety provisions along with a sharp rise in the cost of living has resulted in social unrest. Conflicts between employers and employees over lay-offs are common. Several strikes and labor violence have already been reported. For instance, in April 2000, thousand of workers at Daewoo Motors demanded that the government scrap a plan to sell the operation to a foreign company. The protest resulted in a bloody conflict between demonstrators and the police. Failure to cope with the social implications may lead to large-scale social unrest which is likely undermine the necessary restructuring and program of austerity measures. Thus, a fundamental rethinking of the social dimension of economic development is important as the purely economic issues.[4]

At the same time, the crisis itself is in need of a major economic restructuring and thus can be an opportunity for the nation to push toward new social developmental strategies. As seen in Section 2, the latest economic data for Korea show a more optimistic view of the economy, with strong signs of recovery. Employment-generating schemes and special credit schemes for small companies are expanding. In contrast with Thailand, Indonesia, and Malaysia, Korea is the only 1997 crisis-plagued country in Asia with an unemployment insurance system. Furthermore, a substantially high proportion of those in need in Korea have been covered by the combination of active and passive measures based on the concept of "productive welfare," which came into effect in October 2000 as a newly reformed social assistance system.

However, the contributory unemployment insurance benefits are still beyond the reach of most of the poor people, and a non-contributory public assistance program is vastly limited in terms of coverage of the population and its level of benefits. Facing a daunting task in reconstructing its economy and social safety nets, Korea will probably take some time before it is rid of its economic woes. The impact of the crisis on overall economic and social development may be much larger than previously thought although the exact extent is difficult to measure. In particular, the unemployment rate will remain high for a long period even after the economy recovers from the worst of the crisis. Therefore, special efforts to strengthen the system of social protection are of great necessity.

NOTES

[1] The Human Development Index (HDI) is based on three national indicators of longevity (life expectancy), knowledge (adult literacy and mean years of schooling), and standard of living (purchasing power based on real GDP per capita adjusted for the local cost of living). Yet, although HDI shows basic picture of social development, it focuses on only a few standard indicators, which are closely linked to education and public health. Other indicators such as unemployment, poverty, and income inequality are also important for measuring human development.

[2] Since the Korean government produces national income data covering the whole population every five years. Researchers have a limitation in analyzing an annual national poverty rate. Hence, different researchers present different poverty rates, based on other complementary data sets. Here, Bark (2000) estimates the national poverty rate, based on the Family Income and Expenditure Survey (FIES), which includes only urban workers. He assumes that relationship between national poverty rate and poverty rate of the urban workers' households keeps constant for the year of 1996.

[3] The Gini Coefficient is a popular way of measuring inequality used by economists and policy analysis. It ranges from 0 (perfect equality-income evenly spread across quintiles) to 1 (absolutely inequality): the higher the Gini Coefficient, the more unequal the distribution.

[4] Generally, the economic crisis and structural adjustment policies have created severe hardship in many countries, especially having a severe impact on poor and vulnerable groups. Concern for these groups has led the United Nations Children's Fund (UNICEF) to call for "adjustment with a human face" and to urge governments to devise safety nets and programs to protect those most likely to be harmed by structural adjustment policies. (Cornia et al., 1987).

REFERENCES

Asia Development Bank (ADB): 1999, Asian Development Bank Outlook 1999 (Oxford University Press, Oxford).

Asia Development Bank (ADB): 2001, 'Republic of Korea', http://www.adb.org/Documents/Books/ADO/2001/kor.

Bark, S.I.: 2000, A Study on Causes of the Increasing Income Gap and Policy Measures for the Low Income Classes (Korea Institute for Health and Social Affairs).

Chang, H.J.: 1998, 'Korea: The misunderstood crisis', World Development 26(8), pp. 1555–1561.

Cornia, G.A., R. Jolly and F. Stewart: 1987, Adjustment with a Human Face (Clarendon Press, Oxford).

Garron, R.: 1998, Tigers Tamed: The End of the Asian Miracle (University of Hawaii Press, Honolulu).

Goldstein, M.: 1998, The Asian Financial Crisis: Causes, Cures, and Systemic Implication (Institute for International Economics, Washington, DC).
Haggard, S.: 2000, The Political Economy of the Asian Financial Economy (Institute for International Economics, Washington, DC).
Hoa, T.V.: 2000, The Social Impact of the Asia Crisis (Palgrave, New York).
International Monetary Fund (IMF): 1998, World Economic Outlook (IMF, Washington, DC).
International Monetary Fund (IMF): 2000, Republic of Korea: Economic and Policy Developments, IMF Staff Country Report No. 00/11. (IMF, Washington, DC).
Kim, K.H., and D.M. Leipziger: 1997, Korea: A case of government-led development', in Ed. D. Kim and Danny M. Leipziger (eds.), Lessons from East Asia (University of Michigan Press, Ann Arbor).
Kim, K.W.: 2001, Three Years after the IMF Bailout: A Review of the Korean Economy's Transformation since 1998 (Samsung Economic Research Institute, Seoul).
Ko, J.M., Y.I. So and W.K. Choi: 2000, New challenges of the Korean economy', The Journal of East Asian Affairs 14(2), pp. 364–405.
Kwon, S.H., and M. O'Donnell: 1999, 'Repression and Struggle: The state, the chaebol, and independent trade unions in South Korea', The Journal of Industrial Relations 41(2), pp. 272–293.
Lee, H.K.: 1999, 'Globalization and the emerging welfare state: The experience of South Korea', International Journal of Social Welfare 8, pp. 23–37.
Lee, S.H.: 1998, 'Crisis in Korea and the IMF control', in Eun Mee Kim (ed.), The Four Tigers: Economic Development and the Global Political Economy (Academic Press, San Diego).
Lee, Y.Y. and H.H. Lee: 2000, 'Korea: Financial crisis, structural reform and social consequences', in Tran Van Hoa (ed.), The Social Impact of the Asia Crisis (Palgrave, New York).
Ministry of Finance and Economy (MOFE): 2001, Recent Economic Trends: No. 43 (MOFE, Seoul).
Ministry of Health and Welfare (MOHW): 1999, Yearbook of Health and Welfare Statistics (MOHW, Seoul).
Ministry of Labor (MOL): 1999, Labor Market Policy Measures and Labor Relations Reform in Korea (MOL, Seoul).
Organization for Economic Cooperation and Development (OECD): 2000, 'Korea: Better social policies for a stronger economy', http://oecdobserver.org/news/fullstory.php/aid/372.
Park, T.W.: 1999, 'South Korea in 1999: Swallowing the bitter pills of restructuring', Asian Survey 39(1), pp. 133–147.
Park, S.I.: 1999, 'Labor market reform and the social safety net in Korea', in Korea and the Asian Economic Crisis: One Year Later (Korea Economic Institute of America, Seoul).
Pempel, T.J.: 1999, The Politics of the Asian Economic Crisis (Cornell University Press, Ithaca).

Radelet, S. and J. Sachs: 1998, 'The East Asian financial crisis: diagnosis, remedies, prospects', Brooking Papers on Economic Activity 1, pp. 1–90 (Brookings Institution, Washington, DC).

United Nations Development Programme (UNDP): 1999, Human Development Report (Oxford University Press, New York).

Wade, R.: 2000, 'Gestalt shift: From miracle to cronyism in the Asian crisis', in Leonardo Burlamaqui, Ana Celia Castro and H.J. Chang (eds.), Institutions and Role of the State (Edward Elgar, Cheltenham).

World Bank: 1998, Social Policy and Governance, http://www.worldbank.org/eapsocial/countries/korea/.

World Bank: 1999, World Development Indicators 1999 (Oxford University Press, New York).

Department of Political Science
University of Missouri – Columbia
Columbia, MO 65201
USA
E-mail: Jj41c@mizzou.edu

DOH CHULL SHIN and JUNHAN LEE

DEMOCRATIZATION AND ITS CONSEQUENCES

ABSTRACT. This article addresses the significant consequences of democratic changes in Korea, not only for the way the country is governed, but also the way in which its people lead their lives. Institutionally, the first decade of democratization fully transformed a military dictatorship into a functioning representative democracy. Procedurally, it redirected the goal of policymaking toward the promotion of economic justice, social welfare, and quality of life. Substantively, democratic reforms expanded political freedom and reinvigorated civil society. As in the authoritarian past, however, the country still suffers from the imbalance of power between the president and the National Assembly. There are also serious deficiencies in the rule of law, and a need for a proper restraint on executive power. As a result, the Korean people, as a whole, remain more dissatisfied than satisfied with the way the current system of democratic governance performs.

> Democracy's claim to be valuable does not rest on just one particular merit. There is a plurality of virtues here, including, first, the intrinsic importance of political participation and freedom in human life; second, the instrumental importance of political incentives in keeping governments responsible and accountable; and third, the constructive role of democracy in the formation of values and in the understanding of needs, rights, and duties.
>
> Amartya Sen, 1999

> In repressive regimes, there is not much talk about injustices. In authoritarian regimes, poverty is hidden. In nondemocratic regimes, information tends to be unclear. In open and democratic regimes, in contrast, the insistence on revealing what is wrong, revealing injustices, revealing inequalities, and urging that all this be corrected paves the way for finding solutions to these problems, even if they cannot be solved immediately.
>
> Fernando Henrique Cardoso, 2001

Throughout human history, democracy has most often been regarded as the form of government that is essential to the improvement

Social Indicators Research **62, 63:** 71–92, 2003.

of citizens' lives (Dahl, 1998; Sen, 1999). Unlike other forms of governments, democracy allows individual citizens to pursue freely what they cherish for their own personal lives. Holding competitive and free elections on a regular basis, democracy also requires political leaders to implement policies that would benefit a majority rather than a minority (Cardoso, 2001; Powell, 1982). Citizens of democracies, therefore, tend to experience a significantly greater quality of life than those of non-democracies (Leftwich, 1998; Shin, 1989).

Korea is one of over five dozen countries that have recently transformed autocratic rule into a democracy in order to improve the quality of their citizens' lives. As in many of its peers in the current, third wave of democratization, democracy in Korea evolved out of a military dictatorship (Huntington, 1991). During the period 1987–88, the military dictatorship, headed by former general Chun Doo Hwan, was transformed into a democratic state headed by a popularly elected president. In 1992, the country elected its first civilian political leader, in more than three decades, as its president. In 1997, the leader of an opposition party was elected as the president of the country for the first time in its political history. Obviously, these changes have brought about a number of significant consequences not only for the way the country is governed, but also the way its people live their lives.

This study is intended to examine the democratization of the Korean political system, and its major consequences for the way the country is governed. It will also look at the way ordinary individuals live as citizens of a democratic state. The study will first highlight the distinguishing features of its previous military dictatorship. It will then discuss how much progress the Korean people believe has been achieved in democratizing the institutions and procedures of military rule. It will also examine how well Koreans think the current political system performs as a government by the people and for the people. Afterwards, the study will assess the consequences of democratization for civic life and policymaking. Finally, this chapter summarizes and highlights key findings about the changing nature of political life in Korea.

KEY FEATURES OF AUTHORITARIAN RULE

Korea remained a prototype of the developmental state for nearly three decades prior to the advent of democracy (Moon, 1994). In 1961, Park Chung Hee seized political power through a military coup and instituted a developmental dictatorship, which lasted until 1987. At the time of the military coup, Korea was one of the world's poorest countries, plagued by protracted poverty and unending security threats from the Communist North. In order to achieve economic development and national security, Park created a developmental state by undertaking a series of institutional and policy reforms, which subsequently transformed the subsistence agricultural economy into an economy based on manufactured exports.

Politically, the Korean developmental state provided the president with unprecedented and unlimited powers, both executive and legislative in character (Lim, 1998). By allowing the president to appoint one-third of its members, Park's Yushin constitution (1972–79) guaranteed executive control of the National Assembly. In fact, President Park Chung Hee exercised unlimited power to the extent which he dissolved the National Assembly and took emergency measures, whenever he deemed it necessary for public safety and national security. Under his rule, it was the technocrats and bureaucrats, not elected officials, who played the key role in the policymaking process. Those technocrats and bureaucrats, moreover, were completely insulated from partisan politics and social pressures. Through the Korean Central Intelligence, the police, and other security agencies, Park Chung Hee and Chun Doo Hwan, Park's successor, were also able to control political and civil society. Such harsh authoritarian rule of coercion, intimidation, and threats attained political stability, which, in turn, induced foreign capital and investment for economic development.

Economically, the Korean developmental state was equivalent to the "hard state" described by Gunnar Myrdal. It was capable of actively promoting fast-paced industrialization. It was able to define national priorities through five-year economic plans, and enforce the annual development programs through direct intervention in the private sector. In a single generation, the developmental state controlled by the military, successfully transformed a poverty-stricken country into an economic powerhouse. While authoritarian rule was responsible for economic development, this very process of development hastened its collapse. It sponsored prosperity fueled popular demands for freedom and democratic rule (Shin, 1999). Unlike the Latin American cases, the Korean military rule came to an end not because of economic downturns, but because of economic prosperity.

DEMOCRATIC PROGRESS: PUBLIC ASSESSMENTS

Since the demise of military rule in 1988, however, Korea has been rapidly becoming a politically new state. Over a relatively short period, the country has successfully carried out a series of sweeping democratic reforms (Diamond and Shin, 2000). These reforms expanded civil liberties and political rights by downsizing and overhauling the various security agencies, which meddled in every important decision of both government and private organizations, and controlled the behavior of private citizens. The reforms also firmly established civilian control over the military by purging military generals and disbanding secret societies within the military establishment (Steinberg, 2000).

Accordingly, Korean democracy today meets the criteria of procedural democracy or polyarchy as specified by Dahl (1971) and many other scholars (Rose et al., 1998; Schmitter and Karl, 1991): a political regime characterized by free and fair elections, universal adult suffrage, multiparty competition, civil liberties, and a free press. In the words of Kim Byung-Kook (2000: p. 52), "electoral politics has become the only possible game in town for resolving political conflicts."

Indeed, Korea has been more successful than many of its democratizing predecessors and contemporaries in transforming its authoritarian political institutions and culture (Im, 2000). Unlike many new democracies in Latin America, Korea has fully restored civilian rule by extricating the military from power, and has fully established the minimal infrastructure of procedural democracy. The country has also become the first new democracy in Asia that peacefully transferred power to an opposition party. Therefore, in the Western media and scholarly community today Korea is mentioned increasingly as a possible model of democratization for the emerging post-authoritarian countries in the world (*New York Times*, 1998; *Wall Street Journal*, 1992).

Nonetheless, Korea's remarkable success in democratization still remains largely unexplored from the perspective of ordinary citizens, who have experienced democratic political life on a daily basis. To examine their perceptions and assessments of democratization in Korea, three sets of items were selected from the Korea Democracy Barometer (hereinafter the KDB) survey conducted in November 1999. For this survey, the Gallup Poll in Seoul, Korea conducted face-to-face interviews with a representative sample of 1007 voters age 20 and older (for survey methodology, see Shin, 1999).

Institutional Democratization

The 1999 KDB survey asked respondents to rate their current and past political systems on a 10-point ladder scale (for the wording of this and other questions, see Appendix A). This scale allows participants to respond according to their own understanding of democracy and dictatorship. A score of 1 on this scale indicates "complete dictatorship," while a score of 10 indicates "complete democracy." Responses to this question, as reported in Table I, provide two important pieces of information concerning the perceived character of the old authoritarian and new democratic systems. For the two systems, Table I provides the percentage of respondents who choose each of the ten positions or steps on the ladder scale. As the data in this table reveals, a vast majority (87%) rated the past regime as undemocratic by placing it at 5 or below. In sharp contrast, a substantial majority (68%) rated the current regime as democratic by placing it at 6 or above. These figures, when compared, make it clear that the military authoritarian rule of three decades has been transformed into a democracy.

Table I also gives the average ratings on this scale for the current democratic and past authoritarian systems. Like the percentage ratings, the average ratings for the current system are indicative of the extent to which the mass public embraces it as democratic. The average rating of the past regime was 3.9; for the present regime, however, the average increased to 5.9. This shift in the mean ratings

TABLE I

Perceptions of the Current and Past Political Systems

Scale points	Distribution (%)	
	Past regime (1980–88)	Current regime (1998–present)
1 (complete dictatorship)	10.5	0.9
2	17.3	0.8
3	19.8	5.1
‘4	18.8	5.5
5	20.3	19.3
6	8.8	32.3
7	2.9	22.5
8	1.2	10.5
9	0.3	2.3
10 (complete democracy)	0.1	0.5
(mean score)	3.9	5.9

Source: 1999 Korea Democracy Barometer Survey.

confirms considerable progress in institutional democratization in the wake of the democratic regime change in 1998. The mean rating of 5.9 for the present system on a 10-point scale, however, suggests that Korean democracy is highly limited even after more than a decade of democratic rule.

Substantive Democratization

A second pair of key questions asked in the 1999 KDB survey deals with how well the current political system performs as a democracy. Democratization has to bring about significant improvements in the extent to which a political system responds to its citizens. In addition, it should bring about similar changes to enable the masses to get involved in the making of public policies. The empowerment of ordinary citizens and the responsiveness of a political system to their preferences are at the core of substantive democratization.

Respondents to the 1999 survey were asked: How much influence do you think the votes of people like yourself have on the way our country is governed: a lot, some, a little, or none? To what extent do you think government leaders take the interests and opin-

TABLE II

Citizen Empowerment and System Responsiveness

Scale points	Citizen empowerment	System responsiveness
A lot	32.1%	3.1%
Some	44.3	23.7
A little	20.5	51.1
None	1.6	19.7
(no answer)	1.4	2.4

Source: 1999 Korea Democracy Survey.

ions of people like yourself into account when making important decisions: a lot, some, a little, or none? Table II shows the distribution of respondents across four different levels of empowerment and system responsiveness. Based on the nature of these distributions, we can determine how positively respondents feel about themselves as citizens of a democratic state and their own state as a democracy.

A large majority (76%) reported feeling at least some amount of empowerment under the present system of government. This suggests that Koreans tend to feel that they have a way to express their opinions and promote their interests under the present system. Unfortunately, a large majority (71%), nonetheless, reported that the system is only a little, or not at all, responsive. This suggests that although the people have the ability to express their opinions, they do not perceive the government as being responsive to them.

Table III collapses four different levels of democratic experiences into two broad categories, one affirming and the other denying the experience of those two substantive qualities of democratic governance. By jointly considering these two categories of empowerment and responsiveness, four patterns were discerned to examine the deepening presence of democracy in the substance of policymaking. The first pattern refers to the absence of either quality. The second and third patterns refer to the presence of only one of those two qualities, which indicates a partial achievement of substantive democratization. The fourth pattern, on the other hand, refers to the presence of both qualities, attesting to the achievement of substantive democratization to the fullest degree. The particular

TABLE III

Experience of Substantive Democracy

Types of experience		Distribution
empowerment	responsiveness	(percent)
No	No	17.1
No	Yes	4.8
Yes	No	52.8
Yes	Yes	21.7
(no answer)		3.6

Source: 1999 Korea Democracy Barometer Survey.

pattern in which a majority or a plurality of Korean voters place them indicates how well or poorly the current political system works as the government by the people as well as for the people. Table III reveals that a majority (53%) felt that they were empowered in the new system, but that this system was not responsive to their interests.

To assess the overall quality of its substantive performance as a democracy, the 1999 KDB survey also asked respondents how satisfied or dissatisfied they were with the way democracy works in their country today. On a 10-point scale, where 1 means complete dissatisfaction and 10 means complete satisfaction, respondents were asked to express the degree of their satisfaction or dissatisfaction with the current practice of democratic politics. Table IV provides the mean rating on this scale and the percentages of those placed at each of its 10 scale points. As this figure shows, a minority of 42 percent expressed satisfaction with the present regime with its placement at 6 or above on the scale. The mean score of 5.2 reinforces this qualified response. Being lower than the midpoint (5.5) of the 10-point scale, the mean score indicates clearly that the Korean people as a whole are more dissatisfied than satisfied with the way the present democratic system performs.

Overall Patterns of Democratizing Authoritarian Rule

We can make a comprehensive and balanced account of Korean democratization only when we jointly consider positive and negative

TABLE IV

Evaluation of the Performance of the Present Political System

Scale points	Current regime (1998–present)
1 (complete dissatisfaction)	1.5
2	5.0
3	6.7
4	10.5
5	34.1
6	25.8
7	10.4
8	3.7
9	1.7
10 (complete satisfaction)	0.7
(mean score)	5.2

Source: 1999 Korea Democracy Barometer Survey.

assessments of its substantive performance with democratic and authoritarian perceptions of its institutional character. In Table V, these perceptions and assessments are classified into four distinct patterns of democratization. The first pattern features a lack of progress in either the institutional or the substantive domain of democracy. The second and third patterns represent partial progress with the advancement of one of these two domains. The fourth pattern represents democratic progress on a full scale as evidenced in both domains. These patterns make it possible to unravel the dynamics of democratization and its distinctive characteristics.

As the data in Table V shows, one-fourth (25%) judged their political system as neither democratic nor functioning to their satisfaction. A much smaller minority (7%) judged it as undemocratic, but functioning to their satisfaction. One-third (33%) judged it as democratic, but failing to function to their satisfaction. Slightly over one-third (36%) were fully positive about the character as well as performance of their current political system. To a large majority, the Korean political system today does not represent a well-functioning democracy. If a democratic regime is to become enduringly legitimated in Korea, and thus consolidated, it must be

TABLE V

Overall patterns of Popular Assessments of Democratization in Korea

Democratic character	Satisfying performance	Distribution (percent)
No	No	25.3%
No	Yes	6.8
Yes	No	32.5
Yes	Yes	35.5

Source: 1999 Korea Democracy Barometer Survey.

seen by a larger proportion of its people to be delivering on its political promise of freedom, accountability, responsiveness, and respect for the constitution (Chu et al., 2001).

CONSEQUENCES FOR CITIZENS AND POLITICAL LEADERS

The advent of democracy in Korea has affected the way ordinary Koreans live their lives as citizens of a democratic state. It has also affected the way political leaders respond to citizen preferences and formulate public policy. This section focuses on the consequences of democratization for the mode of civic life among ordinary Koreans, and that of policymaking among politicians and public officials.

Participation of Civic Life

Under the pretext of national security and anti-Communism, the military dictatorships, headed by former generals Park Chung Hee and Chun Doo Hwan, suppressed political opposition and controlled the news media and civic organizations (S. Kim, 2000). By invoking the National Security and Anti-Communist laws, the military regimes substantially curtailed freedom of expression and association among individual citizens and their civic associations. By mobilizing security agencies, such as the Korean Central Agency and the National Security Command, those regimes placed the news media under strict censure, and labor unions and educational institutions under constant surveillance. Moreover, the regimes even controlled opposition parties and other non-political civic and business organizations through a variety of tactics including those of co-optation and intimidation. By suppressing political opposition and not allowing individual citizens and civic groups to take part in the political process, the military dictatorship not only shielded economic policymaking from politicization, but also insulated it from the pressures of social and political groups (Moon and Kim, 1998).

Democracy, as government by the people, is predicated on active involvement in public affairs. Allowing individual citizens and their associations to take part in public affairs, democratization in Korea during the past decade has transformed the way in which policies used to be made under the military regimes. The implementation of various institutional reforms has virtually ended state control over civil society. With the abolition of the Basic Press Laws and other regulations that were used to control public protest and censure the new media, freedom of expression and association has been restored. The institutionalization of free and fair elections in both local and central governments has also expanded the involvement of the mass public in electoral politics and policymaking. Farmers, factory workers, women, the elderly, the urban poor, businessmen, and journalists have all formed new public interests groups as balancing forces against the existing government-controlled representational organization. As of 2000, 6159 non-governmental organizations are known to operate in Korea (Lim, 2000). The unprecedented expansion of civil society has produced a high level of political activism. As a result, civic associations and interest groups have become formidable players in economic policymaking in democratic Korea. In general, democratization has transformed the policymaking process into an open and contentious realm of mass politics by allowing those groups, formerly excluded by the military regimes, to participate in it.

Civic associations and interest groups employ a variety of methods to influence the process of legislation in the National Assembly (Lee, 2001). In every Assembly election, these groups and associations recruit and support as their own candidates, the people who would represent their legislative preferences. In the 15th National Assembly (1996–2000), for example, 82 of 299 lawmakers were known to actively represent associations of lawyers

(20), businessmen (10), educators (10), doctors (7), pharmacists (5), and other citizen groups. These civic associations and interest groups influence the legislative process in the National Assembly by providing political funds to its individual members and their political parties; they also influence the process by regularly attending the Assembly's public hearings, and providing relevant information to its committees.

In addition, they regularly submit petitions to those committees for legislative consideration. The 15th National Assembly received a total of 5426 petitions from various citizen organizations and acted on 5090 (Lee, 2001). Besides submitting petitions for or against a particular piece of legislation under consideration, they adopted and issued public statements or resolutions for the purpose of informing public opinion in favor of their policy position. They sometimes engage in demonstrations or sit-ins to protest the passage of a bill that would be considered harmful to their cause. Environmentalist groups alone, for example, took part in 20 demonstrations or sit-ins, protesting legislative actions during the 1995–2000 period.

Cycles of free and competitive elections have forced politicians to alter their survival strategy. To get re-elected, all office holders have had to seek the support of their hometown voters instead of relying solely on the owners of the *chaebols*. The replacement of the indirect presidential election by a direct one has dissolved the authoritarian ruling bloc known as the growth-oriented coalition composed of industrialists, generals, and bureaucratic elites. Since the ultimate survival of every president and his political party depends on maintaining support from the electorate, the former is compelled to distribute jobs and budget lines to his local supporters in exchange for electing him.

As Jang Soo Chan's (2000) analysis of coalition politics over the past three decades reveals, procedural democracy in Korea since 1988 has developed a new form of coalition politics by inserting pork barrel politics between elected officials and their region-based constituents. Under the existing system of democratic governance, therefore, public policies are now driven, as much by a winning electoral formula of forming region-based coalitions in terms of votes and contributions, as by economic rationality or bureaucratic prerogatives.

In the April 2000 parliamentary elections, a new form of citizen movement was formed to democratize the electoral process by challenging the lawmakers of both the ruling and opposition parties, who thus far had refused to reform the undemocratic election law. Three months before the 16th parliamentary elections held on April 13, 2000, about 500 civic organizations joined together to form the Citizens' Alliance for the 2000 General Elections (hereinafter the CAGE) to reform and democratize the electoral and party systems (Leem, 2000). Specifically, the CAGE, which was often dubbed "a voters' revolution," strove to prevent political parties from nominating "unfit" candidates for the forthcoming elections, and they also tried to discourage citizens from voting for those who were nominated despite being blacklisted (Choi, 2000). It was a direct challenge to the popularly elected National Assembly, one that refused to revise the election law. It was a demand for reforms in the legislature and political parties, entities that failed to serve as effective institutions representing the electorate. It was also a demand that individual members of the National Assembly meet the basic moral standards of democratic political life, not to mention its procedural norms.

The CAGE movement was led by members of the younger generation of the Korean population, those in their 30s, who played a key role in the democratization movement of the 1980s. The movement carried out a two-phase campaign. It first announced a list of politicians "unfit" for membership in the National Assembly. This directly challenged the power of party bosses, who had the ultimate authority to hand-pick the candidates of their party. It led to the breakup of the main opposition – the Grand National Party. In the second phase, the CAGE movement held a series of street rallies to dissuade the voters from supporting candidates, who were on its blacklist. Sometimes the civic activists had to silently endure physical assaults on the campaign trial. The final outcome was a stunning defeat ratio of nearly 70 percent: 59 out of the 86 blacklisted candidates lost their races.

Undoubtedly, this civic movement to create a more effective system of representation had its own limitations. Being a negative campaign to eliminate politicians, who were considered unfit to run for the National Assembly, it fell short of offering more meaningful alternatives. Its criteria for judgment were often challenged because of their lack of objectivity. Still, the movement contributed tremendously to raising awareness of the principle that politicians should keep clean records in their public and private lives. It published the sordid records of candidates, who were convicted of crimes of various kinds, including draft dodging, tax evasion, and domestic assaults. The group also made public important information about the candidates' absences from parliamentary sessions and their opposition to democratic reforms.

Besides defeating unfit candidates, the CAGE played the major role in recalling the lawmakers for an extraordinary parliamentary session to review a legislative bill that they had already passed, involving a readjustment of legislative district lines with blatant instances of gerrymandering. Equally noteworthy, is the fact that CAGE's groups continue to monitor the activities of the National Assembly and its individual members. By demonstrating and instilling good citizenship among ordinary citizens, and encouraging their representatives to be accountable and responsive to themselves, the CAGE opened a new chapter in Korean democratization. Institutionally, the movement is significant for displacing the unsatisfactory reformative role of the state during the period of democratic consolidation (Choi, 2000). Culturally, it is also significant for invigorating the passive political culture that keeps the voters from becoming informed of the legislative activities of their representatives.

Policymaking

Ideology as a new vision or superstructure for a good society shapes the formulation of those policies more consistently and coherently than environmental factors or institutional apparatus (Moon, 1999). As a coherent system of beliefs and values, ideology guides political leaders and experts to the foremost goals and appropriate means of economic policymaking. The ideals of democratic politics are, therefore, highly capable of transforming the particular style of economic management not only by shaping an ideological landscape or a dominant paradigm itself, but also by undermining the legitimacy of old authoritarian institutions.

During the period of rapid economic growth in the 1970s and 1980s, Korea's economic policymaking was guided by the ideology of *dirigisme* that combined developmentalism with Keynesian expansionism. The country had to escape poverty and defend itself against Communist North Korea. President Park Chung Hee adopted economic growth and industrialization as the supreme goals of economic policymaking and President Chun Doo Hwan followed suit. As Moon Chung-in (1999) aptly points out, the old Japanese nationalist ideology of "rich nation, strong army" re-emerged as the dominant paradigm in Korea, dictating the nature and direction of its economic management.

In the wake of the economic slowdown during the early 1980s, the ideology of developmentalism began to lose steam. The founding of the democratic Sixth Republic in 1988 formally put an end to the era of *dirigisme* in Korean politics. Subsequent institutional reforms and competitive elections at the national and local levels occasioned policymakers and ordinary citizens to embrace the ideals of democratic politics and put those ideas into political practice. This shift in new ideological and political templates necessitated fundamental changes in economic institutions and management styles.

Associated with democratic ideology are ideas of economic justice, social welfare, and redistribution. During democratic regime change in 1988, the developmentalist ideology, couched in terms of national prosperity and security, was devalued as economic growth and national security could no longer serve as its political *raison d'etre* (Jang, 2000). Popular demands for redistribution, welfare, quality of life, and environmental safety have constituted new political and ideological mandates. In democratic Korea, the values of individual freedom, equality, justice, and welfare have replaced those of *dirigisme* and mercantilism. The competitive popular election of political leaders required policymakers to incorporate popular demands for economic redistribution as critical components of their economic programs. Consequently, the old economic policy that required the state to intervene actively in strategic industries was relinquished as a way of solving the age-old problems of disparities in income and wealth across the various segments and sectors of the Korean economy.

A careful content analysis of presidential inaugural speeches by Jang Soo Chan (2000) confirms such a shift in policy priorities. Presidents Park Chung Hee and Chun Doo Hwan, under military rule, emphasized "economic growth and stability" as the top policy priority in economic policymaking. Presidents Roh Tae Woo and Kim Young Sam, under democratic rule, on the other hand, were equally devoted to the issues of economic growth and distribution. In several ways, the democratic institutional changes and the expansion of civil society altered the ideological template, and thereby reshaped the nature and direction of economic policymaking and management. While Presidents Park Chung Hee and Chun Doo Hwan were obsessed with economic growth and industrialization, their successors were forced to deal with distributional issues.

As Kim Jun Il and Mo Jongryn (1999) observe, no change in economic policymaking has been as significant as that of redirecting economic policy toward redistribution and social welfare. Democratization has opened the process of policymaking to those groups that were excluded by the authoritarian regime. As soon as labor unions, farmers, and small-and medium-size enterprises were allowed to participate in policymaking processes, social welfare and redistribution became the most salient economic issues. As the policymaking process increasingly became more open, decentralized, participatory, and contentious under democratic rule, elected officials as well as technocrats had to respond to popular demands for equity and welfare.

According to Kim and Mo's recent analysis of governmental expenditures, in the aftermath of the democratic regime change in 1988, these expenditures increased rapidly. From 1990 to 1994, for example, central government expenditures as a share of the GDP rose from 18.5 to 19.7 percent. More notable was the sharp increase in the proportionate share of social services in a short period. Social services, as a share of central government expenditures, rose from 12.5 percent in 1986 to 20.0 percent in 1991. According to an article recently published in the *Chosun Ilbo* (January 27, 2001), the welfare budget had more than doubled over the past three years (J. Lee, 2001). The welfare budge for the fiscal year 2001 is 8.1438 trillion won, which amounts to 8.6 percent of the total national government budget. This percentage figure is more than two times as large as the 4.1 percent figure for the fiscal year 1998. This increase in rate in welfare services is known to be much higher than what has happened to the GDP and tax revenues over the past three years. The main reason for such a steep increase is known to be for "the basic life guarantee subsidy" program introduced October 1997. This program is designed to provide those four-person families in the lowest income bracket with 940000 won ($800) per month.

In addition to this program for the poorest segment of the Korean population, the successive governments under democratic rule have undertaken a series of programs benefiting the middle- and low-income population. First, efficient vocational training programs and a new credit guarantee system for low-income workers was introduced. Second, the mandatory holding period of employee stock-ownership was reduced to provide workers with more money revenue options. Third, low interest rate loans were expanded for farmers and fisherman. Fourth, minimum livelihood benefits for low-income workers, the elderly and physically disabled are now guaranteed. Fifth, employment insurance for all workplaces, regardless of the number of employees, was expanded, and the national fund has been extended to society at large. Other social insurance programs, including medical insurance and industrial accident compensation insurance, have eased their eligibility requirements. Finally, maternity leave for female workers has been implemented.

More recently, the government has implemented various policy measures to address the soaring problems of unemployment and homelessness especially after the outbreak of the economic crisis in November 1997. The trilateral agreement among labor, business, and the government established a special fund in the amount of 5 trillion won for the unemployed in return for the trade unions' concession of the legalization of layoffs. For the unemployed and low-income workers, a total of 10 trillion won was disbursed in 1998, and 9.2 trillion in 1999. Furthermore, two million jobs were created through various programs, such as job training, expansion of an information network connecting job searchers to employers, and promotion of the job supply in venture firms and in the tourism industry.

Since the democratic transition in 1988, the government has made a concerted effort to protect and promote small-and medium-sized firms, a victim of authoritarian rule. It is known that as many as eight laws were enacted to protect these firms located throughout different regions of the country. As many as nine different public funds were created to promote their business activities. For example, local banks are required to allocated 80 percent of every loan increase to businesses, while national banks and financial institutions, are obligated to allocate 45 percent of their annual loan increases to them (Moon, 1999). In addition, the Kim Young Sam government inaugurated the Agency for Small and Medium Industry in January 1996 to institutionalize support for small- and medium-size firms in the areas of technical advancement, structural adjustment, and corporate management. During his presidency, governmental support for these firms soared. From 1993 to 1995, for example, it nearly doubled from 1.1 trillion to 2.1 trillion won.

In summary, democratic changes in Korea during the past decade have significantly shifted the priorities of its economic policies by allocating greater resources to formerly neglected population groups and business sectors (Kim and Mo, 1999). In terms of fiscal policies, the share of central government expenditure by social welfare programs has increased substantially on a steady basis at the expense of national defense. In terms of monetary policies, a high priority has been given to agriculture and the fishing industry as well as small and medium industries, the two economic sectors that were neglected by the regimes of the authoritarian past. At the same time, there have been significant reductions in policy-based loans, which always favored the heavy industries monopolized by the Korean conglomerates called *chaebols*.

SUMMARY AND CONCLUSIONS

Korea has been in democratic transition for nearly one-and-a-half decades. During this period, the country has carried out a large number of institutional reforms, and reshaped the institutions and procedures of military-authoritarian rule into those of a representative democracy. Free and fair electoral contests have been held at all government levels. Three free and competitive presidential elections were conducted, the third of which produced a historic transition of power. Four rounds of parliamentary elections also enabled the people to choose their representatives to the National Assembly. In local communities, popularly elected governors and legislators have taken the place of appointees of the central government.

Korea has, thus, fully restored civilian rule by extricating the military from power. Korea has also fully established the other minimal infrastructure of procedural democracy. Accordingly, in Korea today, there is general agreement that electoral politics has become the only possible game in town. Korean democracy meets the criteria of a robust procedural democracy or polyarchy specified Robert Dahl (1971), Larry Diamond (1999), and many others. For the past several years, the country has received an average rating of 2.0 on Freedom House's scale of political rights and civil liberties, placing it within the ranks of the world's liberal democracies.

The democratization of military rule to date has brought about significant changes in the making of economic policymaking. With the expansion of political freedom and the reinvigoration of civil society, the policymaking process is now open to those who were excluded in the authoritarian past. The goal of economic policymaking has also been redirected to promote economic justice, social welfare, and quality of life. More than ever before, the government provides for those people and businesses that were long neglected under the military regimes of Presidents Park Chung Hee and Chun Doo Hwan. There is no doubt, that more than a decade of democratic rule in Korea, has transformed its economic policymaking process into the one that is more open as well as "kinder and gentler" to ordinary citizens (Lijphart, 1999).

In terms of formulating policies democratically, however, progress has been much slower and less substantial. As in the authoritarian past, the country suffers the imbalance of power between the president and the National Assembly. The constitutional principle of checks and balances rarely applies in the process of policymaking, even though the legislature is elected by the people to represent themselves in that process. Instead, the principle of executive dominance always prevails over the democratic principle of checks and balances. While the democratic principle of popular sovereignty is well practiced at all levels of government through regularly scheduled electoral contests, no progress has been made in institutionalizing the equally important principle of checks and balances. Unevenness in democratic progress is one important feature of Korean democratization.

Unlike his peers in fully consolidated democracies in Western Europe and North America, the Korean president exerts strong leadership unchecked by the National Assembly. As Lim Seong-Ho (1998) aptly points out, the Korean National Assembly, which was once ridiculed as "a rubber stamp" under military regimes, still remains a "peripheral" legislative institution even under a civilian president. While the constitution has been amended to give the people the right to elect their president, enjoy freedom of the press, and establish the rule of law, an all-powerful, imperial presidency has continued. Rule of person, not the rule of law, has persisted. Even the election of Kim Dae Jung, a well-known activist for democracy, has not changed old-style "politics as usual." All other major political leaders, including those of the ruling and opposition political parties, have not shed their authoritarian behavior (Mo and Kim, 1999). Consequently, Korean democracy suffers serious deficiencies in the rule of law and the proper restraint of executive power.

APPENDIX A
1999 KOREA DEMOCRACY BAROMETER SURVEY QUESTIONS

1. Perceptions of the Current and Past Political Systems

Q49. Here is a scale ranging from a low of 1 to a high of 10. On this scale, 1 means complete dictatorship and 10 means complete democracy. The closer to 1 the score is, the more dictatorial our country is; the closer to 10 the score is, the more democratic our country is.

a. On this scale, where would you place our country under the Chun Doo Whan government? Please choose a number on this cared.
b. Where would you place our country under the Kim Young Sam government?
c. Where would you place our country under the Kim Dae Jung government?

2. Citizen Empowerment and System Responsiveness

Q32. How much influence do you think the votes of people like yourself have on the way our country is governed – a lot, some, a little, or none?

Q36. To what extent do you think government leaders take the interests and opinion of people like yourself into account when making important decisions – a lot, some, a little, or not at all?

Q37. To what extent do you think government leaders take into account the interests and opinions of the interest groups and organizations before making decisions?

3. Overall Performance of the Current Political System as a Democracy

Q40. How satisfied or dissatisfied are you with the way democracy works in our country? Please choose a number on this scale ranging from a low of 1 (complete dissatisfaction) to a high of 10 (complete satisfaction).

REFERENCES

Cardoso, F.H.: 2001, 'Democracy as a starting point', Journal of Democracy 12, pp. 5–14.
Choi, J.J.: 2000, 'Democratization, civil society, and the civil social movement in Korea', Korea Journal 40, pp. 26–57.
Chu, Y.H., L. Diamond and D.C. Shin: 2001, 'Halting progress in Korea and Taiwan', Journal of Democracy 12, pp. 122–136.
Dahl, R.A.: 1971, Polyarchy (Yale University Press, New Haven).
Dahl, R.A.: 1998, Democracy and its Critics (Yale University Press, New Haven).
Diamond, L.: 1999, Developing Democracy Toward Consolidation (Johns Hopkins University Press, Baltimore).
Diamond, L. and D.C. Shin (eds.): 2000, Institutional Reform and Democratic Consolidation in Korea (Hoover Institution Press, Stanford).
Huntington, S.P.: 1991, The Third Wave: Democratization in the Late Twentieth Century (University of Oklahoma Press, Norman, OK).
Im, H.B.: 2000, 'South Korean democratic consolidation in comparative perspective', in L. Diamond and B.K. Kim (eds.), Consolidating Democracy in South Korea (Lynne Rienner, Boulder, CO).
Jang, S.C.: 2000, Driving Engine or Rent-Seeking Super-Cartel. Ph.D. Dissertation submitted to Michigan State University (Michigan State University, East Lansing, MI).
Kim, B.K.: 2000, 'Party politics in South Korea's democracy: the crisis of success', in L. Diamond and B.K. Kim (eds.), Consolidating Democracy in South Korea (Lynne Rienner, Boulder, CO).
Kim, J.I. and J. Mo: 1999, 'Democratization and Macroeconomic policy', in J. Mo and C. I. Moon (eds.), Democracy and the Korean Economy (Hoover Institution Press, Stanford).
Kim, S.: 2000, The Politics of Democratization (University of Pittsburgh Press, Pittsburgh).
Lee, J.: 2000, 'Welfare budget doubles in three years', Chosun Ilbo (January 27).
Lee, J.H.: 2001, 'Interest group politics in transition: Its features and tasks', in J.G. Min (eds.), Korean Politics in the 21st Century (Bummoonsa, Seoul).

Leem, K.H.: 2000, 'Back to the future: The politics of economic reform under Kim Dae Jung presidency', paper presented at the Conference on "Korea: Its International and Comparative Contexts", Harvard University, March 3–4.

Leftwich, A. (ed.): 1998, Democracy and Development (Polity Press, Cambridge).

Lijphart, A.: 1999, Patterns of Democracy (Yale University Press, New Haven).

Lim, H.S.: 2000, 'Historical development of civil social movements in Korea: Trajectories and issues', Korea Journal 40, pp. 5–25.

Lim, S.H.: 1998, 'A paradox of Korean democracy', Korea and World Affairs 22, pp. 522–538.

Moon, C.I.: 1999, 'Democratization and globalization as ideological and political foundations of economic policy', in J. Mo and C.I. Moon (eds.), Democracy and the Korean Economy (Hoover Institution Press, Stanford).

Moon, C.I. and Y.C. Kim: 1998, 'A circle of paradox: Development, politics, and democracy in South Korea', in A. Leftwich (ed.), Democracy and Development (Polity Press, Cambridge).

New York Times: 1998, 'Day of hope in South Korea', (February 25): A22.

Powell Jr., G.B.: 1982, 'Social progress and liberal democracy', in G. Almond, M. Chodorow and R. Pearce (eds.), Progress and Its Discontents (University of California Press, Berkeley).

Rose, R., W. Mishler, and C. Haerpfer: 1998, Democracy and its Alternatives (Johns Hopkins University Press, Baltimore).

Schmitter, P.C. and T.L. Karl: 1991, 'What is democracy is and is not', Journal of Democracy 3, pp. 75–88.

Sen, A.: 1999, 'Democracy as a universal value', Journal of Democracy 10, pp. 3–17.

Shin, D.C.: 1989, 'Political democracy and the quality of citizens' lives', Journal of Developing Societies 5, pp. 30–41.

Shin, D.C.: 1999, Mass Politics and Culture in Democratizing Korea (Cambridge University Press, New York).

Steinberg, D.: 2000, 'Continuing democratic reform: The unfinished symphony', in L. Diamond and B.K. Kim (eds.), Consolidating Democracy in South Korea (Lynne Rienner, Boulder, CO).

Wall Street Journal: 1992, 'Democracy wins one', (December 22): A12.

Department of Political Science
University of Missouri at Columbia
Columbia, MO 65211
USA
E-mail: Shind@missouri.edu

AIE-RIE LEE

STABILITY AND CHANGE IN KOREAN VALUES

ABSTRACT. Dramatic changes have taken place in socio-political value orientations in Korea throughout the post-World War II period, primarily as a function of intergenerational change and rising levels of education. This article, by using the three waves of the World Values Surveys conducted between 1982–1996, investigates the changing patterns of basic social values, and analyzes the relationship between these values and their effects on mass political orientations in Korea. The findings indicate that social values have played an important, if not crucial, role in shifting mass political attitudes, and in enhancing the propensity to engage in political action between 1982–1996. What we learned is that Authoritarian-Libertarian (A-L) values have sharply partitioned Korean society largely along the lines of age and education, the latter becoming more important in the later period. It was also shown that the differences in the A-L values are strongly related to contrasting protest potential.

The last four decades in South Korea (hereinafter referred to only as Korea) have been marked by mass social unrest and important internal challenges to the power of government leaders and the political system, especially exemplified by the sudden dramatic emergence of student protest. There may be several reasons why these events have occurred and are still prevalent in Korea. But the bottom line is that Korea has been experiencing dramatic changes in sociopolitical value orientations throughout the post-World War II period, primarily as a function of intergenerational change and rising levels of education.

As early as four decades ago, Harry Eckstein (1961, 1973) suggested that the lack of fit between culture and structure contributes to political instability and democratic breakdown. Almond and Verba (1965) also proposed that congruence or incongruence between structure and culture is related to allegiance or alienation. Looking at Korea, for instance, the young have been socialized to articulate their demands and interests through the Western-oriented educational system and mass media. Conversely, the political system has maintained, to a great extent, non-modern modes

Social Indicators Research **62, 63:** 93–117, 2003.

of government. In view of this lack of fit or congruence between the developing modern political culture among the younger and more educated elements of the society and the existing modes of government, it is natural to expect a high level of cynicism or alienation that is conducive to a decline in system support and protest activity.

A multitude of factors may be involved in the transformation of socio-political value orientations. Among them is a socio-economic change that often becomes a major cause of political value changes. A rapid on-going social changes is likely to accelerate the pace of social mobilization that, in turn, raises political consciousness and participation. Stated differently, not just change by itself, but the pace of change in the material-technological conditions of life has been the motor of this value change in Korea.

Korea has been and is still undergoing an extremely rapid economic transformation and social mobilization. This had been especially noticeable in the last two or three decades. For example, between 1946 and 1995 the proportion of the population living in cities increased from 14 percent to 79 percent. People engaged in the primary sector (e.g., fishing and agriculture) dropped from 75 percent in 1946 to 12 percent in 1995. In the same period, the proportion of the relevant age cohort enrolled in secondary education increased from 20 percent to 96 percent, while the GNP per capita rose by a factor of 108 over the period 1966–1995. As a consequence of these rapid social changes in the past 30 years, there are many conflicting social values among groups in Korea. Thus, I wish to test the hypothesis that social values provide an important clue in understanding the nature of political conflict and its resolution in Korea.

Korea's tremendous economic progress over two-and-one-half decades of military rule not only has brought about social change, but also has increased the pressure for democratization and has facilitated this process. Korea then reached a point in the late 1980s in which its political structure was no longer compatible with its political culture. Over the last decade, it has been pressure from below that has forced Korea's opening to democratic reform (Han, 1989). Koreans no longer condone the continuation of authoritarian rule in part because the predominant values and norms in society have altered overtime to reduce tolerance for repression and concentration of power and have stimulated demands for freedom. Beginning in the late 1980s democracy finally arrived in Korea, according to Samuel Huntington (1991), with the end of the "third wave" of democratization. By 1992, Korea had open elections, legal opposition parties, and electoral procedures that allowed the winners of elections to assume control of the government. Indeed, the 1992 presidential election was considered to be a turning point in Korean political history. It was a peaceful and fair election, unlike the past presidential elections that were marred with voter fraud and vote tampering. Moreover the 1997 presidential election and the victory of Kim Dae Jung, known as the beacon of democracy, symbolized the first peaceful democratic transition in government from a party leader to an opposition leader in 30 years in Korea.

Although the value change literature is a "growth industry" in comparative politics, most of the focus has been on Western Europe, North America, and Japan. Thus it is propitious that we examine Korea, a nation that has undergone tremendous change from the status of a less developed nation to its recent position as a newly industrialized state. I am particularly interested in addressing such questions as: are peoples' values changing?; what kinds of value cleavages do exist and how do they affect political action?; how are values measured?

The object of this paper then is, first, to investigate the changing patterns, if any, of basic social values and, second, to analyze the relationship between these social values and their effects on mass political orientations in Korea between 1982 and 1996. In doing so, I will first review the literature in a discussion of the value change process – why and when it occurs, the form it takes, and its relationship to democratic transition. Then, via survey research conducted in 1982, 1990, and 1996 as part of the World Value Survey (WVS hereinafter) studies, I will identify and analyze systematically to what extent these social values persist and/or are changing and their influence upon political action of Koreans, particularly their protest potential. The last section contains conclusions.

BACKGROUND STUDIES ON VALUE CHANGE

In a series of writings, Scott Flanagan (1979, 1980, 1982, 1987, 1991) introduced one of the most systematic value change models that explain political attitudes and behavior. Later Flanagan and this author (1988, 1990, 1991, 2000a) argued that the Authoritarian-Libertarian (A-L) value change is a product of changes in the underlying material-technological realities of the human condition. These changes begin with the early phases of industrialization and then distance themselves from an agrarian style of life, but do not reach very far into society until that society has reached high levels of education, welfare benefits, technological development and all the other trappings of postindustrial society. Culture provides a value system that enables people at a particular stage of material-technological development to survive, cope, and prosper. In agrarian societies which were characterized by conditions of insecurity, interdependency, and scarcity, this value system necessarily imposed severe constraints on an individual's inherent drive for self-actualization.

We argue that two kinds of changes in the human condition have progressively relaxed the *socio-political constraints* on the individual's drive to realize one's full potential, with the result that younger generations are emerging with altered values. First, a growing *equality* in education, access to information, material life-styles, and life changes is blurring class distinctions and weakening the authority of hierarchic roles and statuses. Equality of circumstances brings with it freedom from personal dependencies on powerful authority figures. Second, the accelerating *pace of change* increasingly rewards innovation, independent thinking, and open-mindedness to what is new and different and penalizes adherence to custom and tradition. These two kinds of changes, then, are replacing hierarchic, deferential, conformist norms, especially among the younger and better educated cohorts, with egalitarian, individualistic, self-assertive norms (for a fuller discussion of the concept, see Flanagan and Lee, 1990).

A second, related type of value change is occurring which is relaxing the *moral constraints* on one's quest for self-realization. This is being driven by another two distinct but interwoven changes in the human condition. The advent of the *welfare state* and social guarantees against loss, old age and impoverishment have weakened one's objective need to keep his/her nose to the grindstone, discipline his/her consumptive urges and maintain a surplus. The other change is the advance of *scientific knowledge* which is undermining mysticism, religiosity and the rationale for the disciplines of pietism. These changes are replacing the traditional values of diligence, austerity and strict moral codes with proclivities towards self-indulgence and permissive values that tolerate a broader range of behavior.

Our basic conceptualization of the authoritarian to libertarian value change is thus that the over-arching concept that integrates the notion of libertarian values is self-actualization. To achieve the goal of self-actualization, the individual requires freedom in three separate but interrelated domains. These are a social domain to provide freedom from the tyranny of authority, a psychological domain to free the individual from rigidly held traditional beliefs and customs, and a physical domain to afford freedom from material limitations. The drive for self-actualization and its expression in the social, psychological, and physical domains then defines the scope of the A-L value change, which occurs along three distinct sub-dimensions: Deference to Autonomy, Conformity to Openness, Austerity to Self-Betterment – the first two sub-dimensions of the A-L cleavage identified as constituting the defining core of the A-L value change are relevant to this study.

A shift from deference to autonomy refers to a growing emphasis on equality rather than hierarchy, on self-assertive individualism rather than a passive compliance or submissive resignation, and a general orientation toward seeking more self-determination and control over one's own life. This dimension captures the general decline modern societies are experiencing in the respect, loyalty, and obedience that authorities and institutions, such as parental authority, the community, the church, one's boss, and even political authorities, can command. What lies behind this shift is the growing equality in incomes, education, information, and lifestyles, which, in turn, has diminished the scope and magnitude of authority that one individual can exercise over another. With these changes in life condition has come a decline in the primacy of the values of respect for authority, obedience, loyalty and passive resignation and a rise in emphasis on autonomy, individual rights, self-assertiveness, and personal and political freedom.

The second dimension of the authoritarian-to-libertarian value change – change in the psychological domain – represents a movement from an emphasis on conformity to an attitude of openness, that is, a seeking of freer environment to facilitate self-actualization by throwing off the constraints of traditional customs and religious beliefs, opening oneself to new ideas, adopting more accepting attitudes toward new lifestyles and a broader range of moral behavior, and displaying more tolerance of and empathy with people or groups different from oneself, including religious or ethnic minorities. Another factor undermining conformity to traditional beliefs is the advance of scientific knowledge and education. The diffusion of knowledge and scientific advances, therefore, has undermined traditional moral codes, and religious beliefs and practices and has increased mankind's ability to understand and control his/her environment. Further, the diffusion has induced a change from pietism and strict moral codes to more permissive values that are tolerant of a broader range of behavior.

In short, libertarian values are values which facilitate self-actualization by assigning a higher priority to autonomy, openness, and self-betterment. It is thus highly plausible that the growth of libertarian values has helped to bring down authoritarian regimes (e.g., Chun and Rho) in Korea, since major components of libertarianism are not only a heightened emphasis of free speech and autonomy, but also linked with mass participation in elite-challenging forms of political action (Flanagan and Lee, 2000a,b).

DATA, VARIABLES, AND METHODS

The data sets employed in this study are derived from the 1982, 1990, and 1996 WVS studies[1] conducted in Korea, the former with a sample of N = 970 and the latter with N = 1251 and 1249, respectively.

In performing this analysis, a total of 5 demographic characteristics are considered control variables. These are: (1) gender; (2) age; (3) education; (4) type of community; (5) family income. The gender variable is measured on a nominal scale. Age is an interval scale ranging from 18 years to 65 years and older. Education is classified into four categories ranging from elementary education or less to some college education. Communities are classified into three types: (1) rural area or village; (2) small or middle size town; (3) big town. Household yearly income is divided into ten categories from less than 3000000 to more than 11000000 won.

Also employed is a whole set of political and social attitudes: system support or trust, nationalism, leftist ideology, psychological involvement in politics, and protest potential.[2] Basically, the psychological involvement (PI) refers to the attitudinal orientations of an individual citizen, including his/her political awareness, his/her sense of political outcomes, and his/her interest in political matters. In fact, several political scientists (such as Almond and Verba, 1965; Hagner and Pierce, 1982; Verba et al., 1971) have found that the higher the PI in politics is, the greater the likelihood that an individual will have an ideological conceptualization of politics. Thus, many conceptual models of political participation and voting behavior, in particular, view psychological factors as the immediate causal influences upon participation.

Several studies also show that distrust of government is an incentive for protest (Flanagan and Richardson, 1980; Lee, 1993; Lie, 1991; Sigelman and Feldman, 1983; Waltz, 1982; White, 1981). One way to measure the degree of distrust in the political system is to ask people directly about the images of political institutions. As far as democratic reform taking place in Korea is concerned, the most important and proximate variable is perhaps protest potential. What I would like to explain in this study is what leads Koreans to develop elite challenging attitudes which foster their willingness to engage in political protest and to espouse change. In this study, political protest is more of a measure of propensity than actual protest experience. The protest potential scale taps the presence of assertive, elite challenging attitudes that are conductive for leading individuals to move beyond simply distrust and cynicism to doing something about it. They feel justified and competent to challenge the legally constituted authorities by various forms of legal and illegal direct action whenever they feel that their interests or preferences are being sufficiently threatened. The system trust and protest potential scales are constructed by standardizing, equally weighting, and combining appropriate items.

It was my intention to use the exact same scale for this analysis. Therefore, I was forced to make several minor changes. First, not all the items were available for all three time intervals. Where an item was completely unavailable for a particular wave of the survey, a dash is indicated on the table. In some cases, not all the questions used to construct a particular item were available at all three time points, and I had to settle for less than optimal number of items.

Seven items are identified for the first of these two value scales – the Conformity/Deference scale. Given the nature and concerns of the surveys, most of these items are related to the private domain rather than the public domain (the latter being almost exclusively utilized by Inglehart). However, other analyses using both have shown that the two are highly intercorrelated (Flanagan, 1987), and there are reasons to prefer private domain items because they lack any political content that could lead to tautologies when trying to use them to predict political attitudes and behavior. These items have a strong face validity and seem to tap well the distinction between hierarchic, deferential attitudes and egalitarian, autonomous ones.

Of the seven Conformity/Deference items, four tap the emphasis that should be placed on independence versus good manners in raising children, and on following one's superiors' instructions versus more respect for authority in the near future. The other two tapped how much one felt that parents should sacrifice their own interests and well-being for their children and whether parents should be loved and respected regardless of their faults. The final variable, public domain items, included in the scale was constructed from the Inglehart four-item Postmaterialist scale recoded in an A-L format.[3] Thus the two Libertarian choices (free speech and participation) were given positive scores, the one Authoritarian item (law and order) a negative score, and the economic item (fighting rising prices), which is argued to be largely orthogonal to the A-L dimension, a zero score (see Flanagan, 1987). The respondents' two choices were then summed into a single variable, with first choices being weighted more heavily than second choices. The resultant variable became the seventh item in the Conformity/Deference scale.

The traditional morality scale was comprised of six items. The first five measured the extent to which respondents felt that there was never any justification for suicide, prostitution, divorce, abortion, or homosexuality. The last tapped traditional family values regarding the importance of having children to a woman's fulfillment.

In Table I the factor loadings of each item on the first unrotated factor are reported for both scales. As can be seen, the fit of these items is not perfect. The weakest fit is found in 1982. However, it appears that the fit is improving over time. A couple of the loadings were fairly low. For example, there was virtually little variance on the respect for authority item, with over 70 percent of the Korean sample for the 1982 data feeling that emphasis on greater respect for authority would be a bad thing in the near future. In spite of these problems, it was decided to include all seven of the Conformity/Deference and all six of the Traditional Morality items in their respective scales and to construct the scales using exactly equivalent simple additive procedures. This enables one to compare the levels of Libertarian orientations across time.

Once the two scales were constructed, they were found to have modest intercorrelations (Pearson's r = 0.31 for 1982, 0.28 for 1990 and 0.36 for 1996). Hence both scales were normalized using z-score procedures and combined. Almost in every case, the resultant combined A-L scale yielded slightly higher correlations with all of the other analytic variables than either of the two individual scales. Thus throughout the remainder of this paper, with one exception where a meaningful pattern of difference was found, it is the combined A-L scale that will be employed.

VALUE CHANGE AND ITS ATTRIBUTES

The study will now turn to dimension by dimension analysis of the associations between values that play important roles in the socialization process and political attitude-building and the set of demographic and attitudinal variables. The study will further employ two statistical steps of data analysis. First, the results of zero-order correlations between the selected demographic variables and the combined A-L scale are examined. Second, the data are subjected to a regression analysis (OLS), from which conclusions

TABLE I

Factor Loadings and Value Scores of Conformity/Deference and Traditional Morality Items

	Loading on first unrotated factor for:			A-L Score		
	1982	1990	1996	1982	1990	1996
Conformity/Deference items:						
Teach child independence	0.382	0.441	0.447	–8	+8	+20
Teach child good manners	–0.459	–0.330	–0.481	–40	–86	–82
Must follow superiors' instructions	0.013	–0.402	–0.286	+18	+66	+36
Respect for authority	–0.001	–0.439	–0.341	+75	+68	+48
Parents should sacrifice for children	–0.676	–0.578	–0.576	–34	+6	+1
Must love and respect parents regardless	–0.319	–0.206	–0.387	–85	–87	–88
Inglehart items coded in Lib. Form	0.631	0.513	0.489	+10	+8	+4
Mean	0.351	0.416	0.430	–8.4	–2.4	–8.7
Traditional morality items:						
Never any justification for:						
Suicide	0.708	0.630	0.685	–26	–28	–36
Prostitution	0.718	0.682	0.720	–30	–56	–22
Divorce	0.794	0.749	0.819	–2	+24	+14
Abortion	0.722	0.651	0.764	+1	+24	–14
Homosexuality	0.621	0.556	0.721	–26	–80	–34
Women need children to be fulfilled	0.335	0.282	0.331	–49	–52	–34
Mean	0.650	0.592	0.673	–22	–28	–21

[a]I gave a weight of –2, –1 for the respondent's choice to 'maintaining order in the nation' as his/her respective top and second choices and treat them as authoritarian, a weight of 2, 1 for their respondent's 'more say in government decisions,' and 'freedom of speech' categories as one's first and second choices, respectively, and consider them as libertarian.

are drawn about the explanatory power of each of the independent variables with the control variables.

To what extent have values of Koreans been changing? The last columns of Table I report the extent of the differences in the overall A-L response distributions for each item.[4] In every case, scores were obtained by subtracting percentages of respondents who offered authoritarian responses from the percentages giving libertarian types of answers. Negative scores, then, indicate a predominance of authoritarian values and positive scores indicate a shift in the libertarian direction.

While scores across four of the seven items of the C-D value dimension showed negative signs in 1982, which indicate a predominance of authoritarian values, by 1996 five of them offered positive signs, which signify a predominance of libertarian values. Overall, the study found virtually no change in values with an average of –8 selecting an authoritarian response across the seven items in 1982 and falling to –2 in 1990; and bouncing back to roughly –9 in 1996. Even in the late 1990s, however, Koreans were still more inclined to think that we must respect parents regardless and that children ought to be taught good manners at home. Meanwhile, contemporary Koreans held more libertarian attitudes on five items: parents should have own life and should not be asked to sacrifice their own well-being for the sake of their children; teaching children independence is more important; "more say in government decision" and "freedom of speech" are more important in our country for the next ten years; emphasis on greater respect for authority is not necessarily a good thing; people should not necessarily follow superiors' instructions. Although difficult to interpret these complex findings, it is safe to say that Koreans have begun to defy some, if not all, of the principles of traditional Confucianism, say, sacrifice of parents' lives.

One of the Korean traditional values is the importance attached to social customs and morality. While the implications of these customs and moral standards may change with time, the principle of upholding them is always there. In this study, the value dimension of traditional morality refers to the difference in the relative emphasis on traditional customs and morals. Here, the main purpose is to discover Koreans' dominant thinking or mental traits: Whether Koreans have retained their moral beliefs and traditional customs or whether they have adopted more liberal outlooks. The study expects to find the libertarian person as one who can more readily acknowledge the process of social transformation taking place around him/her, such as marriage, divorce, abortion, homosexuality, marital affairs, and traditional practices, and who can more freely accept the changed opportunities, and the authoritarian person as one who is likely to offer resistance to all those changes.

At first glance, Table I reports the similar but opposite pattern, in some cases, as the C-D dimension, a very minuscule decreasing trend towards authoritarian values from –22 in 1982 to –21 by 1996.[5] Yet, a closer inspection of the 1996 data shows marked contrasts in the perception of the TM values. What is perhaps most striking is, however, the fact that the pattern for two items (divorce and abortion) is reversed in 1996: a trend toward a rising for the former and diminishing for the latter endorsement of libertarian values. While Koreans are more readily to acknowledge the process of social transformation taking place around them on one item (divorce is somewhat justified), so are they more traditional on five morals and customs/practices items (either prostitution, suicide, abortion or homosexuality is not justified, a woman has to have children in order to be fulfilled). It would seem that attitudes are still strikingly traditional on some morals items in Korea. Evidently, one can argue that no change has taken place on these items in Korea at least over fourteen-year period examined.

Table II provides a more concrete representation of how the levels of value change means. The combined A-L scale was first recoded into four categories selecting cut points that divided the 1982 sample into four groups. These same cut points were used throughout to determine the direction and amount of change over about one-and-half decades. As revealed in Table II, there is a movement from both extremes on the scales to more central positions, with authoritarian categories gaining by 4 percentage points, and the semi-libertarian and libertarian categories declining by 1 and 3 points, respectively across the entire fourteen year period. To put it differently, 49 percent of the sample held authoritarian values in 1982, while about 52 percent did in 1990 and 47 percent held libertarian values in 1996. As we will see in the next section, there

TABLE II

Value Types and Value Change, 1982–1996

Value Types	82	90	96	Change 82–96
Authoritarian	26	22	30	+4
Semi-Authoritarian	23	27	23	0
Semi-Libertarian	26	28	25	–1
Libertarian	25	24	22	–3
Total Percentage	100	101	100	
N	832	1226	1242	

were special contextual problems or period effects that account for this unexpected finding.

One might also argue that the massive changes that have been taking place in Korea over the last four decades as a consequence of the rapid economic development and social mobilization processes have been impacting across all demographic categories. As attitudes have changed, the aggregate profile of Korea's political culture has shifted as well.

As Table III shows, age and education remain strong predictors as expected, a major pattern of intergenerational value change with younger generations holding increasingly libertarian values. Again, as expected, education ranks as a close second in 1990, becoming the strongest predictor in 1996, with the highly educated holding more libertarian values. This suggests that the relatively recent and rapid expansion of educational achievement levels among the Korean population was perhaps the most important engine of value change. Income had much lower but still significant bivariate associations except for 1990 with the wealthy having more libertarian outlooks. Gender is an insignificant predictor of values for all three time periods. For the purposes of data presentation, the percentages for the two authoritarian and libertarian categories were summed, resulting in 100% except in cases of rounding error.

The anomaly is the apparent reversal in the direction of value change, especially among the wealthy and the highly educated. This helps to explain the pattern of change found on the individual A-L

TABLE III

Socio-Demographic Attributes and Changes in Value Types

	Libertarian type				Authoritarian type				Association[a]		
	1982 %	1990 %	1996 %	82–96 change	1982 %	1990 %	1996 %	82–96 change	1982	1990	1996
Generation[b]											
Postwar gen.	—	55	43	–12	—	45	57	+12			
Wartime gen.	—	37	29	–8	—	63	71	+8			
Prewar gen.	—	24	3	–21	—	76	97	+21	—	–0.40	–0.40 (Gamma)
Education											
Primary	—	24	9	–15	—	76	91	+15			
Middle	—	34	18	–16	—	66	82	+16			
High	—	51	31	–20	—	49	69	+20			
College/over	—	62	54	–8	—	38	46	+8	—	0.36	0.58 (Gamma)
Family income											
Low	47	48	31	–16	53	52	69	+16			
Middle	56	54	46	–10	44	46	54	+10			
High	72	51	56	–16	28	49	44	+16	0.31	(0.06)	0.28 (Gamma)
Sex											
Female	48	50	46	–2	52	51	54	+2			
Male	53	54	49	–4	47	46	51	+4	(0.50)	(0.05)	(0.03) (Eta)

[a]For nominal variables the measure of association used was Eta, while for ordinal variables it was Gamma.
[b]The postwar generation for the 1982 survey is operationally defined by those between 18 and 34 years of age; the wartime generation is defined by the age between 35 and 49; and the prewar generation is those 50 and over; for the 1990 data, the upper and lower limit that defines the generations then by 7 years on; for the 1996 data, the upper and lower limit that defines the generations then by 5 years on.
Notes: All measures of association are significant at the 0.05 level except those in parentheses.

items as mentioned in the previous section. The item with the most dramatic reversal was the teaching child good manners item, but the other items, emphasis on greater respect for authority and any justification for suicide, also experienced substantial reversals. I would hypothesize that the social disorder associated with the process of democratic reforms was unnerving to many Koreans (Lee, 1990), especially the wealthy and highly educated, who may have felt that they had the most to lose from any breakdown in social order.

The four variables (sex, age, education, and family income) in Table III and residence are used for multiple regression analysis to test whether the patterns that emerged in the bivariate analysis were substantiated in the multivariate analysis and also to determine their relative contributions to the growth of libertarian values. As shown in Table IV, age and education are, albeit some fluctuations, clearly and consistently the two strongest predictors of libertarian values across the two time intervals. Partial correlation coefficients between education and the A-L scale and between age and the A-L scale, respectively, are 0.35 and –0.10 in 1996. Education, as expected, becomes most strongly associated with the emergence of Libertarian values in the late 1990 Korea. Other factors but residence in 1990 have uniformly low betas, which become insignificant in all three periods.

An intriguing question is: Why are there strong and significant associations between education and values, but not between individual affluence, measured by income, and values in either period? Flanagan and this author argue that a shift of people's values from authoritarian to libertarian is very much a function national affluence, and thus the effects of individual affluence do not induce value change. In the modern "no risk society," even those with rather modest incomes enjoy insurance, entitlement and welfare benefits which free them from concerns about scarcity or dependency on personal benefactors leading them to shed authoritarian orientations nearly, if not quite, as rapidly as their more affluent country counterparts. On the other hand, education has a direct impact on extinguishing authoritarian orientations.

Authoritarian vales are based in part on mysticism, traditions, religious beliefs, sacred symbols, ascriptive status, and a belief in the inherent superiority of those in positions of authority. Educa-

TABLE IV

The Effects of Socio-Demographic Factors on Libertarian Values

Predictors	1982		1990		1996	
	B	Beta	B	Beta	B	Beta
Age	—	—	−0.03	−0.28	−0.00	−0.10
Education	0.18	0.43[a]	0.15	0.18	0.34	0.35
Income	0.04	(0.07)	−0.01	(−0.03)	−0.00	(−0.00)
Sex(female)	−0.02	(−0.01)	−0.02	(−0.02)	0.12	(0.05)
Residence	−0.00	(−0.01)	0.06	0.08	—	—
(Constant)	1.1		4.3		2.4	
Multiple R	0.46		0.39		0.38	
Adjusted R Square	0.21		0.15		0.14	
N	751		1171		1239	

[a]Age finished school.

Note: All coefficients are significant at the 0.05 level except those in partentheses.

tion undermines all those attitudes by replacing mysticism with science and ascription with meritocratic norms. Broadening the attainment of higher education in society becomes only a small step for many to realize that those in positions of authority are probably not brighter, wiser, or nobler than ordinary people like themselves. Education also has a liberalizing effect, relaxing strict traditional moral constraints by increasing one's awareness, tolerance of and empathy with alternate values, customs and life styles. Thus if we conceive of value change as an authoritarian to libertarian spectrum, we should expect to find a much stronger association of values with education rather than with income.

Finally, perhaps the most interesting finding is that with respect to the relationship between a religious denomination and values. Here the value scale is divided into its two original components, the Conformity/Deference and Traditional Morality scales, because of the difference found in the pattern of associations between them. Religion tends to be a conserver of traditional values and hence one would expect to find that adherence to a religion would be more strongly associated with authoritarian values. In the case of Korea, however, the traditional religion is Buddhism. Christianity

TABLE V

The Association Between Religious Denomination and Values

	Normalized (z-score) value scales								
	Conformity/Deference			Traditional morality			Sample percent		
	1982	1990	1996	1982	1990	1996	1982	1990	1996
Buddhist	−0.17	−0.17	−0.11	−0.08	−0.13	−0.01	28	25	26
Other/NA/DK	−0.24	0.02	0.11	−0.08	−0.00	0.17	3	8	4
Christian	0.13	−0.00	−0.00	−0.06	−0.00	−0.12	23	38	32
None	0.06	0.14	0.00	0.08	0.19	0.14	45	29	39
N of cases	855	1230	1242	922	1247	1247			
Eta	0.12	0.08	0.09	(0.07)	0.14	0.13			

Note: A positive sign indicates a group's mean value score is more Libertarian than the sample mean, while a negative sign indicates more Authoritarian values. The all eta are significant at the 0.05 level expect that in parentheses.

is a Western import and therefore, might be associated with more modern, Western values.

In Table V, the two value scales have been normalized with means equal to zero and standard deviations of 1.0 to aid in the interpretation of the differences between denominational group means. Plus scores indicate that the group is more libertarian than the sample mean while negative scores indicate more authoritarian values. On the Traditional Morality scale, the study finds that the Buddhist and Christian categories hold a trend toward an endorsement, albeit diminishing, of authoritarian values, and the Other/DK groups are becoming the most libertarian by 1996, followed by those that reject all religious beliefs and affiliations. This, particularly the Christian category, is not as we might expect. On the Conformity/Deference scale, while the Christian and No affiliation groups fall around the sample mean, the positioning of the Other/DK category once again, remains unchanged, becoming clearly the most libertarian. It may be, then, in the context of Eastern Confucian societies, that Christianity, with its message of individual salvation and its association with the more individualistic and less hierarchic Western cultures, may not play a significant role in socializing their followers into these kinds of more libertarian values.

TABLE VI

The Comparative Associations Between Libertarian and Postmaterialist Values and Demographic and Key Attitudinal Variables (Pearson's r)

	Libertarian values			Postmaterialist values		
	82	90	96	82	90	96
Protest Potential	0.41	0.38	0.33	0.18	0.25	0.19
System trust	−0.30	−0.33	−0.21	−0.18	−0.19	(−0.04)
Leftist ideology	0.13	0.23	0.27	0.10	0.18	0.14
Nationalism	−0.23	−0.20	−0	(−0.04)	(−0.01)	—
Psychological involvement	0.28	0.09	0.15	0.22	0.18	0.16

Note: All coefficients are significant at the .05 level except those in partentheses.

Even more puzzling is why basic values of the Christian group became more traditional, or authoritarian, in the later period. Ironically, religion in Korea might have played a significant role in critically evaluating the existing culture and changing moral values, perhaps because Christians felt more vulnerable with regard to those issues. In other words, it is possible that the Christian group was more concerned about an unstable cultural system which had produced distrust in laws, norms, and human relations. It is equally plausible that these Western religious traditions (Protestantism or Catholicism) also have historically taken strictly moralistic positions on these issues.

Political Implications of Value Change

The shift from authoritarian to libertarian values has important implications for a number of key political attitudes. As one of the intervening variables employed in this study, psychological involvement in politics also plays an important role in determining the scope and intensity of system support or protest potential, those holding libertarian values exhibit higher levels of psychological involvement in polities than those retaining authoritarian values.

Also noted in Table VI is that libertarian values are associated with declining nationalism and more leftist ideological beliefs with the latter having a rather weaker relationship with values in 1982. This might be due to the fact that prior to the advent of legislatively sanctioned party competition in Korea, and the traditional regional rather than ideological basis of Korean politics (Han, 1974; Morriss, 1996; Shin, 1995), the left and the right did not have much meaning to Koreans. Indeed, the left was probably associated with many Koreans' minds with communism, which became abhorrent in the wake of the Korean War (Han, 1974; Henderson, 1968; Kim, 1988). As the public's experience with party competition in open democratic elections increases, one would expect these terms to acquire more meaningful and consistent interpretations. Indeed, the data suggest such a trend. In addition, libertarian values are also associated with a decline in the level of system support. Libertarians, then, are more cynical towards their political institutions and political leaders. These higher levels of cynicism, in turn, are reflected in higher levels of disaffected forms of political behavior, thus observing rather high correlations between libertarian values and protest potential. Libertarians tended to favor protest activity, while authoritarians were strongly against it. Declining political trust, rising reformist ideologies and a growing willingness to protest are inevitably going to put more pressure on elites to respond to populist demands for democratic reforms.

In trying to account for the particular association between A-L values and protest potential, Flanagan and myself argue that there is something inherent in these values that inhibit protest activity. Authoritarians value law and order, are deferential to the traditional symbols and holders of authority and carefully adhere to rules and regulations. These value predispositions, coupled with their conformity to traditional customs and practices, make it unlikely that they would sanction elite challenging activities. In contrast, libertarians value individualism and self-actualization, building a better self and society through self-improvement and social change. Their greater self-confidence and lack of deference towards authority figures enhance their willingness to question the actions of leaders and forcefully press for new policies, even in the face of official opposition.

Table VI also reports, as a comparison, the relationships between Inglehart's post-materialist values and this study's selected key attitudinal variables. Since better conceptualization and measurement of value changes in explaining how and why people engage in political activity have brought on an ongoing debate, particularly between Inglehart and Flanagan (Flanagan, 1987; Inglehart, 1987), it is worth nothing that regardless of time, in every case but two (psychological involvement in 1990 and 96), this study's A-L value scale yields higher correlations than Inglehart's original 4-item scale. As has been noted elsewhere (Lee, 1993, 1996, 1998), this author has held that a multidimensional model of value conflict such as Flanagan and my authoritarian-libertarian model is more applicable to a valid assessment of the underlying patterns of value politics in Korea than Inglehart's materialist/post-materialist model (also see Shin et al., 1989a,b).

Finally, Table VII presents the results of a multivariate analysis of protest potential in Korea, including five demographic variables (age, education, income, sex, and residence), four attitudinal variables (psychological involvement, nationalism, system trust, and leftist ideology), and values. This author holds that libertarian values promote protest activity and also directly increase psychological involvement in politics, which, in turn, relates to protest potential. On the other hand, libertarian values also decrease support for political authorities and institutions, which again increases leftist ideology and political protest. Thus a person's attachment to authoritarian values, his/her support for political authorities and institutions, and his/her low level of psychological involvement in politics will decrease his/her possibility of participating in protest action.

Of all the variables, values and psychological involvement are consistently strong predictors of protest potential across the three time intervals, albeit the former ranks first, second, and third in the predictive power with a beta of 0.21, 0.19 and 0.17 in 1982, 1990, and 1996, respectively. While system trust was a moderate predictor of protest in 1982 and 1990, it became weak in explaining protest potential by 1990, suggesting that support for political institutions became less salient in affecting protest activity in mid-1990 Korea. Age completely disappeared as a factor in 1996, reflecting the weaker role of the younger generation in Korean politics. Also observed is that sex, income, nationalism and leftist ideology exhibit small effects on inclination toward protest activity both in 1990 and 1996. In terms of the percentage of variation explained together, these demographic, attitudinal variables, and values explain roughly

TABLE VII

The Effects of Predictor Variables on Protest Potential

Predictors	1982		1990		1996	
	B	Beta	B	Beta	B	Beta
Age	—	—	−0.01	−0.21	−0.00	(−0.03)
Libertarian values	0.07	0.21	0.08	0.19	0.06	0.17
Psychological involvement	0.18	0.18	0.20	0.17	0.27	0.25
System trust	−0.07	−0.11	−0.14	−0.15	−0.01	−0.08
Education	0.01	(0.08)	0.06	0.14	0.09	0.26
Sex (female)	−0.05	(−0.07)	0.09	0.09	0.03	(0.03)
Income	0.00	(0.02)	−0.01	−0.06	−0.00	−0.05
Leftist ideology	0.01	(0.05)	0.01	(0.04)	0.01	0.06
Nationalism	−0.02	(−0.05)	−0.01	(−0.01)	—	—
Residence	−0.01	−0.09	−0.00	(0.00)	—	—
(Constant)	0.91		0.66		0.28	
Multiple R	0.46		0.55		0.53	
Adjusted R Square	0.19		0.30		0.27	
N	342		1066		1219	

Note: All coefficients are significant at the .10 level except those in parentheses.

29 percent of the variation in protest potential in the 1990s which is a 10 percent increase from the 1982 model.

An immediate puzzle from the findings is why basic values become less important to Koreans in defining their orientations to politics in the mid 1990s than fourteen years earlier. Albeit difficult to prove at this moment, the study underscores one possible explanation: the degree of development of democratic institutions. One possibility for the less impact of values on politicization among Korean mass publics is the very nature of this study's dependent variable. One could argue that the more developed the democratic or conventional forms of mass political action (e.g., voting, attending political meetings and campaigns) are in a nation, the less crucial the role value change may play in providing the individual with the justifying rationale that legitimates his/her participation in protest activities. Obviously, the environment of 1990 Korea was more democratic than a decade ago. In fact, a relatively well institutionalized party system and political opposition were in operation by the early 1990s. Therefore, it is plausible that the institutional devices for democratic participation were on the way in 1990 Korea, thereby values played a much less dominant role in stimulating protest potential. However, this paper cannot document that here.

CONCLUSIONS

The goal of this study has been to examine the extent to which mass public's values have changed and/or persisted, and their impact they had on political orientations in Korea. The findings suggest that values have played an important, if not vital, role in shifting mass political attitudes and enhancing the propensity to engage in political action between 1982 and 1996. Specifically uncovered was the A-L values, albeit diminished in 1996, sharply partitioned Korean society largely along the lines of age and education, the latter becoming more important in the later period. It was also shown that the differences in the A-L values were found to be strongly related to contrasting protest potential.

What are the implications of this study? I would posit that the A-L shift in social values is closely associated with a change in political values. As Inglehart (1997) and Flanagan and I (2000a,b) have argued, economic development, value change and political change go together in a coherent pattern. Economic development and the changes that accompany it – rising education, affluence, security, information, mobility, and leisure have been associated with an important shift in mass attitudes and world view, towards more assertive, independent, and self-seeking attitudes. Citizens who hold libertarian values are no longer in awe of leaders, but are rather cynical of their motives and integrity and no longer willing to passively delegate authority to them. Thus it has been mass pressure from below that has been pushing Korea towards democratic reforms over the past decade, and while it still have some distance to travel, it will continue to be mass pressure that provides the impetuous to put more democratic practices in place.

NOTES

[1] The data used in this study are part of the World Value Surveys study, which is available through the Inter-University Consortium for Political and Social

Research of the University of Michigan (ICPSR 2790). The ICPSR bears no responsibility for my analysis and interpretations.

[2] The psychological involvement scale is composed of two items on the respondent's level of interest in politics and frequency of discussing politics with friends. The nationalism scale is constructed from one item on degree of pride in one's country. Leftist ideology is measured by the standard ten-point left-right self-placement scale. System trust measures the respondent's level of confidence in their nation's legal system, national legislature, civil service, police and armed forces. The protest potential scale is the standard one which asks whether the respondent had done, might do and would never do of four different kinds of activities from signing a petition to occupying a building.

[3] The question asked is: "There is a lot of talk these days about what the aims of this country should be for the next ten years. On this card are listed some of the goals which different people would give top priority. Would you please say which one of these you, yourself consider most important? And which would be the next important?"

[4] Overall authoritarian-libertarian scores are computed for each item by subtracting the percentage of responses classified as authoritarian from the percentage of those classified as libertarian. In the computing process, I standardized the A–L scores so that the fact that some items have more missing data or some items have middle or neutral categories that cannot be classified as either authoritarian or libertarian does not bias the score result. A positive sign indicates a shift in the libertarian direction and a negative sign a shift in the authoritarian direction.

[5] Note that my five items on moral issues are measured on the standard ten-point scale. The problem here is that, in the process of computing the A-L scores, I find a very skewed distribution, with most respondents choosing one of the first three categories as authoritarian and very few picking the last three categories. If I treat the first five categories as authoritarian and the second five as libertarian, the results would tend to show overwhelmingly authoritarian attitudes. The item format employed for this dimension, therefore, does not permit as easy identification of what point on the ten-point scales divides authoritarian from libertarian responses. As one way of overcoming this problem, I compute an average score for each item from the 1982 data, and treat categories below the average as authoritarian and ones above the average as libertarian responses. For instance, in the case of prostitution, I first computed the 1982 mean that was 1.93 and then classified 1 through 1.90 as authoritarian and 2.00 through 10 as libertarian response categories.

REFERENCES

Almond G.A. and S. Verba: 1965, The Civic Culture: Political Attitudes and Democracy in Five Nations (Princeton University Press, Princeton, NJ).

Eckstein, H.: 1961, A Theory of Stable Democracy (Center of International Studies, Princeton University, Princeton).

Eckstein, H.: 1973, 'Authority patterns: A structural basis for political inquiry', American Political Science Review 67(4), pp. 1142–1161.

Flanagan, S.C.: 1979, 'Value change and partisan change in Japan: The silent revolution revisited', Comparative Politics 11, pp. 253–278.

Flanagan, S.C.: 1980, 'Value cleavages, economic cleavages and the Japanese voter', American Journal of Political Science 24, pp. 177–206.

Flanagan, S.C.: 1982, 'Measuring value change in advanced industrial societies', Comparative Political Studies 15, pp. 99–128.

Flanagan, S.C.: 1987, 'Value change in industrial societies', American Political Science Review 81, pp. 1303–1319.

Flanagan, S.C. and A.R. Lee: 1988, Explaining value change and its political implications in eleven advanced industrial democracies. Paper presented at the Fourteen World Congress of the International Political Science Association, Washington, D.C.

Flanagan, S.C. and A.R. Lee: 1990, The causes and socio-political implications of value change in the advanced industrial democracies. Paper presented at the annual meeting of the Midwest Political Science Association, Chicago.

Flanagan, S.C. and A.R. Lee: 1991, Modernization and the emergence of the authoritarian libertarian value cleavage. Paper presented at the annual meeting at the Southern Political Science Association, Tampa, Florida.

Flanagan, S.C. and A.R. Lee: 2000a, 'Value change and democratic reform in Japan and Korea', Comparative Political Studies 33(6), pp. 626–659.

Flanagan, S.C. and A.R. Lee: 2000b, Losing faith: Value change and declining levels of trust and compliance in the United States and Japan. Paper presented at the "Losing Faith in the United States and Japan" Conference, Quebec, Canada.

Flanagan, S.C. and B.M. Richardson: 1980, 'Political disaffection and political stability: A comparison of Japanese and Western findings', in R.F. Tomasson (ed.), Comparative Social Research, 3 (JAI Press, Greenwich Conn., pp. 3–44).

Flanagan, S.C., S. Kohei, I. Miyake, B.M. Richardson and J. Watanuki: 1991, The Japanese Voter (Yale University Press, New Haven and London).

Hahn, S.C.: 1976, Hankook Minjujuui-wa Jungchi Paljun [the Korean Way to Democracy] (Pupmun-sa, Seoul).

Hagner, P.R. and J.C. Pierce: 1982, 'Correlative characteristics of levels of conceptualization in the American public: 1956–1976', Journal of Politics 44, pp. 793–796.

Han, S.: 1974, The Failure of Democracy in South Korea (University of California Press, Berkeley).

Han, S.:1989, 'South Korea: Politics in transition', in L. Diamond, J.J. Linz, and S.M. Lipset (eds.), Democracy in Developing Countries Asia (Lynne Rienner Publishers, Boulder, Colorado, pp. 267–304).

Henderson, G.: 1968, Korea: The Politics of the Vortex (Harvard University Press).

Huntington, S.: 1991, The Third Wave (University of Oklahoma Press, Norman and London).

Inglehart, R.: 1987, 'Value change in industrial societies', American Political Science Review 81, pp. 1290–1303.

Inglehart, R.: 1997, Modernization and Postmodernization (Princeton University Press, Princeton, New Jersey).
Kihl, Y.W.: 1988, 'Party politics on the eve of a gathering storm: The constitutional revision politics of 1986', in I.J. Kim and Y.W. Kihl (eds.), Political Change in South Korea (Paragon House, New York, pp. 75–90).
Kim, C.L.: 1988, 'Potential for democratic change', in I.J. Kim and Y.W. Kihl (eds.), Political Change in South Korea (Paragon House, New York, pp. 44–74).
Lee, A.R.: 1998, 'Politicization of the Korean mass public through value change', in Ilpyong J. Kim (ed.), Two Koreas in Transition: Implications for U.S. Policy (In Depth Books, Rockville, MD, pp. 223–244).
Lee, A.R.: 1996. 'Consistency or change in women's politicization in South Korea', Policy Studies Journal 24(2), pp. 183–200.
Lee, A.R.: 1993, 'Culture shift and popular protests in South Korea', Comparative Political Studies 26(1), pp. 63–80.
Lee, H.: 1990, 'Uncertain promise: Post-1987 democratic consolidation in South Korea', Social Science Research II, pp. 163–178.
Lie, J.: 1991, 'Democratization and its discontents: Origins of the present crisis in South Korea', Monthly Review 42, pp. 38–52.
Morriss, P.: 1996, 'Electoral polities in South Korea', Electoral Politics 15, pp. 550–562.
Shin, D.C.: 1995, 'Political parties and democratization in south Korea: The mass public and the democratic of political parties', Journal of Democratization 2(2), pp. 20–55.
Shin, D.C., M. Chey and K.W. Kim: 1989a, 'Cultural origins of public support for democracy in Korea', Comparative Political Studies 22, pp. 217–238.
Shin, D.C., M. Chey and K.W. Kim: 1989b, 'Left-right polarization and support for democratization among the mass public in Korea. Paper presented for the First World Conference of Korean Political Studies, Seoul, Korea.
Sigelman, Lee and S. Feldman: 1983, 'Efficacy, mistrust, and political mobilization', Comparative Political Studies, pp. 118–143.
Verba, S., N.H. Nie and J.O. Kim: 1971, 'The modes of democratic participation: A cross-national comparison', Comparative Politics Series, No. 01–013(2) (Sage, Beverly Hills, pp. 53–63).
Waltz, S.E.: 1982, 'Antidotes for a social malaise', Comparative Polities, pp. 127–147.
White, J.W.: 1981, 'Civic attitudes, political participation, and system stability in Japan', Comparative Political Studies pp. 371–400.

Department of Political Science
Texas Tech University
Lubbock, TX 79409
USA
E-mail: uqlee@ttacs.ttu.edu

PART II. QUALITY OF LIFE ACROSS LIFE DOMAINS

OK KYUNG YANG

FAMILY STRUCTURE AND RELATIONS

ABSTRACT. This paper aims to evaluate how the Korean family fares in terms of its quality of life. Specifically, it examines the perceived quality of relationships among family members in relation to the objective conditions of family life, and the decision-making process that takes place therein. According to National Census data, family size is becoming smaller, and the divorce rate is increasing, while the marriage rate is decreasing. The nuclear two-parent family has changed little in its relative size, while the incidence or size of the three-generation extended family has continued to decrease. At the same time, there has been a sharp increase in single-person households. According to a recent survey of college students, Korean families, despite the widely held notion of a hierarchical Confucian influence, enjoy a liberal and flexible family environment in everyday life. Such a family atmosphere, together with a large family income, is found to contribute to greater qualities of family life, involving such elements as love, caring, recognition, and acceptance.

In Korea, there is an old saying: "A happy family life leads to successful social achievement (*ga-wha-man-sa-sung*)." As this suggests, Koreans widely recognize the family as a pillar of society, shaping the "habits of the heart" in Korea. Under the strong influence of Confucianism, Koreans also consider the harmony and continuity of the family as the basis for upholding the human community. Central to these Confucian beliefs is the notion that human society should be an extension of the relations found in the family. These beliefs have led Koreans to a "family-first" ideology, meaning that family was considered to be a top priority over the well-being of individual members. An individual's sacrifice for the good of the entire family is taken for granted. This traditional Korean family ideology espouses a form of collectivism, and it leads an individual family member to behave as a member of the family, not as an independent individual. An individual exists only in relation to his or her family.

It is no wonder then that such family ideology is one of the most important values in Korea. In Confucianism, the family is character-

Social Indicators Research **62, 63:** 121–148, 2003.

ized as the most fundamental institution for human life. According to Jae Suk Choe (1976), "the family is a single most important social unit; an individual is not independent of the family; the relationship between members of the family is neither autonomous nor equal, but strictly hierarchical; and this kind of relationship pattern is extended to the whole society." This hierarchical order among family members is apparent, and often observed cross-sexually: that is, the father shows respect and obedience to the grandmother. This domain of family ideology is widely believed to remain intact and serve as the basis of human relations in Korea. The younger members, for example, still respect their elders.

The Korean family is rapidly changing, however, and so is the family ideology. A family does not seem to exist anymore without the recognition of individual members' uniqueness and individuality. The changes in ideology have resulted in changes in the understanding of family function. For instance, the emotional aspect is more emphasized these days than are traditionally defined institutional functions (Shin and Chang, 1997; Yang, 2000). Families that demonstrate love, caring, respect, acceptance, comfort, support, openness, and freedom are increasingly recognized as healthy and functional in Korean society today. Such a new conception of good family life confirms a significant change in family ideology (Kim, 1993; Park and Cho, 1995). These changes in family ideology and function call for a new approach to studying the quality of family life (Rettig et al., 1991; Rettig and Leichtentritt, 1999).

The most essential component of the Confucian family ideology is the inequality of interpersonal relations based on gender and generation. It emphasizes and justifies the need to distribute decision-making authority unequally between generations and between genders. Recent changes in family ideology, however, have contributed to reducing the unequal distribution of such authority. Today, gender inequality, especially between husbands and wives, is much less pronounced and less import than in the past. On the other hand, generation inequality, although changing, is still considered a virtue in Korean culture.

Such liberal trends in the family ideology are, however, often interpreted as a breakdown in the family, and a fracturing of the family relationship. The considerable weakening of Confucian family ideology has recently become a serious issue in the wake of sharp increases in the numbers of divorces, of elderly people living alone, and of families headed by youths. Such breakdowns in family life are often viewed as declines in the overall quality of family life.

This research on the quality of family life is predicated on the premise that psychological satisfaction of the needs in family relations is essential to the overall quality of family life (Retting and Leichtentrill, 1999). The quality of family life is, therefore, equated in this study with the quality of interpersonal relationships among family members. Specifically, it refers to the extent to which each member of a family is loved, cared for, respected, understood, acknowledged, and accepted by other family members.

Only a few earlier studies have addressed the quality of family life in Korea. These studies, moreover, dealt with narrowly specified areas of family life quality, for instance, the stresses and burdens of diseases such as cancer or long-term disabilities placed on family members (Noh and Kim, 1998; Park et al., 1998). To date, little effort has been made in Korea to study the quality of family life from a comprehensive and balanced perspective of relationships within the family.

To what extent do the Korean people experience what they want and expect from other members of their own family? What makes their family relationships satisfying and rewarding to the greatest degree? Is it the objective environment in which their family lives as a unit? Or does it depend largely on the way in which members of their family interact with each other, and decide the important matters affecting their well-being? This paper explores these questions with two sets of survey data.

METHOD

Data

This study involves two distinct sets of data. The first set, from the National Census data (hereinafter the national data), concerns the structural changes in family life. In addition to family type and family size, the national data set dealt with marriage and divorce rates, housing, and income. This data set, however, is insufficient in and of itself to reveal the nature of a family's real life interactions, such as its decision-making patterns and relationship traits among family members. In order to overcome the limitations of the national data, a second set of data was also assembled.

The second set of data came from a survey of college students the author conducted in 2000 (hereinafter, the student data). This data set was analyzed to examine the interpersonal quality of family life and the decision-making patterns within the family as well. Although limited in external validity due to the selection of college students, the student data covered the rich dynamics of everyday forms of a family's life. This student population was purposefully selected because it was intended to capture the dynamics of interpersonal life without being exposed to newly emerging family structures. This sample of 850 never-married students consisted of 587 (69%) females and 263 (31%) males, with an average age of 21 years. Of this sample, about 60 percent of their mothers were homemakers and 40 percent of their fathers were professionals or officials, and the monthly income of the households ranged from below U.S.$800 to U.S.$4800 and above, with an average of U.S.$2400.

Measures

The indicators used to measure the objective conditions of family life in the national data include items for demographics and other social background variables. Those variables are gender, income, family type, housing, and the rates of marriage, divorce, and remarriage. The data on these variables were gathered at the midpoint of each of the past three decades.

To identify the locus of the decision-making power within the family, respondents in the student data were asked to describe the decision making used in nine areas of family life issues. These include: (1) living expenses, (2) investments, (3) leisure and vacation time, (4) family goals, (5) children's education, (6) dating and marriages of the children, (7) children's job selection, (8) choices of religion, and (9) the making of friends. Specifically, they were asked to identify the exact locus of decision-making power by choosing one of five different modes: (1) the father alone; (2) the mother alone; (3) one's self; (4) the parents together; and (5) the family as

TABLE I

Composition of Each Item and Reliability Scores of the Family Relationship Scale

Sub-scales	# of items	Items	Mean (sd)	Cronbach's Alpha
Love & caring	11	Open and clear communication; family leisure time; intimacy; honesty and straightforwardness; supportive; expression of thoughts & feelings	3.4 (0.72)	0.93
Recognition*	7	Isolation; ignorance; blaming; violence; preference of being with others	4.2 (0.61)	0.83
Acceptance	6	Respect; acceptance; acknowledgement; right to speak up; take responsibility	3.5 (0.65)	0.78
Total	24		3.7 (0.56)	0.93

*All the items scored reverse.

a whole. This measure was designed to determine whether a family is either one-person dominant or whether the whole family (or the parents) shares in decision-making responsibilities.

The Family Relationship Scale (hereinafter the FRS), developed by the author, is designed to measure the quality of the relationship among family members on a 5-pont scale, with a higher score indicating a better quality of family relationship. The 24-item scale consists of three sub-scales: "love and caring", "recognition", and "acceptance". Internal consistencies of each of the sub-scales are 0.93, 0.83, and 0.78 respectively, and 0.93 for the whole scale. Table I presents the means, standard deviations, and the items of each sub-scale scale.

The "love and caring" sub-scale consists of 11 items, including the ones on open and clear communication, intimacy, honesty, support, and togetherness. This scale measures the emotional and affective involvement between family members. The average score of 3.4, which is higher than the midpoint on this 5-point scale, means moderate to high involvement in the surveyed Korean families.

The "recognition" sub-scale focuses on the absence of isolation, ignoring, violence, and blaming. It measures the extent to which the family is engaged in the ignoring and violent aspects of the relationship. The relatively high mean score of 4.2 on a 5-point scale indicates that the Korean families surveyed live in a relatively low violent and isolating environment.

The "acceptance" sub-scale deals with respect for differences, no insistence on rules and regulations, acknowledgement of feelings, the right to speak out, and taking responsibilities. This scale measures the cognitive-behavioral aspects of the relationships in a family. This sub-scale scored 3.4, the lowest among the three sub-scales. Yet, it was higher than the midpoint of the scale.

Method of Analysis

A number of different methods were used to examine the various qualities of family life. To analyze the objective dimensions of family life, a frequency tabulation was used. For the subjective aspects of quality of life, methods of frequency tabulation, mean distributions, analysis of variance, and multiple analysis of variance were utilized.

RESULTS

Objective Conditions of Family Life

How has the average size of Korean families been changed? As of 1995, there was a total of 12956000 households in Korea with an average of 3.3 members per household. The Korea National Statistical Office (hereinafter the NSO) released only a preliminary report on the 2000 Census data, which indicates that the average number of family members has declined to 3.1. Of more interest is the fact that this average has continually decreased by about one person every decade, from 5.0 people in 1975, to 4.1 in 1985, and it is currently 3.1.

How has the family structure and household composition changed over the period of 1975–95? Table II compares percentages

TABLE II

Households by Family Type (%)

Family type	1975	1985	1995
Nuclear family			
Married couple	4.8	7.1	10.8
Married couple with child(ren)	53.2	52.8	50.4
Single parent with child(ren)	9.7	8.9	7.4
Extended family			
Married couple with parent(s)	0.5	0.7	0.9
Married couple with parent(s) and child(ren)	10.4	9.1	6.9
Other types*	17.1	12.8	9.6
Single person household	4.2	6.9	12.7
Non blood related household	0.0	1.7	1.4
Total	100.0	100.0	100.0
Average of family members (person)	5.0	4.1	3.3 (3.1)

Source: Korea National Statistical Office, *Population and Housing Census*, 1975–1995.
*Other types include households of siblings, other relatives, and family communities.
( ): Data of 2000, www.nso.go.kr/report/data.

of nuclear, extended, and other types of families over this period. For a typical nuclear family, i.e., a married couple with children, little has changed over the 20 years. This pattern accounted for about 53 percent of families in 1975, and 50 percent in 1995. On the other hand, the family type consisting of childless married couples increased from 5 percent in 1975 to 11 percent in 1995, whereas the typical, traditional extended family type significantly decreased from 10 percent in 1975 to 7 percent in 1995. Unfortunately, the NSO has not yet released a complete report on the 2000 Census, so we cannot determine whether these patterns are continuing.

Table II shows that the "single parent with children" household type decreased, despite an increase in the divorce rate. A possible explanation for this change would be the higher percentage of remarriages and the increasing number of early divorces before having children. Another notable change that appeared over time was an increase in the number of single-person households. In 1995,

TABLE III

Family Formation Through Marriage, Divorce, and Remarriage (%)

Marital status	1970	1980	1990	1995	1999
Total marriage*	9.2	10.6	9.3	8.7	7.7 (7.0)
Divorce**	3.9	5.9	11.4	17.1	32.5 (36.0)
Remarriage**	—	—	10.6	13.7	17.5
Either side remarried***	—	—	55.7	52.6	47.0
Both side remarried***	—	—	44.3	47.5	53.0

Source: Korea NSO, *Annual Report on the Vital Statistics*, 1990–1999. www.nso.go.kr/report/data

*crude marriage rate; **out of total marriage; ***out of remarriage.

( ): Data of 2000.

the proportion was triple that of 1975. Among all family types, the most notable was the approximate 50-fold increase in the non-blood related household type. This group would include unmarried couples or groups of friends living together.

Table III shows that the crude marriage rate (1 out of 1000) has been decreasing, and in 2000, it reached its lowest level, that of 7.0 since 1970. The divorce rate, nevertheless, has been rising. One of three marriages (33%) in 1999 ended in divorce, and the data for 2000 indicates an even higher divorce rate (36%). For the year 2000, this rate was nine times higher than in 1970. Even so, the remarriage rate has also been increasing each year. Of all marriages in 1990, remarriages accounted for 11 percent, and the percentage rose to 18 percent in 1999. Of these remarriages, couples in which both members were remarrying increased from 44 percent in 1990 to 53 percent in 1999, indicating that divorced people were remarrying more often than in the past.

The trend in marital status can be summarized as follows: the total number of marriages is decreasing, while divorces and remarriages are rapidly increasing. This trend indicates that the traditional notion of the family is changing. In the past, once the family was established, it was considered a permanent institution. Today, however, the family seems easily formed, de-formed, and re-formed based on each member's wishes. This change in family life corre-

TABLE IV

Types of Housing Occupancy and Average Monthly Income of the Family (%)

Category	1975	1985	1993	1995	1996
Housing occupancy					
Own	63.6	53.7	—	53.3	—
Rent (long-term)	17.5	23.9	—	29.7	—
Monthly rent	15.7	15.4	—	14.5	—
Other(rent free)	3.3	1.9	—	2.5	—
Monthly income					
Less than $1000	—	92.9	28.1	—	12.8
$1000 ~ less than $2000	—	6.1	48.3	—	40.9
$2000 ~ less than $3000	—	1.0	16.5	—	28.5
$3000 ~ less than $4000	—	—	7.0	—	10.8
$4000 and above	—	—	—	—	6.9
Average monthly expenditure					$1888

Source: KNSO, *Population and Housing Census*, 1975–1995.
KNSO, *Social Statistics Survey*, 2000.

sponds with the societal and cultural changes in Korea, which gear each individual toward mutually beneficial and emotionally satisfying relationships more than strictly blood-oriented family relationships. It is also influenced by the emergence of societal values that emphasize individual free will over endurance or obedience for the good of the family.

To further assess changes in the objective conditions in which Korean families live, this paper considered the housing and income status of these families. As of 1995, more than half of the families resided in their own homes, and about 30 percent lived in rented housing (see Table IV). Living in a rented house, however, does not necessarily mean that the family is financially less well off. For instance, owning an apartment in the Kangbuk area in Seoul (north of the Han River), costs almost the same as renting a similar-sized apartment in the Kangnam area (south of the Han River).

In regard to monthly income at the national level, including both urban and rural, the highest proportion falls into the $1000–$2000

TABLE V

Locus of Decision Making Power: Student Data (%)

Dimensions	Father alone	Mother alone	Self** alone	Parents together	Family as whole
Living expenses	11.5	49.1	9.2	23.6	5.4
Investment	31.3	12.9	4.5	44.1	4.4
Leisure and vacation	12.8	6.5	16.3	20.9	41.1
Family goals	6.1	1.8	22.0	6.1	62.7
Education*	5.8	10.2	22.0	25.3	35.3
Marriage and dating*	2.7	4.1	43.1	15.5	32.7
Job selection*	3.1	1.5	68.9	6.1	18.5
Choosing a religion	2.4	4.1	62.9	7.3	21.3
Making friends	6.0	1.2	92.9	1.1	3.1

*These dimensions target children.
**Self means the student who was responding to the survey.

category. The average monthly income of an urban wage earner's household in 1999 was reported as $2387 (NSO, 2000), and the total average monthly expenditure was $1888. This calculation suggests that the urban household is better off than the rural one.

Locus of Decision-Making Power

The second set of the student data was analyzed to see how Korean family members interact with each other when they make important decisions. Korean families have been traditionally seen as authoritative in nature and father-dominant in the everyday decision-making process. Table V examines the making of nine important family decisions in terms of five different modes. Tables VI, VII, and VIII examine the relationships between the modes of decision making on the one hand and gender, income, and family type on the other hand.

If we look at financial decisions affecting each family's daily life, it is clear that about half of the time, the mother alone (49%) made the decision of allocating living expenses. In nearly one of four families (24%), the parents together made this decision. In the case of investing, the parents made this decision together most frequently (44%), followed by the father deciding alone (31%).

For more general family matters, such as setting family goals and deciding on family leisure and vacation, all family members were involved most frequently. A large majority (63%) reported that all the members of the family were involved in setting family goals. In the case of the leisure and vacation decisions as well, this mode of decision making was most popular, although it was practiced in a little over four out of ten families (41%). Such popularity of collaborative decision making in these matters remains invariant across the categories of gender and income, and the types of families.

To examine the issues that involve the children in a family, this study considered education, marriage and dating, and job selection. Depending on the issues, the parents and children tended to exercise varying levels of influence. On children's education, for example, the parents appeared to have a slightly larger voice than children themselves (25% vs. 22%). In more than one out of three families (35%), educational decisions were made jointly by children and their parents.

In Korea today, the entire family or parents are most often involved in decisions regarding which college to apply to and which major to choose. On the issues of marriage and dating, and job selection, however, children themselves tend to make the final decision without consulting with their parents or other family members. In more than four out of the ten families surveyed (43%), the parents allowed their children to choose their own mates. In more than six out of ten families, the parent allowed the children to choose the job and religion they liked most. Parents did not appear to insist on their personal preferences.

In virtually all areas, considerable differences were observed between the two genders. The most notable differences were observed in four areas: (1) leisure and vacation; (2) education; (3) marriage and dating; and (4) job selection. As compared to their female counterparts, male students were more often allowed to choose what they liked most (see Table VI). Korean parents are still more lenient toward their sons than their daughters. It appears that sons are more respected and trusted in making family decisions.

How does the locus of decision-making power vary across the levels of family income? Table VII shows that family income significantly influences the mode of decision making in four out of nine

TABLE VI

Locus of Decision Making by Gender: Student Data

Dimensions	Category	Male		Female		χ^2
		N	%	N	%	
Living expenses	Father alone	39	14.8	58	10.1	8.17
	Mother alone	123	46.8	294	50.1	
	Self alone	31	11.8	47	8.0	
	Parents together	55	20.9	146	24.9	
	Family as a whole	13	4.9	33	5.6	
Investment	Father alone	82	31.2	184	31.3	11.91*
	Mother alone	37	14.1	73	12.4	
	Self alone	18	6.8	20	3.4	
	Parents together	101	38.4	274	46.7	
	Family as a whole	17	6.5	20	3.4	
Leisure and vacation	Father alone	37	14.1	72	12.3	23.28***
	Mother alone	16	6.1	39	6.6	
	Self alone	65	24.7	74	12.6	
	Parents together	54	20.5	124	21.1	
	Family as a whole	86	32.7	263	44.8	
Family goals	Father alone	15	5.7	37	6.3	2.68
	Mother alone	4	1.5	11	1.9	
	Self alone	65	24.7	122	20.8	
	Parents together	18	6.8	34	5.8	
	Family as a whole	155	58.9	378	64.4	
Education	Father alone	20	7.6	29	4.9	24.55***
	Mother alone	18	6.8	69	11.8	
	Self alone	82	31.2	105	17.9	
	Parents together	60	22.8	155	26.4	
	Family as a whole	80	30.4	220	37.5	
Marriage and dating	Father alone	3	1.1	20	3.4	43.32***
	Mother alone	8	3.0	27	4.6	
	Self alone	156	59.3	210	35.8	
	Parents together	24	9.1	108	18.4	
	Family as a whole	68	25.9	210	35.8	

TABLE VI

Continued

Dimensions	Category	Male		Female		χ^2
		N	%	N	%	
Job selection	Father alone	8	3.0	18	3.1	13.65**
	Mother alone	2	0.8	11	1.9	
	Self alone	202	76.8	384	65.4	
	Parents together	12	4.6	40	6.8	
	Family as a whole	33	12.5	124	21.1	
Choosing a religion	Father alone	3	1.21	17	2.9	4.68
	Mother alone	10	3.8	25	4.3	
	Self alone	175	66.5	360	61.3	
	Parents together	15	5.7	47	8.0	
	Family as a whole	54	20.5	127	21.6	
Making friends	Father alone	2	0.8	3	0.5	3.77
	Mother alone	1	0.4	9	1.5	
	Self alone	245	93.2	544	92.7	
	Parents together	4	1.5	5	0.9	
	Family as a whole	6	2.3	20	3.4	

*$p < 0.05$; **$p < 0.01$; ***$p < 0.001$.

areas. While setting family goals was not influenced by income level, with respect to the issue of leisure and vacation, the lower the income level the more the parents seemed to rely on their children to decide on family vacations. In matters regarding the children's education, the parents of low-income families tended to rely on their children more often than those of high-income families. In making important financial decisions, low- and high-income families also differed significantly. In the former, mothers were more influential than fathers in deciding on investments. In the latter, by sharp contrast, fathers were more influential than mothers. In most areas, however, the parents' as well as the entire family's influence became much stronger with increases in family income.

Table VIII examines the relationships between family types and the locus of decision-making power. Regardless of family types, the

TABLE VII

Locus of Decision Making by Income (U.S. Dollar): Student Data

Dimensions	Category	Below $1000		$1000–$2000		$2000–$3000		$3000–$4000		$4000 and above		χ^2
		N	%	N	%	N	%	N	%	N	%	
Living expenses	Father alone	5	11.4	21	9.3	37	13.5	12	11.7	19	12.3	31.13*
	Mother alone	16	36.4	115	50.9	138	49.8	54	52.4	68	52.3	
	Self alone	12	27.3	19	8.4	15	5.4	12	11.7	13	10.0	
	Parents together	8	18.2	59	26.1	67	24.2	19	18.4	30	23.1	
	Family as a whole	3	6.8	12	5.3	20	7.2	6	5.8	3	2.3	
Investment	Father alone	5	11.9	71	32.7	84	30.4	39	38.2	44	34.4	62.20***
	Mother alone	12	28.6	32	14.7	32	11.6	10	9.8	20	15.6	
	Self alone	10	23.8	10	4.6	10	3.6	4	3.9	1	0.8	
	Parents together	13	31.0	90	41.5	139	50.4	46	45.1	59	46.1	
	Family as a whole	2	4.8	14	6.5	11	4.0	3	2.9	4	3.1	
Leisure and vacation	Father alone	5	11.9	31	14.0	37	13.5	15	14.6	16	12.6	41.11**
	Mother alone	3	7.1	15	6.8	14	5.1	8	14.8	14	11.0	
	Self alone	16	38.1	48	21.6	32	11.6	11	10.7	19	15.0	
	Parents together	2	4.8	35	15.8	74	26.9	28	27.2	26	20.5	
	Family as a whole	16	38.1	93	41.9	118	42.9	41	39.8	52	40.9	

TABLE VII

Continued

Dimensions	Category	Below $1000		$1000–$2000		$2000–$3000		$3000–$4000		$4000 and above		χ^2
		N	%	N	%	N	%	N	%	N	%	
Family goals	Father alone	4	9.5	14	6.3	16	5.7	6	5.8	7	5.4	16.93
	Mother alone	2	13.3	5	2.2	5	1.8	1	1.0	2	1.6	
	Self alone	16	38.1	50	22.4	63	22.5	15	14.6	25	19.4	
	Parents together	1	2.4	17	7.6	17	6.1	8	7.8	8	6.2	
	Family as a whole	19	45.2	137	61.4	179	63.9	73	70.9	87	37.4	
Education	Father alone	3	7.0	13	5.8	18	6.5	6	5.8	5	3.9	29.28*
	Mother alone	3	7.0	21	9.4	29	10.5	10	9.7	19	14.7	
	Self alone	19	44.2	57	25.4	55	19.9	14	13.6	22	17.1	
	Parents together	7	16.3	53	23.7	79	28.5	34	33.0	28	21.7	
	Family as a whole	11	25.6	80	35.7	96	34.7	39	37.9	55	42.6	
Marriage and dating	Father alone	1	2.3	6	2.7	10	3.6	5	4.9	1	0.8	24.59
	Mother alone	2	4.7	6	2.7	10	3.6	2	1.9	9	7.1	
	Self alone	26	60.5	106	47.7	119	42.8	35	34.0	51	40.2	
	Parents together	6	14.0	26	11.7	48	17.3	23	22.3	23	18.1	
	Family as a whole	8	18.6	78	35.1	91	32.7	38	36.9	43	33.9	

TABLE VII
Continued

Dimensions	Category	Below $1000		$1000–$2000		$2000–$3000		$3000–$4000		$4000 and above		χ^2
		N	%	N	%	N	%	N	%	N	%	
Job selection	Father alone	1	2.4	9	4.0	5	1.8	6	5.8	4	3.1	17.89
	Mother alone	1	2.4	2	0.9	3	1.1	1	1.0	5	3.9	
	Self alone	32	76.2	158	70.9	195	70.7	68	66.0	85	65.9	
	Parents together	4	9.5	9	4.0	18	6.5	8	7.8	12	9.3	
	Family as a whole	4	9.5	45	20.2	55	19.9	20	19.4	23	17.8	
Choosing a religion	Father alone	2	4.8	6	2.7	6	2.2	3	3.0	2	1.6	25.19
	Mother alone	1	2.4	10	4.5	6	2.2	5	5.0	10	7.8	
	Self alone	31	73.8	146	65.5	184	66.7	64	63.4	76	58.9	
	Parents together	6	14.3	9	4.0	19	6.9	11	10.9	10	7.8	
	Family as a whole	2	4.8	52	23.3	61	22.1	18	17.8	31	24.0	
Making friends	Father alone	0	0.0	1	0.4	1	0.4	2	1.9	1	0.8	19.73
	Mother alone	0	0.0	1	0.4	3	1.1	2	1.9	3	2.3	
	Self alone	40	95.2	213	95.5	266	95.3	93	90.3	117	90.0	
	Parents together	1	2.4	1	0.4	1	0.4	1	1.0	5	3.8	
	Family as a whole	1	2.4	7	3.1	8	2.9	5	4.9	4	3.1	

$^{*}p < 0.05$; $^{**}p < 0.01$; $^{***}p < 0.001$.

parents, either individually or jointly, monopolized the making of financial decisions. In all types of families, the mother was most influential in managing living expenses, while the father was most influential in deciding on investments. Single parents showed the tendency to rely on the children's decision more often than in a two-parent family in almost all areas of family life. Across all family types, students were most influential in making their own personal choices regarding marriage, job, religion, and friends.

In summary, the survey findings presented above suggest that Korean families tend to practice collaborative decision making contrary to what was once believed. Before this study, Korean families were widely perceived to be so heavily influenced by Confucianism, that family members interacted with each other on a hierarchical rather than collaborative basis. Such perceptions are no longer accurate. An increasing number of families currently allows individual members to choose their own mates, jobs, and religions. The power to decide on investments is also delegated to the married couple, although the husband has more power than the wife. All in all, it is evident that equality is being achieved and the quality of family life is improving, although there is still discrimination against daughters.

QUALITY OF FAMILY RELATIONS

Quality of Family Relationships by Objective Conditions

Is the quality of a family relationship affected by gender, income, and family type? The results of bivariate analysis are reported in Table IX. Only the income level seemed to have a significant positive impact for love and caring. The lower the level of family income is, the lower the level of love and caring among family members. It is, therefore, the lowest income group student, who reported the lowest quality of family life. Both male and female students were equally loved and cared for by their families. Regardless of their family type, moreover, they appeared to be treated equally.

In terms of recognition, Table IX shows significant differences across the levels of family income and the types of families. With respect to income level, for example, lower income class students

TABLE VIII

Locus of Decision Making by Family Type: Student Data

Dimensions	Category	Married couple N	Married couple %	Single parent N	Single parent %	Self sibling N	Self sibling %	Non-blood related N	Non-blood related %	χ^2
Living expenses	Father alone	59	10.4	6	9.7	22	15.7	9	18.0	38.16***
	Mother alone	292	51.3	33	53.2	65	46.4	17	34.0	
	Self alone	41	7.2	13	21.0	14	10.0	8	16.0	
	Parents together	150	26.4	3	4.8	32	22.9	12	24.0	
	Family as a whole	27	4.7	7	11.3	7	5.0	4	8.0	
Investment	Father alone	174	31.2	13	21.3	58	41.3	18	36.0	115.77***
	Mother alone	63	11.3	25	41.0	17	12.1	4	8.0	
	Self alone	13	2.3	9	14.8	6	4.3	9	18.0	
	Parents together	288	51.7	7	11.5	52	37.1	17	34.0	
	Family as a whole	19	3.4	7	11.5	7	5.0	2	4.0	
Leisure and vacation	Father alone	71	12.7	4	6.5	27	19.6	6	11.8	51.16***
	Mother alone	41	7.3	6	9.7	5	3.6	2	3.9	
	Self alone	75	13.4	25	40.3	22	15.9	14	27.5	
	Parents together	127	22.7	2	3.2	35	25.4	10	19.6	
	Family as a whole	245	43.8	25	40.3	49	35.5	19	37.3	
Family goals	Father alone	35	6.2	4	6.5	7	5.0	3	5.9	20.59
	Mother alone	6	1.1	3	4.8	2	1.4	3	5.9	
	Self alone	115	20.3	19	30.6	37	26.4	12	23.5	
	Parents together	36	6.3	0	0.0	11	7.9	3	5.9	
	Family as a whole	375	66.1	36	58.1	93	59.3	30	58.8	
Education	Father alone	34	6.0	3	4.8	8	5.7	3	5.9	32.2***
	Mother alone	67	11.9	9	14.5	10	7.1	1	2.0	
	Self alone	104	18.4	23	37.1	35	24.8	19	37.3	
	Parents together	153	27.1	8	12.9	42	29.8	7	13.7	
	Family as a whole	207	36.6	19	30.6	46	32.6	21	41.2	
Marriage and dating	Father alone	18	3.2	2	3.2	2	1.4	1	2.0	33.66***
	Mother alone	22	3.9	5	8.1	5	3.6	2	4.0	

TABLE VIII

Continued

Dimensions	Category	Married couple N	Married couple %	Single parent N	Single parent %	Self sibling N	Self sibling %	Non-blood related N	Non-blood related %	χ^2
	Self alone	224	39.6	43	69.4	62	44.6	28	56.0	
	Parents together	94	16.6	3	4.8	28	20.1	6	12.0	
	Family as a whole	207	36.6	9	14.5	42	30.2	13	26.0	
Job selection	Father alone	18	3.2	3	4.8	3	2.2	2	4.0	18.94
	Mother alone	10	1.8	1	1.6	2	1.4	0	0.0	
	Self alone	381	67.4	54	87.1	98	70.5	39	78.0	
	Parents together	40	7.1	0	0.0	7	5.0	4	8.0	
	Family as a whole	116	20.5	4	6.5	29	20.9	5	10.0	
Choosing a religion	Father alone	16	2.8	1	1.6	0	0.0	2	3.9	27.94*
	Mother alone	26	4.6	3	4.8	6	4.3	0	0.0	
	Self alone	350	62.2	51	81.0	96	69.6	26	51.0	
	Parents together	41	7.3	2	3.2	10	7.2	8	15.7	
	Family as a whole	130	23.1	6	9.5	26	18.8	15	29.4	
Making Friends	Father alone	4	0.7	0	0.0	0	0.0	1	2.0	9.65
	Mother alone	8	1.4	1	1.6	1	0.7	0	0.0	
	Self alone	529	93.0	61	96.8	135	97.1	46	92.0	
	Parents together	6	1.1	0	0.0	2	1.4	1	2.0	
	Family as a whole	22	3.9	1	1.6	1	0.7	2	4.0	

*$p < 0.05$; ***$p < 0.001$.

perceived significantly less recognition from their families than higher income class students. It is apparent that blaming, ignoring, isolating, and acts of violence occurred more frequently in lower class families than higher income families.

Among the three distinct qualities of family life surveyed in this study, acceptance was the only dimension in which the income level did not matter significantly. Nonetheless, it turned out to be the only dimension in which the variable of gender made a significant

TABLE IX

Quality of Family Relationships by Objective Conditions: ANOVA Mean (sd)

Variables	Categories	Love & caring	Recognition	Acceptance	Total
Gender	Male	3.4 (0.71)	4.1 (0.69)	3.5 (0.64)	3.7 (0.57)
	Female	3.4 (0.73)	4.2 (0.57)	3.4 (0.65)	3.7 (0.56)
	t	**–0.53**	**–0.95**	**2.31****	**0.29**
Income	Blow $1,000	3.2 (0.76)*	4.2 (0.59)	3.5 (0.65)	3.6 (0.58)
	$1,000–$2,000	3.3 (0.73)*	4.1 (0.63)*	3.4 (0.62)	3.6 (0.55)*
	$2,000–$3,000	3.4 (0.71)*	4.1 (0.67)	3.4 (0.64)	3.6 (0.57)*
	$3,000–$4,000	3.6 (0.74)*	4.2 (0.59)	3.5 (0.70)	3.8 (0.59)
	$4,000 & up	3.7 (0.68)*	4.3 (0.51)*	3.6 (0.66)	3.9 (0.54)*
	F	**7.74*****	**3.06***	**2.24**	**5.32*****
Family type	Married couple	3.5 (0.73)	4.2 (0.60)	3.4 (0.65)	3.4 (0.65)
	Single parent	3.4 (0.73)	4.1 (0.58)	3.6 (0.66)	3.6 (0.66)
	Self, sibling	3.4 (0.72)	4.1 (0.61)	3.5 (0.66)	3.5 (0.66)
	Non-blood	3.3 (0.63)	4.0 (0.70)	3.4 (0.60)	3.4 (0.60)
	F	**1.29**	**2.73***	**0.95**	**1.17**

*$p < 0.05$; ***$p < 0.01$.
Significant by Scheffe test.

difference. Male students, as compared to their female counterparts, reported experiencing not only more acceptance and acknowledgment but also more respect. Male students felt as though they had more power to express themselves than female students. This finding indicates that Korea remains a gender-based society in which one's gender status affects the quality of interpersonal life even within one's own family. As in the past, males are still more likely to be recognized as an independent, autonomous, and responsible person.

In the last column of Table IX, all three qualities of family life – love and caring, recognition, and acceptance – were considered together to examine the impact of gender, income, and family type on the overall quality of family. From the data reported in this column, it is clear that gender does not matter much for the overall quality of family life that Korean students experience. It is also clear that family type does not matter as well. What matters most is the amount of financial resources that families command. The greater the level of their incomes are, the better the overall quality of their family lives. Economic deprivations and hardships detract most from the good quality of family life in Korea.

Locus of Decision-Making Power and the Quality of Family Life

Does the way in which the family makes important decisions affect the quality of family life? To explore this question, an analysis of variance was performed on the three sub-scales measuring the quality of family relationships and the nine sub-scales measuring the modes of decision making. Table X presents the mean scores of love and caring, recognition, and acceptance for each of five decision modes.

The results suggest that the liberal atmosphere of the family contributes significantly to the good quality of relationships among its members. Specifically, a democratic environment was an essential element in attaining a quality family relationship among family members. The different levels of quality in their relationships could be predicted by ascertaining who was involved in the process of making important decisions. In all nine areas, when a father alone made decisions, students felt worse about their family life than when either the parents decided together or the whole family decided. In issues directly affecting children a higher-quality relationship was perceived when the whole family (including the students) was involved in decision making, rather than the father deciding alone and then ordering others to follow his decision. Even with respect to decisions on living expenses, both parents' involvement led to a higher-quality family relationship than if the father alone made the decisions. There is little doubt that extensive involvement in family decision making enhances the perceived quality of family relationships.

Predictors of the Quality of Family Life

The description analyses presented above revealed that objective conditions have relatively little effect on the quality of family life. Out of three objective conditions, only family income registered significant differences. In sharp contrast, how each of nine important

TABLE X

Quality of Family Relationship by Locus of Decision Making: ANOVA Mean (sd)

Dimension	Category	Love & caring	Recognition	Acceptance	Total
Living exp.	Father alone	3.2 (0.77)*	4.0 (0.59)	3.3 (0.73)*	3.5 (0.62)*
	Mother alone	3.4 (0.70)	4.2 (0.60)	3.4 (0.64)	3.7 (0.55)
	Self alone	3.4 (0.76)	4.1 (0.65)	3.5 (0.68)	3.7 (0.58)
	Parents together	3.5 (0.73)*	4.2 (0.63)	3.5 (0.61)*	3.8 (0.56)*
	Family as a whole	3.5 (0.62)	4.2 (0.61)	3.5 (0.53)	3.8 (0.50)
	F	**3.59****	**2.28**	**4.02****	**4.20****
Investment	Father alone	3.3 (0.74)*	4.1 (0.60)	3.4 (0.69)	3.6 (0.59)*
	Mother alone	3.3 (0.70)	4.1 (0.61)	3.5 (0.66)	3.6 (0.54)
	Self alone	3.3 (0.70)	4.1 (0.65)	3.5 (0.64)	3.6 (0.56)
	Parents together	3.5 (0.71)*	4.3 (0.59)	3.5 (0.62)	3.8 (0.55)*
	Family as a whole	3.5 (0.62)	4.0 (0.78)	3.5 (0.47)	3.7 (0.50)
	F	**3.93****	**3.37****	**2.64****	**3.54****
Leisure and vacation	Father alone	3.2 (0.72)*	4.0 (0.69)*	3.2 (0.68)*	3.4 (0.59)*
	Mother alone	3.5 (0.59)	4.1 (0.64)	3.5 (0.61)*	3.7 (0.50)
	Self alone	3.2 (0.77)*	4.1 (0.61)*	3.4 (0.67)*	3.6 (0.58)*
	Parents together	3.5 (0.75)	4.2 (0.65)	3.4 (0.62)*	3.7 (0.57)*
	Family as a whole	3.6 (0.67)*	4.3 (0.53)*	3.6 (0.61)*	3.8 (0.51)*
	F	**9.07*****	**7.3*****	**8.82*****	**10.83*****
Family goals	Father alone	3.1 (0.66)*	3.8 (0.62)*	3.0 (0.65)*	3.3 (0.57)*
	Mother alone	3.3 (0.48)	3.5 (0.64)*	3.2 (0.55)	3.4 (0.45)*
	Self alone	3.2 (0.77)*	4.0 (0.63)*	3.3 (0.69)*	3.5 (0.58)*
	Parents together	3.4 (0.69)	4.1 (0.69)*	3.4 (0.57)*	3.6 (0.51)
	Family as a whole	3.6 (0.68)*	4.3 (0.57)*	3.6 (0.61)*	3.8 (0.53)*
	F	**15.05*****	**15.18*****	**13.36*****	**18.82*****
Education	Father alone	3.7 (0.81)*	4.0 (0.67)*	3.1 (0.74)*	3.4 (0.65)*
	Mother alone	3.3 (0.66)*	4.0 (0.67)*	3.3 (0.62)*	3.5 (0.53)*
	Self alone	3.2 (0.70)*	4.1 (0.62)*	3.5 (0.66)*	3.6 (0.53)*
	Parents together	3.5 (0.74)*	4.2 (0.61)	3.4 (0.67)*	3.7 (0.59)*
	Family as a whole	3.6 (0.68)*	4.3 (0.54)*	3.6 (0.57)*	3.8 (0.51)*
	F	**10.25*****	**9.25*****	**9.86*****	**12.18*****

TABLE X

Continued

Dimension	Category	Love & caring	Recognition	Acceptance	Total
Marriage and dating	Father alone	3.0 (0.80)*	3.7 (0.73)*	2.9 (0.77)*	3.2 (0.65)*
	Mother alone	3.5 (0.75)	4.0 (0.74)	3.4 (0.65)	3.6 (0.62)
	Self alone	3.3 (0.70)*	4.1 (0.62)*	3.4 (0.64)*	3.6 (0.55)*
	Parents together	3.5 (0.76)	4.2 (0.63)*	3.4 (0.64)*	3.7 (0.58)*
	Family as a whole	3.6 (0.70)*	4.3 (0.51)*	3.6 (0.63)*	3.8 (0.52)*
	F	**7.86*****	**10.10*****	**6.14*****	**9.94*****
Children's job selection	Father alone	3.0 (0.76)*	3.7 (0.77)*	2.9 (0.69)*	3.2 (0.62)*
	Mother alone	3.4 (0.52)	4.0 (0.62)	3.2 (0.57)	3.5 (0.43)
	Self alone	3.4 (0.72)*	4.2 (0.60)*	3.5 (0.64)*	3.7 (0.56)*
	Parents together	3.5 (0.61)	4.1 (0.64)*	3.4 (0.56)*	3.4 (0.48)*
	Family as a whole	3.6 (0.70)*	4.4 (0.50)*	3.6 (0.63)*	3.9 (0.53)*
	F	**6.24*****	**9.53*****	**7.85*****	**9.88*****
Choosing a religion	Father alone	3.0 (0.70)*	3.5 (0.61)*	2.8 (0.61)*	3.1 (0.50)*
	Mother alone	3.3 (0.59)	4.0 (0.65)*	3.2 (0.64)*	3.5 (0.50)*
	Self alone	3.4 (0.71)*	4.2 (0.59)*	3.5 (0.64)*	3.7 (0.55)*
	Parents together	3.4 (0.70)	4.0 (0.63)*	3.3 (0.66)*	3.6 (0.56)*
	Family as a whole	3.7 (0.70)*	4.4 (0.58)*	3.6 (0.60)*	3.9 (0.55)*
	F	**6.90*****	**13.43*****	**10.83*****	**12.82*****
Making friends	Father alone	2.8 (0.95)	3.6 (0.80)	2.5 (0.70)*	3.0 (0.72)
	Mother alone	3.7 (0.70)	3.8 (1.00)	3.4 (0.41)	3.6 (0.29)
	Self alone	3.4 (0.72)	4.2 (0.59)	3.5 (0.65)*	3.7 (0.56)
	Parents together	3.6 (0.48)	3.9 (0.74)	3.4 (0.43)	3.6 (0.40)
	Family as a whole	3.7 (0.80)	4.2 (0.82)	3.6 (0.67)*	3.8 (0.68)
	F	**2.4***	**2.77***	**3.12***	**2.41***

*$p < 0.05$; **$p < 0.01$; ***$p < 0.001$.
Significant by Scheffe test.

TABLE XI

Quality of Family Relationship by All Variables: Multiple ANOVA

	Love & caring		Recognition		Acceptance		Total	
	F	eta squared (%)	F	eta squared (%)	F	eta squared (%)	F	eta squared (%)
Living exp.	3.27	0.82	3.47***	0.90	7.49	1.75	6.50*	1.63
Investment	1.11	0.28	1.75	0.45	0.13	0.03	0.03	0.01
Leisure	0.46	0.12	3.06	0.79	0.98	0.23	1.77	0.44
Fam. goals	13.13***	3.31	17.79***	4.60	18.61	4.34	23.30***	5.86
Education	2.29	0.58	2.04	0.40	3.19	0.74	3.56	0.90
Marriage	1.51	0.39	1.89	1.36	0.10	0.02	1.36	0.34
Job	0.51	0.13	1.54	0.49	0.07	0.02	0.76	0.19
Religion	4.56*	1.15	5.28*	0.25	4.76	1.11	6.93**	1.74
Friends	0.06	0.22	1.91	1.37	0.00	0.00	0.36	0.09
Gender	0.87	6.17	0.98	0.25	8.83	2.06	3.76	0.95
Income	24.51***	0.33	5.29*	1.37	5.07	1.18	15.11***	0.35
Fam. type	1.32	0.14	4.55*	1.17	0.07	0.02	1.40	
F	9.14***		8.61***		7.61***		11.40***	
R^2	0.14		0.13		0.12		0.16	

$^{*}p < 0.05$; $^{**}p < 0.01$; $^{***}p < 0.001$.
The eta-squared statistic describes the proportion of total variability attributable to a factor, and the 'estimates of effect size' gives a partial eta-squared value for each effect and each parameter estimate. Thus, eta-squared statistic is utilized to estimate the relative power of each estimate in the equation.

issue of family life was decided was found to affect significantly each of three qualities of family life. Which ones of these objective and subjective variables contribute most of those qualities? Multiple analysis of variance was thus performed to address this question. Table XI reports the results of this analysis, including eta-equared values and F values.

Of the 12 independent variables listed in the table, setting a family goal, freedom to choose a religion, and family income appeared to be the most powerful predictors of sharing love and caring. With regard to recognition being felt in the family relationship, both family income and type figured significantly along with the variables of living expenses, setting a family goal, and freedom to choose a religion. With regard to feeling accepted by the family, variables, such as gender and income, along with living expenses, setting a family goal, and freedom of religion were significant. Overall, the variables of income level, living expenses, setting a family goal, and freedom of religion turned out to be the most significant.

On the whole, family income figured most significantly in explaining how family members related to each other. Low-income families seemed to have less time and energy to share love with and show respect to other family members. Family sharing of life events through decision-making processes at different levels also revealed a consistent impact on the family's relationship at both the emotional and the psychological level. The overall quality of family relationships was predicted by income level, family involvement in freedom of religion, and family goal setting.

SUMMARY AND DISCUSSION

How family life has been changing is one of the most compelling issues in Korea today. As Korean society has changed in the wake of industrialization, urbanization, and globalization, families have undergone drastic shifts in their ideology, roles, and structure. There are many widely-held views on how the contemporary Korean family is structured and managed: it is tightly controlled by Confucian ideology, requiring a strong emphasis on education; with clear distinctions of status between old and young, and between male and female.

This paper sought to determine the exact nature of the changes that are shaping today's Korean family life by examining the locus of decision-making power and evaluating the perceived quality of relations among family members. The quality of a family relationship was measured in terms of love and caring, recognition, and acknowledgment. The locus of decision-making power with the family was measured by examining how its members interacted with each other in deciding on nine important issues ranging from living expenses to religion.

One of the most notable findings is that perceptions of good family life are shaped strongly by the consistent involvement of the whole family in many aspect of the decision-making process especially with respect to the children's education. Such involvement attests to the fact that Korean families are no longer as hierarchical as the Confucian family ideology once demanded. It is no longer the husband or the father who plays the dominant role in decision making. The entire family tends to take part in making important decisions. The husband and wife are equal partners in making those decisions. The democratic values of autonomy, freedom, and equality have supplanted the authoritarian values of Confucianism as the family ideology.

Another notable finding of this study concerns the quality of relations among family members. Korean families are found to offer all of the three essential qualities featuring love and caring, recognition, and acknowledgement to varying degrees. Both male and female students are equally loved and cared for, but males are more accepted, respected, and empowered. Whether Korean students live with one or both parents, they experience similar qualities of family relationships. Students from low-income families, however, experience significantly lower qualities of interpersonal relationships than those from high-income families do. The family income level and involvement in decision making are the two most powerful forces shaping the interpersonal quality of family life in Korea today.

In conclusion, the hierarchical ideology and legacies of the Confucian past are no longer dominant influences on the way Korean families live. The families today have begun to share powers and responsibilities equally among their members. They are in the process of creating a new family ideology, and are building sharing, caring, and collaborative relationships within the family. By doing so, they are experiencing a greater quality in their family life.

REFERENCES

Chang, H.S. and H.O. Kim: 1994, 'Defining 'Quality of life' from the perspective of the family', Journal of Health and Social Welfare 14(2), pp. 62–81.

Chang, H.S. et al.: 1994, Quality of Life in Family Dimension and Policy Tasks (Korean Institute of Health and Social Affairs).

Choi, Jae Suk: 1976, Social characteristics of Koreans (Gamun Sa, Seoul).

Cohen, E.H., R.A. Clifton and L.W. Roberts: 2001, 'The cognitive domain of the quality of life of university students: A re-analysis of an instrument', Social Indicators Research 53, pp. 63–77.

Crowley, M.J. and A.E. Kazdin: 1998, 'Child psychosocial functioning and parent quality of life among clinically referred children', Journal of Child and Family Studies 7(2), pp. 233–251.

Cummins, R.A.: 1996, 'The comprehensive quality of life scale: Theory and development', Health Outcomes Bulletin 6, pp. 18–22.

Cummins, R.A.: 2000, 'Objective and subjective quality of life: An interactive model', Social Indicators Research 52(1), pp. 55–72.

Jeffres, L.W. and J. Dobos: 1995, 'Separating people's satisfaction with life and public perceptions of the quality of life in the environment', Social Indicators Research 34(2), pp. 181–211.

Kang, D.S.: 1991, 'A study on the <Quality of Life Indicators>', Journal of Cheju University 33, pp. 437–459.

Kim, B.G. et al.: 1997, 'Study on changes in quality of life and economic development in Korea: Re-evaluation of quantitative indicators for transition to qualitative growth', unpublished report.

Kim, M.H.: 1993, 'Transformation of family ideology in upper-middles-class families in urban South Korea', Ethonology 32, pp. 69–85.

Keith, K.D., M. Yamamoto, N. Okita and R.L. Schalock: 1995, 'Cross-cultural quality of life: Japanese and American college students', Social Behavior and Personality 23(2), pp. 163–170.

Lee, Suni: 1998, 'Marital status, gender, and subjective quality of life in Korea', Development and Society 27, pp. 35–49.

Lever, J.P.: 2000, 'The development of an instrument to measure quality of life in Mexico city', Social Indicators Research 50(2), pp. 187–208.

Lloyd, K.: 1996, 'Planning for leisure: issue of quality of life', Social Alternatives 15(2), pp. 19–22.

Park, E.S. et al.: 1998, 'Study on establishing a model of predicting the quality of life in family of chronic patients', Korean J. of Nusing 28(2), pp. 344–356.

Park, I.H. and L.J. Cho: 1995, 'Confucianism and the Korean family', Journal of Comparative Family Studies 26, pp. 117–134.

Palomar, J.: 1999, 'The relationship between family functioning and quality of life in families with an alcoholic member', Salud Mental 22(6), pp. 13–21.

Rettig, K.D., S.M. Danes and J.W. Bauer: 1991, 'Family life quality: Theory and assessment in economically stressed farm families', Social Indicators Research 24, pp. 269–299.

Rettig, K.D. and R.D. Leichtentritt: 1999, 'A general theory for perceptual indicators of family life quality', Social Indicators Research 47(3), pp. 307–342.

Sam, D.L.: 2001, 'Satisfaction with life among international students: An exploratory study', Social Indicators Research 53, pp. 315–337.

Schumm, W.R., E.E. McCallum, M.A. Bugaighis, A.P. Jurich and S.R. Bollman: 1986, 'Characteristics of the Kansas family life satisfaction scale in a regional sample', Psychological Reports 58, pp. 975–980.

Shin, Y.H. and K.S. Chang: 1997, Korean family and culture of community in 21 Century (Jisik, Seoul).
Yang, O.K.: 2001, 'Study on college students' perception of family', Korean Journal of Family Social Work 7, pp. 175–199.
Yang, O.K. 2000, 'Qualitative research on the concepts of family in Korea', Korean Journal of Family Social Work 6, pp. 69–99.

Department of Social Welfare
College of Social Sciences
Ewha Womans University
11–1 Daehyun Dong
Sudaemun Gu, Seoul
Korea
E-mail: okyang@ewha.ac.kr

ANDREW EUNGI KIM

RELIGIOUS INFLUENCES ON PERSONAL AND SOCIETAL WELL-BEING

ABSTRACT. This paper examines religious influences on personal and societal well-being in South Korea by systematically analyzing recent research on the topic, and by comparing the findings with those of other countries, especially those of North America, to assess similarities and differences. In concert with generally accepted findings elsewhere, the paper shows that Koreans with religious faith generally have higher levels of satisfaction than those without religious faith with respect to such quality of life indicators as income level, interpersonal relationships, job satisfaction, marital life, and health. Among those considered to be religious, Protestants were found to be most satisfied with life, followed by Catholics and Buddhists. It is also clear that individuals with strong religious beliefs, and those who frequently participate in religious activities, are more satisfied with life than those with less strong religious conviction and commitment. With regard to the relationship between religion and societal well-being, this paper shows that religious organizations in South Korea, especially Christian ones, have contributed significantly to societal well-being through their extensive involvement in welfare services, socio-economic activities, such as health care and education, and the democratic movement. What this paper confirms, therefore, is that religious beliefs and practices do matter in the lives of real people: religious resources can help individuals feel more secure, stable and happy; and religious resources also can be mobilized to meet social needs, thereby contribute to societal progress.

INTRODUCTION

Objective life conditions that are often used in measuring quality of life consist of such things as: health, economic resources (income and wealth), social support, education, employment and working conditions, political and legal rights, and housing. In particular, health, financial stability, job satisfaction, a happy marriage and a loving relationship, and good interpersonal relationships are main elements of a sense of well-being. While there are ample studies that measure these objective conditions of life, the role of religion

Social Indicators Research **62, 63:** 149–170, 2003.

in the quality of one's life is relatively less well researched: the potential relationship between the two is often disregarded as being unimportant or is often taken for granted.

Research on the relationship between religion and quality of life is complicated by the fact that both concepts are multifaceted, and the relationships between the two are highly complex (Maton and Wells, 1995; Paloutzian and Kirkpatrick, 1995; Wildes, 1996). A person's religious experience or commitment, for example, can be divided into two categories of "belonging" (church membership) and "meaning" (importance of faith) (Hadaway and Roof, 1978), and can include such religious activities as affiliation with a religious organization, belief in religious dogmas, participation in religious services, and personal spirituality. A person's subjective well-being, used synonymously with quality of life, emphasizes his or her achievements, "dominance over circumstances, ability to overcome adversity, freedom from constraint, and fulfillment of individual aims" (Moberg, 1970: p. 3). In general, researchers have found religiosity to be positively related to higher levels of well-being, including positive self esteem, job satisfaction, general happiness, and life satisfaction (Clemente and Sauer, 1976; McCann, 1962). More specifically, many studies have demonstrated a positive correlation between religiousness and psychological well-being or mental health (Bergin, 1983; Gartner et al., 1991; Ventis, 1995). Similarly, higher levels of religious participation and commitment are also correlated with lower levels of anxiety and depression among the elderly (Johnson, 1995; Koenig, 1998) and the bereaved (Gray, 1987). Being religious is also associated with active and effective coping with problems and crises, such as a terminal illness (Pargament, 1997; Tix and Frazier, 1998). Other studies have approached these relationships from diverse conceptualizations of well-being, including physical health (Dull and Skokan, 1995; Ellison and Levin, 1998; Koenig et al., 1998), marital stability (Call and Heaton, 1997; Lehrer and Chiswick, 1993), and substance non-abuse and recovery (Benson, 1992; Cochran et al., 1988). In these studies, religious beliefs and involvement are found to promote better health, inspire constructive coping mechanisms, enhance marital stability and family cohesion, and/or furnish hope and optimism in times of crisis.

The reasons for the positive influence of religious participation or religiosity on subjective well-being are many, but five explanations are most important. First, religious involvement may provide a coherent frame of reference for understanding events and uncertainties associated with daily experiences (Berger, 1967). Second, religious involvement may help the individual to cope better with stressful situations, including the death and illness of significant others, by providing cogent answers to the "problem of meaning" (see Spilka et al., 1985). Third, religious organizations provide a supportive environment for social relationships, whereby fellowships and friendships are nurtured, and whereby feelings of reassurance and encouragement are enhanced. Fourth, religious involvement allows adherents to enhance their self-esteem by developing a close relationship with the all-loving Supreme Being (Pollner, 1989). Finally, religious involvement may affect the individual's health, as religious norms against smoking and drinking are likely to, among others, lower cancer rates (Levin and Vanderpool, 1991).

The question is: what is the relationship between religiousness and subjective well-being for Koreans? Is there any relationship between religion and societal well-being? Are research results in South Korea (hereinafter Korea) consistent with those found elsewhere, including North America? These questions will be examined in this paper. However, it must be noted that such a task is undertaken in the absence of rich literature, for only a handful of such research products exist, including those focusing on the impact of religiousness on the quality of life of the Korean elderly (Gallup Korea, 1998; Kim, M. and Park, 2000; Lee, W., 1991; Lee, Y., 1994). In stark contrast to the proliferation of research on the topic in North America, sociologists of religion and psychologists of religion in Korea have paid only scant attention to the relationship between religion and well-being. The fact that sociology of religion and psychology of religion remain outside the "mainstream" of sociology and psychology in Korea – much more so in Korea than elsewhere – has not helped the matter either.

This paper begins by presenting a survey of the characteristics of religious life in Korea. It then reviews and analyzes research findings on the effects of religion upon personal and societal well-being in Korea. In the process, the findings in Korea will be compared with those of other countries to highlight similarities and differences. The paper concludes by suggesting that more research undertakings, those which examine the relationship between religion and quality of life among specific age groups, such as adolescents and the elderly, and which analyze the relationship between religion and such quality of life indicators as physical health and marital stability in Korea, are needed to better understand the complexity of the religion-life satisfaction nexus in the Korean context.

RELIGIONS AND RELIGIOUSNESS OF KOREANS

Korea has no "official" religion nor is there one dominant religion: Buddhism, Catholicism, Protestantism, Confucianism,[1] and Shamanism,[2] as well as a whole spectrum of new religious movements, co-exist peacefully in one of the most religiously pluralistic countries in the world (see Cha, 1995; Choi, 1998; Jung, 1986; Kim, T., 1973). What is interesting about the religious situation in contemporary Korea is that, in spite of rapid industrialization and urbanization, a strong religious impulse remains intact. The proportion of the population that is religious has actually increased steadily during the last four decades. Indeed, traditional religions and Christianity remain vibrant in the vastly modernized society. From 1964 to 1994, the "religious population" jumped more than six-fold, while the total population increased by about one-and-a-half times. The increase was especially conspicuous from the early 1960s to the end of the 1980s, the period of the country's remarkable economic development and rapid urbanization.[3] The growth has been particularly pronounced for Protestant Christianity (see Kim, B., 1985; Lee, W., 1992; Ro and Nelson, 1995). Since the early 1960s, when Korean Protestants barely topped the one million mark, the number of Protestant Christians in Korea increased faster than in any other country, more than doubling every decade. By 1997, there were nearly nine million Protestants and approximately 100000 pastors attending to nearly 60000 churches, making the Protestant Church in Korea one of the most vital and dynamic in the world. The remarkable growth of Protestant Christianity is further demonstrated by the fact that five of the ten largest churches in the world, including the world's largest Yoido Full Gospel Church with more than 700000 members,

TABLE I

Religious and Non-Religious Population in South Korea[9]

Religion	Population (in thousands)	%
Buddhists	10388	23.2
Protestants	8819	19.7
Catholics	2988	6.6
Confucians	193	0.5
Won Buddhists	85	0.2
Daesoonjinlihoe	68	0.14
Chondogyo	30	0.06
Daejonggyo	11	0.02
Others	197	0.43
Subtotal	22779	50.85
No religion	22772	49.15
Total population	45551	100

Source: National Statistical Office (1995).

are found in the nation's capital, Seoul, a "city of churches" (Draper et al., 1994).

With regard to the specifics of the religious population, about half of the Korean people identify themselves as belonging to a religious organization. Buddhism is the largest religion with 10.3 million followers; Protestantism is a close second with 8.8 million adherents; followed by Catholicism with about 3 million followers (see Table I) (National Statistical Office, 1995).[4] Together with virtually all other societies, more Korean females than males are religiously committed, the ratio being about 6 to 4, although the difference is slightly larger for Buddhists. The average age of the religiously committed is higher than that of the general population, and the average age of Buddhists is the highest, followed by Catholics and then by Protestants.

In the context of a relatively small religious population, Koreans, in general, are relatively less inclined to believe in religious values.[5] For example, a 1997 Gallup survey showed that only 48.3 percent of Koreans believe in God; 42.2 percent believe in heaven; 52.6 percent believe in spirits; 59.6 percent believe in miracles; and 51.4 percent believe in angels and devils (see Table II).[6] Similar results

TABLE II

Belief in Religious Values

	National average	Buddhists	Protestants	Catholics	No religion
Absolute being/god	48.3%	44.9%	89.0%	75.1%	29.5%
Paradise/heaven	42.2	42.6	86.1	73.0	21.8
Spirits	52.6	54.2	86.4	77.5	36.0
Miracles	59.6	52.6	89.1	82.5	47.7
Devils/angels	51.4	54.5	84.7	67.1	35.1

Source: Gallup Korea (1998: pp. 103–105).

were found in two previous polls by Gallup Korea in 1984 and 1989. These surveys also show that more Christians than Buddhists believe in these religious values, and that a considerable proportion of those professing no religious faith is affirmative as well. The results further indicate that Koreans on average are not any more religious than people of most other nations. For example, a 1985 survey in the United States showed that 95 percent of Americans believe in God; 80 percent believe in life after death and in miracles; 72 percent believe in angels; and 65 percent in the devil (Stark and Bainbridge, 1985). Furthermore, A World Values Survey published in 1994 revealed that 82 percent of American respondents saw themselves as “a religious person,” compared to 55 percent in Britain, and 48 percent in France (*The Economist*, 1995: p. 20).

With regards to the religiosity of Korean Catholics and Protestants, however, they are second to none. For example, 1989–1991 surveys of religious activities in 18 counties, including the United States, England, Hungary, and Australia, showed that about 68 percent and nearly 74 percent of Korean Catholics and Protestants, respectively, attended church each Sunday. The figure for Protestants was the highest by far among the 18 countries, while the result for Catholics was the second highest after Northern Ireland (Gallup Korea, 1998: pp. 216–217). Korean Christians’ strong religiosity is also demonstrated in the frequency of prayer and the reading of scripture. According to the 1997 survey by Gallup Korea (1998: pp. 86–89), 64 percent of Korean Protestants and 41 percent of their Catholic counterparts prayed at least once a day, and more than 50 percent of the former, compared to nearly 34 percent of the latter,

TABLE III

Socio-economic Status and Religiosity

	High-income	Mid-income	Low-income
Attend religious service once a week or more	57.1%	43.9%	32.1%
Pray once a day or more	42.2	41.2	36.3
Read religious texts at least 3–4 times a week	19.8	23.5	21.8

Source: Gallup Korea (1998: pp. 264–266).

TABLE IV

Educational Level and Religiosity

	University degree or higher	High school diploma	Middle school diploma lower	Elementary education or
Attend religious service once a week or more	57.0%	43.0%	36.2%	26.9%
Pray once a day or more	42.8	39.8	37.2	37.3
Read religious texts at least 3–4 times a week	24.0	24.2	25.8	13.6

Source: Gallup Korea (1998: pp. 264–266).

were found to read religious scriptures more than once a week, all of which were among the highest in the world.

As for the relationship between economic status and religious participation in Korea, they are generally found to be positively correlated (see Tables III and IV) (Gallup Korea, 1998; see Lee, W., 1988). For example, both income level and educational attainment are positively correlated with the frequency of praying and attendance at religious services, while such a correlation is not evident for the frequency of scripture-reading.[7] These results generally correspond with the existing research findings in North America (Demerath III, 1965; Fukuyama, 1960) which show that the higher the socio-economic status, the higher the participatory and ritualistic religiosity.

TABLE V

Religious Affiliation and Level of Satisfaction (an average out of 10)

	Income level	Interpersonal relations	Physical health	Marital life/love	Job satisfaction	Overall
Buddhists	5.29	6.38	5.82	6.45	5.81	5.82
Protestants	6.06	7.11	6.72	6.79	6.40	6.48
Catholics	6.05	7.08	6.17	6.57	6.41	6.38
Non-Religious	5.36	6.64	6.33	6.31	5.67	5.92

Source: Gallup Korea (1998: p. 37).

Social class is also positively correlated with the belief in main religious doctrines. Asked about their belief in the existence of God, life after death, spirits, hell, and heaven, mid- and high-income respondents consistently were more affirmative than their low-income counterparts (Gallup Korea, 1990b: pp. 460–471). These results contradict the widely held stereotype that low-income or lower-class individuals are more "religious" than their higher income-earning counterparts.

RELIGIOUSNESS AND PERSONAL WELL-BEING

The 1997 survey by Gallup Korea (1998: pp. 36–37) asked the respondents (N = 1613) to rate their level of satisfaction from 0 (very unsatisfied) to 10 (very satisfied) on such quality of life indicators as income level, interpersonal relationships, physical health, marital life, and job satisfaction (see Table V). The result shows that religious individuals generally profess higher, albeit not significantly higher, levels of life satisfaction than the non-religious by an average of 6.23 to 5.92. Such a small difference is attributable to the low score of Buddhist respondents, who were found to have a lower level of overall life satisfaction than nonreligious respondents by an average of 5.82 to 5.92. Among those with religious faith, Protestant respondents scored the highest average, followed by Catholics, and Buddhists. With the exception of the health indicator, in which the Catholic respondents scored lower than the non-religious respondents, Protestants and Catholics were found to be more satisfied than both Buddhists and the nonreligious in every quality of life indicator. The difference between Protestants and Catholics on the one hand, and Buddhists and nonreligious on the other, was more pronounced in responses for upper levels of satisfaction, i.e., the proportion of Catholic and Protestant respondents who rated their overall life satisfaction in the 8 to 10 range was one-and-a-half times higher than their Buddhist and nonreligious counterparts.

Besides their relatively more frequent religious participation and stronger religiosity, both of which are found to be positively associated with higher levels of satisfaction, the Christians' relatively higher level of satisfaction seem to be due to their relatively higher income level and educational attainment as well as a greater sense of belonging and comfort of fellowship derived from the regularity of religious participation required by their churches. Secular reasons for the Buddhists' relatively lower level of satisfaction, in contrast, seem to be their relatively lower income level and educational attainment, overrepresentation in the old age group, and the irregularity of religious participation. Studies indeed show that regular participation in collective religious activities enhance the quality of life for adherents (Hadaway and Roof, 1978). Survey results also show that younger people and those with higher educational attainment and income are found to be more satisfied with their life than their older counterparts and those with lower educational attainment and income, respectively (Gallup Korea, 1998: p. 117). With regard to the economic status, surveys consistently demonstrate that more Catholics and Protestants comprise the middle class than Korean Buddhists (see Table VI). In a 1991 finding, more than two-thirds of Catholics and Protestants belonged to the middle and upper-middle class strata, while only about a half of Buddhists – as well as those with no religion – did so (Seoul National University Population and Development Research Center, 1991).[8] Buddhists also fared poorly in terms of income level, for they were over-represented in the lower-income bracket: 51.8 percent of Buddhists, compared to 33.4 percent of Protestants and 11.4 percent of Catholics, earned less than 1.5 million won (roughly US$1100) a month (Gallup Korea, 1998: p. 239).

As suggested above, Christians and Buddhists also differ significantly in terms of educational attainment, which is a very signifi-

TABLE VI

Religious Affiliation and Socio-economic Status

	Buddhists	Protestants	Catholics	No religion
Upper-middle class	2.4%	3.5%	11.3%	3.3%
Middle class	48.3	63.1	64.8	51.0
Working class	11.3	15.2	9.9	13.5
Urban Low class	7.9	5.8	5.6	4.3
Farming class	30.1	12.3	8.5	28.0

Source: Seoul National University Population and Development Research Center (1991).

cant element in determining the individual's class status in Korea, perhaps more importantly so than in most other countries. In general, Buddhists are relatively over-represented in the low educational attainment level, while Christians tend to be better educated. For example, nearly 30 percent of Korean Buddhists have an elementary education or less, while only about 3 and 11 percent of Catholics and Protestants, respectively, have the same educational background (Gallup Korea, 1998: p. 56). One-fourth of Korean Protestants have a university degree or better – this figure fits the overall profile of Korean Catholics as well – while just 7 percent of Buddhists have similar educational attainment. As for the reasons why Christians' socio-economic status is higher than that of Buddhists, we could single out the facts that more Christians are found in urban areas and that more upwardly mobile young people have been converted to the imported faith. Still, there is no study which offers definitive answers to the question as to why Korean urbanites and young people prefer Christianity over Buddhism.

Similar to the results of the 1997 Gallup survey, a study by Won Gue Lee (1991) also shows that religious individuals feel a slightly higher level of satisfaction overall than their nonreligious counterparts.[9] Lee's (1991: p. 181) survey, in which the respondents (N = 326) were asked to rate the level of satisfaction from 0 (very unsatisfied) to 5 (very satisfied) in regard to such quality of life indicators as income level, interpersonal relationship, job satisfaction, marital life, and health, shows that Protestants have a higher level of satisfaction, followed by Catholics and Buddhists.

In terms of the relationship between the respondents' religiousness on the one hand, and demographic and socio-economic variables on the other, Lee's study reveals several distinct patterns (Lee, W., 1991: pp. 173–175). First, religion is found to be a bigger contributing factor to older people's sense of well-being than to younger people, which is consistent with the findings in North America (Blazer and Palmore, 1976; Hunsberger, 1985). Specifically, among 30-year-olds or younger respondents, those with no religious faith actually expressed a higher level of satisfaction than their religious counterparts by a margin of 3.50 to 3.00. While there was no real difference in the satisfaction level for the 31–40 and 41–50 age groups, a marked difference was evident for the 51–60 age group, as indicated by an average of 3.60 for the religious and 3.04 for the nonreligious. Second, the low-income respondents with religious faith were found to be more satisfied with life than their counterparts without religious faith, while the opposite was true for the high-income respondents. What this seems to demonstrate is that the function of religion as compensation for felt deprivation is more prominent among the economically underprivileged population. Third, the "religious" respondents living in urban areas, especially large cities, were found to have higher levels of satisfaction than the nonreligious urbanites. As for those living in rural areas, the nonreligious respondents were found to be more satisfied with life than respondents with religious faith.

Lee's study further demonstrates that stronger religiosity generally has a positive impact on levels of satisfaction. Indeed, those identifying themselves as deeply religious and not so deeply religious were found to be more satisfied with life than those identifying themselves as slightly religious. For example, those professing strong beliefs in the existence of God or transcendental being and heaven were found to be markedly more satisfied with life than the less religiously inclined (see Table VII) (Lee, W., 1991: p. 177). It was also found that religious participation, i.e., attendance at religious services and scripture-readings, was positively correlated with the level of life satisfaction (see Table VIII). In addition, those who deemed religion to be important in their lives professed a higher level of satisfaction than those who thought of religion as less important (Lee, W., 1991: p. 180).

TABLE VII

Strength of Faith in God and Level of Life Satisfaction

	Strong	Not very strong	Weak
Very strongly satisfied	10.6%	8.4%	9.1%
Strongly satisfied	47.0	30.5	24.2
Not strongly satisfied	36.4	50.5	51.5
Weakly satisfied	4.5	10.5	15.2
Very weakly satisfied	1.5	0.0	0.0

Source: Lee, W. (1991: p. 177).

TABLE VIII

Frequency of Scripture-reading and Level of Life Satisfaction

	More than once a week/Several times a week	Once a week or less	Very infrequently
Very strongly satisfied	6.0%	11.8%	7.7%
Strongly satisfied	48.0	30.1	30.8
Not strongly satisfied	38.0	49.5	48.1
Weakly satisfied	8.0	7.5	13.5
Very weakly satisfied	0.0	1.1	0.0

Source: Lee, W. (1991: p. 177).

The findings in Korea generally support the research results in North America – that the individual's religiousness has a positive influence on his or her subjective well-being. Among the religious, Protestants are found to be most satisfied with life, followed by Catholics and Buddhists. Interestingly, Buddhists are found to be less satisfied with life than the nonreligious. It seems that such secular characteristics of Korean Buddhists as relatively lower educational attainment and income have contributed to their lower level of life satisfaction. It is also clear that religiosity is positively correlated with life satisfaction, meaning that those with strong religious beliefs and those who frequently participate in religious activities are likely to be more satisfied with life than those with less strong religious conviction and commitment.

RELIGION AND SOCIETAL WELL-BEING

The question of how religion or religious resources can contribute to societal progress or improvement in overall quality of life has been seldom examined. Perhaps the dominance of the currently accepted meanings of secularization, particularly the idea that emphasizes the diminishing social significance of religion in society at large, can be blamed for such oversight. However, the Korean case not only challenges the one-sidedness of the concept, but also demonstrates the centrality of religion in enhancing societal quality of life.

As suggested above, rapid modernization and urbanization have not undermined the influence of religion in Korea. In fact, the Buddhist, Catholic, and Protestant Churches collectively are the nation's most powerful non-governmental organizations, engaging in extensive socio-political activities and operating a wide range of commercial enterprises. These religious bodies publish more than 200 newspapers, magazines and periodicals, and operate dozens of research centers. In addition, each of these major religious bodies has its own cable television and radio network, which broadcast nationally, a feat unmatched in most other countries. Their active social involvement is most compellingly exemplified by their commitment to education. In addition to operating hundreds of kindergartens, primary and secondary schools, they operated, as of 1996, 22 junior colleges and more than 70 four-year universities, which comprised nearly one- fourth of the total number of colleges and universities in Korea (*Hangukjonggyosahoeyeonguso*, 1997). The fact that three of the most prestigious universities in Korea are Christian – Sogang University, Yonsei University, and Ewha Womans University – attests to the powerful presence of religious organizations in Korean education. Local churches also operate large numbers of educational programs that amount to continuing education, offering day or night courses on subjects ranging from theology and philosophy to consumer rights and English conversation.

Religious institutions have also built a considerable number of large hospitals, many of which are affiliated with Christian universities. In addition, they are the largest non-governmental contributors to philanthropic causes in Korea (Kim, M. et al., 1999; Kim, I., 1998). In fact, religious organizations operate more welfare institutions than any other organization, governmental or nongovernmental. It was the Protestant missionaries who first introduced institutional philanthropy by founding the nation's first orphanages and schools for the blind. Korean churches, Protestant and Catholic, have followed in their footsteps by operating an estimated two thousand-plus welfare centers all across the country, including those for the poor, orphans, abandoned children, the elderly, and the mentally- or physically-challenged (Kim, M. et al., 1999: p. 57). The services they provide include, among others, meal provisions for the homeless and poor elderly, recreation and continuing education for the elderly, scholarships for poor children, free or subsidized daycare centers for the poor, vocational training, and job placement services. Religious organizations also provide an extensive array of counseling services, including those related to jobs, martial or family problems, juvenile delinquency, and teenage pregnancy. For some time, Buddhist sects were hesitant to engage in welfare activities, but have become more active of late, setting up, among others, nursing homes, sanatoriums, orphanages, and welfare facilities for the physically challenged. The government, unable to meet the rising demand for these welfare services, has warmly welcomed such active involvement of religious bodies by providing financial support.

As impressive as the religious organizations' involvement in education and philanthropic causes was, so too with their prominence in the nation's democratization process. Against the unprecedented socio-political role of the military and its oppressive rule – which goes back to South Korea's first administration of Rhee Syhngman from 1948 to 1960, and which became most severe during the Park Chung Hee's regime from 1961 to 1979 – religious organizations, especially the Catholic Church, became the strongest supporters of the democratic movement (see Han, 1987). Such prominent religious groups as the Catholic Priests' Association for Justice, the National Council of Churches in Korea, and the Alliance for *Minjung* Buddhist Movement played eminent roles in championing democracy during the 1970s and 1980s. These groups and many churches functioned as primary institutional centers for the movement, collectively questioning the regime's commitment to human rights and democracy, and confronting the government over human rights abuses and political oppression. This is not to say that the religious organizations' stance against the military regimes had been unequivocal, for many large, conservative Protestant churches had maintained neutrality or even a passive support of the authoritarian regimes. Korean religious groups as a whole, however, represented, along with university student associations, the only major organizations to oppose the policies and decisions of the authoritarian regimes. And it was during this period of oppressive political rule that a Korean form of liberation theology called *minjungsinhak*, literally meaning the "theology of the people," became a towering symbol of the rally for democracy, equality, social justice, and human rights (The Commission on Theological Concerns of the Christian Conference of Asia, 1981). Like other variants of liberation theology, *minjungsinhak* views the struggle for democracy, justice and equality as a spiritual struggle to realize God's kingdom on earth. Accordingly, the proponents of the theology became engaged in a variety of religiously based social action to remedy social injustice and inequalities.

The religious groups' role as an agent of democratization was also manifested in their equally strong demand for fairer labor laws and more equal distribution of the nation's newly created wealth amongst the working class. While labor laws in recent times have become more moderate, anti-labor measures of the Korean government from the 1960s through the 1980s were most appealing: labor strikes, staged by desperate workers fighting against sweatshop-like working conditions and pay (60 hour-plus workweek had been the norm), were brutally crushed by riot police; labor organizers were often arrested on outlandish charges of anti-government activities; and missionaries who got involved in the labor movement were deported, while Korean clergy doing the same had to endure imprisonment and even torture. In response, religious groups made strong demands for improvement in working conditions and for more equitable labor laws. A system of industrial evangelism that catered to the needs of the industrial labor force was implemented, most prominently by Protestant denominations. From initiating the program of medical insurance to establishing the workers' credit unions, the industrial mission had been at the forefront of championing the welfare of laborers. The industrial mission also provided labor education to labor leaders and workers, and offered undivided moral support for their cause.

In short, while religion has served as a source of status quo in many instances, religious groups in Korea have played significant roles in trying to build a more democratic, just, equitable, and better society. Their contribution to the overall improvement in societal well-being cannot be underestimated, for their extensive involvement in such areas as medical care and education has been welcomed by the government and needed by the public. It would be difficult to find another country in which religious organizations collectively operate more hospitals, schools and universities, and welfare services than in Korea. It is no secret that the government could not keep abreast of the rising public demand for education at every level and better health care. With the blessing of the government, religious organizations stepped in, investing huge sums of money into those areas that helped improve the standard of living in Korea. In education, profit could not have been their motive for involvement in education, for the education law in Korea grants only non-profit status to private schools and universities. Entrepreneurs, scientists, technicians, and professionals, not to mention a huge pool of the educated labor force, who have been educated at schools and colleges founded by religious organizations have been an important part of the engine that achieved remarkable economic growth – and marked improvement in quality of life – for the last forty years in Korea.

CONCLUSION

This paper has shown that Koreans who practice their religion have higher levels of life satisfaction than their nonreligious counterparts. Such a finding is consistent with comparable legitimate research findings in North America. This paper has also shown that Koreans with religious faith tend to have higher educational attainment and economic status, important determinants of a sense of well-being, than those without religious faith. Among those with religious faith, Protestants have the highest level of satisfaction, followed by Catholics, and then by Buddhists, who are found to be actually less satisfied with life than the nonreligious. It is also evident that those with strong religious conviction and commitment are likely to be more satisfied with life than the less religiously inclined.

As regards the relationship between religion and societal well-being, the paper has shown that religious institutions in Korea, especially Christian ones, have contributed immensely to societal well-being through their extensive involvement in welfare services, socio-economic activities, and the democratic movement. This paper thus draws attention to the need for a greater appreciation of the practical roles religion can play in the life of the community. The Korean case demonstrates how religious resources can be mobilized to meet social needs and contribute to societal progress, thereby enhance societal well-being. The phrase "being at the right place and at the right time" could not have been more apt for the religious institutions in Korea for them to affect the society as they have, leaving lasting impressions on the country's religious landscape as well as in practically every other sphere of society. While there is abundant evidence of religious apathy or opposition to social change in many parts of the world, this has not been the case in Korea. In addition to providing comfort and solace to its members, religious institutions in Korea have been at the forefront of efforts to promote societal progress and well-being.

From our analysis of the above survey, we get a glimpse of the impact of religion on personal and societal well-being in the Korean context. However, more research is needed to consider the relationship between religion and specific age groups in order to better understand the complexity of the issue. For example, research that examines the relationship between religion and quality of life among Korean adolescents and Korean elderly – as well as comparisons between the two age groups – is likely to offer significant insights into the dynamics of religion in the perceived sense of well-being for differently aged individuals. More research on the relationship between religion and more diverse quality of life indicators, such as physical health and marital stability, in the Korean context is also desirable. The findings in Korea could then be compared with those found in other parts of the world to decipher similarities and differences. Finally, research that involves bigger samples and also include balanced representations of both genders in Korea is needed to better understand the richness of the religion-quality of life relationship in a more balanced way.

ACKNOWLEDGEMENT

The author wishes to thank Eunkyoung Kim for her assistance in writing this article.

NOTES

[1] While the pre-modern Confucianism had a sacrificial cult of veneration for Heaven and ancestors, today's Confucianism in Korea survives largely as a set of social ethics emphasizing the importance of the family, education, loyalty, hierarchy, and propriety. In fact, the only "religious" element in contemporary Confucianism is ancestor worship. Koreans still remain Confucianists at heart, for a large majority of Koreans, including a substantial proportion of Christians, perform Confucian-style ceremonies for their dead ancestors on death anniversaries and on culturally significant public holidays, such as *Chusok* (Korean Thanksgiving) and the Lunar New Year's Day.

[2] Central to this folk religion is the notion that spirits, including those of ancestors, nature, and prominent kings and generals in Koreans history, wield power on the shifting fortunes of each individual and that these spirits must be appeased through shamanic rituals to implore their blessings for material wishes such as health, longevity and prosperity (Kim, T., 1972, 1981; Kendall, 1996; Moon, 1982; Howard, 1998). From time immemorial, Korean ancestors held all kinds of shamanic rites for, among others, safe childbirth, cure from illness, village welfare, good harvest, and rain.

[3] As for the socio-historical factors that inspired such rapid expansion of religion, most oft-cited are psychological scars and an overwhelming sense of shame felt by Koreans over Japanese colonial rule (1910–1945); traumatic experience of the Korean War (1950–1953); the anomie arising from rapid industrialization and urbanization; and the profound sense of deprivation borne by widening income gap (Noh, 1989; Kim, J. et al., 1982; Lee, W., 1997). Also, by serving as welfare agencies and as points of contact for displaced individuals – which included millions of North Korean refugees – religious organizations provided for the adherents a sense of belonging, identity and security.

[4] A poll conducted in 1997 actually shows Protestantism to be slightly ahead of Buddhism in terms of membership (Gallup Korea, 1998). Surveys show that Buddhism has experienced a steady, albeit slight, drop in membership since 1989, while the opposite has been true for Protestantism.

[5] There is no cultural bias toward the notion of religion in Korea, and people would not hesitate to identify themselves as having a religion. This is largely because the government and cultural nationalism have extolled traditional religions as integral elements of Korean identity and culture, and because Korean society has largely appreciated Protestantism and Catholicism as agents of modernization (Kim, A., 2000).

[6] For this and other surveys, none of the questionnaires permitted multiple responses.
[7] In the 1989 Gallup survey, both income level and educational attainment did correlate positively with the frequency of scripture-reading.
[8] Social classes were determined on the basis of the respondents' profession. Accordingly, middle and upper-middle classes included professionals (doctors, lawyers, dentists, professors, accountants, etc.), managers and small business owners, whereas the working class consisted of clerical workers, service workers, and industrial workers.
[9] Research on the relationship between religion and the quality of life of the Korean elderly also demonstrates that religious elderly are more satisfied with life and feel happier than the nonreligious elderly (Kim and Park, 2000; Lee, Y., 1994).

REFERENCES

Benson, P.: 1992, 'Religion and substance use', in J.F. Schumaker (ed.), Religion and Mental Health (Oxford University Press, New York, pp. 211–220).

Berger, P.: 1967, The Sacred Canopy: Elements of a Sociological Theory of Religion (Doubleday, Garden City, NY).

Bergin, A.E.: 1983, 'Religiosity and mental health: A critical reevaluation and meta analysis', Professional Psychology: Research and Practice 14, pp. 170–184.

Blazer, D. and E. Palmore: 1976, 'Religion and aging in a longitudinal panel', The Gerontologist 16, pp. 82–85.

Call, V. and T.B. Heaton: 1997, 'Religious influence on marital stability', Journal for the Scientific Study of Religion 36, pp. 382–392.

Cha, S.: 1995, Hangukjonggyosasangui sahoehakjok ihae (A Sociological Understanding of Korean Religious Thoughts) (Moonhakgwajisungsa, Seoul).

Choi, J.: 1998, Hangukuijonggyo moonhwaroikneunda (A Survey of Korean Religions from Cultural Perspectives), Volumes 1 and 2 (Sagyejol, Seoul).

Clemente, F. and W. Sauer: 1976, 'Life satisfaction in the United States', Social Forces 54, pp. 621–631.

Cochran, J.K., L. Beeghley and E.W. Bock: 1988, 'Religiosity and alcohol behavior: An exploration of reference group theory', Sociological Forum 3, pp. 256–276.

The Commission on Theological Concerns of the Christian Conference of Asia: 1981, Minjung Theology: People as the Subject of History (Orbis, Maryknoll, NY).

Demerath III, N.J.: 1965, Social Class in American Protestantism (Rand McNally, Chicago).

Dongailbo (Donga Daily Newspaper): 1997, 'Musok-yoksul yulpoong' (Shamanism and Fortune-telling Craze), January 3.

Draper, E., H. Gorges and K. Petersen: 1994, The Almanac of the Christian World/1993–1994 (Tyndale House Publishers, Wheaton, Illinois).
Dull, V.T. and L.A. Skokan: 1995, 'A cognitive model of religion's influence on Health', Journal of Social Issues 51, pp. 49–64.
The Economist: 1995, 'America and Religion', July 8, pp. 19–21.
Ellison, C.G. and J.S. Levin: 1998, 'The religion-health connection: Evidence, theory, and future directions', Health Education and Behavior 25, pp. 700–720.
Fukuyama, Y.: 1960, 'The major dimensions of church membership', Review of Religious Research 2, pp. 154–161.
Gallup Korea: 1985, Hangukinui jonggyowa jonggyosaengwhal (Religion and Religious Life of Koreans) (Gallup Korea, Seoul).
Gallup Korea: 1990a, Hangukinui jonggyowa jonggyosaengwhal (Religion and Religious Life of Koreans) (Gallup Korea, Seoul).
Gallup Korea: 1990b, Hankukinui ingan gachigwan (The Value System of Koreans) (Gallup Korea, Seoul).
Gallup Korea: 1998, Hangukinui jonggyowa jonggyosaengwhal (Religion and Religious Life of Koreans) (Gallup Korea, Seoul).
Gartner, J.D., D.B. Larson and G.D. Allen: 1991, 'Religious commitment and mental health: A review of the empirical literature', Journal of Psychology and Theology 19, pp. 6–25.
Gray, R.E.: 1987, 'Adolescent response to the death of a parent', Journal of Youth and Adolescence 16, pp. 511–525.
Hadaway, C.K. and W.C. Roof: 1978, 'Religious commitment and quality of life in American society', Review of Religious Research 19, pp. 295–307.
Han, Y.: 1987, '1970nyundaeui hangukgyohoewa jeongchi' (Korea churches and politics in the 1970s), Catholicsahoegwahakyeongu (Catholic Social Scientific Research) 1, pp. 107–130.
Hangukjonggyosahoeyeonguso (Research Institute for Korean Religion and Society): 1997, Hangukjonggyoyeongam 1996–97 (The Yearbook of Korean Religion, 1996–97) (Hangukjonggyosahoeyeonguso, Seoul).
Howard, K.: 1998, Korean Shamanism: Revivals, Survivals, and Change (Royal Asiatic Society, Seoul).
Hunsberger, B.: 1985, 'Religion, age life satisfaction, and perceived sources of religiousness: A study of older persons', Journal of Gerontology 40, pp. 615–620.
Idler, E.L.: 1987, 'Religious involvement and the health of the elderly: Some hypotheses and an initial test', Social Forces 66, pp. 226–238.
Johnson, T.: 1995, 'The significance of religion for aging well', The American Behavioral Scientist 39, pp. 186–208.
Joongangilbo (Joongang Daily Newspaper): 1998, 'Jomboneunsaramdeul' (People who frequent fortune tellers), March 6.
Jung, J.: 1986, Hangukjonggyomunhwaui jongae (Introduction to Korean Religions) (Jipmundang, Seoul).
Kendall, K.: 1996, 'Korean shamans and the spirits of capitalism', *American Anthropologist* 98, pp. 512–527.

Kim, A.E.: 2000, 'Christianity, Shamanism, and modernization in South Korea', Cross Currents 50, pp. 112–119.

Kim, B.: 1985, 'The explosive growth of the Korean church today: A sociological analysis', International Review of Mission 124, pp. 59–72.

Kim, I.: 1998, 'Jonggyogye sahoebokgi chamyeohyunhwang mit hwalseonghwa bangan' (Religious organizations' involvement with social welfare, and measures for expansion), Sahoebokji (Social Welfare) 139, pp. 54–66.

Kim, J., J. Jung and H. Jung: 1982, Hangukgyohoe sungjanggwa shinangyangtaee gwanhanjosayungu (A Study of the Korean Church Growth and Faith) (Hyundaesahoeyeonguso, Seoul).

Kim, M., S. Hong, M. Lee and J. Yu: 1999, Jonggyogyeui sahoebokjihwaldong hyunhwanggwa hwalseonghwa bangan yeongu (A Study on Church Social Welfare Activities in Korea) (Hangukbogeonsahoeyeonguwon, Seoul).

Kim, M. and M. Park: 2000, 'Jonggyoga noinui salmui jile michineun younghyang yeongu' (Research on the impact of religion on the quality of life of the elderly), Journal of the Korean Gerontological Society, pp. 29–47.

Kim, T.: 1972, 'Components of Korean Shamanism', Korea Journal 12(12), pp. 17–25.

Kim, T.: 1973, Hangukjonggyo gaegwan (A Survey of Korean Religions) (Wongwang University Press, Iksan).

Kim, T.: 1981, Hanguk Musok Yungu (A Study of Korean Shamanism) (Jipmundang, Seoul).

Koenig, H.G.: 1988, Religious behaviors and death anxiety in later life', Hospice Journal 4, pp. 3–24.

Koenig, H.G., K.I. Pargament and J. Nielsen: 1998, 'Religious coping and health outcomes in medically ill hospitalized older adults', Journal of Nervous and Mental Diseases 186, pp. 513–521.

Lee, W.: 1988, 'Gyecheungbyul eushikgujowa jonwhanshidaeui gidokkyo' (Class consciousness and Christianity in the changing time), Christian Thought (September Issue), pp. 34–48.

Lee, W.: 1991, 'Jonggyowa inseong tonghap' (Religion and character integration), in W. Lee (ed.), Jonggyo sahoehak (Hanguksinhakyeonguso, Seoul, pp. 153–193).

Lee, W.: 1992, Hangukgyohoeui sahoehakjok ehae (A Sociological Interpretation of the Korean Church) (Sungsuyungusa, Seoul).

Lee, W.: 1997, Jonggyosahoehakuiihae (Understanding the Sociology of Religion) (Nanam Publishing House, Seoul).

Lee, Y.: 1994, 'Jonggyo mit sahoehwaldongi noinui sanghwalmanjokdoe michineun younghyange gwanhan yeongu' (Research on the impact of religion and social activities on the happiness of the elderly), Chungbuksahoebokjiyeongu (Chungbuk Social Welfare Research) 3, pp. 243–273.

Lehrer, E. and C. Chiswick: 1993, 'Religion as a determinant of marital stability', Demography 30, pp. 385–403.

Levin, J.S. and H.Y. Vanderpool: 1991, 'Religious factors in physical health and the prevention of illness', Prevention in Human Services 9, pp. 41–64.

McCann, R.V.: 1962, The Churches and Mental Health (Basic Books, New York).
Maton, K. and E. Wells: 1995, 'Religion as a community resource for well-being: Prevention, healing, and empowerment pathways', The Journal of Social Issues 51, pp. 177–193.
Moberg, D.: 1979, 'The development of social indicators of spiritual well-being for quality of life research', in D. Moberg (ed.), Spiritual Well-Being (University Press of America, Washington, D.C.), pp. 1–14.
Moon, S.: 1982, 'Shamanism in Korea', in S. Chun (ed.), Korean Thought (Sisayongosa, Seoul), pp. 17–35.
National Statistical Office: 1995, Ingujutaek chongjosa (National Census).
Noh, G.: 1989, 'Hangukjonggyosungjangui sahoejokbaegyung' (Social factors in religious growth in Korea), in W. Lee (ed.), Hangukgyohoewa sahoe (Korean Church and Society) (Nadanchulpansa, Seoul), pp. 94–126.
Paloutzian, R.F. and L.A. Kirkpatrick: 1995, 'Introduction: The scope of religious influences on personal and societal well-being', The Journal of Social Issues 51, pp. 1–11.
Pargament, K.I.: 1997, The Psychology of Religion and Coping: Theory, Research, Practice (Guilford Press, New York).
Pollner, M.: 1989, 'Divine relations, social relations, and well-being', Journal of Health and Social Behavior 30, pp. 921–1004.
Ro, B. and M. Nelson (eds.): 1995, Korean Church Growth Explosion, Rev. ed. (Word of Life Press, Seoul).
Ryu, S.: 1987, Gidokgyo Yebaewa Yugyojesa (Christian Service and Confucian Rite) (Yangsuhgak, Seoul).
Seoul National University Population and Development Research Center: 1991, Jonhwangiui hankuksahoe: 1990 kukminuishik josa (Korea at a Turning Point: 1990 Survey of Korean Attitudes).
Spilka, B., R.W. Hood, Jr. and R.L. Gorsuch: 1985, The Psychology of Religion: An Empirical Research (Prentice-Hall, Englewood Cliffs, NJ).
Stark, R. and W.S. Bainbridge: 1985, The Future of Religion: Secularization, Revival and Cult Formation (University of California Press, Berkeley).
Tix, A.P. and P.A. Frazier: 1998, 'The use of religious coping during stressful life events: Main effects, moderation, and mediation', Journal of Consulting and Clinical Psychology 66, pp. 411–422.
Ventis, W.L.: 1995, 'The relationships between religion and mental health', Journal of Social Issues 51, pp. 33–48.
Wildes, K.: 1996, 'Ordinary and extraordinary means and the quality of life', Theological Studies 57, pp. 500–512.

Korean Studies, Graduate School of International Studies
Korea University
Sungbuk-gu Anam-dong 5–1, Seoul, Korea
E-mail: aekim@korea.ac.kr

SOONMAN KWON

HEALTH AND HEALTH CARE

ABSTRACT. Quality of life in the area of health and health care is measured in terms of inputs, throughputs and outcomes in Korea. The national health insurance program has contributed to the improvement of health and health care. However, there are financial barriers to health care utilization because of limited benefit coverage and high copayment. Quality of life, as measured by health outcomes such as life expectancy, has also improved a great deal in thirty years, although there sill exists differential mortality rates among different socio-economic groups. Strengthening the areas of primary health care, accident and disease prevention and health promotion will be essential to improving health outcomes among the Korean population.

INTRODUCTION

Health and the provision of health care are an essential part of the quality of life because they directly affect one's daily activity and psychological as well as physical well-being. It is questionable whether Korea has experienced as much progress in health and social development as compared to the pace of its economic development. With respect to the financing of its health care system, Korea has a national health insurance system with universal coverage of its population. However, the benefit coverage is limited and patients still have a substantial out-of-pocket expense at the point of service. Therefore, the universal coverage of health insurance itself cannot necessarily guarantee better health and an improved quality of life.

The quality of life in health and health care critically depends on what we mean by a healthy life and how we measure it. It can, of course, be measured in several dimensions. The most important aspect of the quality of life associated with health and health care is health status or health outcomes. One needs health care in order to improve the status of one's health, but health care itself is not the goal, but rather a means for achieving better health outcomes. But

Social Indicators Research **62, 63:** 171–186, 2003.

there are technical difficulties in measuring improvements in health status or assessing health outcomes accurately. Therefore, one often relies on indirect measures of health outcomes, such as health care utilization or the availability of health care personnel and medical facilities. In a sense, health status cannot address all relevant aspects of the quality of life in health and health care. For example, not only health outcomes but also how or through what process we achieve those outcomes matters.

In this paper, measures of the quality of life in health and health care are based on three elements: structure, process and outcome. Structure or input measures are based on features or inputs of the health care system that are expected to have impacts on health outcomes. Examples of structure (input) indicators include per capita health care personnel and medical facilities and the existence of a public financing mechanism for health care, such as national health insurance or a tax-based national health service system. Process or throughput measures are based on evidence related to activities to improve health outcomes. Examples of process (throughput) measures include indicators of health care utilization and expenditures. Outcome measures are based on the assessment of evidence related to health status and consumer satisfaction. Indicators of health status include both objective measures (mortality and morbidity) and subjective measures (self-assessed health status). Not only the level of health status but also its distribution across different socio-economic groups is an important measure of the quality of life associated with health.

STRUCTURE INDICATORS

Structure indicators are inputs to produce better health. Korea has experienced a substantial improvement in access to health care thanks to the consistent increase in the supply of health care manpower and medical facilities. From 1976 to 1999, per capita numbers of physicians and traditional medical doctors have tripled (see Table I). The per capita numbers of nurses and dentists have increased by four and five times, respectively. Population per physician has decreased from 2009 to 672, population per traditional medical doctor from 12556 to 4130, population per dentist from

TABLE I

Health Care Personnel (Unit: Persons)

	1976	1981	1986	1989	1992	1995	1997	1999
Population per physician	2009	1631	1304	1067	904	789	735	672
Population per dentist	13064	9811	6875	4919	3877	3296	2990	2712
Population per nurse	552	345	240	201	172	146	135	120
Population per traditional doctor	12556	12360	10199	7810	6397	5175	4951	4130
Population per pharmacist	1730	1530	1315	1187	1106	1042	1004	952

Source: Ministry of Health and Welfare (2000).

13064 to 2712, population per nurse from 552 to 120 population per pharmacist from 1730 to 952.

The per capita number of pharmacists has increased, but at a slower rate than other types of health care personnel. When the supply of medial personnel was scant, Koreans depended on community pharmacists for inexpensive primary care. Before the mandatory separation of prescribing (physicians) and dispensing (pharmacists) was implemented in 2000, there was little division of labor between the physician and the pharmacist. The latter were allowed to dispense prescription drugs without physicians' prescriptions. As the supply of medical personnel increased Koreans substituted physician services for pharmacists, which resulted in a relatively slower growth of pharmacists over time.

The per capita number of beds has also increased substantially. The number of beds per 100000 persons was up by more than four times in 20 years, from 104 to 422 (MOHW, 2000). High-cost medical technology, such as the MRI (Magnetic Resonance Imaging) and CT (Computerized Tomograph) has been adopted and its utilization has increased rapidly as well. However, there are gaps between the demand for and the actual supply of beds in different types of health care institutions.

One of the unique characteristics of the Korean health care system is that physician clinics have inpatient facilities, mostly in surgery and obstetrics. In 1999, a quarter of all beds were owned by physician clinics (MOHW, 2000), which were competing with hospitals for inpatient care. Koreans prefer large general or tertiary care hospitals to small or medium-sized ones, which has led to long waiting lines in the former types of hospitals whereas physician clinics and small hospitals suffer from an excess supply of beds.

The over-reliance on large general hospitals also affects the relative supply of physicians. Most graduates of medical schools are getting training as specialists and Korea is in short supply of primary care physicians. The limited role of primary health care, which is regarded as cost-effective in improving the health of the Korean population, is a barrier to the efficient delivery of health care and cost containment. Most of the office-based physicians are board-certified specialists and compete with hospitals, the latter of which have not only inpatient facilities but also large outpatient clinics. Achieving a division of roles between physician clinics and hospitals will be a critical step in organizing health care delivery in Korea.

The national health insurance system has contributed to the consistent increase in health care personnel and medical facilities. Social insurance for health care was first introduced in 1977 for employees in large corporations, which was incrementally extended to workers in small firms. It covered the self-employed in rural areas in 1988, and provided for universal coverage of the Korean population in 1989. Before the consolidation of the various health plans in 2000, there were three different categories of more than 300 insurance plans: one for employees (industrial workers), one for the self-employed, and one for government and school employees (Kwon, 2003b). The basic features of these insurance plans were the same with some minor differences in contribution rates.

The implementation of national health insurance has enhanced the purchasing power of medical consumers, which in turn has occasioned a growth in the number of health care institutions in the private sector rather than in the public sector. The proportions of public hospitals and beds are less than 15 percent of all hospitals and beds and they have been decreasing over time (NOHW, 2000).

Most hospitals in Korea are for-profit with physician-owners. Many hospitals originated from clinics with small inpatient facilities, which were later expanded by entrepreneurial physicians. The for-profit nature of the hospital industry in Korea is closely related to the fact that most private hospitals depend almost exclusively on patient care for their revenue without philanthropic donations or government subsidies. The government has not been willing to put more resources into the health care sector or invest in the infrastructure of health care delivery. That was one of the rationales that led the government to adopt a contribution-based national health insurance plan rather than a tax-based national health service (NHS) approach as in the United Kingdom (Kwon, 2002).

A health care system consisting of predominantly for-profit providers turned out to be quite vulnerable to the physician strikes that occurred as a result of the mandatory separation of prescribing and dispensing drugs.[1] Physician strikes have caused panic throughout the entire health care system, which caused patients to rush to public health care institutions. Public hospitals can serve as social safety nets even under the national health insurance, particularly when benefits of those programs are stringent. Providing health care through public institutions can be efficient in managing eligibility and benefits (quantity and quality of services) more flexibly. For example, public hospitals can provide medical care to those who are poor but categorically ineligible under the Medicaid program. In other words, they can decide, at the point of service, who is in need and how much care should be provided (Bovbjerg et al., 1987).

PROCESS INDICATORS

Although structure or input measures affect health outcomes, the former is still loosely associated with the latter. The increased supply in health care personnel and medical facilities and the implementation of the national health insurance program may not improve health status as expected if there are other barriers to health care utilization. Furthermore, health care is just one of many inputs to better health, and nutrition, the quality of the environment, and hygiene factors should also contribute to the improvement in health

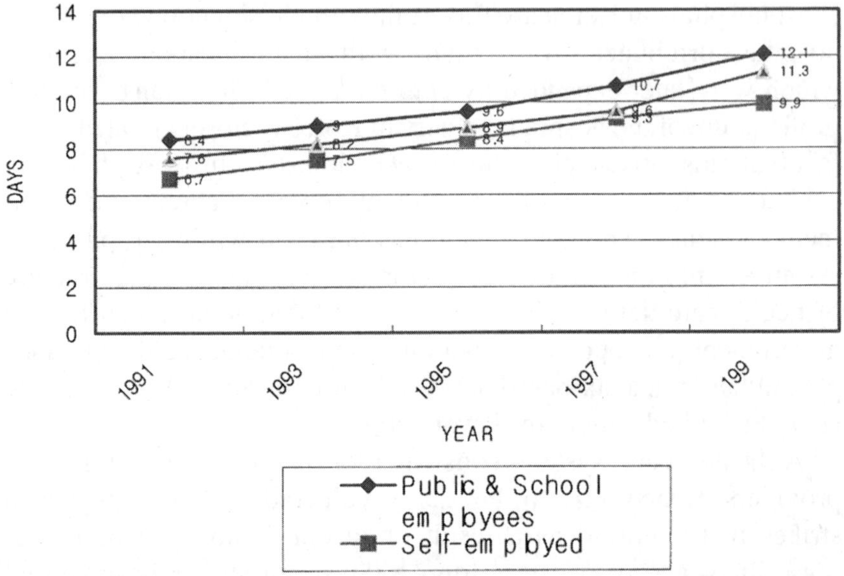

Source: National Health Insurance Corporation (2000).

Figure 1. Outpatient visits per insured (unit: days).

outcomes. That is why process or throughput measures of health, which are closely related to activities to improve health outcomes, are important.

Since 1991, the per capita number of outpatient visits increased substantially although there were differences in health care utilization across the three different types of health insurance plans (see Figure 1).[2] Health care utilization is highest among government and school employees (12.1 visits per insured) and lowest among the self-employed (9.9 visits per insured). The difference in health care utilization across different insurance groups can result from the difference in age structures, such as a larger proportion of those over 70 among government and school employees, and those between 20–29 among industrial workers. Financial barriers also seem to exist for the self-employed. The regional maldistribution of health care personnel and medical facilities also has a negative effect on health care utilization by the self-employed particularly in rural areas.[3]

Increased health care utilization may not necessarily mean an improved quality of life associated with health and health care.

Due to information asymmetry, patients have limited knowledge and influence over health care utilization. Physicians can induce unnecessary health care utilization for reasons of profit or if their income is squeezed by competition. Demand inducement is more likely in Korea because fee-for-service is the predominant form of reimbursement to providers, and the role of public hospitals is very limited.[4] Information asymmetry is less severe in outpatient care than in inpatient care, and hence the former is less vulnerable to physician influence. Nonetheless, the increase in outpatient health care utilization is partially accounted for by physician influence or their desire for financial incentives.

The existence of the national health insurance program itself does not necessarily guarantee better health outcomes. Detailed institutional characteristics of the health insurance program affect health care utilization and health outcomes. One of the major shortcomings of the Korean national health insurance program is its limited benefit coverage. The government has pursued a policy priority in expanding the coverage of the Korean population at the expense of limited benefit coverage along with a low contribution rate (less than 4% of income). Despite having medical insurance with universal coverage, patients must come up with substantial out-of-pocket payments for both insured (cost-sharing) and uninsured services. The proportion of private payments in total health care expenditures has shown a steady decrease, from 73 percent in 1987, to 54 percent in 1998 (Chung, 2001). Patients, on average, still bear more than half of health care expenses at the point of service, which poses a substantial financial barrier for the poor.

A low contribution rate has been accompanied by a rather strict regulation of the fees for medical care. Providers have responded to the fee regulation by increasing the volume and intensity of services and by distorting the mix of treatment inputs (Kwon, 2003a). Providers make profit from the difference between the insurance reimbursement and the acquisition cost of pharmaceuticals and medical supplies. Accordingly, providers have strong incentives to increase the volume of drugs and medical supplies used or substitute more of them for their own services in treatment. The proportion of pharmaceutical expenditures to total health care expenditures in

Korea is around 30 percent, which is much greater than that of other industrialized countries (COHCR, 1998).

Since the fee regulation is applied only to insured medical services, providers also have a strong incentive to substitute uninsured medical services for insured ones to increase their net income. Rapid diffusion and utilization of high-cost medical technology, which is not usually covered by health insurance, are closely associated with the medical suppliers' perverse financial incentives to provide more (and profitable) medical services that are not covered by insurance. The increase in the volume and intensity of both insured and uninsured services has resulted in a substantial financial burden on patients.

The low public coverage of health care expenses has important implications for both efficiency and equity. Due to the limited benefit coverage, health insurance has not provided adequate protection against loss of income due to illness, which contributes to low efficiency in spreading risks. High out-of-pocket payments at the point of service are inequitable (regressive) because it does not depend on the wealth of patients – resulting in an inequity in the economic burden of illness. High co-payments surely affect the poor more, and inequity in access to health care results despite the universal coverage of the health insurance plan. Therefore, it is imperative that the contribution be increased and the benefit package expanded so as to enhance both efficiency and equity in the health care financing mechanism.

The percentage of the national health care expenditure of the GDP (Gross Domestic Product) was 5.1 percent in 1998, which was a rather large increase from 4.7 percent in 1995 (Chung, 2001). After the International Monetary Fund (hereinafter IMF) rescue loan was granted, the Korean economy had a slow recovery. This means that Korea will not enjoy as rapid an economic growth as they have enjoyed in the past. At the same time, Koreans are getting more concerned about their quality of life and better health care. Therefore, the percentage of the national health expenditure of the GDP is likely to increase in the future. The growing proportion of the aged in the population will also rapidly increase health expenditures. The proportion of the elderly (over 65 years of age) was 6.2 percent in 1998, up from 4.9 percent in 1990. Yet health insur-

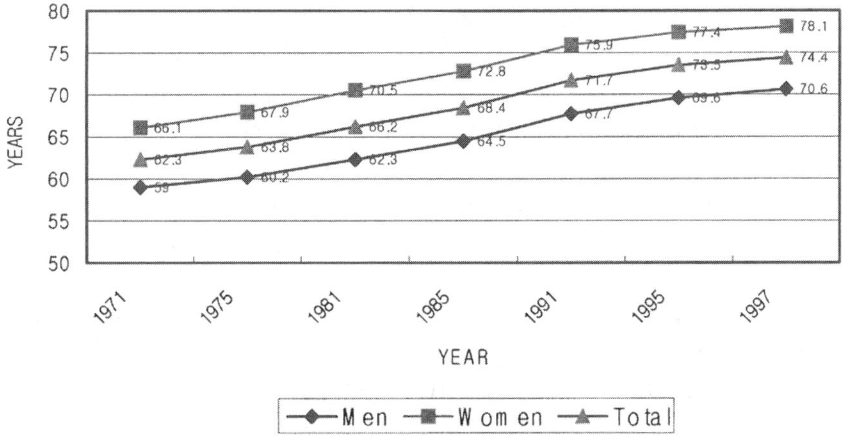

Source: National Statistical Office (1999).

Figure 2. Life expectancy (unit: years).

ance expenditures for the elderly accounted for 15.5 percent of total health insurance expenditure in 1998, up from 8.6 percent in 1990 (NHIC, 2000).

OUTCOME INDICATORS

Outcome indicators of the quality of life in health and health care are related to the level and distribution of health status. The level of health status of the Korean population can be measured both in objective and subjective terms. Life expectancy, morbidity and mortality are primary measures of objective health outcomes. For the past 30 years, life expectancy in Korea has increased by 12 years, from 62.3 in 1971 to 74.4 in 1997 (see Figure 2). The life expectancy of women (78.1) is greater than that of men (70.6) by almost eight years although their improvements over the past 30 years are similar. Life expectancy has been forecasted overall to be 77, 73.3 for men and 80.7 for women, in 2010. WHO (World Health Organization) estimates the DALE (Disability-Adjusted Life Expectancy)[5] to be 65, 62.3 for men and 67.7 for women, in 1999, which is lower than 70.2 of the Organization for Economic Cooperation and Development (OECD) average and 74.5 of Japan (WHO, 2000). High-ranking OECD countries in terms of DALE include

Australia (73.2), France (73.1), and Sweden (73.0), and the other extreme takes in Turkey (62.9), Hungary (64.1), and Mexico (65.0).

The primary cause of restricted activity or disability is illness. According to the survey of MOHW and KIHASA (1999), major diseases with high prevalence per 1000 persons include dental cavities (184), skin diseases including allergies (170), arthritis (80), lower-back pain (64), gastritis and gastric ulcers (60), and hypertension (45). The prevalence rate varies depending on age and sex. For women over 45 years of age, high-prevalence diseases include arthritis (347), lower-back pain (218), skin diseases (173), hypertension (166), dental cavities (162), and gastritis and gastric ulcers (120). For men over 45 years of age, they include skin diseases (237), dental cavities (150), arthritis (124), hypertension (111), gastritis and gastric ulcers (98), and lower-back pain (91). Restricted activity due to illness leads to productivity loss, which was estimated to be 1.7 percent of the GDP in 1998 (MOHW and KIHASA, 1999). Lower-back pain and arthritis are the leading causes of productivity loss, which are 0.30 percent and 0.25 percent of the GDP, respectively.[6] Taking into account the cost of medical treatment, cost associated with waiting and traveling and the cost of caregivers, the social cost of illness will be much greater than the cost of productivity loss alone.

Cardiovascular diseases, cancer, and accidents are three major causes of death in Korea (see Figure 3). Deaths from cardiovascular diseases and accidents have been decreasing steadily over the past ten years although those from cancer have been stable. 58000 persons died of cardiovascular diseases in 1999. Mortality from cardiovascular diseases accounts for 23.3 percent, (20.7% for men, 26.6% for women,) of all deaths, which were down from 29.9 percent in 1990. Among deaths from cardiovascular diseases, 60 percent are from cerebrovascular diseases, 15 percent from ischemic heart diseases, and 6 percent from hypertension. Deaths from ischemic heart disease have increased by 78 percent in ten years, which is expected to increase further in the future due to obesity, a high-fat diet, and the lack of physical exercise.

Cancer is the second leading cause of death in 1999. 54000 persons died of cancer in 1999. Mortality from cancer accounted for 21.9 percent (25.3% for men, 17.8% for women) of all deaths,

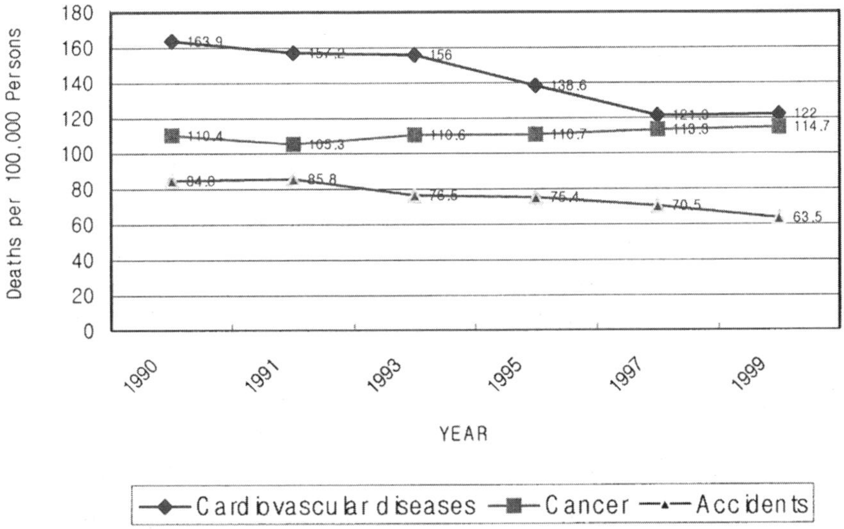

Source: National Statistical Office (2000).

Figure 3. Three major caused of death (unit: deaths per 100,0000 persons).

which were up from 20.1 percent in 1990. Among mortality from cancer, 21 percent are from stomach cancer, 19 percent from lung cancer and 18 percent from liver cancer. For the past ten years, death rates of lung cancer (1.5 times), colon cancer (1.8 times), and pancreatic cancer (1.6 times) have increased rapidly whereas mortality from stomach cancer has decreased. In Korea, mortality from breast cancer for women is still relatively low, 4.8 per 100000 women.

Accidents are the third major cause of deaths in Korea. 30000 persons died as a result of accidents in 1999. Deaths from accidents accounted for 12.1 percent, (15.7% for men, 7.7% for women) of all deaths, which were down from 15.4 percent in 1990. It is noteworthy that the death rate from accidents for men is twice that for women, meaning that men are exposed to a higher risk of accidents. Among deaths from accidents, 41 percent are due to automobiles and 23 percent due to suicide. Mortality from suicide has increased from 9.8 in 1990 to 16.1 per 100000 persons in 1999. The mortality rate from accidents in Korea is one of the highest in OECD countries. In particular, deaths from accidents are the primary cause of early death (for those who die before 40) in Korea.

TABLE II

Self-Evaluation of Health

Sex	Self-evaluation	1986	1989	1992	1995	1999
Men	Very healthy	11.3	14.5	7.8	8.0	8.0
	Healthy	43.4	47.7	46.3	42.5	42.3
	Fair	32.0	24.1	32.8	34.8	35.6
	Unhealthy	11.3	11.7	11.5	12.9	11.8
	Very unhealthy	2.0	2.0	1.5	1.9	2.3
Women	Very healthy	6.7	8.2	3.8	4.2	4.2
	Healthy	36.6	39.8	35.3	33.0	31.3
	Fair	37.0	30.3	37.7	38.9	39.8
	Unhealthy	17.5	19.3	20.9	21.5	21.5
	Very unhealthy	2.2	2.4	2.2	2.4	3.2

Source: National Statistical Office (1999).
*National sample of 30000 households (for those above 15 years of age).

Since consumers have difficulty in assessing health outcomes, objective health indicators have long been regarded as a primary measure of health status, in particular, for health policy. Furthermore, subjective evaluations should depend on surveys and the results can be vulnerable to the sampling method and sample size. Subjective measures of health outcomes or self-assessment of health status are still useful for evaluating quality of life because what people perceive affects their welfare and they make decisions on health and health care based on their perceptions and beliefs. Self-assessed health status has been deteriorating slightly for the past 15 years. In other words, the proportion of Koreans who think they are healthy has decreased (see Table II). In 1986, 55 percent of men responded that they were healthy or very healthy. This figure decreased to 50 percent in 1999. The proportion of women who think they are healthy or very healthy was down from 43 percent to 36 percent. Self-evaluation of health status is higher for men. However, it is not clear whether this trend represents a real deterioration of health status or is due to increased concern on the part of Koreans about their health.

Not only the level of health outcomes, but also their distribution is critical to assessing the quality of life. Equitable distribution of

TABLE III

Mortality by Socio-Economic Status in the Health Insurance for Public and School Employees

	Level	Number of deaths	Number of persons	Age-adjusted mortality*
Income	0–20th percentile	314	187799	27.8
	20–40th percentile	186	194893	20.3
	40–60th percentile	221	214773	16.3
	60–80th percentile	312	220085	12.5
	80–100th percentile	503	181514	10.5
Region	Metropolitan	634	463078	13.6
	Urban	587	393932	14.9
	Rural	315	142062	21.4
Total		1536	999074	15.4

Source: Cho (1997).
*Standardized based on all inured of the health insurance for government and school employees.

health outcomes among different socio-economic groups is essential for a better overall quality of life in a nation. Based on data from public and school employees health insurance, Cho (1997) finds that there is a difference in age-adjusted mortality rates among different income groups. The mortality rate of the lowest-income group (lower 20%) is 27.8 per 10000 persons, which is almost three times that of the highest income group (upper 20%), 10.5 per 10000 persons (see Table III). There also is a difference in mortality rates depending on where people live. The incidence of mortality of those living in rural areas is 21.4 per 10000 persons while that in metropolitan areas is only 13.6 per 10000 persons. Considering the fact that public and school employees who have insurance are more or less homogeneous, the different incidence of mortality among different socio-economic groups is particularly striking. The distribution of the incidence of mortality in different socio-economic groups of the entire population should be more skewed.

Health policy and institutional factors as well as environmental factors affect the level and distribution of health outcomes. Prevention and health promotion are more cost-effective than medical treatment. Primary care is also more cost-effective than more sophisticated and specialized care. To improve the health of Koreans, the government needs to put more public resources in prevention and health promotion programs as well as strengthen the role of primary care, for example, by providing financial incentives. Compared with the fee-for-service payment system, the capitation, which pays a lump sum to health care providers periodically, regardless of the actual cost of treatment, provides a strong incentive for them to invest in prevention and health promotion for their patients. The paradigm of health policy should be changed to emphasize population health outcomes, and the cost-effectiveness of health outcomes should also play an important role in the design of health insurance benefits. For an equitable distribution of health outcomes among different socio-economic groups, the government should lower the financial barrier to medical care, which still exists in the national health insurance program.

CONCLUDING REMARKS

Quality of life in health and health care can be measured in several different dimensions. In terms of the availability of health care personnel and medical facilities, Korea has experienced significant improvements over the past 30 years. The national health insurance program, which provides universal coverage of Koreans, has enhanced the purchasing power of consumers and contributed to the subsequent increase in the supply of (private) health care facilities. However, there still are financial barriers to the access of medical care because of limited benefit coverage and the high out-of-pocket payment that patients should pay in medical care utilization. As a result, the proportion of private payments in total health care expenditure is greater than the payment by national health insurance. There is inequity in terms of health care utilization, which has been lower for the self-employed than for industrial workers. The lesson is that not only the implementation of the national health insurance program but also its institutional characteristics matter for better access to health care, and consequently for better health outcomes.

Quality of life measured by health outcomes, such as life expectancy, has improved a lot in 30 years. Three major causes of death are cardiovascular diseases, cancer and accidents, and the death rate from accidents is much higher than in other industrialized countries. Although the incidence of mortality has been decreasing, there still is a difference in the incidence of mortality in different socio-economic groups. The government now needs to focus on the cost-effectiveness of medical interventions to improve health outcomes subject to the constraint of scarce social resources. Strengthening the role of primary health care; changing the payment system for providers; adopting capitation for them to put more resources in prevention than in treatment; channeling resources for outcomes research and health promotion; and considering cost-effectiveness in the design of health insurance benefits are the examples that public policy should pursue.

NOTES

[1] Until recently, physicians could both prescribe and dispense drugs. This constituted the largest source of their income because the insurance reimbursement to physicians for drugs was much higher than their cost of purchasing them. In order to change these perverse economic incentives of physicians and reduce the overuse of drugs, the government has implemented an historic reform that mandates the separation of prescribing and dispensing drugs, which led to several lengthy physician strikes (Kwon, 2003c).

[2] Reliable data on health care utilization before the national health insurance program was implemented are not available.

[3] The government has established health care centers in rural areas and physicians have to serve in these health care centers for three years in fulfillment of their military duty (Korea has a draft system). Note, however, that most private health care institutions are located in urban areas.

[4] Under the fee-for-service reimbursement, providers can increase their net income by providing more medical care.

[5] DALE (Disability-Adjusted Life Expectancy) is the life span without restricted activity and disability.

[6] Productivity loss from accidents is estimated to be 0.24 percent of the GDP (MOHW and KIHASA, 1999).

REFERENCES

Bovbjerg, R., P. held and M. Pauly: 1987, 'Privatization and bidding in the health-care sector', Journal of Policy Analysis and Management 6(4), pp. 648–666.

Cho, H.: 1997, Mortality by Socio-Economic Class in the Health Insurance for Public and School Employees, Doctoral Dissertation, Seoul National University (in Korean).

Chung, Y.: 2001, 'National health expenditure in Korea', Korean Social Security Review 17, forthcoming (in Korean).

Committee on Health Care Reform (COHCR): 1998, Health Care Reform (in Korean).

Kwon, S.: 2002, Achieving Health Insurance for All: Lessons from the Republic of Korea, ILO (International Labor Office).

Kwon, S.: 2003a, 'Payment system reform for health care providers in Korea', Health Policy and Planning, forthcoming.

Kwon, S.: 2003b, 'Health care financing reform and the new single payer in Korea: social solidarity or efficiency?' International Social Security Review, forthcoming.

Kwon, S.: 2003c, 'Pharmaceutical reform and physician strikes: separation of prescribing and dispensing drugs in Korea', Social Science and Medicine, forthcoming.

Ministry of Health and Welfare (MOHW): 2000, Health Care Statistics (in Korean).

Ministry of Health and Welfare (MOHW) and Korea Institute for Health and Social Affairs (KIHASA): 1999, '98 Survey of Health and Nutrition (in Korean).

Ministry of planning and Budget (MOPB): 2000, Government Budget (in Korean).

National Health Insurance Corporation (NHIC): 2000, Health Insurance Statistics (in Korean).

National Statistical Office (NSO): 2000, 99 Causes of Death (in Korean).

National Statistical Office (NSO): 2000, Social Statistics (in Korean).

WHO (World Health Organization): 2000, The World Health Report 2000 – Health Systems: Improving performance.

Department of Health Policy and Management
School of Public Health
Seoul National University
28 Yonkon-dong, Chongno-gu, Seoul 110-799
Korea
E-mail: Kwons@snu.ac.kr

JUNGHYO KIM and JUNHAN LEE

EDUCATIONAL ATTAINMENT AND POLICY

ABSTRACT. This article focuses on the levels and quality of educational attainment in Korea. To what extent have the Korean people attained a formal education, attending primary, secondary, and higher schools of education? How do they actually feel about their country's educational system? This paper addresses these two and other related questions drawing upon aggregate educational statistics and public opinion surveys. Analysis of these data reveals that the public educational system has produced the most literate of the economically developed countries. Yet, the country remains far from being a nation of citizens endowed with creative spirits and compassionate minds.

More than ever before, education has become indispensable for the improvement of the human lot. A good education equips individual citizens with cognitive skills and practical knowledge so that they can lead a better life. In addition, it provides a society with a competent workforce for economic development and societal modernization. Such socio-economic development, in turn, provides greater opportunities and resources for a better life among individual citizens. Literacy rates and enrollment ratios are, therefore, oftentimes employed as key indicators of life quality, along with life expectancy as well as the Gross Domestic Product (hereinafter the GDP) per capita (Morris, 1979; Hagerty et al., 2001; United Nations Development Programme, 2001).

To what extent have the Korean people attained a formal education, attending primary, secondary, and higher schools of education? What efforts has the Korean government made to improve the general level and quality of their educational system? How do their school enrollment and graduation rates compare with what has been noted in other members of the Organization for Economic Cooperation and Development (OECD hereinafter)? Does the Korean government spend for public education as much as the other OECD countries? What major problems need to be addressed in order to improve public education? This article examines these questions with aggregate educational statistics and recent survey findings.

Social Indicators Research **62, 63:** 187–195, 2003.

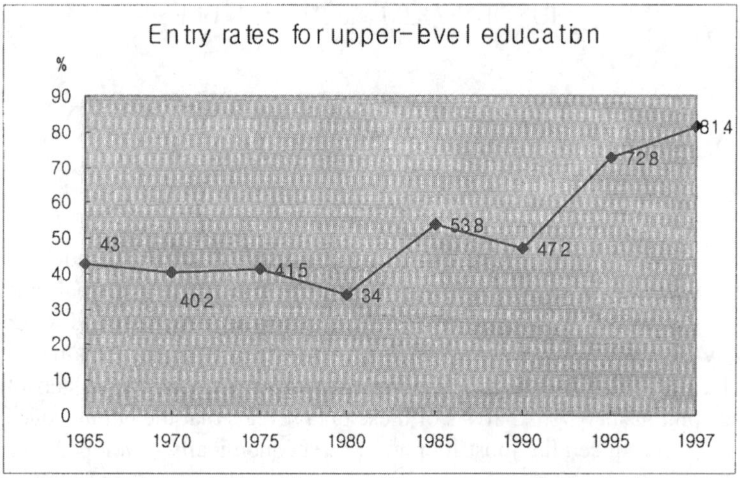

Source: KEDI (1997)

Figure 1. Entry rates for upper-level education in Korea.

LEVELS OF FORMAL EDUCATION

In 1950, Korea adopted the American system of 6-3-3-4 years for primary, lower secondary, upper secondary, and tertiary education. Primary education was mandatory starting in 1950, and lower secondary education became mandatory in 2001. As a result, the mandatory period of formal education has significantly increased over the past five decades. In 1997, Korean males, on average, spent 15 years in school, while their female counterparts 14 years, as compared to 16 years of schooling by American males and females. Korean schooling years became one of the longest as compared to the global standard (World Bank, 2001).

According to *World Development Indicators* (World Bank, 2001), 93 percent of the relevant age group enrolled in primary educational institutions, and 97 percent of the relevant age group enrolled in secondary educational institutions in the year of 1997. The enrollment ratio for primary educational institutions in Korea is nearly the same as the average rate (94%) among upper middle-income world economies. The ratio for secondary educational institutions in the former is, however, significantly higher than that (43%) of the latter (World Bank, 2001).

As of the late 1990s, the Korean educational system appears to be better developed at the levels of upper secondary and higher education. As Figure 1 illustrates, the entry rates for upper level education remained around 40 percent during the 1960s and 1980s. Starting in the mid-1990s, the rates rose sharply and it finally reached 81 percent in 1997. In addition, the average rate of graduation from high schools is also significantly higher for Korea than for the OECD countries (90% versus 79%).

The entry rate for tertiary education is significantly higher for Korea than for the OECD countries. For the former, the rates of participation in tertiary education, for those between the ages of 18–21 and 22–25 years, were 31 percent and 16 percent, respectively. The corresponding figures for the OECD as a whole are 22 percent for those 18–21 years old, and 15 percent for those 22–25 years old (KEDI, 1997).

In 1998, 65 percent of 25–64 year-old Korean adults received upper secondary or higher education. Moreover, 17 percent of the Korean adult population received the tertiary type A (Bachelor, Master, or equivalent degrees) or higher education. According to the *OECD in Figures: Statistics on the Member Countries* (OECD, 2001), these figures are higher than the mean for the OECD countries as a whole. Slightly over three in five adults (61%) in the OECD countries, on average, went on to upper secondary or higher education in 1998. In these countries, only 14 percent received the tertiary type A or higher education in the same year.

Koreans' devotion to a higher education has produced a notably large number of college degree earners and Ph.D. degree holders. Figure 2 clearly indicates that the number of Ph.D. degree holders per 10000 persons almost doubled between 1985 and 1990. It doubled again over a period of five years from 1990 to 1995. In 1997, 11 out of 10000 Koreans were found to hold a Ph.D. degree.

In terms of literacy, how does Korea compare with the countries at a similar stage of economic development? In 1999, only 1 percent of males, and only 4 percent of females aged 15 and over in Korea, were known to be illiterate. These figures are far lower than 9 percent for males and 11 percent for females among the upper middle-income economies in the world (World Bank, 2001). In addition, less than 0.5 percent of the Korean youth, aged between 15 and 24, were illiterate in 1999, which is also far lower than 4 percent among the upper middle-income world economies (World

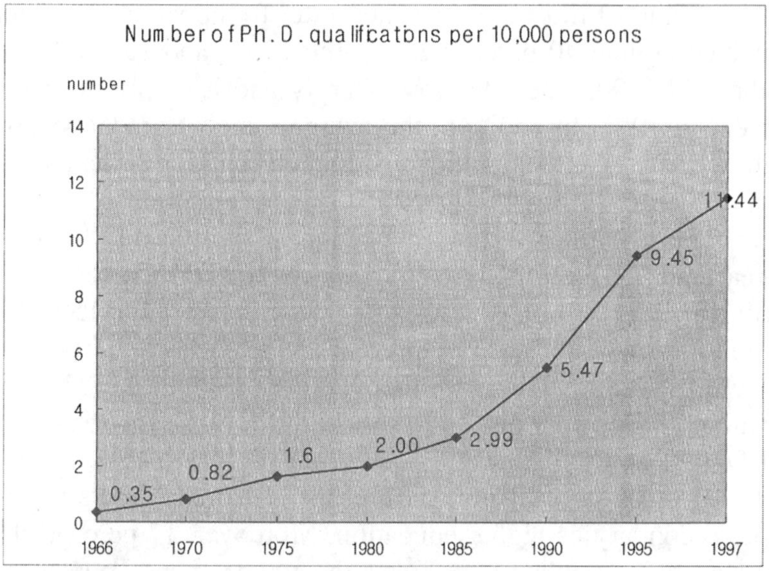

Source: KEDI (1997)

Figure 2. Ratio of Ph.D. qualification in Korea.

Bank, 2001). Undoubtedly, Korea represents the most literate of economically developed countries.

EDUCATIONAL RESOURCES

Governmental Expenditures

Figure 3 shows the governmental expenditures on primary and secondary education per student in 1997 became more than five times as large as that of 1985. Until the mid-1980s, public educational spending accounted for a very small proportion of the government budget. In 1998, the Korean government spent 4.4 percent of its GDP on public educational institutions (OECD, 2001). In the same year, the amounts of annual spending per student at the levels of primary, secondary, and tertiary education were U.S.$3308, U.S.$3518, and U.S.$6844, respectively (OECD, 2001).

These figures, however, are lower than the means of the OECD countries. In 1998, their expenditures on educational institutions averaged 5.1 percent of their respective GDP. Their annual expenditures per student at the level of primary, secondary, and tertiary

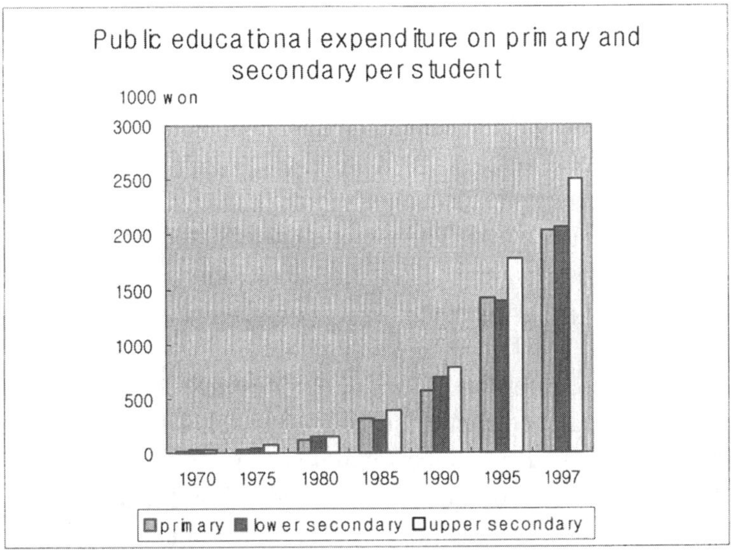

Source: KEDI (1997)

Figure 3. Public educational expenditure on primary and secondary per student.

education were U.S.$3851, U.S.$5274, and U.S.$8601, respectively (OECD, 2001). Although the Korean government expenditures per student on public education has increased enormously since 1985, it has yet to reach the OECD levels.

As a result of a relatively smaller level of governmental spending on education, Korea's ratio of students to teaching staff is much higher than the average for the OECD countries as a whole, which may be responsible for the lower quality of education in Korea. The number of students per primary school teacher was 31 in 1997, and this ratio was significantly higher than 25 for the upper middle-income world economies as a whole (World Bank, 2001). In Korean high schools, teachers, on average, teach 44 students in each of their classes, and 4600 classes are known to have more than 51 students (*Chosun Ilbo*, Dec. 4, 2000). To reduce these ratios between students and teachers, the government estimates that more than 5500 teachers were needed in the academic year 2001 alone.

Household Expenditures

Over the past two decades, individual households have been making greater financial investments and sacrifices for their children's education. The expenditures for the education of their school-age children have risen sharply. The percentage of their family incomes spent on education was 6 percent in 1980, but it rose to 11 percent in 1999 (see official website of the Korean National Statistics Office). The average Korean household is now spending, for private tutoring and formal schooling, nearly twice as much as they did two decades ago. The private tutoring fees, therefore, have become highly burdensome to family life, although they are widely considered to be absolutely necessary for admitting children to good colleges (KEDI, 1999; 2001).

More than three-quarter (79%) of students are currently known to take various kinds of private tutoring after school and to subscribe to commercially devised educational materials (*Chosun Ilbo*, Dec. 4, 2000). This extra school work is intended solely for the preparation of university entrance examinations, not for the enhancement of cognitive skills and general knowledge. This is because university education is increasingly regarded as the key to personal success – a better job, a larger income, and greater social status – in Korean life by the parents of the post-Korean War generation. Their children currently spend their entire period of primary and secondary education in school as well as elsewhere for the preparation of college entrance examinations. The excessive practice, of private tutoring for university entrance examinations, strains both students and their parents, both psychologically as well as financially.

SUBJECTIVE EVALUATIONS OF EDUCATIONAL ENVIRONMENT

Then, how do Korean adults actually feel about the educational system in their country? To address this question, the Korea Educational Development Institute (hereinafter the KEDI) conducted a survey in 1999 with a sample size of 1500 adults, between the ages of 20 and 65 across the nation. According to the survey, a majority (86%) of the respondents expressed dissatisfaction with the level of the government's financial support for education (see Table I). One in eight respondents (13%) reported that the government spent about the right amount of money on education. In terms of private tutoring, the same survey revealed that as many as four out of five Koreans

TABLE I

Degree of Satisfaction with Government Investment in Education

	(M)	Primary & secondary school parents
Too small	22.9%	21.7%
Small	62.5	64.0
Fit	12.7	12.3
Much	1.3	1.6
Too much	0.6	0.4

Source: KEDI (1999).

TABLE II

Degree of Burden for Private Tuitions

	Parents				
	(M)	Pre-school	Primary school	Lower secondary	Upper secondary
Not at all	1.4%	0.4%	1.2%	2.1%	1.1%
Not so much	4.9	4.4	4.2	3.2	3.8
A little bit	6.5	10.2	7.2	4.8	4.6
Much	47.7	53.3	57.8	53.4	43.7
Very much	28.2	38.9	26.5	31.2	35.4

Source: KEDI (1999).

(82%) viewed private tutoring fees as a financial burden at least to some degree (see Table II).

In addition, the KEDI survey sought to identify the specific level and substantive area of formal education with which the Korean people were most dissatisfied. Of the three levels of schooling, ranging from primary to tertiary levels, the Korean people were most dissatisfied with the way upper secondary schools teach students. Substantively, they remain most dissatisfied at failing to not only enhance creativity and individuality, but also inculcate the values of citizenship and morality.

The Korean National Statistics Office (hereinafter the KNSO) also reported that a majority of Koreans were not satisfied with their educational system. In 1999, eight in every ten Koreans (80%)

refused to rate positively their educational environment and opportunity structure. In 1996, a nearly identical proportion (79%) refused to do so. They cited educational expenses as the primary cause of their dissatisfaction with the education system. They tend to believe that the Korean government has failed to allocate enough money for public education, although a greater level of spending is required for the introduction of new educational technology, such as computers. As a result, they tend to believe that individual households have had to spend a greater portion of their incomes on education than they ought to.

SUMMARY AND CONCLUSIONS

The past two decades have witnessed significant improvements – quantitative and qualitative – in Korean education. These changes have undoubtedly improved the quality of Korean life in may ways. Korea's literacy rate is, for example, one of the highest in the world, and its expected schooling years are one of the world's longest.

Nonetheless, the country's public educational system has failed to produce a nation of citizens endowed with creative spirits and compassionate minds. Instead, it has merely produced a nation obsessed with the acquisition of college degrees especially from prestigious institutions. It is, therefore, urgent that the Korean government and its citizens redefine the meaning of education in such a way that it could enrich the human lot by serving its various needs, including those of a non-material and spiritual nature.

According to Sirgy (1998), there is no end to the process of improving life quality from the perspective of materialism. To date, Korean education has primarily served individuals in a way that it can help them to obtain more material things than others. But education can contribute to the quality of life more meaningfully and enduringly by motivating them to explore and experience goodness in human life in a variety of ways (von Wright, 1972).

What should be done to improve the quality of Korean education? First, the government should formulate a consistent policy that would reduce the level of obsession with university entrance examinations. The government should also increase educational spending to the extent that individual households' financial burden can be eased substantially. Classroom size should be reduced; the ratio of students to teacher needs to be lowered; and school facilities need to be adequately equipped.

At the same time, the school system at all levels should expend great effort to develop students' mental skills as well as to promote emotional maturity and moral judgment. It also needs to inspire students to explore various life goals and styles, and encourage them to pursue what they think is in their own best interest, and not only for their parents and their prospective employers.

REFERENCES

Chosun Ilbo, Dec. 4, 2000.
Hagerty, M.R. et al.: 2000, 'Quality of life indexes for national policy: Review and agenda for research', Social Indicators Research 55(1), pp. 1–96.
KEDI: 1997, Trace of Education in Korea (KEDI, Seoul).
KEDI: 1999, Analyses of Demand for Life-long Education (KEDI, Seoul).
KEDI: 2001, http://www.kedi.re.kr.
Korean National Statistics Office. www.nso.go.kr.
Morris, M.D.: 1979, Measuring the Condition of the World's Poor: The Physical Quality of Life Index (Pergamon, New York).
OECD: 2001, OECD in Figures: Statistics on the Member Countries.
Sirgy, M.J.: 1998, 'Materialism and quality of life', Social Indicators Research 43, pp. 227–260.
United Nations Development Programme: 2001, Human Development Report 2001 (Oxford University Press, Oxford).
Wright, G.H. von: 1972, The Varieties of Goodness (London, Routledge and K. Paul, New York).
World Bank: 2001, World Development Indicators (The World Bank, Washington, D.C.).

Department of Elementary Education Junghyo Kim
Ewha Womans' University
11-1 Daehyun-dong, Seodaemoon-gu, Seoul
Korea # 120-750
E-mail: junghyo@ewha.ac.kr

University of Missouri at Columbia Junhan Lee
Columbia, Missouri 65211, USA
E-mail: Junhanlee@hotmail.com

JOUNG-WOO LEE

INCOME, CONSUMPTION, AND POVERTY

ABSTRACT. This article examines changes in economic welfare within Korea in terms of income, consumption, and poverty. Analyses of government statistics reveal that it has been extraordinarily successful in raising the average level of both income and consumption, while reducing the incidence of poverty during the last four decades. In reducing the unequal distribution of income during the same period, however, the country has been much less successful. In the aftermath of the 1997 economic crises, the level of poverty has risen due to sharp increases in unemployment. The lives of the poor are at risk since the social safety net system in Korea is only minimal. The heavy concentration of land and wealth in a few hands is a major obstacle to the further enhancement of the quality of economic life among the Korean people.

1. INTRODUCTION

Nobody would deny the importance of income and consumption in human life. Conventional indicators of economic development, such as the Gross Domestic Product (hereinafter the GDP) per capita, however, are of limited value in measuring the quality of economic life, not to mention the quality of human life as a whole. The GDP, for example, is not capable of measuring the distribution of income, which affects the economic welfare of the citizenry as a whole. Nor is it capable of addressing the problem of poverty. A comprehensive and dynamic account of the quality of economic life, therefore, requires use of indicators capable of directly measuring both the level and distribution of income and consumption.

This paper examines the changing quality of economic life especially among Korean workers with systematic analyses of time-series data on income, consumption, and poverty. The analyses are based on two assumptions. The first is what John Rawls characterizes as "maximin principle," i.e., the quality of life in a given society cannot be regarded as satisfactory when some of its citizens are in a miserable state of life. The second premise is that Korean

Social Indicators Research **62, 63:** 197–209, 2003.

workers have yet to receive their fair share of economic development, although it is internationally regarded as more equitable than what is observed in other developing countries (World Bank, 1993).

INCOME GROWTH

Korea has displayed unprecedented rapid economic growth from the mid-1960s up until the late 1990s, when an abrupt economic crisis hit the country. Per capita national income increased 80-fold from U.S.$125 in 1966 to over U.S.$10000 in 1995. This kind of rapid economic growth could be found only in few East Asian countries like Hong Kong, Singapore, and Taiwan. Another notable feature of economic growth in Korea is that it has not been accompanied by a worsening distribution of income, as witnessed in many Latin American countries.

Over a prolonged period of time, Korea was able to combine unusually high rates of economic growth with a reasonably equitable distribution of the fruits of that growth. This puts Korea in the prestigious category of "economic miracles," which only a small number of countries in East Asia have attained according to an evaluation of the World Bank (World Bank, 1993). More notable is that Korea, as a member of the Organization for Economic Cooperation and Development (hereinafter the OECD), is the most prominent of the economic miracle states in East Asia.

Fast economic growth coupled with a fair distribution of income suggests that the process of rapid industrialization has brought about significant improvements in the standard of living for most Koreans. Laborers appear to have enjoyed the fruits of economic growth as much as other groups within the society. According to the data reported in Table I, nominal wages of full-time workers in the non-farm sector have increased 86 times during the period 1970–99. After accounting for the rise in the consumer price level, real wages have increased 6.5 times over three decades. An annual rate of real wage growth of 6.7 percent, which has lasted for three decades, is a remarkable achievement, which few countries have been able to emulate.

How do Korean workers compare with other groups in receiving the fruits of economic growth? Table II provides the directly relevant

TABLE I

Wages, Prices, and Productivity (Full-time Workers, Non-farm Sector)

Year	Nominal wages		CPI	Real wages		Labor productivity	
	(won)	(index)	Index	(won)	(index)	(1) Physical	(2) Value added
1970	17831	(100)	(100)	17831	(100)	(100)	
1980	176058	(987)	(451)	39063	(219)	(259)	(100)
1990	642309	(3602)	(828)	77574	(435)	(722)	(302)
1999	1544365	(8661)	(1329)	116205	(652)	(2056)	(762)
Growth rates (%)							
1970–80	25.7		16.3	8.2		10.0	
1980–90	13.8		6.0	7.1		10.8	11.7
1990–99	10.2		5.4	4.6		12.3	10.8
1970–99	16.6		9.3	6.7		11.0	11.3

Sources: Bank of Korea, *Yearbook of Economic Statistics*, various years. Ministry of Labor, *Yearbook of Labor Statistics*, various years.
Note: labor productivity is measured for mining, manufacturing and electricity only.
(unit: Korean Won).

data to this question, i.e., the relative income share of total national income by workers in general. Historically, it is known that labor's share of income in a given country rises with its economic growth. Cross-nationally, it is also known that the values of this statistic in developed countries hover around 75–80 percent.

The first column of Table II shows that the labor income share has grown from around 40 percent in 1970, to around 60 percent in 1998. The second column provides the number of employees divided by the total workforce, thus indicating the share of individual workers among the total workforce. It shows basically the same pattern of growth as that of the labor income share, viz., from 40 to 60 percent during the same period. In other words, the working class constituted about 40 percent of the workforce, and was rewarded with about 40 percent of the national income in 1970. In 1998, this class constituted about 60 percent of the workforce, and received 60 percent of the national income. When these figures

TABLE II

Relative Economic Position of the Working Class

Year	Labor income share (1)	Share of workers among workforce (2)	Wage parity ratio (3) = (1)/(2)
1970	39.5	38.9	101.5
1975	39.6	40.6	97.5
1980	50.1	47.3	105.9
1985	50.3	54.2	93.0
1990	57.8	58.8	98.3
1995	61.0	62.6	97.6
1998	60.0	61.0	98.4

Sources: The Bank of Korea, *Yearbook of Economic Statistics* and National Statistical Office, *Yearbook of Economically Active Population.*

(1) = employee remuneration/factor cost domestic income (wL/yN).

(2) = no. of employees/no. of total workforce (L/N).

(3) = employees' per capita income/per capita domestic income at factor cost

= w/y=(wL/yN)/(L/N)=(1)/(2).

are considered together, it is apparent that the past three decades brought about little change in the relative place the Korean working class occupied in the distribution of national income.

The third column of Table II shows the wage parity ratio, which is simply derived by dividing the figure in Column (1) by the one in Column (2). As might be expected, the wage parity remained near 100 throughout the entire period of three decades. This indicates that the relative position of workers changed little during this period. A wage parity ratio of around 100 means the working class has been rewarded with about an average income within the society. The Korean working class was rewarded an average income thirty years ago, and they are rewarded the same now. Evidently, the economic growth of Korea over the last three decades has been "neutral," favoring neither the working class nor the non-working class.

Table III provides another relative measure of economic welfare among Korean workers. Over the period 1971–99, it compares the

TABLE III

Wage Differentials by Occupations (non-farm sector)

Year	Manager	Prof. tech.	Clerical	Sales	Service	Production
1971	359	250	204	118	90	100
1976	474	292	222	112	103	100
1980	395	246	162	89	100	100
1985	340	234	153	136	99	100
1990	256	173	120	98	87	100
1995	218	147	113		89	100
1999	202	150	110		92	100

Sources: Ministry of Labor, *Occupational Wage Survey*, 1971–99.
Relative wages of various occupations as compared to production workers (=100) in all industries.
Prof = professionals, Tech = technicians.

average wage earned by production workers with that of managers, professionals and technicians, clerks, sales personnel, and service workers. In 1976, managers were, on average, paid five times more than production workers, but they are now paid only two times more. Professionals and technicians were paid three times more than what those workers received two decades ago, but they are now paid only one-and-a-half times as much. Clerical workers, who were once paid more than double that of production workers, are now paid just slightly more. The wage gaps between different occupations have been reduced significantly during the past two decades. During this period, the economic standing of production workers has significantly improved relative to those with higher levels of education and training.

2. INCOME DISTRIBUTION

Individual scholars and research institutes have reported that income distribution in Korea has improved during the last couple of decades. The Korea National Statistical Office (hereinafter the NSO) (2000) and Dr. Hakchung Choo (1982, 1992) of the Korea Development Institute are in agreement that income inequality has been lowered in both rural and urban areas since the late 1970s. According to the Farm Households Economic Survey (hereinafter the FHES, which is conducted annually by the Ministry of Agriculture and Fishery, the Gini coefficient was estimated to be 0.324 for 1967, and 0.288 for 1988. This strongly suggests a lowering of income inequality in rural areas over the past decades. When combining the urban and rural income survey data, it is evident hat income distribution in Korea has been moving in the direction of lesser inequality before the economic crisis hit the country in 1997.

Nonetheless, the Gini coefficients based on these survey data have recently been called into question (Ahn, 1995; Lee and Whang, 1998). These surveys were not capable of properly incorporating the unearned incomes stemming from the soaring prices of land, houses, and stocks. The windfall gains from those sources occur only once or twice in life, so that people tend to regard them as "abnormal" income, that should not be counted as income in the social surveys. Therefore, it is highly unlikely that occasional income surveys could capture the vast amount of unearned income, which explored in the late 1980s. This is one reason why there is a lingering doubt about the findings of improving income distribution, even though existing official statistical data provide us with supporting evidence.

For 1988 alone, for example, the realized capital gains from land were around 20 percent of the Gross National Product (hereinafter the GNP), and those from the stock market added another 5 percent. The Gini coefficient of 1988, reported by the NSO, was given as 0.336. However, the Gini coefficient is actually estimated to be 0.388, one the capital gains arising from land in the late 1980s are taken into account (Lee, 1991). The gains from the booming stock market in the late 1980s further raised the coefficient to 0.412, a figure that is significantly higher than what the NSO originally estimated the coefficient to be. In reality, therefore, it is highly probable that income inequality in Korea is much higher than what is known from the governmental household surveys, and it has been worsening during the past decade.

TABLE IV

Relative standard of Living between Working and Non-working Class

Year	Relative consumption				Engel coefficient			
	white collar	blue collar	laborers	non-laborers	white collar	blue collar	laborers	non-laborers
1963	128.5	64.4	89.5	100	51.0	60.1	55.1	53.1
1964	120.1	67.0	88.4	100	52.7	63.4	57.6	56.2
1970	104.5	68.8	87.9	100	38.5	44.0	40.6	40.3
1975	116.4	73.3	92.3	100	40.5	48.9	44.2	42.9
1980	124.8	76.2	91.0	100	32.7	38.6	36.1	36.2
1985	119.7	72.7	89.7	100	33.8	39.7	36.8	37.0
1990	108.2	70.7	85.8	100	30.0	34.8	32.7	31.2
1995	106.5	82.5	92.9	100	27.5	29.9	29.0	28.8
2000	116.2	84.1	97.6	100	25.6	29.4	27.5	27.2

Sources: National Statistical Office, *Urban Household Income and Expenditure Survey.*

3. CONSUMPTION PATTERN

How does the working class compare with the non-working class in terms of what they consume on a daily basis? The present study addressed this question with the Urban Household Income and Expenditure Surveys (hereinafter the UHIES) conducted by the NSO for the period of 1963–2000. Table IV compares the relative levels of consumption of three working classes – blue collar, white collar, and laborers – with that of non-laborers. In addition, the table provides the Engel coefficient, i.e., the ratio of food consumption as a part of total consumption, for these four classes. There is no strict criterion, but often an Engel coefficient over 70 percent means "extremely poor," and over 50 percent "poor."

According to the Engel coefficients reported in Table IV, both the working and non-working classes were poor during the 1960s. They had to spend more than half of their living expenses on food items. In 2000, however, they were spending less than one-third of those expenses for the same purpose. Their Engel coefficients have declined to the high 20s, by as much as 50 percent over the past four

TABLE V

The Consumption Structure of Worker Households (after adjusting the housing cost)

Year	Total	F	H	C	U	M	E	T	Other
1963	100	55.1	14.2	6.1	6.1	2.8	4.3	2.4	9.0
1970	100	40.6	18.2	10.5	5.8	3.1	5.3	4.7	11.8
1975	100	44.2	12.2	9.0	5.7	4.1	5.6	4.3	14.9
1980	100	36.1	19.9	9.2	6.3	5.5	4.6	4.9	13.5
1985	100	29.8	22.7	6.2	5.9	6.2	5.1	5.2	18.9
1990	100	26.2	23.0	6.8	3.6	4.2	5.8	6.5	23.9
1995	100	21.6	27.6	6.0	3.1	3.6	6.8	8.7	22.6
2000	100	20.5	27.8	4.3	3.8	3.1	8.1	12.2	20.2

Source: National Statistical Office, *UHIES*
(1) The portions of various categories of consumption.
Total = total consumption F = food, H = housing, C = clothing, U = utilities, M = medical cost, E = education, T = transportation and communication.
(2) Housing cost includes the monthly rents, lump-sum payments, and the imputed cost for owner-occupied housing.

decades. This indicates a remarkable improvement in the standard of living among all classes of the Korean population.

Of the three classes surveyed, blue-collar workers remain the least well off, still spending the most on food items, the same as they did four decades ago. When improvements in the overall levels of consumption are considered, however, it is the blue-collar workers, who have achieved the greatest level of improvement in their standard of living. In 1963, they were 35 percentage points behind non- laborers. In 2000, however, they were only 16 percentage points behind, indicating a gain of 19 percentage points over the period in question.

Table V examines changes in the consumption structure of worker households after adjusting for the housing costs that were underestimated in the analysis reported by the government. Specifically, the opportunity cost of the lump-sum deposits and the imputed rents of owner-occupied housing were taken into account in order to estimate, accurately, the percentage figures for food and other consumption items. The most notable feature of Table V concerns steady and significant declines in the Engel coefficients from 55 in 1963, to 21 in 2000. As a result of such declines in food consumption, Korean workers have been able to spend more on such items as medical care, education, transportation, and communications.

Of all those non-food items, the relative level of spending has increased to the greatest extent in the "other" consumption category, which covers furniture, electronic equipment, and entertainment expenses. These items are generally considered to be luxuries rather than necessities. The six-fold rise in this category from 2 to 12 percentage points is evidence of the remarkable improvement in the standard of living of the Korean working class during the past four decades. Nonetheless, it should be noted that housing costs have become the single most important item in the worker's household budget. Housing and food costs together constitute almost half of this budget.

How does the Korean workers' standard of living compare with what has been observed in the other developed and developing countries? The *World Development Report* (hereinafter the WDR), published by the World Bank, provides relevant data for a cross-national comparison. Table VI summarizes the consumption structures of sixty-three countries grouped into four categories: the low-income countries; lower-middle-income countries; upper-middle-income countries; and high-income countries. According to the World Bank, Korea currently belongs to the upper-middle income group.

Table VI contains three separate estimates for Korea by line. Line (1) contains the original figures reported in the 1990 *WDR* in which Korea was listed as upper-middle-income-economy. Line (2) lists the figures derived from the 1985 UHIES data, which cover the same period as the *WDR*. Line (3), on the other had, reports the figures adjusted for housing costs. Of these three estimates, the third is widely considered the most realistic one.

In terms of housing costs, Korea tops countries in the upper middle income group, and joins the ranks of the high income group (12.5% versus 12.9%). In terms of food costs, Korea looks more like the upper income group (34% versus 31%) than the high income group. In terms of expenses for luxury items, listed in the "other" category, Korea resembles the low middle income group (21.6%

TABLE VI

Consumption Structures of the World

Country groups	No.	F	H	C	U	M	E	T	Other
Low Income	16	51.1	7.2	9.1	4.4	3.1	4.0	6.2	15.9
Lower Middle	20	36.9	9.6	8.5	2.4	5.5	5.9	8.4	22.4
Upper Middle	7	31.3	8.9	8.4	3.0	5.6	5.3	9.7	26.3
High Income	20	15.3	12.9	6.1	4.1	9.7	7.9	12.6	31.6
Korea (1)		35.0	6.0	6.0	5.0	5.0	9.0	9.0	25.0
(2)		36.8	4.6	7.6	7.3	7.7	6.3	6.4	23.3
(3)		33.7	12.5	7.0	6.7	7.0	5.7	5.8	21.6

Source: World Bank, *World Development Report*, 1990.
Korea (1) is the original figures in *World Development Report*, 1990.
Korea (2) is based on worker households' budget in *UHIES*, 1985.
Korea (3) is after adjusting the housing cost of lump-sum deposits.
F = food, H = housing, C = clothing, U = utilities, M = medical cost, E = education, T = transportation and communication.

versus 22.4%) more than the upper income group. This finding makes it clear that Korea's appearance as a high or upper middle income country is highly deceptive as far as the overall quality of economic life among workers is concerned. As compared to their peers in affluent countries, Korean workers have relatively less to spend for items other than basic necessities. In this sense, the quality of economic life or standard of living of Korean workers does not compare favorably with that of other countries with similar and higher levels of the GDP per capita.

4. POVERTY

Poverty is an issue closely related to income distribution. Its magnitude tells us about the state of life quality among the bottom ranks of people including blue-collar workers. The rate of poverty in Korea, which was once over 40 percent in the early 1960s, has declined to a significant extent during the 1960–80 decades of rapid industrialization. Table VII shows recent trends in and the current status of poverty in terms of two conventional measures. The first is the head count ratio that divides the number of poor people divided

TABLE VII

Absolute Poverty and Poverty Gap (%)

Year	Head count ratio	Poverty gap
1993	13.4	2.4
1994	13.9	2.3
1995	10.0	1.7
1996	8.7	1.3
1997	7.3	1.0
1998	13.1	2.3

Source: Daewoo Economic Research Institute, *Korea Households Economic Survey*, 1993–1998.
Head Count Ratio (HCR) = The number of poor people divided by all people.
Poverty Gap = The size of income needed to raise the incomes of poor households to the poverty line divided by the total income.

by all people. The second is the poverty gap that divides the amount of income needed to raise the incomes of poor households to the poverty line by total income. In the two measures, the poor is defined as members of households, whose incomes fall below the minimum cost of living, as estimated by the Korean Institute for Health and Social Affairs.

According to the panel data gathered by the Daewoo Economic Research Institute and reported in Table VII, the head count ratio of the poor declined steadily from 13 percent in 1993, to 7 percent in 1997. Right after the outbreak of the economic crisis in November 1997, however, the ratio rose sharply to 13 percent, the figure reported in the early 1990s. Similarly, the poverty gap, the proportion of household income needed to pull the poor households out the poverty, declined steadily until the outbreak of the crisis, and then rose sharply. Nonetheless, the gap remains at a very low level of 2 percent. From this finding, it is evident that the real issue of poverty in Korea has more to do with the unequal distribution of incomes than with the absolute scarcity of material resources. Accordingly, a little improvement in income distribution may greatly contribute to the reduction of poverty.

Who are the poor in Korea? According to a recent survey (Kwon et al., 1998), the poverty rates in Korea are especially high among families headed by persons with little or no educational background, and those headed by unemployed or underemployed persons. The incidence of poverty is also high among families headed by young or old persons. The highest rates of poverty, however, are found among families of single mothers with dependent children. The official records also show that 63 percent of those who receive public assistance from the government, are women thus suggesting 'feminization of poverty' in Korea.

5. CONCLUDING REMARKS

Korea has been extraordinarily successful in raising the average level of both income and consumption for working class as well as others during the last four decades. The country has also been successful in providing a reasonably equitable distribution of the fruits of rapid economic growth, and in reducing the incidence of poverty. Undoubtedly, few countries can rival Korea in improving the quality of economic life among ordinary citizens. For all these successes, blue-collar workers as a whole remain significantly worse-off than any other occupational group. The outbreak of the recent economic crisis has put them at a greater disadvantage (the adverse effects of the economic crisis on the quality of Korean life are documented in Jiho Jang's article in this special issue).

In addition to the economic crisis, the disparity in the distribution of land and wealth remains a major barrier to the further improvement of the quality of economic life among ordinary Koreans. In Korea today, land is heavily concentrated into a relatively few hands, and its per acre price is the highest in the world (Lee and Lee, 2001). The heavy concentration and high price of land are responsible for the highly unequal distribution of wealth in Korean society. These factors are also responsible for rising housing and a multitude of other problems, including a shortage of affordable housing costs and roads. In short, the concentration of land and wealth in a few hands constitutes the most serious threat to the further enhancement of the quality of life of the Korean people at this time. It is, therefore, fair to conclude that the future quality of life in Korea will depend on the values and distribution of land as much as the degree of household income and consumption.

REFERENCES

Ahn, K.S.: 1995, 'Economic development and income distribution in Korea', Korean Journal of Development Economics 1, pp. 53–76.

Choo, H.: 1982, Income Distribution and Its Determinants in Korea, vol. 1 & 2 (Korea Development Institute, Seoul).

Choo, H.: 1992, Income distribution and social equity in Korea. Paper presented at Korea Development Institute/China Institute for Economic Research Joint Seminar in Seoul, Korea.

Korea Institute for Health and Social Affairs (KIHASA): 1998, Korea Human Development Report (KIHASA, Seoul).

Kwon, S.W. et al.: 1998, Combating Poverty: The Korean Experience (United Nations Development Programme, Seoul).

Lee, J.W.: 1991, 'Wealth, capital gains, and income inequality in Korea', Korean Economic Journal 23, pp. 327–362.

Lee, J.W. and S.H. Whang: 1998, 'Policy issues of income and wealth distribution in Korea', KDI Policy Studies 22, pp. 153–214.

Lee, J.W. and S. Lee: 2001, 'Estimating wealth inequality in Korea', Korea Development Economics Journal 7/1, pp. 1–28.

World Bank: 1990, World Development Report (Oxford University Press, New York).

World Bank: 1993, The East Asian Miracle (Oxford University Press, New York).

Department of Economics
Kyungpook National University
Daegu 702-701
Korea
E-mail: joulee@knu.ac.kr

JAE-YOUNG SON, YUN-HI WON and CHOON-GEOL MOON

CHANGING CONDITIONS AND QUALITY OF HOUSING

ABSTRACT. This article analyzes the major trends and features of the housing market. It also reviews governmental programs and policies in light of the critical issues facing this market. Our analysis reveals that the quantity and quality of housing stock for the average Korean has improved greatly over the past four decades due partly to the government's extensive involvement in land development and price regulation. The onset of the economic crisis in November 1997 prompted the government to abolish the various forms of regulations and encourage house financing by the private sector. Since then, housing types have become more diversified and a closer linkage has been established between the capital market and the housing industry. At the same time, the stock of small houses for the poor has fallen off sharply. Accordingly, the government should consider providing more financial resources for low-income housing.

Since the end of the Korean War in 1953, the housing situation in Korea has steadily improved. The sheer number of housing units has increased dramatically, and a greater proportion of these units have been equipped with modern conveniences. More than ever before, the average Korean today lives in a larger, more comfortable, and safer home. The purpose of this paper is to examine the trends in and the current state of the Korean housing market by reviewing the relevant literature (Son, 1997; Kim, 1993; Renaud, 1989). Specifically, this paper will first examine the major trends in the housing market, and highlight the more notable of its quantitative and qualitative changes over the past four decades. We will then look at the important role the government has played in the market. Finally, we will discuss the pressing issues affecting the present and future state of Korea's housing market, and then explore their policy implications.

Social Indicators Research **62, 63:** 211–237, 2003.

LONG-TERM TRENDS IN HOUSING CONDITIONS

Housing Stock

Table I shows trends in housing stock in terms of type, size, and supply ratio. Over the 40-year period from 1960 to 2000, the total number of dwelling units increased 2.3 times. The housing supply ratio, a popular indicator of housing stock adequacy,[1] was 86 percent in 1995. The Ministry of Construction of Transportation estimated the ratio to be 94.8 percent in 2000, and expects it to reach 100 percent in 2002. In the mid-1980s, the housing supply ratio declined to less than 70 percent, but it subsequently bounced back to its current level. The declining housing supply ratio, until the mid-1980s, was mainly an urban phenomenon due to a number of factors, including rapid urbanization and insufficient investment in housing. In the mid-1980s, the housing shortage in the Capital region became acute because the government was reluctant to accommodate the influx of people into the area.

An Increasing Share of Apartments and Loss of Small-Scale Houses

Table I also shows that, of the various housing types, the number of apartment houses and their share of the total housing stock have increased dramatically. The "apartment" (rather, *Aa-part* in Korean vocabulary) is considered attached housing in a building five stories or taller where each unit is individually owned.[2] Apartments are usually built as a complex of multi-story buildings; during an earlier period each building consisted of five stories, but currently they run from 13 to 30 stories. Each apartment complex usually contains 500 or more units. As land became scarce and building skills improved, this type of dwelling unit became popular in the major cities during the 1970s. Currently, many apartment buildings are constructed in rural areas, where there is no shortage of land, because rural residents prefer convenient heating, a modern kitchen, easy maintenance, and the kind of security provided by apartment life. Between 1995 and 2000, apartments accounted for 81 percent of new housing construction, much higher than the 29 percent registered during the latter half of the 1970s. In contrast, single detached houses constituted 37.3 percent of all housing units in 2000, down from 95.3 percent in 1970. Except for enclaves for the rich, many of these

TABLE I

Trends in Housing Stock

	1970	1980	1985	1990	1995	2000
Total	4,359	5,318	6,104	7,374	9,570	11,493
	(100%)	(100%)	(100%)	(100%)	(100%)	(100%)
(1) by Type						
Single detached	4,154	4,652	4,719	4,726	4,490	4,289
house	(95.3%)	(87.5%)	(77.3%)	(64.1%)	(49.9%)	(37.3%)
Town house	146	161	349	602	1,122	1,319
	(3.3%)	(3.0%)	(5.7%)	(8.2%)	(11.7%)	(11.5%)
Apartment	33	373	821	1,628	3,610	5,498
	(0.8%)	(7.0%)	(13.5%)	(22.1%)	(37.7%)	(47.8%)
Others[1]	25	131	213	202	348	387
	(0.6%)	(2.5%)	(3.5%)	(2.7%)	(3.6%)	(3.4%)
(2) by Size						
less than 14 pyong	—	1,856	1,581	1,403	1,464	—
($46.2m^2$)	—	(34.9%)	(25.9%)	(19.6%)	(15.9%)	—
14 ~ less than 29	—	2,787	3,473	4,146	5,735	—
pyong ($95.7m^2$)	—	(52.4%)	(56.9%)	(57.9%)	(62.3%)	—
29 ~ less than 49	—	532	806	1,146	1,408	—
pyong ($161.7m^2$)	—	(10.0%)	(13.2%)	(16.0%)	(15.3%)	—
49 pyong and over	—	149	256	465	589	—
	—	(2.8%)	(4.2%)	(6.5%)	(6.4%)	—
Housing supply ratio(%)[2]	78.2	71.2	69.8	72.4	86.0	—

Source: National Statistical Office, Population and Housing Census, each year. Preliminary counts for the year 2000.

[1]Mostly houses within non-residential buildings.

[2]Total housing stock in 1960 was 3,464 thousand units with housing supply ratio of 84.2%.

detached housing units are in poor condition, and are located in older sections of the cities or rural areas.

As family income rose and as apartments gained popularity, the average family moved into a larger and better home. Small houses of less than 14 pyong (46.2 m^2) decreased not only in terms of the

TABLE II

Trends in Housing Quality

	Unit	1970	1980	1985	1990	1995
Average size of a house	m^2	47.9	68.4	72.6	80.8	83.0
Dwelling area per person	m^2	6.8	10.1	11.3	13.8	17.2
Dwelling area per household	m^2	35.9	45.8	46.4	51.0	58.6
Persons per room	persons	—	2.1	1.9	1.5	1.1
Households						
occupying one room	%	—	—	32.6	25.8	12.3
with hot and cold running water	%	—	9.9	19.9	34.1	74.8
with flush toilet	%	—	18.3	33.1	51.3	75.1

Source: National Statistical Office, Population and Housing Census, each year.

share of the total housing stock, but also in sheer numbers. They accounted for 49.4 percent of the housing stock (2.33 million units) in 1975, and 34.9 percent or 1.86 million units in 1980, but the ratio plummeted to 15.9 percent (1.46 million units) in 1995. This loss of small houses is not an indication that all those who once lived there are now able to afford larger houses. Instead, many small houses were demolished to make room for mid- to large-scale houses, with little regard for the poor, who were dislocated. The loss of small houses, however, translates into fewer housing opportunities for low-income households, and this partly explains why housing prices for small houses increased more than large-scale ones.

Housing Quality and Residential Satisfaction

Various housing quality indicators show that an average Korean family has enjoyed improved housing conditions over the years. Table II shows that the average size of a house and dwelling area, per person and per household, has increased, while the number of persons per room, and the ratio of households crammed into one room have decreased. About three-quarters of all families in 1995 lived in a house with hot running water and modern toilet.

Table III shows how Koreans evaluate their individual housing units and neighborhood. In the five-year period between 1992 and

1997, the ratios of people who were satisfied with their residence and location increased, but in 1997, 40.8 percent of all households in the sample were still not content with their residence, and 28.6 percent were not satisfied with their location. For all households, the small size of a residence was frequently a cause for complaint, but cases of dilapidation were a more important concern for rural households. With respect to location, schools and crime were less of a problem for both rural and urban households. Rural households, however, complained most about inconvenient transportation, while inferior natural environments, pollution, and parking problems were problems for urban households.

Tenure: Owner-occupancy and the Chonsei Rental Contract

Trends in housing tenure are shown in Table IV. The ratio of families residing in their own homes decreased from 63.6 percent in 1975, to 49.9 percent in 1990, and then it rose to 53.3 percent in 1995. The decline in the owner-occupancy ratio until 1990 was due to rapid urbanization as well as failure to supply a sufficient number of dwelling units in urban areas. There has been a wide difference between owner-occupancy ratios in urban and rural areas; in 1990, the ratio was 40.5 percent in urban areas as compared to 77.5 percent in rural areas. Later on, the owner-occupancy ratio increased mainly in the urban areas where massive housing construction had been concentrated.

When speaking of housing tenure, one has to mention Korea's peculiar Chonsei rental system. All segments of the Korean real estate rental market involve rental contracts called Chonsei. With a Chonsei rental contract, the tenant makes a large deposit in lieu of monthly rent payments, and the interest income that accrues to the landlord constitutes the rent. At the end of the usual two-year rental term, the deposit is returned in full to the tenant. Because of steady inflation in housing prices, capital gains are an additional, and traditionally more important source of income for the landlord. This form of rental contract is universal in the mid- and upper level residential rental market. Evidence for this can be found in a report that estimated total Chonsei deposits outstanding in 1992 to be 50 trillion Won nationwide, double the amount of the total official housing loans outstanding (Lee and Huh, 1993).

TABLE III
Subjective Assessment of Housing and its Location

	1992			1997		
	Nation	Rural	Urban	Nation	Rural	Urban
(1) About Housing Unit						
Much satisfied	5.4	5.8	7.1	6.6	11.2	5.5
Moderately satisfied	15.6	17.7	19.5	15.9	18.7	15.1
Acceptable	35.3	33.6	36.0	36.7	34.3	37.3
Moderately dissatisfied	35.3	31.1	28.5	33.5	29.0	34.7
Much dissatisfied	8.4	11.8	8.9	7.3	6.7	7.4
(1-2) Reasons for dissatisfaction						
Lack of sunshine and fresh air	6.2	1.5	7.7	8.6	2.8	9.9
Dilapidation	23.7	39.0	18.8	25.5	41.8	21.9
Small size	28.0	19.9	30.5	33.8	25.5	35.6
Inadequate heating, bathroom, etc.	40.5	39.5	41.2	23.9	24.8	23.7
Excessive maintenance costs				2.3	0.9	2.6
Lack of economic value, and others				5.8	4.2	6.1
(2) About location						
Much satisfied	7.0	8.1	6.6	8.5	12.0	7.6
Moderately satisfied	18.6	19.5	18.3	20.2	24.1	19.2
Acceptable	42.1	42.2	42.0	42.6	41.1	43.0
Moderately dissatisfied	27.4	25.8	28.0	25.1	19.9	26.5
Much dissatisfied	4.9	4.4	5.1	3.5	2.8	3.7
(2-2) Reasons for dissatisfaction						
Bad schools	7.3	13.7	5.3	6.4	13.3	5.0
Inconvenient transportation	24.8	32.6	22.3	22.2	39.8	18.7
Inferior natural environment	12.1	4.0	14.6	22.5	12.0	24.6
Pollution	26.2	13.6	30.1	9.8	2.7	11.1
Lack of neighborhood facilities	23.5	33.3	20.4	16.2	25.2	14.4
Crime	3.9	0.6	4.9	2.6	0.4	3.0
Parking difficulty				15.0	2.4	17.5
High commodity prices				4.5	2.7	4.8
Others	2.3	2.1	2.4	0.9	1.3	0.9

Source: National Statistical Office, Social Statistics Survey, each year.

TABLE IV

Trends in Housing Tenure (unit: %)

	Total	Owner occupied	Chonsei rental	Monthly rental	Free or other arrangement
1975	100	63.6	17.5	15.7	3.3
1980	100	58.7	23.9	15.4	1.9
1985	100	53.7	23.1	19.7	3.6
1990	100	49.9	27.8	19.1	3.2
1995	100	53.3	29.7	14.5	2.5

Source: National Statistical Office, Population and Housing Census, each year.

For the period spanning from 1975 to 1995, approximately 30 to 35 percent of urban households held a Chonsei tenancy, but the ratio has increased significantly among rural households. Monthly rental contracts tended to increase until 1985, but decreased thereafter, reflecting a stabilization of the housing market during the 1990s.

Price Trends

From the 1960s to the early 1990s, housing prices, together with land prices, rose faster than real income or general inflation. Official housing price statistics, since 1985, are shown in Table V.[3] Among the size categories of housing, prices for small houses rose more rapidly than large ones, mainly because of a decrease in the number of small houses. With respect to housing types, apartments underwent much higher price increases than others, which reflected the popularity of apartment style living. Most notably, the Chonsei rent increased much faster than the sale price for all housing types and size categories. Even during the 1990s, when house sale prices stagnated, Chonsei deposits rose continuously until the onset of the economic crisis in late 1997. Tenants, who are less wealthy than homeowners, have suffered from relatively rapid increases in housing expenses.

There was a sudden jump in housing prices between 1988 and 1990. Compared to 1987, the sale price of all houses rose 57 percent by 1990, while the Chonsei rent for small houses rose 63.6 percent.

TABLE V

Trends in Housing Price by Size and by Type (end of 1985 = 100)

	1986	1988	1990	1992	1994	1996	1997
(1) All houses							
Sale Price Index	97.3	118	163.6	154.9	150	151.2	153.5
Chonsei Rent Index	105.4	142.9	196.1	214.1	230.2	245.0	245.9
(2) By size							
Sale Price Index							
Large	96.6	109.3	148.2	139	133.8	134.0	136.6
Medium	97.6	117.7	163.7	152.2	146.5	146.3	151.7
Small	97	122.3	170.7	162.2	158	158.0	163.7
Chonsei Rent Index							
Large	107.5	140.6	185.3	189.3	194.5	195.2	205.4
Medium	105.3	140.9	197.9	208.8	217.2	218.3	233.7
Small	106.4	150.9	212.5	239.3	258.6	260.3	277.6
(3) By type							
Sale Price Index							
Single detached	72.5	85.4	109.6	104.7	100.7	99.8	99.2
Town house	95.1	111.1	162.6	152.7	148.9	149.3	150.2
Apartment	95.8	125.8	200.0	186.6	182.9	190.6	199.6
Chonsei Rent Index							
Single detached	104.6	140.6	183.4	196.4	205.1	217.3	217.1
Town house	104.8	138.4	206.6	236.0	253.4	278.8	280.7
Apartment	107.5	149.9	221.6	248.4	275.2	317.6	322.8
(4) CPI	102.8	113.5	130.2	151.1	168.3	184.5	192.8

(1) Small houses are less than 85 m^2 in private residence area, medium size houses are between 85 and 132 m^2, and the large houses are above 132 m^2. This classification is different from Table II, which shows total floor area including area for communal use. Small houses in this table roughly correspond to units less than 29 pyong in Table II.
(2) See Figure 1 for price trends after 1997.
Source: Korea Housing Bank, Monthly Economic Review, March, each year.

This period was characterized by an acute housing shortage, which prompted the creation of the Two Million Housing Construction Drive. Housing prices began to fall in late 1991, as the first batch of mass produced housing units began to flood the market, and macroeconomic conditions stabilized. Nevertheless Chonsei rents, especially for small houses, continued to rise, aggravating housing conditions of the poor.

In real terms, however, both sale prices and Chonsei deposits feel substantially from their peaks in 1990. At the end of 1997, the nationwide sale price index was 63.3 percent of 1990, and the Chonsei index was 84.7 percent in real terms. This pattern of gradual decline in real housing prices was much different from that of Japan and other countries, where a sharp rise and sudden collapse of property prices was attributed to a property price bubble.

Affordability: Price Income Ratio

Affordability of housing can be measured by various measures: the ratio of housing sale prices over annual income (hereinafter the PIR); rent to income ratio (hereinafter the RIR); the ratio of principal and interest payment for housing loan over income (that is, payment-to-income ratio); and debt-to-income ratio. Since the Chonsei contract dominates the Korean rental market, the RIR is not relevant for a majority of tenants. The PIR, however, should be considered an important indicator of housing affordability in Korea in light of the fact that most houses are built for outright sale. The PIR was estimated to vary between 9 and 10 at the peak of housing price inflation (1990–91), but it came down to between 5 and 6 during the mid-1990s. This latest figure is still higher than the ratio of the United Sates (3.9), the United Kingdom (3.4), and most other industrialized countries except Japan (where it was 4.9 for attached housing, but 6.8 for detached housing).

The PIR varies across different regions of the country since housing prices vary more than income across regions. For example, a recent estimate by the Housing and Commercial Bank shows that the nationwide PIR in 1999 was 4.58, but in Seoul it was 6.67 (Park and Kim, 1999). According to the Korea Development Institute (2000), in all regions except Seoul and its immediate vicinity, an urban worker with an average income can now buy a mid-sized apartment house, and pay back a 15-year mortgage with a 50 percent loan-to-value ratio using less than 30 percent of his income.

Housing Expense Ratio

Another measure of housing affordability is the ratio of housing expenses to income. Table VI shows the total income and housing expenses for an average urban household in different years and for different income groups in 2000. We added imputed rent (i.e., interest on a Chonsei deposit or on the sale price of an owned home)[4] to cash income and to housing expenses, arriving at the total figures for income and for housing expenses.

Table VI shows that income and housing expenses of the average owner-occupant are higher than those of the average Chonsei tenant, who, in turn, enjoys a higher income than the average monthly renter. This indicates a hierarchy of housing tenure preference among different income groups. The housing expense ratio has stayed within a narrow range of 21 to 22 percent for owner-occupants, but it has gradually increased for Chonsei tenants. This reflects the fact that Chonsei deposits have increased faster than the sale price. Currently, an average Chonsei renter pays 21 percent of his income for housing, while an owner-occupier pay 22.2 percent, indicating that the latter lives in a larger and better unit than the former. Even though the household budget survey may not be absolutely accurate,[5] it is fair to conclude that housing expenses are a heavy burden for Korean families. To buy a house, Koreans had to adopt the "save-first, buy-later" pattern in contrast to the "buy-first, pay-back-later" pattern dominant in Western countries, where mortgage payments are classified as a housing expense.

Among income groups, the housing expense ratio is greater for lower income groups than for higher income groups.[6] A typical household in the lowest income decile spends around a quarter of its total income and about 30 percent of its cash income for housing, while a typical household in the highest income decile spends between 5–10 percent of its total income and a slightly higher ratio out of its cash income. Differences in expense ratios between a Chonsei tenant and a home owner are smaller in lower income groups than higher income groups.

TABLE VI

Housing Expenses Ratio: Trend and Cross-section

(1) Trend for average urban households (unit: 1,000 won)

Year	Total monthly income			Housing expenses			Housing expense ratio (with respect to total income)		
	Owner occupant	Chonsei tenant	Monthly renter	Owner occupant	Chonsei tenant	Monthly renter	Owner occupant	Chonsei tenant	Monthly renter
1985	649	457	260	136	80	63	20.9%	17.6%	24.2%
1990	1,379	996	593	306	163	111	22.2%	16.4%	18.8%
1995	2,671	2,200	1,304	582	439	241	21.8%	20.0%	18.4%
2000	3,406	2,687	1,352	755	563	290	22.2%	21.0%	21.5%

(2) Cross-section by income deciles (2000)

Income decile	Total monthly income		Housing expenses		Housing expense ratio (with respect to total income)	
	Chonsei tenant	Owner-occupant	Chonsei tenant	Owner-occupant	Chonsei tenant	Owner-occupant
1	842	861	199	217	23.6%	25.3%
2	1,299	1,309	231	241	17.8%	18.4%
3	1,564	1,612	220	268	14.1%	16.6%
4	1,833	1,901	239	308	13.1%	16.2%
5	2,103	2,166	264	328	12.6%	15.1%
6	2,373	2,493	250	370	10.5%	14.8%
7	2,726	2,857	272	402	10.0%	14.1%
8	3,111	3,341	253	484	8.1%	14.5%
9	3,726	3,994	286	554	7.7%	13.9%
10	6,298	6,660	321	683	5.1%	10.3%

Total Income = Cash Income + Imputed Rent as reported by National Statistical Office.

Housing Expenses = Reported Housing Expenses (not including utility expenses) + Imputed Rent.

Source: Calculated from National Statistical Office, Household Budget Survey, each year.

Profiles of First-time Home Buyers

Table VII shows the profile of first-time homebuyers from 1987 to 1997. In 1987, about 20 percent of all households already had a home before marriage, but the ratio for this gradually declined to 14.4 percent in 1997. The ratio of households that purchased a first home later than ten years after marriage increased from 36.6 percent in 1987, 41.3 percent in 1992, and to 47.8 percent in 1997. This shows that it takes more time than before for an average Korean household to purchase its first home. Inflation in housing prices in general is not the reason for this trend, since the price of a house in real terms was lower in 1997 than in 1992. Perhaps, first-time homebuyers may now purchase larger and better (thus more expensive) houses than before, or they may be putting off their purchase since their consumption priority has changed to something else, such as a car, travel, or children's education. However, the number of moves one might make before his first purchase has decreased; 49.1 percent of all households moved less than three times in 1997, compared to 45.4 percent in 1992. Nevertheless, more than a quarter of families moved five times or more before they purchased a home during the two years compared.

The last section of the table shows the primary source of funds for acquiring a first home. 80–90 percent of families making a purchase relied on either their own savings (including returned Chonsei deposits) or family support. Yet the number of those relying mainly on family support is decreasing. Instead, the ratio of households that finance by loans is rising rapidly. Of course, most households must draw upon various resources to finance their home purchase as shown in the next section.

House Financing

Until recently, Koreans could not rely on financial institutions to provide adequate housing loans when they purchased a home. Sources of housing loans were limited to the National Housing Fund (hereinafter the NHF) and the loans issued by Korean Housing Bank (hereinafter the KHB). The NHF, a government fund managed by KHB for a fee, is restricted to subsidized low-interest loans to builders of small houses, which are then assumed by homebuyers once they move into the houses. The KHB, until it was privatized

TABLE VII

When and How Korean Households Purchase Their First Home (unit: %)

	1987	1992	1997
(1) When			
Before marriage	19.9	16.8	14.4
Less than 1 year after marriage	10.4	11.4	7.8
2 to 3 years	15.7	12.8	11.5
4 to 5 years	16.8	14.9	12.5
6 to 9 years	20.8	19.6	20.4
10 to 14 years	19.8	21.8	22.2
15 years or later	16.5	19.5	25.6
Average years after marriage	8.4	9.1	10.9
Estimated age of male head of household	35	37	40
(2) Number of moves before the first home purchase (married couple)			
None	—	14.7	21.6
1 to 2	—	30.7	27.5
3 to 4	—	25.1	21.1
5 to 10	—	23.2	23.5
11 or more	—	6.2	6.3
Average moves	—	3.6	3.4
(3) Primary source of fund for the first home purchase			
Savings	42.3	49.2	43
Inheritance and family support	44.6	40.5	36.2
Loans	8.7	6.4	16.1
Sale of other assets	2.9	2.6	2.5
Others	1.4	1.3	2.2

Source: National Statistical Office, Social Statistics Survey, each year.

and renamed as the Housing and Commercial Bank (hereinafter the HCB) in 1997, was fully owned by the government with a mandate to allocate at least 80 percent of its lending funds to housing loans. Even though its current business is the same as other commercial banks, the HCB still dominates in financing private sector housing. The HCB lends to builders and buyers of houses, which are larger in size than those houses which qualify for NHF loans. The interest rate on the NHF loans is below the market rate of interest.

According to Park and Kim (1999), an average HCB borrower got a loan of 20.7 million Won (22.6 million Won in Seoul) in 1999, which amounted to only 28.0 percent (23.4 percent in Seoul) of the price of the house purchased with the loan. The rest of the purchase price had to come from a returned Chonsei deposit, other savings, loans from other sources, and a gift from the family. The purchase price was 3.67 times the annual income (4.18 times in Seoul), and the combined monthly payment of the principal and the interest to the HCB and other lenders was 15.1 percent of total income.

Yoon (1995) reports that financial institutions funded less than one-third of construction costs excluding the cost of land. Total housing loans outstanding amounted to 11.6 percent of the Gross National Product (hereinafter the GNP), as compared to 53.9 percent in the United States (1993), 56.9 percent in the United Kingdom (1992), and 29.6 percent in Japan (1994). Due to lack of funds, the loan-to-value ratio has been in most cases less than 30 percent. Obviously, the financing sector of the housing market has not performed its intended function successfully.

GOVERNMENTAL INVOLVEMENT IN THE HOUSING MARKET

Two Million Housing Construction Drive (1988–92)

The shortage of housing units in the Capital region became increasingly acute during the 1980s. In response to this problem, the government launched a new program to build two million housing units. The program, called the Two Million Housing Construction Drive (hereinafter the Drive) was intended to remedy the failure of the rigidly managed housing supply structure during the earlier decades. During the 1980–87 period, for example, the housing industry built about 220000 houses annually, roughly 130000 units short of the estimated annual need.[7]

When the government announced its intention to build two million homes over a five-year period, which was equal to one-third of the existing housing stock in 1987, many people were skeptical. There was concern, particularly, about the availability of land. Yet, the plan accomplished more than its original goal; housing starts between 1988 and 1992 exceeded the target by 717,682 units (see Table VIII). The land problem was solved instantly when the government decided to develop new towns in the Capital region, and building regulations were relaxed in the old sections of urban areas.

Five new towns were developed in the Capital region as part of residential land supply measures. Three of them were smaller new towns within existing urban areas, while the other two large ones were completely new cities. All of these new towns were located within 20 Km from the center of Seoul so that the housing needs of the Capitol region could be met. The size of these new towns ranged from 5 Km^2 to 20 Km^2 in land area, and from 170000 to 390000 in population. Building five new towns with a total of about 300000 housing units within five years required large-scale land development and managerial skills. Unlike old urban areas with narrow access roads and few parking spaces, the five new towns were reasonably laid out, and had a sufficient micro- and macro infrastructure to deal with increasing car ownership.

The units built in these five new towns constituted one small component of the government plan to build 2.7 million housing units during the period 1988–1992. Another significant element of the plan was to build public rental housing for low-income families. These families would be left out as long as newly built houses were intended for those who could purchase them. The government, therefore, decided to assume the responsibility for taking care of those who could not afford to buy a house. With funds from the central and local government budgets, 250000 "permanent rental houses" were built to accommodate families in the lowest 10 percent income bracket.

If mass construction was a successful housing policy, it was a failed macroeconomic policy. The share of housing investment had long been less than 5 percent of the GNP, and around 15 percent of total capital investment. Yet, these figures suddenly jumped to over 8 percent of the GNP, and 22 percent of capital investment in both 1990 and 1991. Increases in wages and the price of materials were inevitable, and they hit the manufacturing sector hard. In addition, the construction industry was not prepared for the sudden expansion. Skilled workers could not be found at any wage, and

TABLE VIII

Trends in Housing Starts by Sector and by Type

Year	Total units	By sector[1]		By type			Housing investment in GNP[2]
		Public	Private	Single detached	Town house	Apartment	
1978~1982	1103949	485737	618212	541601	116047	446492	5.26%
1983~1987	1207952	647895	560057	310962	244629	652073	4.83%
1988~1992	2717682	905454	1812228	363659	471903	1884224	6.94%
1993~1997	3125797	1173051	1952746	264424	355707	2506362	7.05%
1998~2000	1144234	422376	721370	92322	112109	939803	5.43%

[1] In addition to houses built by public sector suppliers, such as the KNHC and local governments, those built by private firms are also classified as public sector construction if they are, even partly, financed by NHF loans.
[2] Average of annual ratios. Percentages of Gross National Income for 1998–2000.
Source: Korea National Housing Corporation, Yearbook of Housing Statistics, each year.

building materials of all kinds were in short supply. The residents of houses built in this period worried about the safety of their buildings. These and other negative consequences of the Drive were blamed largely on the new town development. In response, the government stopped building large-scale new towns, and switched to relatively small-scale development projects scattered around major cities.

The capacity of the construction industry was enlarged during the Drive, and coupled with deregulation measures, the industry built even more houses during the mid-1990s rather than during the Drive itself. Housing prices stabilized after 1991, however, and a low prospect of capital gains curtailed demand for new houses. As a result, a large number of houses could not be sold. In 1995, 152000 units remained unsold, putting a great strain on the construction industry even before the onset of the economic crisis.

Deregulation of Land Use Control During the Mid-1990s

The government relaxed land use regulations in the mid-1990s, partly following a worldwide deregulation trend, and partly responding to loud complaints from the industry that could not find suitable land upon which to build factories. The centerpiece of the land market deregulation was the introduction of the semi-agricultural area in 1994 as one of the five National Planning Zones. The semi-agricultural area consisted of farmland and forestland that were judged as not being critical to the cause of preservation. A positive list of permitted uses was replaced by a negative list of restricted uses in the semi-agricultural area; small-scale developments involving less than 30000 m^2 of land were allowed in this area if water and air pollution was not a concern. With this deregulation, the area where urban land use was allowed amounted to 41.7 percent of all national land. This figure is in sharp contrast to the 15.6 percent under the previous regulatory system. With this deregulation measure, the government expected that the land shortage problem would be over once and for all.

Some deregulation measures, nonetheless, were limited in nature and some others produced negative side effects. A number of key policies, such as greenbelt zoning, had hindered land development for a long time, and the housing supply remained intact by and large. These policies were deemed too controversial to be subject to a substantial deregulatory reform. Other deregulation measures, on the other had, began to produce unintended negative consequences during the late 1990s. Residential land development and housing construction in the semi-agricultural area were allowed, for example, if the size of the site did not exceed 30000 m^2, an area that could accommodate roughly 250–300 housing units.

The architects of the deregulation drive presumed that such minor developments would neither put a strain on the existing infrastructure nor cause excessive congestion in the neighborhood. Hundreds of homebuilders, however, rushed out to the semi-agricultural area around Seoul, and applied for development permits for their "small scale" apartment complexes. They did this without giving any due consideration to the provision of infrastructure, such as roads linking Seoul to other cities, schools, public offices, and pollution abatement facilities. In retrospect, deregulation was only a necessary condition to increase the supply of urban land. Good planning and infrastructure investments required in meeting the demand for urban land were neglected by the deregulation drive.

Reviving the Depressed Housing Market

The outbreak of the economic crisis in November 1997 depressed the real estate and housing markets severely. From the last quarter of 1997 to the end of 1998, the nationwide land price index fell by 13.8 percent, and the nationwide house sale price index and the Chonsei rent index fell by 13.2 percent and 20.1 percent, respectively. New housing starts in 1998 were about half of those in 1997, and other indicators of the construction market such as construction investments, building permits, and new construction contracts all collapsed.[8] Naturally, an unprecedented number of construction firms went bankrupt; 522 general contractors (13.4% of all such firms in early 1997), 433 homebuilders (15.8%), and 1,321 specially contractors (6%) failed in 1998.

To revive the depressed housing market, emergency measures were introduced to the housing industry. First, several real estate taxes were reduced temporarily. Especially taxes on the purchase of new small houses were reduced significantly. Secondly, emergency financial assistance was provided to housing market participants. A total of 10 trillion Won was provided to homebuilders, new buyers, and Chonsei landlords for the purchase of unsold apartments, installment payments for home purchases, and the return of Chonsei deposits.[9] Thirdly, price regulation of new housing sales was finally lifted. With a massive stock of unsold houses around the country, the government abolished the regulation on the price of new housing sales in 1998.[10]

In addition to these deregulation measures and tax incentives, other measures are being discussed. First, the government wants to change the greenbelt regulation. The initial policy proposal stipulated that greenbelt designation of small and medium cities would be totally lifted. Parts of the greenbelt around major cities would be deregulated if such deregulation was judged to be not detrimental to the environment. Secondly the government is seriously considering dropping the anti-speculation thrust behind real estate taxes, which distinguish between land essential for business operations and land for speculative purposes. The government wants to penalize the latter.

CURRENT PROBLEMS AND FUTURE PROSPECTS

Public and private sectors of the housing market in Korea still face a variety of problems in their operation. In this section, two of these problems are selected for a careful review.

Uncontrolled Development

The deregulation in 1994 allowed private sector developers to build small residential estates in semi-agricultural areas. As a consequence, a large number of apartment estates sprang up in formerly agricultural or forest area around Seoul. These developers were required to provide adequate living conditions within their project sites. However, what constitutes "adequate living conditions" cannot be delineated for a small neighborhood, nor to mention a single housing estate.

By 1999, it became clear that a disaster was looming as tens of thousand of housing units neared completion in these "uncontrolled development" locations. For instance, in Yongin Country, located just south of Bundang new town, 171581 houses (mostly apartments), almost twice the number of houses in Bundang, were under construction or planned to be built. Most new residents are expected to commute to Seoul or nearby cities, since little else but housing is located there. However, no new inter-city roads and rails are being built, and schools and other facilities are expected to be in extremely short supply. Ensuing public concern forced the government to announce a series of new plans and budget commitments to alleviate the problem, but residents are expected to endure inconvenience and unsafe environment for a long time to come.

Several lessons were learned from the "uncontrolled development" of small-scale new towns. First, from the planners' point of view, a fundamental cause of the problem was that development was executed without adequate plans covering more than the development site. Some urban planners would like to introduce a European-style planning regime in Korea, and "no development without plans" is a popular motto. The government is moving in that direction by requiring comprehensive land use planning in potential problem areas, and by introducing more regulations in the semi-agricultural areas. There are worrisome elements in this trend. Korean cities are much more dynamic than European ones in terms of inter-regional migration, economic growth, and increases in housing demand. Korea's lax planning system may have been one of the hidden contributing factors for high economic growth. A tighter planning system may severely restrict the supply of urban land required for industrial development and housing construction.

Secondly, large-scale new town development seems to be a better, or at least not a worse, choice than other alternatives experimented during the 1990s. A comparison between large-scale new towns of the 1980s and small housing estate developments in the 1990s, makes it clear that the former is preferable to the latter in the following respects: government budget requirements; the range of infrastructure funded by the development itself; the mix of urban functions; and general living conditions. There still are diehard opponents against new town development. These opponents often cite the possibility of a number of detrimental consequences: accelerating population concentration in the Capital region; loss of open space; and environmental deterioration. But they cannot ignore the fact that new town residents are quite satisfied with their living environments.[11] Shaking off negative perceptions on the large-scale new town development, the government is considering two new sites, both of them in the southern parts of the Capital region, as candidates for new towns.

Housing for the Poor

Most countries have a large number of families that cannot afford to buy a home. Given this situation, assisting the poor so that they might enjoy decent and stable housing is a very important housing policy objective. The Korean government has shown a degree of concern on the housing conditions of the poor, but it has provided neither persistence nor sufficient resources. The net result is that, of all the housing units, only 6.5 percent (754000 units) were built for rental purposes. But, of these, 58 percent were to be sold after a 5-year mandatory rental period required for preferential NHF loans. Only 235000 units, about 2 percent of the total housing stock, were built with government funding, and thus will remain rental units over the long run.[12]

In the private sector, most rental units are those originally built for sale, but the individual owners for some reason decided to rent on a temporary basis. The rental market is active and lively, but few houses were built for the permanent commercial rental business. Depending on market conditions, the rental housing supply and the terms of contracts are subject to sudden fluctuations, and as a result housing conditions for tenants may become unstable. Building a commercial rental sector is possible only when profitability is ensured. Stable housing prices, low interest rates, and spreading acceptance of monthly rental contracts work favorably to the renters in the private sector at the present time. In addition, the government is providing tax benefits as well as low interest rate loans to private rental operators.

The role of the commercial rental sector to date has been disappointing; many shaky construction companies started to build long-term rental houses in order to receive subsidized loans but only with a disastrous consequence. In the year 2000, 786 rental housing projects, about 39 percent of all subsidized projects, were in trouble because the developers went bankrupt. This affected the construction and operation of 220694 housing units. About half of them were completed with the developers taking large amounts of deposits from the tenants. In many cases, asset values turned out to be less than the sum of the National Housing Fund loans and the tenants' deposits. Under a worst-case scenario, after a foreclosure sale, tenants may be evicted without being able to recover their deposits.

The role of the public sector seems to be important in the current rental market development. The first large-scale government effort to build up public rental housing stock was the permanent rental housing program as a part of the Two Million Housing Construction Drive. To the dismay of well-meaning planners, however, this program was not popular among the intended beneficiaries even though the new houses were larger and better than their current residences. At one large site in Seoul, 40 percent of the selected recipients canceled their applications. This response was due in part to heightened expectations on the part of the target group; many complained that they were not given ownership. Other, however, had legitimate complaints. Permanent rental houses were built where land was found, at times far away from where low-income families earned their income. Also, many poor households felt that they would not be able to continue to pay monthly rents, even though the rent amounted to no more than operating expenses. As a result the government had to allow higher income tenants into the permanent rental housing units, but the total number still had to be scaled down from the originally planned 250000 to 190000 units.

With the completion of the permanent rental housing program, the government experimented with various other programs including: employee's rental housing; 5-year public rental housing; 50-year public rental housing; and currently a 10- and 20-year citizen's rental housing program. Each program was given a specified budgetary subsidy and/or financial assistance from the NHF. Even so, the enthusiasm behind the permanent rental housing program has waned. A surprising fact in these programs is that subsides were given without any legal provisions. Being a response to the contemporary political and social problems relating to low-income housing, they were no more than arbitrary and short-lived budget commitments. Social activists have demanded a universal right to decent and affordable housing be written into law, which would require the government to take continuing steps to improve housing conditions for the poor. In line with this effort, there are proposals for establishing minimum standards for decent and safe housing (Ha, 2000), but such an idealistic approach may produce side effects unless the problem of "Who pays for it?" is adequately addressed.[13]

The experience of the permanent rental housing program must be familiar to the United States and other countries that witnessed a large number of public housing projects turn into a fermenting ground of a so-called social underclass. These countries no longer develop large-scale low-income housing projects, and have switched to various demand side approaches such as providing housing allowances. In light of the absolute lack of the public rental housing stock, however, Korea has to build more public rental houses in the future, but hey should be built at more carefully chosen locations with proper designing and tenant selection.

SUMMARY AND CONCLUSIONS

Both in terms of quantity and quality, housing conditions in Korea have improved greatly. The current housing stock almost matches the number of households that require an independent residence. Various housing quality indicators show that the average household is living in a larger and better house than in the past. Until the early 1990s, housing prices rose faster than other prices, mainly because land use regulations restricted residential land supply. There also were occasional sharp rises in housing prices, notably between 1987 and 1990, due to the excess liquidity in the economy. In some sense, home ownership has been an excellent investment for those who could afford to buy one, especially at the low regulated price.

Government policy has strongly affected these trends, but without consistent budgetary or financial commitments. The government corporations developed and provided inexpensive land to homebuilders, who in turn were required to sell houses at regulated prices to qualified buyers. Many bought a house to benefit from this scheme while low-income households, that could not afford to buy, were left out. Worse yet, the poor suffered from the loss of the stock of small-scale houses and the relatively rapid price increases. The price regulation on new houses also resulted in high-density apartments of similar design and materials, making Korean cities esthetically unappealing. The state of housing finance reflects the low priority of the housing sector in resource allocation. Because of lack of funds from official sources, construction firms sell houses before they are built, and many homebuyers rely on their Chonsei deposits. A Chonsei rental contract is arguably an inefficient and inequitable arrangement, but it still dominates the mid to upper housing markets.

After the peak of 1990–91, as housing prices stabilized and instant capital gains were no longer certain, a large number of newly built houses remained unsold nationwide. Then came the economic crisis at the end of 1997, and property prices collapsed. In the past, the expectation of capital gains forced households to: patiently wait in the queue of prospective homebuyers; save up for their Chonsei deposits and house purchase funds; and accept the prior sale of unfinished houses. With the prospect of capital gains gone, consumers became hesitant to purchase a home, and many homebuilders encountered difficulties. The government tried its best to revive the housing industry, abolishing the price regulation on new houses.

Freed from regulation, the housing industry experimented with a variety of housing types, designs, and materials, and has achieved several notable successes by appealing to consumer tastes and needs. Houses are now more of a durable good than an asset to sell in the future. This change appears to be permanent given the long-term trends in population, inter-regional migration, and economic growth prospects. Also, the development of private sector housing finance, together with low interest rates and stable housing prices, will help a large number of Chonsei tenants to purchase a home. Under the new market environment, many of the rental contracts will turn into monthly rentals. The increasing acceptance of the monthly rental contract will eventually spawn an institutionalized private rental housing sector. For the time being, however, government initiatives in building up public rental housing stock seems inevitable.

The government should provide more budgetary support and financial resources for the low-income housing sector. However clever the regulations on housing supply might be, the benefit given to low-income households is limited if the houses are built only to be purchased. The government should consider restarting the permanent rental housing program or its equivalent. Although the program is costly, and bad planning may create more problems than it solves, the stock of small houses for the poor has fallen far too much. If the government adopts budget allocation as the main policy tool for improving housing conditions for the poor, many regulations in the housing market can be further relaxed, and the housing supply structure will become more market-oriented.

ACKNOWLEDGMENT

The authors wish to acknowledge the financial support of the Korean Research Foundation made in the program year of 1997.

NOTES

[1] The housing supply ratio, which is calculated as the number of housing units divided by the number of households, while excluding one-person households and non-blood related households, is a controversial measure of housing stock adequacy. On the numerator side, each so-called multi-household house, which provides independent living spaces to more than one household, but is legally owned and traded as a single unit, is counted as one housing unit. On the denominator side, many one-person households need an independent living space. Overall, the housing supply ratio overestimates the housing supply at the national level, but underestimates it in Seoul where multi-household housing units are concentrated. The Ministry of Construction and Transportation still uses the housing supply ratio as a key indicator in formulating housing policies, but, because of the controversy, National Statistical Office no longer places emphasis on the ratio.
[2] The apartment in Korea is similar to the high-rise condominium in the U.S. Another form of attached housing in a one to four story building, also individually owned, is termed as the Town House in this paper.
[3] Housing price increases in the Capital region, not shown here, were much more pronounced than these national averages.
[4] Estimated by the National Statistical Office. If a homeowner's capital gains (losses) are subtracted from the estimated monthly rent, the owner-occupier's housing expense ratios will decline (increase).
[5] Accuracy is questioned since Korea has had a high PIR and high interest rates until 1999, and sharp housing price inflation in the late 1980s, which would raise the housing expense ratio, and market crash after 1997, which would decrease the ratio, are not reflected in the table.
[6] The first part of Table VI is based on results from separate surveys of households in each tenure category. The second part uses the same income and housing

expenses for each income decile. Only imputed rents are different between owner-occupants and Chonsei renters. Since the Chonsei rent is less than the sale price, the housing expense ratio of an owner occupant is always higher than that of a Chonsei renter.

[7] Planners estimate the need for new houses by the sum of the number of households being formed and the number of demolished houses. This is a useful but crude planning tool. Economists prefer to use "demand" rather than "need", since the latter does not reflect the effects of changes in income and price on consumer behavior.

[8] For instance, public and private contracts in total construction orders were 44 percent vs. 57 percent in 1997, but as the private sector retrenched because of high interest rates and mounting uncertainty, the ratio changed to 66 percent vs. 34 percent.

[9] Timely inflow of installment payments is important since it amounts to the construction finance for homebuilders. If that financing does not take place, homebuilders cannot continue their work, and buyers would panic and stop making any further installment payments.

[10] With this deregulation, the rationing scheme of new houses is also being phased out. For instance, buyers of a new apartment can sell the unit for a profit at any time, even before completion, and homebuilders will no longer be required to build a specified percentage of small houses for low-income households. Currently, homebuilders frequently run advertisements on how easily their new apartments can be sold at a premium. Such a practice would have been viewed as immoral and unethical, if not illegal, in the past.

[11] In a survey conducted by the Korean Research Institute for Human Settlements, New Town residents rated their living environments as an overall score of 3.67 at the scale of 1 (dissatisfied) to 5 (satisfied), which was higher than the scores for Seoul (3.06) and other cities (3.23 to 3.29) in the Capital region (Shin and Min, 1999).

[12] In comparison, public rental housing stocks in major European countries amount to around 20 percent of their respective total housing stocks (Park, 2001).

[13] For instance, strict enforcement of ideal housing standards may be detrimental to the housing welfare of the low-income households who can afford substandard housing only.

REFERENCES

Ha, S.K.: 2000, 'Evaluation of housing policies and new insights', in S.K. Ha (ed.), Housing, City, and Public Interest (in Korean) (Park Yong Sa, Seoul).

Kim, K.Y.: 1993, 'Housing policies in the 1990s', in K.Y. Kim and Werner Puschra (eds.), Housing Policy in the 1990s: European Experiences and Implications for Korea (KDI Press).

Korea Development Institute: 2000, Changing Environments of Housing Finance Market and Management of National Housing Fund (in Korean) (Korea Development Institute, Seoul).

Lee, J.H. and J.S. Huh: 1993, 'Institutionalizing Chonsei deposit finance', Housing Finance (162) (in Korean), pp. 1–29.

Park, S.Y.: 2001, 'An analysis of Korean public rental housing: In comparison to advanced countries', mimeo (in Korean) (Korean National Housing Corporation, Seoul).

Park, W.A. and K.Y. Kim: 1993, 'Homeownership, savings and Chonsei system in Korea', Review of Finance (15) (in Korean), pp. 81–111.

Park, Y.T. and S.O. Kim: 1999, '1999 housing finance demand analysis', Housing Finance (218) (in Korean), pp. 60–80.

Renaud, B.: 1989, 'Compounding financial repression with rigid urban regulations: Lessons of the Korea housing market', Review of Urban and Regional Development Studies 1(1), pp. 3–22.

Shin, J.C. and B.S. Min: 1999, Evaluation of the Capital Region New Towns (in Korean) (Korea Research Institute for Human Settlements, Seoul).

Son, J.Y.: 1997, 'A review of the Korean housing market and related policies', Review of Urban and Regional Development Studies 9(1), pp. 80–99.

Yoon, H.I.: 1995, 'Housing finance in Korea: Current state and future challenges', mimeo (in Korean), (Korea Housing Bank, Seoul).

Department of Real Estate Studies
Konkuk University
Seoul, 143-701, Korea
E-mail: jyson@kkucc.konkuk.ac.kr

Jae-Young Son

Department of Tax Studies
The University of Seoul
Seoul, 130-743, Korea
E-mail: Yhwon@uos.ac.kr

Yun-hi Won

Department of Economics
Hanyang University
Seoul, 133-791, Korea
E-mail: mooncg@unitel.co.kr

Choon-Geol Moon

HEE-JONG JOO

CRIME AND CRIME CONTROL

ABSTRACT. This article provides an overall picture of crime and crime control in Korea over the past 30 years. By using official crime data, we examined general trends and characteristics of crime, crime rates, and crime control practices in each stage of the criminal justice system in Korea during that period. The relative seriousness of crime problems in Korea is also examined from a comparative perspective by engaging in a cross-national comparison. The findings of this research indicate that the overall crime problem in Korea is not as serious as that in Japan and in the United States. Recent data, however, show an alarming increase in the crime rates in Korea during the past several years. These results are interpreted within a social context, and we can determine that economic, political, and socio-cultural factors have played and continue to play a crucial role in crime and crime control practices. Recent phenomena, such as the financial crisis that hit Korea in the late 1990s, and the current political stalemate in Korea, seem to have contributed to the disturbing increase in crime and crime rates.

INTRODUCTION

Crime is no longer viewed as only one problem to a given society. Rather it is an integral part of understanding a nation's socio-cultural, political, and economic situation. Korea is no exception. Until the mid-twentieth century, Korea's crime rate was lower than those in other Asian countries as well as most Western nations. Having been an agrarian society, a majority of the Korean population were farmers and primary relationships tended to be strong. Korea's crime rate back then was lower than in a society characterized by secondary relationships. In addition, Korean have long been under the influence of Confucian moral codes that emphasize conforming to authority and the natural order and avoiding friction with others (Chang and Janeksela, 1996: p. 416). As Korean society has become increasingly industrialized and urbanized, however, crime rates have been rising.

Social Indicators Research **62, 63:** 239–263, 2003.

Sometimes various social problems stem from 'uncoordinated and unsystematic' social changes, particularly among those who are unable to adapt to ever-changing new environments. Rapid social change always tends to produce social disorganization, which includes crime. Although every society experiences various degrees of social change and consequent increases in crime and crime rates, rates of change differ from one society to another. If this is indeed the case, then it is possible to understand a society by examining changes in crime and crime rates where they are used as an index for measuring societal changes and their characteristics.

Accordingly, this paper will attempt an overview of the trends and characteristics of crime and crime control in Korea, and in doing so will provide a general understanding of crime in Korean society. To begin with, we will present an overall picture of crime in Korea by examining the trends and patterns of crime over the past three decades. We will then explore crime problems in Korea from a comparative perspective by conducting cross-national comparisons of crime problems in two other countries. By examining the crime data, we can get a better picture of how safe it is to live in Korea. This will be followed by an overview of crime control practices of the criminal justice system in Korea. This article will conclude with a discussion of the case of Korea as it experiences rapid change. We will also look at how these changes influence crime and crime control practices.

DATE AND METHOD

The present analysis will cover crime, the crime rate, and four subsequent rates in each successive stage of the criminal justice system in Korea. They include: the arrest rate by the police; the prosecution rate by the public prosecutor's office; the conviction rate by the courts; and, the incarceration rate by the Department of Corrections. This analytical framework was employed in a previous study on crime and social control in Korea (Yoon, 1998: pp. 55–65). Our relying on this framework will make it possible to examine crime and crime control practices in a single frame of reference.

The data on crime, arrests, and prosecutions, upon which we rely, come in large part from the Analytical Report on Crime, published by the Supreme Public Prosecutors' Office. Annual publication of a White Paper on Crime, published by the Legal Research & Training Institute, was used in part to calculate the crime rates and arrest rates. The data on convictions and incarcerations came from the Judiciary Yearbook, which is published annually by the Administrative Office of Courts.

The Analytical Report on Crime is the most comprehensive compilation of statistical data on crime, police activity, and the dispositions of public prosecutors in Korea. Although official crime statistics are not entirely accurate, they are the most reliable sources available and do provide an indication of crime trends. The report divides crime into two broad categories: offenses that violate the Criminal Code and offenses that violate many special Laws (Yoon, 1998: pp. 83–86).

According to the Criminal Code, offenses are classified into seven sub-categories: violent crimes, property crimes, forgeries, crimes by government officials, crimes against public morals, crimes of negligence, and others. Of these, violent and property crimes consist of approximately four-fifths of all Criminal Code Offenses. The violent crime category is composed of criminal homicide, robbery, arson, rape, assault, aggravated assault, intimidation, kidnapping, and illegal confinement. Property crimes consist of larceny-theft, stolen property, fraud, embezzlement, breach of trust, and destruction of property.

Violations of Special Laws include various laws regulating all aspect of society. In 1999 there were approximately 200 Special Laws. The Act concerning Punishment for Violent Offenses; the Special Act on Disposition of Traffic Accidents; and the Road Traffic Act are typical examples of these laws. These three comprise approximately 80 percent of all violations of the Special Laws in 1999.

Official crime data of the United States and Japan were used for cross-national comparisons of crime rates. Included in the official data is the Uniform Crime Report (UCR) issued by the Federal Bureau of Investigation (FBI) and the White Paper on Crime issued by the Japanese Department of Justice.

TRENDS IN CRIMES

General Trends in Crimes

This section presents an overall picture of crime trends in Korea. Korean society has experienced rapid industrialization and urbanization as well as a notable increase in population (about 45%) over the past 30 years. As a consequence, both the total number of crimes and the crime rate have increased.

The total number of crimes occurring in Korea has increased 5.2 times over the past three decades, from 333537 in 1970 to 1732522 in 1999. The crime rate, which is defined as the total number of crimes that take place per 100000 people, has also increased 3.6 times over the same period, from 1035 in 1970 to 3697 in 1999. If we narrow our focus to just the last decade, the total number of crimes that occurred in Korea increased 1.5 times, between 1990 and 1999. The crime rate also increased 1.4 times over the same period. The total number of crimes remained stable from 1970–1975. After that it steadily increased to 810416 in 1985; to 1171380 in 1990; and then, steeply, to 1765887 in 1998 (Legal Research & Training Institute, 2000: p. 28).

The total number of arrest increased 5.7 times as well, from 289,637 in 1970 to 1,651,896 in 1999. The proportion of total arrests to the number of incidences of crime, which is known as the clearance rate,[1] hovered around 87 percent during the 1970s and 1980s. It has hovered around 90 percent since 1991. In 1993, it reached 95.7 percent, the highest rate ever.

In order to properly understand and interpret these changes and trends in crime over time, we need to take a multidimensional view. This view encompasses the interrelationships between the crime itself and the various social forces and responses to crime. Although crime control activities are practiced mainly by criminal justice agencies, they also constitute social phenomena closely associated with other social forces outside criminal justice agencies (Welch, 1996; Yoon, 1998: p. 55). This should be kept in mind when trying to understand crime patterns and trends in Korea.

Korean society has experienced a myriad of political climates and instability over the past three decades. This is not to say, however, that in focusing on the social determinants of crime and crime

TABLE I

Total Number of Incidences of Crime and Arrests (1970–1999)

Year	Category					
	Number of incidences of crime	Number of arrests	Number of arrestees	Clearance rate (%)	Crime Rate	Total population (unit: 1,000 people)
1970	333537	289637	415504	86.8	1035	32241
1971	351574	293279	395467	83.4	1069	32883
1972	369839	330890	442274	89.5	1104	33505
1973	323363	298157	398431	92.2	948	34103
1974	337535	292839	400266	86.8	978	34692
1975	387207	335944	462908	86.8	1097	35281
1976	504630	450059	609177	89.2	1408	35849
1977	506545	448168	600197	88.5	1391	36412
1978	513165	438265	589008	85.4	1388	36969
1979	555793	491567	651998	88.4	1481	37534
1980	595277	475353	697629	79.9	1561	38124
1981	625934	549532	734981	87.8	1616	38723
1982	658371	575029	784564	87.8	1674	39326
1983	786553	656204	859097	83.4	1971	39910
1984	803792	693387	888105	86.3	1989	40406
1985	810416	693270	885765	85.5	1986	40806
1986	809660	704874	902895	87.0	1966	41184
1987	946390	825601	1054407	87.2	2276	41575
1988	968965	856517	1114468	88.4	2308	41975
1989	1073997	949308	1179156	88.4	2534	42380
1990	1171380	1047760	1326775	89.4	2737	42793
1991	1230118	1130262	1418168	91.9	2843	43268
1992	1241102	1135146	1451942	91.5	2842	43663
1993	1356914	1298637	1656113	95.7	3080	44056
1994	1373407	1246582	1582428	90.8	3090	44453
1995	1399085	1269375	1599930	90.7	3119	44850
1996	1494846	1358982	1681321	90.9	3304	45248
1997	1588613	1452097	1802720	91.4	3454	45991
1998	1765887	1632678	2010814	92.5	3803	46430
1999	1732522	1651896	2081797	95.3	3697	46858

[1]Source: Adapted from the Analytical Report on Crime, published by the Supreme public Prosecutor's Office, various years.
[2]Clearance rate means the proportion of crimes that result in arrest.
[3]Crime rate means the number of incidences of crime per 100000 people.

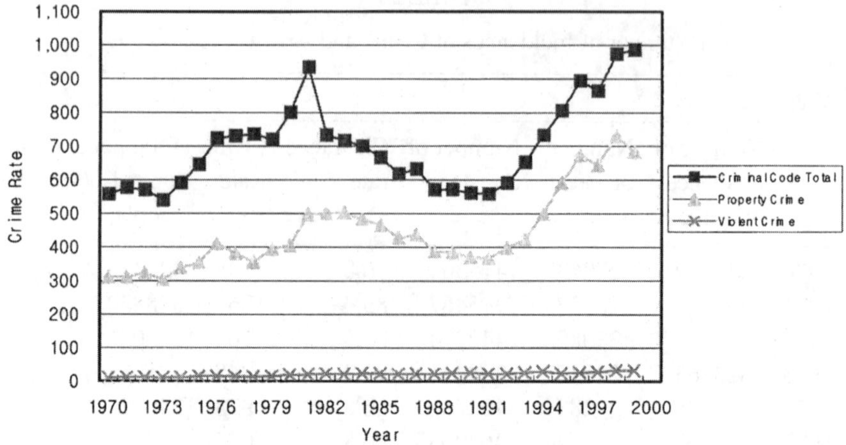

Figure 1. Crime rates of criminal code offenses.

control one ought to ignore the relationship between crime and crime control. Keeping all of this in mind, we will try to explain the changing nature and trends in crime as we analyze the subject matter in more detail.

Trends in Criminal Code Offenses and Their Characteristics

The term Criminal Code Offense (CCO) is a broad category of crimes. Violent and property crimes consist of approximately four fifths of all CCOs.[2] As Figure 1 shows, the total number of CCOs increased 257 percent, from 179608 in 1970 to 462253 in 1999. The crime rate of CCOs also increased 1.77 times over the same period, from 558 in 1970 to 986 in 1999. Between 1990 and 1999, the total number of CCOs increased 192 percent. With the exception of 1990 and 1997, CCOs have increased every year.

It is interesting to note that increases in crime rates, as well as in the total number of CCOs, show three different patterns over the past three decades: a notable increase in the 1970s; a slow down during the 1980s; and, another steep increase since 1990. Along with the notable increase in crime during the 1970s, we need to understand it in a social context. Korean society experienced rapid structural changes brought on by industrialization and modernization over the same period. Major institutions like the family, schools, government, churches, and others were undergoing rapid transformations. As an increasing number of Koreans moved to urban areas, the society became increasingly heterogeneous.

Social changes always tend to produce social disorganization, some of which is crime. In Korea, the rapid growth in the urban population; the increase in the stress and strains of urban life; the higher standard of living; and, the changes in the existing value systems, were some of the factors contributing to the rapid increase in the crime rate during the 1970s (Chang and Janeksela, 1996: pp. 415–416).

While property crimes normally show a rapid rise with increased industrialization in most countries, it was violent crimes, rather than property crimes, that increased in Korea during the 1970s. Economic growth and an increase in employment opportunities, brought on by industrialization and modernization in the cities, seemed to contribute to a moderate increase in property crimes during that time.

With regard to the decline in crime and arrest rates during the 1980s, it is interesting to note that it took place after former president Doo-Whan Chun's authoritarian and repressive regime (1980–1987) came to power as a result of a military coup. Militaristic authoritarian governments, faced with a crisis of legitimacy, tend to use coercion and force against those who resist. As some have convincingly argued, the security of authoritarian regimes is heavily dependent on maintaining social stability and social order. Of necessity, such a regime strengthens its social control functions in order to keep the social order intact (Barberet, 1994; Chang and Iacovetta, 1996; Deng et al., 1994). Crime control is a form of social control and all disruptive behaviors are likely to be subjected to punitive state control.

Right after Chun seized political power (1980–1981), his government launched a massive program to crack down on hooligans, thieves, and violent offenders. Thousands of people, for example, who committed crimes of violence, including fraud, smuggling, drug trafficking and illegal drug use, were sent to boot camp as part of a "Social Purification Movement." The decline in the crime rate during the 1980s appears to be closely related to this existing repressive and coercive social atmosphere, in which the threat of severe punishment was used to deter crime (Koo, 1993; Lee, 1990; Park, 1996; Yoon, 1998).

The crime and arrest rates, however, rose again in the 1990s. Faced with nationwide demonstrations for democratic reforms at the end of 1980s, Tae-Woo Roh, the successor of the Chun regime, made a public declaration that he would fully accept public demands for a democratic government. He chose to abandon repressive and coercive ways of social control, and he removed the existing restrictions on the basic rights of freedom of the press, publication, assembly and association (Bedeski, 1993; Paik, 1994).

In the early 1990s, Korea took steps toward participatory democracy even though a lot of unstable political and social conditions continued to exist. In this regard, the sharp increase in the number of crimes and arrests that took place might be partly explained by the government's "war on crime" in the early 1990s when the Roh regime faced turbulent sociopolitical upheavals. For example, the police arrested over 1.9 million suspects in 1991. This is strong evidence indicating that there might be a relationship between political situations and crime control practices. The massive number of arrests might easily account for the dramatic increases in crime as well as the arrest rate for crimes of violence and crimes against property during that era.

As shown in Figure 2, property crime rates, by crime type, increased sharply during the 1990s. Fraud in particular increased steadily in that decade, and the incidence of larceny-theft rose sharply after 1995. As Korean society increasingly put greater emphasis on material success as a means of determining personal worth, there was a correspondingly higher rate of property crime. As Korea enjoyed enormous economic growth, and the overall size of the Korean economy rapidly expanded during the 1990s, the number of available targets for property offenses increased as well.

There had been a steady increase in the violent crime rate as well. In the case of robbery, there was a steady increase in the incidence of this crime between the 1970s and the 1980s. It has been fluctuating since 1990, showing a big increase from 2.9 (per 100000 people) in 1970 to 10.1 in 1999 (see Figure 3). There was also an increase in the incidence of rape during the 1970s. It declined slowly during the 1980s, and peaked in 1993 at 16.0 (per 100000), and then hovered

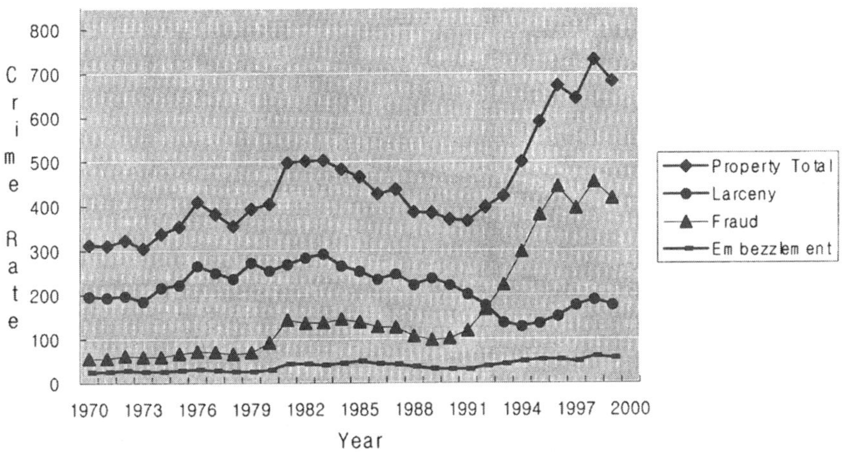

Figure 2. Crime rate: property crime within CCOs.

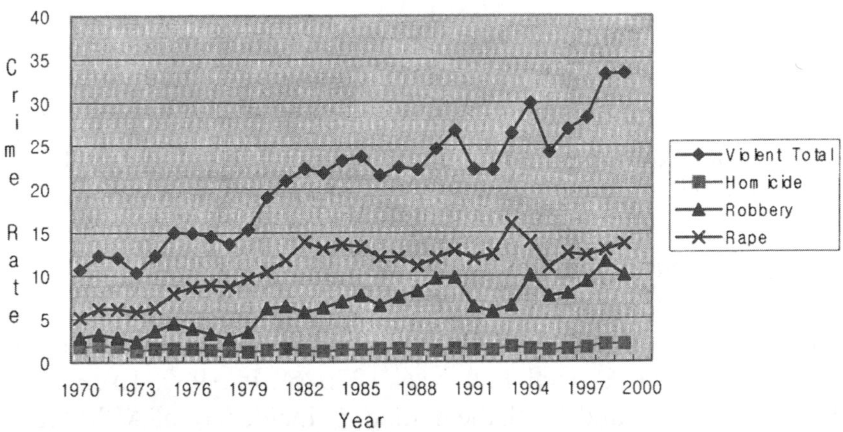

Figure 3. Crime rate: violent crime within CCOs.

at around 11.0 to 13.9 (per 100000) during the 1990s. There has, however, been little change in the crime rate for criminal homicide over the past three decades.

Trends in Violations of Special Laws and Their Characteristics

Violations of Special Laws (VSL) include such laws as an "Act concerning Punishment for Violent Offenses" (APVO); a "Special Act on Disposition of Traffic Accidents" (SADTA); and a "Road Traffic Act (RTA)." They are considered the big three, and they

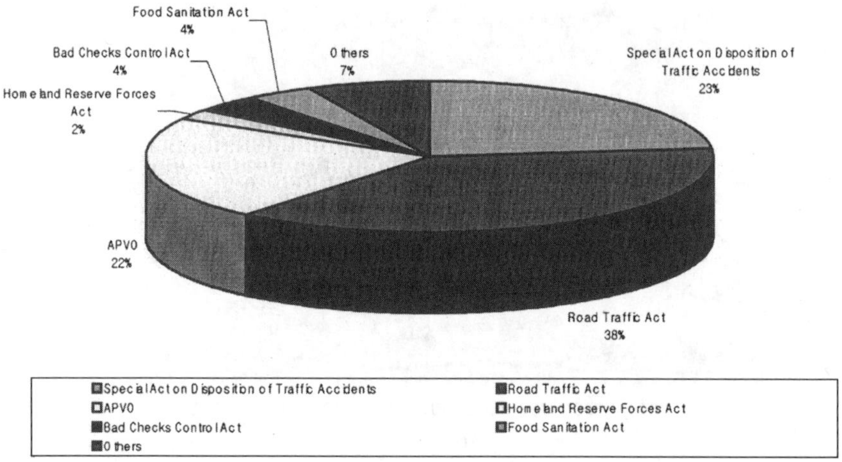

Figure 4. Composition of offenses violating special laws, by categories of crimes (1999).
[1]Source: White Paper on Crime, 2000. Legal Research & Training Institute.
[2]Total number of APVO (Act concerning Punishment of Violent Offences): 1028335.

comprise approximately 80 percent of all violations of Special Laws in 1999, as shown in Figure 4.

In terms of the number of incidences of crime, offenders who violated Special Laws were more numerous than those who violated Criminal Code offenses (CCOs). For example, while the total number of incidence of CCOs was 462253, the total number of violations of the Special Law was 1270269 in 1999. Except for 1992, 1994, 1995 and 1999, the number of incidences of APVO rose steadily from 1990 through 1999. The total number of violations of the Special Laws in 1999 (931235 cases) far outstripped the number in 1999, which soared to 1270269 cases, an increase of 36.4 percent (Legal Research & Training Institute, 2000: pp. 36–39).

One of the main reasons for the sustained trend in the increase in the number of major criminal offenses may be attributed to a continued increase in the number of violations of special legislation such as the 'Special Act on the Disposition of Traffic Accidents.' The other reason may be due to revisions and improvements of the criminal justice system, laws and regulations. The improved regulations represent an attempt to exert more efficient control over Korea's increasingly complex society. This social phenomenon is manifested in the rapid expansion of the scope of activities engaged in by the public, together with the various ways in which these activities are pursued as Korean society progresses.

If we narrow our focus to the APVO, which we will examine as a separate category of violent crime, the total number of incidences of crime increased 1.5 times, from 150013 in 1990, to 230434 in 1999. The crime rate also increased 1.4 times, from 351 to 492, over the same period.

COMPARISON WITH OTHER MAJOR COUNTRIES

Comparison of Overall Crime Rates

An overall comparison of crime rates with the United States and Japan, with respect to the number of major crimes[3] that occurred per 100000 people during the 1990s, reveals that figures for both Korea and Japan are substantially lower than those of the United States (see Table II). While the crime rate in the U.S. has declined since 1990, the crime rate in Korea has risen rapidly over the same period. When it comes to comparing the crime rate between Japan and Korea, Korea had a much lower one until 1992. Korea began to surpass Japan in 1993, when Roh's government was in the middle of waging a war against crime. The accuracy of the figures below, however, cannot be attested to, given the differences between the countries in terms of the provisions of the crimes that were subject to statistical analysis, as well as of the statistical methodology employed by each country.

Comparison of Crime Rates of Criminal Code Offenses

Relying on the official crime statistics of the U.S., Japan, and Korea, we will examine overall trends in Criminal Code Offenses over the past three decades. We will then focus on the trends in five major types of Criminal Code Crimes that receive the most attention from criminal justice agencies. The five crime categories to be covered here include criminal homicide, forcible rape, robbery, aggravated assault, and larceny-theft.

TABLE II

Crime Rate Comparison with Major Countries

Year	Country		
	U.S.A.	Japan	Korea
1990	5820	1324	910
1991	5898	1377	896
1992	5660	1400	911
1993	5483	1566	1918
1994	5374	1540	1959
1995	5269	1420	2015
1996	5079	1440	2028
1997	4930	1506	2033
1998	4616	1608	2330

[1]The statistics of each country are based on the following sources.
U.S.A.: Crime in the United States, Federal Bureau of Investigation, various years.
Japan: The White Paper on Crime, Research and Training Institute, Ministry of Justice, various years.
Korea: The White Paper on Crime, Legal Research and Training Institute, Ministry of Justice, various years.
[2]Crime rate: Number of crimes per 100000 people.

Trends in the Overall Crime Rate in Criminal Code Offenses

Compared to the U.S. and Japan, the overall crime rate in Korea has been relatively low during the past three decades. The overall crime rate of Criminal Code Offenses in 1999, for example, numbered only 987, compared to 2292 in Japan, and 4276 in the U.S. However, the ratio of increase in the crime rate of Criminal Code Offenses is higher in Korea than in the other two countries (see Figure 5). For instance, the incidence of crimes per 100000 people in Korea increased by 75 percent, from 557 in 1970 to 987 in 1999. The percentage of increase was 32 percent in Japan, and 25 percent in the U.S., over the same period.

The crime rate in Korea has fluctuated over the past three decades. It showed a steep increase in the 1970s, then declined

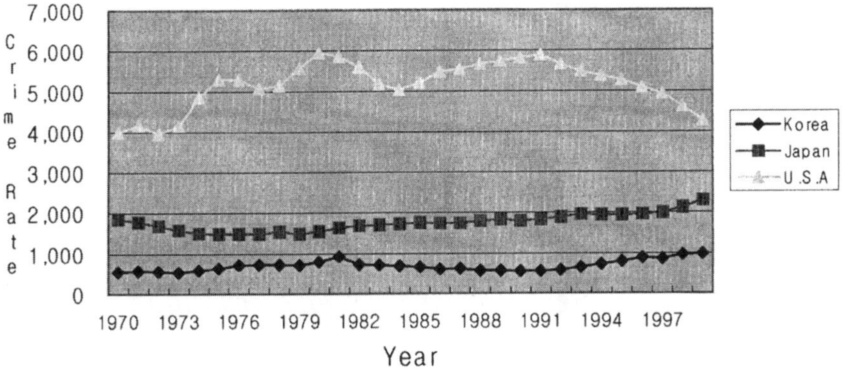

Figure 5. Trends in crime rates among the U.S.A., Japan and Korea: total criminal code offenses.

during the 1980s, and rose again in the 1990s. As mentioned previously, rapid industrialization and urbanization during the 1970s precipitated a social environment that gave rise to criminal behavior. On the other hand, the authoritarian rule of the Chun regime in the 1980s put a strong emphasis on social order and control, which seems to have deterred people from committing crime. In the 1990s, as the Korean economy expanded, the crime rate and property crimes in particular, rose sharply.

In Japan, the crime rate registered minor increases up until the 1980s. As was the case in Korea, however, it is noteworthy that increases in the crime rate were larger during the 1990s. The crime rate in the U.S. has been fluctuating over the past 30 years. Crime increased during the 1970s, but then began decreasing during the mid-1980s and most of the 1990s. This remarkable decrease in the crime rate during the 1990s in the U.S. is notable in that the crime rates in Japan and Korea were increasing during the same period.

Trends in Major Criminal Code Offenses of Three Countries

In line with the crime rates of the U.S., it is interesting to note that crimes of violence, such as criminal homicide, forcible rape, and burglary as well as crimes against property have all decreased since the early 1990s (FBI, 1999). These decreases can be attributed to a number of factors. They include the economic boom which occasioned the fall in unemployment; the demographic shift of

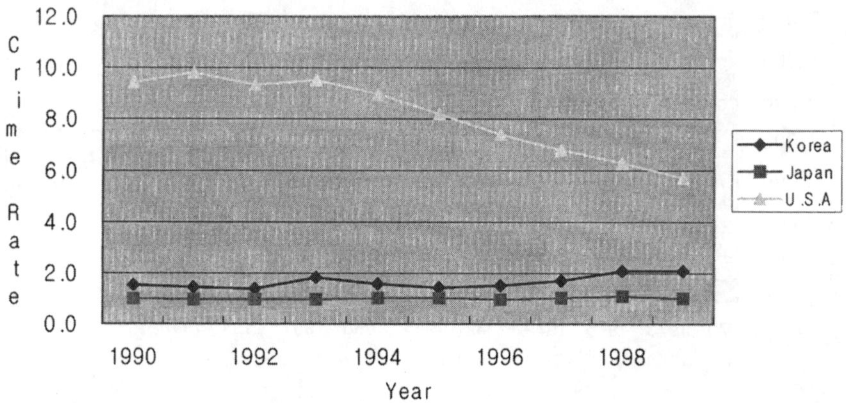

Figure 6. Trends in crime rates among the U.S.A., Japan and Korea: criminal homocide.

baby boomers from the crime-prone age to middle-age; the success of community-policing strategies; and various crime prevention programs (Coleman and Cressey, 2000; Dunham and Alpert, 1993).

When it comes to comparing property crimes between Korea and Japan, the crime rate of larceny/theft in Japan is noticeably higher than that of Korea. The economic recession in the 1990s in Japan seems to have caused reductions in the number of jobs and income; this perhaps led to an increase in property crimes (Shikita and Tsuchiya, 1992; Thornton and Endo, 1992). On the other hand, the rates of crimes of violence, such as robbery, rape, and criminal homicide, in Japan is much lower than that in Korea. The high crime rate of violent crimes in Korea has a strong impact on society in that violent offenses are seen as more threatening to public safety and intensity fear of crime among the public. These trends are clearly evident in Figures 6 through 9.

CRIME CONTROL PRACTICES IN KOREA

This section identifies overall trends in crime control in Korea. With Yoon's (1998: pp. 55–65) pioneer study[4] serving as background, we will examine changes in criminal justice practices over the past three decades. We will rely on up-to-date data and some revisions in the four classifications of crime date: total, violent,

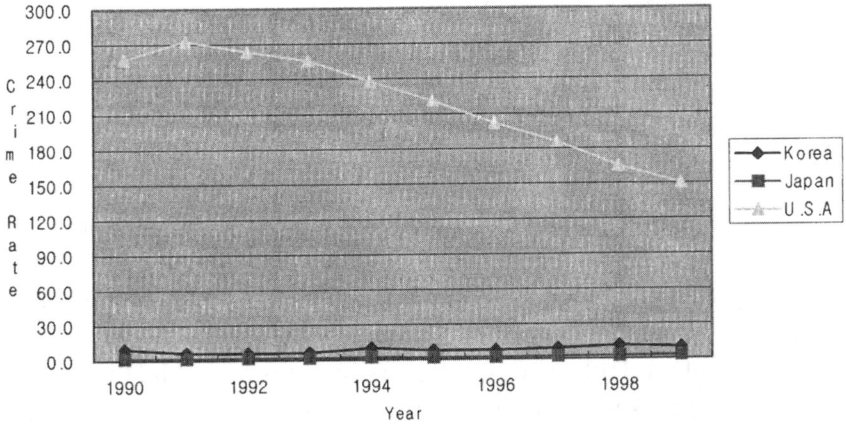

Figure 7. Trends in crime rates among the U.S.A., Japan and Korea: robbery.

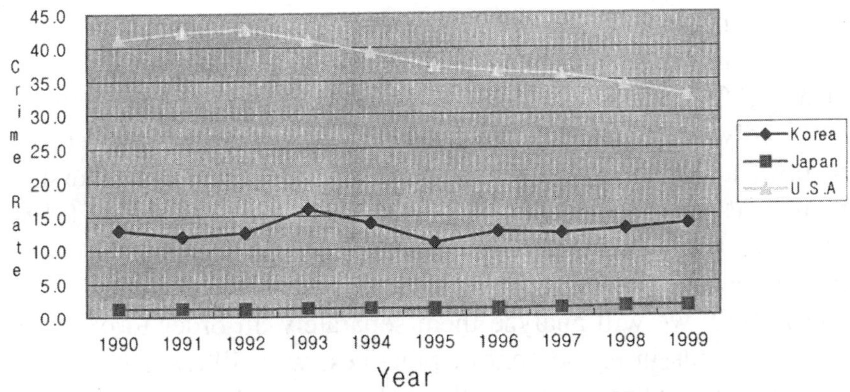

Figure 8. Trends in crime rates among the U.S.A., Japan and Korea: rape.

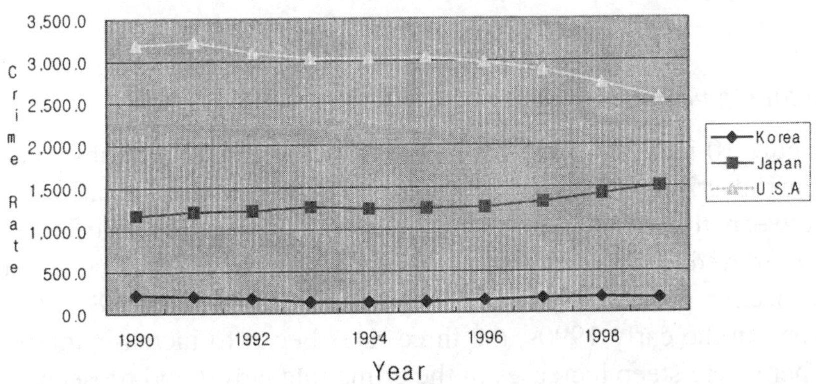

Figure 9. Trends in crime rates among the U.S.A., Japan and Korea: larceny/ theft.

property, and a specific category crime of violence (a crime violating the "Act concerning Punishment of Violent Offenses" or APVO). The criminal justice system consists of several subsystems that are independent of each other as well as interdependent (Rather and McMullan, 1987). Given the complexity of the criminal justice system and the influence of internal and external factors on the operation of the entire system, crime and crime control practices need to be examined in a social context.

To do this, we need to examine violent and property crimes separately as well as together. In such an analysis, there are two categories of violent crimes. The first is prescribed in the Criminal Code. The second consists of violations of the APVO. This latter act regulates a wide range of violent offenses and identifies certain types of offenses and certain conditions that deserve greater punishment. The purpose of the act is to punish people who commit collective or habitual violent offenses or commit such acts at night. Offenders who commit these crimes either habitually or repeatedly, collectively with more than two people, or after sunset receive, at maximum, a punishment one-and-a-half time harsher than that prescribed in the Criminal Code. Since Yoon's (1998) research revealed that there are considerable differences between the two categories of violent crimes prescribed in the Criminal Code and APVO, we will analyze them separately. In order to examine general trends in crime control practices, we will trace the crime rate and four subsequent rates in each stage of the criminal justice system in Korea over the past three decades.

Total Crime and Crime Control

Figure 10 identifies changes in the crime rate and four subsequent rates of crime control of all crime.[5] There is a close relationship between the crime rate, arrest rate and prosecution rate.[6] Each rate moved upward with some fluctuation in the 1970s, reached its respective peak in 1981, and then decreased between 1981–1990. Then in the early 1990s, the three rates began to increase sharply. There were steep increases in the crime rate, arrest and prosecution rate after 1991. However, the ratio of increase in the arrest rate was higher than that of the other two.

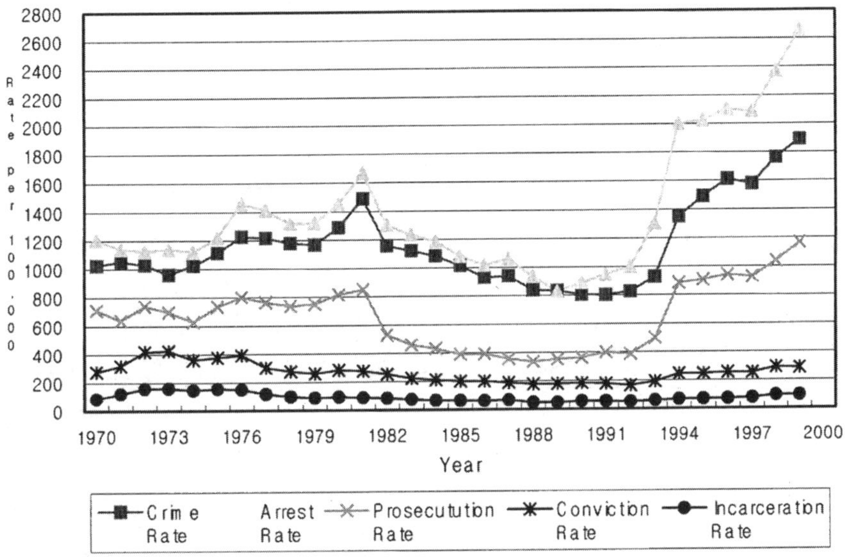

Figure 10. Total crime and crime control.

The crime rate, arrest rate, and prosecution rate in 1990 were 806, 889 and 362 respectively. They increased to 928, 1305, and 499 respectively in 1993, and then to 1890, 2656, 1165, respectively, in 1999. This sharp increase in the crime rate, arrest rate and prosecution rate between 1990 and 1993 might be partly explained by the "war on crime" campaign by Roh's government in the early 1990s. The subsequent increase during the remainder of the 1990s also seems to be related to the "get tough on crime" policy that occurred at that time (Yoon, 1998: p. 56).

Both the conviction rate and the incarceration rate showed the highest increase in 1972 and 1973. They declined until the early 1990s and then posted an increase. It is interesting to note that the two rates declined even when the crime rate, arrest rate, and prosecution rate had been increasing with some fluctuation between 1973 and 1981. These two measures of court practices reveal relatively few changes over time except in the early 1970s.

Property Crime and Crime Control

As shown in Figure 11, the crime rate and the arrest rate are almost parallel for property crimes. The two rates fluctuated up until

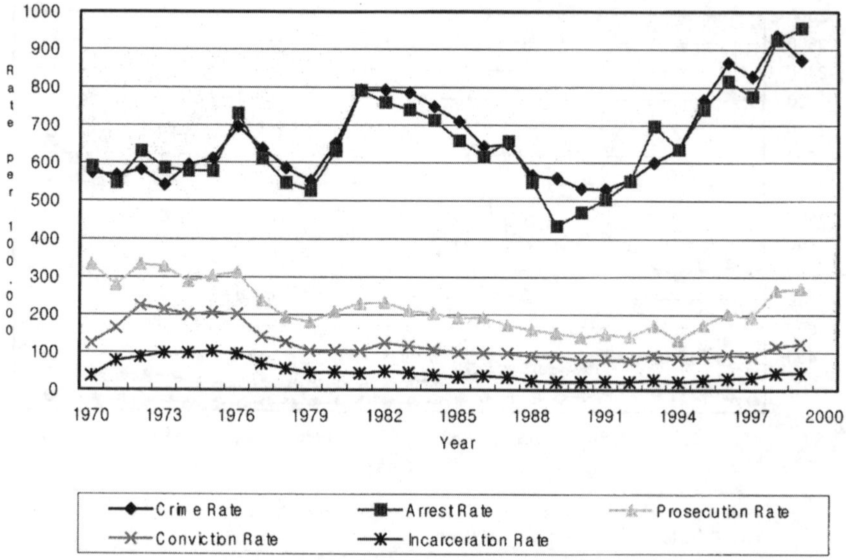

Figure 11. Property crime and crime control.

the middle of 1976 when a sharp increase took place. They then declined up until 1979, when afterwards both rates recorded their second peak in 1981. Fraud in particular was known to be responsible for this rapid increase in the property crime rate in the early 1980s. This was the time when unprecedented political changes were occurring after Chung-Hee Park's 18 years of authoritarian rule, and when Korean society suffered from transitional turmoil and instabilities (Kim and Cha, 1994).

During most of the 1980s, however, both the crime rate and arrest rate declined. Beginning in 1991, the property crime rate began to rise sharply and continued to increase during the rest of the 1990s. This increase in property crimes might help explain the increase in the total number of criminal code crimes given in Figure 10.

The prosecution, conviction and incarceration rates of property crimes showed an overall decline until 1992. Since then, all of the three rates have risen again. As we indicated in the previous study (Yoon, 1998: p. 60), there seems to be a relatively minor correlation between the conviction rate and the property crime rate and between the incarceration rate and the property crime rate.

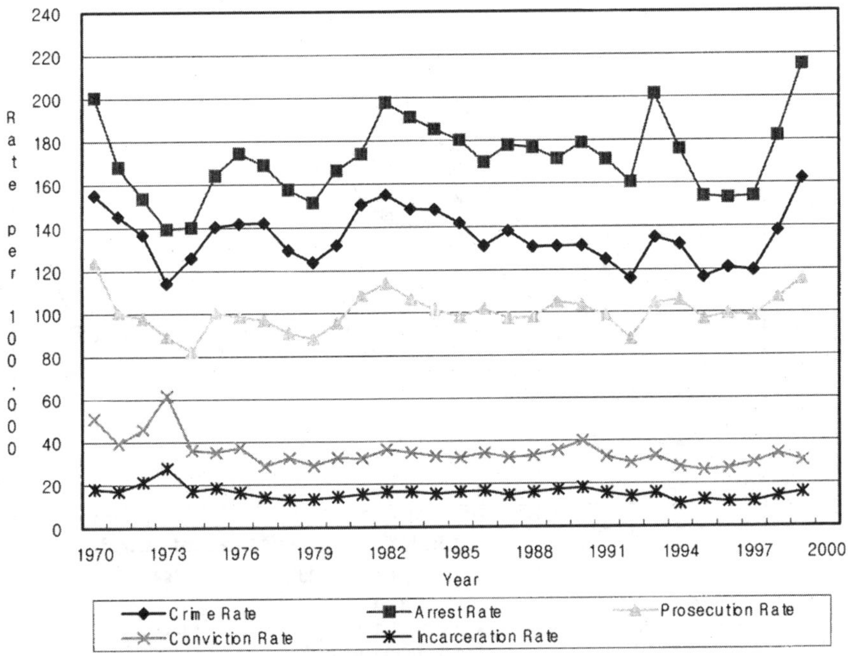

Figure 12. Violent crime and crime control.

Violent Crime and Crime Control

Crimes of violence, the crime rate, arrest rate and the prosecution rate are almost identical in pattern (see Figure 12). The three rates started off very high in the early 1970s, and then dropped sharply. They then fluctuated and increased drastically in the early 1980s. During the 1990s they increased rapidly. The patterns of the conviction rate and incarceration rate were also parallel. Both rates were very high in 1974, and then turned stable. Both rates rose again between 1987 and 1990. Thereafter, they declined until 1995, and then rose again. Unlike property crimes, the violent crime rate appears to be highly correlated with the arrest rate, prosecution rate and conviction rate.

These fluctuations can be attributed to the volatile economic, political, and socio-cultural conditions that have existed during the past 30 years. The financial crisis of the late 1990s, and all the turmoil in society that it caused apparently had a particularly major impact on the rate of violent crime.

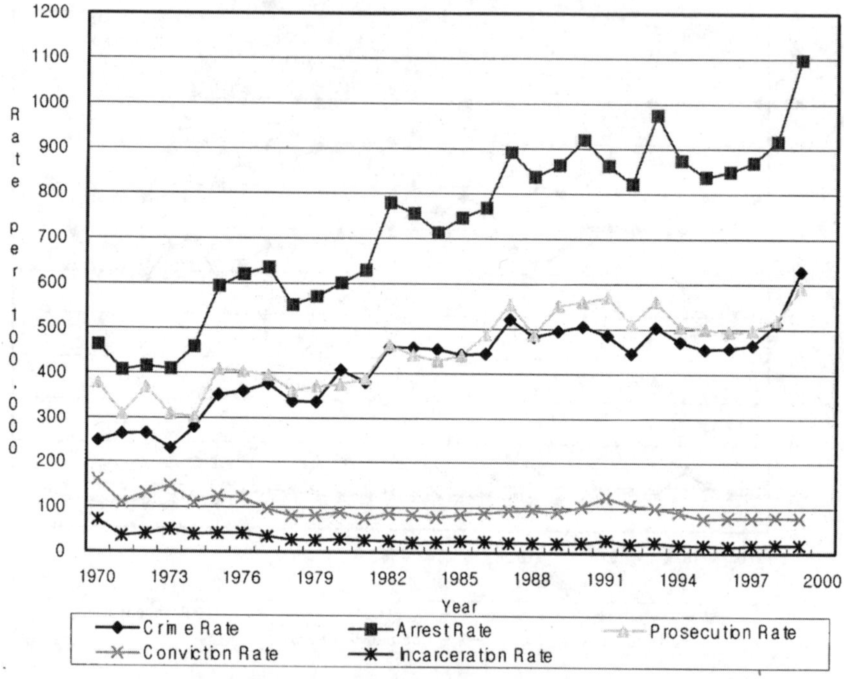

Figure 13. APVO crime and crime control.

APVO Crime and Crime Control

Figure 13 depicts trends in the crime rate and the four subsequent rates of crime control for the special category of violent crime, which are violations of the APVO. As mentioned earlier, this special law was enacted to control the prevalence of violence by handing out harsher punishment than that provided for in the Criminal Code. These offenses constitute a large proportion of all crime. For example, there were 230434 incidences of APVO in 1999, and this accounted for 13.3 percent of all crime (1732522) of that year. Compared to the incidences of Criminal Code violations, this amount was as much as fifty percent of the total number of Criminal Code offenses (462253) in 1999 (Legal Research & Training Institute, 2000).

Figure 13 shows a notable characteristic for the APVO. As was noted in Yoon's (1998) previous study, the APVO rates of crime, arrest and prosecution are quite different from the violent crimes under the Criminal Code. While the three (crime, arrest and prosecution) rates of violent crime prescribed in the Criminal Code (see Figure 12) fluctuated most of the time and showed relatively minor increases, the three rates of APVO increased sharply most of the time.

The conviction rate and the incarceration rate, however, did not show parallel trends with these three rates. As was the case with the conviction and incarceration rate for violent crimes under the Criminal Code, these two rates did not show much change in their patterns, and were almost identical with crimes of violence under the Criminal Code. Although the APVO crime rate and subsequent arrest and prosecution rates have also risen during the past three decades, both rates of conviction and incarceration for APVO crimes have declined. As mentioned earlier, one of the major reasons for a continued increase in the APVO crime rate may be attributed to the improved laws and regulations, which exert more efficient control over various violent offenses in an increasingly complex society.

SUMMARY AND CONCLUSIONS

Trends in crime and the crime rate in Korea over the past three decades can be summarized as follows. The incidence of crimes fluctuated during that time. One exception to this trend was the APVO crime rate, which displayed a general pattern of increase. However, it is especially noteworthy that the overall crime rate rose during the 1990s. This increase appears to be attributable to the increase in the crime rate of both property crime and APVO crime in the 1990s. A cross-national comparison reveals that overall rates of crime in both Korea and Japan were substantially lower than that in the U.S. While rates of crime of the U.S. have declined or leveled off since 1990, the crime rate in Korea rose rapidly over the same period.

The crime rate in Korea was much lower than in Japan until 1992; thereafter, Korea began to surpass Japan. This indicates that social disorganization in Korean society took place much faster than in Japan. In addition, it indicates that the safety of the Korean society in terms of crime is not so good as it used to be. In fact, it became worse than that of Japan after the middle of the 1990s in that crime rates of violent offenses became higher than those in Japan.

Compared to the U.S. and Japan, the overall crime rate of Criminal Code Offenses (CCO) in Korea has been relatively low over the past three decades. However, the ratio of increase in the crime rate of CCO is higher in Korea than in the other two countries. It is also noteworthy that the crime rates of violent crimes, as well as of property crimes, have all decreased in the U.S. since the early 1990s.

For the past 30 years, there has been a close relationship between the crime rate, arrest rate and prosecution rate. Steep increases in the three rates were found after 1991. However, the ratio of increase in the arrest rate was higher than that of the other two. The sharp increase in the crime rate, arrest rate and prosecution rate between 1990 and 1993 is attributable to the "war on crime" or the "get tough on crime" policies during the 1990s in Korea. The increase in property and APVO crimes might explain most of the increase in the total number of crimes during the 1990s.

When it comes to the conviction rate and the incarceration rate, both rates have declined even while the rates of crime, arrest, and prosecution have been increasing. These two features of court proceeding have revealed relatively few changes over time. There seems to be a relatively minor correlation between the crime rate and conviction rate, and between the crime rate and incarceration rate for property crimes. Although the APVO crime rate and subsequent arrest and prosecution rates rose during the period we studied, both rates of conviction and incarceration for APVO crimes declined. This might explain the relatively low levels of change in the rates of conviction and incarceration.

According to this study, the overall crime problem in Korea is not as serious as that in Japan and the U.S. However, recent data indicate an alarming increase in the crime rate. From the data analyzed, we can determine that economic political, and societal factors have played a crucial role in the occurrence of crime and crime control practices in Korea. Recent phenomena, like the financial crisis and the current political stalemate in Korea, seem to have contributed to this recent disturbing increase in crime. If these factors can be stabilized, then we may anticipate the improvement of the crime situation in Korea.

NOTES

[1] Clearance rate refers to the number of arrestees over the number of incidences of crimes multiplied by 100. The number of crimes refers to those crimes that took place in the relevant year, and the number of arrestees includes the arrests of suspects that had occurred in the year immediately preceding the year of computation.
[2] As stated in the Data and method section, violent offenses include criminal homicide, robbery, rape, arson, assault, aggravated assault, intimidation and kidnapping. Included among property crimes are larceny-theft, stolen property, fraud, embezzlement, breach of trust, and destruction of property.
[3] Crime categories that are subjected to this statistical analysis in each country are as follows:

U.S.A.: Crime Index Offense (homicide, rape, robbery, bodily injury, illegal entering, car theft, larceny. Arson was added in 1979, but was not included in the number of crimes that occurred).
Japan: Penal Code offenses include violations of the Law for the Punishment of Violent Crimes, Explosives Control Law, Law Relating to Duel and Law Concerning the Prevention and Punishment of Burglary, Robbery, Larceny, etc. Excluded from Penal Code offenses is professional or gross negligence causing death or bodily injury by traffic accident.
Korea: The violations of the Laws concerning Punishment of Violent Crimes are included. However, the violations of the Special Acts on Disposition of Traffic Accidents and the Road Traffic Act are excluded.

[4] Yoon's (1998) study made a unique contribution to the issues of crime and social control in that it attempted to incorporate crime and various crime control practices in a single frame of analysis for the first time in criminological studies in Korea. She examined trends and patterns of crime and crime control practices from 1964 through 1993. This analysis is, in part, an attempt to update and extend Yoon's study from 1970 through 1999.
[5] In this analysis, total crime means total criminal code crime.
[6] In most cases, the arrest rate is higher than the crime rate because a crime can have more than one offender and the arrest rate measures the number of arrestees.

REFERENCES

Administrative Office of Courts: various years, Judiciary Yearbook (written in Korean) (Seoul).

Barberet, R.L.: 1994, Modernization, Criminal Sanctions and Crime in Spain. Unpublished dissertation, University of Maryland.

Bedeski, R.E.: 1993, The Transformation of South Korea: Reform and Reconstruction in the Sixth Republic under Roh Rae Woo, 1987–1992 (Routledge, New York).

Chang, D.H., and R.G. Iacovetta: 1996, 'Organized crime in South Korea,' Comparative Criminal Justice, pp. 115–128.

Chang, D.H., and G.M. Janeksela: 1996, 'An analysis of the Korean criminal justice system', Comparative Criminal Justice, pp. 411–425.

Choi, I.S., and S.J. Park: 1993, Social Structure and Crime (written in Korean) (Korean Institute of Criminology).

Chung, G.S.: 1998, 'Urbanization and urban crime' (written in Korean) (Korean Association of Pubic Safety and Criminal Justice Review 7).

Coleman, J.W. and R.C. Donald: 2000, Social Problems, 7th ed. (Longman, New York).

Deng, F., M.S. Vaughn and F.F.Y. Hung: 1994, 'Correlates of crime in Taiwan: A time-series analysis from 1964 to 1990', Crime, Law & Social Change 21, pp. 267–285.

Dunham, R.G. and G.P. Alpert: 1993, Critical Issues in Policing (Waveland Press, Inc., IL).

Federal Bureau of Investigation (FBI): Various years, Uniform Crime Report.

Fields, C.B. and R.H. Moore Jr.: 1996, Comparative Criminal Justice Traditional and Nontraditional Systems of Law and Control (Waveland, Prospect Heights, Ill).

Japanese Department of Justice: various years, White Paper on Crime.

Kim, J.H. and J.C. Cha: 1994, On Fraud in Korea (written in Korean) (Korea Institute of Criminology, Seoul).

Koo, H.: 1993, 'The state, Minjung, and working class in South Korea', in Hagen Koo (ed.), State and Society in Contemporary Korea (Cornell University Press, Itaca, pp. 131–162).

Lee, M.W.: 1990, The Odyssey of Koran Democracy: Korean Politics, 1987–1990 (Praeger, New York).

Legal Research and Training Institute: various years, White Paper on Crime (written in Korean) (Woori Printing Company, Seoul).

Messner, S.F.: 1986, 'Modernization, structural characteristics and social rates of crime: An application of Blau's Macrosociological Theory', Sociological Quarterly 27(1).

Paik, Y.C.: 1994, 'Political reform and demographic consolidation in Korea', Korea and World Affairs 18(4), pp. 730–748.

Park, H.K.: 1996, 'Developmental dictatorship and human rights: Ideology of national security and Human rights violation', Democratic Legal Studies 10, pp. 196–221 (Kwanak, Seoul).

Ratner, R.S. and J.S. McMullan: 1987, State Control: Criminal Justice Politics in Canada (University of British Columbia, Vancouver).

Samsung Economic Research Institute: 1996, Transformation of Korean Society and Response: Social Development and Crime (written in Korean). Policy Report No. 96-15-052.

Shikita, M. and S. Tsuchiya: 1992, Crime and Criminal Policy in Japan (Springer-Verlag, New York).

Supreme Public prosecutor's Office: various years, Analytical Report on Crime (written in Korean) (Seoul).
Thornton, R.Y. and K. Endo: 1992, Preventing Crime in America and Japan (M.E. Sharpe, Inc., New York).
Welch, M.; 1996, Corrections: A Critical Approach (McGraw-Hill).
Yoon, O.K.: 1998, The Economy, Political Repression and Crime Control: A Time-series Analysis of Korean Case, 1964–1993. Ph.D. dissertation, University of Georgia.

Southwest State University
E-mail: hjoo@southwest.msus.edu

MEESOOK KIM

SOCIAL WELFARE SYSTEM

ABSTRACT. The social welfare system in Korea has become a public issue recently. Before the 1997 financial crisis, policy makers as well as the general public were mainly interested in pursuing economic growth and largely downplaying welfare needs. In the wake of the crisis, however, the demand for welfare increased significantly, and this in turn has brought changes in the welfare structure, along with an expansion in welfare expenditures. This paper highlights the features of the Korean welfare system in terms of social insurance, pubic assistance, and social service. It examines the basic limitations and key issues surrounding the system. It compares the size of social welfare expenditures in Korea to other Organization for Economic Cooperation and Development (hereinafter the OECD) countries. In sum, welfare coverage, expenditures, and benefit levels are among the barriers to surmount especially in these times of high aspirations toward national unification and globalization.

I. INTRODUCTION

As in all other civilized societies, a welfare state has been adopted in Korea as a basic principle of its constitution. Yet, the country failed to make any significant progress in building a welfare state for five decades since its independence from Japan in 1945. Faced with constant threats from the Communist North and the pressing problem of extreme poverty, policymakers and the general public remained preoccupied with issues of national security and economic development. As a result, the responsibility to help the poor and others in need was left to individual citizens, their family, and the marketplace.

In November 1997, Korea was stricken with the worst economic crisis since the end of the Korean War a half century ago. In the wake of this crisis, social welfare emerged as an important and urgent policy issue for the first time in its history. Soaring unemployment and the increasing incidence of poverty and homelessness forced the government to confront the vitally urgent and overriding chal-

Social Indicators Research **62, 63:** 265–289, 2003.

lenge of reorganizing and strengthening its meager welfare system. The social security budget, as a percentage of the Gross Domestic Product (hereinafter the GDP), had increased from 5.2 percent in 1995, to 11.1 percent in 1998. In 1999, the Livelihood Protection law, enacted in 1961, was replaced by the National Basic Livelihood Guarantee (hereinafter the Basic Guarantee law), and both the pension system and heath insurance were reformed to extend coverage.

This paper attempts to offer an overview of Korea's social security system from historical and comparative perspectives. To this end, it will first examine the structure and programs of social insurance, public assistance, and social services. It will then compare Korea's social welfare expenditures and programs with those of the Organization for Economic Cooperation and Development countries. Finally, it will discuss the current problems and future challenges facing the country's welfare system.

II. SOCIAL INSURANCE

Social insurance is a welfare system that helps the insured to get prepared of times of little or no income, disease, disability, old age, or death. Korea's social insurance fund is financed by contributions from employees, employers, and the government. In Korea, as shown in Table I, there are four social insurance components: work injury compensation insurance, health insurance, public pensions, and unemployment insurance. Work injury compensation insurance, introduced in 1964, is the oldest among them. Health insurance has been widely adopted since 1977, and the public pension program was established in 1988. Unemployment insurance, adopted in 1995, is the latest social insurance (Lee, 1998). Korea laid the groundwork for its social insurance with its four major components over a short period of time. There are, however, several tasks remaining to be tackled to achieve a more complete role for social insurance.

TABLE I

Types of Social Insurance of Korea, 2001

Type	Recipients	Number of participants	Ministry, year established
Work injury compensation insurance	All workplaces	9.50 million workers (2002)	MOL* 1964
Health insurance	All people	Over 96% of population	MOHW* 1977
National pension	All people	16 million (2000)	MOHW 1988
Unemployment insurance	Almost all workplaces	9.27 million workers	MOL 1993

MOL: Ministry of Labor; MOHW: Ministry of Health and Welfare.

1. Work Injury Insurance

Work injury insurance is the older insurance in Korea. After the enactment of the Work Injury Compensation Law in 1964, the number of beneficiaries was expanded. Now, employees at any workplace with 1 or more workers, and the injured, stick, disabled, or the relatives of those, who die in the course of their employment, benefit from the insurance (In, 1998). Since the work injury insurance is being financed exclusively by contributions from employers, employees are not required to make contributions to the fund (In, 1998; Kim, 1996). This social insurance system provides the insured with benefits for treatment of work-caused diseases and injuries, compensates for income losses, while treating disease and injury, and helps in preventing work-related injuries (In, 1998). In addition, occupation-related diseases, which develop over time, are also covered by the insurance (In, 1998). The government pays for the administrative cost of the system.

The range of beneficiaries of work injury insurance has been expanded over time. In 1964, only miners, assembly workers, and employees, who worked at firms with more than 500 employees, were covered (Chang et al., 1999). As a result of amendments made to the law in 1972, the insurance was extended to cover workplaces with 30 or more workers (Chang et al., 1999). The insurance was further extended in 1992 to cover workplaces with 5 or more employees, and after the financial crisis, it was extended to all workplaces in the country (Change et al., 1999). As of 2000, the total number of beneficiaries amounted to 9.50 million workers at 706231 workplace nationwide (Chang et al., 1999).

Benefit types consist of: sick leave benefits; a sickness compensation pension; and a disability benefit (In, 1998). In addition, there are two special benefits: supplementary benefits for sever disability and for survivors. These benefits are of a case and in-kind nature.

2. *Health Insurance*

Health insurance is a social security system designed to reduce the financial onus imposed by accident, disease, delivery of a baby, or death, by having all participants share in the burden. When the Health Insurance Law was enacted in 1963, the coverage was too minimal to function as a social security system. It was only during the 1970s that health insurance became a social issue. Witnessing the need for health insurance, while the country was in the throes of economic development, president Chung Hee Park turned his attention to developing a social welfare program including health insurance (Choi et al., 1998). Against this backdrop, the national health insurance system was adopted in 1977 for firms with more than 500 employees (Choi et al., 1998). At the same time, medical assistance for the absolute poor was adopted. In 1989, twelve years after its inception, the health insurance system was extended to cover everyone, including rural residents and the urban self-employed. (Chang et al., 1999).

Benefits of health insurance consist of both cash payment and in-kind benefits. In-kind benefits provided by health service centers include: medical consultations, drugs and other therapeutic materials, medical and surgical treatments, hospitalization, operations, and other services, such as nursing care and transportation costs (The Editing Committee of White Paper on Welfare Reform, 1998). To prevent unnecessary utilization of health care services/resources, and to save health care fees, insured persons are required to make co-payments, when receiving medical care services (The Editing

Committee of White Paper on Welfare Reform, 1998). As for hospitalization, the patient has to pay 20 percent of the total fee (Choi et al., 1998). Cash benefits are paid to reimburse for medical care and costs of delivering a baby that are paid by insured persons or by their dependents. A fixed cash benefit is also paid to cover a portion of funeral expenses (Choi et al., 1998).

There used to be three types of health insurance programs for different target groups: (1) for government employees, private school employees, military servicemen and their dependents; (2) for rural or urban self-employed individuals; and (3) for employees of industrial or commercial companies (Choi et al., 1998). In 1998, the first and the third health insurance programs were combined into one, and in 1999, all three were incorporated into a single system under the National Health Insurance Act (Chang et al., 1999). The health insurance system is financed by contributions from the insured, employers, and the government.

In the year 2000, prescription services were separated from dispensing services for the first time in Korean medical history. The separation mandate was adopted to prevent overuse/misuse of drugs, as well as to reduce drug expenses by suppressing the over-prescribing of drugs (The Editing Committee of White Paper on Welfare Reform, 1998a). Eight months after the inception of the separation mandate, the National Health Insurance Corporation was confronted with a serious financial imbalance due to the increasing medical insurance fees that medical service centers require. The Korean government had to come up with a way of easing the financial burden on medical insurance.

3. *National Pension*

Korea's first pension system was adopted in 1988 with the amendment of the once unworkable, ineffective 1973 National Pension Law. Before 1973, only government employees (government employees pension), military personnel (military personnel pension), and private school teachers (private school teachers pension) had pensions. As the National Pension system was adopted, all people, including farmers and fishermen, and the self-employed, became eligible for public pensions. The National Pension Scheme (hereinafter the NPS), the centerpiece of public pensions within Korea, provides the insured with financial security against aging, disability, and death.

The target group of the NPS comprises those between the ages of 18 and 60, who are not included in any one of the three insurance plans. NPS participants are divided into two groups: workplace-based participants and residential area-based participants. As for the workplace-based group, employees at firms with 10 or more workers are eligible for participation in the NPS. Since 1991 those employed at businesses with 5 or more workers were included in the pension scheme. Since 1994, rural dwellers were able to participate in the NPS along with the previously insured urban dwellers. As of 1998, there were 5.06 million workplace-based participants, and 2.11 million regional participants in the pension scheme (Yoon, 1998). In 1999, the urban self-employed, those employed at workplaces with 5 or less employees, and part-time workers were added (Chang et al., 1999). Full-time housewives, and those aged under 23, who are not working, are not covered by the pension scheme (Chang et al., 1999). They can, however, voluntarily participate in it.

The average income replacement level used to be 70 percent for those with 40 or more years of participation, but it was reduced to 60 percent when the law was amended (Chang et al., 1999). Pension benefits are provided to insured persons for life. To achieve financial stability in the pension fund, the minimum age of pension benefits will be raised from the current 60 to 65 in 2033 (Chang et al., 1999). To provide for financial security of the elderly, the minimum period of insurance was reduced from 15 to 10 years (Chang et al., 1999).

4. Unemployment Insurance

Among the four types of social insurance, Unemployment Insurance is the newest. It was launched in 1995, two years after the enactment of the Unemployment Insurance Act (hereinafter the UIA), when the unemployment rate in Korea was fairly low. The purpose of unemployment insurance is to secure income for workers during times of unemployment, and to promote employment through job training and human development.

All workers, with the exception of those working part-time, are covered by insurance. As of 2001, 9.27 million workers from

1208000 workplaces were covered (MOL, 2001). There are three types of benefits of unemployment insurance: support for employment security; unemployment benefits; and job training and human development. Unemployment benefits amount to 50 percent of the average income before unemployment with a minimum of 250000 won per month and a maximum of 900000 won (Chang et al., 1999). To be eligible for unemployment insurance, the insured is required to have worked at an insured company for at least 6 months. The unemployed can be covered by the insurance for between 2–7 months (NSWC, 2000).

III. PUBLIC ASSISTANCE

1. Public Assistance

In Korea, for over 38 years, the public assistance system used to be called "Livelihood Protection" until the enactment of the National Basic Livelihood Guarantee Law in 1999. The public assistance system was officially launched in 1961, when the Basic guarantee Law took effect. This Law provided the poor with six types of public assistance: livelihood aid, self-support aid, educational aid, maternity aid, burial aid, and medical aid. There used to be two types of Basic Guarantee recipients: Home and Institutional Care recipients and Self-support Care recipients. Home and Institutional Care recipients were those without the ability to work. Included in this group were the elderly, children, the disabled (demographic eligibility criteria for Home Care), and those who were cared for at welfare institutions. Self-support Care recipients were those who were able to work, but lack sufficient resources for living. Livelihood aid, maternity aid, and burial aid were provided only to Home Care and Institutional Care recipients (Ministry of Health and Welfare, 1997). Livelihood aid, educational aid, and medical aid were provided to both recipient groups.

The Livelihood Protection system is widely criticized because of its several limitations, including low benefit levels, unreasonably narrow selection criteria, and other structural problems. In 1999, the Livelihood Protection Act was replaced with the Basic Guarantee law due to the rising demand for public assistance after the economic crisis hit the country. During the economic crisis, the unemployment rate rose sharply from 2.6 percent in 1997, to 6.8 percent in 1998, and 6.3 percent in 1999. The mass unemployment resulted in many social problems including poverty. The poverty rate increased twice over its pre-crisis level, and Korea's social safety net was too weak to protect all of the poor with proper social support. For example, the Livelihood Protection system could cover only 60.4 percent of the absolute poor before the new poverty law was enacted (Kim, 2001).[1] In other words, because Korea's social safety net for poverty had not been fully established, it could not handle the drastically increasing poor population. Self-support Care recipients and the low-income unemployed were not entitled to livelihood aid, and hence, they, not the lowest class, were the ones who suffered most.

Under these circumstances the Basic Guarantee law was enacted. This Law is a pivotal element in Korea's social welfare system, in the sense that it was the first legal mechanism to guarantee a "National Minimum" and self-sufficiency for the poor, which the Livelihood Protection system could not provide. The major goals of the new law are to: (1) enhance people's rights to claim benefits by renaming the law; (2) modernize the institutional framework by abolishing the demographic eligibility criteria (65 or older, or children under 18); (3) achieve equity by introducing the concept of Estimated Household Income (household head's monthly income + monthly tariff income); and (4) enhance the productivity of the welfare system by providing the unemployed with incentives and systematic self-support programs to promote motivation to work (Kim, 2001).

People who fall under the following categories are eligible for benefits: (1) elderly persons, who are unable to support themselves, children under 18, expectant mothers, and those who are unable to work due to disease or mental and/or physical disability; (2) those who have no one to support them, or who have no household members, who can support them; and (3) those, who have a family per capita income and a household with property with the value below a certain level (in 2000, to be eligible for the system, family income should be no more than 930000 won, and with household property valued at 32 million won or less for a family with four members).

TABLE II

Percentage of Livelihood Aid Beneficiaries

Classification	1997	1998	1999	2000
Total beneficiaries of public assistance (A)	1410000	1470000	1920000	1510000
Number of persons covered with livelihood aid (B)	370	440000	540000	1510000
B/A∗100	26.2	29.9	28.1	100

Source: Mee-Gon Kim, 2001, "Basic Livelihood Guarantee System as a Social Safety Nets", Workshop on Securing Social Safety Nets, KIHASA, p. 77.

There are seven types of protection: livelihood aid, housing aid (newly added), medical aid, educational aid, self-support aid, maternity aid, and burial aid. According to the new law, the demographic eligibility criteria (65 and older, children under 18) have been lifted, and anyone, who fits the family income and property criteria, is entitled to receive livelihood aid. Under the new law for the first time in the Korean welfare system, housing aid is provided, suggesting that every aspect of living is now protected.

Since the adoption of the new law, the Korean social safety net has been strengthened. Owing to the Basic Guarantee Law, over 1.5 million people in poverty were provided with livelihood aid in 2000, whereas only 0.5 million people were covered by the same program in 1999, when the new law was not yet in effect (see Table II) (Kim, 2001). Moreover, the overall benefit level, per beneficiary, has risen. As for Home Care recipients, the percentage of recipients has risen by 9.0 percent. As for Self-support Care recipients, who were not eligible for the livelihood aid according to the old law, the percentage has risen by as much as 40.9 percent (Kim, 2001).

The Korean government has markedly increased the budget for basic livelihood aid. In 1997, the per capita basic livelihood aid budget was 639000 won, but in 2001 it was increased to 1980000 won, having increased by as much as 210 percent (Kim, 2001).

2. *Medical Assistance*

Medical assistance is provided to those who are eligible for public assistance. The medical assistance system was first adopted in 1961, when the Livelihood Protection law was enacted. The government, however, had to stop providing the assistance due to a lack of funds. Thereafter, the medical assistance program was managed separately from the Livelihood Protection law. The system is more closely linked to the health insurance system, unlike other countries, where medical assistance programs are part and parcel of public assistance.

To be eligible for benefits one must be proven to live under the poverty line. There are two kinds of medical assistance depending on the degree of the beneficiary's poverty, viz., first class and second class assistance. First class medical assistance, which is given to those in the lowest-income class, provides various medical services, including hospitalization or outpatient services free of charge. Second class medical assistance, which is provided to people from the second lowest-income class, offers medical services with minimal charge, viz., when hospitalized, recipients pay 20 percent of fees, and when receiving outpatient services, they pay 1,500 won per visit (MOHW, 2000b). Only in-kind benefits are provided to them.

IV. SOCIAL SERVICES

1. *Welfare for the Elderly*

Due both to the low fertility and mortality rates in Korea, the elderly population is increasing. The total fertility rate has decreased from 4.5 in 1970 to 1.7 in 1995 (National Statistical Office, 1970, 1995). Life expectancy at birth has increased from 63.2 in 1970, to 73.5 in 1995, and to 74.3 in 2000 (national Statistical Office, 1995). As shown in Table III, in 1960 the proportion of the elderly over 65 was only 2.90 percent, but after 30 years, in 1990, increased almost twice as much, reaching 5.12 percent. Korea became an aging society in 2000 with 7.13 percent of the elderly over 65.

Due to the increase in the elderly population and the decrease in family responsibility for supporting the elderly, at a time when the family experienced both structural and thus functional changes,

TABLE III

Elderly Population by Year

Year	1960	1970	1980	1990	2000	2001	2025
%	2.90	3.21	3.82	5.12	7.13	7.43	14.33

Source: National Statistical Office, The Future Estimated Population, 1996.

elderly care became an important social issue. Problems that the Korean elderly are facing – including financial insecurity, ill health, early retirement, and loneliness – cannot be treated solely within the family. Societal involvement is absolutely necessary. Furthermore, after the economic crisis the financial situation of the elderly only worsened. Most of the elderly lost one or more of their sources of income, and were not able to depend upon their adult children, who were also struggling with financial difficulties. As a result, the life of the elderly became harder. Governmental policies are mainly geared toward protecting low-income elderly. There are several types of programs provided by the government for the elderly, which provide financial security, health protection and housing.

Public policies for financial security of the elderly include pensions, public assistance, and old age pensions. Public pensions involve four separate programs: the national pension launched in 1988, the Government Employees Pension in 1960, the Military Personnel Pension in 1963, and the Private School Teachers Pension in 1975. The main public pension program in Korea is the NPS, which covers all citizens regardless of their occupations, unlike the other three pension schemes. Since its recent implementation, the NPS covers only 1.1 percent of the elderly aged 65 and older. Even the other pension scheme does not cover much of the aged population, as shown in Table IV (Suk, 2000).

Public assistance is available to the low-income elderly. The public assistance system in Korea has been changed from the Livelihood Protection to the Basic Guarantee in 2000, as mentioned earlier. According to the new public assistance system, people living below the poverty line are eligible for public assistance benefits. In 1999, 7.5 percent of the aged population received public assistance (Suk, 2000).

TABLE IV

The Elderly Covered by Public Income Security Scheme (1999)

Type	Public pension				Old age pension	Public assistance	Total
	National pension	Government employee pension	Private school teachers pension	Military personnel pension			
%	1.06	0.84	0.13	0.50	20.6	7.53	23.1

Source: Suk, 2000, Analysis of Income Sources and Income Maintenance Schemes for the Elderly in Korea, p. 150.

An old age allowance is provided to those who are eligible for public assistance, but are not covered by a pension plan. The purpose of an old age allowance, serving as a supplementary noncontributory pension, is to protect the aged not participating in the NPS (Suk, 2000). As of 2000, 584976 elderly, 17.3 percent of the total aged population, were covered by it (Suk, 2000). Among them, 53.2 percent are public assistance recipients, and the remaining 46.8 percent are low-income elderly (Suk, 2000).

The benefit level of the old age allowance varies across the different ages and financial situations of the elderly. The elderly, between the ages of 65 and 79 receive public assistance in the amount of 40000 won a month; those over 80 receive 50000 won a month; the low-income elderly receive 30000 won a month; and if a couple is eligible for public assistance, one member of the couple receives only 22500 won a month, while the other receives the full amount (MOHW, 2000b). In other words, the benefit level of the old age allowance is too low to serve as a social safety net for one's later years.

The recent health care policies for the elderly primarily deal with health insurance, medical assistance, free health examinations, treatment for dementia, and chronic disease and health care services for the home-ridden elderly (MOHW, 2000b).

With the implementation of National Health Insurance in 1977, 96.2 percent of the elderly were covered by the insurance, and the rest were covered by medical assistance (Chung, 1999). With health insurance, the elderly need to pay only 20 percent of all hospitalization fees, and 30–55 percent of all medical fees (Chung, 1999). Due to the well-established health security system in Korea, the elderly are able to utilize hospitals more often. Since many of the elderly suffer, however, from more than one chronic disease, and the insurance covers a limited number of them, the elderly are burdened by high medical costs.

To improve the health of the elderly by diagnosing geriatric diseases at an early stage, the Korean government has been providing free health examinations to the low-income elderly since 1983. The free health examinations were extended, in 1992, to cover various geriatric diseases, including diabetes and cataracts. A further expansion, including general examinations including blood tests and X-ray examinations to special geriatric diseases, such as cancer, occurred in 1996 (Editing Committee of White Paper on Welfare Reform, 1998a). In 1999, 33661 elderly received free health examinations (MOHW, 2000b).

Currently, 8.3 percent (280000 persons) of the elderly suffer from dementia, and this number is expected to increase over time (MOHW, 2000b). The government established comprehensive long-term health and welfare policies, and built consulting offices for the treatment of dementia nationwide. As of 1999, there were 21 hospitals for the elderly. By 2003, there will be a total of 60 (MOHW, 2000b). For the elderly with dementia, 15 hospitals that treat dementia are now open, and by the year 2001, in every city and province, at least one additional hospital will be built to treat it (MOHW, 2000b).

Since one-third of the elderly are not able to conduct daily living activities without help from other (KIHASA, 1999), the government has promoted home care services for the elderly with mental and physical disabilities. There are three types of home care service in Korea: home help services, such as helping with eating, bathing, being escorted to a hospital; day care services through which the elderly are cared for during the day time; and short-term care services by which the elderly are protected while away from home for several days (2–3 days or 10–40 days).

The elderly, who need housing, can live in welfare facilities. There was seven types of welfare facility for the elderly in Korea: free elderly homes, free nursing homes, low-cost elderly homes, low-cost nursing homes, general elderly homes, and nursing homes, and facilities for those with dementia. As of 1999, there were 229 elderly welfare facilities, protecting 12751 elderly (MOHW, 1999).

In the year 2000, 0.4 percent of the elderly (337000 persons), lived in welfare facilities (MOHW, 2000c). It is expected that the number of the elderly, who need housing, will increase due to the rise in nuclear family households and the changing attitude of the elderly towards living arrangements. The number of elderly people with resources, who want to live separately from their adult children, is increasing at an accelerating rate. Accordingly, the government plans to expand various types of welfare facilities, whether free or at cost, to meet such demand.

Post-retirement leisure and social activities are becoming an increasingly important social issue as life expectancy after 65 rises. The government of Korea encourages the elderly to participate in volunteer as well as leisure activities for active aging. In 1997, the Welfare Act for the Elderly was amended to appoint the elderly to serve as community volunteer leaders. Also, the elderly are encouraged to have a vital life through volunteer activities in the fields of traffic control, resource conservation, and social activities. As for leisure facilities, there were 38452 elderly activity centers in 1999 (MOHW, 2000b). The government provides each of them with 44000 won a month for managing them, and 250000 won a year for heating costs (MOHW, 2000b). In addition, there are 527 elderly schools, 6 resort centers, and 118 multi-purpose senior centers, all of which are built for the active aging (MOHW, 2O00b).

2. *Welfare for the Disabled*

There are 1449500 disabled persons as of 2001, comprising 3.09 percent of the total population (Byun et al., 2001). The number of people with a disability at birth is gradually decreasing, whereas the number of people with a disability after birth, due to various accidents, including car or industrial accidents, is increasing. The number of the elderly, who have become disabled due to age related diseases, is increasing as well. In 1985, the rate of acquired disabilities was 81.2 percent, but the percentage increased to 89.4 percent in 2000 (Byun et al., 2001).

Still, the rate of the disabled in Korea is much lower than that in developed countries. This is because the range of disabilities in Korean is far narrower than in other OECD countries, where more types of disabilities are included. In 1999, the category of legal disabilities was expanded to include serious, chronic intestinal disorders, and mental disabilities (Korea Welfare Committee for the Disabled, 1999).

Welfare for the disabled started in 1981, when the Welfare Act for the Mentally and Physically Disabled was enacted. The Act further matured in 1988, when the Para-Olympic Games were held in Seoul, and in 1989, when the act was amended and called the "Welfare Act for the Disabled" (Editing Committee of White Paper on Welfare Reform, 1998a). From that point on, welfare for the disabled underwent dramatic development with the instituting of other measures, which in turn served as a basis for understanding the disabled and living closely with them (Editing Committee of White Paper on Welfare Reform, 1998a).

The main objective of welfare for the disabled in Korea is to achieve their complete social integration by activating their social participation, and providing them with equal opportunities (Editing Committee of White Paper on Welfare Reform, 1998b). Accordingly, welfare for the disabled has focused on creating a social environment in which the disabled can mix with other people, as well as by creating the necessary social conditions, so that they might participate in social activities including work (MOHW, 2001). Policies for the disabled include income support, tax and other fee exemptions, medical support, education support, a technical devices provision, occupational rehabilitation, welfare facilities, and the providing of easy access to relevant facilities.

Those disabled, who have financial difficulties (viz., Basic Livelihood Aid recipients), class 1 and class 2 types,[2] who are not capable of working, receive disability allowances in addition to livelihood aid. In 1997, 42000 disabled persons, 15 percent of the disabled total, received an allowance of 45000 won per person (Park and Kim, 1998). In the year 2000, to those who could work, the government provided loans with a low interest rate (8.25% yearly interest rat, repayment within five-years with a five-year grace period), amounting to 12 million won per household (MOHW, 2001). To promote the financial independence of the disabled, the government gives priority approval to the disabled, when they apply for work in retail stores or running vending machines in public facilities.

To alleviate the financial burden of the disabled and to support them with income, various fees and tax example programs are available, including the exemption of public facility fees, railroad and subways fees, telephone and television bills, and income inheritance, customs, and vehicle related taxes (MOHW, 2001).

Since 1996, the number of days of medical insurance covering the disabled was extended to one year, and therefore, the registered[3] disabled could receive medical care service throughout the year (Editing Committee of White Paper on Welfare Reform, 1998a). the disabled need to pay only 50 percent of their medical fee due the primary medical service providers,[4] and only 20 percent to the secondary or tertiary medical service providers (MOHW, 1999a).

In 1992, educational support was extended to school-age students from lower class disabled families. This was done to break the cycle of poverty with younger generations of disabled families (MOHW, 2000b). Junior high and high school students of low income disabled families had their entrance fees and tuition covered.

The government provides technical devices free of charge to the low-income disabled. For other disabled individuals, health insurance covers about 80 percent of their cost (MOHW, 2000a). In addition, the low-income disabled can receive a solidly built wristwatch and a TV caption box (MOHW, 2001).

The Employment Promotion Act for the Disabled requires companies with over 300 workers to hire disabled persons amounting to not less than 2 percent of their employee pool. Disregarding or not complying with this mandate is subject to a fine. In 1998, disabled persons employed at businesses within the private sector, with more than 300 workers, constituted only 0.54 percent of the employee pool. In conjunction with this it should be noted that the employment rate for the disabled in the public sector has increased to 1.23 percent (Byun et al., 2000). To support the financial independence of the disabled, the government runs 150 workplaces and 12 work facilities for them as of the year 2000 (MOHW, 2000b).

TABLE V

Social Assistance for the Low-Income Disabled (2000)

Item	Number of recipients	Contents	Budget	Recipients
Income Support	76899	45000	40.9 billion	The Low class Disabled (class 1 and class 2)
Medical Support	93251	Primary care: 50% Secondary Care: 80%	9.3 billion	Low Income Disabled
Education Al Support	6894	Entrance fees and tuition	4 billion	Junior Middle and High-school students from low income disabled family
Loan	1500 households	12 million	18 billion	Low income Household
Technical Devices[1]	3000	Prosthesis and brace	630 thousand	Low income Disabled

[1]The figures of the technical devices are from 1999.
Source: The Ministry of Health and Welfare: 2000a, 'Guide to Welfare for the Disabled', 1999a.

There are two types of welfare facilities for the disabled: welfare centers that provide those living at home with medical treatments, occupational rehabilitation programs and lifelong education; and welfare institutions that provide them with housing and medical treatment. There are 184 welfare centers and 188 welfare institutions for the disabled in Korea as of 2000 (MOHW, 2000b). Until recently, most welfare policies for the disabled have been geared toward institutionalized disabled persons, who constitute only 2 percent of the total number of disabled persons in the country. Now, however, that is changing. Current policies are being made increasingly sensitive to the needs of disabled persons living at home. Various types of home care arrangements, such as day care and short-term care services, have been increased since 1997.

Since 1991, the government has been making access to a wide range of facilities convenient, including government offices, police stations, post offices, and department stores (Editing Committee of White Paper on Welfare Reform, 1998a). In 1997, the "Convenience Facility Installation Law for the Disabled, Elderly and Pregnant Woman" was enacted, and easier to facilities began to be provided.

3. *Welfare for the Lone Parent Family*

A lone parent family is defined as a single parent household – a household led by a male without a wife being present or by a female without a husband being present – with one or more children under 18 years of age. Despite the increase in the number of lone parent families, the proportion of this group, to the total number of households in the country, has decreased from 8.9 percent in 1985, to 7.4 percent in 1995 (National Statistical Office, 1998). This results from the fact that the number of total households including single member households has been increasing at a higher rate.

The lone parent family group is divided into two subgroups: the fatherless family and the motherless family. In Korea, fatherless families constitute most (82.1%) of the lone parent families. The disproportionately large number of fatherless families is traceable to several factors. First, single male household heads have a higher tendency to remarry, compared to single female household heads, because there has been continuing social prejudice against a mother being remarried (Kim et al., 2000). Second, women have a longer life expectancy than men. In addition, their lower participation is social activities means, that they are less exposed to risks of accidents that may result in death. In recent years, the high death rate among men, in their 40s, brought about a marked increase in the number of fatherless families (National Statistical Office, 1998). The death rate of men, in their 40s, is double that of women (National Statistical Office, 1998).

The main causes of a lone parent family are death of a spouse 54.8%, 1995), divorce or separation, or abandonment (22.5%, in 1995), and having children outside of marriage (12.9%, 1995) (National Statistical Office, 1998). The divorce rate is on the rise in Korea. In 1980, the crude divorce rate, (a rate calculated on the basis of the number of divorces per 1000 population), was only 0.6, but it increased to 0.9 in 1985, 1.0 in 1990, 1.5 in 1990, and 2.0 in 1997 (National Statistical Office, 1998). The latest statistics show that the current crude divorce rate in Korea is behind the rate in Great Britain (3.0), the highest among the OECD countries. Due to the rise in the divorce rate within Korea, the number of lone parent families is expected to increase in the years to come.

Policies for lone parent families in Korea consist of social insurance and public assistance. Social insurance includes a pension, and public assistance consists of the Basic Guarantee, Veteran Protection, and low-income lone parent family protection. Although there are some policy provisions in place for middle/upper income lone parent families, most social policies are directed toward low-income families. Currently, the number of low-income lone parent families covered by government protection measures is 68815, most of whom are families without a father (81.6%, in 1999) (MOHW, 1999b).

Lone parent families living below the poverty line are eligible for the Basic Guarantee and medical assistance. Low-income lone parent families living above the poverty line are protected under the Fatherless Family Act (enacted in 1989). Not only fatherless families, but also motherless families are covered by the Act. Benefits include a child allowance, education fees for junior high and high school, loans, job training, housing, and medical fees. To ease the financial burden of lone families, the government has provided for the reimbursement of educational fees (tuition and entrance fees) for 14989 students, and has provided child allowances (525 won per day) to 6202 children under 6 years of age. (MOHW, 1999b). Lone parent families are also eligible to get welfare loans from the government. The amount is 12 million won for 5 years, with a low-income interest rate of 8.75 percent (MOHW, 1999b). They are also entitled to rent dwelling units (for example, an apartment), as long as they want. As of 1999, a total of 742 families were living in permanent rental apartments (MOHW, 1999b).

Additionally, lone parents can receive job training, when they are unemployed (MOHW, 2000b). While they are receiving job training, living expenses are provided for them. Another service that a lone parent family can receive is counseling. Whenever lone parents have problems associated with work, family, or children,

TABLE VI

Social Security Expenditure as a Percentage of GDP (1990–1998)

Year	Rate
1990	4.52
1991	4.28
1992	4.63
1993	4.71
1995	5.23
1996	5.47
1997	6.65
1998	11.09

Source: Korea Institute for Health and Social Affairs, Health and Welfare Indicators in Korea, 2000, pp. 436–37.
Note: This is based on OECD Estimation of Social Security Expenditures.

they can visit counseling offices with no charge for the service. Professional counselors not only counsel them, but also provide them with information on child-rearing methods, and link them to community resource persons and organizations.

V. WELFARE EXPENDITURES

Until the recent economic crisis, social welfare benefits in Korea were low, as compared to the other OECD countries. As shown in Table VI, in 1990, a total of 8 trillion won, or only 4.52 percent of the GDP, was spent for social security, according to the OECD estimate of social security expenditures on social insurance, public assistance, and social services (expenditures from the voluntary sector are excluded) (KIHASA, 2000b). Social security expenditures, as a percentage of the GDP, was increased in 1997 to 6.65 percent (30 trillion won) (Choi and Ko, 2000). In 1998, right after the financial crisis, social security expenditures under went a drastic increase to 11.09 percent of the GDP (KIHASA, 2000). The continuous increases in social expenditures came from growth in the budgets devoted to social assistance and unemployment insurance (Choi and Ko, 2000).

Current social security expenditures for Korea, in comparison to the other OECD countries, have still not reached an adequate level. Korea's social security expenditures in 1995 were the second lowest (5.23%) among the OECD countries, followed by Mexico (3.67%). Even for some of the OECD countries like Japan and the United States, where the social security expenditures as a percentage of GDP is comparatively lower than other developed countries, the ratio of the social security budget to the GDP was over 14 percent, almost three times as high as Korea (Choi and Ko, 2000).

Expenditures on health, which includes expenditures for health insurance and medical assistance, constituted the largest share (37.0%) of total social security expenditures, followed by unemployment (34.9%), pensions (18.0%), work injuries (3.7%), social services (3.7%), and public assistance (2.7%) (Choi and Ko, 2000). Korea's social expenditures, in comparison with some of the OECD countries, were lower in every social security category with the exception of work injuries. In the near future, however, expenditures on health and pensions are projected to reach the level of the developed countries (Choi and Ko, 2000).

Social security expenditures in Korea will inevitably rise due to the ever-accelerating process of population aging, and the increasing demand for social welfare. The underprivileged and the elderly will call for more protection from the government as the country's economy grows. The elderly and children are bearing the brunt of the changing social mores that weaken the sense of familial responsibility. One of these has been the fact that women are increasingly entering the labor force. This has led to further dissolution of the family and an increase in the number of divorces. All of these factors will make welfare for children, the elderly and family a more important social issue in the years to come.

Meeting the increasing demand for social welfare would require the Korean government to raise social security expenditures over time in a prudent manner. Social welfare areas that are in need of urgent expansion include public assistance and healthcare, areas whose budget allotments are strikingly insufficient when compared to the other OECD countries. Choi and Ko (2000) claim that the proper ratio of gross expenditures on social security to the GDP should be 15 percent. To achieve this level would require the Korean government to reserve welfare funds by drawing on the financial resources of both the public and voluntary sectors (Choi and Ko, 2000).

VI. FUTURE CHALLENGES TO THE KOREAN WELFARE SYSTEM

Korea has undergone a bewildering array of social changes – the aging of the population, the 1997 economic crisis with its adverse impacts, and the high expectation of unification between the two Koreas. All of this has called attention to the necessity of strengthening social security and the country's social safety net.

Due to the rapid aging of its population, Korean society will have to meet the welfare and health needs of the elderly, because they are the ones who suffer most from poor health and financial difficulties. Over 90 percent of the elderly in Korea suffer from chronic disease, and their financial situation is much worse than that of the younger generation (Chung et al., 1998). As a result of the diminishing role of the family as an informal elderly care mechanism, along with the increasing participation of women in the labor force, the buck of protecting the elderly has been passed on to society as a whole.

The economic crisis occasioned an unemployment rate that is still lower than the OECD average, but much higher than the pre-crisis level. Before the crisis, Korea was approaching full employment with an unemployment rate of 2.0 percent. Now, as a result of trace instances of unemployment in many of the developed countries, Korea is likely to face yet higher unemployment rate with its advancing economy. Thus, social protection for the unemployed will become an increasingly important issues, and Korea will need to establish a social safety net with broad coverage to protect them in the aftermath of the crisis.

Also, Korea should be prepared for raising the living standard of people in North Korea before taking further steps towards unification, because the poverty level in North Korea is very high, and its GNP is much lower than that of South Korea. In the event of unification, Korea would require a welfare system buttressed by increased expenditures, and an appropriate combination of social safety measures to protect all the needy people in North Korea.

In addition, welfare expenditures need to be increased, and public sector participation in financing welfare funds needs to be strengthened. The current contribution rate for the private sector in Korea is much higher than that for the other OECD countries (the United Kingdom: 1.0%; the United States: 3.0%; Germany: 4.6%; and Sweden: 4.5% as of 1993), constituting 26.5 percent in 1996 (Ademan and Einerhand, 1998; KIHASA, 1998). Meanwhile, the private sector should continue to be involved in strengthening the social welfare system through volunteer activities and donations. In sum, in the midst of globalization and torrential social changes, the Korean welfare system should adopt new strategies to increase budget allocations to enhance programs, benefit levels, and coverage.

NOTES

[1] In developed countries the coverage of the social safety net is much higher. In Canada 112 percent of the absolute poor are covered by social assistance; in Finland 112 percent; in France 98 percent; in New Zealand 92 percent; in Germany 89 percent; and in Australia 82 percent.

[2] In Korea, the disabled are categorized into several classes according to the degree of their handicap. The lower the number of classes, the more serious is their handicap.

[3] The disabled should register to get covered by various policies. However, the registration rate was only 62.6 percent in 2000 (Byun et al., 2001).

[4] In the Koran medical system, if one is sick, he/she needs to first go to a primary medical service provider or clinic; then a secondary one, a medium size hospital, to a tertiary one, a large hospital.

REFERENCES

Ademan, W. and M. Einerhand: 1998, 'The growing role of private social benefits', Lobour Market and Social Policy: Occasional Papers, No. 32.

Byun, Young-Chan, D. Suh, S. Lee, S. Kim, J. Hwang, S. Kwon and H. Kye: 2000, A 2000 Survey on the Disabled (KIHASA, 2001).

Change, In-Hyup, H. Lee and J. Oh: 1999, Social Welfare (Seoul National University, Seoul).

Choi, Eunyoung, J. Kim and W. Lee: 1998, Health Care System in Korea (Korea Institute for Health and Social Affairs, Seoul).

Choi, Byug-Ho and K. Ko: 2000, 'Social security expenditure in korea and ways to improve its level', Health and Welfare Policy Forum 49, pp. 48–58.

Chung, Kyung-Hee, Y. Cho, Y. Oh, J. Byun, Y. Byun and H. Moon: 1998, A National Survey on the Elderly Life and Their Welfare Need (KIHASA).

Chung, Kyung-Hee (ed.): 1999, Living Profiles of Older Persons and Social Policies on Aging in Korea (KIHASA).

Editing Committee of White Paper on Welfare Reform: 1998a, Welfare Reform in Korea Toward the 21st Century: To Enhance the Quality of Life in the Globalization Era (Ministry of Health and Welfare, Seoul).

Editing Committee of White Paper on Welfare Reform: 1998b, National Welfare: Opening a New Horizon (Ministry of Health and Welfare, Seoul).

In, Kyung-Suk, 1998: The Korea Welfare State: Ideals and Realities (Nanam Publishing Corp., Seoul).

Korea Institute for Health and Social Affairs: 2000, Health and Welfare Indicators in Korea.

Kim, Mee-Gon: 2001, 'Basic livelihood guarantee system as a social safety nets', Presented at the Workshop on Securing Social Safety Nets (KIHASA, Seoul).

Kim, Meesook, M. Park, S. lee, S. Hong, B. Cho and Y. Won: 2000, The Life of Low Class Lone Parent Family and Policy Issues (KIHASA, Seoul).

Korea Welfare Committee for the Disabled: 1999, Method of Expanding the Range of the Disabled and Classifying the Disabled Level.

Kwon, Sun-Jin: 1998 'Welfare for the disabled', in Chang-Young Park (eds.), Establishing Long-term Social Welfare Plan and Policy Issues (KIHASA Seoul).

Lee, In-Jae: 1998, 'Evaluation on social welfare policies and tasks', in Korea Social Science Research Council (eds.), Reality of Social Welfare In Korea and Policy Issues (Human and Welfare Publish, Seoul).

Lee, Ka-Ok (eds.): 1999, Current Welfare for the Elderly and Tasks (Nanam Publisher, Seoul).

Ministry of Health and Welfare: 1999a, A Survey on Lone Parent Family (Unpublished Paper).

Ministry of Health and Welfare and KIHASA: 1999b, Estimation of Korean Social Security Expenditures: 1990–1997.

Ministry of Health and Welfare: 1997, Guide to Welfare for the Disabled Ministry of Health and Welfare: 1999a, Annual Report on Welfare Facilities for the Elderly.

Ministry of Health and Welfare: 1990b, Survey on Low Income Lone Parent Family.

Ministry of Health and Welfare: 2000a, Guide to Welfare for the Disabled.

Ministry of Health and Welfare: 2000b, White Paper on Health and Welfare.

Ministry of Health and Welfare: 2000c, Annual Report on Welfare Facilities.

Ministry of Health and Welfare: 2001, White Paper on Health and Welfare.

Ministry of Labor: 2001, White Paper on Labor.

National Statistical Office: 1996, The Future Estimated Population.
National Statistical Office: 1996, Population and Housing Census, 1995 (National Statistical Office, Daejun).
OECD: 1999, Social Expenditure Database, 1980–1996.
Park, Chang-Young and M. Kim: 1998, Current Poverty Issues and Counter Policies in Korea (KIHASA and UNDP, Seoul).
Shin Dong-Myeon: 2000, 'The Recent Development of Welfare System in Korea: Transition to a Welfare State from a Welfare Society?' Social Security Research 16, pp. 187–209.
Suk, Jae-Eun and T. Kim: 2000, Analysis of Income Sources and Income Maintenance Schemes for the Elderly in Korea (KIHASA, Seoul).
Yoon, Suk-Myung, 1998: 'National Pension' Goal Set-up for Social Security Development and Current Issues (Korea Institute for Health and Social Affairs, Seoul).

Korea Institute for Health and Social Affairs
E-mail: Mskim@kihasa.re.kr

CHONG-MIN PARK

QUALITY OF LOCAL GOVERNMENT AND DEMOCRATIC CITIZENSHIP

ABSTRACT. This paper attempts to describe the quality of local government and democratic citizenship in Korea through an analysis of political and social attitudes as well as the behavior of local residents in five selected cities. The analysis, which is based on an interview survey, reveals that there is broad support for local self-governance. Nonetheless, public perceptions of the efficiency and autonomy of local government are largely negative in nature. Popular involvement in local politics and voluntary associations is low, and a sense of citizen empowerment is lacking. Overall, the quality of local government and democratic citizenship in Korea is found to remain far short of democratic ideals. These findings, of the undergrowth of civic culture and social capital, indicate that grassroots democracy in Korea is still at the electoral stage, and not yet fully consolidated.

1. INTRODUCTION

South Korea is now widely known as one of the third-wave democracies. The transition from authoritarian rule to democracy has ultimately changed the character, not only of national politics, but local politics as well. In 1995, for the first time in the last 35 years, Koreans had an opportunity to elect their mayors and governors. This historic event signified the beginning of an era of local self-governance in Korea. Electoral democracy at the local level was finally institutionalized in 1998, when Koreans once again freely made meaningful choices as to whom would govern their communities.

It is widely held that the introduction of free elections is indispensable for developing democracy. According to a minimalist definition, democracy is a political system in which governmental accountability is secured through free elections with universal suffrage (Schumpeter, 1952). Therefore, much of the political transition literature tends to emphasize free elections as the essence of democracy. However, it is also pointed out that the introduction

Social Indicators Research **62, 63:** 291–319, 2003.

of free elections does not necessarily bring about a high-quality democracy, and that they are not sufficient in themselves for democratic consolidation to occur (Linz and Stepan, 1996; Rose and Shin, 2001). It is convincingly argued that the growth of democratic culture as well as the development of democratic institutions are both necessary for deepening democracy. Consequently, the recent comparative study of democratic consolidation has intensively and extensively focused on popular beliefs, attitudes and values about democratic governance (Diamond, 1999; Huntington, 1991; Norris, 1999).

Following this line of reasoning, this paper attempts to examine the nature of mass political orientations in Korea, on the basis of the assumption that active democratic citizenship is required for high-quality local democracy. It is postulated that deepening local democracy requires an alert and active citizen body, and that without a participatory citizenry, local government will not be accountable, responsive and representative. That is to say, developing local democracy needs the growth of democratic citizenship consistent with democratic institutions and practices.

With this point in mind, we will explore the degree to which local democracy has been consolidated in Korean localities, where grassroots democratic experiments have been going on since 1995. Using a personal interview survey, we will attempt to describe mass local political life through an analysis of political and social attitudes and behavior of local residents. By doing so, we hope to assess the quality of local government and democratic citizenship in local politics in Korea.

2. LOCAL DEMOCRACY AND DEMOCRATIC CITIZENSHIP

Local democracy requires that local government officials are popularly elected, accountable, responsive, and representative. Hence, it is not unreasonable to say that the election of mayors and governors in 1995 signified the first step toward the establishment of democracy at the local level. The degree of democracy present at the local level can be determined by the extent to which a system of collective decision-making is subject to popular control by all local residents considered as coequals. Therefore, popular control and political equality can be regarded as the key basic components of democracy. It should be noted that the electoral process is whole and complete only if popular control and political equality are effectively secured.

The principles of popular control and political equality are closely linked to four criteria, namely, popular authorization, accountability, responsiveness, and representativeness of government (Beetham, 1996). The criterion of popular authorization requires that key governmental decision-makers are chosen through elections with universal suffrage. The criterion of popular accountability requires that elected decision-makers are held accountable to the people for their policies and actions. The criterion of responsiveness requires that governments take note of the full range of public opinion in making and implementing policy decisions. Finally, the criterion of representativeness requires that all sections of society are guaranteed an equal chance to have their voices heard. In brief, local democracy requires that local governments are popularly authorized, accountable, responsive, and representative through a set of institutions and processes including free elections. It should be stressed, however, that for local democracy to be developed beyond the stage of electoral democracy, a fully participating citizen body is a sine qua non.

There are two influential works on the development of democratic citizenship for effective democratic governance. First, Gabriel Almond and Sidney Verba's study, *The Civic Culture* (1963), attempts to explain differences in democratic governance in the United States, Great Britain, Italy, Mexico, and Germany by examining democratic citizenship within a "civic culture." Based on cognitive, affective, and evaluative orientations toward the political system in general, its input and output aspects, and the self as political actor, they identify three types of political culture: parochial, subject, and participant. Although the civic culture is a mixed political culture, it is an allegiant participant culture, in which the members of the participant polity tend to be explicitly oriented to the system as a whole, and to both the input and output aspects of the political system. Furthermore, they tend to be oriented toward an "activist" role of the self in the polity. Almond and Verba also emphasize social relations, organizational membership and socialization as sources of democratic citizenship. They argue that the propensity of civic cooperation is rooted in social attitudes, such as having faith in people, which is directly related to the development of voluntary associations that infuse their members with habits of cooperation (Tocqueville, 1969). Hence, voluntary associations are viewed as playing a major role in developing democratic citizenship.

Second, Robert Putnam's study, *Making Democracy Work* (1993), specifically suggests socio-cultural sources of democratic citizenship. He employs the concept of social capital to explain effective democratic governance in Italy. He finds that similar democratic institutions work very differently in different regions of Italy. Regions with a dense network of secondary associations have more effective democratic governance. He uses social capital to refer to "features of social organization, such as trust, norms and networks, which can improve the efficiency of society" by facilitating coordinated action. Social trust is seen as an essential component of social capital because it facilitates civic cooperation. The greater the level of trust within a community, the greater the likelihood of cooperation. He points out that social trust can arise from two sources: norms of reciprocity and networks of civic engagement. Civic associations as social structures of cooperation internally instill in their members' habits of cooperation, solidarity, and public-spiritedness. A dense network of civic associations also enhances the effectiveness of interest articulation and interest aggregation. Thus, he argues, the formation of social capital is conducive to the development of democratic citizenship, which is essential for effective and stable democratic governance.

Both the civic culture and the social capital perspectives may be seen as independent of each other. However, since social capital can be viewed as a precondition of the civic culture, both perspectives may well be regarded as complementary, rather than competitive in explaining sources of democratic citizenship for democratic governance. In line with this reasoning, we will examine popular beliefs, attitudes, and values for local democratic governance suggested by the civic culture and the social capital perspectives. By doing so, we hope to assess the quality of local government and democratic citizenship in Korea.

3. METHODOLOGY

Let us briefly note the main method of data collection for this study. The data were collected during the summer of 1999. It was a survey of 1482 adults, age 20 and over, who were personally interviewed. The interviews were administrated to a sample of individuals residing in five selected ordinary cities – Seongnam, Bucheon, Pyeongtaek, Cheongju and Jinju. The cities that were chosen were by no means representative of all the Korean cities. In light of this, a probability sample of the residents of each city was drawn so as to achieve representativeness within each individual city.

The sample for each city was selected through a multistage stratified cluster sampling method. On the basis of economic and social characteristics, the primary sampling units for each city, Dongs, the lower-level administrative units, were stratified. Then, an average of 15 Dongs was randomly selected from each city. From each selected Dongs, one Tong or Ri, the lowest administrative unit, was selected. Then from each selected Tong or Ri, two Bans or villages were selected. From each selected Ban or village, an average of ten households was randomly selected. In each household the interviewers listed all members 20 years of age and over, and from among them selected the one whose birthday came first. The interview was conducted under the supervision of the Survey Research Center of the Institute of Governmental Studies at Korea University. A total of 1,482 interviews was completed – 350 from Seongnam, 349 from Bucheon, 242 from Pyeongtaek, 291 from Cheongju, and 250 from Jinju.

4. THE QUALITY OF LOCAL GOVERNMENT

Support for Local Self-governance

As noted above, popular authorization of local government is a minimum condition for local democracy. In fact, such a condition for local democracy came into being in Korea in 1995, when mayors and governors were popularly elected through local elections. Prior to the first elections, the head of the local or regional government was appointed by the central government in Seoul. Local administration directed by the central government was finally replaced by local self-government through popular elections. Currently mayors, the heads of local governments, are chosen in partisan elections, while councilmen, the members of local councils, are chosen in non-partisan elections.[1] How supportive are Koreans of local self-governance?

First, commitment to local self-governance appears to be widespread. As we see in Table I, less than 5 percent of the respondents were supportive of the previous local administrative system in which mayors were appointed by the central government. In contrast, almost nine in ten of those sampled were supportive of a system in which mayors are chosen indirectly by local councils. A widespread commitment to a popularly elected mayor system suggests that the belief in the legitimacy of electoral local democracy is widely held.

Second, despite broad support for local self-governance, there is widespread opposition to its politicization. As we see in Table I, a majority of Koreans are opposed to an election system in which mayoral candidates run under the banner of their political parties. Only one in five is supportive of such an election system. In all the Korean cities surveyed, the proportion of those opposing party involvement is three to four times as high as that of those supporting it. This finding manifests not only popular cynicism toward party politics at the local level, but also apparent discontent with the current mayoral election system.

Third, the endorsement of the de-politicization of local self-governance can also be found in broad opposition to party involvement in the nomination of council candidates. As we see in Table I, nearly 60 percent are opposed to an election system in which council candidates run in the names of their political parties. Less than 20 percent are supportive of such an election system. In all the cities we examined, the proportion of those opposing party involvement is three to four times as high as that of those supporting it. This finding may be seen as support for the current non-partisan local council elections. It could be interpreted, however, somewhat differently. Although party involvement in local council elections is officially prohibited, informal party nomination of council candidates is a prevailing practice. This finding could be viewed, therefore,

TABLE I

Support for Local Self-governance

	Seongnam	Bucheon	Pyeongtaek	Cheongju	Jinju	Total
1. Which is a better method to choose mayors?						
Popular voting	84.8%	85.9%	88.8%	83.4%	88.0%	86.0%
Election by local council	1.7	4.3	2.9	2.8	1.2	2.6
Appointment by central government	4.9	5.7	2.5	4.8	2.0	4.2
Don't know	8.6	4.0	5.8	9.0	8.8	7.2
(N)	(349)	(348)	(242)	(291)	(246)	(1477)
2. Which is better – to allow for political parties to nominate mayor candidates or not to allow it?						
To allow	20.6	21.6	16.5	20.6	13.8	19.0
Not to allow	56.0	61.5	60.7	56.4	45.5	56.4
Don't know	23.4	17.0	22.7	23.0	40.7	24.6
(N)	(350)	(348)	(242)	(291)	(246)	(1477)
3. Which is better – to allow for political parties to nominate council candidates or not to allow it?						
To allow	18.6	19.2	14.1	16.8	12.1	16.6
Not to allow	55.7	62.8	63.1	59.8	44.9	57.6
Don't know	25.7	18.1	22.8	23.4	42.9	25.8
(N)	(350)	(349)	(241)	(291)	(247)	(1478)
4. Are local councils necessary, don't they make any difference or would it be better without them?						
Necessary	39.8	44.7	38.9	42.4	39.1	41.2
Don't make any difference	32.7	31.2	34.7	36.6	27.4	32.5
Would be better without them	17.2	12.6	11.6	10.3	13.7	13.3
Don't know	10.3	11.5	14.9	10.7	19.8	13.0
(N)	(349)	(349)	(242)	(290)	(248)	(1478)

as evidence of broad dissatisfaction with such a practice More evidently, it exhibits popular support for the continuing de-politicization of local self-governance.[2]

Fourth, a plurality of Koreans appears to be supportive of the existence of councils as governing institutions at the local level. As we see in Table I, 41 percent believe that local councils are necessary for local self-governance. Only 13 percent believe that it would be better without them. In the cities surveyed, the proportion of those accepting local councils is almost three times as high as that of those rejecting them. It should be noted, however, that one in three of those surveyed believes that local councils make no difference. This finding evidently shows that many Koreans do not regard local council as the essence of local democracy. It should not be accepted, however, as evidence against local self-governance. Rather it may be viewed as popular dissatisfaction with the performance of current local councils.

In short, the broad picture presented thus far shows that Koreans appear to have somewhat ambivalent attitudes toward their local governments. They seem to have little confidence in their local councils as major governing institutions. Yet, they are overwhelmingly in favor of the current popularly elected mayoral government. They are opposed, moreover, to any partisan local elections. All of these findings suggest that Koreans are supportive of a de-politicized local government headed by a popularly elected mayor.

Perceived Performance of Local Government

As Almond and Verba (1963) argue, cognitive and affective aspects of government output are important components of democratic citizenship. When affect is lacking and cognition is vague, the motivation to get involved in politics tends to be weak. Therefore, if citizens are not aware of, and do not evaluate favorably the impact of local government, they are less likely to be involved in local self-governance.

To what extent do Koreans perceive local government as having an impact on their daily lives? As we see in Table II, the impact of local government is not widely acknowledged. Only 8 percent see their local governments as having much impact on their daily lives. Nearly 40 percent attribute little or no effect to their local

TABLE II

Perception of the Impact of Local Government

	Seongnam	Bucheon	Pyeongtaek	Cheongju	Jinju	Total
1. How much impact do the activities of local government have on your daily lives?						
Much	7.7%	9.8%	7.0%	7.6%	7.6%	8.0%
Some	36.7	28.7	36.8	36.8	36.4	34.8
Little + None	46.1	48.3	41.3	45.4	37.0	44.1
Don't know	9.5	13.2	14.9	10.3	19.2	13.0
(N)	(349)	(348)	(242)	(291)	(250)	(1480)
2. Do the activities of local government improve or deteriorate local conditions?						
Improve	17.4	29.0	18.7	23.4	12.9	20.8
Neither improve nor deteriorate	56.9	50.3	49.4	46.7	56.2	52.0
Deteriorate	6.6	5.7	11.2	12.7	12.0	9.3
Don't know	19.1	14.9	20.7	17.2	18.9	18.0
(N)	(350)	(348)	(241)	(291)	(249)	(1479)

governments. This finding shows that large majorities of the cities' inhabitants examined here are not cognitively oriented to local government action.

Whether or not the impact of local government is perceived as favorable is likely to influence support for local self-governance. As we see in Table II, popular evaluation of the impact of local government is somewhat favorable. When asked whether "the activities of local government improve or deteriorate local conditions," 21 percent chose the former, while 9 percent the latter. We obtained more positive than negative responses in the cities surveyed here. The fact, however, that slightly more than half of the respondents said that local government makes no difference shows that there is considerable skepticism about the efficacy of local self-governance.

The findings presented thus far show that a plurality of Koreans are not aware of, and do not evaluate favorably, policy outputs of their local governments. These local residents are "isolated" or

TABLE III

Evaluation of Local Government's Efficiency and Autonomy

	Seongnam	Bucheon	Pyeongtaek	Cheongju	Jinju	Total
1. The central government is more efficient than local governments in providing public services.						
Agree	36.3%	33.2%	34.3%	42.8%	29.4%	35.4%
NA/NDA	10.7	10.7	13.2	12.1	15.1	12.1
Disagree	36.0	38.5	36.0	23.1	26.9	32.6
Don't know	17.0	17.6	16.5	22.1	28.6	20.0
(N)	(347)	(346)	(242)	(290)	(245)	(1470)
2. Local governments pay too much attention to the central government's intention and just follow its order.						
Agree	60.7	67.2	52.7	74.6	56.9	63.0
NA/NDA	15.7	12.1	14.5	9.6	9.8	12.4
Disagree	9.7	6.1	10.0	6.9	6.5	7.5
Don't know	15.0	14.7	22.8	8.9	26.8	17.0
(N)	(346)	(347)	(241)	(291)	(246)	(1471)

NA/NDA: Neither agree nor disagree.

"alientated" in the output sense. If so, it is hard to expect them to possess participatory orietnations toward local self-governance.

The advocates for local self-governance tend to justify their views for three reasons (Stoker, 1996). First, local government provides an opportunity for participation in politics. Second, it helps to ensure efficient delivery of public services. Third, it expresses a tradition of opposition to an over-centralized government. These advocates regard local government as a relatively autonomous, multiple-purpose institution providing public services. Table III specifically shows how Koreans evaluate their local governments in terms of the efficiency of service delivery and their autonomy from the central government.

First, the perception of local government's efficiency in delivering public services is apparently split: 35 percent agree that "the central government is more efficient than local governments in providing public services," while 33 percent do not agree. Similar response patterns are found in all the cities surveyed with one exception. This finding suggests that the advocacy of local self-governance, on the basis of its efficient delivery of services, is not a cogent argument for many Koreans.

Second, the perception of local government's autonomy from the central government is highly negative. Two in three agree that "local governments pay too much attention to the central government's intention and just follow its order," whereas fewer than one in ten disagrees. Similar response patterns are found among those surveyed within the cities. This finding is evidence of the fact that Korean local governments are perceived as being submissive to the central government. It suggests that a vast majority of Koreans see their local government as being more responsive to the central government than their communities, despite the fact that they are popularly elected.

Local self-governance in Korea appears to be judged unfavorably in terms of the efficient delivery of services and opposition to a centralized government. In particular, the finding that local governments are perceived as more subservient to the central government demonstrates that the current local government system is not truly self-governance. Nevertheless, the findings should not be accepted as evidence for the lack of a broad commitment to local self-governance. As indicated earlier, since an overwhelming majority of Koreans are supportive of a popularly elected local government rather than a centrally appointed local administration, it could be said that the legitimacy of local self-governance is widely upheld. These findings only suggest that local government in Korea is still far short of the ideal of efficiency or autonomy. Therefore, it is fair to say that many Koreans currently have some doubts about the efficacy of current local self-governance.

As we see in Table IV, any evaluation of local bureaucratic output turns out to be mixed. We asked respondents a hypothetical question: "How do you think you would be treated if you visited a city government office seeking an answer to a tax question or a construction permit?" Almost 30 percent said they would expect equal treatment, while 20 percent said unequal treatment. Although the proportion of those expecting equal treatment is almost 10 percent higher than that of those expecting unequal treatment, nonetheless, it should be noted that two in five said that it would depend on the situ-

TABLE IV

Assessment of Local Bureaucratic Output

	Seongnam	Bucheon	Pyeongtaek	Cheongju	Jinju	Total
1. How do you think you would be treated if you visit a city government office for some question?						
Equal treatment	30.9%	25.8%	26.0%	30.2%	34.1%	29.3%
Unequal treatment	28.0	20.6	19.0	12.7	17.7	20.1
Depending on situation	36.0	42.7	40.5	48.1	34.5	40.4
Don't know	5.1	10.9	14.5	8.9	13.7	10.2
(N)	(350)	(349)	(242)	(291)	(249)	(1481)
2. What do you think city bureaucrats would do if you tell them about your point of view?						
Give it serious consideration	11.1	16.0	19.0	11.7	28.1	16.6
Give it a little consideration	44.9	45.8	32.6	49.7	33.7	42.2
Ignore it	35.1	28.7	34.7	28.3	26.1	30.7
Don't know	8.9	9.5	13.6	10.3	12.0	10.6
(N)	(350)	(349)	(242)	(290)	(249)	(1480)

ation. This finding suggests that a plurality of Koreans perceive local bureaucratic behavior as less predictable or more particularistic.

Second, we asked respondents another hypothetical question: "What do you think bureaucrats would do if you visited a city government office to tell them about your point of view on some matter?" Only 17 percent said that the bureaucrat would give it serious consideration, while 31 percent said they would ignore it. Negative assessments of local bureaucratic responsiveness were found in all of the examined cities except one. Since local democracy is supposed to increase responsiveness of administrative bureaucracy by institutionalizing popular control of local government, positive evaluation of local bureaucratic output is expected to increase correspondingly. Contrary to such an expectation, however, Koreans do not feel favorably toward local bureaucratic output. This finding suggests that Koreans are also "alienated" from the administrative output process.

The larger picture presented thus far shows that a majority of Koreans are not cognitively and affectively oriented toward the output side of local self-governance. They are less confident in the capacity of local government to deliver services efficiently, and to express the opposition to over-centralized government. The overall negative assessment of the performance of local government may in time erode the current commitment to grassroots democracy.

Trust in Local Government

Despite some debate over the meaning of trust in government measures, it is likely that prolonged political distrust may undermine the belief in the legitimacy of a political system (Citrin, 1974; Easton, 1975; Miller, 1974). Likewise, local political cynicism or distrust may erode popular commitment to a grassroots democracy, and this in turn may lead to the rejection of local self-governance itself. Table V reports the extent to which Koreans trust their local governments.[3] First, the perception of the trustworthiness of local government appears to be negative in nature. When asked "how much of the time do you think your local government does what is right?" only 12 percent said "most of the time," while 29 percent, said "rarely." As PDI (Percentage Difference Index)[4] values indicate, the proportion of those distrusting their local government is higher than that of those trusting them in all the cities surveyed here.

Second, the perception of the fairness of local government is largely negative in nature. When asked whether "your local government is run for a few big interests or for the benefits of most of the people," 45 percent chose "a few big interests," while 37 percent chose "the benefit of most of the people." As PDI values indicate, the proportion of those perceiving their local government as unfair is slightly higher than that of those perceiving their local government as fair in three of the cities surveyed. Contrary to a general expectation that local self-governance would increase popular control

TABLE V
Trust in Local Government

	Seongnam	Bucheon	Pyeongtaek	Cheongju	Jinju	Total
1. How much of the time do you trust local government to do what is right?						
Most of the time (A)	8.0%	13.2%	13.2%	7.2%	17.4%	11.5%
Sometimes	50.3	43.3	36.0	48.5	42.9	44.7
Rarely (B)	31.4	28.1	32.6	29.2	21.1	28.7
Don't know	10.3	15.5	18.2	15.1	18.6	15.1
PDI (B-A)	–23.4	–14.9	–19.4	–22.0	–3.7	–17.2
(N)	(350)	(349)	(242)	(291)	(247)	(1479)
2. Is local government run for a few big interests or for the benefit of most of the people?						
Most of the people (A)	49.9	45.4	33.6	56.6	35.6	45.1
A few (B)	36.7	35.9	48.1	25.9	42.5	37.2
Don't know	13.5	18.7	18.3	17.6	21.9	17.7
PDI (B-A)	–13.2	–9.5	14.5	–30.7	6.9	–7.9
(N)	(349)	(348)	(241)	(290)	(247)	(1475)
3. How much money we pay in taxes does local government waste?						
Not very much (A)	1.4	3.2	5.0	3.4	2.4	3.0
Some	39.4	41.5	38.0	41.2	39.8	40.1
A lot (B)	47.1	39.8	32.2	44.0	34.9	40.3
Don't' know	12.0	15.5	24.8	11.3	22.9	16.6
PDI (B-A)	–45.7	–36.6	–27.2	–40.9	–32.5	–37.3
(N)	(350)	(349)	(242)	(291)	(249)	(1481)
4. How many people in local government are corrupt?						
Hardly any (A)	1.1	3.2	4.5	2.8	5.2	3.0
Some	56.7	57.8	54.5	61.0	50.6	56.4
Many (B)	32.1	29.6	21.9	23.4	20.5	26.2
Don't know	10.0	10.3	19.0	12.8	23.7	14.4
PDI (B-A)	–31.0	–26.4	–17.4	–20.6	–15.3	–23.2
(N)	(349)	(348)	(242)	(290)	(249)	(1478)

TABLE V

Continued

	Seongnam	Bucheon	Pyeongtaek	Cheongju	Jinju	Total
5. How many people in local government know what they are doing?						
Many (A)	41.7	35.5	29.5	37.8	38.9	37.0
Some (B)	38.6	39.0	39.0	38.5	28.3	37.0
Don't know	19.7	25.6	31.5	23.6	32.8	26.0
PDI (B-A)	3.1	−3.5	−9.5	−0.7	10.6	0.0
(N)	(350)	(344)	(241)	(288)	(244)	(1467)

of local government, a plurality of citizens appear to consider their local governments as unfair in representing their interests in policy-making.

Third, the perception of the wastefulness of local government is overwhelmingly negative in nature. When asked whether "your local government wastes a lot of money that we pay in taxes, or wastes some of it, or doesn't waste very much of it," 40 percent chose "a lot," while only 3 percent chose "not very much." As PDI values indicate, the perception of the efficiency of local government is predominantly unfavorable across all the cities that were surveyed.

Fourth, the perception of the integrity of local government turns out to be negative in character. When asked whether "many people in your local government are corrupt, or not very many are, or hardly any of them are corrupt at all," 26 percent chose "many" while only 3 percent chose "hardly any." As PDI values also indicate, there were more people who saw their local government as corrupt than those who saw them as uncorrupt.

Lastly, the perception of the competence of local government appears to be polarized: 37 percent believe that "most of the people in your local government usually know what they are doing," while 37 percent believe that "some of them don't seem to know what they are doing." There are some slight cross-city differences in the perceived competence of local government.

The findings presented thus far evidently show that Koreans have more or less negative assessments of their local governments in terms of trustworthiness, fairness, efficiency, and integrity.

Although they have ambivalent attitudes toward their local governments' competence, they are particularly critical about their local governments' wastefulness and corruption. On the whole, there is widespread local cynicism or distrust in local government. Even if cynicism may reflect the negative assessment of local incumbents, rather than local self-governance itself, chronic popular cynicism caused by frequent local political scandals and bureaucratic corruption could ultimately undermine the belief in the legitimacy of local self-governance itself. If local democracy in Korea is to be consolidated, then, it will be necessary to improve the rationality and transparency of the local administration.

5. THE QUALITY OF DEMOCRATIC CITIZENSHIP

Political Knowledge

Democratic citizenship is related to having information about political institutions and processes. We may assume that if citizens are informed about politics, they are likely to be politically competent and active in the political process. Our survey contained two types of measures of political knowledge or information. The first type was based on one's ability to recall the names of local and national office holders, such as mayor, governor, National Assemblyman, and councilman. The second type was based on one's ability to comprehend the nature of local elections.

First, 55 percent correctly recalled the names of their mayors while 60 percent, the names of their respective governors. The proportion of those who correctly recalled the names of their National Assemblymen or councilmen was, however, far lower than those figures. For instance, only 15 percent correctly recalled the names of their councilmen, while 33 percent recalled those of their National Assemblymen. The identification of public representatives, whether they are local or national, appears to be poor. Second, only 23 percent correctly answered that party nomination of council candidates is prohibited. Furthermore, less than 50 percent correctly answered that the nomination of a mayoral candidate by a political party is allowed. A plurality of citizens appear to be poorly informed about the current local election system.

TABLE VI

Psychological Involvement in Local Politics

	Seongnam	Bucheon	Pyeongtaek	Cheongju	Jinju	Total
1. Levels of local political knowledge						
Low (0–2)	58.6%	58.0%	47.6%	63.9%	42.3%	54.9%
Medium (3–4)	32.5	33.4	39.6	30.6	44.0	35.4
High (5–6)	9.0	8.6	12.9	5.5	13.7	9.6
(N)	(345)	(348)	(240)	(291)	(248)	(1472)
2. How interested are you in local politics?						
Very much	4.9	8.3	4.5	6.2	7.3	6.3
Some	22.9	25.6	31.4	34.8	29.0	28.3
Little + None	72.3	66.0	64.1	59.0	63.7	65.4
(N)	(350)	(348)	(242)	(290)	(248)	(1478)
3. How often do you talk about local public affairs with neighbors?						
Often	4.0	9.2	5.4	4.1	7.3	6.0
Sometimes	14.3	15.2	19.8	24.1	19.0	18.1
Seldom + Never	81.7	75.6	74.8	71.8	73.6	75.9
(N)	(350)	(349)	(242)	(291)	(247)	(1479)

Table VI reports levels of political knowledge measured by a single composite index based on all of the six questions mentioned above. The cumulative political knowledge index has seven values ranging from 0 to 7. These values are re-coded as low (0–2), middle (3–4), and high (5–7). As we see in the table, 55 percent gave fewer than three correct answers, while only 10 percent gave more than four correct answers. There are some cross-city differences in levels of political information, perhaps because some mayors and governors are in office longer than others. Thus, the former are likely to be more easily identified than the latter.

On balance, ordinary citizens' levels of knowledge about local politics are considerably low. A majority of Koreans do not know who their mayors or councilmen are. They do not know whether party nomination of candidates for local offices is allowed or not. These findings illustrate the lack of popular interest in local governing processes and institutions. Perhaps, since people have little motivation to acquire political information, their understanding about local politics appears to be unclear or ambiguous.

Interest in Local Politics

As Almond and Verba (1963) argue, awareness of politics is a minimal degree of political involvement. Although following governmental and political affairs constitutes minimal involvement, there would be no democratic citizenship without it. It is widely demonstrated that persons, who are less interested in and concerned about political matters, are less likely to be activists. Interest in politics reflects a psychological involvement that determines exposure to political stimuli. It is evident that persons, who are interested in politics, are more likely to follow what is going on in politics, and to participate in the process by which decisions are made. Hence, measures of interest in local politics get at the dimension of attentiveness to local political input.

As we see in Table VI, popular levels of interest in local politics are considerably low. When asked "how interested are you in local politics?" only 6 percent say "very much," whereas 65 percent say "little' or "none." Similar response patterns were observed in all the cities that were surveyed. This finding shows that a majority of citizens prefer to be bystanders, not active participants in local political processes. For them local politics is not a major concern.

The lack of interest in local politics is also found in the pattern of responses to another question, as shown in Table VI. When asked "how often do you talk about local public affairs with your neighbors?" only 6 percent say "often," whereas nearly 76 percent say "seldom" or "never." Only one in four says they discuss local public affairs with their neighbors. It is obvious that the input orientations of a vast majority of Koreans fall far short of the level required by the ideal of democratic citizenship.

In general, since local government is supposed to be more immediate, accessible, and familiar than the central government, people are expected to be more interested in local rather than national politics. Yet, the findings presented above are inconsistent with such an expectation. Perhaps, since local government in Korea is new, it may still be unfamiliar to the minds of local residents. Or, since centralized inter-governmental relations constrain power of local government to such a degree that people may still not be aware of the impact of local government. In these situations, it is hard to assume that local government is more advantageous than a central government in immediacy, accessibility, and familiarity. The lack of interest in local politics shows that people are psychologically distant from their local government. Unless citizens come to recognize that decisions of their local government directly and greatly influence their daily lives, they will tend not to get involved in local politics to influence local public decisions.

Citizen Empowerment

It is widely accepted that political efficacy, defined as the feeling that one is capable of influencing the public decision-making process, has significant behavioral consequences (Barnes and Kaase, 1979; Campbell et al., 1960). It can be demonstrated that people who are politically efficacious, are more interested in politics, more informed about public affairs, and more involved in political activities, than those who are not politically efficacious. The concept of political efficacy has two components, internal and external. The former refers to the image of oneself as politically effective or confident, while the latter is the image that the government is responsive (Abramson, 1983; Lane, 1959).[5] Thus, it can be said that internal efficacy or citizen empowerment is the input side of efficacy, while external efficacy or system responsiveness is the output side. By using two standard items of internal political efficacy, we seek to determine whether ordinary Koreans are politically empowered.

Before presenting the findings, it should be kept in mind that our measures of political efficacy reflect national competence rather than one of local character.[6] It is pointed out that people feel more politically efficacious in relation to local government than to a central government (Almond and Verba, 1963). This is so because of the proximity and general accessibility of local government in comparison to a central government. Such an argument assumes the institutional availability of being able to participate at the local level.[7] Such a line of reasoning, however, may not be applicable to the Korean situation. Since a period of local self-governance in Korea started just a few years ago, local government still remains less proximate and accessible in relation to the central government. Consequently, Koreans may not be expected to be more competent locally than nationally. Although we are not able to determine whether this conjecture is true, we will present the findings with this caveat in mind.

As we see in Table VII, levels of citizen empowerment are relatively low. First, 64 percent agree that "politics and government seem so complicated that a person like me can't really understand what's going on," whereas only 16 percent do not agree. It turns out that a large majority of Koreans feel unable to express their demands effectively in the input process. They seem cognitively impotent, confronted by a complexity of politics and government activities. Second, 72 percent agree that "voting is the only way that people like me can have any say about how the government runs things," whereas only 13 percent do not agree. It turns out that an overwhelming majority of Koreans do not have confidence in the means of input into influencing the decisions of government. These findings suggest that there is a sense of powerlessness among ordinary citizens, when dealing with control within democratic government.

As mentioned above, political efficacy as used here appears to measure national competence rather than one local in nature. Hence, these findings may not be an accurate report on citizen empowerment in relation to local government. However, local competence would not be higher than national competence, because local government still remains more foreign or less familiar than the national government in Korea. If this is the case, we would expect many ordinary citizens to see themselves as locally ineffective or powerless.

It is fair to conclude that a majority of ordinary Koreans are politically cynical or distrustful. A widespread sense of political powerlessness is likely to cause ordinary citizens to remain bystanders in local governing processes. As political democratization at the local level begins to provide opportunities for participation, levels of citizen empowerment in relation to local government would gradually increase. Nonetheless, the findings presented above suggest that the development of local democracy in Korea may not go beyond the stage of electoral democracy unless as empowered citizenry is formed.

TABLE VII

Citizen Empowerment

	Seongnam	Bucheon	Pyeongtaek	Cheongju	Jinju	Total
1. Politics and government seem so complicated that a person like me can't really understand what's going on.						
Agree	54.7%	63.9%	67.3%	76.7%	59.7%	64.1%
NA/NDA	17.8	16.6	11.6	10.3	21.4	15.6
Disagree	25.0	17.2	13.2	10.3	9.7	15.8
Don't know	2.6	2.3	7.9	2.7	9.3	4.5
(N)	(349)	(349)	(242)	(291)	(248)	(1479)
2. Voting is the only way that people like me can have any say about how the government runs things.						
Agree	68.8	75.3	73.5	73.9	65.8	71.6
NA/DNA	7.7	9.2	8.3	9.6	10.1	8.9
Disagree	18.9	13.2	10.8	10.6	11.3	13.4
Don't know	4.6	2.3	7.5	5.6	12.9	6.2
(N)	(349)	(349)	(241)	(291)	(248)	(1478)

NA/NDA: Neither agree nor disagree.

Organizational Membership and Social Trust

The civic voluntarism model of political participation suggests some sources of democratic citizenship (Verba et al., 1995). According to this model, citizens may be inactive because they lack resources, such as time, money and civic skills; because they lack psychological engagement with politics such as interest in politics and political efficacy; or because they are not linked to the networks that mobilize them politically. It is specifically pointed out that social institutions play a major role in stimulating citizens to participate in politics. It is also shown that the institutions with which individuals are associated – families, schools, non-political organizations, and religious institutions – foster political participation. Almond and Verba (1963) and Putnam (1993) similarly contend that organizational membership and civic engagement influence political competence and participation.

How high are ordinary Koreans' levels of social participation? As we see in Table VIII, the extent of membership in voluntary associations is extremely limited. Nearly four in five individuals are not affiliated with any social organization. Less than one in five people give indication of only one affiliation. The proportion of those indicating two or more affiliations is less than 6 percent. Furthermore, the types of organizations with which they are affiliated tend to be alumni associations or trade organizations. No one indicated membership in any civic association related to any of the recent social movements. This finding shows that a vast majority of Koreans are outside the networks of intermediary groups, which could provide them with participatory skills and political opportunities. Overall, Koreans are neither linked to politics through intermediary groups nor socially organized, so that they tend to be politically atomized (Henderson, 1968). Even joining once flourishing mutual loan circles is also quite limited. As we see in Table VIII, more than half of the respondents indicated no affiliation with any such circle or club. Only 30 percent indicated one or two affiliations. It seems that social life in the Korean localities hardly approximates the ideal of a civic community. It is no wonder that the civil society, largely consisting of atomized individuals, is found powerless in relation to the state at the local level (Park, 2000).

It is widely believed that voluntary civic cooperation is facilitated by social capital (Almond and Verba, 1963; Putnam, 1993). And social trust is essential for the formation of social capital. It is claimed that social trust can come from two sources: norms of reciprocity and networks of civic engagement. In this regard, it is pointed out that social trust is associated with dense networks of social exchange. The denser such networks in a community are, the more likely its citizens will cooperate for mutual benefit. Hence, the vitality of associational life in a community can be seen as a key indicator of civic sociability. As presented above, associational life in the Korean localities is hardly vital. Nearly three in four indicated no affiliation with any social organization. No one indicated four or more affiliations. Furthermore, the extent of membership in informal mutual loan circles is also quite limited. A majority of Koreans indicated no membership in rotating credit circles. It is fair to conclude

TABLE VIII

Membership in Organizations and Loan Circles

	Seongnam	Bucheon	Pyeongtaek	Cheongju	Jinju	Total
1. The number of memberships in organizations						
0	78.0%	83.7%	63.2%	79.7%	85.6%	78.5%
1	16.6	12.3	26.4	15.1	10.0	15.8
2	4.0	3.2	6.6	4.1	2.4	4.0
3 or more	1.4	0.9	3.7	1.0	2.0	1.7
(N)	(350)	(349)	(242)	(291)	(250)	(1482)
2. The number of memberships in mutual loan circles						
0	65.7	62.2	67.8	38.1	48.0	56.8
1	16.3	13.2	13.6	16.2	18.0	15.4
2	11.4	13.8	11.6	18.9	18.8	14.7
3	3.7	5.7	5.4	12.4	10.0	7.2
4 or more	2.9	5.2	1.6	14.3	5.2	6.0
(N)	(350)	(349)	(242)	(291)	(250)	(1482)

that membership in voluntary organizations is rare among Koreans. This finding suggests that a vast majority of ordinary Koreans are not effectively linked to the social networks that infuse them with democratic citizenship. Evidently, most Koreans are hardly joiners.

As mentioned above, social trust is essential for the formation of social capital. Social trust makes it easier to form social groups and to facilitate civic cooperation, which ultimately brings about political action. On the other hand, social distrust retards the development of such political capacity. As Banfield (1958) reports, "amoral familism" which reflects the lack of social trust causes the inability of people to act together for their common good. To determine levels of social trust in Korea at the local level, we employed modified "faith in people" measures developed by Rosenberg (1956).

As we see in Table IX, 38 percent agreed that "most people can be trusted," whereas 55 percent disagreed with this. Furthermore, 75 percent agreed that "if you don't watch yourself, people will take advantage of you," whereas only less than 10 percent disagreed. However, 74 percent agreed that "human nature is fundamentally

TABLE IX

Social Trust: Faith in People

	Seongnam	Bucheon	Pyeongtaek	Cheongju	Jinju	Total
1. Most people can be trusted.						
Agree	31.1%	33.6%	49.4%	40.2%	34.2%	37.0%
NA/NDA	30.3	25.9	18.8	23.4	29.8	25.9
Disagree	36.9	37.9	28.8	34.0	29.4	34.0
Don't know	1.7	2.6	2.9	2.4	6.5	3.1
(N)	(347)	(348)	(239)	(291)	(245)	(1470)
2. If you don't watch yourself, people will take advantage of you.						
Agree	71.4	76.0	76.4	75.0	69.4	73.7
NA/NDA	11.8	12.3	12.8	8.9	16.7	12.3
Disagree	16.1	10.0	9.5	15.8	8.6	12.3
Don't know	0.6	1.7	1.2	0.3	5.3	1.7
(N)	(347)	(349)	(242)	(291)	(245)	(1474)
3. Human nature is fundamentally cooperative.						
Agree	69.2	72.5	79.7	70.8	71.5	72.4
NA/NDA	18.7	15.8	12.4	15.5	15.9	15.9
Disagree	10.6	9.4	6.2	12.1	7.7	9.5
Don't know	1.4	2.3	1.7	1.7	4.9	2.3
(N)	(348)	(349)	(242)	(291)	(246)	(1476)
4. No one is going to care much what happens to you.						
Agree	19.2	20.1	16.1	19.6	22.0	19.5
NA/NDA	7.2	8.6	14.5	8.6	14.6	10.2
Disagree	73.1	68.8	66.9	70.4	56.9	67.8
Don't know	0.6	2.6	2.5	1.4	6.5	2.5
(N)	(349)	(349)	(242)	(290)	(246)	(1476)

NA/NDA: Neither agree nor disagree.

cooperative," whereas only less than 10 percent disagreed with this. Moreover, only 20 percent agreed that "no one is going to care much what happens to you," while 63 percent disagreed. Overall, the analysis reveals a mixture of social trust and distrust in the Korean localities. Koreans appear to be overwhelmingly optimistic about human nature. In contrast, their realistic judgement of human behavior seems far less optimistic. Their responses to the desirability of caution in dealing with others reveal that they are far less positive about the safety and responsiveness of the human environment. The lower frequency of expression of social trust may be related to the absence of social participation presented earlier. Both a lack of social participation and a paucity of general social trust attest the undergrowth of democratic citizenship in Korea.

6. CONCLUSION

Local democracy in Korea came about when mayors and governors were elected in 1995. It is fair to say that electoral democracy at the local level was established as local government officials began to be popularly elected. It needs to be noted, however, that the introduction of local elections is a minimum condition for local democracy. The consolidation of local democracy requires the growth of democratic citizenship at the local level. Although popular beliefs, attitudes and values about democratic governance may not determine the transition to democracy, they certainly constrain the functioning of democratic institutions. With this point in mind, we primarily endeavor to portray the mass local political life in Korea through an examination of political and social attitudes and behavior. By doing so, we hope to assess the quality of local government and the prospect of grassroots democracy in Korea.

Overall, our analysis shows that despite considerable differences in their sizes, histories, locations, demographic compositions, and socio-economic conditions, the cities surveyed here appear to share some common features about local governance. First, there is overwhelming support for local self-governance. The belief in the legitimacy of local government, headed by a popularly elected mayor, is widely accepted. Even so, broad opposition to the political party's involvement in local elections displays strong support for the de-politicization of local self-governance. Furthermore, a lack of full support for the necessity of local council shows that any local self-governance system increasing the role of a council may not be widely endorsed.

Second, awareness of the impact of local government appears to be considerably vague. Local government still remains alien to a majority of ordinary Koreans. Moreover, any evaluation of the nature of the impact appears to be equivocal in nature. Many Koreans are not aware of the difference a local government would make. It seems that popular confidence in the usefulness of local government does not remain strong.

Third, perception of the efficiency of local government in delivering public services, and its autonomy from the central government, are largely negative in nature. It suggests that both efficiency and autonomy, which serve as normative criteria often used for justifying local self-governance, may not be appealing to many Koreans. Fourth, perceptions of local government in terms of wastefulness and corruption are particularly negative in nature. The widespread local political cynicism and distrust in local government may undermine popular commitment to grassroots democracy. Moreover, negative assessments of local bureaucratic output suggest that modern public administration, based on the rule of law and impersonal rationality, has not been fully established, despite the apparent increasing popular control of the local bureaucracy.

Fifth, the current level of local political knowledge and interest in local politics indicates low psychological involvement in local politics. A vast majority of Korean seem apathetic to local politics, and only a few appear to be active in local politics. Furthermore, the current level of citizen empowerment reflects potentially low democratic citizenship at the local level. It is no wonder that it is difficult to find an empowered citizenry in relation to local self-governance.

Lastly, the extent of membership in voluntary organizations is exceedingly limited. Even the extent of membership in mutual loan circles, once popular credit sources for the average citizen, is quite narrow. We also learned that social trust and distrust are mixed together. Yet, a large majority of Koreans turn out to be so cautions in dealing with others that they seem less likely to form social and political groups for the common good.

In summary, the current local political life in Korea can be characterized, not by the participant political culture of involvement and activism, but by the parochial or subject political culture of alienation and passivity. Democratic citizenship suitable to local democracy has not been fully developed. The introduction of local elections surely is the first step toward the establishment of democracy at the local level. However, deepening local democracy requires more than the introduction of local elections. Without democratic citizenship, electoral democracy may not effectively ensure the accountability, representativeness, and responsiveness of local government. If the current political life in Korean localities is largely parochial or subject oriented, the quality of local democracy cannot be great. The undergrowth of civic culture and social capital or the absence of democratic citizenship would retard the development of a full-fledged grassroots democracy. Our analysis evidently demonstrates that the present system of local self-governance in Korea is still far short of the ideal of democracy at the local level.

ACKNOWLEDGEMENTS

The author would like to express his appreciation to B. Bae, H. Choi, S. Choi and J. Yoo for their participation in the development and administration of the survey.

NOTES

[1] Local council elections are supposed to be non-partisan. However, the practices of informal party nomination of candidates make them actually less non-partisan.
[2] For the purpose of de-politicizing local governance, 40 percent of local governments in the United States maintain reform mechanisms like non-partisan election, city-manager system, and at-large election (Chandler and Clark, 1995).
[3] Our measures of trust in local government are based on five traditional standard items to measure the trust in government.
[4] The PDI values are computed by subtracting the percentage of the low category from that of the high category. The magnitude of a negative value indicates a preponderance of distrust, while a positive value indicates a higher degree of trust.
[5] These two concepts have different objects of attitude. Nevertheless, both components are used together because a democratic government tends to be responsive to politically active citizens. Consequently, it is widely demonstrated that both are highly correlated. However, there may exist negative or no correlation between them in authoritarian political systems (Coleman and Davis, 1976). For instance, those who are internally efficacious may perceive the responsiveness of an authoritarian government as negative.
[6] We use terms like “politics” and “government” in the questionnaire. There is

a possibility that our respondents may regard those terms as meaning the central government rather than a local one.

[7] This upholds the classic argument that political participation crucially influences the development of civic capacity at the local level.

REFERENCES

Abramson, P.R.: 1983, Political Attitudes in America (Freeman, San Francisco).

Almond, G.A. and S. Verba: 1963, The Civic Culture (Princeton University Press, Princeton).

Banfield, E.C.: 1958, The Moral Basis of a Backward Society (Free Press, Chicago).

Barnes, S.H., Max Kaase et al.: 1979, Political Action: Mass Participation in Five Western Democracies (Sage, Beverly Hills).

Beetham, D.: 1996, 'Theorizing democracy and local government', in D. King and G. Stoker (eds.), Rethinking Local Democracy (Macmillan, London).

Campbell, A., P.E. Converse, W.E. Miller and D.E. Stokes: 1960, The American Voter (Wiley, New York).

Chandler, J.A. and T.N. Clark: 1995, 'Local government', in S.M. Lipset (ed.), The Encyclopedia of Democracy (Congressional Quarterly, Washington, D.C.).

Citrin, J.: 1974, 'Comment: The political relevance of trust in government', American Political Science Review 68, pp. 973–988.

Coleman, K.M. and C.L. Davis: 1976, 'The structural context of politics and dimensions of regime performance', Comparative Political Studies 9, pp. 189–206.

Diamond, L.: 1999, Developing Democracy: Toward Consolidation (Johns Hopkins University Press, Baltimore).

Easton, D.: 1975, 'A reassessment of the concept of political support', British Journal of Political Science 5, pp. 435–457.

Henderson, G.: 1968, Korea: The Politics of the Vortex (Harvard University Press, Cambridge).

Hunginton, S.P.: 1991, The Third Wave: Democratization in the Late Twentieth Century (University of Oklahoma Press, Norman).

Lane, R.E.: 1959, Political Life (Free Press, New York).

Linz, J.J. and A. Stepan: 1996, 'Toward consolidated democracies', Journal of Democracy 7, pp. 14–33.

Miller, A.H.: 1974, 'Political issues and trust in government: 1964–1970', American Political Science Review 68, pp. 951–972.

Norris, P. (ed.): 1999, Critical Citizens: Global Support for Democratic Government (Oxford University Press, Oxford).

Park, C.M.: 2000, 'Local politics and urban power structure in South Korea', Korean Social Science Journal 27(2), pp. 41–67.

Putnam, R.D.: 1993, Making Democracy Work (Princeton University Press, Princeton).

Rose, R. and D.C. Shin: 2001, 'Democratization backwards: The problem of third-wave democracies', British Journal of Political Science 31, pp. 331–354.
Rosenberg, M.: 1956, 'Misanthropy and political ideology', American Sociological Review 21, pp. 690–695.
Schumpeter, J.A.: 1952, Capitalism, Socialism and Democracy (George Allen & Unwin, London).
Stoker, G.: 1996, 'Introduction: Normative theories of local government and democracy', in D. King and G. Stoker (eds.), Rethinking Local Democracy (Macmillan, London).
Tocqueville, A. de.: 1969, Democracy in America (Anchor Books, Garden City, N.Y.).
Verba, S., K.L. Schlozman and H.E. Brady: 1995, Voice and Equality (Harvard University Press, Cambridge).

Department of Public Administration
Korea Univesity
Seoul, Korea
E-mail: cmpark@mail.korea.ac.kr

DONG-KI MIN

ENVIRONMENTAL CONDITIONS AND GOVERNMENTAL FISCAL POLICY

ABSTRACT. The purpose of this paper is to review and analyze the Korean government's financial policy regarding the environment and its resulting effects on domestic environmental quality. The Korean government has adamantly pursued economic growth since the 1960s and only recently has it begun to focus on the serious environmental problems that have arisen as a result of economic growth and industralization. In so doing they have begun to invest seriously in the environmental sector. This present empirical study, using data sets collected in the 1990s, shows that these financial investments in the environmental sector have reduced harmful emission and waste discharge levels.

INTRODUCTION

The government of Korea has tirelessly pursued and achieved economic growth during the past four decades. Unfortunately, this commendable feat was accomplished without any consideration being given to the possible impact that this would have on the environment. As a result, Korea's economic success story has been bittersweet, as the county is presently paying dearly for its neglect of the environment. It has only been recently that Korea has come to realize that the deterioration in the environment has only aggravated the quality of Korean life. It has also, however, hindered future economic growth potential. It is anticipated that the financial cost for improving environmental conditions will increase greatly.

Over the past four decades, Korea's environmental conditions have gone through many changes due to the many stages of the county's national economic development. The early 20th century can be characterized as an era of massive deforestation of national lands in order to provide for sufficient fuel supplies. As a result of the extensive deforestation, Korea was faced with devastating soil erosion problems. It should be noted, however, that Korea's forest ecosystems have been revived through reforestation efforts

Social Indicators Research **62, 63:** 321–344, 2003.

implemented in the late 1960s. Soon after, however, Korea began to experience yet another environmental catastrophe. In the early 1960s, the Korean government adopted and strongly encouraged an export-oriented industrialization strategy in its pursuit of economic development. In the late 1970s, the Korean government focused heavily on the promotion of the heavy-metal and chemical industries. During this key development period, such industrialization schemes brought about serious industrial pollution problems. Even as environmental conditions greatly deteriorated in the country's big push for industrialization, public concerns regarding the environment were not vocalized until the early 1980s. Once Korea achieved economic prosperity, the public's concern shifted to safeguarding the environment as well as reducing existing environmental pollution.

ENVIRONMENTAL LAWS

To deal with environmental problems associated with industrialization, the Korean government enacted the Pollution Prevention Act of 1963 (hereinafter the Pollution Prevention Act) as its first piece of environmental legislation. This legislation, however, proved ineffective because the government pursued a growth-oriented economic policy as its first priority. Little attention was paid to the environmental impact that this policy was having. As a consequence, the Pollution Prevention Act was not properly implemented and national environmental quality deteriorated even further with the process of rapid industrialization.

As environmental problems worsened, the government enacted the Environmental Conservation Act in 1977 (hereinafter the Environmental Conservation Act) to replace the moribund Pollution Prevention Act in an effort to finally deal with the mounting environmental problems. This comprehensive law dealt with most of the environmental trouble-spots by establishing guidelines, such as the promulgation of all encompassing emission standards for air and water. It is this Act that spawned the environmental policy movement in Korea. In 1980, the concept of environmental rights as a basic human right was written into the Korean Constitution. Even though there had been significant developments in the domestic environmental policy and government environmental system, these policy and system were not properly implemented until the early 1980s due to the low priority given to these policies and weak administrative capacities.

During the 1980s, environmental conditions continued to get worse as a result of rapid industrialization. The Korean government recognized the need for more stringent environmental regulations and investment in the environmental sector with the goal of tackling environmental problems. In 1990, in response to this recognition, the Basic Environmental Policy Act (hereinafter the Basic Environment Act) was enacted to replace the Environmental Conservation Act, and is regarded as the cornerstone for all environmental law in Korea. The Basic Environmental Policy Act clearly sets forth the principal requirements and objectives of environmental policy. In addition, five new laws were enacted in 1990: the Air Quality Preservation Act; the Water Quality Preservation Act; the Noise and Vibration Control Act; the Toxic Chemical Control Act; and the Environmental Dispute Settlement Act. The first and second of these laws were enacted: (1) to reduce air and water pollution by setting emission standards for emitters of pollution; and (2) to impose penalties for particular pollutants that are discharged into the environment. The Noise and Vibration Control Act was enacted to reduce noise and vibration to healthy levels for humans and the environment.

As a result of rapid economic growth and industrialization, there was a corresponding increase in the quantity and variety of toxic chemicals that were being introduced into the environment. This prompted the Korean government to formulate a policy to control them. The Toxic Chemical Control Act was the result. Its purpose was to establish a management system to properly control toxic chemicals and enhance the effectiveness of safety inspection programs. In response to the increase in public attention to and concern for the environment in the 1980s, the Korean government enacted the Environmental Dispute Settlement Act. This Act outlines the necessary measures required in settling disputes related to environmental issues.

As a result of the growing complexity and expanding nature of environmental problems and the ever-increasing public concern, the government took additional steps and enacted additional environmental legislation. As of the year 2000, there were 31 environmental laws that fell under the jurisdiction of the Ministry of Environment. This total did not include environment-related laws that fell under the jurisdiction of the other Ministries (see Table I).

ORGANIZATION OF ENVIRONMENTAL ADMINISTRATION

The first administrative office for the environment was established in 1967 titled as the Pollution Prevention Section under the Ministry of Health and Social Affairs. In 1980, this office was upgraded and subsequently referred to as the Environmental Agency. Then, in 1994, it was called the Ministry of Environment, and along with the name change, the authority of its enforcement arm was significantly strengthened.

This Ministry, which functions as the central hub of the environmental management system, is primarily in charge of maintaining and developing environmental policies that address air and water quality, and waste management issues. In this regard, it is empowered to formulate comprehensive plans for preserving and improving the environment. There are several organizations that serve under the Ministry of Environment: the Central and Regional Environmental Dispute Settlement Commission; the National Institute of Environmental Research; the Environmental Officials Training Institute; and eight Regional Environmental Management Offices. The Central and Regional Environmental Dispute Settlement Commissions, established as outlined in the Environment Dispute Settlement Act, are located in major cities and provinces and exist to settle disputes over environmental problems. The National Institute of Environmental Research performs surveys and research projects primarily of environmental pollution problems to support the environmental policies developed by the Ministry of Environment. The Environmental Officials Training Institute was established to educate and train environmental officials to understand and properly handle environmental problems that are more specialized and diversified. The Environmental Management Offices were established to share in the duties of the Ministry of

TABLE I

List of Environmental Laws in Korea

Field	Act
Environmental management	• Basic Environmental Policy Act • Environmental Dispute Settlement Act • Special Act Relating to the Control of Environmental Crimes • Act Relating to Support and Development of Environmental Technologies • Environmental Improvement Account Act • Act Relating to Environmental Improvement Charges • Environmental Management Corporation Act • Korean Resources Recovery and Reutilization Corporation Act • Natural Environment Conservation Act
Natural environment management	• The Wildlife Protection and Hunting Law • Natural Parks Act • Act for Environmental, Traffic and Disasters Impact Assessments • Special Act Relating to the Conservation of Island Ecosystems such as Tokdo, etc. • Soil Environment Preservation Act • Wetlands Preservation Act
Air and noise management	• Air Quality Preservation Act • Noise and Vibration Control Act • Air Quality Management Act for Underground Living Spaces
Water management	• Water Quality Preservation Act • Act Relating to Treatment of Sewage, Night Soil and Livestock Wastewater • Drinking Water Management Act • Inland Water Body Water Quality Management Act • Water Supply and Waterworks Installation Act • Sewage Treatment Act • Act Relating to Water Resource Quality Improvement and Local Resident Support in the Han River Watershed

TABLE I

Continued

Field	Act
Waste management	• Waste Management Act • Act Relating to Promotion of Resource Saving and Reutilization • Act Relating to the Trans-boundary Movement of Waste and its Disposal • Act for Promotion of Waste Treatment Facilities and Local Communities • Toxic Chemicals Control Act • Act Relating to Establishment and Operation of the Metropolitan Area Landfill Management Corporations

Source: Ministry of Environment, http://www.me.go.kr, 2001.

Environment and deal with regional environmental problems more efficiently.

Local government is also responsible for dealing with environmental problems within their jurisdiction in conjunction with the respective Environmental Management Office in their region. As public concern over environmental quality increase, the roles of the environmental section in local government bureaus take on vital importance. It has only been recently that local governments have been put in charge of environmental policy implementation. They have had little experience in this area, and consequently need more support in the financial and technical assistance areas.

In the Korean governmental system, several Ministries, including the Ministry of Construction and Transportation, the Ministry of Agriculture and Forestry, and the Ministry of Government Administration and Home Affairs, are working together with the Ministry of Environment in implementing environmental policies (see Table II).

ENVIRONMENTAL FISCAL POLICY AND EXPENDITURES

Since the 1980s, the amount of government spending on the environmental sector has continuously increased in size and its share of the total budget. This increase is a direct result of the growing demands

TABLE II

The Environmental Administration of the Central Government

Min. of Science & Technology	• Coordination of nuclear safety control • Establishment and implementation of radioactivity preventive measures • Regulations on transportation, handing and disposal and treatment of nuclear and radioactive industrial wastes
Min. of Government Administration & Home Affairs	• Designiation and supervision of national and provincial parks
Min. of Agriculture & Forestry	• Measure for agriculture and forestry pollution • Planning and technical guidance on the development of agricultural water
Min. of Trade Industry & Energy	• Import/export toxic substances and import restriction on industrial wastes • Allocation and management of industrial sites • Supply of low sulfur oil • R&D on new and alternative energy • Safety management of nuclear power generators and disposal and treatment of nuclear wastes
Min. of Construction & Transportation	• Formulation and coordination of a comprehensive plan for national land use • Designation of areas subject to the National Land Use and Management Act • Designation of areas where development is restricted • Establishment and coordination of a comprehensive plan for water resources development • Management of rivers, reclamation and use of rivers and lakes • Type approval and performance tests of motor vehicles • Designation and development of tourist attractions
Min. of Labor	• Countermeasures against occupational diseases and improvement of working conditions

TABLE II

Continued

Min. of Culture and Sports	• Designation, protection and management of national monuments such as rare plants, animals, etc.
Min. of Maritime Affairs and Fisheries	• Protection of marine resources and countermeasures against marine pollution • Reclamation and management of public sea waters • Countermeasures against pollution of coastal waters • Supervision and prevention marine pollution
The Office of Forestry	• Formulation of Basic Forestry Plan • Protection of wild animals and restrictions on hunting • Protection of forests and supervision of forest destruction activities
Agriculture Promotion Administration	• Improvement of agricultural land and provision of guidance on soil improvement

Source: Ministry of Environment, *Environmental Protection in Korea*, 1997.

for investments in the environment. Table III provides central government expenditures for the environmental sector. Although the total expenditure on the environment in 1991 was only 486.3 billion won, it has increased every year since then except in 1999, and it rose to 3058.1 billion won in 2000.

In late 1997, Korea experienced an economic crisis, and in 1999 the government temporarily reduced its expenditures for the environment. The percentage of total environmental expenditures to total government expenditures also has grown steadily during the 1990s. That is, the percentage has increased significantly from 1.24 percent in 1991 to 2.44 in 2000. At the same time, the percentage of total environment expenditures to the Gross Domestic Product (hereinafter GDP) has risen from 0.22 percent in 1991 to 0.59 percent in 2000.

Since several Ministries, including the Ministry of Environment, are involved in the implementation of environmental policies, all are separately responsible for their respective government expendi-

TABLE III

Central Government Expenditures for Environmental Sector (unit: billion won)

	’91	’92	’93	’94	’95	’96	’97	’98	’99	2000
Total Environment Expenditure (A)	486	614	727	1161	1780	2241	2775	2812	2764	3058
Total Government Expenditure (B)	39367	43842	51188	64458	74534	85308	98330	110314	120021	125179
(A/B, %)	1.24	1.40	1.42	1.80	2.39	2.63	2.82	2.55	2.30	2.44
GDP	216511	245700	277497	323407	377350	418479	453276	444367	482744	517097
(A/C, %)	0.22	0.25	0.26	0.36	0.47	0.54	0.61	0.63	0.57	0.59
Min. of Environment	272	140	189	472	673	885	1080	1113	1154	1302
Min. of Construction and Transportation	175	215	238	192	302	375	407	578	471	523
Min. of Government Administration and Home Affairs	29	244	285	407	513	601	898	827	830	992
Min. of Agriculture and Forestry	0	0	0	0	40	40	40	34	36	36
Min. of Maritime Affairs and Fisheries	0	0	0	0	0	12	26	20	22	45
Min. of Finance and Economy	10	15	15	91	253	328	323	240	251	160
Exchange rate (won/dollar)	760.8	788.4	808.1	788.7	774.7	844.2	1415.2	1207.8	1145.4	1259.7

Source: Ministry of Environment, http://www.me.go.kr, 2001.

tures. Most government environmental expenditures are allocated to the Ministries of Environment, Construction and Transportation, and Government Administration and Home Affairs. Their share of expenditures out of the total government expenditure for the environment was 98 percent (470 billion won) in 1991 and 92 percent (2,817 billion won) in 2000. Although government expenditures for the environment have steadily increased, the public's demand for investments in this area have increased more rapidly than what the government has been spending, thus, the government has not been able to keep up with public demand.

Table IV shows the budget of the Ministry of Environment divided into its different sectors. Total expenditures have risen significantly from 272 billion won in 1991 to 1,302 billion won in 2000. The Ministry of Construction and Transportation managed the piped water sector until 1993. After 1993, the Ministry of Environment began to share the responsibility for this sector. One-fourth of the budget in 1994 and one-fifth of the budget in 2000 was allocated to this sector. The sewage and wastewater treatment sector received 68 percent of the budget. However, since the Ministry of Government Administration and Home Affairs began to share the responsibility for this sector in 1992, their budget share decreased to 8.95 percent in 1992. Up to that time, the budget share of this sector had been increasing on as regular basis to 31.42 percent in 2000.

Thus, more than 50 percent of the Ministry of Environment budget was allocated to these two sectors in 2000. If the expenditures on these sectors by other ministries are added together, the government expenditure on these sectors is more than 70 percent of the total government expenditure in this area. Looking at the government's spending pattern in the environmental area, it can be inferred that it has focused primarily on water quality. In the waste treatment sector, 24.5 billion won was allocated from a grand sum of 272 billion won in 1991 and the budget for this sector has steadily increased to 286.5 billion won in 2000. The share of the budget for this sector in 2000 was 22.0 percent.

As for the air quality preservation sector, its share of the budget has been trivial, around 1 percent or less during 1990s except in 2000. This does not mean that the total expenditure for this sector

TABLE IV

Ministry of Environment Budget by Sector (unit: billion won)

	'91	'92	'93	'94	'95	'96	'97	'98	'99	2000
Total expenditure	272	140	189	472	673	885	1,080	1,113	1,154	1,302
– Piped water supply	—	—	—	125.1	221.2	238.6	272.7	217.1	241.6	244.2
	—	—	—	(26.53)	(32.87)	(26.96)	(25.25)	(19.50)	(20.94)	(18.75)
– Sewage and wastewater treatment	184.8	12.5	18.3	57.2	172.6	243.8	295.7	352	355.2	409.2
	(67.99)	(8.95)	(9.70)	(12.13)	(25.65)	(27.54)	(27.37)	(31.62)	(30.79)	(31.42)
– Waste treatment	24.5	28.9	35.1	43	145.6	188.1	271.7	266.6	268.6	286.5
	(9.01)	(20.70)	(18.60)	(9.12)	(21.64)	(21.25)	(25.15)	(23.95)	(23.28)	(22.00)
– Air quality preservation	3.1	2	2.4	2.7	2.9	10.5	8.9	7.4	9.5	46.5
	(1.14)	(1.43)	(1.27)	(0.57)	(0.43)	(1.19)	(0.82)	(0.66)	(0.82)	(3.57)
– Preservation of natural	0.3	0.3	0.3	0.9	3	4.9	6.3	48.3	59.2	74.2
environment	(0.11)	(0.21)	(0.16)	(0.19)	(0.45)	(0.55)	(0.58)	(4.34)	(5.13)	(5.70)
– Environmental and technology	1.9	4.3	7.4	18.4	74.7	121.7	133.5	118.4	114	126.7
policy and development	(0.70)	(3.08)	(3.92)	(3.90)	(11.10)	(13.75)	(12.36)	(10.64)	(9.88)	(9.73)
– Environmental management et al.	57.2	91.6	125.2	224.3	52.9	77.5	91.4	103.3	105.5	115
	(21.04)	(65.62)	(66.35)	(47.56)	(7.86)	(8.76)	(8.46)	(9.28)	(9.15)	(8.83)

Source: Ministry of Environment, http://www.me.go.kr, 2001.

is small. Most expenditure for this sector has been derived from collection efforts from the business sector under the polluter-pays-principle.

The Korean government created a Special Account for Environmental Improvement in order to manage environmental investment financial resources more efficiently. In addition, to protecting the environment in the most cost effective way, the Korean government adopted an economic incentive system as a supplement to the command and control method. This latter method may result in cost burdens that are distributed between both the industrial and governmental sectors.

As a result, five economic instruments have been implemented. First, an Environmental Improvement Charge was established in order to reduce pollution from the commercial and consumption sectors in order to raise financial resources for environmental investments. It consists of levying fees on commercial building owners and on diesel powered vehicle owners based on the amount of water and fuel that are used. Second, an Emission Charge was put into effect in 1983 to prevent environmental damage by imposing charges on the emissions or discharges of certain pollutants (viz., 10 specific air pollutants and 17 specific water pollutants) that exceed permissible limits. Third, a Deposit-Refund System for Waste Disposal went into effect in 1992 to promote waste recycling by collecting deposits from producers and importers of recyclable products. Under this system, when producers and importers collect and treat the wastes, they are reimbursed in accordance with their performance in collecting and recycling the wastes. Fourth, a Waste Treatment Charge, with the purpose of promoting waste reduction and resource conservations, was established in 1993. This charge is levied on producers and importers of products and containers which are difficult to collect and hard to recycle. Fifth, under the Drinking Water Management Act, Water Quality Improvement Charges were levied on producers or importers of bottled water since 1986 to fund protection efforts of public ground water resources as well as improvements to drinking water quality.

Table V provides available revenue figures from the Special Account for the Environmental Improvement measure. The total revenue from economic instruments implemented in 1995 was 419

TABLE V

Revenue from Special Account for Environmental Improvement (unit: million won, %)

	'95	'96	'97	'98	'99	2000
Total revenue	419355	358318	463134	544061	563432	615220
Environmental	97610	159184	221688	290869	310369	356361
improvement charge	(23.28)	(44.43)	(47.87)	(53.46)	(55.09)	(57.92)
Emission charge	17163	20787	42174	60541	59765	50722
	(4.09)	(5.80)	(9.11)	(11.13)	(10.61)	(8.24)
Deposit-refund for	45231	33680	63338	51218	37667	44040
waste disposal	(10.79)	(9.40)	(13.68)	(9.41)	(6.69)	(7.16)
Waste treatment charge	22404	36422	58364	47166	47697	51406
	(5.34)	(10.16)	(12.60)	(8.67)	(8.47)	(8.36)
Water quality	—	26177	25588	26944	25747	15664
improvement charge	—	(7.31)	(5.52)	(4.95)	(4.57)	(2.55)
Others	236947	82068	51982	67323	82187	97027
	(56.50)	(22.90)	(11.22)	(12.37)	(14.59)	(15.77)

Source: Korea Environment Institute, *Environmental Budget and Policy Objectives* (D. K. Min, eds.), 2001.

billion won or 67 percent of the Ministry of Environment budget. Such revenue has steadily increased to 615 billion won in 2000. The ratio of this revenue to the Ministry of Environment budget was 47 percent in 2000 because of an accelerated increase in the budget for the Ministry of Environment.

Revenue raised from the Environmental Improvement Charge (hereinafter the Charge) accounted for 23 percent of the total revenue collected in 1995. The ratio of revenue from the Charge increased to 57.92 percent of total revenue in 2000. The amount of reveneue from this same Charge increased to 356 billion won in the same period. Thus, the revenue raised from the Charge has become the main source of financing for the Special Account for Environment Improvement.

CURRENT ENVIRONMENTAL STATUS

Air pollution. Air quality has improved since the late 1980s as a result of the expanded use of cleaner fuels, low-sulfur oils, and

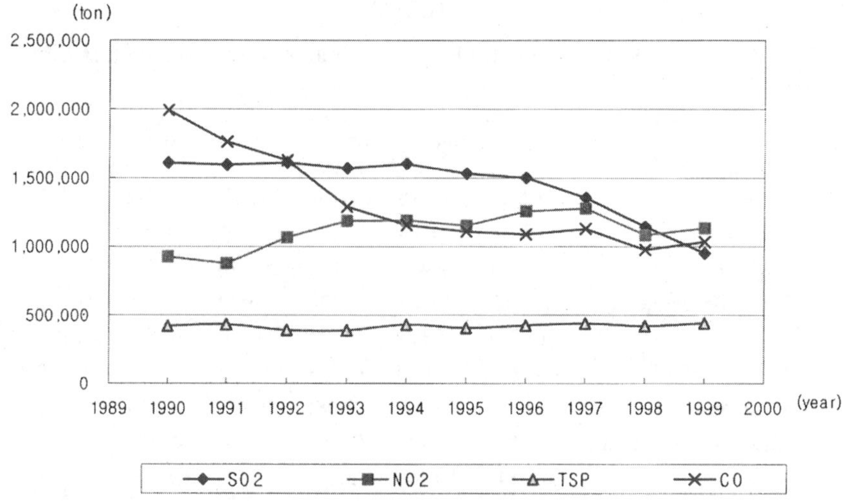

Figure 1. Trends of air pollutant emission.

through the introduction of low emission vehicles. Figure 1 illustrates clearly this trend. Sulfur dioxide (hereinafter represented by the chemical formula SO_2) levels have been lowered as a result of the declining use of low-sulfur oils and liquefied natural gas from 1610960 tons in 1990 to 951183 tons in 1999. Concentrations of SO_2 have also experienced a decline during this same period. There are some cities, however, whose air quality still exceeds the national ambient air quality standards.

In the case of Nitrite (hereinafter represented by the chemical formula NO_2) concentrations have increased slightly from 926065 tons in 1990 to 1135503 tons in 1999. This rise can be attributed to the increase in the number of motor vehicles traveling the roads. Concentrations of NO_2 within cities also have not improved in the last ten years. Ambient levels of NO_2, however, in major cities currently satisfy air quality standards. In the case of Total Suspended Particle (hereinafter represented by the chemical formula TSP), it has been steadily below the national standard during the past ten years. It should be mentioned, however, that concentrations of TSP are unusually high in the spring due to winds that bring yellow sand and dust from China and Mongolia.

Water pollution. Since rainfall occurs mostly during the summer, there are water shortage problems in Korea. In addition, the annual

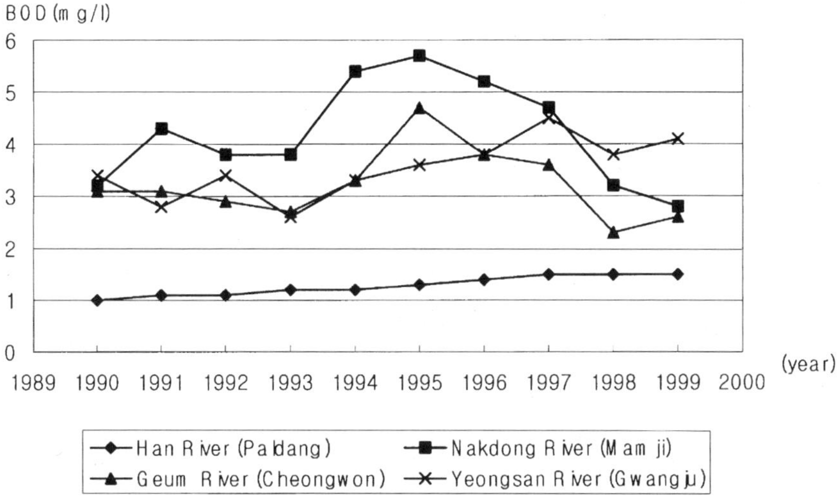

Figure 2. Trend in water quality in major rivers (BOD).

average precipitation rates for some years in the 1990s were much lower than historical annual averages. As expected, these factors exacerbated the water pollution problem. The levels of pollution within the country's four major rivers have not shown any significant improvement. The Han River, which passes through the capital city of Seoul, is the least polluted among the four as a result of the policy of continuous investments that were made in the environmental infrastructure for the preservation of water quality. The Biochemical Oxygen Demanded (hereinafter represented by the chemical formula BOD) level of the Han River is around 1 to 1.5 mg/*l*, however, it increased slightly during the 1990s.

The Nakdong River is the most polluted and its BOD level has fluctuated every year. Recently, the level was recorded at a low 2.8 mg/*l* in 1999, as compared with the highest level of 5.7 mg/*l* recorded in 1995, as a result of environmental protection efforts. The Geum River has experienced fluctuations in BOD levels over the years. Its highest level was recorded in 1995 at 4.7mg/*l* and recently, it has improved to a level of 2.6 mg/*l* as recorded in 1999. In regards to the other rivers, with the single exception of the Yeongsan River, BOD levels have shown recent improvements. The BOD level measurement of the Yeongsan River was found to be 4.1 mg/*l* in 1999 and is the highest among the four rivers.

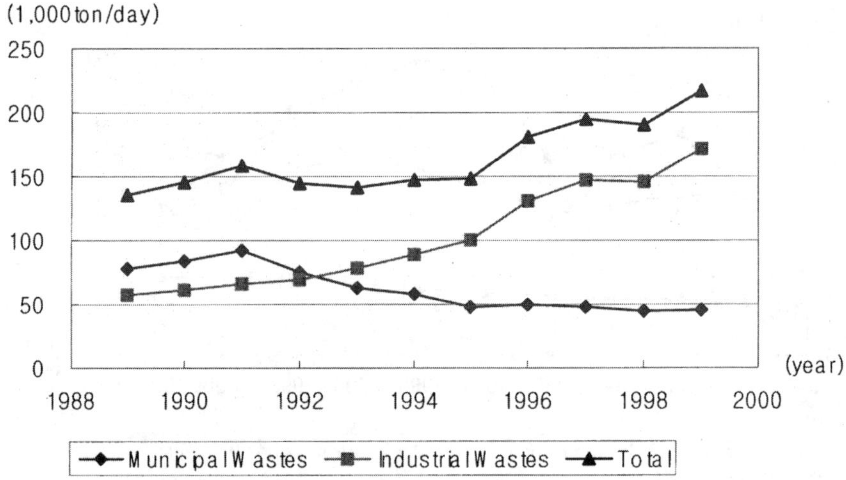

Figure 3. Trend in generation of wastes.

Waste management. Waste is categorized into two types, municipal and industrial waste. Non-hazardous industrial waste is classified as general waste and hazardous industrial waste is classified as specified waste. Figure 3 reports that total amount of generated waste has steadily increased except for a slight decrease in 1992 and 1993. In addition, the total amount of municipal waste has decreased every year except in 1996 as a result of the use of a volume-based charging system and the switch from coal to other fuels such as liquefied natural gas (see Table VI). The amount of industrial waste, however, has increased over the years except in 1998. In 1998, Korea experienced an economic crisis and thus, industrial waste decreased. In 1994, the criteria for classifying specified waste and general waste were changed and most specified wastes were shifted to the general waste category. Consequently, the total amount of specified waste was reduced greatly since 1994.

POLLUTION ABATEMENT AND CONTROL EXPENDITURES

The Bank of Korea has estimated the amount of Pollution Abatement and Control (hereinafter PAC) expenditures every year since 1993. Table VII shows PAC expenditure trends for different economic agencies and for different type of expenditures. Total PAC expenditures have increased over the years from 4,608 billion won

TABLE VI

Generation of Wastes (Unit: ton/day)

	Total	Municipal waste	Industrial waste		
				general	specified
1989	135600	78000	57600	—	—
1990	145400	84000	61400	—	—
1991	158300	92200	66100	—	—
1992	144535	75096	69439	48058	21381
1993	141383	62940	78443	55969	22474
1994	147049	58118	88931	85229	3702
1995	148042	47774	100268	95823	4445
1996	180573	49925	130648	125409	5239
1997	195275	47895	147380	141305	6075
1998	190255	44583	145672	140406	5266
1999	219217	45614	173603	166114	7489

Source: Ministry of Environment, *Environmental Statistics Yearbook.*

in 1993 to 7834 billion won in 1999 with the exception of 1998 when Korea experienced the economic crisis. The governmental and industrial sectors finance most of the PAC expenditures and the amount financed by the government has been usually a little higher than that for the industrial sector. Among PAC expenditures, the amount expended for investment has been similar to that for maintenance.

Table VIII shows PAC expenditures for each type of pollution. Among PAC expenditures, approximately one-half was for the water sector in the 1990s. Around 30 percent was used for waste management and less than 20 percent was used for air pollution management. For each sector, PAC expenditures have increased steadily except in 1998.

THE EFFECT OF EXPENDITURES ON ENVIRONMENTAL QUALITY IMPROVEMENTS

Using the data for PAC expenditures and the amount of emitted or discharged pollution levels as explained in previous sections, the

TABLE VII

Pollution Abatement and Control Expenditure (Unit: million won)

	1993	1994	1995	1996	1997	1998	1999
Total expenditure (A)	4608470	5351638	6306027	7239096	8420630	7266832	7834268
(A/GDP, %)	(1.66)	(1.65)	(1.67)	(1.73)	(1.86)	(1.64)	(1.62)
Type of economic agency							
Government	2188932	2498554	2928079	3366876	4327135	4032488	4312903
		(14.14)	(17.19)	(14.99)	(28.52)	(–6.81)	(6.95)
Industry	2145507	2546617	2966579	3329040	3521883	2883349	3185066
		(18.70)	(16.49)	(12.22)	(5.79)	(–18.13)	(10.46)
Household	274031	306467	411369	543180	571612	350995	336299
		(11.84)	(34.23)	(32.04)	(5.23)	(–38.60)	(–4.19)
Type of expenditure							
Investment	2268859	2662373	3130503	3507031	4244819	3353703	3564929
		(17.34)	(17.58)	(12.03)	(21.04)	(–20.99)	(6.30)
Maintenance	2339611	2689265	3175524	3732065	4175811	3913129	4269339
		(14.94)	(18.08)	(17.53)	(11.89)	(–6.29)	(9.10)

Source: Bank of Korea, http://www.bok.or.kr, 2001.

Note: ( ) indicates growth rate in each year, %.

TABLE VIII

Pollution Abatement and Control Expenditure by Type of Pollution (Unit: million won)

	1993	1994	1995	1996	1997	1998	1999
Total expenditure (A)	4608470	5351638	6306027	7239096	8420630	7266832	7834268
Air pollution (B)	803432	918035	1035387	1071089	1400696	1025433	1242608
(A/B, %)	17.4	17.2	16.4	14.8	16.6	14.1	15.9
Growth rate (%)		14.26	12.78	3.45	30.77	–26.79	21.18
Water Pollution (C)	2168983	2471627	3075304	3608221	4260231	3479619	3610473
(A/C, %)	47.1	46.2	48.8	49.8	50.6	47.9	46.1
Growth rate (%)		13.95	24.42	17.33	18.07	–18.32	3.76
Waste (D)	1452013	1705658	1928719	2291236	2520370	2562670	2774833
(A/D, %)	31.5	31.9	30.6	31.7	29.9	35.3	35.4
Growth rate (%)		17.47	13.08	18.80	10.00	1.68	8.28
Others (E)[1]	184042	256318	266617	268550	239333	199110	206354
(A/E, %)	4.0	4.8	4.2	3.7	2.8	2.7	2.6
Growth rate (%)		39.27	4.02	0.73	–10.88	–16.81	3.64

Source: Bank of Korea, http://www.bok.or.kr, 2001.
[1]Noise and Vibration, etc.

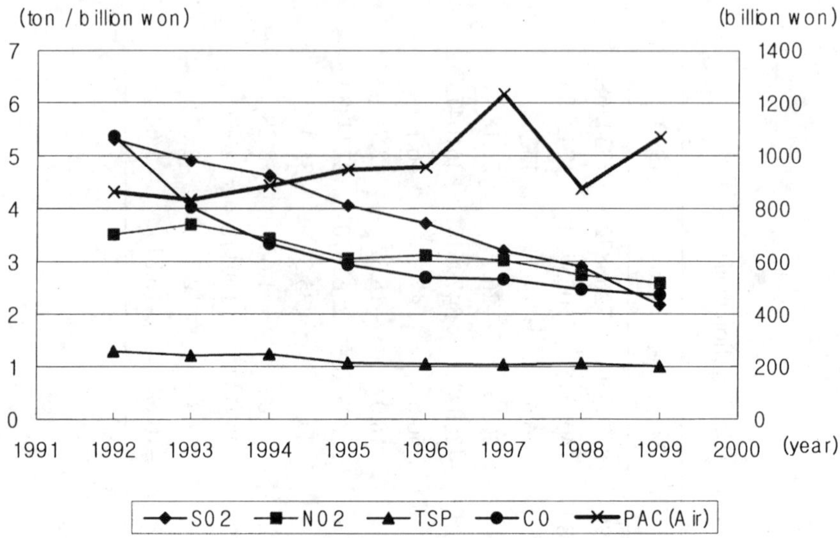

Note: 1) SO_2, NO_2, TSP, and CO represent the ratio of emission to real GDP.

Figure 4. The ratio of emission to real GDP and PAC expenditure for air quality.

effect of environmental expenditures on the amount of air pollution emission or waste water discharge reduction can be estimated. Figures 4 and 5 show the ratio of emission to real GDP, the ratio of industrial waste water discharge o real GDP and PAC expenditure for each sector using the above data set. In Figure 4, the ratio of each type of air pollutant to real GDP has been declining, while PAC expenditures have been increasing slightly. In Figure 5, the ratio of industrial waste water discharge to real GDP is usually decreasing (increasing) when PAC expenditure is increasing (decreasing). In Figure 6, the relationship between the ratio of generation of municipal waste to real GDP and PAC expenditure is also usually negative.

Using the following simple regression formula, the effect of environmental expenditures on the amount of air pollution emission, industrial waste water or waste discharge reduction can be accurately estimated.

$$\log\left(\frac{X_i}{realGDP}\right) = \alpha_0 + \alpha_1 \log Y_j$$

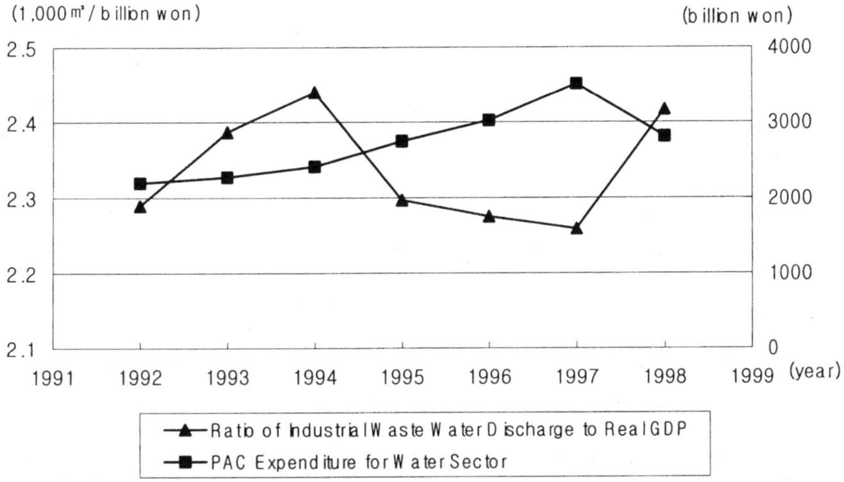

Figure 5. The ratio of industrial waste water discharge to real GDP and PAC expenditure for water quality.

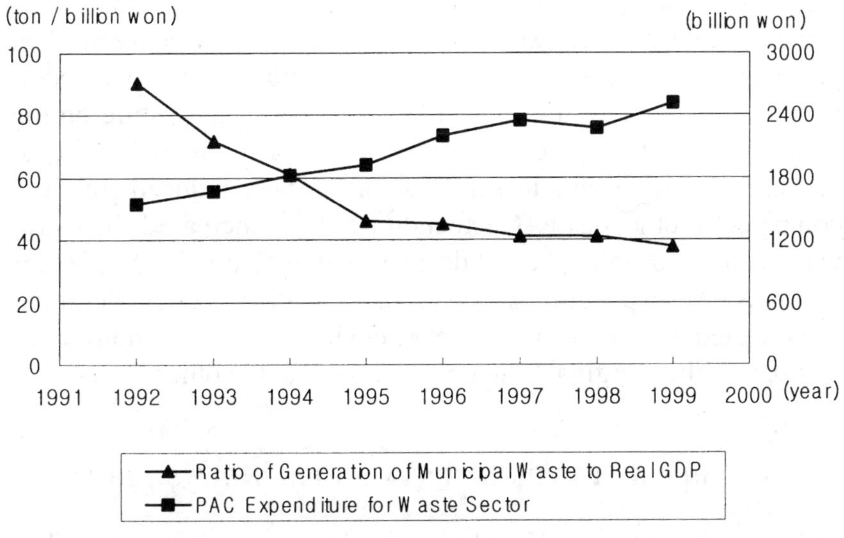

Figure 6. The ratio of generation of municipal waste to real GDP and PAC expenditure for the waste sector.

TABLE IX

The Elasticity of PAC Expenditures on the Amount of Emission or Discharge

	SO_2	NO_2	TSP	CO	Industrial waste water	Municipal waste
Elasticity	−1.18	−0.44	−0.41	−0.78	−0.16	−1.48
	(−1.5)	(−1.2)	(−2.1)	(−1.5)	(−2.4)	(−6.4)

Note: The figures in parentheses are t-statistics.

X_i: The amount of emission for each type of air pollutant such as SO_2, NO_2, TSP, CO, waste or industrial waste water discharge

Y_j: Real PAC Expenditure for air, water, or waste sectors

The elasticity of PAC expenditures on the amount of emission or discharge can be defined as the percentage change in the amount of emission or discharge due to the percentage change in PAC expenditure. Table IX describes the results of the regression formula to test for elasticity. It should be duly noted that all elasticities are negative. The results show that during 1990s, the correlation between the amount of emission or discharges and PAC expenditures is a negative one, viz., the amount of emission or discharges decreases when PAC expenditures increase and vice versa. The percentage of reduction is highest in the municipal waste sector, which shows that a 1 percent increase in PAC expenditure on this sector reduces 1.48 percent of the amount of municipal waste. In the case of SO_2, the amount of emission has been reduced greatly as compared to others as PAC expenditures have increased. Industrial waste water, however, did not decrease significantly as compared to others as PAC expenditures increased. Since the Korean government has invested more than 50 percent of environmental expenditures on this sector, the marginal efficiency is less than the other sectors.

TOWARDS AN ENVIRONMENTALLY-FRIENDLY SOCIETY

In recent decades, the Korean government has slowly opened its eyes to the seriousness of environmental degradation and has made great strides in improving the environment. This in turn has enhanced the quality of life for the Korean people. As a result, several indexes, which serve as indicators for the quality of the environment, have registered slight improvements in the 1990s. Monumental environmental problems, however, still persist in Korea. Efforts to safeguard the environment, which include addressing environmental problems that result from reckless economic development, must go on.

In order to ensure effective environmental policies, the Korean government must implement various policy initiatives and encourage financial investment in the environment. Environmental problems cannot be abated solely with government money. Accordingly, the following policy recommendations must be incorporated into the environmental agenda to insure the quality of life among the Korean people.

First, the Korean government has paid a significant amount in subsidies to environmentally-unfriendly activities by charging them fees that are lower than the actual costs involved. The government does this ostensibly for the purposes of subsiding those of lower income levels or in order to control price levels. The data show that this policy has failed to achieve its goals. What has happened is that it has resulted in an excessive demand for products that are damaging to the environment as well as causing serious environmental problems. In order to achieve both a healthy environment and economic growth, the Korean government must engage in proper pricing of activities that are harmful to the environment, and at the same time it needs to reduce several types of subsidies given for these activities.

Secondly, in order to encourage the development of environmentally-sound technologies, it will be necessary for the government to create enabling conditions and incentives to induce the industrial sector to make investments in relevant research and development. By adopting environmentally-sound technologies, the industrial sector will utilize less energy and raw materials to produce the same equivalent in products, and thus, minimize harmful emissions and production of waste.

Thirdly, in order to promote an environmentally-friendly country, the roles of international organizations will prove vital. International organizations must monitor the cross-boundary movements of harmful emissions and waste. They must also develop policy measures that will facilitate cooperation among nations in resolving international environmental disputes.

Fourthly, public awareness of environmental issues needs to be heavily promoted. To raise public awareness, the government needs to effectively utilize all appropriate channels of the mass media including the press, radio, television, and various publications. By involving the mass media, the government will communicate the importance of environmental policies to the people of Korea.

Finally, environmental education and training programs are pivotal tools to preserving the environment. Through environmental education and training opportunities, the government will achieve a healthy balance in priorities taking into consideration the importance of both economic growth and environmental preservation.

ACKNOWLEDGEMENT

I would like to acknowledge financial support from the Konkuk University research fund.

REFERENCES

Bank of Korea, Quarterly National Accounts: 2001, 3.

Korea Institute for Health and Social Affairs: 1998, Korea Human Development Report 1998.

Min, Dong-Ki: 1999, 'Consumption trends with economic growth in Korea', Sustainable Consumption Patterns (Korea Environment Institute).

Min, Dong-Ki: 2000, 'Environmentally-unfriendly subsidies in Korea', Green Tax Reform Towards a Sustainable Society.

Ministry of Environment (ROK): 1997, Environmental Protection in Korea.

Ministry of Environment: 1995~1999, Generation & Treatment of Industrial Waste Water.

Ministry of Environment: 1989~2000, Environmental Statistics Yearbook.

National Statistical Office Republic of Korea: 2000, Major Statistics of Korea Economy, 3.

Korea Environment Institute: Environmental Budget and Policy Objectives (D. K. Min eds.).

Konkuk University
Department of Economics
E-mail: dkm2@konkuk.ac.kr

HUN SHIK KIM

MEDIA, THE PUBLIC, AND FREEDOM OF THE PRESS

ABSTRACT. This article examines the diversification of the news media in Korea since the 1990s as a result of deregulation and democratization. It also examines the impact of media diversity on the public's use patterns and its trust in the media, and evaluates the current state of freedom of the press in Korea. Contrary to scholarly research, which holds that freedom of the press has increased significantly over the last decade, this study found that the Korean press still faces a variety of restraints despite improvements in a few areas.

Since the founding of the Republic of Korea in 1948, the fate of the South Korean (hereafter, Korean) press has mirrored the political changes in the country. During the past five decades, from the early days of an authoritarian regime to the more recent democratic governments in the 2000s, the path of the Korean media has been dictated by the government and various political elites.

The unprecedented political and social changes of the 1980s and 1990s have ushered in dramatic transformations in the Korean media industry. In June 1987, a series of nationwide popular movements and democratic uprisings successfully pressured the repressive, military-led government of Chun Doo Hwan into launching sweeping political reform programs. This experiment with democracy gave birth to a transition to democracy and an increasing liberalization of media activities up to the present day.

This paper traces the development of the Korean media since the 1987 democratization drive, and surveys daily media use by Koreans, as well as evaluates the extent of freedom of the press in the country, which is vital not only for news professionals, but also for the enhancement of the public's quality of life.

EXPANSION OF KOREAN MEDIA INDUSTRY

The 1987 liberalization drive initiated by Roh Tae Woo, Presidential candidate for the ruling Democratic Justice Party and close

Social Indicators Research **62, 63:** 345–364, 2003.

friend to then-President Chun Doo Hwan, transformed the Korean news media from a government-controlled enterprise to a more autonomous entity in line with the country's changing sociopolitical circumstances (Yang, 1999). In their Freedom Forum survey of East Asian media, Heuvel and Dennis (1993) noted that the Korean press was living through a golden age. "The media have been freer than ever to criticize the government, address formerly taboo issues, and expand with virtually no restraint" (p. 13).

The 1987 reform, thereafter, paved the way for a significant expansion of the mass media industry, thus occasioning greater commercial competition unprecedented under the rule of the authoritarian governments of Park Chung Hee and Chun Doo Hwan. During the five-year period between 1987 and 1992, the number of daily newspapers increased more than threefold from some 30 to 100. As of 2001, there are 60 daily newspapers, including 10 national, 39 local, five business, four sports and two English dailies. *Yonhap News* is the only national news agency. There are three television networks, five independent local television stations, and 27 smaller television stations airing programs ranging from traffic information, weather, education to religions (Newspaper and Broadcasting Yearbook, 2000/2001). In addition, there are more than 2000 weekly and monthly magazines that trumpet headlines of the momentous to the mundane. The number of people working with these media is approximately 38000 (Journalism and Broadcasting Yearbook, 2001/2002). This figure topped 42000 in 1997 before the Asian economic recession hit the media industry in late 1997, slashing more than 4000 jobs.

With the increased number of print media outlets, only a few national daily newspapers have thrived while other mid- to smaller-sized newspapers struggled to capture a slice of the market. The national dailies have engaged in fierce wars of circulation running into the millions of issues, to the extent of provoking complaints from readers about pushy vendors plying them with gifts in return for subscriptions (Lee, 2001). Seoul, the capital city, is home to almost a dozen daily newspapers, and another dozen business and sports dailies. The big three dailies are *Chosun Ilbo, JoongAng Ilbo* and *Dong-a Ilbo*.

The three major national television networks include the state-owned public Korean Broadcasting System (hereinafter the KBS), the partly public Munhwa Broadcasting Corporation (hereinafter the MBC) and the commercial Seoul Broadcasting System (hereinafter the SBS). The launch of the commercial television network SBS in 1991 ushered in a new era of a multi-channel broadcasting system. It represented a departure from the monopolistic broadcasting system represented by KBS and MBC for more than three decades. With the introduction of a second commercial network, SBS, Korean broadcasters opened themselves to the influences of advertisers and commercialism. For example, more than 60% of state-run KBS's revenue comes from advertising rather than a monthly household reception fee of about U.S.$20. MBC funds 98% of its operation through advertising revenue. A 1998 survey by the Korean Broadcast Producers' Association shows that 78.1% of producers acknowledged that they are under increasing pressure to boost the ratings of their programs (Kim, 2001c).

Since 1995, cable television has provided viewers with more than 30 channels through its 27 regional program providers and 54 local system operators throughout the country (Ma, 1998). The cable television offerings feature news, entertainment, sports, home shopping, and movie channels. In the same year, the government approved the launching of local private television stations in the five major cities of Inchon, Taegu, Taejon, Kwangju and Pusan. These local television stations further contributed to the diversification of news media in the country.

The three major television networks have offered High Definition Television (hereinafter HDTV) broadcasting since late 2001. The impact of digital HDTV broadcasting with the advantages of a vastly improved picture and sound quality better than analog programs, has already signaled the home electronics industry to shift their production from analog sets to digital HDTV sets. Consumer interest is also evident; many are looking for new digital television sets that receive the HDTV signals. The first programming in HDTV includes entertainment shows, dramas and sporting events. The full conversion, however, from analog to HDTV programming for the three networks is expected to be completed in 2010. The conversion will be slow as long as the prices for HDTV sets remain beyond the reach of the average consumer.

Satellite digital television debuted in March 2002. *SkyLife*, Korea's first satellite broadcasting company, airs 120 television channels with digital audio-video signals from a geostationary *Mukungwha* satellite (located at 5786 kilometer above the earth). The satellite digital television transmission also provides two-way data services to subscribers including home shopping, e-mailing, home banking and other online-based multimedia services (Hwang, 2001). It is likely that the satellite broadcasting will overtake the traditional "wired" cable television industry with more advanced technology and software features as well as with more than three times the number of channel choices for viewers.

KOREAN AUDIENCES AND MEDIA USE

Who constitutes the audiences for the Korean news media and how do these listeners/viewers use the media as a source of news and information? Koreans have achieved an almost 100-percent literacy rate as a result of a strong public school system and high career aspirations on the part of society. The use of the news media by Koreans, therefore, far exceeds the UNESCO minimum that separates the "developed" from the "developing" nations (Kim, 2001b). During the 1990s, several revolutionary changes, including the leap in the number of daily newspapers and the advancement in broadcasting technologies, helped heighten the public's use of the mass media.

For example, every Korean household owns at least one television set, with many households owning two or more sets. Some 35% or more of families own two or three cellular phones as a lifestyle necessity (Kim, 2001b). In a 2001 survey, 67.1% of middle and high school students (between the ages of 13–18) carry cellular phones (Digital Chosun, 2001a). Most people get their news from ten national daily newspapers and three network television news programs that air either at eight or nine o'clock every night. The majority of Koreans subscribe to daily newspapers, which provide an impressive diet of news. A survey by the Korea Press Foundation (2000) indicated that people use television as their major source

TABLE I

Use of Mass Media by Koreans (N = 1200; in percent)

Media type	Users	Non-users
Newspaper	81.4	18.6
Television	98.7	1.3
Radio	48.3	51.7
Magazine	33.1	66.9
Internet	41.8	58.2

Source: Media Audience Survey, Korea Press Foundation (2000).

of news and information (98.7%); followed by daily newspapers (81.4%); radio (48.3%); and the Internet (41.8%). The percentage of television use exceeds that of newspapers, confirming the primacy of the television as the most pervasive medium.

In tandem with the Internet explosion worldwide, Internet access in Korea by individuals has exploded from 10.3% in 1998 to 56% in 2002. It is expected that the use of the Internet will continue to grow, at the expense of television viewership and newspaper readership in the years to come.

In terms of time spent on the media, Koreans spend the most time watching television, followed by use of the radio, the Internet and newspapers. As seen in Table II, the average Korean spends almost three hours watching television on a daily basis, 35 minutes reading newspapers, and about one hour listening to the radio.

When compared to earlier surveys, the total time devoted to newspapers and radio has decreased year after year, while the time spent on the Internet has increased. Audiences have also reported that their primary motivations for using television, radio and magazines are to satisfy their interests as well as for entertainment and relaxation. They reported reading newspapers and accessing the Internet to acquire new information and knowledge. Audiences ranked television as their primary source for news (22.2%), followed by newspapers (13.9%), radio (2.9%), magazines (1.0%) and the Internet (0.4%). While television and newspapers are rated as major sources of information, the reliance on newspapers is declining steadily. The staple diet for newspaper readers is

TABLE II

Daily Length of Media Use by Koreans (N = 1200; in minutes)

	Year		
	1996	1998	2000
Newspapers	43.5	40.8	35.1
Television	172.0	193.6	174.1
Radio	72.9	68.3	61.2
Magazine	11.8	7.6	10.5
Internet	NA	30.4	42.2

Source: Media Audience Survey, Korea Press Foundation (2000). NA = Not available.

TABLE III

The Priorities of the Korean Press (N = 1200; in percent)

	Year	
	1998	2000
Reporting political and civic events fairly and objectively	44.7	49.2
Helping audience to understand/evaluate issues	32.2	32.3
Voice the audience's concerns	16.3	12.2
Present ways to solve problems	6.7	6.1
Don't know	0.2	0.3

Source: Media Audience Survey, Korea Press Foundation (2000).

crime and accidents followed by weather, sports, politics, the television guide and entertainment, and business news. On the other hand, the main attractions on television are news, investigative reports, drama, comedy/sitcoms, music, entertainment, and sports. Respondents unequivocally rated television as the most influential medium.

According to respondents, the most important role of the press was to report political and civic events fairly and objectively. This response is believed to reflect the audiences' yearning for a free and democratic press more than anything else.

TABLE IV

Areas for Improvement for the Korean Press (N = 1200; in percent)

	Year	
	1998	2000
Ownership by conglomerates	14.4	14.3
Irresponsible reporting	30.7	26.3
Pro-Government stand	32.7	28.8
Protecting interests of media organization	15.7	17.2
One-sided reporting to protect corporate advertisers	5.7	7.0
Other	0.2	5.4
Don't know	0.8	1.3

Source: Media Audience Survey, Korea Press Foundation (2000).

When asked which areas need improvement, respondents cited the press' pro-government stand as the most pressing issue (28.8%); followed by irresponsible reporting (26.3%); protecting the interests of press firms (17.2%); ownership of the press by business conglomerates (14.3%); and one-sided reporting which protects corporate advertisers (7.0%).

When asked, "Who are the most powerful and influential group in Korean society," the respondents identified politicians (56.1%); followed by journalistis (9.6%); government officials (9.2%); businessmen (7.5%); and civic activists (3.2%). For many years, journalists have been rated as the second most influential group after politicians in Korean society. The ratings for businessmen as an influential group, however, have increased significantly over the last few years.

In terms of credibility, most democratic societies rate television as the most influential and trusted medium. For example, Graber (1997) noted that television is the primary source of news and entertainment for average citizens. It is also the most trusted source of information. Until 1996, however, Korean audiences rated newspapers as the most trusted source of news. Korean audiences began rating television as the most trusted source of news only in the late 1990s, as seen in the 1998 survey by the Korea Press Foundation. In its latest survey, the gap in perceived media trustworthiness between

TABLE V

The Most Trusted Media When Reporting the Same Issue (N = 1200; in percent)

	Percent saying "trusted"
Newspapers	24.3
Television	61.9
Radio	2.5
Magazines	0.4
Internet	10.8

Source: Media Audience Survey, Korea Press Foundation (2000).

newspapers and television has widened considerably. When asked which media's reporting they trust the most in reporting on the same issue, the audiences reported that they trust television's reporting more than any other medium.

Internet use in Korea has shown a most dramatic growth in the last few years. Most Koreans use the Internet at home (49.2%) while "PC Bhang" (PC café or lounge), work, and school comprise 26.3%, 19.1%, and 4% respectively. On average, people pay U.S.$25 as monthly Internet service fees. Apart from gathering information and data, other popular uses of the Internet include e-mailing and online gaming. The primary reasons given for Internet use include the indispensability of the Internet for children's education and "to get recognition at work."

Koreans are reportedly the world's most avid Internet surfers, spending an average of 17 hours per month on the Internet as of May 2000 (Digital Chosun, 2001b). According to a survey by A.C. Nielsen, Koreans spend five hours more than Hong Kong citizens who ranked second in time spent surfing the Net*. Americans, Canadians, Mexicans and Singaporeans surf the Internet for nine hours 38 minutes, eight hours 55 minutes, eight hours 38 minutes, and eight hours and 13 minutes per month respectively.

Despite the financial losses incurred by several channels, cable television has reached most Korean homes. The majority of Koreans subscribe to community cable television as well as national cable television and the Internet.

TABLE VI

Use of new media technologies (N = 1200; in percent)

Type of new media	Percent
Community Cable TV	67.4
National Cable TV	24.1
Internet	39.2
Satellite Antenna TV	2.9
Community Satellite Antenna TV	7.6

Source: Media Audience Survey, Korea Press Foundation (2000).

A satellite broadcasting company, *SkyLife*, began its operation in 2002. *SkyLife* features about 120 channels including movies, sports, and over-the-air network broadcasting (KBS, MBC and SBS). The company is run on subscription fees from more than 400000 subscribers. Whether Korean audiences will add satellite broadcasting to their media diet is still open to question.

FREEDOM OF THE PRESS IN QUESTION

Although many scholars have suggested that freedom of the press in Korea has vastly improved since 1987, it is questionable whether it has reached a level optimal for democratization. Chaudhary and Chen (1995) maintain that Korea's media system was allowed to flourish, in the economic sense, as long as journalists steered away from challenging its undemocratic government. This statement indeed captures the essence of the five turbulent decades of Korean media history.

From the First Republic of Syngman Rhee to the military regimes of Park Chung Hee and Chun Doo Hwan, the Korean press has suffered from a lack of freedom, and ethical crises that eroded public trust until recent years. In 1961, President Park Chung Hee banned news stories critical of his government and stationed intelligence agents in newsrooms (MacIntyre, 2001). Under Park's dictatorship, all journalistic activities, including news products, were placed either under the close scrutiny of government censors or "voluntary self-censors" within the news organizations. A few journalists, who challenged the system, were either fired or prosecuted.

After President Park Chung Hee's assassination in October 1979, the Korean press enjoyed a brief respite. Under the interim government of President Choi Kyu Ha, between 1979 and 1980, many Korean journalists chorused the principles of freedom of the press and democracy, without reflecting on their support for the dictatorial government during the earlier dark era.

When General Chun Doo Hwan rose to power in 1980, after a series of political upheavals and a military coup, the Korean news media quickly reverted to their position of so-called "social responsibility" and, unabashedly curried favor with the new government. During the notorious overhaul of the media industry in 1980, more than 800 journalists were dismissed from their jobs on charges of incompetence or unethical conduct (Lee, 1997; Yang, 1999). In the broadcasting industry alone, KBS and MBC fired 135 and 111 employees respectively (Kim, 2001c).

The authoritarian governments used "carrot and stick" strategies with the Korean news media; the ruling elite promised various favors ranging from massive tax-breaks and business opportunities to cooperative news media owners. Similar privileges in the forms of long-term low-interest bank loans and rights of apartment ownership were given to acquiescent journalists as well. An ambiguous slogan of social responsibility replaced the idea of the press as a watchdog. Adjusting itself to the changed political situation, rather than insisting on its freedom, the Korean press accepted its role as a "voluntary servant" of the ruling government.

After the 1987 democratic reform under Roh, the Korean news media enjoyed unprecedented freedom of the press and autonomy from government influence (Heuvel and Dennis, 1993; Yang, 1999). Lee (1997) noted, however, that this freedom and autonomy in the Korean broadcasting media was still questionable, given hierarchical newsroom cultures and veiled threats from government and political elites as perceived by news professionals. Despite the abolition of authoritarian restraints on the news media, Lee argued there remained a complicated interplay between politicians and veteran journalists who control newsroom gatekeeping. Specific news items are carefully selected, positioned, weighed or rejected based on intricate behind-the-scene deals between government officials and senior editors and news directors. It is well known that a phone call from the presidential Blue House can change the angle and placement of specific news items, and sometimes even result in a story being dropped altogether.

How free is the Korean press? The Freedom House in the United States has consistently ranked Korea as "Free" among more than 180 countries in its annual freedom of the press surveys (Freedom House, 1999, 2000, 2001). This is consistent with a 1999 survey by the Korea Press Foundation, in which Korean journalists reported enjoying the autonomy to choose and write their own stories (90.7%), although they indicated that challenges to professional autonomy usually come from media owners (81.9%).

The annual surveys by Freedom House, however, have also consistently pointed out that the Korean news media have not fully enjoyed freedom of the press. The 1999 survey noted that "the mainly private newspapers still self-censor. They are far more subtly pressured than years ago when daily telephone calls from the information ministry demanded particular coverage and even specific placement of stories (p. 20)." In 2000, the survey concluded, "[O]fficials now use persuasion to prevent critical and unflattering reports of the government (p. 22)." In the 2001 Freedom House survey, Korea scored 27, which positioned her among the lower rungs of the category of "Free" countries. The New York-based organization, however, also criticized Korean politicians and businesses for taking advantage of libel laws to punish journalists for publishing articles that are critical, although factually accurate, of the ruling elites. The Korean Public Prosecutors' Office, for example, has filed more than 12 libel suits since 1999 against journalists, who reported embarrassing stories about investigations by prosecutors. It was alleged that the journalists wrote inaccurate stories with malicious intent. For all 12 suits the prosecutors are seeking over U.S.$10 million in punitive damages (Kim, 2001a), which would be sufficient to have a chilling effect on journalists. Freedom House also noted that, "[Korean] journalists also censor themselves with regard to the business interests of media owners (p. 24)."

Another obstacle to freedom of the press originates from the Korean government's practice of appointing the top managers of media organizations, directly or otherwise. For example, the heads of two major Korean television networks, KBS and MBC, are always hand-picked by the Korean President. Similarly, heads of the state-owned *Yonhap News Agency* and the daily *Taehan Maeil Shinmun* are not free from government affiliation. The *Yonhap News Agency* is the only Korean wire service that deals with foreign news. Consequently, government influence is instituted through this channel of "political appointees." To some extent this limits the diversity of perspectives in the coverage of foreign news.

Old habits die hard; in late 1998, then newly-elected Korean President Kim Dae Jung chose the presidents of the two television networks from among his close associates. These new network chiefs then inevitably replaced their respective news directors with their personal favorites. In 2000, the president of the *Yonhap News Agency* was also replaced with an associate of President Kim. It is, therefore, quite reasonable to assume that the Korean network news services toe the line in accordance with the government's agenda. Through the government's insistence on retaining power over appointments of media managers, the pro-government tradition of Korean journalists and media organizations persists. That tradition is one of supporting the political regime in power by remaining silent at times and serving willingly as the mouthpiece of government at other times.

Is the government the only obstacle to freedom of the press? During the 1980s, Korean journalists felt that the most influential factor restraining freedom of the press was the government (Korea Press Foundation, 1993). In the 1990s, however, a majority of journalists listed business pressures, specifically from media owners and advertising sponsors, as the most influential factors. While print journalists perceived influences from media owners and business constraints to be the strongest, broadcast journalists at network television stations noted that government influence is still the most salient factor restricting their freedom (Korea Press Foundation, 1999).

The debate over the issue of freedom of the press also involves the Internet. In August 2000, thousands of Korean *Netizens*, or

TABLE VII

Factors Restricting the Freedom of the Press (N = 703)

Types of restraints	Level of restraint on press freedom*
Press laws and regulations	6.41
Government influence	7.69
Advertisers' pressures	9.03
Media organizational pressures	8.50

Source: Korean Journalists, Korea Press Foundation (1999).
*Level of restraint measured on a 0–14 scale, with zero representing no restraint and 14 for maximum restraint.

Internet users, protested the new Internet regulations by swarming onto the Ministry of Information's website and shutting it down for several hours. The proposed Internet laws, effective as of 2002, will tighten regulations and impose penalties on the misuse and leakage of personal information on the Web. Although the stated aim is to keep teenagers away from pornographic websites, the laws are seen by many as a means of prosecuting people who post messages critical of the President and his administration. The laws would enable the government to raise censorship levels and control information on the Web.

One notable characteristic of the Korean press system is the practice of the *chonji*, which is a cash gift in an envelope, or other kinds of gifts from news sources to journalists. A case can be made for eliminating this deep-rooted corrupt practice. Chaudhary and Chen (1995) noted that "although most Korean journalists agree that the *chonji* is ethically unacceptable, many habitually accept it," believing it to be a custom. A 1999 survey by the Korea Press Foundation found that 18.9 percent of Korean journalists admitted they had received a *chonji* in the form of cash. Other forms of the *chonji* include free gifts (67.1%); free meals (39.5%); free tickets (15.5%); and overseas tours (13.1%). According to the survey, journalists with the local media tend to receive the *chonji* more than journalists with the national media. Recently, most of the major news organizations, because of their codes of ethics and the resolutions of their labor unions, are rejecting the *chonji*.

The maintenance of *Kijadan*, or press club system, is another outdated practice that impedes the professional development of Korean journalism. The *Kijadan* controls the release of specific news items from various government offices, and denies non-member journalists' access to the same news sources. Despite much criticism, Korean journalists, who cover the various government offices, insist a certain level of control by the *Kijadan* is desirable. They contend it provides for an equitable distribution of news, and curbs excessive competition among members, who may attempt to get the news at any cost. The *Kijadan* at the Supreme Court and Ministry of Justice, for example, has maintained a tradition of banning any member, who releases embargoed stories from its press room for a certain period of time. Ironically, with the *Kijadan* practices, the Korean journalists themselves adopt the role of news censors, the very roles they most openly resist. Denial of access to information has also been the practice of the government as well. On June 20, 2000, the press department of the Korean president banned a *JoongAng Ilbo* journalist from an official building after he reported that the North Korean government was considering amending the Code of the Workers' Party that regarded South Korea as an "enemy." The article was seen as being interpreted by South Korean authorities as jeopardizing the ongoing dialogue between the two countries (International Press Institute, 2001b).

More subtle but intricate form of government pressure was imposed on the Korean media since 1999, when the National Tax Administration announced it would investigate two daily newspapers, the *JoongAng Ilbo* and the *Chosun Ilbo*, on suspicions of tax evasion. As a result, Hong Suk Hyon, president of the *JoongAng Ilbo* was arrested and prosecuted. He later pleaded guilty to tax evasion charges. By 2001, the tax investigation and audits were expanded to include 23 other media outlets in the country, creating a furor over the real political intentions of the Korean government. Journalists and various freedom of press organizations criticized these actions as a new and updated form of press control as they were launched shortly after President Kim Dae Jung announced he was considering a media reform to root out corruption in the country's free-wheeling press (International Press Institute, 2001a). The government and citizen groups, in defense of their actions, maintained that there was no political motive behind the tax investigations. They insisted that the operation of media organizations, like other businesses, must be open and above board by adhering to tax laws.

In June 2001, the Korean government's National Tax Service levied U.S.$390 million in back taxes and penalties on six news media, of which three were the country's top three dailies, the *Chosun Ilbo*, the *JoongAng Ilbo* and the *Dong-a Ilbo*, all known for being most critical of President Kim's policies (Lee, 2001; MacIntyre, 2001). In August, a panel of judges ordered the arrest and detention of three newspapers' owners – Bang Sang Hoon, president of the *Chosun Ilbo*, Kim Byung Kwan, joint owner of the *Dong-a Ilbo*, and Cho Hee Joon, who controls the *Kukmin Ilbo* (Lee, 2001). The charges included embezzlement and tax evasion. In October, all three media magnates were out on bail pending trial.

As for the legitimacy of the unprecedented four-month tax probe, the public as well as the journalists appear evenly divided. The pro-government camp argues that the newspaper industry in general needs reform in order to banish its deep-rooted practices of unfair and sensational news reporting. This group also claims that the news media in the past have attempted to evade taxes by threatening to write embarrassing stories about tax officials. Those who oppose the investigations, however, insist the charges are politically motivated. Calling President Kim a "press dictator," they point out that smaller pro-government newspapers and television stations have not been targets of the tax probes (Lee, 2001). This camp also alleges that the move is an attempt by the President to crush media opponents of his controversial "Sunshine Policy," one of engaging North Korea (MacIntyre, 2001).

In light of this ongoing battle, the International Press Institute warned the Korean government that it believes the media tax probe was only a prelude to a campaign to muzzle the independent press in Korea under the guise of "press reform" (International Press Institute, 2001c). In September 2001, the organization sent a freedom of the press mission to Seoul, and later put Korea on its Watch List of those countries against freedom of the press.

CONCLUSION: CHALLENGES AND PROSPECTS

For the last five decades, the Korean media has gone through various challenges and hardships – from the dark days of suppression under dictatorial governments to the vibrant and competitive commercial market of today. The news media in Korea are undergoing a transformation from the traditional dichotomous print and broadcasting industry to a more diversified multi-media operation that includes the Internet, cable television and satellite television. Over the last 15 years, the Korean media industry has also seen multiple expansions in numbers, thanks to democratic reforms and deregulation policies in the country. As far as the number of media outlets is concerned, Korea now enjoys more than a sufficient number of channels of news media through which public opinion can be conveyed.

As the media are diversifying their form and content, so do also the audience's perceptions of media. Media consumption patterns of the audience, as seen in surveys (i.e., Korea Press Foundation, 2000), confirmed the Korean audiences' changing lifestyles and attitudes toward the mass media. For instance, the traditional reliance on daily newpapers has shifted to television and online media. Newspapers still enjoy a significant influence over the formation of public opinion, but they continue to give way to television, cable TV and online publications over the last few years. The multi-media and multi-channel environments now available to most Koreans will provide even more challenges to newspapers as well as the broadcast television industries. The dramatic growth of the Internet, together with its synergistic marriage to other media, is expected to continue into the next decade. Korea already is the world's most wired country with a fith of its population of 48 million broadbound Internet connections. The Korean government aims to offer broadbound access to all household by 2005. The use of the Internet, however, is sometimes controversial because of the ease with which teens can access pornography and the use of online chat rooms for teen prostitution. A reality of this new age of the Internet, as Hachten (1999) observed, is that even government authorities are unable to control these individual "information seekers," who can select or choose his/her news or information from a widening variety of sources.

Freedom of the press has been an unending proposition in Korea. Since the birth of the Republic, the news media have been subject to constant suppression up until the mid-1980s. The 1990s have seen a twofold quantum leap in the number of news media outlets, thus enabling a more diversified public voice to be heard.

That optimism, however, falls short of a free and responsible press. Apart from explicit suppression through the firing of journalists and stationing of government agents inside news organizations by the dictatorial governments of Park Chung Hee and Chun Doo Hwan, the more democratic governments of Kim Young Sam and Kim Dae Jung also have tried to control the news media by way of implicit coercion, by changing, downplaying and dropping certain stories. More recently, the government and its agencies have been suing journalists and news media firms for reporting specific stories against their wishes. In 2001, a tax probe that led to the arrests of three media magnates culminated in the reality of government control over the news media. The arrests were said to give the government power to muzzle the vocal press from voicing dissent against President Kim Dae Jung for his unpopular policies as well as to give his administration a break at a time when the Presidential election was about a year-and-a-half away. Television, on the other hand, was given a respite from the harsh tax probes, although broadcasters were asked to pay overdue taxes as well. The reason for this mild treatment is that television still lacks an independent editorial stand due to successful political interference from the government. Korean television has been a major player in mobilizing the public with its wide reach and diversity of messages packaged in a variety of programs. As the news medium providing objective and impartial news editorials and interpretations on political and civic matters, television still has a long way to go.

The character of these news media audiences, is also changing. Korean audiences are evolving from passive and muted consumers to more diversified and assertive individuals, who want a voice. The Korean public flexed its mussels during the television reception fee boycott movement in the 1980s and "turn-off TV movement" in the 1990s, when the pro-government news media failed to represent the people's will and demands for democracy. The Presidential election in 2002 has demonstrated how Internet – sawy voters in their 20s and 30s ae at the forefront of political reform. It is this audience, who will provide the energy for reforming the daily news gathering practices of journalists and the news media in the country.

NOTE ADDED IN PROOF

The Internet has become the most important forum for political debates among the younger generation, thus making it a key apparatus in Presidential election campaigns. The power of the Internet was demonstrated well during the latest Presidential election in December 2002. Apart from setting up homepages for a presidential candidate, each camp initiated online campaigns by sending campaign messages to the electorates through email, chat channels, and message boards. Among the four major candidates, none benefited from the Internet as much as ruling party candidate Roh Moo-Hyun (and the eventual victor) whose 7000000 online supporters launched a sympathy campaign to shape up his image (Reuters, 17 December, 2002). During the Presidential campaign, young Korean votors aged between their 20s and 30s, dubbed as "Generation 2030," were identified as the driving force behind Roh's victory. Generation 2030 not only formed an online group called "Rohsamo" or "people who love Rho," they also rallied other young voters to go vote for Roh on the day of election.

The Internet is also a means of mobilizing demonstrations. In June 2002 when a U.S. Army's armored vehicle accidentally ran over and killed two Korean schoolgirls, no major newspapers or television reported the incident. However, Internet chat channels and discussion groups played a key role in spreading the news and mobilizing young Koreans to initiate candlelight vigils in protest of a U.S. military court's acquittal of two American soldiers involved in the accident. The widespread demonstrations further sparked off calls for a revision to the Status of Forces Agreement (SOFA) governing the legal status of U.S. soldiers in Korea.

REFERENCES

Chaudhary, A.G. and A.C. Chen: 1995, 'Asia and the Pacific', in J.C. Merrill (ed.), Global Journalism: Survey of International Communication, 3rd ed. (Longman, New York, NY, pp. 269–328).

Digital Chosun: 2001a, 67.1 percent of middle school and high school students carry cell phones. [Online]. Available: http://www.chosun.co.kr/w21data/html/news.html (November 26, 2001).

Digital Chosun: 2001b, Koreans, the world's number one time spent on the Internet. [Online]. Available: http://www.chosun.co.kr/w21data/html (June 23, 2001).

Freedom House: 1999, Press Freedom 1999: News of the World. Press freedom survey 1999.

Freedom House: 2000, Censor Dot Gov: The Internet and Press Freedom 2000. Press freedom survey 2000.

Freedom House: 2001, How Free? Press freedom survey 2001.

Graber, D.A.: 1997, Mass Media and American Politics, 5th ed. (Congressional Quarterly Press, Washington DC).

Hachten, W.A.: 1999, The World News Prism, 5th ed. (Iowa State University Press, Ames, IA).

Heuvel, J.V. and E.E. Dennis: 1993, The Unfolding Lotus: East Asia's Changing Media (Freedom Forum Media Studies Center, Columbia University, New York, NY).

Hwang, K.S.: 2001, October 31, 'Satellite broadcasting is to send test signal in January next year', Maeil Business Daily, p. 42.

International Press International: 2001a, IPI concerned over apparent administrative pressure on South Korean media. [Online]. Available: http://www.freemedia.at/index1.html (June 17, 2001).

International Press Institute: 2001b, World press freedom review: South Korea. [Online]. Available:http://www.freemedia.at/wpfr/southkor.htm (June 17, 2001).

International Press Institute: 2001c, IPI sends press freedom mission to South Korea. [Online]. Available: http://www.freemedia/dia/at/prKorea03.09.01.htm (November 20, 2001).

Kim, D.J.: 2001a, November 17, 'The power elites who enjoy suing', Chosun Ilbo, p. 7.

Kim, S.J.: 2001b, World press review: South Korea: a literate society devours the news. [Online]. Available: http://www.worldpress.org/cover16W.htm (May 31, 2001).

Kim, Y.H.: 2001c, 'The broadcasting audience movement in Korea', Media, Culture & Society 23, pp. 91–107.

Korea Press Foundation: 1993, The Korean Journalists: The Third Biennial Survey of Newspaper, Broadcast and Wire Service Reporters. Research Report, 93-3 (in Korean).

Korean Press Foundation: 1999, The Korean Journalists: The Sixth Biennial Survey of Newspaper, Broadcast and Wire Service Reporters. Research Report, 99-3 (in Korean).

Korea Press Foundation: 2000, Media Audience Survey. Survey Analysis 2000-2 (in Korean).

Korea Press Foundation: 2001, Newspaper and Broadcasting Yearbook 2000/2001 (in Korean).

Lee, B.J.: 2001, August 27, 'Breaking some news: A president picks a dangerous fight with the media', Newsweek, p. 13.

Lee, J.K.: 1997, 'Press freedom and democratization: South Korea's experiment and some lessons', Gazette 59, pp. 135–149.

Ma, D.H.: 1998, 'New media', in J.M. Kang et al. (eds.), Mass Media and Society (Segyesa, Seoul, pp. 227–268) (in Korean).

MacIntyre, D.: 2001, July 16, 'Stomping the presses', Time, p. 14.

Nam, I.S.: 2002, December 17, 'Voters are just a click away in South Korean election', Reuters.

Yang, S.M.: 1999, 'Political democratization and the news media', in D.C. Shin and L. Diamond (eds.), Institutional Reform and Democratic Consolidation in Korea (Hoover Institution Press, Stanford University, Stanford, CA, pp. 149–170).

Korean Broadcasting System
E-mail: newspro2000@hotmail.com

PART III. QUALITY OF LIFE ACROSS POPULATION GROUPS

GYEONGJOON YOO

WOMEN IN THE WORKPLACE: GENDER AND WAGE DIFFERENTIALS

ABSTRACT. The purpose of this study is to clarify the real causes of gender wage differentials in Korea by analyzing changes over the period 1988–1999. The participation rate of women in the Korean labor force has gradually increased since 1963, reaching 47.4 percent as of 1999. This increase can be attributed to more active participation by women of all ages, except those between the ages of 15–19, as a result of their enrollment in higher level education. In particular, a remarkable rise in labor market participation was achieved by those between the ages of 25–29. On the other hand, the gender gap in terms of pay has gradually decreased – the ratio of female workers' earnings to that of male workers has increased from 45.1 perecent in 1972, to 63.1 percent in 1999. However, when the gender wage differentials were broken down into their various categories, it was found that discrimination against female workers, compared to the gender gap, played a greater role in human capital endowment as it relates to productivity for the 1988–1999 period.

1. INTRODUCTION

In Korea, women were paid approximately 60 percent of male workers' earnings in 1999. Gender wage differentials remain considerable, although they have been diminishing. It would be wrong to argue that the differentials result entirely from gender discrimination. A certain part of wage differentials may result from different individual characteristics including education and prior working experiences, which often lead to a productivity gap between men and women. Noteworthy here is that the gender productivity gap differs from gender discrimination.

This paper examines the magnitude and sources of gender differences in earnings. Section 2, that follows immediately, reviews the current state of the Korean female labor force. Section 3 presents detailed facts on gender wage differentials, and Section 4

Social Indicators Research **62, 63:** 367–385, 2003.

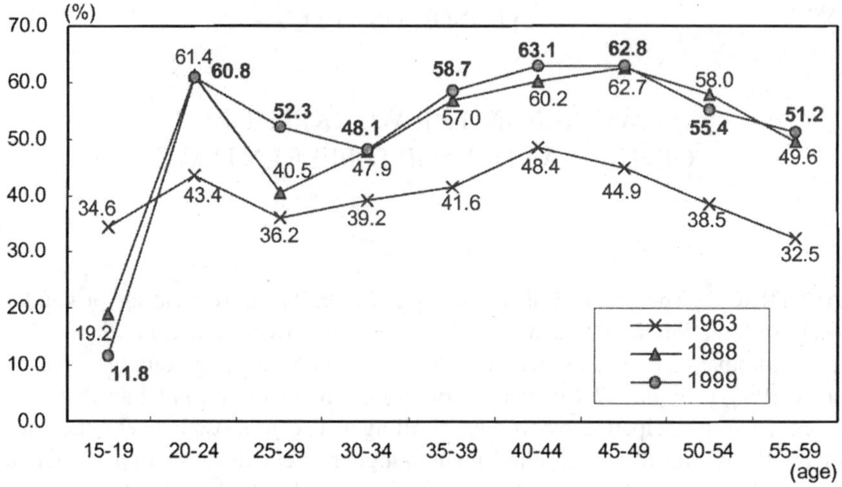

Source: National Statistical Office, KOSIS.

Figure 1. changes in female economic participation by age.

pinpoints their causes. The last section introduces a wage equation to decompose gender wage differentials.

2. FEMALE LABOR FORCE TRENDS

In 1999, women comprised about 40 percent of the entire economically active population in Korea, compared to 35 percent in 1965. A similar trend was also seen in total employment. This increase in women's participation in the labor market over the past decades was mainly due to the rise in the economically active participation among two age groups, 20–24 and 30 or over, as shown in Figure 1. On the other hand, the higher education enrollment rate has contributed to a decrease in the labor force participation rate by those aged 15–19, from 34.6 percent in 1963 to 11.8 percent in 1999. Those aged 15–19 had once played an important role in boosting the Korean economy during the 1960s, which was based on labor-intensive industries.

The overall increase in female participation in the labor market has contributed to a threefold increase in the number of female workers between 1963 and 1999, while male participation doubled over the same period. This active participation by female workers has been a main source of labor force supply for the last 30 years,

TABLE I

Gender Wage Differentials Over Time (Unit: won, %)

	Men's wage (A)	Women's wage (B)	B/A
1972	29319	13222	45.1
1975	65908	27167	41.2
1980	222957	95692	42.9
1985	386346	173319	44.9
1989	603259	315995	52.4
1994	1194821	678779	56.8
1999	1681216	1060098	63.1

Monthly wage including irregular bonus payments.
Source: Ministry of Labor, *Survey Report on Wage Structure*.

a remarkable period of speedy economic growth in Korea. Since the financial crisis in 1997, growth of the economically active population as well as that of total employment in Korea have been somewhat stagnant. As in many other countries, the importance of women in the Korean labor market will continue to increase.

3. GENDER WAGE DIFFERENTIALS

As mentioned earlier, the female labor force has played a vital role in boosting gthe Korean economy, and its importance will continue to increase. While fair treatment in the labor market cannot be overemphasized, gender discrimination in current labor practices is likely to pose barriers to new entrants into the labor market and also to render existing women participants facing difficulties.

In this context, this section examines the current state of gender wage differentials. Although we cannot simply say that the sole cause of gender wage differentials is discriminatory treatment of women, which is often institutional and historical in nature, one may surmise that a certain extent of the wage differentials are indeed due to gender discrimination.

As shown in Table I, the average wage of female workers was less than 45 percent that of male workers until the mid-1980s. This situation has somewhat been ameliorated since the late 1980s mainly due to the labor force shortage in the manufacturing industry. As a

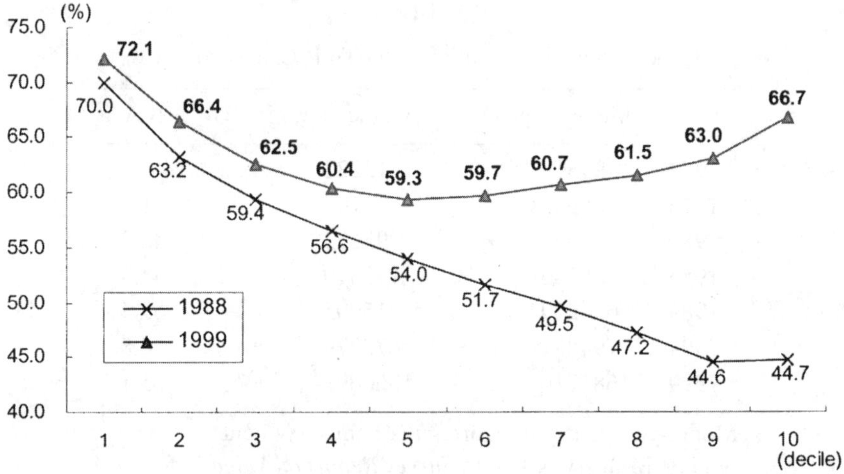

Source: Author's calculation from the Ministry of Labor's *Survey Report on Wage Strucutre Tape*.

Figure 2. Average wage and gender differentials by decile distribution.

result, the average monthly wage of female workers in 1999 reached 63.1 percent that of male workers, or 1060 thousand won.

Figure 2 shows a distinct change in the average wage differentials between male and female workers by decile distribution between 1988 and 1999. In 1988, female workers were paid remarkably less than their male colleagues in every decile. It is worth noting that wage differentials were larger in higher deciles. In fact, in the 1st decile, female workers earned 70 percent of male workers' wages, while the figure dropped to as low as 45 percent in the 9th and 10th deciles. In 1999, the overall gender wage gap relatively narrowed, with the lowest ratio in the 5th decile standing at about 60 percent. Another change from a decade ago is the fact that women in higher deciles were receiving higher wages in 1999.

Figure 3 shows the change in the earnings profile by gender. It is evident that, in 1999, the average wage of male workers increased as they got older until the ages of 45–49, while female workers received their highest wages at the ages of 30–34, with their wages gradually decreasing thereafter. This means that men's experiences are valued properly, whereas those of women are not.

Figure 4 shows the ratio of male and female workers to the total labor force by decile distribution as of 1999. Thirty-eight percent of male workers belonged to the 8th, 9th, and 10th deciles while

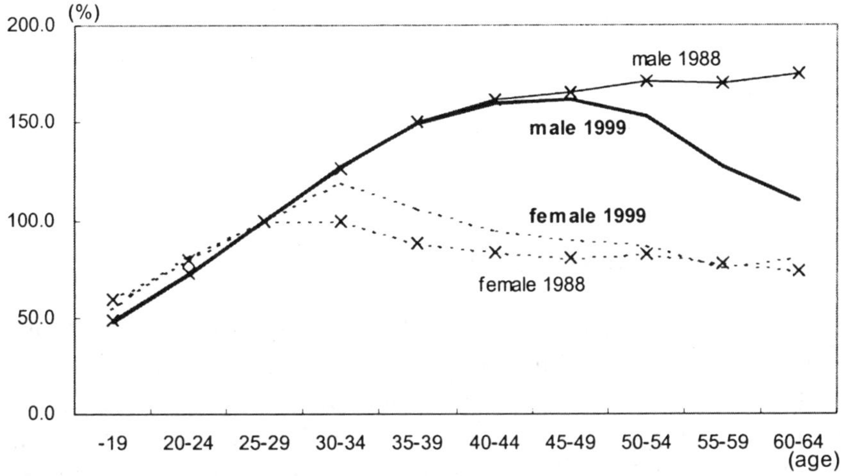

Note: Wage of workers aged 25–29 = 100.
Source: Ministry of Labor, *Survey Report on Wage Structure.*

Figure 3. Age-wage profiles by gender.

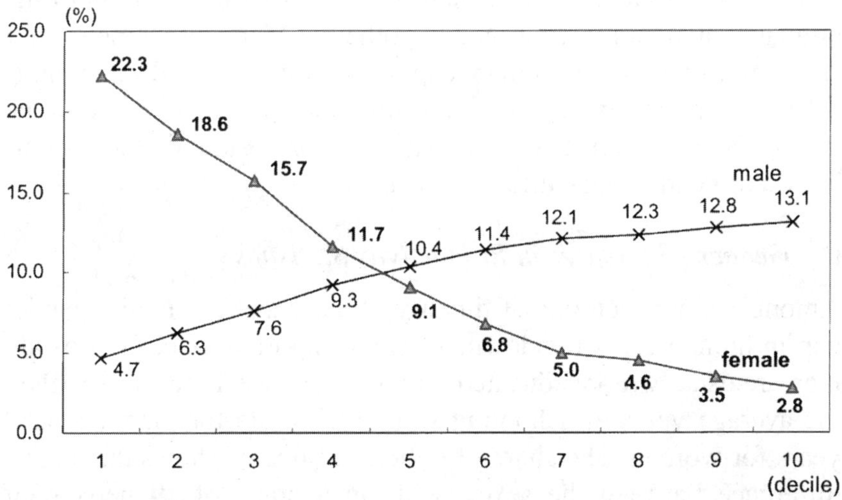

Source: Author's calculation from the Ministry of Labor's *Survey Report on Wage Strucutre Tape*.

Figure 4. Ratio of male and female workers to total labor force by decile distribution (1999).

only 10.9 percent of female workers were included in these highly paid groups. On the other hand, more than half of the total female workers belonged to the 1st, 2nd, and 3rd deciles, the poorly paid groups in which less than 20 percent of male workers were included. Thus, Figure 4 clearly illustrates the sharp contrast between men and women in wage distribution.

4. CAUSES OF GENDER WAGE DIFFERENTIALS

What are the causes of wage differentials between male and female workers? The human capital theory hypothesizes that men and women alike are paid the value of their productive contribution, implying identical wage determination structures, and that gender wage differentials are attributable to differences in human capital investment between the sexes. In comparison, institutionalists contend that the labor market is segmented according to sex due to intentional discrimination against women and that this discrimination is the major source of gender wage inequality.

What then are the causes of gender wage differentials in Korea? In the Korean labor market, there is evidence supporting both the human capital and institutional hypotheses. Men and women differ substantially in their human capital endowment. Administrative rules and practices in Korean firms also articulate institutional discrimination against women. This section examines the various causes of gender wage differentials in Korea.

(1) *Gender Differences in Productivity Statistics*

Amongst other factors that directly affect wage levels, the gender gap in human capital endowment is an important one. First of all, men are usually more educated than women (see Table II). In 1999, the average years of schooling were 13.2 years for men and 12.2 years for women. The share of college graduates shows the largest difference between the sexes, with an average of 29 percent of men and 13.3 percent of women completing this level of higher education. Such a large difference reflects women's lower college enrollment rate, their concentration in majors, such as literature and humanities, whose graduates are less preferred by employers, and the lack of employment opportunities for highly educated women.

TABLE II

Gender Differences in Individual Characteristics (1999)

	Men			Women		
	Single	Married	Total	Single	Married	Total
Education (%)						
Elementary school & under	0.7	3.8	3.0	0.6	14.6	7.4
Middle school	3.9	13.2	11.0	2.4	23.1	12.4
High school	53.0	43.2	45.5	61.6	41.1	51.7
Junior college	15.9	10.1	11.5	21.5	8.6	15.2
College & over	26.5	29.8	29.0	14.0	12.6	13.3
Years of schooling (in years)	13.5	13.1	13.2	13.0	11.2	12.2
Tenure (in years)	3.2	7.4	6.4	3.1	5.1	4.1
Pre-Co. exp. (in years)	9.1	21.3	18.4	5.8	22.6	14.0
Monthly working Hours (in hours)	213.4	213.7	213.6	203.7	208.5	206.0

Pre-Company Experience = age – ages of schooling – 6. Source: Author's calculation from the Ministry of Labor's *Survey Report on Wage Structure Tape*.

In addition, the average company tenure for men was 6.4 years, which was approximately 1.5 times that of women. Differences in tenure between unmarried men and women were greater than the average, with men showing two times longer tenure. However, the average pre-company experience for men was 18.4 years, while that of women was 14 years. Table II shows that the average for married women was longer than that of men, but this was because women's intermittent labor force participation was not properly taken into account. Many women, in fact, tend to discontinue working for various reasons, including marriage. The labor force participation rate of men aged 25–49 was over 90 percent in 1999, whereas that of their female counterparts ranged from 48.1 percent to 62.8 percent. Pre-company experience of married women is exaggerated because the definition (age – years of schooling – 6) often includes the periods when they were economically non-active or unemployed.

For a fairer comparison, it is necessary to compare the *actual* pre-company experience, without including the periods of temporary

TABLE III

Gender Differences in Pre-Company Experience and Skills (1999) (Unit: %)

	Men			Women		
	Single	Married	Total	Single	Married	Total
Pre-Co. experience						
One year or less	17.9	4.7	7.9	18.4	9.3	14.0
1-3 years	29.9	9.3	14.2	32.7	17.6	25.4
3-5 years	24.8	12.9	15.7	25.2	18.6	22.0
10 years or more	8.8	48.6	39.0	5.0	28.3	16.3
Skills						
Certificates holders	46.0	43.5	44.1	21.9	26.1	23.9
No certificates	13.6	12.7	12.9	12.6	32.8	22.4
Probationers	40.3	43.8	43.0	65.4	41.1	53.6
Other workers	0.0	0.0	0.0	0.0	0.0	0.0
N.A.	0.1	0.1	0.1	0.1	0.0	0.1

Source: Author's calculation from the Ministry of Labor's *Survey Report on Wage Structure Tape*.

lay-off, between male and female workers. It is noteworthy that pre-company experience did not include the years of work experience irrelevant to the present one. When considering gender differences in human capital endowment in view of the five different groupings of pre-company experience as shown in Table III, the percentage of men with more than 5 years of pre-company experience accounted for 62.2 percent of the men's total, whereas it was only 38.7 percent for women. On the other hand, women with less than 3 years of pre-company experience accounted for 39.4 percent, in striking comparison with the 24.1 percent for that of men. Furthermore, in the case of married individuals, 73.2 percent of married men had more than 5 years of pre-company experience, while the percentage of married women with the same years of experience was only 44.5 percent. In short, the average years of pre-company experience were longer for men than for women.

In addition, possession of skills is considered another index of human capital. As shown in Table V, 55.1 percent of male workers possessed various skill certificates, thus rendering them professional technicians, engineers, etc. Only 23.9 percent of female workers held such certificates. Hence, a great portion of gender wage differentials can be attributed to differences in human capital investment between men and women. This means that even with no discrimination against women (implying that wage is solely determined by personal contribution to production), women are more likely to be paid less than men.

(2) *Discrimination Against Women in Employment*

Neoclassical economists argue that wage is determined by interplay of labor demand and labor supply. Employers demand labor to the point where their returns are maximized under given conditions, in other words, where wage meets the marginal revenue productivity (MRP) of labor. Workers supply labor as a way of maximizing their utility, distributing their available time among work and leisure. It is in the competitive market where these decisions of labor demand and labor supply meet, and at the same time, where wage and employment are determined accordingly. Wage determined in the competitive market through this process would thus be equal for workers with the same productivity or relevant human capital. In turn, in the competitive market, the wage differentials between workers would purely result from differences in the workers' productivity, and not from discrimination.

On the other hand, institutionalists argue that there is a certain degree of discrimination in the labor market. According to them, wage is not determined by interplay of labor supply and demand, but rather by internal institutional rules and practices of firms. Furthermore, there are diverse types and classes of occupations, which actually determine wage. Thus, if some workers are excluded from being assigned certain duties or promoted even though they possess sufficient capability, we can presume that institutional discrimination exists. In this case, workers with the same productivity may be paid differently.

Gender differences in the types and classes of occupation from the viewpoint of institutionalists will be examined next. Table IV lists differences in occupational and hierarchical composition between male and female workers. More men were engaged in executive and managerial as well as professional and technical jobs than in clerical, service and sales, or production positions in

TABLE IV

Gender Differences in Occupational and Hierarchical Composition (Unit: %)

	1988			1999		
	Men	Women	Women/ total	Men	Women	Women/ total
Occupation						
Exceutive – managerial	5.5	0.1	1.3	7.4	1.0	5.7
Professional – technical	10.5	5.9	22.8	29.6	19.2	21.7
Clerical	22.3	22.4	34.7	16.1	37.6	50.0
Service – sales	5.5	7.3	41.1	3.0	11.2	61.8
Production	56.1	64.2	37.7	44.0	31.0	23.2
Hierarchical position						
Executive officer – General manager	3.6	0.1	1.8	8.4	1.3	6.1
Manager	4.4	0.1	1.5	8.5	1.4	6.5
Depute manager – team leader	3.2	1.0	13.4	3.5	1.8	18.4
Others	88.7	98.8	37.1	79.6	95.5	34.0

'Men' and 'Women' refer to their respective ratio in each occupational or hierarchical composition. 'Women/Total' refers to the ratio of female workers to the total number of workers regardless their sex.
Source: Author's calculation from the Ministry of Labor's *Survey Report on Wage Structure Tape.*

1999 than in 1988. The share of female workers increased in all types of occupations except production. However, by calculating the ratio of female workers in each type of occupation, it can be noted that the highest-paid and socially respectable occupations are often over-represented by male workers. In particular, the ratio of female workers in executive and managerial occupations stood at a mere 1 percent, meaning that the highest-paid jobs are nearly monopolized by men. Similar gender differences were found in hierarchical positions as well. Almost all top positions, such as executive officers and general managers, are held by men.

Although Table IV shows gender differences in types of occupation and hierarchical position, it is difficult to say that there was discrimination against women in job assignment or promotion. This

TABLE V

Gender Job Segregation (Unit: %, 1000 won/month)

		Male-dominated	Female-dominated	Mixed
1988	Share of job categories	52.5	26.0	21.5
	Male workers			
	Composition	74.4	7.0	20.0
	Average wage	567	372	438
	Female workers			
	Composition	11.3	60.9	27.8
	Average wage	359	253	276
1999	Share of job categories	65.3	8.5	26.5
	Male workers			
	Composition	77.5	1.8	20.7
	Average wage	2197	1647	1945
	Female workers			
	Composition	27.0	28.2	44.9
	Average wage	1584	1310	1260

Sample includes only firms with 500 or more employees.
Source: Author's calculation from the Ministry of Labor's *Survey Report on Wage Structure Tape.*

is because, even for the same occupation or same position, there are, in fact, diverse duties. Therefore, any discrimination by gender may not be detectable just by looking at the overall classification of occupational and hierarchical positions between men and women.

Table V divides all occupations into three categories: male-dominated, female-dominated, and mixed jobs. If an occupational category is more than 70 percent occupied by one gender, it is defined as being dominated by this gender. If the share of one gender is 30–70 percent, it is defined as a mixed job. According to this categorization, 52.5 percent of all jobs in 1988 were dominated by men and 26 percent by women, resulting in 79.5 percent of jobs being dominated by one gender. This means that there existed very serious gender job segregation. Moreover, female-dominated jobs involved poor compensation.

This phenomenon has been changing since 1999, with about 73.5 percent of jobs being segregated by gender. When compared to the figures from 1988, male-dominated jobs have increased and female-dominated positions have decreased. The average wage of female workers in the female-dominated occupational category was slightly higher than that of female workers in the mixed jobs category, but it was generally lower than that in the male-dominated category. Gender job segregated and the crowding of female workers within a limited range of unskilled job at the bottom rung of the job hierarchy raise the question of discrimination against women in the course of job assignment and promotion. It also supports the crowding hypothesis, which states that the low wage of women often results from intensive competition among female workers due to their crowding within a limited range of jobs. This situation also reduces women's opportunity for on-the-job training and promotion, and results in a lower level of attachment to the firm and relatively shorter tenure.

(3) *Pay Discrimination Against Women*

Another cause of gender wage differentials is pay discrimination against women, which is defined as occurring when a female worker doing the same job with the same level of human capital is paid less than her male counterpart. Korean companies, in particular the conglomerates, pay their employees based on internally established pay-steps or salary classes, which result in institutional discrimination against women. Table VI shows starting wages by worker group of one of Korea's big companies. Institutionalization of discrimination based on education and gender of workers is particularly noteworthy. From this pay-steps table, company A's new employees are first classified by their education level. Workers with the same education level usually fall into non-competing groups, but starting steps may be assigned differently to workers by gender, resulting in 4–14 percent lower wage for women than men with the same education level.

Starting pay-steps and wage differentials are not necessarily evidence of pay discrimination against women because men and women with the same education level may be assigned to different jobs. Rather, starting pay-step differentials by education level and by gender may be regarded as employment discrimination rather than pay discrimination.

TABLE VI

Starting Wages by Worker Group (Company A, 1999) (Unit: 1000 won, %)

	Starting wage	Starting wage index (male college graduates = 100)
College graduates		
Men	1553	100.0
Women	1484	95.6
Junior college graduates		
Men	1279	82.4
Women	1164	75.0
		(91.0)
High school graduates		
Men	1186	76.4
Women	1026	66.1
		(86.5)

(1) Company A is one of Korea's largest firms in the machinery and equipment industry.
(2) Numbers in parentheses indicate the female workers' starting wage index when the starting wage of male workers with same education level equals 100.
Source: Korea Employers Federation, *Case Studies on Personal Management and Wages*, 2000.

Pay discrimination by gender can only be proven when men and women with the same human capital, and who perform the same duties in a company, are paid differently. Table VII presents cases where women with the same education level age, pre-company experience, and tenure as men have been paid approximately 20 percent less than men. The 20 percent gap between men and women has not changed for the 1988 to 1998 period. The table does not include all types of duties, and therefore it may not be correct to assume that all of the wage differentials from the table reveal gender discrimination. Nonetheless, it would not be too much of an exaggeration to suggest that some portion of wage differentials is in fact due to discrimination against women.

TABLE VII

Gender Wage Differentials of Workers with the Same Human Capital (Unit: won, %)

	Individual characteristics	Men's wage (A)	Women's wage (B)	(B/A)
1998	High school, 19-years old, 1 year tenure, 1–2 years pre-co. exp.	485678	370330	76.3
	High school, 22-years old, 1 year tenure, 3–4 years pre-co. exp.	526431	426315	81.0
	High school, 23-years old, 4 years tenure, 1–2 years pre-co. exp.	543573	428473	78.8
	High school, 21-years old, 3 years tenure, 3–4 years pre-co. exp.	1691250	1275333	75.4
	High school, 23-years old, 1 year tenure, 2–3 years pre-co. exp.	1426917	1187667	83.2
	High school, 25-years old, 7 years tenure, 5–10 years pre-co. exp.	1881500	1223417	65.0

(1) Electrical and electronic equipment mechanics and fitters were surveyed.
(2) Pre-company experience includes only those relevant to the current job.
Source: Author's calculation from the Ministry of Labor's *Survey Report on Wage Structure Tape.*

5. DECOMPOSITION OF GENDER WAGE DIFFERENTIALS

As seen in the previous sections, women are often less endowed in human capital, which according to human capital theorists, directly relates to productivity. Female workers are also discriminated in the course of job assignment, promotion, and compensation. How significantly, then, do these factors compose the total gender wage differentials? The answer to this question can be very critical in suggesting policies to effectively deal with the problem. If gender wage differentials are mainly due to the differences in human capital investment, the government should promote policies that facilitate human capital investment in women. On the other hand, if discrimination is the main cause of gender wage differentials, then the government should take measures to deter companies' internal discrimination in the decision-making process for job assignment, promotion, and compensation.

This section decomposes the overall gender wage differentials into various factors and clarifies their roles and importance respectively. Sources of wage differentials include differences in human capital endowment relating to productivity and discrimination against female workers. The latter in turn includes discrimination in employment and in pay. Discrimination in employment means that women are unfairly treated in terms of occupation types, while discrimination in pay relates to female workers' lower rate of return than their male counterparts to the same human capital investment, such as education and tenure.

The wage equation used in this section is as follows

Wage per hour = F (years of schooling, years of schooling squared, tenure, tenure squared, years of pre-company experience, years of pre-company experience squared, job type dummy, job position dummy).

Regression analysis shows the estimated coefficients to be decomposed into three parts: a constant; a coefficient relating to human capital variables such as education, tenure, and pre-company experience; and men are denoted as "m" and women as "f." Therefore, each estimated coefficient can be denoted as follows:[1]

C: constant

G_{ff}: vector composed of all female estimated coefficients except the constant

G_{fm}: vector composed of female estimated coefficients for human capital variables and male estimated coefficients for job type and position variables

G_{mf}: vector composed of male estimated coefficients for human capital variables and female estimated coefficients for job type and position variables

G_{mm}: vector composed of all male estimated coefficients

F_1: vector composed of average years of women's schooling, their square, years of women's tenure, their square, women's years of pre-company experience, and their square

F_2: vector composed of women's job types and positions

$F =$ $(1, F_1, F_2)$

M_1: vector composed of average years of men's schooling, their square, years of men's tenure, their square, men's years of pre-company experience, and their square

M_2: vector composed of men's job types and positions

$M =$ $(1, M_1, M_2)$

From the above, Average wage of female workers = $(C_f, G_{ff}) \cdot F$
Average wage of male workers = $(C_m, G_{mm}) \cdot M$
Overall gender wage differentials = (C_m, G_{mm}) *cdot* $M - (C_f, G_{ff}) \cdot F$
Gender wage differentials resulting from differences in human capital endowment

$$= G_{mm} \cdot (M_1, F_2) - G_{mm} \cdot (F_1, F_2)$$

Gender wage differentials resulting from differences in the rate of returns to human capital investment, that is, wage discrimination

$$= (C_m, C_f) + \{G_{mf} \cdot (F_1, F_2) - G_{ff} \cdot (F_1, F_2)\}$$

Gender wage differentials resulting from discrimination in job types and positions

$$= G_{fm} \cdot (F_1, M_2) - G_{ff} \cdot (F_1, F_2)$$

Table VIII, which includes the decomposition results of gender wage differentials calculated using the above method, shows the differences between 1988 and 1999.

The disparity in human capital investment accounted for 51 percent and 43 percent of total gender wage differentials in 1998 and 1999, respectively. On the other hand, discrimination accounted for 49 percent in 1988 and 57 percent in 1999, implying that discriminatory factors have become more important. Among other human capital, level of education and tenure are the key causes of gender wage differentials in human capital investment between men and women. From the table, it can be seen that pay discrimination

TABLE VIII

Decomposition of Gender Wage Differentials (Unit: won, %)

	1988	1999
Total gender wage	216,941	530,253
Differentials	(100.0)	(100.0)
Human capital endowment	50.8	43.0
Level of education	14.7	11.5
Tenure	22.0	23.0
Pre-Co. experience	14.2	8.5
Discrimination	49.2	57.0
Pay	47.5	71.0
Job assignment & promotion	1.7	–14.0

(1) Gender wage per hour differentials.
(2) Pre-company experience does not include tenure at present firm, and is computed as (age – years of schooling – tenure at present firm – 6).
Source: Author's calculation from the Ministry of Labor's *Survey Report on Wage Structure Tape.*

against women has been aggravated, whereas the situation in job assignment and promotion improved greatly in 1999.

6. CONCLUSIONS

This study has examined the dynamics and sources of gender wage differentials in Korea by analyzing changes in workers' wage between 1988 and 1999. As in other societies, the wage differentials between the two genders in Korea have been reduced considerably during the process of economic development. Yet, there still remained notable wage differentials in Korea. More notable in that discrimination against female workers has replaced human capital endowment as their main cause of the wage gap between the two genders.

In order to solve the problem of gender wage differentials, therefore, policies aimed at eliminating wage discrimination must be promoted. At the same time, efforts should be made to facilitating women's human capital investment should be promoted. Usually, women's low level of education results from the Korean custom of favoring boys, as well as from difficulties in employment faced by highly educated women. Female workers' relatively short tenure and pre-company experience are due to the typically simple and repetitive nature of their jobs as well as the established practice of laying-off female workers upon marriage. It is thus necessary to combat institutional discrimination against women, which is in fact more important than what is revealed by the statistical analysis presented above. Important policies to effectively deal with this problem may include forbidding gender wage discrimination and providing more job training opportunities for female workers.

APPENDIX

Data Set

Since 1971, the Korean government has conducted an Occupational Wage Survey (OWS hereinafter). This paper used the surveys from 1988 and 1999, which were the latest statistics available.

The survey first selects sample companies from a list of companies with 10 or more employees. The survey covers all workers in the selected companies with 10–99 employees; 70 percent of those in companies with 100–299 employees; 50 percent of those in companies with 300–499 employees; and (depending on the year) up to 50 percent of those in companies with 500 or more employees. All industries and regions are included except for government offices, army and police, and educational institutions. The OWS covers about 60 percent of total employees and about 7 percent of total establishment.

The labor income variable used in this study is worker wage and salary income, including base salary, overtime pay, and bonuses. In the Korean context, the latter two are increasingly important components of income.

The OWS is not without its limitations, however. By the very nature of the sampling design, workers in small companies, the self-employed, and the unemployed are excluded. Furthermore, the OWS gathered information only on the labor earnings of sampled workers. Thus, information is not available on the individuals' other income sources or on the incomes of other family members. These factors of the data set should be kept in mind for future studies.

NOTE

[1] More details about this decomposition method can be found in Lee, W.D. (1987).

REFERENCES

Bibb, R. and W.H. Form: 1977, 'The effects of industrial, occupational, and sex stratification on wages in blue – collar markets', Social Forces 55(4), pp. 974–997.

Burris, V. and W. Amy: 1982, 'Sex segregation in the U.S. labor force', RRPE 14(3), pp. 43–56.

Doeringer, P.B.: 1983, Segmenting Forces in Labor Market – Towards a Theory of Work Groups and Employment System, Mimeo (Department of Economics, Boston University).

England, P.: 1982, 'The failure of human capital theory to explain occupational sex segregation', The Journal of Human Resources XVII(3), pp. 358–370.

Halaby, C.N.: 1982, Job-Shift Differences between Men and Women in the Workplace, Vol. 11, No. 1 (Academic Press, Social Science Research, New York and London, pp. 1–29).

Halaby, C.N.: 1979, Sexual in the Workplace: An Employer – Specific Analysis of Pay Differences, Vol. 8, No. 1 (Academic Press, Social Science Research, New York and London, pp. 790–104).

Lee, Won-Duck: 1987, Earnings Distribution and the Role of Enterprises in Korea. Unpublished Ph.D. Dissertation, Boston University.

Mincer, J.: 1974, Schooling, Experience, and Earnings (National Bureau of Economic Research, New York).

Osterman, P. (ed.): 1979, Sex Discrimination in Professional Employment. A Case Study. ILRR, Vol. 32, No. 4, pp. 451–464.

Park, S. and F. Park: 1984, Wages in Korea (in Korea) (Korean Development Institute).

Roos, P.A.: 1981, Sex Stratification in the Workplace: Male – Female Difference in Economic Returns to Occupation, 10. Social Science Research (University of Massachusetts, pp. 195–224).

Korea Development Institute
P.O. Box 113 Chongnong
207-41 Chongnayanu-dong
Dongdalmun-Ku, Seoul 130-120
Korea
E-mail: yoogj@kdi.re.kr

MEESOOK KIM and KYUNG-HO CHO

QUALITY OF LIFE AMONG GOVERNMENT EMPLOYEES

ABSTRACT. The main purpose of this study is to examine distinctive aspects of the quality of life (QOL) of Korean government employees utilizing in large part many features of the 1999 QOL survey of Korean government and private sector employees. To this end, responses of government and private sector employees regarding various dimensions of QOL are compared. This study finds that the QOL of government employees is significantly lower than that of private sector employees. The result of regression analysis of QOL dimensions shows that the level of satisfaction with one's work environment is the most influential determinant of the overall QOL of Korean government employees. Based on this finding, this study recommends that the government agencies consider improving their employees' work-related environment.

I. INTRODUCTION

The roles of Korean government employees are very much in transition. Their behavior had always been in conformity with the demands of policymakers and politicians. Recently, they became more assertive, however, about their own views and opinions in designing various economic and political initiatives. It is becoming clear, furthermore, that many of the past human-resource management policies and programs in the public sector are inadequate for any future work environment. Considerable attention is being paid, in particular, to the needs and expectations of government employees regarding their attempts to balance their work and private lives (Kim and Cho, 2000). Some observers and managers have found that current government employees behave in their own interests in the workplace, and perceive their job as not a mere part of public affairs, but as a place to enhance their individuality and personal development (Cho, 1997; Lim, 1995).

The importance of QOL in Korean government agencies is accentuated, more than ever before, in the current era of globalization. If the government fails to respond to the demand for

Social Indicators Research **62, 63:** 387–409, 2003.

QOL enhancement of public employees, it will eventually be placed at a competitive disadvantage compared private counterparts. As Cho (1997) pointed out, government manger typically regard themselves as captives of a series of cumbersome internal management "systems" over which they have no control, and they believe that they are suffering form a lack of discretion, freedom, and individuality, some evidence suggest that the resulting erosion of the morale and confidence among government employees may cause disruption of public responsibilities and self-trust (Cho and Kim, 2000; Park and Won, 2000). Many studies warn, moreover, that the current system of government workers is losing high-quality employees due to its declining pay levels as well as the declining prestige of their occupation (Cho, 1997; Kim, 1994). For these reasons, Korean public administration today faces a number of overriding issues; increasing one's sense of personal commitment to their respective agencies.

The challenge of the Korean government is to respond to social changes that places emphasis on non-material benefits, especially social relationships. QOL within many agencies today is much more than a composite of material incentives for their employees; it is increasing perceived as a pivotal element in fulfilling employees' need for self-actualization in an organization. Keeping this social context in mind, the Civil Service Commission of Korea (hereinafter the CSC of Korea), the government's primary personnel management agency, conducted a nationwide survey in 1999 to assess the level of QOL of government employees, and the results were made public (Kim and Cho, 2000). With limited funding arranged by the National Assembly, the CSC of Korea provides government-wide human resource management policies, guidance, and oversight for some one-half million central government employees.

This paper attempts to delineate the major dimensions of QOL from a subjective perspective, and thereby evaluate the quality of life experienced by government employees. What constitutes the QOL people themselves experience on a daily basis? How do government employees compare with private sector employees in the experience of it? Do government employees really experience a lesser QOL than private sector employees? If so, in what domains of QOL do the two groups show a significant difference, and to what extent?

What factors determine the QOL government employees? These are the specific questions we attempt to address in this paper.

There has been considerable research on the public-private differences in work-related behaviors and attitudes (Cho, 2000; Cho and Kim, 2000; Chubb and Moe, 1988; Posner and Schmidt, 1996; Rainey et al., 1995; Schmidt, 1996; Rainey et al., 1995; Schneider and Vaught, 1993). Yet, few studies have investigated the differences in QOL scores between the public and private sectors. The present study, therefore, seeks to fill this gap in the literature by examining the QOL differences between the two sectors, and also by investigating the various forces affecting the perceived QOL among Korean government employees.

II. MODELS OF QUALITY OF LIFE

Approaches

The quality of life at community and individual levels has been measured and evaluated from a variety of perspectives (Haas, 1999; Seed and Lloyd, 1997). In Korea, local governments have recently increased their efforts to measure QOL by using objective indicators, such as average income, employment rate, and crime rates (Ha, 1996). Kim et al. (1998) examined the changing QOL in local communities by focusing on six domains, including educational opportunity, sports and recreation, health, and safety. According to the objective indicators of these life domains, the QOL in many of those communities has deteriorated since the local autonomy system was introduced in 1995. Unlike these studies that deal with the objective conditions of local communities, Cho and Oh (1993) focused on the life experiences or perceptions of community residents. They examined how residents of Kyungju perceived the heath and pleasure of their living environment, the providing of public and private services, and neighborhood safety.

There have also been two approaches to the study of QOL among employees of the private and public sectors. The first one is widely regarded as "objective" because it is based on a range of the economic and other resources those employees command. The second approach involves efforts to understand to what degree these employees are satisfied with particular organized policies and living conditions. There have been, however, discrepancies in the QWOL between employees' self-ratings and government statistics (or the statistics of employing organizations). Despite the inconsistency between the objective and subjective results, many scholars agree with the view that the employees' subjective evaluation of QOL is very important for continuing improvement in government administration (Poister and Henry, 1994; Gold and Wooldridge, 1995; United States Merit Systems Protection Board, 1991). Between these two approaches, we employ the subjective one because people choose or do not choose to work in government agencies on the basis of their perceptions of what is offered in those agencies.

A Multi-Dimensional Model

Under the guidance of its Civil Service Commission, the Korean government recently began an innovative effort to enhance the QOL of its employees. Two projects have been initiated according to this plan. One was to assess the needs for reinventing personnel practices in Korea (Korean CSC, 1999); the other was to compare the perceptions of the QOL of government and private sector employees (Kim and Cho, 1999). These QOL programs were designed in order to achieve three specific goals. They were to: (1) increase the ability of government agencies to attract and retain employees in critical occupations and positions, such as technical and scientifically research; (2) provide increased benefits for severely underrepresented individuals, such as women and the handicapped; and (3) provide diverse opportunities to balance work responsibilities and family needs, which have generally been neglected in the study of personnel administration.

Private firms in Korea are beginning to respond to the needs of working parents with new policies respecting child care, flexibility in the workplace and scheduling, and other concerns. Government agencies rarely address these QOL issues through reforms in the area of personnel and the work environment. Therefore, government agencies are at a competitive disadvantage in recruiting and maintaining qualified employees. To redress this problem, the CSC developed a multi-dimensional model of QOL among government employees. This model, which reflects the private sector model of QOL, consists of ten life domains. These domains include

TABLE I

This Study's QOL Survey Items

Clusters	Indicators
Commuting	Commuting time
Work	Income, working hours, job satisfaction in 10 dimensions, and fear of unemployment
Health	Current Health condition and stress and anxiety
Family	Understanding between spouses
Family finances	Average monthly family income, and situation of family finances
Housing	Home ownership
Leisure	Length of summer vacation
Social life	Number of friends
Community	Contact frequency with neighbors
Country	Pride in Korea and emigration intention

commuting, work, health, family, family finances, housing, leisure, social life, community, and country.

III. METHODOLOGY

Sample

For the present study, two sets of samples were developed, one of which was drawn from 47 ministries and independent agencies, and the other from 53 private firms. Trained interviewers distributed a structured questionnaire to the respondents. They were asked to fill it out by themselves. The survey was conducted from October 27 to November 2, 1999.

This study utilized two separate sampling methods. With respect to government sector employees, a purposive quota sampling method was employed. The sample size of each agency was determined in proportion to the size of its employee pool. The gender and rank distributions in each sample were based on the total number of government employees (female: 20%, ranks, 1st~9th). Then, the purposive sampling method was utilized with the help of the director of the human resources department in each agency. The directors assisted the interviewers in selecting respondents fitting into the gender and rank distributions.

As for private sector employees, two-stage cluster sampling and purposive sampling methods were used. First, from a list of 679 "outstanding firms" each with more than 100 full-time workers, 150 private firms, all in cities where the government ministries and agencies were located, were selected randomly. After classifying them into three groups based on the number of employees (large, medium, and small size firms), fifty-three firms were chosen for the survey: 14 firms with 100–499 employees (small); 16 firms with 300–499 employees (medium); and 23 firms with 500 or more employees (large). From each firm, respondents were selected in proportion to the gender and rank distributions within the public sector.[1] The number of selected employees varied depending upon the number of employees in the firm: (19–21 respondents form lager firms, 9–11 respondents from medium-sized firms, and 4–5 respondents from small firms). With the assistance of the directors of the respective departments of human resources, respondents fitting into the gender and rank distribution were selected.

Characteristics of the Sample

The two sectors were found to be slightly different from one another in terms of socio-demographic variables (see Table II). Government employees were found to be older than their private sector counterparts (the average age of government employees was 37.9, while that of private sector employees was 32.4). More female employees were selected from private firms than the government (18.6% for the government sector and 21.6% for the private sector). Government employees outstripped private sector employees in terms of years of educational and degrees earned. As for educational attainment, the proportion of those without a college education among government employees was much lower than that of the private sector employees (10.3% versus 20.2%). The percentage distribution of college degrees was similar between the two groups: (government employees 68.2%; private employees 70.8%). With respect to graduate school, however, over 20 percent of government

TABLE II

Socio-demographic Characteristics of Respondents

	Government employees		Private employees		Total	
	Freqency	Percent	Freqency	Percent	Freqency	Percent
Total	1002	65.7	524	34.3	1526	100.0
Sex						
Male	815	81.4	411	78.4	1226	80.4
Female	186	18.6	113	21.6	299	19.6
No answer	1	—	—	—	1	—
Age						
20s	122	12.2	193	36.8	315	20.7
30s	467	46.8	250	47.7	717	47.1
40s	335	33.6	68	13.0	403	26.5
50s +	73	7.3	13	2.5	86	5.7
No answer	5	—	—	—	5	—
Education						
High school	103	10.3	106	20.2	209	13.7
2-year college	70	7.0	58	11.1	‘128	8.4
College	613	61.2	313	59.7	‘926	60.7
Graduate school	206	20.6	43	8.2	249	16.3
Others	9	0.9	4	0.8	13	0.9
No answer	1	—	—	—	1	—
Martial Status						
Married	849	84.9	306	58.4	1155	75.8
Single	146	14.6	208	39.7	354	23.2
Divorced	1	0.1	7	1.3	8	0.6
Widowed	4	0.4	3	0.6	7	0.5
No answer	2	—	—	—	2	—
Rank						
Street level	118	11.8	86	16.4	204	13.4
Low level manager	547	54.6	254	48.5	801	52.8
Middle manager	310	30.9	168	32.1	478	31.3
High level manager	27	2.7	16	3.1	43	2.8
Income						
Less than 1 mill	40	4.0	28	5.5	68	4.6
1–2 million	477	48.4	177	34.9	654	43.8
2–3 million	351	35.6	151	29.8	502	33.6
3–4 million	75	7.6	83	16.4	158	10.6
4–5 million	30	3.0	40	7.9	70	4.7
5 million +	13	1.3	28	5.5	41	2.7
No answer	16	—	17	—	33	—

employees had a graduate school degree, while only 8.2 percent of private sector employees did.

With respect to martial status, government employees have a higher marriage rate than private sector employees, which may be attributable to the age differences between the two groups. In terms of rank, public employees are crowed at the middle range ranks, whereas private employees are more evenly distributed. Government employees report a lower income than their private sector counterparts. Another difference between the two groups was that government employees were found to be in the middle income range, while private sector employees were more likely to earn either a low or high income.

In sum, government employees were: older; had a higher marriage rate, and a higher education level; but earned less than their private sector counterparts. Since these group characteristics are likely to affect people's QOL, a careful interpretation is necessary when comparing the two groups. Accordingly, we will take a look at the QOL of government employees in ten life domains.

IV. THE QOL OF GOVERNMENT EMPLOYEES IN TEN DOMAINS

Commuting

Since commuting affects the daily lives of workers, commuting time is widely considered to be one of several important factors of QOL. One may assume at this point that a long commuting time is closely related to high stress and fatigue, and thus may lead to poor QOL. The comparison of commuting time between the two groups has revealed that government employees spend less time on commuting than their private sector counterparts. While 73.7 percent of government employees spend less than one hour on commuting, only 69.5 percent of private employees spend the same amount of time on it. This indicates that government employees live closer to their workplaces. Meanwhile, the proportion of employees, who spend more than one-and-a-half hours commuting, is higher among government sector employees (6.3%), than among private sector employees (4.2%). This, however, constitutes only a small portion of the overall distribution of commuting time.

Work

The fact that employees spend most of their daytime hours at work requires us to take a comprehensive look at their work environment. Here we measured work-related factors such as income levels, working hours, satisfaction levels and fear of unemployment in various aspects of work and job security.

Income. The current survey shows that government employees earn less than private employees. The former earn about 1.2 million won a month on average, while the average income for the latter stands in the range of 1.8 million won a month (see Table III). The proportion of those who earn less than one million won, however, is higher among private employees. This may stem from the fact that the private sector, in comparison with the government sector, has more female workers, who are younger and less educated, than their male counterparts. In the second lowest income level, the proportion of government employees (66.4%) is much higher than that of private employees (48.0%), which means that most government employees earn a comparatively lower income. Furthermore, while only 2.6 percent of government employees earn more than 3 million won, as much as 8.9 percent of private employees earn such an income. There are no government employees who earn more than 5 million won, but 1.1 percent of private employees earn that amount. Interestingly, the income distribution among government employees is much more concentrated than that among private employees.

Hours of work. Korean workers are known for working the longest hours in the world. When comparing work hours between government and private sector employees, the former work longer than the latter. While only 18.7 percent of government employees stopped working within an hour after the end of working hours, as many as 40.3 percent of the private employees stopped working within the same period. In addition, the proportion of government employees, who worked four hours overtime was 20.4 percent, but the figure for private employees was only 7.6 percent. In other words, government employees, despite their longer hours of work, received less income than the private sector workers did. Government employees face a doubly unfavorable work situation.

TABLE III

Average Monthly Income Comparison between Government and Private Employees

	Government employees (%)	Private employees (%)	Total (%)
Less than 1 million won	9.1	17.4	11.9
1–2 million won	66.3	48.0	60.0
2–3 million won	22.0	25.6	23.2
3–4 million won	2.4	5.5	3.5
4–5 million won	0.2	2.3	0.9
over 5 million won	—	1.1	0.4
Total	100.0	100.0	100.0
(persons)	(1.001)	(523)	(1.524)
Average	1.2 million won	1.8 million won	

$\chi^2 = 78.364^{***}$, $^{***}p < 0.001$.

Job satisfaction. Table IV shows the levels of satisfaction towards ten work dimensions including: work duties, income, relations with coworkers, promotion opportunities, overseas business trips, departmental worksites, facilities, participation in decision making, freedom and authority, and the level of public respect. Government employees were less satisfied than private employees with respect to seven of these dimensions: work duties, income, promotion opportunities, department, participation in decision-making, freedom and authority, and public respect. There were no significant differences, meanwhile, in three of the work dimensions: relations with coworkers, opportunities for business trips overseas, and facilities. Both groups showed similarly low satisfaction with the last two dimensions. There was no work dimension with which government employees showed more satisfaction than private employees.

Fear of unemployment. Job security is one of the important factors affecting QOL, because it provides a secure income, and a sense of belonging to workers. Job security used to be a high in the public sector, but after the 1997 financial crisis it bottomed out. Job insecurity was measured by fear of unemployment. Less than half of

TABLE IV

Average Satisfaction Level with Ten Dimensions of Work

	Total	Government employees	Private employee	Difference	T value
Work duty	4.06	3.99	4.19	−0.20	−3.413***
Income	2.54	2.24	3.11	−0.87	−14.097***
Relation with coworkers	4.64	4.62	4.68	−0.06	−1.401
Promotion opportunities	2.88	2.63	3.37	−0.74	−10.799***
Overseas business trip	2.54	2.52	2.59	−0.07	−0.912
Department	3.71	3.56	3.99	−0.43	−6.431***
Facilities	2.67	2.71	2.59	0.12	1.673
Participation in decision making	3.45	3.38	3.59	−0.21	−3.369***
Freedom and authority	3.44	3.33	3.66	−0.33	−4.916***
Respect from public	3.13	2.89	3.58	−0.69	−10.417***

6 point scale (1: highly unsatisfied–6: highly satisfied).
*** $p < 0.001$.

government employees (40.7%) revealed anxiety about unemployment. Since the 1997 economic crisis, 80000 government employees were laid off during the two restructuring episodes (Cho Sun Daily Newspaper, Oct. 7, 1999). Moreover, not only public employees, but also private employees have been suffering from job insecurity since the inception of the crisis. Over 45 percent of private sector employees responded that they fear being unemployed.

Unless there is job security, it is hard to promote employee morale, which may lead to increased productivity and job satisfaction. When employees feel uncertain about job security, they tend to compete with their coworkers in order to survive in the workplace. Interestingly enough, however, the current survey showed that employees were highly satisfied with their work relationships with their colleagues. In other words, it seems that up until now fear of being unemployed had very little, if no, negative effect on employees' relationships with their colleagues.

Health

Current health condition. An overall review of their respective health conditions was achieved by utilizing a six-point scale questionnaire (1: very poor, 6: excellent). Over 70 percent of workers responded that they were in good health, (70.9% for the government employees, and 73.3% for the private employees). There are no statistically significant differences between the two groups regarding their respective states of health.

Stress and anxiety. Four factors – frequencies of stress, loss of motivation, depression, and fear of the future – were measured to examine the negative aspects of their states of health. The result is that to a certain degree both groups had stress, lacked motivation, and worried about the future. As shown in Table V, out of the four negative health indicators, "stress" was first (the average was 3.65, based on a 5-point scale ranging from "no stress at all" to "stress all the time"), followed by "worry about the future" (3.23), and "loss of motivation" (3.01). It is only in the area of depression that these workers achieved a comparatively low score (2.35) with no group differences. What may be inferred from this is that job insecurity, at least after the massive restructuring in the public as well as private sectors, had a negative effect on the psychological well-being of employees in both sectors. In addition, government and private sector employees were shown to have different levels of anxiety. For example, government employees suffered a significant loss in motivation as compared to their private sector counterparts, while private employees were more stressed and apprehensive about their future. Even so, we learned that both of these groups "often" or "always" experience mental health problems.

Family

In the domain of family life, the interaction between husband and wife is believed to affect QOL. The study found that both government and private sector employees have a relatively high level of mutual understanding with their respective spouses, showing no group differences. Only 5.9 percent of all the respondents had a lack of or minimal degree of understanding with their respective spouses.

TABLE V

Negative Aspects of Mental Health Condition

Total		Government employees	Private employees	Total	T value
Stress	3.65	3.60	3.71	−0.11	−2.379*
Loss of motivation	3.01	3.09	2.95	0.14	2.708**
Depression	2.35	2.39	2.33	0.06	1.070
Worry about the future	3.25	3.20	3.40	−0.20	−3.647***

5 point scale (1: not at all–5: all the time), $^{***}p < 0.001$, $^{**}p < 0.05$, $^{*}p < 0.01$.
Higher score means higher negative mental health condition.

Family Finances

Family income. There are differences in family income between government and private sector employees, as shown in Table VI. While family income of public sector employees was clustered in the range of 103 million won per month, that of private sector employees was scattered across various levels of family income, as in the case of work income. In the case of family income of less than 2 million won a month, as much as 52.4 percent of government employees fell within this category. Only 40.4 percent of private employees fell with the same category, about 10 percentage points less than government employees. Furthermore, the proportion of private employees earning over 3 million won a month (29.8%) was 2.5 times as many as that of government employees (11.9%).

Perception of family finances. With regard to the perception of family finances, only a few employees responded positively: 8.7 percent said "good" or "very good," and 21.0 percent said "fair". The rest, almost 70 percent, felt that their family financial situation was not favorable: 39.4 percent said "a little poor," 23.2 percent said "poor," and 7.6 percent said "very poor." The overall financial situation of employees was not good for the government and private sectors alike.

The financial situation for government employees, however, was found to be more unfavorable than that for their private sector counterparts. The proportion of government employees, who rated their

TABLE VI

Monthly Family Income in 1999

	Government employees (%)	Private employees (%)	Total (%)
Less than 1 million	4.0	5.5	4.7
1–2 million	48.4	34.9	43.8
2–3 million	26.6	29.8	33.6
3–4 million	7.6	16.4	10.6
4–5 million	3.0	7.9	4.7
over 5 million	1.3	5.5	2.7
Total	100.0	100.0	100.0
(persons)	(986)	(507)	(1,493)

$\chi^2 = 89.728^{***}$, $^{***}p < 0.001$.

family financial situation as being "very poor," was almost four times (10.4%) as high as that of the private sector employees (2.3%). In addition, 27.3 percent of the government employees rated their family financial situation as being "poor," while only 15 percent of their private sector counterparts did the same. Meanwhile, only 23.3 percent of government employees indicated that their family finances were "little good" or better, while 40 percent of private employees did the same. Therefore, as in other domains of life, it can be said that in the financial domain, the situation of government employees was worse than that of their counterparts.

Housing

Home ownership was measured to ascertain QOL in the domain of housing. The proportion of government employees, who own homes, amounted to only 49.0 percent, whereas that of private employees amounted to 55.3 percent. As for rent, the proportion of the former is twice as large as the latter, indicating that government employees' QOL, in terms of home ownership, is comparatively less pleasant than that of private sector employees. Even though government sector employees are older and have higher marriage rates and educational attainment, their home ownership state was viewed as less favorable than their private sector counterparts.

Leisure

In the domain of leisure, the length of summer vacation was measured. Here we learned that government employees (84.3%) had either 1–5 days or 6–10 days of vacation per year, and less than two-thirds of private employees (69.5%) had a similar number of vacation days. Over twice as many private employees (26.3%) spend more than 11 days on vacation, while only 10.3 percent of government employees did so. Moreover, the proportion of government employees, who had no vacation time, was slightly higher than their private counterparts (government employees: 5.9%, private employees: 4.2%). This shows that government employee' vacation days were shorter, and the number of vacation days of private sector employees was longer as well as relatively more widely spread out.

Social Life

With regard to one's social life, the number of friends was measured. The two groups were significantly different in terms of number of friends to turn when having trouble. The percentage of employees with "a fair" number of friends was higher for government employees (70.1%) than for private employees (60.8%), but the percentage of those with "many or very many" friends, to whom they could turn to, was higher for private employees (25.1%) than for government employees (14.5%). Since government employees spend a longer time at work, they may not have enough time to spend with their friends.

Community

As is the case with relationships with friends, government employees had fewer contacts with their neighbors than private employees. Even though both groups did not have frequent contact with their neighbors (frequent contact: 15.4%), more private employees had frequent contact with their neighbor than the former. For instance, only 13.8 percent of government employees had contact with their neighbors "very often or often," while as many as 18.2 percent of private employees did. This lesser degree of contact seems to be related to some extent to the fact that government employees lack free time due to a tight working schedule.

Country

Pride in Korea. Both employee groups show fairly strong pride in Korea. Over 70 percent of employees from both sectors indicate a little or fairly strong degree of pride in Korea. There are no statistically significant differences between the two sectors in the level of pride individuals feel about their own country.

Emigration intensions. As for emigration intentions, as many as 43.5 responded positively on emigration, indicating that a significant number of employees would like to go abroad. More private sector employees (51.8%), than government employees (39.2%), were found to want to move to another country. This is a very interesting result because private sector employees tend to experience more favorable conditions in most domains of life than their government sector counterparts. This may reflect the fact that private employees are more open to changes in life than government employees.

V. SATISFACTION LEVELS IN TEN DOMAINS

Satisfaction levels regarding ten domains of QOL were compared to identify domain(s) with group differences. Seven domains (commuting, work, family, family finances, housing, leisure, and social life) show statistically significant group differences; the domain of family finances revealed the greatest difference between the two groups (see Table VII). Although satisfaction with family finances was the lowest in both groups, government employees' satisfaction with income was much lower than that of private employees (2.81 versus 3.37 based on a 6-point scale). This indicates that the financial situation of government employees was much worse than that of their private sector counterparts. The only domain in which government employees outscored their private sector counterparts was in the domain of commuting. Their shorter commuting time indicated that they were more satisfied with commuting. In the domains of community and country, however, there are no statistically significant differences between the two groups. Both have a fairly high satisfaction level regarding the two domains.

As for overall life satisfaction, the average score stood slightly above the midpoint (3.5) at 3.80. Government employees (3.75) had

TABLE VII

Comparison of Satisfaction between Government and Private Employees in Ten Domains[1]

	Total	Government employees	Private employees	Differences	T value
Commuting	4.12	4.20	3.97	0.23	3.142**
Work	3.78	3.66	4.00	−0.34	–5.911***
Health	3.78	3.74	3.87	−0.13	–2.192*
Family	4.34	4.28	4.47	−0.19	–3.614***
Family finances[2]	3.00	2.81	3.37	−0.56	–10.009***
Housing	3.73	3.66	3.87	−0.21	–3.237***
Leisure	3.66	3.55	3.86	−0.31	−4.683***
Social life	4.23	4.14	4.40	−0.26	−4.972***
Community	3.94	3.97	3.89	0.08	1.301
Country	3.86	3.86	3.88	−0.02	−0.325
Overall life satisfaction	3.80	3.75	3.90	−0.15	–3.305***

[1]6 point scale (1: Very unsatisfied to 6: very satisfied), $^{***}p < 0.001$, $^{**}p < 0.01$.
[2]Family finances are measured not with satisfaction level but with current financial status using 6 point scale, 1 being very bad through 6 being very good.

a little lower overall life satisfaction level compared to private sector employees (3.90), indicating that the overall QOL of government employees was slightly lower than that of private sector employees. The quality of government employees' life based on the above findings was less favorable than that of private employees in seven domains as well as overall life satisfaction.

VI. DETERMINANTS OF QOL

Table VIII reports the results of a multivariate regression model to explore the determinants of QOL among government employees. We found that the factors affecting QOL of government employees consisted of satisfaction with seven domains of life: work, family, family finances, leisure, social life, community, and country. Out

TABLE VIII

Regression Analysis of Government Employees' Satisfaction with Life

Independent variables	B	Sampling error	Beta	T value	P value
Constant	0.155	.227	—	0.774	0.495
Domains					
Commuting	−0.004	0.019	−0.006	−0.234	0.815
Work	0.177	0.026	0.213***	6.750	0.000
Health	0.048	0.025	0.055	1.888	0.059
Family	0.010	0.027	0.105***	3.492	0.001
Family finances	0.183	0.029	0.198***	6.257	0.000
Housing	0.044	0.024	0.054	1.820	0.069
Leisure	0.070	0.022	0.090**	3.313	0.002
Social life	0.124	0.026	0.131***	4.716	0.000
Community	0.080	0.027	0.084**	2.977	0.003
Country	0.101	0.025	0.119***	4.071	0.000
Socio-demographic factors					
Gender (Male= 1)	−0.051	0.072	−0.021	−0.703	0.482
Age	−0.004	0.004	−0.029	−0.935	0.350
Education	0.027	0.015	0.046	1.725	0.085
Martial status	0.210	0.078	0.081**	2.786	0.005
N					893
F					39.439***
R^2					0.403
Adjusted R^2					0.393

*** $p < 0.001$, ** $p < 0.01$.

of seven statistically significant determinants, the most influential predictor was satisfaction with work (Beta: 0.213), followed by satisfaction with family finances (Beta: 0.198), social life (Beta: 0.131), country (Beta: 0.119), family (Beta: 0.105), leisure (Beta: 0.090), and community (Beta: 0.084). In other words, to improve the QOL of government employees, it would be necessary to raise satisfaction in these domains. Satisfaction with commuting, health, and housing, however, do not affect QOL significantly.

Among five socio-demographic variables, martial status was found to be the only significant determinant. Married government employees were more satisfied with their lives than unmarried government employees. The other four socio-demographic variables – gender, age, education, and family income – were found to have no significant impact on QOL. There were no gender differences with respect to satisfaction with life. Also, various age groups and groups of various educational levels showed no differences in term of satisfaction with life. In addition, family income had no significant impact on life satisfaction. Interestingly, even though satisfaction with family finances, a subjective indicator of QOL, affected life satisfaction positively, the amount of family income, an objective indicator of QOL, had no impact on life satisfaction. Thus, we can conclude that the subjective perception of the life situation, rather than the objective condition, is an important factor in determining QOL.

VII. DISCUSSION

Based on the above research findings, we can conclude that the QOL of Korean government employees was lower than that of their private sector counterparts. In both objective and subjective aspects of QOL, their QOL is less pleasant than that of their counterparts in the private sector. Government employees earn less income, work longer hours, have less family income, are more likely to rent housing, and have fewer summer vacation days than private sector employees. In addition, the satisfaction level of government employees was lower than that of private sector employees in seven out of the ten life domains (work, health, family, family finances, housing, leisure, and social life). Only in the domain of commuting were they more satisfied than private employees.

The results of the regression of QOL show that satisfaction with work was the most influential determinant of QOL. Other significant factors were satisfaction with family finances, family, leisure, social life, community, and country. This implies that attention should be given to improving work-related factors in order to better the QOL of government employees. The second influential determinant of government employees' QOL was satisfaction with family finances. Family income, however, did not significantly affect QOL. Subjective perception was more important than objective condition. The level of satisfaction with family finances, however, could be improved by raising income, because the lack of income leads to dissatisfaction with family finances. In turn, this would lead to dissatisfaction with leisure and family life. Therefore, to improve satisfaction with family finances, raising income would be the first step to take.

Other statistically significant determinants were satisfaction with social life, country, family, leisure, and community. In the United States, the federal government provides its employees with various options of working arrangements so that they can maintain a healthy balance between work and family. This practice is called "family-friendly policy." Flexible work hours and workplace, and childcare facilities at work are specific examples of these policy arrangements. Both the production rates of government employees, and their levels of work satisfaction, were reported to have increased in the United States since the inception of this policy (United States Office of Personal Management, 1998). We can infer that this can also be conducive to job mobility and enhancement of satisfaction levels with work.

In Korea, family life is becoming an increasingly important social issue. The government, therefore, should consider developing policies that help government employees manage work and family life, harmoniously. It may be too early at this juncture for Korea to follow all the policy initiatives, that the United Sates has taken on behalf of its employees. Korea, however, should consider accepting these family-friendly policies over time after weighing their merits. Policies concerning telecommuting, a flexible workplace, and work sharing are not easy to implement in Korea. Even so, on-site/near-site childcare centers, flexible work schedules, and part-time employment are among important policy measures to be considered. With flexible working schedules, for instance, employees can have time for a social life and leisure. On the other hand, on-site childcare centers should be more accessible for the increasing number of double-income families.

As for leisure, even though Korean government employees have vacation days guaranteed by regulations, they are unable to use all their vacation time. There is a disparity between the legal system and the reality, where invisible office conventions forbid the using of all the vacation days guaranteed by the regulations. Employees should be allowed to use all their vacation days. They should, also, be permitted to take their vacation at any time. Currently, most vacation days are taken during the summer, between July and August.

Lastly, satisfaction with one's country affected QOL significantly. Many government employees wanted to emigrate to another country. This may result from economic hardships that the 1997 economic crisis brought about, and the difficulties associated with raising school-aged children in Korea. The latter occurs as a result of increasing fees for private after-school education that come about because of the fierce competition for gaining entrance to college. In addition, a stressful work life without much social life may contribute to dissatisfaction within the country. To increase the desire of government employees to remain in Korea would require a wide range of changes in many areas including education.

NOTE

[1] Classes 1, 2, 3 in government sector are equivalent to the management in private sector; classes 4 and 5 to director position, classes 6 and 7 to entry level positions with college degree; and classes 8 and 9 to entry level positions with high-school diploma.

REFERENCES

Cho, K.H.: 1997, The Values of Public Employees in the Era of Transformation (Jibmoon, Seoul, Korea).

Cho, K.H.: 2000, 'An analysis of the prospects of success of entrepreneurial reform efforts in the public personnel administration', Korean Public Administration Review 34(3), pp. 39–56.

Cho, K.H. and M.S. Kim: 2000, 'A comparative study of quality of life satisfaction between the public and private sector employees', Korean Public Administration Review 34(3), pp. 27–45.

Cho, S.H. and W.Y. Oh: 1993, 'An analysis of citizen satisfaction about urban environments', Land Development 28(4), pp. 161–182.

Chubb, J.E. and T.M. Moe: 1988, 'Politics, markets, and the organization of schools', American Political Science Review 82, pp. 1065–1088.

Gold, M. and J. Wooldridge: 1995, 'Surveying consumer satisfaction to assess managed-care quality: Current practices', Health Care Financing Review 16(4), pp. 155–173.

Ha, H.S.: 1996, '"Local governments" policy outcomes', unpublished doctoral dissertation (Seoul National University).

Haas, B.K.: 1999, 'Clarification and integration of similar quality-of-life concepts', Journal of Nursing Scholarship 31, pp. 215–220.

Kim, B.S.: 1994, 'Psychological burnout and job involvement for public officials', Korean Public Administration Review 28, pp. 1279–1299.

Kim, M.S. and K.H. Cho: 2000, Administrative Reform and the Quality of Life of Public Employees (Nanam Publishing House, Seoul, Korea).

Kim, J.H. and associates: 1998, 'A comparative study on the quality of urban life', Regional Studies 14(1), pp. 21–45.

Korea Civil Service Commission: 1999, Improvement of Public Sector Classification System (Seoul, Korea).

Lane, R.E.: 1994, 'Quality of life and quality of persons: A new role for government?' Political Theory 22(2).

Lee, S.M.: 1997, 'The quality of working life and the quality of life: A search of an comprehensive model', Social Science (Sung Kyun Kwan University, Seoul) 45, pp. 107–131.

Lim, H.S.: 1995, Korean Social Change and the Values (Naman Publishing House, Seoul, Korea).

Park, T.H. and S.Y. Won: 2000, 'Interpersonal trust and connections based on the social categorization in organizations', Korean Public Administration Review 34(2), pp. 101–121.

Posner, B.Z. and W.H. Schmidt: 1996, 'The values of business and federal government executives', Public Personnel Management 25(3), pp. 277–289.

Poister, T.H. and G.T. Henry: 1994, 'Citizen ratings of public and private service quality: A comparative perspective', Public Administration Review 54(2), pp. 155–160.

Rainey, H.G., S. Pandey and B. Bozeman: 1995, 'Research note: Public and private managers' perception of red tape', Public Administration Review 55, pp. 567–574.

Schneider, D.S. and B.C. Vaught: 1993, 'A comparison of job satisfaction between public and private sector managers', Public Administration Quarterly, Spring, pp. 68–83.

Seed, P. and G. Lloyd: 1997, Quality of Life (Jessica Kingsley Publishers, London).

Shin, D.S.: 1981, 'A study of quality of life of Koreans', Jung-Kyung Moonwha, pp. 26–47.

United States Merit Systems Protection Board: 1991, Balancing Work Responsibilities and Family Needs: The Federal Civil Service Response.

United States Office of Personnel Management: 1998, A Review of Federal Family-Friendly Workplace Arrangements.

Webb, K. and H.P. Hatry: 1973, Obtaining Citizen Feedback: The Application of Citizen Surveys to Local Governments (The Urban Institute, Washington, D.C.).

San 42–14, Eunpyung-Gu, Bulkwang-Dong
Korea Institute for Health and Social Affairs
Seoul, Korea
E-mail: mskim@kihasa.re.kr

Meesook Kim

Department of Public Administration
Kookmin University
Seoul, Korea

Kyung-Ho Cho

EUN-YEONG NA and JOHN DUCKITT

VALUE CONSENSUS AND DIVERSITY BETWEEN GENERATIONS AND GENDERS

ABSTRACT. A sample of 366 Koreans (200 younger and 166 older people) was surveyed in May 2001 to investigate consensus and diversity between generations and genders in basic values. Because prior research had indicated that rating abstract value items could produce misleading findings, concrete belief and behavioral practice items were used from which four value dimensions were extracted using principal components analysis. These were: Openness to change, Conformity and Benevolence, Exclusiveness and Self-direction, and Relationship-focused Security. Value consensus between generations and genders was found only for the Conformity and Benevolence factor, while the other three factors revealed value diversity with significant interactions between gender and generational groups. The interactions typically involved traditional gender differences in the older generation either disappearing (Openness to change, Exclusiveness and Self-direction) or being reversed (Relationship-focused security) in the younger generation. In addition, irrespective of gender, younger participants were higher in openness to change than older ones, though the difference was considerably greater for females. Discussion focused on possible reasons for these effects and their possible social implications.

Human values have been defined as desirable goals and guiding principles in life (Rokeach, 1973; Schwartz and Sagiv, 1995). It is believed that people's values will powerfully influence their everyday attitudes and behavioral practices. Thus, people who value harmony more than winning will tend to yield to others in social situations involving conflict.

In general, value consensus seems more likely in homogeneous societies and value diversity in more heterogeneous societies. Thus, members of homogeneous societies would tend to show greater agreement with each other on the important goals and guiding principles in their lives, while members of heterogeneous societies would show greater variability in their basic values and life goals. Korean society has been viewed as relatively homogenous, because it is composed of one race, has only one language, and

Social Indicators Research **62, 63:** 411–435, 2003.

is characterized by collectivistic norms. Inglehart (1997), however, recently noted that Korea had the greatest generation gap in a survey of 43 industrialized countries. His findings have generally indicated that most developed countries are characterized by postmodern values, while most underdeveloped countries have modern values. In Korea, however, both modern and postmodern values may coexist, with older generations retaining modern values, and the younger generations rapidly adopting postmodern values.

Korea has been extremely quick in adopting rapidly changing information technologies, and this might be facilitating rapid shifts in the society as a whole. It seems likely that during a massive social transition such as this, certain sections of society might accept change and new ways of life more rapidly and readily than others. Such social changes should therefore generate value diversity or heterogeneity in a society. Shifts to postmodern values typically involve greater emphases on self-expression and individual freedom (Inglehart, 1990, 1997), so that openness to change and tolerance for diversity would become more important.

VALUE CONSENSUS AND VALUE DIVERSITY

Value consensus is defined as "concurrence among members of a society concerning their values" (Comte, cited in Schwartz and Sagie, 2000: p. 469). In other words, if "agreement among individual members of a society concerning the importance they attribute to different types of values" is high (Schwartz and Sagie, 2000, p. 469), we can say that value consensus is high. In contrast, the larger the disagreement between members of a society in the importance of their values, the greater the *value diversity*.

Schwartz and Sagie (2000) found that value importance in openness to change (including the value types of stimulation, self-direction, and hedonism) and self-transcendence (including the value types of universalism and benevolence) were positively related to economic development and democratization (see Table I for their categorization of values), and that economic development increased value consensus, while political democratization decreased it. Therefore, modernization, in general, presumably results in progressively greater realms of experience becoming

TABLE I

Schwartz's Motivationally Based Values

Higher order value types	Value types	Contents of motivational types of values
Self-enhancement	Power	Social status and prestige, control or dominance over people and resources. (Social Power, Authority, Wealth)
	Achievement	Personal success through demonstrating competence according to social standards. (Successful, Capable, Ambitious, Influential)
Openness to change	Hedonism	Pleasure and sensuous gratification for oneself. (Pleasure, Enjoying Life)
	Stimiulation	Excitement, novelty, and challenge in life. (Daring, A Varied Life, An Exciting Life)
	Self-direction	Independent thought and action-choosing, creating, exploring. (Creativity, Freedom, Independent, Curious, Choosing Own Goals)
Self-transcendence	Universalism	Understanding, appreciation, tolerance and protection of the welfare of all people and for nature. (Broadminded, Wisdom, Social Justice, Equality, A World at Peace, A World of Beauty, Unity With Nature, Proceeding the Environment)
Conservation	Conformity	Restraint of actions, inclinations, and impulses likely to upset or harm others and violate social expectations or norms. (Politeness, Obedient, Self-Discipline, Honoring Parents and Elders)
	Tradition	Respect, commitment and acceptance of the customs and ideas that traditional culture or religion provide the self. (Humble, Accepting My Portion in Life, Devout, Respect for Tradition, Moderate)
	Security	Safety, harmony, and stability of society, of relationships, and of self. (Family Security, National Security, Social Order, Clean, Reciprocation of Favors)

Schwartz and Sagiv (1995: pp. 95–96).

widely shared in a society, and this provides a fundamental basis for value consensus. According to Inglehart (1997), however, the social transition into a postmodern era should generate greater diversity in values and lifestyles, with their roots in a greater acceptance of freedom of expression and a higher valuation of uniqueness.

Inglehart (1990, 1997) has investigated the cultural change occurring as modern industrial societies move to post-materialism. Given his focus, on postmodern changes occurring in already-modernized advanced countries, his data have been collected mainly from 43 advanced industrial societies. He has argued that "economic development leads to stable democracy mainly (though not entirely) insofar as it brings in political culture and social structure" (Inglehart, 1997: p. 184). Fukuyama (1995), in contrast, has suggested that the association of economic development and democracy involves exactly the opposite direction of causality; that is that economic prosperity is caused by social trust culture.

In general, therefore, it would appear that researches differ markedly in their estimation of how culture, values, economic development, and political democracy impact casually on each other. They do, however, appear to agree in expecting strong relationships among these variables. While these issues are not primary focus of the present investigation, an examination of the degree of value consensus and diversity in Korea, a country in which both modern and postmodern values maybe held by different generations, may have significant implications for understanding the degree to which value convergence and divergence may occur in the transition to postmodernism.

Dimensions of Values

Schwartz and his colleagues have proposed a theoretical framework of 10 value types for individuals derived from universally human motivational goals, which are summarized in Table I (see Schwartz, 1992; Schwartz and Bilsky, 1987, 1990; Schwartz and Sagiv, 1995). These ten primary values are organized as circumplex around two higher order dimensions. Crossing two higher order dimensions produces four higher order value types with openness to change located opposite to conservation, and self-enhancement located opposite to self-transcendence. Previous research has shown that economically advanced countries tend to be high on openness to change and self-transcendence, while economically underdeveloped countries tend to be high on conservation and self-enhancement (see Schwartz, 1992; Schwartz and Sagiv, 1995; Schwartz and Sagie, 2000).

Dimensions of Culture

Culture involves the values and beliefs of members of a society, and as such, would profoundly influence their psychological processes and behavioral practices. Culture and values, therefore clearly overlap and very substantially but are not isomorphic.

Hofstede (1980, 1991) extracted four dimensions of culture from the responses of IBM employees in 53 countries: power distance, individualism-collectivism, masculinity-femininity, and uncertainty avoidance. *Power distance* was defined as "the extent to which the less powerful members of institution and organizations within a country expect and accept that power is distributed unequally" (Hofstede, 1991: p. 28). Thus, people in a country high in power distance accept the unequal distribution of power as natural. Authority figures are viewed as powerful experts who take the initiative in communication and decisions, and obedience is expected from subordinates. In contrast, people in low power distance cultures feel freer to express opinions opposing their authorities or seniors. The power distance dimension of culture, thus, seems to be opposite to Schwarz's universalism and benevolence value dimensions.

Individualist societies were described as "societies in which the ties between individuals are loose." In such societies, "everyone is expected to look after himself or herself and his or her immediate family." In contrast, *collectivist* societies were described as "societies in which people from birth onwards are integrated into strong, cohesive ingroups, which throughout people's lifetime continue to protect them in exchange for unquestioning loyalty" (Hofstede, 1991: p. 51). In individualist societies people tend to be treated as individuals regardless of their background, and in collectivist societies as part of a group. In the former, diplomas guarantee economic worth and self-respect, while in the latter they ensure entry to a higher status group. Low context communication styles (where almost everything is explicitly expressed) prevail in the former, while high context communication styles (where implicit intentions and backgrounds have to be inferred from restrained explicit expressions) are prevalent in the latter (see Hall, 1976). Cultural collectivism is highly related to the value priorities of security, conformity, and tradition.

The *Masculinity-femininity* dimension of culture determines whether assertiveness or modesty is viewed as virtues. Masculine societies are those where social gender roles are clearly distinct and men are expected to be assertive, tough, and focused on material success, whereas women are expected to be modest, tender, and concerned with the quality of life. Feminine societies are those where social gender roles overlap, and both men and women are supposed to be modest, tender, and concerned with the quality of life (Hofstede, 1991: pp. 82–83). Masculine societies consider power to be the most important and effective tool for the resolution of conflicts, while feminine societies emphasize peaceful negotiation. In the former societies the major courses of male and female students tend to be quite different, while in the latter the boundaries between males' and females' areas of wok are blurred. The masculinity-femininity dimension of culture seems relevant to Schwartz's achievement and power value dimensions.

Finally, *uncertainty avoidance* is described as "the extent to which the members of a culture feel threatened by uncertain or the unknown situations" (Hofstede, 1991: p. 113). Students in high uncertainty avoidance cultures feel comfortable in structured learning situations, while those in low uncertainty avoidance cultures prefer open-ended discussions. The former think what is different is dangerous, while the latter consider what is different to be interesting. Thus, the latter are more open to cultural differences. Because change involves uncertainty, the uncertainty avoidance dimension of culture would seem to be opposite to the Schwartz's openness to change value dimension.

Value Shift and Increasing Value Diversity in Recent Korean Culture

The rapid social changes occurring in Korea seem likely to be impacting differentially on different social groups, and particularly on gender and generational groups. For example, the shift from marked gender inequality in educational opportunities for earlier generations, to greater gender equality for more recent generations, seems likely to produce greater shifts in the values of females than in males. On the other hand, however, it is also possible males may be showing greater value changes than females in those areas in which males were traditionally more conservative than females. Thus, males seem to have shown greater value change in family centered individualism than females. This seems to have lead to greater value convergence between genders in younger persons, as opposed to the traditional value divergence that seems still apparent for older persons (Na and Cha, 2000).

Na and Cha's (2000) findings from nation-wide surveys in 1979 and 1998 suggest that differential values change for males and females over this period in Korea have reduced certain gender differences in values. In 1979, the proportion of those who said they placed their highest value on the well being of their "country" was higher than those who selected "self or family," and a large gender difference was observed with 16 percent more males than females selecting "country" in 1979. In 1998, however, the proportion of those selecting "self and family" over "country" increased by 22.5 percent and 38.4 percent for female and male respectively, resulting in a similar proportion selecting "self" and "family" (male 71.7%; female 71.8%). Men had, therefore, shifted to less conservative values. In 1979, there was also a large gender difference (male 81.0%, female 48.0%) in those agreeing that relationship problems should be corrected rather than just accepted. In 1998, however, the proportion of those who believed that relationship problems should be corrected had decreased to 65.8 percent among men, and increased to 66.4 percent among women producing value convergence between the genders.

On the other hand, value differences between generations also seem to have increased in certain areas, because value changes seem to be occurring much faster among younger generations than among older generations (see Inglehart, 1997; Na and Cha, 2000). For example, Na and Cha (2000) found that while only 12 percent of the respondents agreed that there was no need to be chaste before marriage in 1979, this had increased to 28.85 percent in 1998

(Na and Cha, 2000). This trend seemed more pronounced in the younger generation (20-year-olds), where the proportion rose from 19.3 percent to 45.2 percent, than among the older generation (50-year-olds), in which it rose from 4.7 percent to 12.6 percent. While the generation gap was already large in 1979 (14.6%), the gap had widened to 32.6 percent in 1998.

In addition, the belief that loyalty and filial piety is important has generally decreased during the past two decades. This has occurred particularly for younger generations, and more so in females than males, and among those with higher than those with lower education. More specifically, while the generational difference (calculated as the difference in the ratio of those answering that loyalty and filial piety were not important) was high in 1979 (11.3%), it was much higher in 1998 (29.0%). This indicated a substantial increase in the generation gap. In these cases, therefore, value diversity seems to have increased because of different rates of value change between generations.

Where the pace of change is similar in different categories of people in a society (as seems to be the case in the United States), or where different rates of change lead to a convergence in beliefs (as for certain gender differences in Korea), conflicts between different groups may be reduced. On the other hand, when different rates of change create divergence in values (as for the different generations in Korea), this could lead to conflict and communication difficulties between these groups.

Value diversity resulting from differential value shifts may be a more serious problem in a society with a cultural tendency to high uncertainty avoidance such as Korea (Hofstede, 1991). In a society characterized by high uncertainty avoidance, people tend to believe "what is different is dangerous" rather than "what is different is interesting." A certain degree of tolerance for and acceptance of difference and variety may be an important condition of the reasonably harmonious existence of marked value diversity in a single society. Korean people have traditionally valued "a single pure ethnic group" and cultural homogeneity, and this emphasis may function as a weakness rather than a strength in the present period of globalization and diversification.

OBJECTIVE OF THE STUDY

The primary objective of this study was to investigate the degree of value consensus and diversity between generations and genders on basic dimensions of value and belief in everyday social behavior and practices in Korea. Previous studies (Inglehart, 1997; Na and Cha, 2000; Na and Min, 2000) have shown a greater generation gap in Korea than in other industrialized countries. This study will focus, therefore, particularly on the degree of value diversity between generations, and the degree of value consensus between genders on basic value dimensions.

MEASUREMENT OF VALUES WITHIN A SPECIFIC CULTURE

Most research on values has followed Rokeach (1973) in using ratings or rankings of highly abstract value concept such as "ambition," "peace," and "equality," (see Rokeach, 1973; Schwartz, 1992; Schwartz and Bilsky, 1987, 1990). In measuring cultural differences, however, researchers have often used more concrete concepts, with some exceptions such as Schwartz and his colleagues who have studied highly abstract value items cross-culturally (e.g., Schwartz, 1992; Schwartz and Sagiv, 1995; Schwartz and Sagie, 2000). According to Hofstede (1980, 1991), national cultures are better studied through differences in *values*, and organizational cultures through differences in *practices*. This suggests that in order to investigate differences among *subgroups* (i.e., different age groups, genders, or organizations) within one country, it may be advisable to compare their concrete everyday practices and behaviors, and derive from these more abstract value dimensions. It has been suggested that cultures are manifest at various levels with values at the core and practices at the surface (Hofstede, 1991). Core structure of culture (i.e., values) cannot be changed easily, but surface structures (i.e., practice) can be changed relatively easily.

Several previous studies have indicated that older generations in Korea experience value conflicts characterized by behavioral conservatism contrasting with ostensibly more liberalized social attitudes and beliefs (see Na and Cha, 2000; Na and Min, 2000). These findings show that younger generations in Korea seem to be characterized by both postmodern beliefs and behaviors, while older generations maintain traditional habitual behaviors but express postmodern beliefs, possibly reflecting the perceived social desirability of these newer more liberal beliefs (see also Cha, 1985). For example, Korean elders "think" that males and females should have equal rights to professional jobs, but should still "behave" as if males have more rights. Such discrepancies are not as apparent among younger generations.

In order to reveal underlying values as guiding principles more effectively among Koreans (especially among older Koreans), it would seem more useful to ask them about their behavioral tendencies and practices in everyday life situations, than to ask them to rate socially desirable abstract value terms. More general and more abstract value dimensions could then be statistically extracted from such concrete behavioral practice items.

METHOD

Subjects and Date of Survey

Questionnaires were completed by 200 college students aged from 18 to 25 years (105 males and 95 females), and 166 older adults aged from 40 to 55 years (68 males and 98 females). The mean age of the college students was 21.8 years (SD = 1.8), and that of the older adults 48.7 years (SD = 3.9). All participants were Korean living in or near Seoul. The survey was conducted in May 2001. Convenience sampling was used and the samples, therefore, not representative of the general population. The older participants, however, were recruited from college students' acquaintances so that the two generational groups would be similar in social status and educational background.

The Questionnaire

Forty-three items expressing concrete behavioral practices in everyday life were written derived from previous studies of cultural value dimensions by Triandis et al. (1985), Hofstede (1980, 1991), and Schwartz and Sagiv (1995). Items were formulated and selected to reflect value dimensions such as idiocentrism-allocentrism (i.e., psychological levels of individualism-collectivism), uncertainty avoidance-acceptance, masculinity-femininity (i.e., assertiveness-humility), communication difficulty, and conformity and benevolence to others. The items were formulated in terms of various areas of everyday life, focusing on social and interpersonal situations. These items are listed in Table II.

The participants were requested to rate their degree of agreement to each of the 43 items on 5-point scales ranging from "never" (1), "a little" (2), "moderately" (3), "considerably" (4), to "very much" (5)." Principal components analysis was used to extract factors from the items, after which factor scores were calculated for each participant. Mean factor scores were then compared for generations and genders.

RESULTS AND DISCUSSION

Results of Factor Analysis

Principal components analysis with varimax rotation was performed on the 43 items to reduce the data into meaningful components, and to extract broader and more abstract value dimensions for further analyses. Kaiser's criterion did not prove useful for selecting the number of factors, as 11 factors had eigenvalues greater than 1, producing a number of factors that were not clearly or meaningfully defined by an adequate subset of items. Cattell's (1966) scree test was therefore used to select the number of factors. The graph of eigenvalues showed substantial drops after four and five factors, after which the graph leveled off to form a scree. Both four- and five-factor solutions were tested, but the four-factor solution proved to be clearly more meaningful theoretically, and was therefore used.

Eleven of the 43 items loaded the first factor, which was labeled "***Openness to Change.***" This factor is similar to Schwartz and Sagiv's (1995) "*stimulation*," in which "excitement, novelty, and challenge in life, daring, a varied life, and an exciting life are included as guiding principles of one's life" (Schwartz and Sagiv, 1995: p. 95). Impatience with waiting can be seen as reflecting a desire to experience novelty and new horizons, and enter new worlds as soon as possible, and therefore seems an integral aspect of "openness to change." Openness to change also includes being

TABLE II

Factor Loadings for Each Item on the Four Factors Extracted

Items loading on the four factors	Factor 1 (11 items) *Openness to Change*	Factor 2 (13 items) *Conformity and Benevolence*	Factor 3 (14 items) *Exclusiveness and Self-direction*	Factor 4 (5 items) *Relationship-focused Security*
Factor 1: Openness to change				
Novelty interests me	0.593	0.139	−0.176	0.171
If I want to know something, I find it intolerable if I can't know it immediately	0.518	0.132	0.165	−0.049
Despite the risks, I try to do things in new ways	0.497	0.154	0.134	−0.243
I find it difficult to tolerate ambiguity	0.468	0.109	0.242	−0.126
It is best to express oneself directly, even when one is saying something unpleasant	0.438	−0.030	0.109	−0.012
I want to solve problems immediately	0.416	0.102	0.322	−0.072
I am not comfortable when there are rules that have to be obeyed	0.400	−0.218	0.037	−0.002
I usually start a conversation when everyone is silent in a meeting	0.384	0.324	0.057	0.041
Competition is necessary to make a good society	0.368	0.299	0.072	0.055
I am a unique person who is different from others	0.348	0.074	0.197	−0.010
I like having friends who differ from me in many ways	0.314	0.063	−0.078	0.067
Factor 2: Conformity and benevolence				
I don't feel free to oppose my elders	−0.034	0.572	0.083	−0.106
I don't feel it easy to reject requests from others around me	0.107	0.532	0.002	0.109

TABLE II

Continued

Items loading on the four factors	Factor 1 (11 items)	Factor 2 (13 items)	Factor 3 (14 items)	Factor 4 (5 items)
	Openness to Change	*Conformity and Benevolence*	*Exclusiveness and Self-direction*	*Relationship-focused Security*
I frequently get together with my colleagues after work	0.247	0.485	−0.128	−0.033
To be comfortable in my job, I feel I cannot avoid having drinks with my colleagues after work	0.254	0.464	0.011	−0.213
I am happier being with others than working on my own	0.261	0.449	−0.037	−0.042
My happiness depends on the happiness of those around me	−0.029	0.447	0.050	−0.136
I feel very awkward having lunch alone	0.244	0.433	0.020	−0.013
I feel comfortable when there are rules to obey	−0.398	0.421	0.235	0.037
It is important for me to be similar to others	−0.311	0.385	0.138	0.140
It is important for me to have many friends	0.060	0.377	−0.038	0.103
I feel I cannot miss a social meeting even though I am busy with my work	−0.098	0.350	−0.030	0.055
I am more comfortable with friends who are similar to me	0.056	0.266	0.013	0.102
Some people emphasize winning, but I am not one of them	−0.080	0.233	0.176	−0.215
Factor 3: Exclusiveness and self-direction				
I don't like being bothered by someone else when I am talking to a close friend	0.161	0.025	0.533	0.078

TABLE II

Continued

Items loading on the four factors	Factor 1 (11 items) *Openness to Change*	Factor 2 (13 items) *Conformity and Benevolence*	Factor 3 (14 items) *Exclusiveness and Self-direction*	Factor 4 (5 items) *Relationship-focused Security*
When someone tells me I am wrong, my first reaction is to get angry	0.129	−0.091	0.509	−0.016
I worry about changes that may come in the future	−0.392	0.195	0.487	−0.047
I feel a psychological distance towards people who are higher in status than me	0.114	0.137	0.451	0.221
I rely on myself than relying on others	0.013	−0.047	0.420	−0.089
Competition is the law of nature	0.356	0.039	0.392	0.294
Thinking issues through oneself usually produces a better solution than discussing them with others	−0.080	−0.267	0.385	−0.084
My job is more important than my family	0.269	0.121	0.357	−0.260
In this country, cooperating with others is difficult	0.199	0.080	0.351	−0.271
It is important that one be different from others in any kind of way	0.341	−0.038	0.349	−0.133
It is better to try and change something that is wrong in a relationship rather than just accepting it for the sake of living together happily	−0.134	0.004	0.326	0.188
My work has a higher priority for me than social occasions	0.137	−0.233	0.293	−0.144

TABLE II

Continued

Items loading on the four factors	Factor 1 (11 items)	Factor 2 (13 items)	Factor 3 (14 items)	Factor 4 (5 items)
	Openness to Change	*Conformity and Benevolence*	*Exclusiveness and Self-direction*	*Relationship-focused Security*
I just hang up the phone when I hear an answering machine	0.097	0.120	0.293	0.103
I think one's present satisfaction is more important than happiness in the future	0.007	0.004	0.186	0.067
Factor 4: Relationship-focused security				
Parents and children should spend as much time with each other as possible	−0.029	0.200	0.055	0.762
Despite the sacrifices it might involve, families should keep together	0.043	0.082	0.202	0.668
It irritates me if someone else outperforms me	0.187	0.302	0.123	−0.646
It is important to consult close friends before making a decision	−0.048	0.046	0.335	0.578
It is important to have close friends, even if they are few	0.247	0.216	−0.194	0.343

uncomfortable with routine and structure, particularly when these are governed by old-fashioned rules.

The second factor was labeled "***Conformity and Benevolence***," with 13 items loading on it, and seems similar to the *allocentrism* of Triandis et al. (1985) and the *benevolence* and *conformity* values of Schwartz and Sagiv (1995). According to Schwartz and Sagiv (1995) conformity includes "restraints of actions, inclinations, and impulses likely to upset or harm others and violate social expectations or norms" such as politeness, obedience, self-discipline, honoring parents and elders (p. 95). Schwartz and Sagiv

(1995) define "benevolence", which is their value directly adjacent to and therefore more highly related to conformity, as involving the "preservation and enhancement of the welfare of people with whom one is in frequent personal contact" such as being helpful, honest, forgiving, loyal, responsible, true friendship, and mature love (p. 95).

The third factor, on which 14 items loaded, was labeled "***Exclusiveness and Self-direction***," and seems similar to Schwartz and Sagiv's (1995) *self-direction* (see Table I) and Triandis et al.'s (1985) *idiocentrism*. Schwartz and Sagiv's (1995) self-direction includes "independent thought and action-choosing, creating, exploring" such as creativity, freedom, independence, curious, and choosing own goals and self-respect (p. 95). Some of the items in the third factor such as "I worry about changes that may come in the future", "Competition is the law of nature," and "It is important that one be different form others in any kind of way" have strong loadings for factor 1 as well. This suggests that self-direction or exclusiveness may also involve openness to change and pursuit of uniqueness as well. This is consistent with Schwartz and Sagiv's (1995) higher order Openness value type, which includes the primary value types of self-direction, stimulations, and hedonism. Preferring one's own judgment to discussing issues with others, and putting a greater emphasis on individual performance than on cooperative work, are representative behavioral tendencies included in the third factor.

The fourth factor, on which 5 items loaded, was labeled "***Relationship-focused Security***." These items emphasize security and dependence on close relationships with a particular emphasis on family and parents and children being together as much as possible, and an unconcern about others outperforming oneself. Among the Schwartz and Sagiv's (1995) values, "*security*" seems closest to this factor. They specified security as "Safety, harmony, and stability of society, or relationships, and of self" such as family security, national security, social order, clean, reciprocation of favors, sense of belonging, and healthy.

Thus, overall, it seems that while the present study used concrete behavioral and life practice items rather than abstract

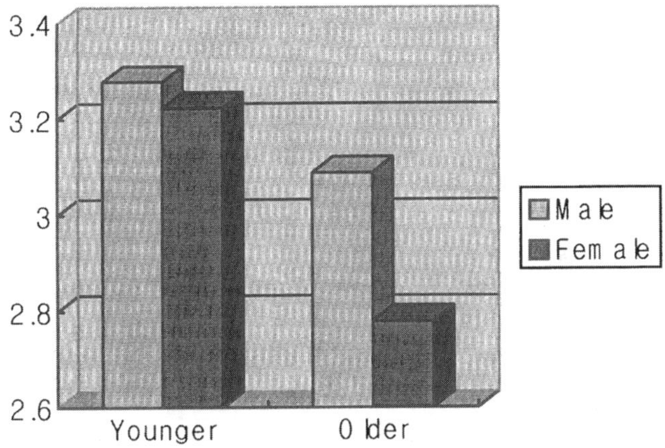

Figure 1. Mean scores on Factor 1 (*Openness to Change*) for younger and older males and females.

value concepts, the broader value dimensions that were extracted statistically were clearly similar to those identified in prior research.

Results of Analyses of Variance on Each of the Four Factors

Openness to change. Figure 1 shows the means scores on factor 1 (Openness to Change, Uniqueness and Variety) for gender and two generations. A 2*2 ANOVA indicated that both main effects and the interaction were significant. The younger group (M = 3.252) showed significantly greater openness to change than the older (M = 2.907), $F(1358) = 36.736$, $p < 0.001$, while males (M = 3.204) were significantly higher than females (M = 3.002) $F(1358) = 12.005$, $p < 0.01$.

These main effects, however, were qualified by the significant interaction $F(1358) = 5.915$, $p < 0.05$. Males and females did not differ in the younger group, but did differ significantly in the older group (Ms = 3.088 for males and 2.780 for females), $F(1160) = 16.731$, $p < 0.001$. This seems to have resulted form the particularly low scores of older females on openness to change, which is consistent with the previous findings of Na and Cha (2000), who found that older females and rural residents had least value change across the two decades they studied. The younger generation, overall, was more open to change regardless of gender (for males, $F = 6.121$, $p < 0.05$; for females, $F = 39.011$, $p < 0.001$)

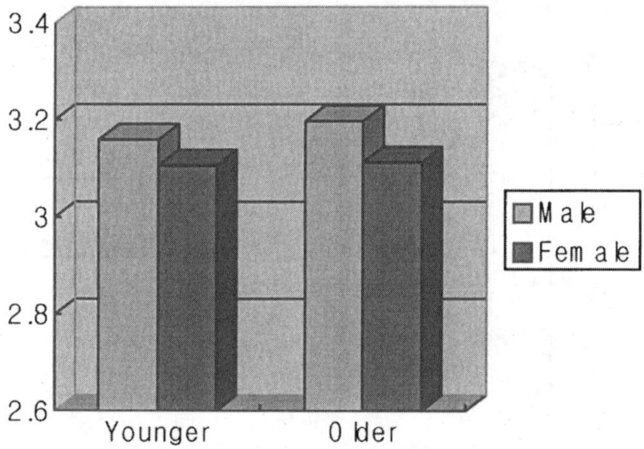

Figure 2. Mean scores on Factor 2 (*Conformity and Benevolence*) for younger and older males and females.

than the older generation, with the older females especially low in openness to change.

Conformity and benevolence. Figure 2 shows the mean scores of younger and older males and females on factor 2 (Conformity and Benevolence). A 2*2 ANOVA indicated no significant effects, indicating that both genders and age groups obtained very similar means on this factor.

This finding suggests a high degree of *value consensus* among generations and genders on conformity, benevolence and a general endorsement of collectivist values. Thus, it seems that the younger generation, despite accepting more individualistic norms and values, still endorse collectivist norms and values of taking other persons into accounts in many social situations, and in showing consideration to others.

When these items, however, were examined separately, there was some value diversity between genders and generations on factor 2. For example, *t*-tests indicated significant differences between generations on 5 of the 13 conformity items. On two of these items (i.e., "I frequently get together with my colleagues after work." And "I feel very awkward having lunch alone") the generational differences were in the opposite direction to that expected; that is with younger persons (M = 3.06 and 3.20) showing greater conformity than their

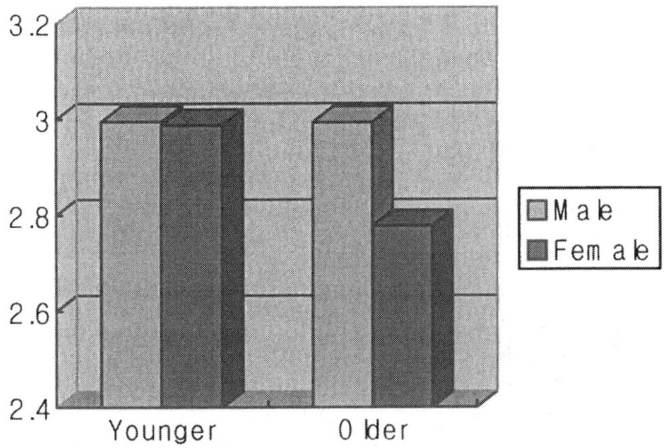

Figure 3. Mean scores on Factor 3 (*Exclusiveness and Self-direction*) for younger and older males and females.

elders (M = 2.71 and 2.74), ts = 3.254, 3.357, ps < 0.01, 0.001, respectively. The differences on the other three items were in the direction expected with older persons being more collectivist than the younger ones ("It is important for me to be similar to others"; "My happiness depends on the happiness of those around me"; "I feel comfortable when there are rules to obey"). There were no significant differences for the remaining 8 items.

The unexpected effects for the first two items might be due to college students usually having lunch together, while older persons would more typically have lunch on their own, particularly in the case of housewives, who would usually eat alone at home.

Exclusiveness and self-direction. Figure 3 shows the gender and generation mean scores on factor 3. Inspection of the figure indicates that older females obtained lower scores than all three other groups, whose scores were very similar. The 2*2 ANOVA produced significant main effects for gender, $F(1361) = 5.305$, $p < 0.05$, and age group, $F(1361) = 4.706$, $p < 0.05$, and a significant interaction, $F(1361) = 4.659$, $p < 0.05$.

Multiple comparison tests indicated that males and females did not differ significantly in the younger group, while older females were significantly lower in exclusiveness and self-direction than older males, $F(1361) = 4.659$, $p < 0.01$. There was a significant

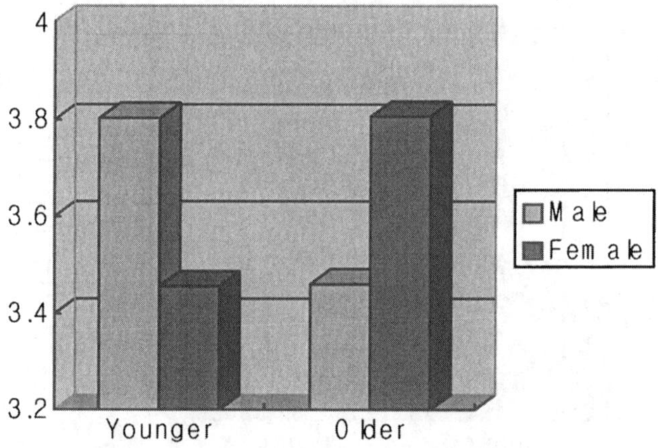

Figure 4. Mean scores on Factor 4 (*relationship-focused Security*) for younger and older males and females.

generation gap for females, $F(1190) = 10.787$, $p < 0.01$, but not for males.

Relationship-focused security. Figure 4 shows the mean scores for gender and generation on factor 4. The 2*2 ANOVA indicated that the main effects for gender and generations were nonsignificant, while the interaction was significant, $F(1362) = 7.633$, $p < 0.01$. The mean scores for younger males ($M = 3.803$) and elder females ($M = 3.806$) were very similar and higher, than the scores for younger females ($M = 3.456$) and older males ($M = 3.461$). Multiple comparison tests showed a marginally significant generation gap for males [$F(1171) = 3.676$, $p = 0.057$], with younger males higher in relationship-focused security than older males. The generation gap for females was significant, $F(1191) = 4.050$, $p < 0.05$, with younger females lower on relationship-focused security than older females.

This generation gap for females was expected since it would reflect older females' greater conservatism. The generation gap, however, in exactly the opposite direction for males was unexpected. It seems that the younger males were higher on openness to change and in exclusiveness and self-direction, but in contrast put a highly conservative emphasis on relationship-focused security, and even did so to a greater extent than older males. A possible explanation for this might be that the older male would have tended to be persons very deeply involved in professional and executive jobs, leading them to de-emphasize close and secure family relationships and friendships for themselves, personally. Younger males, in contrast being mainly unmarried, might be strongly oriented towards future goals of marriage and having a family.

The younger females' de-emphasis of the importance of close and secure family and friendly relationships compared to younger males does suggest that an important change in gender relations may be occurring in Korea. Younger females may be focusing more on their prospects for personal advancements and professional career rather than on traditional goals of marriage and a family. Thus, the traditional pattern, existing in the older generation for females to emphasize the importance of family and close relationships more than males, seems now to have been reversed.

CONCLUSIONS

The main findings of this study can be summarized as follows:

1. *Value consensus* was found between generations and genders for factor 2 *(Conformity and Benevolence)*.
2. There seemed to be greater *value consensus* between genders in the younger generation than in the older generation, with the latter being characterized by relatively greater *value diversity* on factor 1 (*Openness to Change, Uniqueness & Variety)* and factor 3 (*Exclusiveness and Self-Direction*).
3. In the case of factor 4 (*Relationship-focused Security*), the traditionally greater emphasis of women on relationship-focused security was found for the older generation, but reversed for the younger generation. Younger males seemed to place more emphasis on relationship-focused security than females. This suggests that an entirely new kind of value diversity may have arisen between genders.

The most interesting and dramatic findings from this study concern the greater intergenerational value diversity for females than for males. This is shown in traditional gender differences in the older generation either disappearing or being reversed in the younger. One possible methodological reason for this might have been the existence of greater SES (socio-economic status) differences between the older males and females than between their younger counterparts. All the analyses were therefore recomputed using SES as a covariate. The effects already reported, however, remained substantially unaltered in these analyses, indicating that they could not be due to SES.

These greater value shifts for women seem likely to be due to the impact of urbanization and education on women's status, roles and opportunities in Korean society. The findings on factor 4 (relationship-focused security) seemed particularly intriguing, with the traditional pattern for relationship-focused security to be more important for women than men being completely reversed in the younger generation. Younger women seem less oriented to close family and friendship relationships than young men. Social commentators in Japan have in recent years expressed concern about an apparent reluctance of young women, particularly more urban and educated young women, to commit themselves to marriage and rearing families, resulting in lower rates of marriage, a higher age of marriage, women having fewer children, and having them later. This may also be happening in Korea, and young men's greater emphasis on relationship-focused security than the older male generation might in part reflect their desire to find and marry a wife, who will devote herself to having children and rearing them in a social climate in which such women may be becoming more difficult to find.

While the overall findings for factor 2 (conformity and benevolence) suggested value consensus between generations and genders, there were some differences within this factor. Two of the items loading on this factor showed greater allocentrism for the younger generation, while three other items showed greater allocentrism for the older generation. There were no differences on the majority of items, however, so this clearly was the factor on which there was greatest values consensus, with both males and females and younger and older generations agreeing in placing a high value on conformity and benevolence.

Several limitations of this study should be noted. First, because of the focus on concrete behavior and practices in everyday interpersonal situations, certain aspects of values and kinds of values were probably not adequately represented or measured. Examples would be dimensions such as achievement and performance, and authoritarianism and power distance. Second, the samples were not representative of the general population. The younger generation consisted of college students, and the older generation was recruited from persons acquainted with college students. This helped to match the two samples on social background, education and SES. The results overall, however, were derived form samples of urban persons of a generally higher level of SES, and it is quite likely that the results might hold only for such populations, and not for lower SES or non-urban populations.

Overall therefore, gender and generational diversity in values was found in openness to change, pursuit of uniqueness and variety, and intolerance for slowness, as well as in pursuing exclusiveness, self-direction, and relationship-focused security. Younger people in Korea seem to be more open to change, pursue uniqueness and variety, be intolerant to slowness, exclusive, and self-directed than their older counterparts. Younger females, moreover, seem to have shown particularly dramatic shifts in these directions.

Openness to change seems to be an important factor distinguishing younger from older generations in Korea. Thus, as Schwartz and his colleagues have pointed out (Schwartz, 1990, 1992, 1996; Schwartz and Bilsky, 1987, 1990; Schwartz and Sagie, 2000; Schwartz and Sagiv, 1995), the individualism-collectivism dimension, or its psychological counterpart idiocentrism-allocentrism, is not sufficient to adequately classify human cultures or values. Over the past decade there seems to have been growing agreement that other dimensions of culture or cultural values, such as Hofstede's (1980, 1991) uncertainty avoidance and masculinity-femininity dimensions (concerning assertiveness and self-direction), and Schwartz and Sagiv's (1995) openness to change dimension, may be as important as the individualism-collectivism dimension of Triandis et al. (1988). The present finding thus provide additional support for this by indicating that these other dimensions are critical in understanding value differences and similarities between genders and generations in Korea.

REFERENCES

Cha, J.-H.: 1985, 'Generational gaps in values, attitudes, and beliefs a the end of the 1970's', Research in Social Psychology 2(2), pp. 129–168.

Cattell, R.: 1966, 'The scree test of the number of factors', Multivariate Behavioral Research 1, pp. 245–276.

Fukuyama, F.: 1995, Trust: Social Virtues and the Creation of Prosperity (Free Press, New York).

Hall, E.T.: 1976, Beyond Culture (Doubleday Anchor Books, Garden City, NY).

Hofstede, G.: 1980, Cultures' Consequences: International Differences in Work-related Values (Sage, Beverly Hills, CA).

Hofstede, G.: 1991, Cultures and Organization: Software of the Mind (McGraw-Hills, London).

Inglehart, R.: 1990, Culture Shift in Advanced Industrial Society (Princeton University Press, Princeton, NJ).

Inglehart, R.: 1997, Modernization and Postmodernization: Cultural, Economic and Political Change in 43 Societies (Princeton University Press, Princeton, NJ).

Na, E.-Y. and J.-H. Cha: 2000, 'Changes in values and the generation gap between the 1970s and the 1990s in Korea', Korea Journal (UNESCO) 40(1), pp. 285–324.

Na, E.-Y., and K.-H. Min: 2000, 'Discrepancies between formal/explicit and informal/implicit norms in Korea and generation gaps: Theoretical points and evidence from existing survey data', Korean Social Science Journal 27(1), pp. 113–142.

Rokeach, M.: 1973, The Nature of Human Values (Free Press, New York).

Schwartz, S.H.: 1990, 'Individualism-collectivism: Critique and proposed refinements', Journal of Cross-Cultural Psychology 21(2), pp. 139–157.

Schwartz, S.H.: 1992, 'Universals in the content and structure of values: Theoretical advances and empirical tests in 20 countries', in M. Zanna (ed.), Advances in Experimental Social Psychology, Vol. 25 (Academic Press, Orlando, FL, pp. 1–65).

Schwartz, S.H.: 1996, 'Value priorities and behavior: Applying a theory of integrated value systems', in C. Seligman, J. Olson and M. Zanna (eds.), The Psychology of Values: The Ontario Symposium, Vol. 25 (Academic Press, San Diego, pp. 1–65).

Schwartz, S.H. and W. Bilsky: 1987, 'Toward a psychological structure of human values', Journal of Personality and Social Psychology 53, pp. 550–562.

Schwartz, S.H. and W. Bilsky: 1990, 'Toward a theory of the universal content and structure of values: Extensions and cross-cultural replications', Journal of Personality and Social Psychology 58, pp. 878–891.

Schwartz, S.H. and G. Sagie: 2000, 'Value consensus and importance: A cross-national study', Journal of Cross-Cultural Psychology 31(4), pp. 465–497.

Schwartz, S.H. and L. Sagiv: 1995, 'Identifying culture-specifics in the contents and structure of values', Journal of Cross-cultural Psychology 26(1), pp. 92–116.

Triandis, H.C., R. Bontempo, M.J. Villareal, M. Asai and N. Lucca: 1988, 'Individualism and collectivism: Cross-cultural perspectives on self-ingroup relationships', Journal of Personality and Social Psychology 54, pp. 323–338.

Triandis, H.C., K. Leung, M.J. Villarea and F. Clack: 1985, 'Allocentric vs. idiocentric tendencies: Convergent and discriminant validation', Journal of Research in Personality 19, pp. 395–415.

Department of Communications
Sogang University
Seoul 121-742, Korea
E-mail: ena@sogang.ac.kr

Eun-Yeong Na

Department of Psychology
Univeristy of Auckland
New Zealand
E-mail: j.duckitt@auckland.ac.nz

John Duckitt

IK KI KIM and CHEONG-SEOK KIM

PATTERNS OF FAMILY SUPPORT AND THE QUALITY OF LIFE OF THE ELDERLY

ABSTRACT. This study addresses the issue of the quality of life of the Korean elderly in the present day by looking at the relationship between the patterns of support exchange across generations and the subjective well-being of the elderly as measured by the overall life satisfaction index. Relying on equity or exchange theory, we formulated the following hypotheses: in contrast to the elderly who only receive, the elderly who both give and receive are more satisfied with life; while the elderly, who only give or the elderly, who do not exchange any support with their children, are less satisfied. The multiple regression analysis based on the Survey of Living Environment and the Quality of Life of the Korean Elderly in 1997 (n = 1056) appears to support these hypotheses as a whole. The findings suggest that the elderly as well as the younger generations put more value on two-way intergenerational relations based on mutual care and assistance, rather than simply following the traditional norm of filial piety.

INTRODUCTION

Having reached the end of the demographic transition, Korea has evolved into an aging society.[1] The absolute numbers of the elderly, as well as their relative share of the total population, have started to increase. This trend is likely to continue with further improvements in living conditions and advances in medical technology. These demographic changes have been accompanied by rapid social changes that are characterized by urbanization and industrialization and have profound implications for the social conditions and living circumstances of the elderly. The forces of the demographic and socioeconomic changes as a whole are thought to have a detrimental effect. As a result, the well-being or the quality of life of the elderly has drawn increasing attention from policy planners and has become a salient subject of recent studies in Korea.[2]

In this study, we address the issue of life quality of the Korean elderly today by looking at the relationship between the patterns of

Social Indicators Research **62, 63:** 437–454, 2003.

support exchange across generations and the subjective well- being of the elderly. In particular, we are interested in the effect of the flow of intergenerational support on the overall life satisfaction among the older generation. The majority of studies on intergenerational support involving elderly parents in Korea as well as in many other Asian countries focus on the support received by the elderly parents as opposed to the support provided by the elderly to their children (Ofstedal et al., 1999; Shi, 1993). Indeed, in these regions, including Korea, children continue to support their elderly parents in later life fro both normative and practical reasons (Kim and Choe, 1992; Yoon and Cha, 1999). However, the fact that elderly parents, even at advanced ages, are also providers of various types of support to their children is often overseen. It is found that many elderly parents still provide a great deal of support to their adult children. Furthermore, some studies reveal that the elderly perceive the role of support provider as a continuation of parental responsibility (Kim and Rhee, 1999).

Adopting the dual roles of elderly parents, both as providers and receivers of support, we have conceptualized four types of relations that the elderly parents would have with their children in terms of flow in support: (1) both giving and receiving (2) only receiving (3) only giving, and (4) no exchange at all. Based on this typology, we raise three research questions. The first question concerns whether involving a reciprocal relation (versus only receiving) is positively associated with the extent of the life satisfaction of the elderly. The second question involves the relative effect of only giving compared to only receiving on the extent of the life satisfaction of the elderly. The third question is about whether the absence of intergenerational support exchange (versus only receiving) is negatively related to the extent of the life satisfaction of the elderly. In the present study, we attempt to answer these questions form the perspective of equity or exchange theory that has guided much of the work on the effect of support exchanges on the psychological well-being of the elderly.[3] Equity or exchange theory suggests that reciprocity in support relations is a key issue in successful aging and either extreme of non-reciprocity would result in negative outcomes (Antonucci, 1990; Dowd, 1975; Walster et al., 1978).

CONCEPTUAL FRAMEWORK

Exchange theory, the main idea of which is found in the work of Homans (1961), Blau (1964), and Emerson (1962), emphasizes that social interaction is the process of exchange of materialistic or psychological rewards between actors on the basis of a norm of reciprocity (Turner, 1986). This theory views that a relation of balanced exchange would occur if the actors involving exchange were dependent on each other to a similar extent. If such is not the case, then it will establish a relation of power and dependency and result in the equity problem. Such a view was adopted by Dowd (1975) to explain the relations of elderly parents and adult children and are involved in less social interaction, as their resources and values diminish.[4]

The perspective of the exchange theory contains an important implication for understanding the intergeneration support and psychological well-being of the elderly at the individualistic level. The elderly, as age advances, come to the point where they accept the beneficence of their children and depend on them. In the meantime, the elderly parents establish social credit through their contribution to their children over the course of life in exchange for support from them later in life. Besides the individual level of social credit and expectation, the norm of filial piety at the societal level in Korea strongly dictates that the adult children should support their elderly parents. The social credit of elderly parents and the strong norm of filial piety may temper their psychological burden when receiving support from their children. Nonetheless, even in this situation, reciprocating or compensating the support provided by children can be still important to their psychological well-being. On the one hand, reciprocation or compensation may enhance the feelings of usefulness and self-worth which the elderly parents would have. This expectation is consistent with the perception of the lifetime enduring parental role as providers of support among the elderly in Korea. On the other hand, being only a recipient of support from their children may result in having feelings of guilt in burdening them, particularly if they are in need of extensive support form their children (Kim and Rhee, 1999). Therefore, we hypothesize that the elderly, who both give and receive support, would be more satisfied with life than the elderly who receive only support from their children.

If forced to choose between the two extremes of non-reciprocity – only giving and only receiving, equity or exchange theory suggests that receiving is better than giving. The situation in which the elderly parents continue the role of provider without receiving any support from their children deviates from the social expectation and value that the adult children should support their elderly parents instead of being supported. Such a situation may reflect the fact that children may not be able to support themselves but are rather in need of assistance from their elderly parents. Thus, it would lead to psychological distress for the elderly parents as well as their children. Therefore, we hypothesize that the elderly, who give only assistance tot heir children, would be less satisfied with life than the elderly who receive only help from their children. With respect to the absence of support exchange, we hypothesize that the elderly who do not exchange support with their children show a lower level of life satisfaction than the elderly who receive only support from their children. This is because the absence of support exchange between generations may imply a disconnection of intergenerational ties or reflect the situation in which both generations are unable to offer any support to each other for their own difficulties.

The extent to which the elderly are satisfied with their life can be affected by many factors. For an empirical test of the hypotheses established above, we introduced two sets of control variables building on previous studies (i.e., Kim et al., 1998; Won, 1995; Yoo, 1997; Yoon and Lee, 1997). The first set of variables reflects the resources of the elderly parents, indicating financial status, health, and demographic availability of their children. The resources that the elderly parents may have affect the degree of life satisfaction, independently of intergenerational support exchange. At the same time, the resources of the elderly parents may contribute in shaping the patterns of support exchange (i.e., those with fewer resources would be more likely to receive support from their children than provide support to the children). For these reasons, we first controlled for the variables reflecting resources of the elderly. Another set of control variables would be demographic background variables, such as place of residence, age, gender, martial status, and education. We posit that these variables may influence the degree of life satisfaction, but their effect is not as clear as that of the resource variables. The grouping of the control variables into two sets is mainly for the convenience of discussion and it is not based on any clear-cut distinction. Given our focus on the effect of different types of support exchange, we assume that the way we categorize the control variables should not be a serious fault, at least in the present study.

We acknowledge that the typology of intergenerational relations used in the present study is based on a rather simplistic view. Treating the support given and received for the different domains separately would help us to understand which types of support would be most relevant to the psychological well-being of the elderly. In addition, the relative amount of the support exchanged between generations rather than the presence of intergenerational transfer would provide a more refined measure of reciprocity (i.e., to what degree support is reciprocated versus whether it is reciprocated or not). However, this treatment is beyond the scope of the present study. The multidimensional aspects of the intergenerational exchange and the changes in the types of support exchanged over the life course of different generations make it difficult to empirically assess their objective balance (Murtan and Ritzes, 1984; Rossi and Rossi, 1990).

DATA AND METHODS

The data for this study come from the Survey of Living Environment and the Quality of Life of the Korean Elderly that was conducted in 1997 by a group of Korean scholars.[5] This national probability sample consisted of non-institutionalized individuals aged 60 and over at the time of the survey. A Total of 1199 completed face-to-face interviews were obtained. The current study limits its analysis to 1056 males and females who had at least one surviving child and who gave valid answers to the questions of interest in this study. The restriction of the analysis to those with at least one child alive is inevitable since the main concern lies in the patterns of intergenerational support that necessitates the presence of a child.

Table I presents a listing of the variables and the distribution of the sample used in the Ordinary Least Square (hereinafter OLS) regression analyses performed in this study. Additional explanations of the variables are provided below. Life satisfaction is measured with the 6 survey items.[6] The respondents were asked to indicate the extent to which they agreed with the statement in each item on a 10-point scale. The scale ranges from 1 to 10, with the highest being complete agreement to the given item. Unlike other items, the 4th item, "*I often feel isolated or lonely,*" was stated in a negative tone. The score of this item was reversed so that a high score should denote greater life satisfaction. A life satisfaction index was constructed from summing the scores on the reversed 4th item and other items. This brief index ranges from 6 to 60 with a high score representing greater life satisfaction.

Flow of intergenerational support, which is the key independent variable, is derived from a set of items reflecting exchange activities between the respondents and their children. For the provision of support by the elderly for their children, the respondents were asked: (1) whether they contribute to living expenses; (2) whether they give pocket money including gifts; (3) whether they help with household chores (i.e., preparation of family ceremony and child care); (4) whether they help in making family decisions or are consulted with regard to family matters or personal worries; and (5) whether they keep their children company. The responses were coded in a binary format. Then, with the same coding scheme, parallel questions were out to the respondents to ascertain whether the elderly receive support from their children. Based on a total of 10 binary format items (five items for giving and five items for receiving), intergenerational support is categorized into four groups that distinguish its flow direction. The first category, "no flow," refers to the respondents who reported "no" to all of the 10 items described above and involves 8.0 percent of the sample. The second category, "only receiving," is composed of the respondents who said "yes" to any of the five items for receiving, but "no" to the five items for giving. This category for "only receiving," constituting 25.2 percent of the sample, is used as the reference group in the multivariate analysis. The third category, "only giving" consists of the respondents who said "yes" to any of the five items for giving, but "no" to the five

TABLE I

Variables and Characteristics of Sample (n = 1056)

Variables	Definition	Mean/Proportion
Dependent variable		
LSI	Life Satisfaction Index which added the scores of the 6 items (range from 6–60)	36.8
	1. I am satisfied with my life	
	2. I feel that in the future happy things will occur	
	3. I am a valuable person	
	4. I often feel isolated or lonely	
	5. As I look back on my life, it has been successful	
	6. I am happy now	
Independent variables		
Flow of intergenerational support	Patterns of intergenerational support based on the direction of flow	
Only receiving (reference group)	only from the children to R	25.3%
No flow	neither from children to R nor from R to children	8.0%
Only giving	only from R to children	1.6%
Both giving and receiving	both from children to R and from R to children	65.2%
Control variables (1)		
ADL impairment	1 if R needs any help in performing 5 ADL items; else 0 (5 items: getting up/sitting, bathing, dressing/undressing, walking up stairs, crossing street)	10.4%

TABLE I

Continued

Variables	Definition	Mean/Proportion
Monthly pocket money	4 categories of average amount of pocket money per month 1. 0–90000 Korean Won 2. 100000–190000 Korean Won 3. 200000–290000 Korean Won 4. 300000 Korean Won and above	1.85
Number of children	Number of children alive (Range from 1–9)	4.0
Coresidence with child	1 if R coresides with any child; else 0	52.8
Control variables (2)		
Place of Residence		
Rural Areas (reference group)	1 if R lives in rural areas; else 0	46.8%
Metro-city	1 if R lives in metro-city; else 0	40.3%
Mid-sized city	1 if R lives in mid-sized city; else 0	13.9%
Age	Age in single years (range from 60–90 years)	72.8
Female	1 if R is female; else 0	50.4%
Married	1 if R is currently married; else 0	56.5%
Education		
No formal school (reference group)	1 if R never attended school; else 0	45.3%
Primary School	1 if R had attended in the primary school; else 0	33.9%
Secondary or above school	1 if R had attended in the secondary school or above; else 0	20.8%

R indicates the respondent.

LSI, Age, Monthly pocket money, and Number of children are continuous variables. All other variables are dummy variables.

items for receiving. Only a negligible proportion of the sample (1.6%) belongs to this category. The last category, "both giving and receiving," consists of those responding "yes" to any of the five items for giving, and "yes" to any of the five items for receiving. About two-thirds of the sample are in this category.

The first set of control variables reflects the resources of the elderly in terms of finance, health and demographic availability of the children. These include Activities of Daily Living (hereinafter ADL) impairment, the amount of monthly pocket money, the number of children and whether the respondent lives with the children or not. The ADL impairment refers to whether the respondent needs help in performing any of the following activities of daily living (ADL): getting out of bed and sitting, taking a bath or shower, dressing and undressing, walking up stairs, and crossing the street. Of the sample, about 10.4 percent reported that they need assistance in performing any of the ADL items described above. The amount of monthly pocket money is used to assess the financial status of the respondent. There were other items in the survey that can be used as indicators of their financial condition including such items as household income and living expenses. However, in measuring the financial status of the individual elderly, the amount that the elderly can spend on their own is as important as, perhaps more important than, the household level income or expense. In addition, a substantial proportion of the respondents appeared not to be aware of household income or living expenses since other household members (i.e., children) managed these. For these reasons, the amount of pocket money per month is employed in the analysis. This variable, although it constitutes an ordinal scale ranging from 1 to 4, is treated like a continuous one in the regression analysis. Cohabiting with children is coded 1 if the elderly live with any adult child and 0 if elsewhere. About 52.8 percent of the elderly in the sample currently cohabited with their children.

Another set of control variables includes several demographic background variables, such as place of residence, age, gender, martial status and education. Of the elderly in the sample, 40.3 percent lived in metro-cities; 13.9 percent, in mid-sized cities; and 46.8 percent, in rural areas. The average age of the elderly was 72.8 years. Almost half of the elderly were female. About 56.4

percent of the elderly were currently married. In terms of education, 55.3 percent never attended school; 33.9 percent attended primary school; 20.8 percent attended secondary or above level school.

We conducted an OLS regression analysis of the scores on overall life satisfaction among the elderly. Some independent variables are categorical ones. For these variables, several sets of indicator variables were created and included in the regression model. The multiple regression models established in the present study are incremental in nature. We start with a simple regression model, which shows only the effect of flow in intergenerational support, and then we expanded the model by including two sets of variables in cumulative manners. Correspondingly, our interpretation of the results focuses on the effect of the flow in intergenerational support and its changes as the statistical model expands to include other control variables. This strategy is consistent with our main interest in finding whether the effect of flow in intergenerational support would be found even after controlling for the two sets of control variables.

ANALYSIS

Table II presents regression coefficients and standard errors from OLS regression models of the life satisfaction score of the elderly parents. Three statistical models, Model 1, 2, and 3, are presented. In each model, the first column represents unstandardized regression coefficients while the second one indicates standardized regression coefficients. The standard errors are presented in a smaller font under the unstandardized regression coefficients.

Model 1 shows the simple regression model in which the overall life satisfaction score is regressed only on the flow of intergenerational support. According to this model, the overall life satisfaction score of the elderly parents is significantly higher for those both giving and receiving support than for those only receiving (b = 3.950**), while the score is significantly lower for those who do not involve any intergenerational support exchange (b = –5.098**). No significant difference was found between those only giving and those only receiving.

Model 2 allows us to examine the effect of flow in intergenerational support after controlling the variables representing the

TABLE II

Coefficients and Standard Errors from OLS Regression Analysis of Life Satisfaction of the Elderly in Korea (n = 1056)

	Model 1		Model 2		Model 3	
	b	beta	b	beta	b	beta
Constant	34.729**	—	29.823**	—	23.366**	—
	0.592		0.997		3.969	
Flow of int. support (ref. = only receiving)						
No flow	–5.098**	–0.137	–4.690**	–0.126	–4.713**	–0.127
	1.208		1.173		1.169	
Only giving	–3.259	–0.041	–4.337*	–0.054	–4.004*	–0.050
	2.414		2.336		2.326	
Both giving and receiving	3.950***	0.187	3.185**	0.151	3.182**	0.151
	0.697		0.681		0.692	
ADL impairment (vs. no impairment)	—	—	–3.996**	–0.122	–3.879**	–0.118
			0.952		0.967	
Monthly pocket money	—	—	1.952**	0.201	1.922**	0.198
			0.281		0.300	
Number of children	—	—	0.384**	0.073	0.319**	0.060
			0.153		0.157	
Coresidence w/ child (vs. noncoresidence)	—	—	1.243**	0.062	1.853**	0.092
			0.586			
Place of residence (ref. = rural area)						
Metro-city	—	—	—	—	–2.210**	–0.108
					0.660	
Mid-sized city	—	—	—	—	1.074	0.037
					0.907	
Age	—	—	—	—	0.057	0.038
					0.048	
Female (vs. male)	—	—	—	—	2.069**	0.103
					0.716	
Married (vs. unmarried)	—	—	—	—	2.002**	0.099
					0.716	
Education (ref. = no formal schooling)						
Primary school	—	—	—	—	1.479**	0.070
					0.719	

TABLE II

Continued

	Model 1		Model 2		Model 3	
	b	beta	b	beta	b	beta
Secondary or above school	—	—	—	—	1.659* 0.921	0.067
R-Square	0.079		0.112		0.171	
F-Statistics	29.959**		13.208**		15.229**	
Degrees of freedom	(31052)		(101045)		(141041)	

*$p < 0.10$; **$p < 0.05$.
Numbers in a smaller font represent standard errors.

resources of the elderly. When we controlled for these variables, the association between the flow of intergenerational support and the life satisfaction found in Model 1 changed to some extent. The effects of "both giving and receiving" (b = 3.185**) and of "no flow" (b =–4.690**) become slightly smaller, while their statistical significance remains at similar levels. The effect of "only giving" (b = –4.690**) becomes marginally significant ($p < 0.10$), suggesting that the elderly who only give support to their children are less satisfied with their life than the elderly who receive only support from their children. Such findings indicate that the flow of intergenerational support exerts influence on the life satisfaction score independently of resource variables.

All the resource variables added in Model 2 have significant effect s on the life satisfaction score. The score of life satisfaction is higher for the elderly who do not report any difficulty in performing the ADL items than the elderly who have difficulty. Also, the score is positively associated with the amount of monthly pocket money that the elderly have. With respect to the demographic resources, the score is positively related to the number of children. In addition, the score is higher for the elderly who live with their children than the ones who do not.

Model 3 expands Model 2 by including another set of control variables – demographic background variables. The patterns reported from Model 2 are found in Model 3. Given the demographic variables as well as the resource variables, the negative effect of "no flow" (b = –4.713**) and the positive effect of "both giving and receiving" (b = 3.182**) are statistically significant, while the negative effect of "only giving" (b = –4.004*) is marginally significant. Thus, in contrast to those who only receive support from their children, the elderly who both give and receive support are more satisfied, but the elderly who only give support to their children and the elderly who do not exchange support with their children are less satisfied with their life.

The resource variables remain significant, when we considered the demographic background variables. As in Model 2, the life satisfaction score is negatively related to having difficulty in performing the ADL items, and positively associated with the amount of monthly pocket money, number of children and cohabitation with children. With respect to the demographic background variables, all the variables except age have significant effects on the life satisfaction score. The elderly in metro-cities are less satisfied than the elderly in rural areas, while no significant difference was found between the elderly in rural areas and the elderly in mid-sized cities. Female elderly are more satisfied than male elderly. At the present time, married elderly are more satisfied than currently unmarried elderly. Compared to the elderly who had never attended school, the elderly who attended primary school and the elderly who attended secondary or higher level of school are more satisfied.

CONCLUSION

Relying on equity or exchange theory, we formulated hypotheses pertaining to the effect of intergenerational support exchange in the life satisfaction of the elderly. They included: in contrast to the elderly who are only receiving, the elderly who both give and receive are more satisfied with life, while the elderly who only give or the elderly who do not exchange any support with their children are less satisfied. The results from the multiple regression analysis based on survey data obtained form the elderly in Korea appear to support these hypotheses as a whole. After controlling for variables reflecting the resources of the elderly and their demographic background characteristics, the score of life satisfaction is significantly higher among the elderly who both provide and receive support than among the elderly who only receive; the score is significantly lower among the elderly who do not exchange any support with their children than among the elderly who only receive; and the score is marginally lower among the elderly who only give than among the elderly who only receive. These results indicate that the reciprocity of support within family relations contributes to the psychological well-being of elderly parents in Korea, while the unidirectional provision of support to the children as well as the absence of support exchange has a detrimental effect.

The finding that the balanced exchange relation between generations is a crucial aspect of the subjective well-being of the elderly in Korea suggests that being only a receiver of support from their children without being able to reciprocate may lead to a depressed effect, although the filial piety dictates that the elderly parents should be cared for regardless of their ability to compensate for the support form the children. In reality, the elderly as well as the young generations in Korea may place more value on bi-directional intergenerational relations based on mutual care ad assistance rather than simply following the traditional norm of filial piety. The practical implication of this finding is somewhat obvious: to enhance the quality of life of the elderly in Korea, the elderly parents should balance their relations with their children. However, given that the financial resources of the elderly (i.e., wealth) decline as they age, such ability on the part of the parents should not be expected to be acquired or easily maintained at the individual level.

We propose that the efforts to help the elderly to achieve balanced intergenerational relations should be made by expanding the resources that the elderly can access beyond familial level. Although such efforts should be made at various levels, the effort at the government level appears to be most urgently in need. The welfare policy toward the elderly in Korea, based on the principle of "family first, then the government" has given rise to the view that family members should take the primary responsibility for the problems of elderly. As many scholars contend (i.e., Choi, 1996; Kim et al., 1996), the government needs to share more actively with families the responsibility for the elderly and provide comprehensive policy initiatives. Income security and health protection provided by the welfare policy could become the foundation on which elderly parents maintain their autonomy and build balanced relations with their children.

We started with a rather simplistic measure of intergenerational support exchange. As discussed earlier, the investigation of patterns of exchange across specific life domains and the use of more refined measurements of the support exchanged would deepen our understanding on the relations of intergenerational support exchange and the subjective well-being of the elderly parents. In addition, we highlighted the support exchange between elderly parents and their children, since the exchange of support exchange between elderly parents and their children, since the exchange of support mainly occurs within family relations in Korea. Nonetheless, it would offer valuable insights about the support exchange and would broaden research interest to include other informal social networks (such as friends). For future research endeavors, we believe that it is worthy to apply this approach to the children who constitute one of the parties in intergenerational exchange relations and compare these results with those from elderly parents. It remains unexplored whether and to what extend balanced relations with their elderly parents (versus only providing assistance to elderly parents) would result in positive outcomes for the adult children.

ACKNOWLEDGEMENT

This study was supported by Dongguk University Research Fund.

NOTES

[1] An aging society refers to one where the proportion of those aged 65 and above is at least 7% of the total population. According to the preliminary report of the year 2000 census, Korea has become an aging society.

[2] For examples, Chung et al (1998), Kim et al. (1999), Rhee et al. (1994), and Rhee et al. (2000). While these works deal with various aspects of elderly Koreans based on nation-wide surveys, they are written in Korean. For those in the English language, the authors recommend Choi and Suh (1995), Chung (1999), and Kim et al. (1996). These works briefly describe the aging process and overall status of the Korean elderly.

[3] Examples include Ferraro and Su (1999), Lee et al. (1995), Silverstein and Bengston (1994), Stevens (1992), and Umberson (1992).
[4] The validity of exchange theory in explaining the changes in intergenerational relations in Korea are discussed in Choi (1985) and Park (1991).
[5] See the report by Kim et al. (1999) for further information on this survey.
[6] The survey asked 7 items to assess life satisfaction. The items include "7. *I am afraid of death*" in addition to the 6 items listed in Table I. We thought that there was a conceptual distance between the last item and others. In addition, the test of internal consistency reliability revealed that the deletion of the 7th item improved the alpha value significantly from 0.723 to 0.807. Therefore, the study decided to exclude the item reflecting fear of death in constructing a life satisfaction index.

REFERENCES

Antonucci, T.C.: 1990, 'Social supports and social relationships', in R.H. Binstock and L.K. George (eds.), Handbook of Aging and Social Sciences (Academic Press, New York).

Choi, S.J.: 1991, 'Problems of the aged in Korea from the perspective of exchange theory', Korean Journal of Social Welfare 7, pp. 147–165 (in Korean).

Choi, S.J.: 1996, 'The family and ageing in Korea', Ageing and Society 16, pp. 1–25.

Choi, S.J. and H.S. Suh: 1995, Ageing in Korea: Today and Tomorrow (Federation of Korea Gerontological Societies, Seoul).

Chung, K.H.: 1999, Living Profiles of Older Persons and Social Policies on Ageing in Korea (Korea Institute for Health and Social Affairs, Seoul). Working Paper 99-01.

Chung, K.H. et al.: 1998, Living Profile and Welfare Service Needs of Older Persons in Korea (Korea Institute for Health and Social Affairs, Seoul) (in Korean).

Dowd, J.J.: 1975, 'Aging as exchange: A preface to Theory', Journal of Gerontology 30, pp. 584–594.

Ferraro, K.F. and Y. Su: 1999, 'Financial strains, social relations, and psychological distress among older people: A cross-sectional analysis', Journal of Gerontology: Social Sciences 54B(1), pp. S3–S15.

Kim, C.S. and K.O. Rhee: 1999, 'Living arrangements in old age: Views of Korean elderly and middle aged adults', Hallym International Journal of Aging 1(2), pp. 94–111.

Kim, I.K. and E.H. Choe: 1992, 'Support exchange patterns of the elderly in Korea', Asia-Pacific Population Journal 7(3), pp. 89–104.

Kim, I.K. et al.: 1999, The Quality of Life of Korean Elderly (MiRaeIlluk Yunku Center, Seoul) (in Korean).

Kim, I.K., J. Liang, K.O. Rhee and C.S. Kim: 1996, 'Population aging in Korea: Changes since the 1960s', Journal of Cross-Cultural Gerontology 11(4), pp. 369–388.

Kim, T.H. et al.: 1998, 'A study on the improvement of the quality of life for the aged', The Journal of Korean Gerontological Society 18(1), pp. 150–169 (in Korean).

Lee, G.R., K.K. Netzer and R.T. Coward: 1995, 'Depression among older parents: The role of intergenerational exchange', Journal of Marriage and the Family 57, pp. 823–833.

Murtan, E. and D.C. Reitzes: 1984, 'Intergenerational support activities and well-being among the elderly: A converge of exchange theory and symbolic interaction perspectives', American Sociological Review 49, pp. 117–130.

Ofstedal, M.B., J. Knodel and A. Chayovan: 1999, 'Intergenerational support and gender: A comparison of four Asian countries', University of Michigan Population Studies Center, Elderly in Asian Research Report No. 99-54.

Park, J.H.: 1991, 'Problems of the aged in Korea: An exchange perspective', Korean Journal of Sociology 25, pp. 1–20 (in Korean).

Rhee, K.O. et al.: 1994, Livelihood Status and Its Policy Implications of the Korean Elderly (Korea Institute for Health and Social Affairs, Seoul) (in Korean).

Rhee, K.O., H.S. Lee and C.S. Kim: 2000, Quality of Life in Old Age: Development of Index and Evaluation. Manuscripts presented at the 6th Seminar for the Elderly Studies, Seoul, 2000 September (in Korean).

Rossi, A.S. and P.H. Rossi: 1990, Of Human Bonding: Parent-Child Relations across the Life Course (Aldine DeGruyter, New York).

Shi, L.: 1992, 'Family financial and household support exchange between generations: A survey of Chinese rural elderly', The Gerontologist 33(4), pp. 468–480.

Silverstein, M. and V.L. Bengston: 1994, 'Does intergenerational social support influence the psychological well-being of older parents? The contingencies of declining health and widowhood', Social Science and Medicine 38, pp. 943–957.

Stevens, E.S.: 1992, 'Reciprocity in social support: an advantage for the aging family', Families in Society 73, pp. 533–541.

Turner, J.H.: 1986, The Structure of Sociological Theory (Dorsey Press, Chicago).

Umberson, D.: 1992, 'Relationship between adult children and their parents: Psychological consequences for both generations', Journal of Marriage and the Family 54, pp. 664–674.

Walster, E.G., W. Walster and E. Berscheid: 1978, Equity: Theory and Research (Allyn and Bacon, Boston).

Won, Y.H.: 1995, 'Living arrangement and psychological well-being of the elderly in Korea', The Journal of Korean Gerontological Society 15(2), pp. 97–116 (in Korean).

Yoo, S.H.: 1997, 'Effects of number of children and coresidence with married adult children on life satisfaction among elderly Korean', The Journal of Korean Gerontological Society 17(2), pp. 38–50 (in Korea).

Yoon, C.H. and J.K. Lee: 1997, 'The effect of self-esteem, health status, family relationship and social participation on the life satisfaction of aged widows', The Journal of Korean Gerontological Society 17(1), pp. 289–304 (in Korean).
Yoon, H.S. and H.B. Cha: 1999, 'Future issues for the family care of the elderly in Korea', Hallym International Journal of Aging 1(1), pp. 78–86.

Department of Sociology
Dongguk University
Seoul, Korea
Ik Ki Kim

Department of Sociology
Dongguk University
Seoul, Korea
E-mail: chkim108@dongguk.edu
Cheong-Seok Kim

KYEONG-HO CHA

SUBJECTIVE WELL-BEING AMONG COLLEGE STUDENTS

ABSTRACT. This study examined the subjective well-being of Korean college students and its relation with personality constructs, such as self-esteem, collective self-esteem, and optimism. The subjective well-being and personality constructs of 350 Korean students were assessed with self-report measures. The relative contributions of personality constructs in predicting subjective well-being were examined by regression analyses and dominance analyses. Korean students scored low in life satisfaction and affective well-being compared to students of other nations. All personality constructs were significantly correlated with life satisfaction, positive affect, and negative affect.

Subjective well-being (SWB) research focuses on how and why people experience their lives in positive ways (Diener, 1984). SWB researchers have identified two facets of SWB: a cognitive judgment of life satisfaction (Andrews and Withey, 1976) and an emotional aspect consisting of independent positive affect and negative affect components (Diener and Emmons, 1984). Life satisfaction has been defined as "a global assessment of a person's quality of life according to his or her chosen criteria" (Shin and Johnson, 1978: p. 478), and an emotional aspect has been defined as the amount of positive or negative affects a person experiences (Diener, 1984). Although measures of life satisfaction are correlated with both positive affect and negative affect, research has shown that the affective and cognitive components can diverge, behaving differently over time and having differing relations with other variables (Diener, 1994; Lucas et al., 1996). Thus, SWB is defined by three correlated but distinct factors: the relative presence of positive affect, absence of negative affect, and satisfaction with life. The present study examined SWB of Korean college students and whether the factors just mentioned were present in them.

A number of correlates of SWB have been examined in the search for an understanding of the causes of SWB, for example: (a) biosocial variables, such as gender and age; (b) personality variables,

Social Indicators Research **62, 63:** 455–477, 2003.

such as self-esteem and extraversion; and (c) social support variables, such as family satisfaction (Diener, 1984). Several reviews of the SWB literature have suggested that most of biosocial variables account for only a small portion of SWB variance, and that personality may be one of the strongest influences, if not the major determinant of SWB (DeNeve and Cooper, 1998; Diener, 1984; Diener et al., 1999; Myers and Diener, 1995). However, most studies that were reviewed had been conducted with samples from western cultures and little attention has been given to whether the predictors of SWB differ in various cultures. It seems likely that the variables that influence people's SWB do vary across cultures (e.g., Diener and Diener, 1995; Suh et al., 1998). The purpose of the present study was to examine how well personality variables, such as self-esteem, collective self-esteem, and optimism, could predict life satisfaction, positive affect, and negative affect in a culture quite different from western culture.

Several researchers have shown that self-esteem is one of the strongest predictors of SWB. Campbell (1981), for example, found that self-esteem correlated 0.55 with life satisfaction in a normal U.S. probability sample and Lucas et al. (1996) reported correlations of 0.29 to 0.65 between life satisfaction and self-esteem. Diener and Emmons (1984) found that self-esteem correlated (across two studies) 0.46 and 0.34 with positive affect and −0.40 and −0.46 with negative affect. In a large study of college students from 49 countries, Diener and Diener (1995) found mean within-country correlations between life satisfaction and self-esteem of 0.44 and 0.43 for men and women, respectively. The relation between the two was consistent and robust across countries. However, Diener and Diener illustrated that across cultures, the strength of this relation was moderated by the degree to which a country was individualistic or collectivist in nature. In individual countries, such as the United States, self-esteem and life satisfaction were highly correlated, whereas in collectivist cultures they were less so. Diener and Diener explained these findings in terms of the difference in socialization (see also, Diener and Suh, 1999; Suh et al., 1998). In the individualistic culture independent or private aspects of self re emphasized, whereas in the collectivist culture interdependent a or collective aspects of self are emphasized (Markus and Kitayama,

1991; Triandis, 1989). Personal and individualistic aspects of self, that are derived from or related to an individual's personal attributes, competencies, and stand relative to other individuals, may be more salient and important and thus more related to life satisfaction in individualistic cultures than in collectivist cultures.

Although personal, individualistic aspects of the self may be important sources of self-esteem for most people, particularly those in individualistic cultures, self-esteem may also be derived from collective aspects of the self (e.g., Tajfel, 1982). The social or collective self is defined in social identity theory as "that aspect of an individual's self-concept which derives from his knowledge of his membership in a social group (or groups) together with the value and emotional significance attached to that membership" (Tajfel, 1981: p. 255). Those collective aspects of self may be more salient and important and thus more related to life satisfaction in collectivist cultures than in individualistic cultures. Crocker, Luhtanen et al. (1994) indirectly support this possibility. They examined collective self-esteem and SWB among three racial groups. Collective self-esteem refers to the positivity of the self-concept derived from identifying oneself as a member in one or more social groups. Crocker et al. found that collective self-esteem was a stronger correlate of life satisfaction for Asians (*r*s ranging from 0.08 to 0.47) than for either Blacks or Whites (*r*s ranging from −0.01 to 0.33). However, the participants from these groups were all from the United States and it could be that racial differences themselves rather than cultural differences accounted for the differential pattern of findings.

Kwan et al. (1997) examined the relative importance of self-esteem and relationship harmony in predicting life satisfaction for U.S. samples and Hong Kong samples. The relationship harmony was a construct that was related to interdependent aspects of self. They found that self-esteem was more powerful than relationship harmony in predicting life satisfaction for the U.S. samples, whereas, for the Hong Kong samples, self-esteem and relationship harmony were of equal importance in predicting life satisfaction. These findings indicate that collective aspects of self are relatively more influential predictors of life satisfaction in collectivist cultures than in individualist cultures. The present study examined the relative influence of self-esteem and collective self-esteem on not only life satisfaction but also positive affect and negative affect of Korean students. Because Korean culture is collectivist (Hofstede, 1991), it was expected that in predicting SWB, collective self-esteem would be as important as self-esteem itself.

Optimism is also related to SWB (Scheier and Carver, 1992). Scheier and Carver (1985) developed a theory of dispositional optimism, in which one's characteristic thoughts about the future affect one's circumstances and therefore one's SWB. According to their theory, optimism represents a generalized tendency to expect favorable outcomes in one's life. If one expects positive outcomes, he or she will work for the goals that he or she has set, whereas, if one expects failures, he or she will disengage from them. This pattern of behavior leads to more successful achievement of goals by optimists than by pessimists. Several studies reported that optimism was positively related to SWB (Scheier and Carver, 1992). For example, Aspinwall and Taylor (1992) found that college students who scored high on optimism at the start of their first semester demonstrated higher SWB and less psychological distress three months later. Aspinwall and Taylor showed that the effects of optimism on SWB were not only direct but also indirect by adaptive coping methods. Harju and Bolen (1998) also reported similar findings.

Self-esteem, collective self-esteem and optimism are all related with SWB. These personality constructs are theoretically distinct but moderate correlations have been established between them (Lucas et al., 1996; Luhtanen and Crocker, 1992; Scheier et al., 1994). In order to assess their unique contributions to predicting SWB, it is necessary to include these constructs as predictors of SWB in a single study. The present study examined the relative importance of these personality constructs in predicting SWB.

The purposes of this study are: (1) to gain first-hand knowledge of SWB in Korean students – both global life satisfaction and affective well-being; (2) to assess the structural invariance of SWB in a culture quite different from western cultures; (3) to assess the relative contributions made by self-esteem, collective self-esteem, and optimism in predicting SWB.

METHOD

Participants

A total of 379 college students in Korea participated in the current study. Of these, 29 participants failed to complete the whole set of questionnaires, so their responses were eliminated from the analyses. Thus, the final data set included 350 college students. There were 205 men and 143 women. Two participants failed to indicate their gender. The mean age of the entire sample was 21.40 years old (SD = 2.48). All participants were enrolled at Hoseo University located in Asan, Korea. They received extra credits for completing the questionnaires.[1]

Measures

Life satisfaction. Life satisfaction was assessed by the Satisfaction With Life Scale (SWLS; Diener et al., 1985). The SWLS is a five-item measure that asks respondents to rate their global life satisfaction from their subjective perspective. The response scale ranges from 1 (strongly disagree) to 7 (strongly agree), yielding a possible total score range of from 5 to 35. A score of 20 represents the neutral point on the scale, at which the respondent is about equally satisfied and dissatisfied. The SWLS has adequate psychometric properties (Pavot and Diener, 1993). The SWLS was translated into Korean for the current study. The alpha coefficient of the Korean version of the SWLS in this study was 0.77.

Affective well-being. Affective well-being was measured by asking how much of their time during the past month they felt four pleasant (joy, affection, pride, and contentment) and four unpleasant (fear, anger, guilt, and sadness) emotions. Participants used a 7-point scale that ranged from 1 (never) to 7 (always) to indicate how frequently they felt each emotion. The positive affect (PA) score was obtained by averaging the scores of the four pleasant emotion items. Similarly, the average for the four unpleasant emotion items was used as the negative affect (NA) score. The alpha coefficients for the PA and NA scale were 0.74 and 0.67, respectively. An affective balance score (ABS) was obtained by subtracting the NA score from the PA score.

Self-esteem. Self-esteem was assessed by the Self-Rating Scale (SRS; Fleming and Courtney, 1984), a 36-item self-esteem questionnaire. The scale has high reliability, with a test-retest coefficient of 0.82 and an internal consistency (alpha) of 0.92 (Fleming and Courtney, 1984). This scale also has considerable validity data to support its use as a measure of global self-esteem (Blascovich and Tomaka, 1991). The SRS was translated into Korean for the current study. Four items were eliminated because item-total correlations were lower than 0.20 in the preliminary study with the Korean version of the SRS. Thus, total 32 items were used. The Korean version used a 6-point scale. The factor analysis of the Korean version produced the factor structure similar to that of the English version. The alpha coefficient of the SRS in this study was 0.92. This scale includes five subscales: Self-Regard, related to typical self-esteem; Social Confidence, related to self-consciousness in public situations, shyness, and the ability to deal with people in groups general; School ability, concerned self-evaluation of scholastic abilities; Physical Appearance; and Physical Ability. The internal consistencies in the present study were 0.84, 0.88, 0.72, 0.70, and 0.83 for the Self-Regard, Social Confidence, School Ability, Physical Appearance, and Physical Ability subscales, respectively.

Collective self-esteem. Collective self-esteem (CSE) was assessed by The Korean Collective Self-Esteem Scale (KCSES; Kim, 1994). The KCSES is the Korean version of the Collective Self-Esteem Scale (CSES; Luhtanen and Crocker, 1992). The KSES is a 14-item 6-point Likert-type measure that asks respondents to think of a variety of social group memberships based on ascribed category memberships, such as sex, race, religion, and ethnicity. It includes four subscales: Private CSE, measuring one's personal judgments of how good one's social groups are; Public CSE, assessing one's judgments of how positively other people evaluate one's social groups; Membership Esteem, assessing individuals' judgments of how worthy they are as members of their social groups; and Importance to Identity, assessing the importance of one's social group memberships to one's self-concept. Kim (1994) reported full scale alphas of 0.86 and 0.81, and subscale alphas of 0.60s and 0.70s. The full scale alpha in this study was 0.85. The internal consistencies in the preset study were 0.77, 0.64, 0.71, and 0.46 for the Private,

Public, Membership, and Identity subscales, respectively. Because the alpha coefficient of the Identity subscale was lower than 0.60, this subscale was eliminated from the analyses.

Optimism. Optimism was measured by the revised Life Orientation Test (LOT-R; Scheier et al., 1994). The LOT-R requires students to indicate the degree to which they are favorable in their approach to the world; in other words, the degree to which they are optimistic rather than pessimistic. The LOT-R consists of 6 items plus 4 filler items to disguise the underlying purpose of the test. Of the 6 items, three are keyed in a positive direction and three are keyed in a negative direction. Scheier et al. (1994) reported an alpha coefficient of 0.78. The LOT-R was translated into Korean for the current study. Filler items were not used in this study. One of the six items was eliminated because the item-total correlation was lower than 0.20 in the preliminary study with the Korean version of the LOT-R. Thus, 5 items were used to measure optimism. The Korean version used a 6-point scale. The principal components factor analysis for the Korean version, using a varimax final rotation technique, produced one-factor solution. The alpha coefficient of the Korean version of the LOT-R in this study was 0.81.

Procedure

All participants were classroom volunteers. They were required to provide their student numbers in order to receive extra credit. All the questionnaires were conducted in large groups in a one-hour regular class session. Participants were instructed to answer as accurately and honestly as they could. They were also told that there were no right or wrong answers. All data were collected during October and November 1999.

RESULTS

Levels of SWB

Means and the statistical results of the major scales are summarized in Table I. The total mean score for the SWLS was 19.88 that was about the neutral point (20). Korean students seemed to be equally

TABLE I

Descriptive Date

Measure	Total		Men		Women		*t*-value
	Mean	*SD*	Mean	*SD*	Mean	*SD*	
SWLS	19.88	4.96	20.36	4.90	19.17	4.99	2.21*
PA	4.14	1.03	4.22	1.04	4.02	1.01	1.76
NA	2.85	0.90	2.72	0.85	3.04	0.93	–3.30**
ABS	1.29	1.48	1.50	1.43	0.99	1.50	3.23**
Self-esteem	4.00	0.61	4.11	0.63	3.86	0.56	3.75***
Collective self-esteem	4.27	0.58	4.36	0.54	4.15	0.62	3.23**
Optimism	4.50	0.77	4.48	0.80	4.53	0.73	–0.68

*$p < 0.05$; **$p < 0.01$; ***$p < 0.001$.

satisfied and dissatisfied. The difference between men (20.36) and women (19.17) in the SWLS was significant ($t = 2.21$, $p < 0.05$). Men appeared to be slightly satisfied with their lives and women appeared to be slightly dissatisfied with their lives. Comparison means for the SWLS of Korean students with normative data for the SWLS (Pavot and Diener, 1993) shows that the mean for Korean students was lower than American college students (with means such as 23.5, 24.5 and 25.3). However, the mean for Korean students was higher than Soviet college students (with means such as 16.3 and 18.9) and Chinese college students (with means such as 16.1).

The total mean scores for the PA and NA scales were 4.14 and 2.85, respectively. The neutral point of the PA and NA scales was 4. The total mean score for the affective balance score was 1.29. These results indicate that Korean students experience relatively more positive affect than negative affect. The differences between men and women were significant for NA (2.72 and 3.04, respectively; $t = -3.30$, $p < 0.01$) and the affective balance score (1.50 and 0.99, respectively; $t = 3.23$, $p < 0.01$). However, the difference between men (4.22) and women (4.02) for PA was not significant ($t = 1.76$, $p > 0.05$). Men and women seemed to experience equal amount of positive affect, but women appeared to experience more negative affect than men. Thus, the affective well-being of men was higher than that of women. Diener et al. (1995) reported that in the same PA and NA scales, means for American students were 5.0 and 2.5, respectively, and that means for Chinese students were 4.3 and 2.3, respectively. The mean for PA of Korean students was lower than those of American and Chinese students and the mean for NA of Korean students was higher than those of American and Chinese students. These results suggest the affective well-being of Korean students is lower than that of American and Chinese students.

Means and the statistical results of the personality measures are also summarized in Table I. The neutral point in all personality scales was 3.5. Means for all personality scales were higher than the neutral point. The differences of men and women in self-esteem (4.11 and 3.86, respectively; $t = 3.75$, $p < 0.001$) and collective self-esteem (4.36 and 4.15, respectively; $t = 3.23$, $p < 0.01$) were significant, but the difference of men and women in optimism was not significant (4.48 and 4.53, respectively; $t = -0.68$, $p > 0.05$). Men appeared to have higher self-esteem and higher collective self-esteem than women. However, men and women seemed to be equally optimistic about their future.

Structure of SWB

In order to explore the structure of SWB, the principal components factor analysis, using a varimax final rotation technique, was performed on all items of the SWLS, PA, and NA. Three factors were extracted. The factor structure was presented in Table II. The three factors were identified as life satisfaction, positive affect, and negative affect. The first factor, life satisfaction, had an eigenvalue of 3.86 and this factor accounted for 30 percent of the total variance. The second factor, positive affect, had an eigenvalue of 1.81 and this factor accounted for 14 percent of the total variance. The third factor, negative affect, had an eigenvalue of 1.47 and this factor accounted for 11 percent of the total variance. The factor structure was similar to that found in the United States (Andrews and Withey, 1976).

Relations among Personality Variables and SWB

Pearson correlations were calculated between all scales and were summarized in Table III. All correlations in Table III were significant ($p < 0.01$). The SWLS showed a moderate correlation with the PA scale ($r = 0.40$) and a weak correlation with the NA scale

TABLE II

Factor Loading for the Three-factor Model of SWB

Items	Factor 1	Factor 2	Factor 3
SWLS1	0.59	0.18	0.00
SWLS2	0.78	0.08	−0.06
SWLS3	0.75	0.22	−0.21
SWLS4	0.74	0.05	−0.09
SWLS5	0.66	0.16	−0.05
Affection	0.02	0.66	0.19
Joy	0.27	0.72	−0.07
Contentment	0.22	0.79	−0.21
Pride	0.19	0.77	−0.22
Fear	−0.12	−0.03	0.65
Anger	−0.03	−0.19	0.64
Sadness	−0.07	−0.02	0.78
Guilt	−0.07	0.02	0.72

($r = -0.23$). The PA scale showed a weak correlation with the NA scale ($r = -0.18$). Correlations between subscales of self-esteem were 0.31 to 0.58, stronger than correlations of the subscales with the other scales. Correlations between subscales of collective self-esteem were 0.56 to 0.66, and also stronger than correlations of the subscales with the other scales. These results indicate self-esteem and collective self-esteem can be distinguished from SWB and optimism. With the SWLS, optimism showed the strongest correlation ($r = 0.45$) and self-esteem showed the weakest ($r = 0.38$). With the PA scale, optimism showed the strongest correlation ($r = 0.37$) and self-esteem showed the weakest ($r = 0.27$). With the NA scale, self-esteem showed the strongest correlation ($r = -0.42$) and optimism showed the weakest ($r = -0.21$).

In terms of subscales of self-esteem, Self-Regard showed the strongest correlations with the SWLS ($r = 0.40$), the PA scale ($r = 0.33$), and the NA scale ($r = -0.44$). In terms of subscales of collective self-esteem, Membership Esteem showed the strongest correlations with the SWLS ($r = 0.40$), and the NA scale ($r = -0.27$)

and Private CSE showed the strongest correlation with the PA scale ($r = 0.34$).

Regression Analyses

In order to examine the relative influence of self-esteem, collective self-esteem, and optimism on each SWB measure, the regression analyses predicting each SWB measure from self-esteem, collective self-esteem, and optimism were conducted. Results of the regression analyses for each SWB measure were summarized in Table IV. The standardized beta values of three predictors of life satisfaction were all significant ($p < 0.001$). The relative size of the standardized beta values in predicting life satisfaction indicates that optimism ($\beta = 0.293$) was associated much more closely with life satisfaction than collective self-esteem ($\beta = 0.203$) and self-esteem ($\beta = 0.186$). In predicting positive affect the standardized beta values of collective self-esteem ($\beta = 0.245$, $p < 0.001$) and optimism ($\beta = 0.233$, $p < 0.001$) were significant. The standardized beta value of self-esteem was 0.083 and not significant ($p > 0.05$). Collective self-esteem and optimism appeared to be equally influential predictors of positive affect. In predicting negative affect, however, only the standardized beta value of self-esteem ($\beta = 0.377$, $p < 0.001$) was significant. The standardized beta values of collective self-esteem ($\beta = -0.102$, $p > 0.05$) and optimism ($\beta = -0.014$, $p > 0.05$) were not significant. Only self-esteem appeared to be an influential predictor of negative affect.

In order to examine the influence of self-esteem and collective self-esteem in detail, the step-wise regression analyses were conducted using optimism and the subscales of self-esteem and collective self-esteem as predictor variables of each SWB measure. The final results of these regression analyses for each SWB measure were summarized in Table V. In predicting life satisfaction, optimism ($\beta = 0.33$, $p < 0.001$), Private CSE ($\beta = 0.27$, $p < 0.001$), and Physical Appearance ($\beta = 0.20$, $p < 0.001$) were significant predictors ($F = 51.22$, $p < 0.001$). In predicting positive affect, optimism ($\beta = 0.23$, $p < 0.001$), Private CSE ($\beta = 0.22$, $p < 0.001$), and Self-Regard ($\beta = 0.15$, $p < 0.01$) were significant predictors ($F = 30.64$, $p < 0.001$). In predicting negative affect, only the subscales of self-esteem, Self-Regard ($\beta = -0.31$, $p < 0.001$) and Social Confid-

TABLE III

Pearson Correlations for All Major Scales

Scales	1	2	3	4	5	6	7	8	9	10	11	12	13	14
1. SWLS														
2. Positive Affect	0.40													
3. Negative Affect	−0.23	−0.18												
4. Affective Balance	0.42	0.80	−0.73											
5. Self-Esteem	0.38	0.27	−0.42	0.44										
6. Self-Regard	0.40	0.33	−0.42	0.49	0.79									
7. Social Confidence	0.29	0.16	−0.38	0.34	0.87	0.58								
8. School Ability	0.33	0.20	−0.25	0.29	0.71	0.52	0.48							
9. Physical Appearance	0.29	0.20	−0.25	0.29	0.69	0.49	0.49	0.45						
10. Physical Ability	0.16	0.17	−0.24	0.26	0.63	0.38	0.43	0.31	0.34					
11. Collective Self-Esteem	0.39	0.37	−0.25	0.41	0.37	0.44	0.26	0.30	0.13	0.29				
12. Membership Esteem	0.40	0.33	−0.27	0.39	0.47	0.53	0.35	0.39	0.22	0.27	0.81			
13. Private CSE	0.38	0.34	−0.20	0.36	0.26	0.33	0.15	0.23	0.06	0.23	0.88	0.60		
14. Public CSE	0.32	0.29	−0.24	0.35	0.37	0.36	0.30	0.30	0.15	0.26	0.79	0.60	0.66	
15. Optimism	0.45	0.37	−0.21	0.38	0.42	0.47	0.32	0.36	0.21	0.21	0.41	0.46	0.31	0.38

All correlations are significant at $p < 0.01$ level; CSE = Collective Self-Esteem.

TABLE IV

Predicting SWB from Self-esteem, Collective Self-esteem, and Optimism

Variables	*B*	*SE B*	β	R^2
Life satisfaction				
				0.283
Self-esteem	1.503	0.418	0.186***	
Collective Self-esteem	1.730	0.438	0.203***	
Optimism	1.890	0.339	0.293***	
Positive affect				
				0.199
Self-esteem	0.139	0.091	0.083	
Collective Self-esteem	0.432	0.096	0.245***	
Optimism	0.311	0.074	0.233***	
Negative affect				
				0.188
Self-esteem	−0.553	0.081	−0.377***	
Collective Self-esteem	−0.158	0.084	−0.102	
Optimism	−0.016	0.065	−0.014	

$^{**}p < 0.01$; $^{***}p < 0.001$.

ence ($\beta = -0.20$, $p < 0.01$) were significant predictors ($F = 44.40$, $p < 0.001$).

Dominance Analyses

To gain a more precise understanding of the relative importance of the three predictors in each of the three SWB measures, a dominance analysis (Budescu, 1993) was performed separately for each SWB measure. The merit of dominance analysis is that it allows one to statistically decompose the total predicted variance of the regression model according to the importance of each predictor. Although a detailed statistical discussion of this method is available in Budescu's article, consider one case, in which life satisfaction was regressed on self-esteem (SE), collective self-esteem (CSE), and optimism (O). Is this case of p = 3 predictors, one can conceive of 7 different regression models; 3 submodels with a single predictor; 3 submodels with 2 predictors (SE/CSE, SE/O,

TABLE V

Predicting SWB from Optimism and Subscales of Self-esteem and Collective Self-esteem

Variables	B	$SE\ B$	β	R^2
Life satisfaction				
				0.308
Optimism	2.119	0.310	0.328***	
Private CSE	1.671	0.297	0.265***	
Physical Appearance	1.393	0.314	0.203***	
Positive affect				
				0.210
Optimism	0.306	0.073	0.229***	
Private CSE	0.292	0.067	0.224***	
Self-Regard	0.191	0.071	0.149**	
Negative affect				
				0.204
Self-Regard	−0.345	0.066	−0.309***	
Social confidence	−0.226	0.068	−0.196**	

**$p < 0.01$; ***$p < 0.001$; CSE = Collective Self-Esteem.

and CSE/O); and a submodel including all 3 predictors (SE/SCE/O). Dominance analysis compares the squared multiple correlation of the 7 submodels and determines the mean contribution of each of the predictors in all models.

Table VI summarizes the results of the dominance analysis for each of the three SWB measures. The first two columns represent the variable(s) included in the submodel and the R^2 in that particular submodel. The next three columns (one for each predictor) show the increase in R^2 as a result of adding that particular predictor into the model. For instance, the first row of Table VI shows that the R^2 when predicting life satisfaction from self-esteem is 0.147 when self-esteem is the only predictor in the regression model. However, the two right columns show that R^2 increased by 0.072 when collective self-esteem was added and increased by 0.104 when optimism was added in the single-predictor model. The following rows show the additional contribution of each predictor, this time,

TABLE VI

Dominance Analysis: Contributions of Self-Esteem, Collective Self-esteem, and Optimism In Predicting SWB

Variable(s)	R^2	Additional contribution		
		SE	CSE	O
Life satisfaction				
SE	0.147	—	0.072	0.104
CSE	0.153	0.066	—	0.103
O	0.205	—	—	—
SE/CSE	0.219	—	—	0.064
SE/O	0.251	—	0.032	—
CSE/O	0.256	0.027	—	—
SE/CSE/O	0.283	—	—	—
Decomposition of R^2		0.077	0.082	0.124
Positive affect				
SE	0.074	—	0.084	0.078
CSE	0.137	0.021	—	0.056
O	0.135	0.017	0.058	—
SE/CSE	0.158	—	—	0.041
SE/O	0.152	—	0.047	—
CSE/O	0.193	0.006	—	—
SE/CSE/O	0.199	—	—	—
Decomposition of R^2		0.033	0.085	0.081
Negative affect				
SE	0.178	—	0.010	0.001
CSE	0.062	0.126	—	0.002
O	0.045	0.134	0.032	—
SE/CSE	0.188	—	—	0.000
SE/O	0.179	—	0.009	—
CSE/O	0.077	0.111	—	—
SE/CSE/O	0.188	—	—	—
Decomposition of R^2		0.140	0.031	0.016

SE = Self-Esteem; CSE = Collective Self-Esteem; O = Optimism.

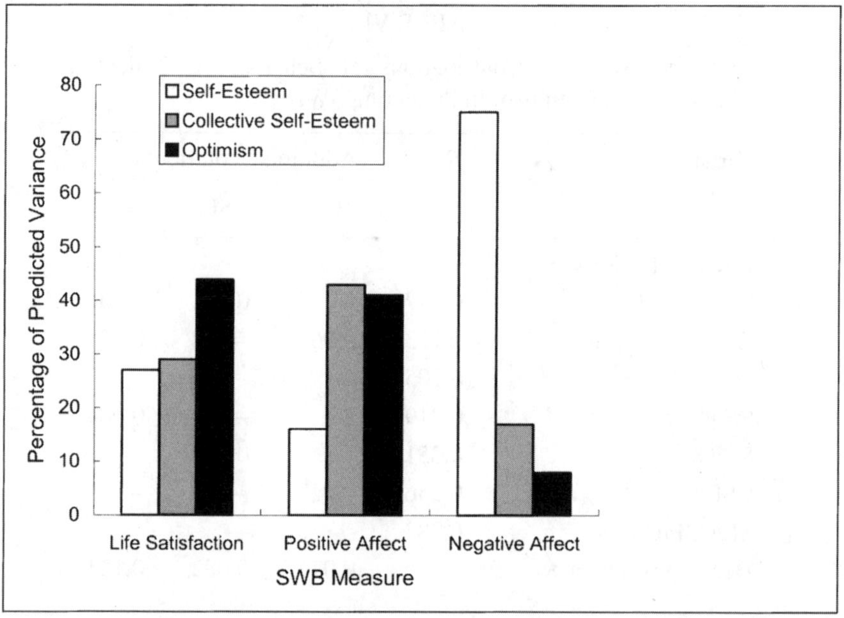

Figure 1. Relative contributions of self-esteem, collective self-esteem, and optimism in predicting SWB.

to each of the 3 two-predictor models (SE/CSE, SE/O, and CSE/O). The SE/CSE/O row presents the full model's R^2, for instance, which is 0.283 in predicting life satisfaction. By averaging each predictor's contribution across all possible models, the full model's R^2 can be decomposed into components that reflect the relative importance of each predictor. For example, in predicting life satisfaction, self-esteem, collective self-esteem, and optimism can be scaled, respectively, as 0.077, 0.082, and 0.124. Because these three values add up to the full model's R^2 (0.283), the average contribution of each predictor can be determined more precisely than in traditional regression methods.

Figure 1 summarized the main findings of the dominance analysis. The figure summarized the percentage of predicted variance attributed to self-esteem, collective self-esteem, and optimism when predicting each SWB measure. In predicting life satisfaction, 27 percent of the predicted variance can be attributed to self-esteem, 29 percent of the predicted variance can be attributed to collective self-esteem, and 44 percent of the predicted variance can be attributed to optimism. Different patterns were observed in predicting positive affect and negative affect. In predicting positive affect, 16 percent of the predicted variance can be attributed to self-esteem, 43 percent of the predicted variance can be attributed to collective self-esteem, and 41 percent of the predicted variance can be attributed to optimism. In predicting negative affect, 75 percents of the predicted variance can be attributed to self-esteem, 17 percent of the predicted variance can be attributed to collective self-esteem, and only 8 percent of the predicted variance can be attributed to optimism.

DISSCUSION

The present study examined the level and structure of SWB of Korean college students and the relations between their SWB and personality variables, such as self-esteem, collective self-esteem, and optimism. The factor analysis of SWB measures produced the same three-factor solution that was found in the United States (Andrews and Withey, 1976): life satisfaction, positive affect, and negative affect. The results from SWB measures showed that Korean students were equally satisfied and dissatisfied, and that they experienced slightly more positive affect than negative affect. Men appeared to have higher SWB than women but the differences were relatively small. These results are consistent with the findings of previous studies (Cha, 1999; Diener, Suh et al., 1995; Kim et al., 1997). Kim et al. (1997) reported a mean for the SWLS of 19.2 in a representative Korean college student sample, and Cha (1999) reported a mean for the SWLS of 18.8 in a student sample similar to this study. Using the same positive affect and negative affect scales that were used in the present study, Cha reported a mean for positive affect of 3.8 and a mean for negative affect of 2.9, and Diener, Suh et al. (1995) reported a mean for positive affect of 4.2 and a mean for negative affect of 3.5 in Korean student samples. These results suggest that the levels of SWB of Korean college students are relatively stable across time.

Because the current study did not include samples from other nations, it is difficult to compare SWB of Korean students to SWB of students of other nations. However, the findings of other studies (Diener, Suh et al., 1995; Pavot and Diener, 1993) using the same

SWB measures suggest that the levels of the life satisfaction and affective well-being of Korean students are very low compared to SWB of college students samples from western countries. Michalos (1991) reported the global life satisfaction and happiness of college students for 39 nations. According to his study, only three nations have life satisfaction scores lower than Korea: Portugal, Japan, and Cameroon. Only four nations have happiness scores lower than Korea: Portugal, Cameroon, Thailand, and South Africa. More important, many countries with lower levels of wealth than Korea have much higher levels of reported well-being. This fact suggests that material aspects of life may not account for low SWB of Korean students.

Diener, M. Diener et al. (1995) examined which factors reliably predicted SWB of various nations. They found that high income, individualism, human rights, and societal equality correlated strongly with SWB of these nations. However, only individualism persistently correlated with SWB when other predictors were controlled for. Individualistic nations have higher SWB than collectivist nations. These findings suggest that national differences in SWB may be accounted for by cultural differences among nations. The fact that Korea has a collectivist culture (Hofstede, 1991), it is not surprising that Korean college students have low SWB. However, the important research question is why collectivist cultures and the Korean culture have negative effects on SWB.

Low SWB of Korean students may be partly accounted for by cultural factors (Diener and Suh, 1999; Suh et Al., 1998). Korea has a Confucian culture. In Confucian cultures, such as Korea, China and Japan, moderate states tend to be preferred to extremes. Good life is defined as the life that is balanced between positive and negative events. Extreme happiness and extreme satisfaction are not ideal states. Thus, cultural norms or ideal levels for SWB may be lower in Confucian cultures than in other cultures. This possibility is supported by the findings of Diener and Suh (1999) who found that norms for SWB were very low in Korea and China. Korea also has a collectivist culture. In relations with others, norms and obligations are emphasized in collectivist cultures, whereas with self-reliance, personal needs and emotions are emphasized in individualistic cultures (Markus and Kitayama, 1991; Triandis, 1989).

Thus, cultural norms for SWB may have more effects on reported SWB in collectivist cultures than in individualistic cultures. This possibility is supported by the findings of Suh et al. (1998), who found that personal emotions were far superior predictors of life satisfaction to norms in individualistic cultures, whereas norms and emotions were equally strong predictors of life satisfaction in collectivist cultures. These findings suggest that low reported SWB of Korean students may be partly accounted for by the Confucian and collectivist culture of Korea. Undoubtedly, other explanations for low SWB of Korean students may be possible, such as societal equality, human rights, and economic equality. Future research is required for this inquiry.

The present study also examined the relations between SWB measures and personality variables, such as self-esteem, collective self-esteem, and optimism. The results showed that all personality variables were moderately correlated to life satisfaction, positive affect, and negative affect. These results are consistent with the findings of previous studies in western cultures (DeNeve and Cooper, 1998; Diener et al., 1999). However, an additional note is necessary for collective self-esteem. Crocker et al. (1994) found that when self-esteem was controlled for, collective self-esteem was not correlated with life satisfaction in a White American college student sample, whereas collective self-esteem was still moderately correlated with life satisfaction in an Asian American college student sample. In this study of Korean students, collective self-esteem was still significantly correlated with life satisfaction ($r = 0.29$ $p < 0.001$), positive affect ($r = 0.30$ $p < 0.001$), and negative affect ($r = 0.11$, $p < 0.05$), when self-esteem was controlled for. These results are consistent with the findings of Crocker et al. (1994), and support that interdependent and collective aspects of self are relatively more important in collectivist culture than in individualistic culture (Markus and Kitayama, 1991; Triandis, 1989).

The relative contributions of self-esteem, collective self-esteem, and optimism in predicting SWB were examined using regression analyses and dominance analyses. The results of these analyses were quite interesting. According to which component of SWB was predicted, the relative contributions of three personality variables were quite different. In predicting life satisfaction, though all three personality variables were influential predictors, optimism was the most influential predictor. In predicting positive affect, optimism, and collective self-esteem were equally influential predictors, but self-esteem was not an influential predictor. In predicting negative affect, only self-esteem was an influential predictor. These results suggest that self-esteem, collective self-esteem, and optimism are correlated with each other but are also clearly discriminable constructs (Lucas et al., 1996; Luhtanen and Crocker, 1992; Scheier et al., 1994), and also that life satisfaction, positive affect, and negative affect are correlated with each other, but are also distinct factors of SWB (Diener, 1984; Lucas et al., 1996).

The result that collective self-esteem and self-esteem were equally important predictors in predicting life satisfaction is consistent with the findings of Kwan et al. (1997). They found that self-esteem was a far superior predictor of life satisfaction to relationship harmony in U.S. student samples, whereas self-esteem and relationship harmony were equally strong predictors of life satisfaction in Hong Kong student samples. These findings indicate that in addition to individualistic aspects of self, collective aspects of self is more closely associated with SWB in collectivist culture than in individualistic culture.

Optimism appeared to be the most important predictor of life satisfaction. Scheier and Caver (1992) suggest that the effect of optimism on SWB may be partly meditated by active coping methods, such as problem-focused coping and positive reinterpretation (see also, Aspinwall and Taylor, 1992). Because optimists tend to use more constructive coping methods then pessimists, optimists are more adaptive to stressful events than pessimists. Thus, optimists report higher life satisfaction than pessimists.

In terms of affective well-being, optimism and collective self-esteem was closely associated with positive affect, whereas only self-esteem was closely associated with negative affect. These results suggest that high self-esteem may reduce the amount of negative emotional experience, but may not increase the amount of positive emotional experience. In order to increase the amount of positive emotional experience, collective self-esteem and optimism need to be high.

The present study examined the relationships between SWB and self-esteem, collective self-esteem, and optimism in Korean college students. Future research is definitely needed to examine how self-esteem, collective self-esteem, and optimism are related with SWB in other age groups.

NOTE

[1] All participants were students who attended one of psychology-related courses. They obtained 5 extra points in the final exam on the course for completing the questionnaires.

REFERENCES

Andrews, F.M. and S.B. Withey: 1976, Social Indicators of Well-Being: America's Perception of Life Quality (Plenum, New York).

Aspinwall, L.G. and S.E. Taylor: 1992, 'Modeling cognitive adaptation: A longitudinal investigation of the impact of individual differences and coping on college adjustment and performance', Journal of Personality and Social Psychology 63, pp. 989–1003.

Blascovich, J. and J. Tomaka: 1991, 'Measures of self-esteem', in J.P. Robinson, P.R. Shaver and L.S. Wrightsman (eds.), Measures of Personality and Social Psychological Attitudes (Academic Press, San Diego, California, pp. 115–160).

Budescu, D.V.: 1993, 'Dominance analysis: A new approach to the problem of relative importance of predictors in multiple regression', Psychological Bulletin 114, pp. 542–551.

Campbell, A.: 1981, The Sense of Well-being in America: Recent Patterns and Trends (McGraw Hill, New York).

Carver, C.S., M.F. Scheier and J.K. Weintraub: 1989, 'Assessing coping strategies: A theoretically based approach', Journal of Personality and Social Psychology 56, pp. 267–283.

Cha, K.: 1999, 'Relationships between subjective well-being and indiocentrism-allocentrism of college students', Korean Adolescence Study 10, pp. 193–216 (in Korean).

Crocker, J., R. Luhtanen, B. Blaine and S. Broadnax: 1994, 'Collective self-esteem and psychological well-being among white, black, and Asian college students', Personality and social Psychology Bulletin 20, pp. 503–513.

DeNeve, K.M. and H. Cooper: 1998, 'The happy personality: A meta-analysis of 137 personality traits and subjective well-being', Psychological Bulletin 74, pp. 197–299.

Diener, E.: 1984, 'Subjective well-being', Psychological Bulletin 95, pp. 542–575.

Diener, E.: 1994, 'Assessing subjective well-being: Progress and opportunities', Social Indicators Research 31, pp. 103–157.

Diener, E. and M. Diener: 1995, 'Cross-cultural correlates of life satisfaction and self-esteem', Journal of Personality and Social Psychology 68, pp. 653–663.

Diener, E., M. Diener, M. and C. Diener: 1995, 'Factors predicting the subjective well-being of nations', Journal of Personality and Social Psychology 69, pp. 851–864.

Diener, E. and R.A. Emmons: 1984, 'The independence of positive and negative affect', Journal of Personality and Social Psychology 47, pp. 1105–1117.

Diener, E., R.S. Emmons, R.J. Larsen and S. Griffin: 1985, 'The Satisfaction With Life Scale', Journal of Personality Assessment 49, pp. 71–75.

Diener E., E. Suh, H. Smith and L. Shao: 1995, 'National differences in reported subjective well-being: Why do they occur?', Social Indicator Research 34, pp. 7–32.

Diener, E. and E.M. Suh: 1999, 'National Differences in subjective well-being', in D. Kahneman, E. Diener and N. Schwarz (eds.), Well-being: The Foundations of Hedonic Psychology (Russel Sage Foundation, New York, pp. 434–450).

Diener, E., E. Suh, R. Lucas and H. Smith: 1999, 'Subjective well-being: Three decades of progress', Psychological Bulletin 125, pp. 276–302.

Fleming, J.S. and B.E. Courtney: 1984, 'The dimensionality of self-esteem: II. Hierarchical facet model for revised measurement scales', Journal of Personality and Social Psychology 46, pp. 404–421.

Harju, B.L. and L.M. Bolen: 1998, 'The effects of optimism on coping and perceived quality of life of college students', Journal of Social Behavior & Personality 13, pp. 185–201.

Hofstede, G.: 1991, Cultures and Organizations: Software of the Mind (McGraw Hills, London).

Kim, H.S.: 1994, 'Korean collective self-esteem scale', Korean Journal of Social Psychology 8, pp. 103–116 (in Korean).

Kim, J.E., E.S. Lee and S.H. Kang: 1997, Life Satisfaction of Korean College Students (Jibmandang, Seoul, Korea) (in Korean).

Kwan, V.S.Y., M.H. Bond and T.M. Singelis: 1997, 'Pancultural explanations for life satisfaction: Adding relationship harmony to self-esteem', Journal of Personality and Social Psychology 73, pp. 1038–1051.

Lucas, R.E., E. Diener and E. Suh: 1996, 'Discriminant validity of well-being measures 71', Journal of Personality and Social Psychology 71, pp. 616–628.

Luhtanen, R. and J. Crocker: 1992, 'A collective self-esteem scale: Self-evaluation of one's social identity', Personality and Social Psychology Bulletin 18, pp. 302–318.

Markus, H. and S. Kitayama: 1991, 'Culture and self: Implication for cognition, emotion, and motivation', Psychological Review 98, pp. 244–253.

Michalos, A.C.: 1991, Global report on student well-being (Springer-Verlag, New York).

Myers, D.G. and E. Diener: 1995, 'Who is happy?', Psychological Science 6, pp. 10–19.

Pavot, W. and E. Diener: 1993, 'Review of the Satisfaction with Life Scale', Psychological Assessment 5, pp. 164–172.
Scheier, M.F. and C.S. Carver: 1985, 'Optimism, coping and health: Assessment and implications of generalized outcome expectancies', Health Psychology 4, pp. 219–247.
Scheier, M.F. and C.S. Carver: 1992, 'Effects of optimism on psychological and physical well-being: Theoretical overview and empirical update', Cognitive Therapy and Research 16, pp. 201–228.
Scheier, M.F., C.S. Carver and M.W. Bridges; 1994, 'Distinguishing optimism from neuroticism (and trait anxiety, self-mastery, and self-esteem): A reevaluation of the life orientation test', Journal of Personality and Social Psychology 67, pp. 1063–1078.
Shin, D.C. and D.M. Johnson: 1978, 'Avowed happiness as an overall assessment of the quality of life', Social Indicators Research 5, pp. 475–492.
Suh E., E. Diener, S. Oishi and H.C. Triandis: 1998, 'The shifting basis of life satisfaction judgments across cultures: emotions versus norms', Journal of Personality and Social Psychology 74, pp. 482–493.
Tajfel, H.: 1981, Human Groups and Social Categories: Studies in Social Psychology (Cambridge University Press, Cambridge).
Tajfel, H.: 1982, 'Social psychology of intergroup relationships;, Annual Review of Psychology 33, pp. 1–59.
Triandis, H.C.: 1989, 'The self and social behavior in differing cultural contexts', Psychological Review 96, pp. 506–520.

Division of Economics and Business
Hoseo University
Cheonan, Korea 330-180
E-mail: chakh@office.hoseo.ac.kr

PART IV. THE QUALITY OF KOREAN LIFE IN COMPARATIVE PERSPECTIVE

HYUN SONG LEE

OBJECTIVE QUALITY OF LIFE IN KOREA AND THE OECD COUNTRIES

ABSTRACT. This study attempts to compare the current state of Korea's quality of life with that of more developed countries in their past, and seeks to derive suggestions for Korea's further development towards a more balanced quality of life. To this end, it analyzes income and five other objective indices of life quality by means of principal components analysis. Korea's real income in 1995 corresponds to the per capita income of many of the Organization for Economic Cooperation and Development (hereinafter the OECD) countries in the late 1960s. Education is the aspect of life in which Korea compares most favorably to the developed countries, approaching the level they experienced in the mid-1980s. In terms of Equity and Work, Korea's current state is much worse than that of the OECD countries in the late 1960s – the years marking the beginning of the time series data used in this study. In light of the OECD countries' past experiences, our analysis clearly indicates that improvements in work conditions and gender equality should be given priority for Korea's further social and economic development.

INTRODUCTION

Rapid economic growth over the past three decades has transformed Korea from one of the world's poorest countries to an upper-middle income country. During the thirty-five years between 1960 and 1995, its economy expanded at an average annual rate of nearly 9 percent. However, in terms of income, and especially quality of life, Korea appears to still lag far behind the developed countries. Despite its economic success, many people are still struggling to secure the necessary means for a basic livelihood (Ministry of Health and Welfare, 1999).

In the field of social indicators research, it is widely understood that economic growth alone does not adequately indicate the overall development of a society, and that monetary income alone does not reflect the multi-dimensional aspects of quality of life (Land, 1983).

Social Indicators Research **62, 63:** 481–508, 2003.

This argument applies both to the developing and developed countries. The United Nations Development Program's (hereinafter the UNDP) Human Development Report (hereinafter the HDR) gives many examples of developing countries, whose quality of life has advanced above their respective levels of income, and vice versa (UNDP, 2000). A study comparing income growth and improvement of quality of life in the developing countries revealed that maximization of income and enrichment of human lives do not necessarily move together in developing countries (Mazumdar, 1999).

This study attempts to diagnose Korea's current state of objective quality of life from the perspective of the past experiences of a specific group of advanced countries, viz., the members of the OECD. It reviews Korea's current state and process of development regarding quality of life during the past thirty-five years, dating back to the start of its all-out industrialization efforts in the early 1960s. A key question here is whether Korea's economic development has been appropriately transformed into actual development of its society. More pointedly, the issue is how much and in which ways Korea's objective quality of life has been advanced or neglected during its process of economic growth, compared to the advanced countries' past experiences. According to the HDR, among developing countries, Korea is recognized as a relatively well-balanced country in terms of both economic growth and social development. Korea's ranking in terms of human development is a little bit higher than its income ranking (the 31st vs. the 35th, respectively, among a total of 174 countries in 2000).[1]

In light of the advanced countries' past experiences, has Korea been passing through a similar tandem process of social development and economic growth? Korea has economically grown much faster than the developed countries have within a very short period of time. Yet it would appear that it has neither had sufficient time nor the means to translate its rapid income growth into an equally rapid improvement in its quality of life. Until the early 1960s, Korea's Gross National Product (hereinafter the GNP) per capita was less than U.S.$500, and more than two-thirds of its workers labored in the agricultural sector. In the span of less than half-a-century, what was once a poor, predominately agrarian country has transformed itself into an industrialized one with income per capita exceeding U.S.$10000. Accordingly, again in comparison to the more developed countries' past experiences, it is not surprising to find that such fast economic growth was not matched by a comparable social development.

On the other hand, there are reasons to expect that in many of the developing countries, quality of life may increase faster than income. The advanced technology in medicine and other domains of life of the Western countries have been introduced into the developing countries, often in the absence of accompanying economic growth. Therefore, we can conjecture that the developing countries' quality of life might be better in certain respects compared to their respective levels of income, than could be inferred from the developed countries' past experiences. In other words, when the developed countries arrived at a given level of income in their past, their quality of life might have been much worse than that of the current developing countries at the same level of income. There might be some "late comer advantages" with regard to quality of life for developing countries – advantages that by definition were not available in the past to the advanced countries.

Income growth outpacing quality of life, and quality of life outpacing income growth – both cases seem quite plausible. Which case, then, is more prevalent for the currently developing countries? With regards to the specific case of Korea, this study finds that the former condition prevails. That is, Korea's social development lags behind its economic growth from the perspective of the developed countries' past experiences. According to a recent study, this is also the case for other East Asian newly industrializing countries (Tang, 1999). Which particular area of social development lags more behind economic growth is considerably dependent upon a country's peculiar development process and historical context. For example, in the case of Korea, educational levels do not lag much behind the advanced countries due to its cultural and historical background. This study attempts to identify which aspects of quality of life lag behind income growth, and offers possible explanations for these gaps.

BACKGROUND

A principal tenet of social indicators research is that objective quality of life cannot be reduced simply to income. However, devising a mean to measure the many facets of quality of life is no easy task. How many summary measures are to be conceptualized and made operational? Which individual indicators are to be chosen for constructing a valid measure of quality of life? And how should they be weighted? These are the main questions that need to be addressed in order to capture an objective quality of life.

There seems to be agreement among scholars that there are no hard and fast rules, which one can apply uniformly to all countries concerning these questions (Diener and Suh, 1997). The initial purpose of social indicators research in its start-up stage, the 1950s, was to monitor social development independently of economic growth, because the latter, it was posited, did not automatically accompany the former in advanced countries in the post-war period. Researchers attempted to provide guidance toward a desirable direction of social development by means of monitoring such development directly (Estes, 1999; Terleckyi, 1975; Zapf, 1987).

Guidance of social development for developing countries may be different from that for advanced countries. This is because the development strategy with regards to quality of life for countries with U.S.$5000 income per capita may not be the same as that for countries with income per capita exceeding U.S.$20000. Accordingly, perhaps a measure of quality of life for the developing countries should be different from that for the developed countries. The United Nations (hereinafter the UN), which developed the most basic system of social indicators, the "System of Social and Demographic Statistics (hereinafter the SSDS)," recommended a set of indicators focused on the necessities of human material survival. This reflects one of the UN's primary concerns, which is the satisfaction of the basic necessities of life for all people in the world (UN, 1993). In contrast, a group of advanced countries, the OECD, recommended more sensitive measures of quality of life for pursuing a better quality of it beyond the minimum level of material survival (OECD, 1976; Davis and Fine-Davis, 1991; Boelhouwer and Stoop, 1999). Therefore, it is hard to determine a common set of social indicators for measuring social development of both developing and developed countries' at the same time – as is attempted in this study.[2] Since the major subject of this study is a developing country, viz., Korea, which could not satisfy minimum material life for the majority of its people until three decades ago, the most basic social indicators are primarily used for measuring objective quality of life, though supplemented by a few of the more sensitive indicators appropriate to the advanced countries.

There are various ways to summarize individual indicators into a measure of quality of life. The Human Development Index (hereinafter the HDI) and Physical Quality of Life Index (hereinafter the PQLI) are examples of measuring it by means of one composite index. Despite their strength of simplicity, overarching indices have serious weaknesses in terms of reflecting the multi-dimensionality of quality of life. They do not indicate which domain of life is better or worse than others, and which domain of life should deserve more emphasis in further development.[3] Indices vary considerably regarding the number of dimensions of quality of life, or in other words, the domains of life they intend to measure. Morris's PQLI and the UNDP's HDI divide a human's life into 3 domains. The OECD's Social Concerns as well as the Japanese government's People's Life Indices (hereinafter the PLI) divide it into 8 domains. The UN's SSDS divides it into 11, and Zapf's study divides it into 16 (Bureau of Economic Planning, 1993; Morris, 1979; OECD, 1976; UN, 1993; UNDP, 1990; Zapf, 1987). As a society becomes more complex, or as people lead more complicated and affluent lives, life domains become, accordingly, more diversified. In this study, a middle position is taken, and life is divided into six domains. This decision is made in consideration of data availability and comparability, as well as conceptual validity of the domain division. The six domains are Income, Health, Education, Work, Culture & Information, and Equity. Each domain of life includes a cluster of individual indicators. The environment, security, and leisure are domains missing in this study due to the problem of data availability or comparability.

Both flow and stock indicators should be included in measuring each domain of life. A flow indicator is a measure to address the amount of resources newly obtained as a result of activities during a given period of time, while a stock indicator is a measure of the amount accumulated from the continued activities thus far. For example, enrollment ratio is a flow measure of education, while the ratio of high school graduates to the whole population is a stock measure. In the case of rapidly developing countries like Korea, their current state measured by stock indicators is prone to be worse than that measured by flow indicators. Therefore, including both kinds of indicators is important for a valid comparison of the developing and the developed countries.

There are various ways to give weight to individual indicators for constructing a composite index of quality of life. Some studies give equal weight to each domain of life or to each individual indicator, as is done in the HDI. This weighting is based on the deductive argument, that each domain of life is equally important for a well-rounded human life. On the other hand, some studies choose an inductive strategy to summarize information from data by using multivariate statistical methods, such as principal components analysis or regression analysis with proxy variables (ex. Boelhouwer and Stoop, 1999; Slottje et al., 1991). Both approaches have advantages and disadvantages. A deductive approach takes composite indices through a somewhat arbitrary process, while indices thus constructed are easy to understand intuitively, as far as the deductive grounds are persuasive. On the other hand, an inductive approach brings out indices by using complicated statistical methods; while these indices are harder to understand, they are less subject to the criticism of arbitrariness. In this study, principal components analysis is used to combine a set of indicators into a composite index for each life domain, except for Income. This method maximizes the sum of variance explained, and the factor score coefficient of each component become weights of indicators to make composite indices. Income represents an exceptional case, as only one indicator, the GDP per capita, is used for simplicity of understanding.

MEASURE OF OBJECTIVE QUALITY OF LIFE

The data used in this study are collected from publications from the UN and other international organizations. Starting in the late 1960s, six time periods at five-year intervals are selected for longitudinal comparison: 1969–70, 1974–75, 1979–80, 1984–85, 1989–90, and 1994–95.[4] Data for the twenty-three OECD countries and Korea are collected on these six time intervals, which makes a total of 144 time-country cases.[5] Objective quality of life is measured by income and five composite indices in this analysis. The five composite indices are constructed by using principal components analysis. The principal components displaying eigen values exceeding 1 are selected. In the case of principal components analysis, the problem of missing values should be dealt with carefully, since all the data for a variable are excluded in an analysis if only one case of the variable is missing. The problem of missing observations is particularly evident in the data for the 1969–70 timeperiod, and more generally, for a few of the variables (such as mortality rate for children under five years old, indices of income inequality, and ratio of the government welfare expenditures). These missing cases are replaced by estimates calculated from regression models, in which those missing variables are set apart as dependent variables.

When more than one principal component is selected for a domain of life, interpretation of those multiple components is problematic. Two principal components with eigen values exceeding 1 were selected in the domains of Education, Work, and Equity. In order to simplify the analysis, two components are combined into one index by giving weight of variance explained to each component.[6]

A major method of analysis in this study is to compare the extent of development between advanced countries and Korea in the context of various domains of life. Standardization of unit of measurement across different composite indices is required for a comparison among those indices. Units of composite indices are standardized by replacing raw scores with the standard deviation from the mean. Setting the lowest and the highest value observed in the advanced countries as the lower and the upper boundary of each composite index, provides a useful means to compare Korea with more developed countries. This is because the upper and the lower limits provide a benchmark enabling us to know intuitively how far Korea lags behind the standard of the advanced countries.[7] The lower boundary is set at 0 by using the lowest value observed, and the highest boundary is set at 100 by using the highest value observed. From these two stages of standardization, the five composite indices are uniformly transformed into variables having values ranging from 0 to 100. Table I provides factor loadings together with brief descriptive statistics for Korea and the OECD countries for each individual indicator.

A BRIEF DESCRIPTION OF EACH INDEX

Income. This index roughly indicates an individual's purchasing power of goods and services, as measured by the GDP per capita. Income is the most important means of enhancing overall quality of life and is closely related to other indices. In order to keep comparability of income across different periods of time, all income values are expressed in terms of constant 1990 US dollars by using the consumer price index.

Health. The index is constructed from six individual indicators: (1) life expectancy at birth, for males and females respectively; (2) infant mortality per 1000 births; (3) mortality of children under the age of 5 years per 1000 children born; (4) percentage of population aged 65 and over; (5) physicians per 100000 persons; and (6) percentage of population with access to safe drinking water. One component with an eigen value exceeding 1 emerged, and it explains 75.9 percent of the total variance. The factor loadings are in the expected direction and of a substantial size, which suggests that the index is valid and reliable.

Education. This index is constructed from four variables: (1) enrollment ratio in post-secondary education for males; (2) enrollment ratio in post-secondary education for females; (3) percentage of population of age 25 and over with post-secondary schooling; and (4) pupil-teacher ratio in primary education. Two components with eigen values more than or close to 1 emerged from the analysis. The first component, explaining 69.1 percent of the total variance, displays relatively high factor loadings on variables indicating quantitative aspects of education, such as enrollment ratio on post-secondary schooling and percentage of population with some post-secondary education. The second component, explaining

TABLE I

Results of the Principal Components Analysis and the Descriptive Statistics

Domain of life – Individual indicators	The 1st/2nd components	Korea 1994–95	OECD 1994–95	OECD 1969–70
Income GDP per capita		$10124	$20417	$8165
Health Life expectancy, Male	0.412	69.5	74.8	68.5
Life expectancy, Female	0.422	77.4	80.7	74.3
Infant morality rate	−0.397	12	6.8	22.7
Under 5 infant mortality rate	−0.405	13	6.5	22.1
% pop. Aged 65 or over	0.302	5.9	16.8	11.0
Physicians rate	−0.365	893	336	755
Access to safe drinking water	0.330	93	99.3	88.8
Eigen value/ variance explained	5.64 / 0.759			
Educ. Enrollment ratio, post-second., Male	0.558 / 0.308	67.9	40.2	20.9
Enrollment ratio, post-second., Female	0.570 / 0.154	40.9	44.4	12.2
% pop. w/ post-secondary educ.	0.512 / 0.098	21.1	19.7	8.3
Pupil/teacher ratio – primary educ.	−0.318 / 0.940	28	14.1	23.5
Eigen value/ variance explained	2.75; 0.82 / 0.691; 0.210			
Work Labor force participation rate, Male	0.559 / 0.392	76.1	77.6	56.9
Labor force participation rate, Female	0.610 / 0.151	48.7	58.6	27.5

TABLE I

Continued

Domain of life – Individual indicators	The 1st/2nd components	Korea 1994–95	OECD 1994–95	OECD 1969–70
Unemployment rate	0.261 / −0.092	2.0	8.6	3.1
Deaths from accidents at work in mfg.	−0.459 / 0.316	17	5.4	14.8
Work hours per week in mfg.	−0.179 / 0.892	49.2	38.3	41.3
Eigen value/ variance explained	2.28; 1.15 / 0.462; 0.228			
Culture Number of TV receivers	0.460	334	449.7	255.7
& Info. Number of book titles published	0.251	74.2	131.2	73.2
Number of telephones	0.493	41.2	52.7	28.3
Circulation of daily newspapers	0.458	407	320.3	307.0
Scientists and technicians per 100	0.509	2	4.2	1.5
Eigen value/ variance explained	3.03 / 0.608			
Equity Income ratio of the highest 20% to lowest	−0.598 / 0.231	5	6.0	7.9
Income share of lowest 40%	0.587 / −0.279	21	19.8	17.1
Sexual inequality in education	0.060 / 0.640	0.60	1.07	0.58
Sexual inequality in labor participation	0.238 / 0.601	0.64	0.75	0.48
Gov. expenditures on soc. security and welfare	0.479 / 0.287	10	36.2	25.6
Gov. expenditures on education and health	0.133 / −0.128	17.4	24.5	21.9
Eigen value/ variance explained	2.32; 1.88 / 0.390; 0.325			

21.0 percent of the total variance, displays high factor loadings on variables indicating qualitative aspects of education, such as pupil-teacher ratio. These two components are combined into one composite index by using amount of variance explained as the weighting.

Work. This index is constructed from five variables: (1) labor force participation rate for males; (2) labor force participation rate for females; (3) unemployment rate; (4) average annual deaths as a result of accidents at work in the manufacturing sector per 100000 workers; and (5) work hours per week in the manufacturing sector. Two components with eigen values exceeding 1 emerged from the analysis. The first component, explaining 46.2 percent of the total variance, displays relatively high factor loadings on variables indicating quantitative aspects of work, such as the labor force participation rate. The second component, explaining 22.8 percent of the total variance, displays high factor loadings on variables indicating inferiority of working conditions, such as work hours per week and industrial accident rate. These two components are combined into one composite index by using amount of variance explained for the weighting, with the second factor's direction being reversed.

Culture and Information. This index indicates the availability, access, and the development of cultural and informational facilities. It is constructed from five variables: (1) number of TV receivers in use per 1000 inhabitants; (2) number of book titles published per 100000 people; (3) number of telephones in use per 100 inhabitants; (4) circulation of daily newspapers per 1000 inhabitants; and (5) number of scientists and technicians per 1000 persons.[8] One component with an eigen value exceeding 1 emerged, explaining 60.8 percent of the total variance.

Equity. The index captures several dimensions of equity in a society. It includes a cluster of variables measuring income and gender inequality, as well as measuring the government's efforts at redistribution and general state of welfare policy. Specific variables include: (1) the ratio of the highest quintile's income to the lowest quintile's income; (2) income share of the lowest 40 percent; (3) enrollment

TABLE II

Correlations of Six Life Domains

	Income	Health	Education	Work	Culture & Info.
Health	0.635				
Education	0.601	0.642			
Work	0.456	0.704	0.742		
Culture & Info	0.769	0.672	0.642	0.470	
Equity	0.287	0.368	0.619	0.523	0.289

*All the coefficients are significant at $p < 0.01$.

ratio of males to females in post-secondary education; (4) ratio of labor force participation rate of males to females; (5) government expenditures on social security and welfare as a percentage of total government expenditures; and (6) government expenditures on education and health as a percentage of total government expenditures. Two components with eigen values exceeding 1 emerged from the analysis. One indicates income inequality, while the other indicates gender inequality. Factor loadings show that the two components are substantially independent from each other. The amounts of variance explained are not much different between the two components; 39.0 percent for the first component, and 32.5 percent for the second one. These two components are combined into one composite index by using amount of variance explained as the weighting.

Table II shows zero-order correlations among these six indices. As expected, these indices display a large degree of correlation with each other, with correlation coefficients typically exceeding 0.60. On the other hand, Equity shows less correlation with other indices, apart from Education and Work. Equity, in particular, shows a low degree of correlation with Income (r = 0.287).

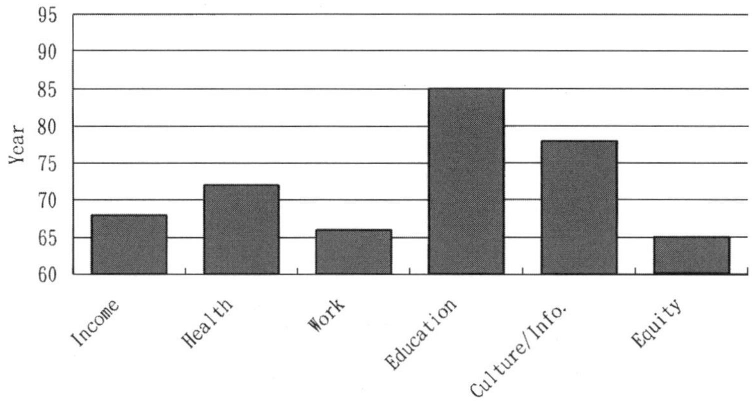

Figure 1. Korea's current condition relative to other OECD countries' experiences (1995).

RELATIVE STANDING OF KOREA IN COMPARISON TO THE OTHER OECD COUNTRIES

In order to diagnose Korea's current state of social development from the perspective of the advanced countries' past experiences, this analysis initially attempts to identify the year when the developed countries arrived, on average, at Korea's current level of quality of life in each domain of life. Figure 1 shows the point in time when the OECD countries approached Korea's current level of quality in each life domain.

The figure shows that except for Education and Culture / Information, Korea's current level is lower in all life domains, than that of the other OECD countries in the early 1970s. In the case of Education and Culture/Information, Korea's current level corresponds to that of the OECD countries in the mid-1980s and mid-1970s, respectively. In the case of Health, Korea appears to be at the level the other OECD countries experienced in the early 1980s. On the other hand, in terms of Income, Work, and Equity, Korea's current levels are lower than those of the OECD countries in the late 1960s.

We can compare development trends between the other OECD countries and Korea in each domain of life from the late 1960's through the mid-1990's. The OECD countries' average income, in the 1990 constant US dollars, has increased 2.1 times, from $8165 in 1969 to $17518 in 1995, while Korea's income has increased 9.8 times, from $885 to $8686 during the period in question (Figure 2a).

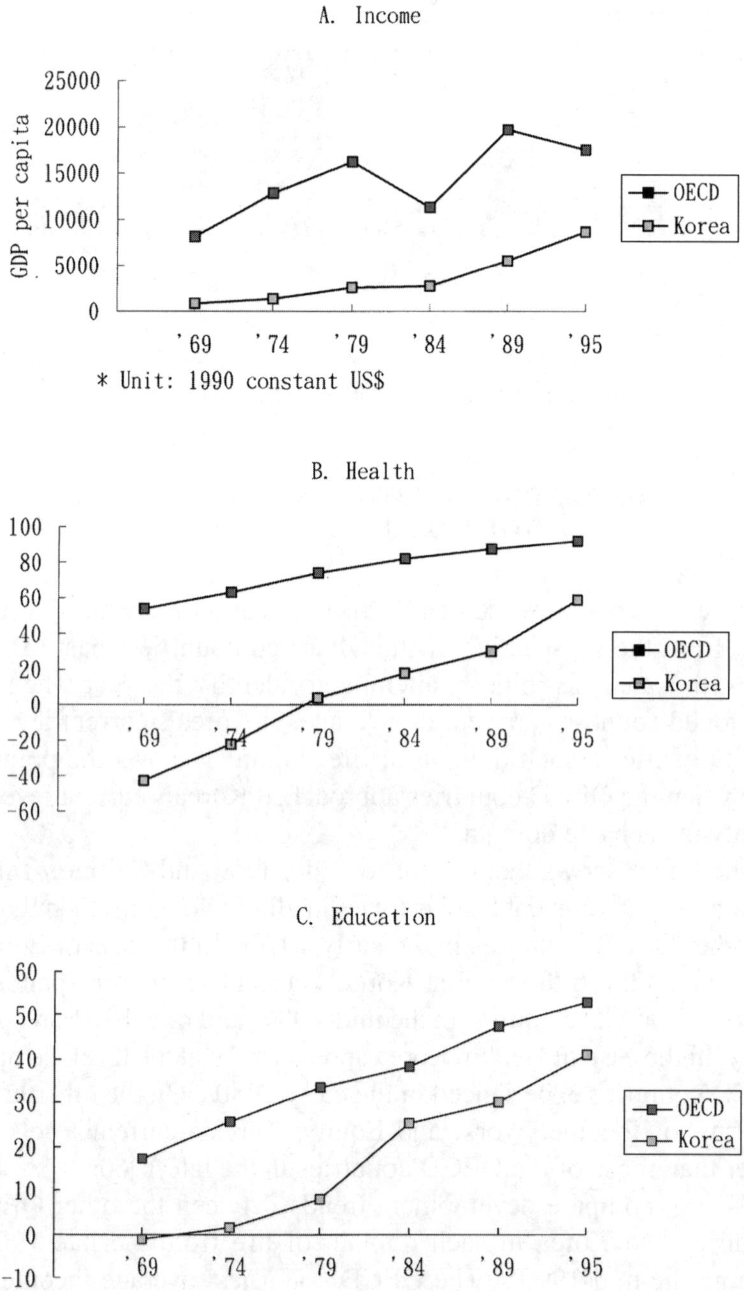

Figure 2. Trend of development in each area of life.

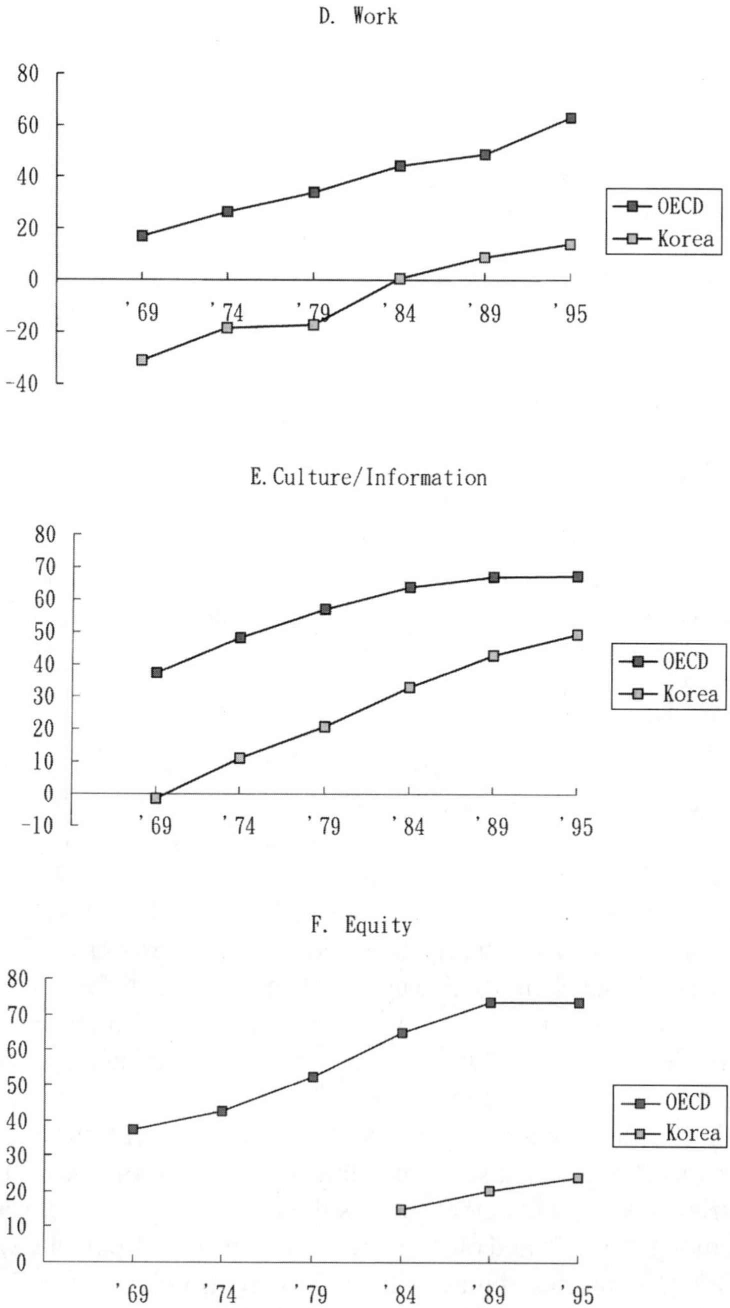

Figure 2. Continued.

When we take into account the huge gap in income between Korea and the OECD countries in 1995, it is clear that Korea should continue efforts to increase income in order to enhance its general quality of life.

Health has interesting characteristics different from other domains of life. That is, gaps in health levels among the OECD countries have narrowed in recent years. Their state of Health was relatively homogeneous in the late 1960s in comparison to other domains, and then became much more homogeneous by 1995. This is reflected in Figure 2b, where the OECD countries' value on the vertical axis is close to 100 in 1995, which means that the OECD countries' mean is close to the highest value observed among all the OECD countries. It also suggests that, relative to past experiences, further improvements in Health for the developed countries will be harder to achieve (at least in terms of the measures employed here). Korea's state of Health in 1995 arrived at the OECD countries' early 1960s levels, even though its level of Health has improved rapidly so far. We can expect that the gap between the other OECD countries and Korea will decrease faster in Health than in other domains of life, because the developed countries appear to be reaching a plateau, while Korea's improvement has yet to slow down.

It is noteworthy that Korea started at a relatively high level of Education even in the late 1960s, and has been consistently narrowing the gap with the OECD countries since then. Figure 2c indicates that Korea's level of Education in the late 1960s was comparable to the lowest level observed among the OECD countries at the time. Particularly in the quantitative aspect of Education, Korea's level in 1995 was equal to or even higher than the OECD countries' mean. For example, Korea's enrollment ratio in higher education, one of the representative flow indicators, was 67.9 percent for males, and 40.9 percent for females in 1995, while the OECD countries recorded 40.2 percent, and 44.4 percent, respectively. In 1995, Korea also displayed a better record than the OECD countries in stock indicators such as the ratio of high school graduates among those 25 and older. Korea's ratio was 21.1 percent, while the OECD countries' figure was 19.7 percent. On the other hand, Korea is still far behind the level the OECD countries experienced in the late 1960s in the qualitative aspects of Education, such as pupil-teacher ratio (23.5 pupils per teacher for the OECD countries in 1969, versus 28 pupils for Korea in 1995).

From Figure 2d, we can ascertain that Work is the most inferior domain of life in Korea compared to the OECD countries' past experiences. The current level of Korea's Work life remains at a much lower level than that of the OECD countries in the late 1960s. Moreover, the gap is not narrowing significantly, as Korea's pace of improvement during the past thirty-five years appears not to be higher than that of the OECD countries. Each individual indicator of Work was examined in an effort to determine the cause of this huge gap. Korea's labor force participation rate is not much lower than the OECD countries. The rate of participation of Korean males in 1995 approaches the early 1990s levels of the OECD countries, and the rate of participation of Korean females in that year approaches the OECD countries' levels of the late 1980s. On the other hand, Korea's rate appears to be extremely inferior to the OECD countries in the qualitative aspects of work life, such as deaths from industrial accidents and work hours per week. There is a large gap between, the 17 deaths per 100,000 manufacturing workers Korea experienced in 1995, versus the 14.8 deaths experienced by the OECD countries in 1969. A similarly large gap persists in work hours per week in the manufacturing sector, with Korean workers averaging 49.2 hours per week in 1995, while the comparable figure of the OECD countries in 1969 was 41.3 hours. Korea's difficult working conditions reflect a long-standing, if unspoken, policy to sacrifice workers' well-being (and indeed suppress their political power) for the sake of rapid economic growth.

In the domain of Culture and Information, Korea has been improving rapidly and consistently, while the OECD countries' development appears to have slowed down as of the 1990s. This is because this index is composed of indicators reflecting the use of basic facilities for information and cultural dissemination, such as televisions, telephones, books, and newspapers, and the OECD countries seem to have approached a stage of saturation with regards to their availability and use. On the other hand, there is a huge gap between the OECD countries and Korea in terms of the ratio of scientists and professionals to the general population, a ratio cited by Daniel Bell (1973) as a representative indicator of an information-based society (2.0 per 1000 persons in Korea, and 4.2 in the OECD countries in 1995).

In Figure 2f, we can infer that the developed countries in recent years have been converging in terms of Equity, as in the case of Health. The OECD countries' values on the vertical axis in the figure are close to 80 in 1995, which are higher than in any other life domain, except for Health. Korea's level of Equity is much worse than that of the OECD countries. Since the Equity index is a combination of two relatively independent dimensions of inequality, income inequality, and gender inequality, we need to examine which aspect of inequality accounts for the poor state of Equity in Korea. The OECD countries and Korea do not show any meaningful difference in income inequality in 1995 (refer to Table I). On the other hand, gender inequality in Korea is enormous compared to the OECD countries, even though it has been improving slowly during the past thirty-five years. According to the recent UNDP HDR's Gender Empowerment Measure (hereinafter the GEM), Korea ranked close to the lowest level of all the observed countries (ranked 63rd out of 70 countries) (UNDP, 2000). This indicates that Korea's inferior state of Equity is principally due to the very poor status of women relative to men.

GAPS BETWEEN THE OECD COUNTRIES AND KOREA

There are various ways to longitudinally compare the OECD countries and Korea in each domain of life. A simple way is to compare the serial trends between the two groups of countries for each life domain as was done above. However, this type of straightforward comparison suffers from a weakness. This is because it ignores casual influences among variables, particularly the impact of income on other variables. Income has considerable influence on other domains of life, and income growth is a principal means to enhance the general quality of life, especially in developing countries, such as Korea. Therefore, a comparison of quality of life can be more meaningful among countries of comparable income, than among those showing great differences in income. This type of comparison can show in which domains of life Korea is better or worse, given a certain level of income, than the advanced countries.

TABLE III

Comparison of Korea and OECD Country Cases with Income $7000–$9000 (Unit: 1990 constant US$, percentile of principal component value)

Domain of life	Korea 1995	OECD (24 cases)	
		Mean	S.D.
Income (GDP/person)	$8686	$7402.1	$1034.2
Health	59.0	65.2	13.6
Education	41.0	20.9	9.4
Work	14.1	24.7	12.7
Culture & Info.	49.3	33.9	12.4
Equity	22.9	44.8	23.8

In order to compare Korea and the other OECD countries, when the latter experienced income levels comparable to Korea's current income level, 24 cases out of the 138 OECD time-countries data points were chosen. These correspond to income between $7000 and $9000 (1990 constant US$).

Table III shows a comparison of Korea in 1995 and the mean values for the OECD countries' 24 cases in each domain of life. It is noteworthy that Korea displays a much better state of Education than the OECD cases. Korea's cheap but well-educated workers are often cited as one of the most important factors having contributed to her rapid economic development. Korea's good state of Education is a result of the people's strong demand for education, which is often attributed to a Confucian cultural tradition, which places great emphasis on both studying and the role of scholars. Another important factor lies in Korea's historical background. Korean society is unusually homogeneous in terms of language, ethnicity, and culture. Moreover, its traditional social class system was largely destroyed in the long period of socio-economic and political upheavals that accompanied colonial subjugation and the Korean War. These series of historical events weakened substantially the influence of heritage, that strongly conditions social mobility in other countries, and left education as a uniquely important means of individual advancement. For this reason, to this day, people strive for as much schooling as possible, which results in an extremely high level of Education in comparison to Korea's income (Kim and Hong, 1997; McGinn et al., 1980).

Given a comparable level of income, Korea displays a relatively better state in the domain of Culture and Information than the OECD cases. This probably reflects the high level of Education, since people's capability to read and write leads to more familiarity with, and demand for, cultural and information facilities. Another reason might be due to different time periods in question. That is, since real unit costs of those informational means have declined over time due to technological development, more Koreans are likely to enjoy those facilities at a cheaper price in 1995, than did the OECD countries' of two or three decades ago.

Korea's state of Health is worse than that of the OECD cases in a similar income range. When we take into account the fact that unit costs associated with improving Health have also typically declined due to medical advances, the large gap is troubling. One could infer that Korea has not made due effort to improve health in its development process in comparison to the advanced countries' past experiences.

Korea's state of Work is much worse in 1995 than that of the OECD cases at a similar level of income. This is because Korea's economy has been driven, until recently, by laborers working long hours under dangerous working conditions. Combining this with significant gender discrimination against women, and the result is a large gender gap in terms of health, in which males fare poorly. Life expectancy at birth shows a great differential of 7.9 years between males and females, and the probability of dying between the ages of 40–45, the peak period for a person's social and economic participation, is 2.87 times higher for males than females (National Statistical Office, 2000b). Job insecurity and long, stressful working hours are partly responsible for the high risk of death among economically active men, to which women are less exposed due to gender discrimination in the labor market.

Finally, Korea's state of Equity is also worse than that of the OECD's 24 cases. As mentioned above, this is principally due to gender inequality rather than to income inequality. The improvement of women's social status has been minimal during the process of economic growth in Korea. This is attributable to discrimination against women, which stems from a deeply rooted Confucian, male-oriented cultural tradition and patriarchal family system. Women's social status has improved more rapidly in terms of ability development than in the *use* of these abilities in social participation (Sen, 1993). Gains, made by women in Health and Education, have outpaced those made by men over the same period. However, opportunities for educated and healthy women to participate in social, economic, and political life have increased very slowly. Less educated, less healthy women remained largely blocked from social participation, and have shown little improvement relative to men during the period in question (Korea Women's Development Institute, 1998).

In truth, the comparisons above – of countries of similar income at different time intervals – are implicitly based upon a suspect assumption. Implied is the argument that Korea should take a path of development similar to the developed countries' past experiences. However, Korea might be placed in a developmental context that differs from the developed countries' past, even though the two groups of countries enjoyed comparable levels of income. Even though industrialization and improvement of quality of life generally tend to move together, in the case of developing countries, latecomer's advantages (or disadvantages) might enhance (or worsen) its quality of life compared to the advanced countries of an identical level of income (Inkeles, 1993; Tang, 1999). To obviate comparability problems associated with this period effect, it is necessary to make a comparison between nations of similar income during the same period of time. Thus, this study also compares quality of life between Korea and those OECD countries with similar income levels in 1995. Greece and Portugal are the OECD countries whose real incomes are close to Korea's in 1995. Results are displayed in Table IV.

As indicated in the table, overall, Korean's quality of life seems to be worse in general than that of Greece or Portugal. On the one hand, in the domain of Culture/Information and Education, Korea looks better than the two countries. On the other hand, we can ascertain a huge gap in Health, Work, and Equity between Korea and the other two countries. This comparison suggests that Koreans enjoy

TABLE IV

A Comparison of Korea, Greece, and Portugal in 1995. (Unit: PPP$, percentile of principal component value)

	Income	Health	Education	Work	Culture & Info.	Equity
Korea	$11,594	61.1	41.2	14.3	50.2	22.3
Greece	$11,636	96.7	30.2	54.1	37.1	64.8*
Portugal	$12,674	81.9	38.1	41.3	28.4	—

*data for 1984.

a much worse quality of life than the level possible from Korea's income level. This is most probably the result of Korea's development strategy, which first emphasizes increasing the sheer size of the economic pie. Moreover, Korea's extremely rapid economic growth has not allowed sufficient time and energy for the transformation of income growth into an improved quality of life.

Even though the effects of Income on other domains of life draw attention in most studies, there exist reciprocal effects of other life domains on Income, as well as among each other. For example, improvement in Education contributes to income growth, and improvement in Work or Equity can also lead to income growth. When a country departs from absolute poverty, and arrives at a substantial level of income, the transformation of income growth into improved quality of life is necessary for continued development towards a still higher level. At the current stage of Korea's development, emphasis should be put on this transformation as well as income growth itself. The priority of improvement should be placed, appropriately, on various domains of life besides Income for Korea's further economic and social development.

In much the same way as Korea can be compared to the other OECD countries with similar Income, matching according to other domains can be done, and the remaining domains compared. For example, countries matching the Education level Korea enjoyed in 1995 can be chosen, and then a comparison of their Work and Equity levels can be done as well. Table V presents the results of such domain-wise comparisons. When Health is chosen as the reference domain for comparison, fifteen OECD countries/time periods with

TABLE V

Priorities for Korean Social Development (as indicated by domain-wise comparison)

Reference domain	Priority for improvement*
Income	Work, Equity, Health
Health	Equity, Work, Income
Work	Equity, Income
Culture & Info.	Equity, Income, Work, Health
Equity	Health, Work, Income, Culture & Info

*After matching by reference domain, the domain in which Korea most lagged behind the other countries is listed first, followed in order by domains in which Korea lagged behind less, suggesting an ordering of priorities for the sake of further social development.

Health levels similar to Korea's in 1995 are chosen for comparison. The results of the comparison indicate that Korea is the furthest behind these 15 countries in terms of Equity, and lags somewhat less behind in terms of Work conditions. Korea compares least invidiously to these countries in terms of Income. Thus, on the basis of this comparison alone, Korea's highest priority for social development would be improving Equity, followed by Work, and then Income.

When matching is done on the basis of the Education level Korea enjoyed in 1995, forty-four OECD country cases are selected. Given comparable levels of Education, Health is shown to be the most inferior domain of life in Korea, followed by Work, Equity, Income, and Culture. When Korea's 1995 Work level is used as the reference domain, 13 country cases are selected. Given a similar Work index score, Korea's Equity compares most invidiously, followed by Income. In the same way, if Culture and Equity are set to the level of Korea in 1995, thirty-two cases and 7 cases, respectively, are selected for comparison. To summarize the results of all these domain-wise comparisons, the following ordering of priorities for social development emerges: Equity, Work > Health, Income > Culture & Information > Education.

In other words, on the basis of the other OECD countries' past experiences, it would appear that Korea lags furthest behind the norm in the domains of Equity and Work. Thus, these are the domains in which Korea would be well advised to focus its efforts for further social and economic development. The next highest priorities are Health and Income. After that follow Culture/ Information and then Educational improvement. To conclude, gender inequality and poor working conditions should be given the highest priority in terms of improving the current state of Korea's quality of life.

SUMMARY AND DISCUSSION

This study attempts to compare the current state of Korea's quality of life with that of more developed countries in their past, and seeks to derive suggestions for Korea's further development towards a more balanced quality of life. Toward this end, in addition to income, five composite indices are constructed and analyzed by means of principal components analysis.

Korea's real income in 1995 corresponds to the per capita income of many OECD countries in the late 1960s. In other words, there exists a gap of about 30 years between the OECD countries and Korea, as far as income is concerned. Education is the aspect of life in which Korea compares most favorably to the developed countries, approaching the level they experienced in the mid 1980s. With respect to the domain of Culture and Information, Korea corresponds to the developed countries' levels of the mid 1970s. In terms of Equity and Work, Korea's current state is much worse than that of the OECD countries in the late 1960s, the years marking the beginning of time series data used in this study.

Since Korea's pace of economic growth has been very fast, there has not been sufficient time and energy to transform income growth into improved quality of life. This is particularly true of the life domains of Health, Work, and Equity. A growth-at-all-costs development strategy is mainly responsible for the seriously poor state of Work life in Korea. A Confucian cultural ethos, and a number of historical upheavals in this century, have contributed to an exceptionally high level of Education. The analysis makes clear that improvements in Work conditions and gender Equity should be given the highest priority for Korea's further social and economic development, in the light of OECD countries' past experiences.

Finally, it should be noted that a painful economic crisis struck Korea, along with several other East Asian countries, in 1997. The crisis created a great deal of unemployment and homelessness. In the span of a year, the GDP per capita fell by one-third – from U.S.$10363 in 1997 to U.S.$6920 in 1998. As a matter of fact, this precipitous decline was partly due to a tremendous decline in the value of the Korean *won* vis-à-vis the US dollar, so the nominal decline in income does not necessarily mean that purchasing power and standards of living fell to a similar extent. Nevertheless, the standard of living is reported to have substantially declined, particularly among lower income groups, while the impact of the crisis on higher income groups was minimal (Korea Institute for Health and Social Affairs and Korea Labor Institute, 1999). By 1999, the national economy had begun to significantly recover. Income and consumption for middle- and high-income groups had largely returned to pre-crisis levels, though there is evidence that a similar recovery for lower income groups has yet to materialize fully.

In keeping with these developments, many recent surveys suggest that income distribution worsened during the crisis and is likely to worsen further (National Statistical Office, 2000a). In addition, the economic crisis has led many people to reduce consumption and redouble their work efforts. Increasing length and intensity of work effort has been the norm for many in the wake of the crisis. Resulting stress from overwork, and an increasingly harsh and insecure labor market, have led to deterioration in health, and more cases of illness among lower income people (Ministry of Health and Welfare, 1999). Thus, unfortunately, the recent economic crisis would only seem to have worsened the problem areas of poor Work conditions and Inequality that were highlighted in the analysis. This further underscores the need to give priority to improving these areas of quality of life.

NOTES

[1] Refer to UNDP and KIHSA (1998) for a review of Korea's current state of human development.
[2] This problem is attributable to cultural differences as well as to the huge gap in income. Particularly, in a comparison of East and West, this problem is concerned with the matter of which domain of life is given more weight in their definition of quality of life (Mukherjee, 1989; LeeKakulthanit and Day, 1993).
[3] This is the same reason why many researchers of practical orientation studying subjective quality of life prefer multiple measures of life satisfaction to one overarching measure of happiness (Campbell et al., 1976).
[4] For each time period, data are collected for one year, for example, 1969 or 1970 (not the two-year period of 1969–70). The choice of the year was largely dependent on data availability and reporting conventions of the organization publishing the data.
[5] Among the OECD countries, Mexico, the Czech Republic, and Hungary are excluded in this analysis since those countries entered the organization in the 1990s. Turkey is also excluded since it is an outlying case in every indicator, which reduces the validity of measurement.
[6] Combining more than one component in this way is controversial since those components are not related to each other (orthogonal). Nevertheless, since the purpose of principal component analysis lies in summarizing information, this combination method can be justified as an extended way of summarizing information (Slottje et al., 1991). As a matter of fact, interpretation of an index constructed in this way should be made with caution.
[7] Refer to Desai (1990) concerning various methods of standardization for comparison.
[8] The inclusion of this last variable is intended to capture the extent to which Korea lags behind these more information and knowledge-based societies wherein scientists and technicians occupy an increasingly important role. Moreover, unlike the first four included variables, which are of the more basic type of indicator typically used to assess developing countries, and in which developed countries have largely experienced saturation, this last variable is a more sensitive one in which variation among developed countries indeed exists.

REFERENCES

Bell, D.: 1973, The Coming of Post-industrial Society (Basic Books, New York).

Boelhouwer, J. and I. Stoop: 1999, 'Measuring well-being in the Netherlands', Social Indicators Research 48, pp. 51–57.

Bureau of Economic Planning: 1993, New People's Quality of Life Index (Bureau of Economic Planning, Tokyo).

Campbell, A., P.E. Converse and W.L. Rodgers: 1976, The Quality of American Life (Russel Sage Foundation, New York).

Davis, E.E. and M. Fine-Davis: 1991, 'Social indicators of living conditions in Ireland with European comparisons', Social Indicators Research 25, pp. 103–365.

Desai, M.: 1990, 'Income and alternative measures of well-being', in D.G. Westerndorff and D. Ghai (eds.), Monitoring Social Progress in the 1990s (Avebury, Aldershot, UK).

Diener, E. and E. Suh: 1997, 'Measuring quality of life: Economic, social, and subjective indicators', Social Indicators Research 40, pp. 189–216.

Estes, R.J.: 1999, 'Social development trends in Europe, 1970–1994: Development prospects for the new Europe', Social Indicators Research 47, pp. 1–19.

Inkeles, A.: 1993, 'Industrialization, modernization and the quality of life', International Journal of Comparative Sociology 32(1–2), pp. 1–23.

Kim, K.S. and S.D. Hong: 1997, Accounting for Rapid Economic Growth in Korea, 1963–1995 (Korea Development Institute, Seoul, Korea).

Korea Women's Development Institute: 1998, Statistical Yearbook on Women (KWDI, Seoul, Korea).

Korea Institute for Health and Social Affairs and Korea Labor Institute: 1999, Survey Report of Unemployment and Welfare Need (KLI, Seoul, Korea).

Land, K.: 1983, 'Social indicators', Annual Review of Sociology 9, pp. 1–26.

Leekakulthanit, O. and R. Day: 1993, 'Crosscultural comparisons of quality of life of Thais and Americans', Social Indicators Research 30, pp. 49–70.

Mazumdar, K.: 1999, 'Measuring the well-being of the developing countries: achievement and improvement indices', Social Indicators Research 47, pp. 1–60.

McGinn, N.F., D.R. Snodgrass, Y.B. Kim, S.B. Kim and Q.Y. Kim: 1980, Education and Development in Korea (Council on East Asian Studies, Harvard University Press, Boston).

Ministry of Health and Welfare: 1999, White Paper for Health and Welfare (MHW, Seoul, Korea).

Moriss, M.D.: 1979, Measuring the Condition of the World's Poor: the Physical Quality of Life Index (Pergamon, New York).

Mukherjee, R.: 1989, The Quality of Life, Valuation in Social Research (Sage, New Delhi, India).

National Statistical Office: 2000a, Annual Report on Urban Household Expenditure (NSO, Seoul, Korea).

National Statistical office: 200b, Social Indicators in Korea (NSO, Seoul, Korea).

OECD: 1976, Measuring Social Well-being: A Progress Report on the Development of Social Indicators (OECD, Paris).

Sen, A.: 1993, 'Capability and well-being', in M. Nussbaum and A. Sen (eds.), The Quality of Life (Oxford University Press, New York).

Slottje, D.J., G.W. Scully, J.G. Hirschberg and K.J. Hayes: 1991, Measuring the Quality of Life across Countries (Westview Press, Boulder, Co).

Tang, K.L.: 1999, 'East Asian newly industrializing countries: economic growth and quality of life', Social Indicators Research 47, pp. 69–96.

Terleckyi, N.: 1975, Improvement in the Quality of Life: Estimates of Possibilities in the United States, 1974–1983 (National Planning Association, Washington, D.C.).
UN: 1993, Report on the World Social Situation (UN, New York).
UNDP: 1990, Human Development Report 1990 (Oxford University Press, New York).
UNDP: 2000, Human Development Report 2000 (Oxford University Press, New York).
UNDP and KIHASA: 1998, Korea Human Development Report 1998 (Korea Institute for Health And Social Affairs, Seoul, Korea).
Zapf, W.: 1987, 'German social report: living conditions and subjective well-being, 1978–1984', Social Indicators Research 19, pp. 1–171.

Anglo-American Studies, School of English
Hankuk University of Foreign Studies
San 89, Wangsan-ri, Mohyun-myun, Yongin-si, Kyunggi
Korea (449-791)
E-mail: hyunslee@hufs.ac.kr

DOH CHULL SHIN and CONRAD P. RUTKOWSKI

SUBJECTIVE QUALITY OF KOREAN LIFE IN 1981 AND 2001

ABSTRACT. Over the past two decades, Korea has been transformed into an economic powerhouse, a maturing democracy, a nation of cities, and a society of mixed cultures. How have these changes affected the quality of life that ordinary Koreans experience in the private and public spheres of their lives? In their eyes, what specific domains of Korean life have changed for the better? What life domains have changed for the worse? This paper explores these questions with two sets of national sample surveys conducted, respectively, in 1981 and 2001. Analyses of these surveys reveal that the Korean people, as a whole, tend to feel that they are worse off than they were 20 years ago. Over this same period, they felt that the domains of health, education, work, and community have changed for the better, while the three domains of leisure, the government, and the country have changed for the worse. Notwithstanding all the significant improvements in the standards of their living, Koreans do not express a significantly greater sense of well-being about the domains of income and housing. Most surprising is that they feel worse about the freely elected democratic government, than they did about the repressive military regime of 20 years ago. Why has the perceived quality of the Korean government deteriorated rather than improved in the wake of democratic regime change? This remains unanswered.

On all fronts Korea today is a country different from what it was twenty years ago. As the 11th largest economy in the world, Korea has been transformed from a low-income country into an economic powerhouse. Politically, it has been transformed from a repressive military dictatorship into a maturing democracy. Socially, it has been transformed from a nation of mostly rural people into one of urbanites. Culturally, Korea has also been transformed from a nation with a predominantly traditional Confucian culture into a multicultural nation with one of the fastest growing Christian populations in the world. Unquestionably, these changes have affected the way the Korean people live their lives privately and publicly. As compared to 20 years ago, for example, they now eat much better and live a longer life. They also live in more comfortable homes and travel far more extensively beyond their country's own borders. These changes stemming from increasing affluence,

Social Indicators Research **62, 63:** 509–534, 2003.

however, cannot be assumed to have created a nation of greater well-being (Lane, 2000: p. 4).

How differently do the Korean people feel about the way in which they now live in the wake of economic, political, and other transformations that have taken place in their country during the past two decades? How has their quality of life changed during this period? What specific feelings of well-being do Koreans experience, and do they do so to a greater extent than they did twenty years ago? What specific feelings of well-being do they feel to a lesser extent than previously? In what specific life domains do they feel more satisfied than in the past? In what specific life domains do they feel less satisfied? None of these questions can be addressed with any degree of confidence by the amount of family income they command or the size of the house in which they live because these measures of life conditions are surrogate indicators of quality of life experiences (Campbell, 1981; Campbell and Converse, 1972). Feelings of well-being can be estimated precisely only when we actually count the number of people who report experiencing those feelings directly. By comparing the number of those people in 1981 and 2001, this study seeks to highlight the magnitude and trajectories of changes in the subjective quality of life in Korea during the past two decades.

The present paper is organized into six sections. In the section that immediately follows an effort is made to explicate the notion of life quality and identify its principle constituent elements. The next section examines how the concept is measured at the various levels of life as a whole and in its specific domains. The third section briefly describes how the two sets of survey data analyzed in this paper were gathered. The fourth section is devoted to what is generally known as general assessments of life quality in their entirety. The fifth section reports evaluations of life as a whole from specific qualities. The sixth section presents assessments of the various aspects or domains of life. The final section summarizes and highlights the notable features of the quality of Korean life in flux.

CONCEPTUALIZATION

Quality of life is widely known as the most difficult concept to define in the social sciences (Dannhauser, 1976; Csikszentmihalyi, 1990; Cuminns, 1998; Nussbaum and Sen, 1993; Szalai and Andrews, 1980). People living in different situations see different things as essential to a meaningful existence. As a consequence, the concept of life quality has been defined in many different ways. Aristotle (Baker, 1962) and McCall (1976), for example, viewed it as a life of happiness. Other scholars have equated life quality with a sense of satisfaction (Campbell et al., 1976). Still others identified it with the realization of life goals and hopes (Milbrath, 1982; Millis, 1990; Schmuck and Sheldon, 2001). As such, quality of life means different things to different people. Unidimensional approaches to the concept of life quality, therefore, only portray a partial picture of the quality which people really seek to bring to their lives (Cuminns, 2000).

In view of the widely known fact that humans value different things for their personal lives, quality of life is considered in the present study as a multi-dimensional concept. Specifically, it refers to the extent to which happiness, enjoyment, satisfaction, and accomplishment are experienced to any significant degree (Allard, 1975; Andrews, 1986; Diener et al., 1999). Happiness and enjoyment represent what von Wright (1972) characterizes as the affective or hedonic dimension of human goodness. Satisfaction and accomplishment, on the other hand, represent what he calls the cognitive or welfare domain of human goodness (Rescher, 1972). By comparing the extent to which these two most important components of human goodness were experienced at two different points in time, this inquiry seeks to portray a comprehensive and balanced account of improvements and declines in the subjective quality of life in Korea. Underlying this inquiry is the notion that quality, like beauty, lies in the eyes of the beholder.

MEASUREMENT

The past two decades have witnessed a variety of approaches to measuring quality of life by subjective indicators (Diener et al.,

1999; Hagerty et al., 2001; see also Cuminns, 1995, 2000). These approaches are built on divergent modes in which people feel about and evaluate their lives. In judging their life experiences, for example, people take into account all those experiences at the same time. Or they focus on each distinguishable component of those experiences at a given point in time. When they consider their life experiences as a whole, they make general evaluations of their well-being from a global or holistic perspective. When they consider only one identifiable aspect of life experience, they make specific evaluations of their well-being from a particular concern of life. As the substantive scope of human evaluations varies from individual life domains to the aggregate or whole of those parts, indicators of those evaluations vary in the level of their specificity (Andrews and Withey, 1996).

To estimate the general level of well-being among the Korean people and the degree to which it changes over time, we selected two sets of indicators that have been frequently used as measures of global well-being in other national and cross-national surveys. The first of these two sets is the 11-point life ladder scale developed by Hadley Cantril (1965). Unlike many other measures of global well-being, this particular scale allows respondents to evaluate their life experiences as a whole according to all the criteria or standards that matter in their own lives. It allows for global evaluations of the human lot in its entirety (see Appendix Q1 & Q2 for the wording of this scale). It also allows for estimating the experienced and expected changes in the overall sense of well-being by asking the same respondents to make such evaluations at different points in time, including those of the past and future.

In addition to the ladder scale, we selected another set of items to estimate the extent to which the Korean people experienced specific qualities or goodness – affective and cognitive – in their lives as a whole. These items, unlike the ladder scale, were verbal scales tapping feelings of happiness, enjoyment, satisfaction, and accomplishment (see Appendix Q3, Q4, and Q5 for the wording of these 4-point verbal scales on happiness, enjoyment, and accomplishment. See Q6-O for the wording of the 7-point general life satisfaction scale, which is collapsed into a 4-point verbal scale). Happiness and enjoyment represent the hedonic goodness of human life while satisfaction and accomplishment represent cognitive goodness.

Besides these two sets of indicators measuring global well-being, we selected 13 items in which we asked respondents to evaluate a different domain of their lives on a separate basis (see Appendix A-3 for the wording of these items). Included in such evaluations are: (1) health; (2) education; (3) leisure; (4) marriage; (5) family; (6) children; (7) friendship; (8) income; (9) housing; (10) work; (11) government; (12) community; and (13) country. Each of these life domains was evaluated on a 7-point verbal scale developed by Campbell et al. (1976). The scale ran from being "completely dissatisfied" to being "completely satisfied."

DATA SOURCES

Basic data from this study came from two national sample surveys. During the month of July in 1981, when the military was back in power after a brief period of democratic emergence, the Institute of Social Sciences (hereinafter the ISS) at Seoul National University in Korea conducted a social development survey, the first of these two surveys. The ISS carried out face-to-face interviews with a national random sample of 1,215 Korean people age 20 and older (Chey et al., 1989). The Korea-Gallup poll (hereinafter Gallup poll) conducted the 2001 Korea Democracy Barometer survey, the second survey during the month of March 2001 when the democratic rule was 13 years old. The Gallup poll carried out face-to-face interviews with a national sample of 1,006 Korean voters age 20 and older, and it used the aforementioned three sets of life quality items that the ISS had asked 20 years before. Both surveys chose a representative sample of the Korean adult population by means of multi-stage area probability sampling. The sample interviewed in each survey was large as well as representative enough to generalize about the Korean population as a whole.

GLOBAL ASSESSMENTS OF LIFE QUALITY

More often than not people make general and summary evaluations of their life experiences as a whole (Andrews and Withey, 1976). How does life fare? How is life treating you? How are things going? How have you been? In everyday conversation, people in Korea, like those in other countries, ask these questions and answer them without much difficulty. This section focuses on the global or holistic assessments of life quality among the Korean people.

In the 1981 and 2001 surveys, respondents were asked to evaluate their own personal lives and their country's on an 11-point ladder scale at three different points in time: at the present time, five years ago, and five years hence. On this ladder scale, the bottom step with a score of 0 referred to the worst possible situation each respondent could imagine for one's own life or that of the country, while a score of 10 referred to the best possible situation he or she could imagine. Table I reports the complete distribution of respondents to the two surveys across 11 scale points. It also reports the mean rating on the scale and percentages expressing positive and negative feelings about their private and public life as a citizen within a nation.

One notable feature of the data reported in Table I is that the Korean people as a whole feel more negative than positive about what they experience currently in their private as well as public spheres of life. When the 2001 KDB survey asked them to rate the quality of their *public life*, 55 percent chose the bottom five steps on the 11-point ladder scale while 21 percent the top five steps. When the same survey asked them to rate the quality of their *private life*, a similar pattern emerged: 50 percent chose the bottom five steps while 25 percent the top five steps. In both the private and public spheres of life, twice as many chose the bottom steps to express varying degrees of ill-being than those of well-being. In terms of the mean statistic on the scale, moreover, the two life spheres averaged 4.3 and 4.4 on a 11-point scale, the scores that are significantly lower than its midpoint (5.0). Judging from the percentage and mean figures reported in the table, it is clear that among the Korean people feelings of ill-being are more prevalent than those of well-being.

When the separate assessments of the two different life spheres are considered together, over one-third (35%) feel *fully negative* about the quality of life in Korea, experiencing varying degrees of

TABLE I

Perceptions of the Quality of Public and Private Life on a 11-point Ladder Scale

Scale points	Public life		Private life	
	1981	2001	1981	2001
0 (worst)	0.0%	1.4%	2.3%	2.4%
1	0.6	2.6	4.3	4.1
2	1.4	7.7	9.1	6.5
3	9.0	19.8	15.0	17.5
4	16.2	23.3	2 0.8	19.7
5	28.3	24.0	27.9	25.3
6	18.1	13.6	11.9	14.5
7	14.2	4.9	5.6	6.3
8	8.1	2.4	2.1	3.0
9	1.9	0.4	0.7	0.4
10 (best)	2.1	0.0	0.2	0.4
Negative (0–4)	27.2	54.8	51.5	50.2
Positive (6–10)	44.4	21.3	20.5	24.6
(mean)	*(5.5)*	*(4.3)*	*(4.3)*	*(4.4)*

Sources: 1981 Social Development Survey and 2001 Korea Democracy Barometer Survey.

ill-being in its private as well as public spheres. Nearly half (45%) feel negative about one of the two life spheres while feeling positive about the other. Only a small minority of one-tenth (11%) feel *fully positive* about the quality of Korean life, expressing at least some degrees of well-being in both spheres. Among the Korean people, a vast majority (89%) feel negative about at least one of the two life spheres. More noteworthy is that those who feel *fully negative* about Korean life are over three times as many as those who feel *fully positive* about it.

The percentage and mean ratings in Table I are compared across the two surveys conducted in 1981 and 2001 in order to determine whether Koreans feel better-off or worse-off than two decades ago. In the *private sphere*, in which the Korean people experience on an individual basis, little has changed over the period in either the negative or positive direction. Its mean score (4.3) remains almost the same as it was before (4.4). Across the survey years, no significant differences are found between the ratings of positive changes or between those of negative changes. These findings indicate that the quality of *private life* among a majority of the Korean people has changed little during the past two decades.

In the *public sphere* of life in which ordinary Koreans are involved as members of the national community, however, notable changes have taken place. In 1981, life in Korea was rated far more positively than negatively. While about a quarter (27%) expressed varying degrees of ill-being, nearly half (44%) expressed ones of well-being. Those experiencing well-being outnumbered those experiencing ill-being by a substantial margin or 17 percentage points. Currently, in sharp contrast, the former are outnumbered by the latter by a larger margin of 34 percentage points (21% vs. 55%). In the eyes of the Korean people, life in Korea has significantly changed for the worse during the past two decades. For a majority, the country has become an unattractive place to live.

Twenty years ago a little over a quarter (27%) felt negative about the country as a place to live. Today more than half (54%) the Korean population feels the same about it. Compared to over two-fifths (44%) in 1981, only one-fifth (21%) feel positive about it. To put it differently, the proportion rating Korea as a bad place to live has increased by 23 percentage points while the proportion rating it as a good place has decreased by 28 percentage points. Why is it that the quality of public life in Korea has declined so much during the last two decades particularly when the country has been transformed into an economic powerhouse and a democratic state? This is the most puzzling question concerning the dynamics of life quality perceptions among the Korean people. It appears that Koreans no longer value economic prosperity and political freedom as much as they once did.

Because of significant declines in the quality of *public life* during the past two decades, the proportion experiencing ill-being in the public as well as private spheres of Korean life has risen sharply. Compared to 17 percent in 1981, 35 percent currently feel negative about their life experiences in both spheres. Those *fully negative* about the quality of Korean life have doubled over the last twenty years. Those *fully positive* about Korean life, on the other hand, have changed little. As they did twenty years ago, only a small minority of one-tenth (11%) express varying degrees of well-being in both private and public life. When these findings are considered together, it becomes evident that democratization, globalization, industrialization, urbanization, and many other changes taken place in Korea during the past two decades have not contributed to the building of a nation of greater well-being. Instead, those changes have transformed the country into a nation of lesser well-being.

How do the Korean people feel the quality of life in their country has changed in the recent past? How do they feel the quality of Korean life will change in the future? Do they feel a greater sense of progress in their private and public lives currently than they did twenty years ago? Do they also feel a greater sense of optimism about these realms than they did before? To explore these, the 2001 Korea Democracy Barometer survey used two questions that were asked in the Social Development survey conducted in 1981. One question in this pair asked respondents to locate on the 11-point ladder scale the quality of life they experienced five years ago. The second question asked them to locate on the scale the quality of life they expect to experience in five years. These past and future numeric ratings are compared to the present ratings to determine the nature – positive, neutral, and negative – of experienced and expected changes in life quality. Table II reports for each of other two survey years the percentages expressing feelings of progress and retrogression about the past. It also reports the percentages expressing feelings of optimism and pessimism about the future.

In terms of the positive and negative changes the Korean people experienced over the past five years, Table II shows significant differences between the two survey years. In 1981, significantly greater proportions reported varying degrees of improvements rather than those of retrogressions in both public and private life. According to the percentage differential index presented in the last column of Table II, 41 percent more experienced improvements in their private life and 70 percent more realized those changes in their public life. In 2001, however, those who experienced retrogressions outnumber those who saw improvements in both spheres of life. The

TABLE II

Experienced and Expected Changes in the Quality of Public and Private Life

Life sphere/ survey year	Types of changes Progress	Retrogression	Balance
A. Experienced changes in life quality			
Public life			
1981	79.1%	8.8	+70.3%
2001	36.1	42.2	–6.1
Private life			
1981	59.7	19.0	+40.7
2001	24.9	47.3	–22.3
B. Expected changes in life quality			
Public Life			
1981	91.1%	2.3%	+88.8
2001	83.0	6.0	+77.0
Private life			
1981	83.7	4.7	+79.0
2001	81.6	3.7	+77.9

Sources: 1981 Social Development Survey and 2001 Korea Democracy Barometer Survey.

former lead the latter in public life by 6 percentage points and in private life by 22 percentage points.

Among Koreans, currently, a plurality report declines in the two spheres of life, and they number nearly twice as many as those reporting improvements in those life spheres (31% vs. 17%). Two decades ago, a majority (52%) reported improvements in both private and public life. Those reporting declines in the private and public life compromised a very small minority (5%). In short, the prevailing mood among the Korean people in the early 1980s was a sense of progress. In sharp contrast, a sense of retrogression is the prevailing mood among Koreans in the early 2000s.

In terms of the changes Koreans expect to experience in the next five years, there is not much difference between 1981 and 2001. As

TABLE III

Patterns of Changes in the Quality of Public and Private Life

Nature of changes		Public life		Private life	
Past	Future	1981	2001	1981	2001
Negative	negative	1.1%	1.5%	1.9%	1.3%
Negative	neutral	0.8	3.7	2.1	5.6
Negative	positive	6.5	36.8	14.9	40.3
Neutral	negative	0.3	2.0	0.9	1.5
Neutral	neutral	2.2	3.1	4.7	5.5
Neutral	positive	9.5	16.6	15.2	20.9
Positive	negative	0.9	2.5	1.9	0.9
Positive	neutral	3.6	4.2	4.7	3.5
Positive	positive	75.1	29.6	53.6	20.5

Sources: 1981 Social Development Survey and 2001 Korea Democracy Barometer Survey.

they did two decades ago, a large majority still expect the quality of their private and public lives to improve in the future. More than four out of five Koreans, (83% in their public life and 82% in their private life), are optimistic about the future, regardless of how they feel about what has recently happened in their private or public lives. Nonetheless, the Korean people as a whole are now significantly less optimistic about their country's life than their own (82% vs. 91%).

What is the most common pattern of life quality that the Korean people experience in their private and public lives at the present time? How does this pattern compare with the one that existed two decades ago? To address these questions, three different categories (negative, neutral, and positive) of the experienced and expected changes in private and public life are jointly considered to construct nine distinct patterns of life quality. Table III provides the percentages of respondents falling into each of these types. In 1981, a majority fell into the pattern in which the quality of life improved over the past five years and was expected to continue to improve over the next five years. In 2001, however, a plurality fell into the pattern in which the quality of life declined in the past, but was expected to improve in the future. Currently, it is relatively

TABLE IV

Specific Feelings of Well-being: Happiness, Enjoyment, Satisfaction and Accomplishment

Degree of well-being	Categories of well-being			
	Happiness	Enjoyment	Satisfaction	Accomplishment
None	8.1%	13.1%	44.3%	21.0%
Little	48.1	57.1	31.9	61.2
Some	41.3	28.2	20.2	17.1
A lot	1.0	1.6	3.5	0.7

Source: 2001 Korea Democracy Barometer Survey.

small minorities of less than one-third, (21% in private life and 30% in public life), who are experiencing continuing progress in their private and public life. Over the past two decades, there has been a drastic shift away from the prevailing pattern of continuing improvements in private and public life.

SPECIFIC FEELINGS OF WELL-BEING

Many Koreans make an evaluation of their lives primarily by focusing on those experiences that are of an affective character – pleasant and unpleasant feelings. Many others rely mostly on their cognitive experiences involving comparisons to criteria such as aspirations and expectations. Still many others consider both the affective and cognitive aspects of their life experiences when making an overall judgment of their life quality. While reflecting on the diverse ways in which the Korean people judge their life experiences, this section examines the experiences of both affective and cognitive natures. Specifically, it focuses on those of happiness, enjoyment, satisfaction, and accomplishment.

From Table IV, it is clear that the Korean people today tend to live without experiencing much well-being. In all four categories of well-being listed in the table, a minority report that they live with "some" or "a lot" of that experience. The percentages reporting such degrees of well-being are 42 percent in happiness, 20 percent in enjoyment, 24 percent in satisfaction, and 18 percent in accom-

TABLE V

Changes in Specific Feelings of Well-being

Categories of well-being	Survey year 1981	2001	Change
Happiness	46.7%	42.3%	–4.4%
Enjoyment	50.3	29.8	–20.5
Satisfaction	19.8	23.7	+3.9
Accomplishment	31.6	17.6	–14.0

Sources: 1981 Social Development Survey and 2001 Korea Development Survey.

plishment. Those reporting a great deal of well-being are miniscule, ranging from less than 1 percent in the specific feeling of accomplishment to a little over 3 percent in that of being satisfied with life as a whole. In Korean life today, every category of affective and cognitive well-being is in short supply.

From Table V, it is evident that the Korean people as a whole feel that they are much worse-off than they were 20 years ago. In three of the four categories surveyed, the percentages expressing feelings of well-being are smaller in 2001 than 1981. Only in one category, do more people express such feelings than before. Over the past two decades, there has been a small increase in the percentage feeling satisfied with their lives as a whole. Yet they now experience happiness, enjoyment, and accomplishment to lesser degrees. The most dramatic change over the last two decades has taken place in the specific feeling of enjoying life. The numbers of those experiencing joy in their lives have fallen sharply by 20 percentage points from 50 percent to 30 percent. As a result, one-fifth (20%) more are presently living a joyless life than in the past.

Table VI compares across the 1981 and 2001 surveys the extent to which the Korean people experienced the four categories of well-being. By counting the number of these categories, a 5-point index is constructed to estimate the overall level of well-being for each of the two survey years. The 1981 and 2001 mean scores on this index are compared to discern the direction and magnitude of change in the overall level of well-being over the past two decades. According to these scores reported in the table, the average person in Korea

TABLE VI

Changes in the General Levels of Well-being

Index score	Survey year	
	1981	2001
0	32.5%	46.9%
1	22.4	18.9
2	20.1	15.2
3	17.0	12.2
4	8.1	6.8
(mean)	*(1.5)*	*(1.1)*

Sources: 1981 Social Development Survey and 2001 Korea Democracy Barometer Survey.

experienced in 1981 1.5 of the four components of well-being. In 2001, the same Korean realized 1.1 of the four components. During the 20-year period, the mean level of overall well-being has fallen by nearly half a point. The downward movement becomes more evident when the two survey years are compared in terms of those experiencing none of the four categories of well-being. Compared to one-third (33%) of the respondents to the 1981 survey, nearly half (47%) of those to the 2001 survey reported a complete failure to experience feelings of happiness, enjoyment, satisfaction, and accomplishment in their lives. This finding constitutes another piece of evidence to confirm a downward trend in the overall subjective quality of Korean life.

In Table VII, four different patterns of well-being are identified for each survey by considering whether the Korean people experience one of both dimensions of well-being. A careful scrutiny of the data in the table reveals that the most common pattern has shifted drastically over the period from the most positive to the least positive one. In 1981, a plurality of one-third (34%) experienced the pattern featuring the most desirable life of both affective and cognitive well-being. Twenty years later, a greater plurality (47%) are living in the pattern that represents the least desirable life fully devoid of the affective and cognitive well-being. As a result of this downward

TABLE VII

Changing Patterns of Well-being

Patterns		Survey year	
Affective	Cognitive	1981	2001
No	No	32.5%	46.9%
No	Yes	6.5	6.9
Yes	No	26.7	20.5
Yes	Yes	34.3	25.8

Sources: 1981 Social Development Survey and 2001 Korea Democracy Barometer Survey.

shift in the most common pattern of experiencing well-being, Korea can no longer be considered a nation of well-being.

In terms of the least common pattern, the country has experienced little change over the past two decades. Experiencing the cognitive dimension of well-being was and still is the least common pattern of living among the Korean people. As in 1981, one in fourteen (7%) individuals lives a satisfying or fulfilling life without experiencing any feeling of happiness or enjoyment. This indicates that the cognitive dimension of well-being remains in shorter supply than that of the affective dimension.

ASSESSMENTS OF LIFE DOMAINS

Human beings, regardless of time and place, live their lives in bits and pieces. These bits and pieces of human life are too numerous to identify comprehensively. And their numbers vary a great deal from one person to another. Yet they form the bases from which human feelings of well-being and ill-being develop. By examining such feelings about the important domains of human life, it can be determined how and why we humans succeed or fail to experience a good quality of life.

In this section, we describe how the Korean people feel about their own experiences in the life domains that refer to specific aspects or areas of life. The domains chosen for evaluation include: (1) health, (2) education, (3) leisure, (4) marriage, (5) family, (6) children, (7) friendship, (8) income, (9) housing, (10) work, (11) the government, (12) the community, and (13) country. Obviously, these thirteen domains do not encompass all the important concerns of the Korean people whose values and beliefs are constantly being transformed and challenged in the process of democratization, globalization, and urbanization. Nonetheless, they include all those concerns that the largest majority of the Korean people consider important to their respective lives. Moreover, they encompass not only materialistic and non-materialistic areas of human life but also both their private and public spheres of life in Korea.

Each of the thirteen domains was evaluated for feelings of satisfaction or dissatisfaction which respondents experienced with that particular domain at the time of their personal interviews. Such feelings of satisfaction or dissatisfaction, unlike those of happiness or pleasures, involve an act of judgment or comparison, and are shaped by a variety of criteria and standards (Campbell, 1981: p. 22; Campbell, Converse and Rodgers, 1976: pp. 31–32). Expectations, aspirations, and other criteria used in evaluating tend to be highly personal, and differ markedly from individual to individual even when the same life domains are being evaluated. As a result, it is not uncommon that a sense of satisfaction stems from low standards rather than high achievement, nor is it uncommon that a sense of dissatisfaction results from high standards rather than low achievement. The ratings of satisfaction and dissatisfaction, therefore, should be interpreted and compared across space and time with caution.

For each of the thirteen domains chosen in the present analysis, Table VIII provides the complete distribution of respondents within the 2001 survey statistics including the mean rating on a 7-point satisfaction-dissatisfaction scale and the percentage differential index (PDI) scores measuring the direction and magnitude of the difference between those who are satisfied and dissatisfied within each life domain.

Among the thirteen domains of life, the Korean people are likely to find themselves more satisfied than dissatisfied in ten domains. These include the domains of health, education, marriage, family, children, friendship, housing, work, community, and country. They tend to be most satisfied and least dissatisfied, especially, with their

TABLE VIII

Satisfaction and Dissatisfaction in Life Domains

Life domains	Completely dissatisfied 1	2	3	4	5	6	Completely satisfied 7	Percentage statistic: Satisfied (A)	Percentage statistic: Dissaatisfied (B)	PDI (A-B)	Summary statistics: Mean	Summary statistics: Ranks	(N)
Health	2.5%	7.1%	10.9%	17.7%	23.3%	25.1%	13.4%	61.8%	20.5%	+41.3%	4.8	10	(1005)
Education	3.6	9.3	15.7	27.1	23.6	14.6	6.0	44.2	28.6	+15.6	4.3	5	(963)
Leisure	9.8	15.9	19.6	22.1	16.9	12.2	3.5	32.6	45.3	−12.7	3.7	3	(994)
Marriage	1.8	3.5	5.9	17.8	24.9	30.3	15.7	70.9	11.2	+59.7	5.1	11	(775)
Family	1.3	3.4	6.2	18.5	27.4	29.4	13.8	70.6	10.9	+59.7	5.1	11	(1003)
Children	2.8	7.3	11.7	26.3	25.5	19.2	7.1	51.8	21.8	+30.0	4.5	7	(749)
Friendship	1.3	2.1	4.7	17.2	27.3	31.1	16.3	74.7	8.1	+66.6	5.3	13	(1005)
Income	11.1	17.2	19.2	23.0	20.8	7.5	1.3	29.6	47.5	−79.9	3.5	2	(847)
Housing	4.4	10.0	14.7	25.8	24.2	15.2	5.8	45.2	29.1	+16.1	4.2	4	(1005)
Work	3.1	7.0	15.6	24.4	24.3	19.0	6.7	40.0	25.7	+24.3	4.4	6	(585)
Government	16.6	21.9	24.7	22.7	10.6	2.8	0.7	14.1	63.2	−49.1	3.0	1	(993)
Community	1.3	5.5	9.8	26.8	28.9	22.1	5.7	55.7	16.6	+39.1	4.7	8	(1004)
Korea	4.6	6.9	10.3	20.6	21.6	22.1	14.5	58.2	21.8	+36.4	4.7	8	(1004)

Source: 2001 Korea Democracy Barometer Survey.

friendships, marriage, and family. In these domains that comprise interpersonal life, a large majority of over 70 percent express satisfaction and a small minority of 10 percent or so express dissatisfaction. In the case of friendship, for example, three quarters (75%) are satisfied and one-twelfth (8%) are dissatisfied. As its PDI score indicates, those satisfied outnumber those dissatisfied by the largest margin of 66 percentage points.

In all four domains of interpersonal life in Korea, Koreans are more satisfied than dissatisfied, as the positive scores of their PDI indicate. The preponderance of satisfaction over dissatisfaction, however, varies a great deal across these domains. Friendship registers the highest level of such preponderance. This is followed by marriage, family, and children in that order. The finding that friendship is rated ahead of the other three domains of family life can be interpreted to suggest that a significant qualitative change is taking place in Korean society built on the Confucian principle that emphasizes the importance of family life over all other aspects of human relationships.

In three of the thirteen domains surveyed, the Korean people as a whole express more dissatisfaction that satisfaction. These include the domains of leisure, income, and the government. The extent to which those dissatisfied outnumber those satisfied is largest in the domain of government and smallest in that of leisure. In the government domain, the former lead the latter by 48 percentage points. This PDI score is over two-and-a-half times as large as what is found in the domains of income (18%) and leisure (17%). Moreover, the government is the only domain with which a majority express dissatisfaction. In the eyes of the Korean people, there is no doubt that their government, currently, represents the worst arena of living in their country.

From the data presented in Table VIII, it is difficult to determine whether Korean life fares better in the private sphere than public sphere, or vice versa. In both spheres, no overwhelming pattern of satisfaction or dissatisfaction exits across their domains. In the private life sphere, which is represented by the first nine of the thirteen domains presented in the table, and the public life sphere, which is represented by the rest, at least two-thirds of the domains are rated more positively than negatively. Within the private life sphere, there is no notable difference between the domains of material life and non-material life. The two material life domains of income and housing, for example, are not any more satisfying than the non-material domains of leisure and education. Nor are the former any more dissatisfying than the latter.

Table IX compares the percentage and mean ratings of 13 domains to identify the domains that have changed for the better and the worse during the past two decades. It also compares their rankings to ascertain changes in their relative standing. By 5 percentage points or more, the levels of satisfaction have increased in eight domains (health, education, marriage, friendship, income, housing, work, and community) and decreased in two domains (the government and country). By the same degrees, the levels of dissatisfaction have increased in three domains (leisure, government, and the country) and decreased in three domains (health, education, and community). When these positive and negative changes are considered together, seven domains experienced the magnitude of changes exceeding 10 points or more on the PDI. Of these seven, the four domains of health, education, work, and community have changed for the better while the three domains of leisure, government, and the country have changed for the worse.

On the basis of these findings, three points can be made about the shifting quality of Korean life over the past two decades. First, the quality of Korean life has changed considerably in a majority of its major domains. Excluded from these domains in considerable flux are all those constituting interpersonal life. The assessments of marriage, family, children, and friendship all remain, by and large, unchanged, indicating considerable stability in the quality of human relationships in Korean society even in the midst of cultural, economic, and technological transformations. More surprising is the lack of any notable increases in the favorable assessments of income and housing, the two core domains of material life. For all the favorable improvements in the objective conditions of these domains during the past twenty years, Koreans do not feel much better about those areas than before.

Second, the major domains of Korean life tend to have changed for the better rather than for the worse. According to the mean ratings reported in Table IX, six domains (health, education, friend-

TABLE IX

Changes in Satisfaction and Dissatisfaction in Life Domains

Life domains	Satisfied			Dissatisfied			Mean			Rank order		
	1981	2001	change	1981	2001	change	1981	2001	change	1981	2001	change
Health	50.5%	61.8%	+11.3%	26.1%	20.5%	–5.6%	4.5	4.8	+0.3	8	10	+2
Education	37.1	44.2	+7.1	34.5	28.7	–5.8	4.0	4.3	+0.3	2	5	+3
Leisure	35.2	32.6	–2.6	35.1	45.3	+10.2	4.0	3.7	–0.3	3	3	0
Marriage	64.5	71.0	+6.5	10.9	11.2	–0.3	5.1	5.1	0.0	10	11	+1
Family life	73.8	70.4	–3.4	7.9	10.8	+2.9	5.4	5.1	–0.3	12	11	–1
Children	50.3	51.8	–1.5	25.8	21.9	–3.9	4.5	4.5	0.0	6	7	+1
Friendship	68.8	74.5	+5.7	8.2	8.1	–0.1	5.2	5.3	+0.1	11	13	+2
Income	22.6	29.4	+6.8	47.8	47.6	–0.2	3.5	3.5	0.0	1	2	+1
Housing	39.5	45.2	+5.7	32.6	29.1	–3.5	4.1	4.2	+0.1	4	4	0
Working	42.0	49.9	+7.0	29.4	25.6	–3.8	4.2	4.4	+0.2	5	6	+1
Government	53.8	14.2	–39.6	16.1	63.1	+47.0	4.7	3.0	–1.7	9	1	–8
Community	50.3	56.7	+6.4	24.6	16.5	–8.1	4.5	4.7	+0.2	7	8	+1
Korea	75.3	58.3	–17.0	6.5	21.1	+14.6	5.5	4.7	–0.8	13	8	–5

Sources: 1981 Social Development Survey and 2001 Korea Democracy Barometer Survey.

ship, housing, work, and community) are rated more positively, while four domains (leisure, family life, the government, and the country) are rated more negatively than twenty years ago. In terms of the breadth of these changes, positive ones have taken place across a wider array of life domains than negative ones. In terms of magnitude, however, negative changes have taken place with greater intensity than positive ones. Only in two of the domains experiencing negative changes (the government and the country), has the mean rating decreased by more than half a point on a 7-point scale. In Korea, positive changes tend to be extensive while negative changes tend to be intensive.

Finally, the past two decades have witnessed considerable changes in the rankings of life domains. Of the thirteen domains ranked in the Table IX from the 1st (worst) to the 13th (best), only two (leisure and housing) remain intact as the third and fourth worst domains of Korean life, respectively. Among the eleven others, eight domains (health, education, marriage, children, friendship, income, work, and community) have moved upward and three domains (family, the government, and the country) have gone downward. More notable changes concern those in the best and worst domain. In 2001, friendship became the best one while government became the worst. In the case of the government, it has moved downward by eight steps from the 9th to the 1st to become the worst domain of life in Korea. It is difficult to understand why the quality of the Korean government has deteriorated rather than improved after the demise of the military dictatorship.

SUMMARY AND CONCLUSIONS

At the dawn of the 21st century, Korea is seen as a respected member of the international community. This is in significant contrast to its position 20 years earlier when it was under the yoke of a repressive military dictatorship. Since that time it has become an economic powerhouse, a maturing democracy, a nation of cities, and a society of mixed cultures. Yet in the midst of all of this, there appears to be something amiss. It is not something readily apparent. It lies just beneath the surface. We have discovered what it is by entering the psyche of the Korean people. For it is within them, and only them, that we learn what is wrong.

The beginning and the end of these two decades have proven to be a study in stark contrasts. In 1981 the ISS at Seoul National University obtained a fairly detailed glimpse of what Koreans were feeling at the time (Shin, 1984). With this set of survey data in hand, we have contrasted those feelings with ones plumbed most recently by the Korea-Gallup poll.

Today, the Korean people as a whole feel more negative than positive about what they experience in their private and public lives. Their feelings of ill-being are more prevalent than those of well-being. During these two decades, moreover, there has been a drastic shift away from the prevailing pattern of experiencing continuing improvements in both private and public life. The Korean people as a whole feel that they are much worse-off than they were 20 years ago. In the early 1980s, Koreans enjoyed a genuine sense of progress. Yet 20 years later their mood is one of retrogression. Now they are also significantly less optimistic about their country's life than they were two decades ago when they lived under a military dictatorship.

This is the puzzle, that is amiss. It is what we have been seeking. Korea, an economic powerhouse and a maturing democracy, is seen through the eyes of its citizens in largely negative terms. It would appear, therefore, that the powerful forces of democratization, globalization, industrialization, technocratic advances, and urbanization have transformed Korea into a nation of lesser well-being.

Over the 20 years, the quality of Korean life has changed considerably in a majority of its 13 major domains. Koreans today are more dissatisfied than satisfied with two more life domains that they were before. In 1981, they expressed more dissatisfaction than satisfaction with the only one domain of income. Nowadays they do the same with three life domains including those of government and leisure. More to our interest is the fact that they feel much worse about as many as four domains, which accounts for nearly one-third of the life domains surveyed. They are leisure, family life, government, and the country.

In addition, the past two decades have witnessed considerable changes in the rankings of the life domains. In 1981, the domain of the country was rated as the best while income was the worst. In

2001 friendship became the best while government was the worst. Why has the quality of the Korean government deteriorated rather than improved over the two decades in question? Could Koreans be defining democracy in *economic* rather than *political* terms? And if indeed they are doing this, could the political system be paying the price of the recent severe economic downturn? Future additional research may provide the answer to this puzzle.

ACKNOWLEDGEMENT

The 2001 life quality survey reported in this paper was supported by a grant from the University of Missouri Research Board (RB 99-105). The financial support of the Research Board is gratefully acknowledged.

APPENDIX A
SURVEY QUESTIONS

1. Global Assessments of Life Quality

(Q1) [**SHOW CARD**] Here is a picture of a ladder. Imagine that the top of the ladder represents the best possible place to live and the bottom of the latter represents the worst possible place to live.

_____a. Where do you think our country stands on the ladder at the present time?
_____b. Where do you think our country stood three years ago when Kim Doe Jung was our president?
_____c. Where do you think our country stood five years ago when Kim Young Sam was our president?
_____d. Where do you think our country will stand five years from now?

(Q2) [**SHOW CARD**] Looking at the ladder again, suppose the top represents the best possible life for you; and the bottom, the worst possible life for you.

_____a. On which step of the ladder do you feel you personally stand at the present time?
_____b. On which step do you think you stood three years ago when Kim Dae Jung was our president?
_____c. On which step do you think you stood five years ago when Kim Young Sam was our president?
_____d. Where do you think you will stand five years from now?

2. Specific Feelings of Well-Being

(Q3) During the past five years, how happy have you been?

1. Very happy
2. Fairly happy
3. Not much happy
4. Not at all happy
8. Don't know

(Q4) How are you enjoying life these days?

1. Very much
2. Somewhat
3. Not very much
4. Not at all
8. Don't know

(Q5) During the past five years, when considering your plans for life, how much have you accomplished?

1. All of it
2. Most of it
3. Little of it
4. None of it
8. Don't know

3. Assessments of Life Domains

(Q6) **[SHOW CARD]** Next I would like you to tell me how much you are satisfied or dissatisfied with the various aspects of your life. For each aspect, please choose the number on this card that comes closest to he way you feel about it where 1 is very dissatisfied and 7 is very satisfied.

a. Health	1	2	3	4	5	6	7	8
b. Marriage (if married)	1	2	3	4	5	6	7	8
c. Family life	1	2	3	4	5	6	7	8
d. Friendship	1	2	3	4	5	6	7	8
e. Income	1	2	3	4	5	6	7	8
f. Education	1	2	3	4	5	6	7	8
g. The elected government	1	2	3	4	5	6	7	8
h. Housing	1	2	3	4	5	6	7	8
i. Neighborhood	1	2	3	4	5	6	7	8
j. Living in Korea	1	2	3	4	5	6	7	8
l. Work	1	2	3	4	5	6	7	8
m. Leisure and recreation	1	2	3	4	5	6	7	8
n. Educating children (if any)	1	2	3	4	5	6	7	8
o. Your life as a whole	1	2	3	4	5	6	7	8

REFERENCES

Allard, E.: 1975, Dimensions of Welfare in a Comparative Scandinavian Study. Research Report No. 9 (University of Helsinki, Helsinki).
Andrews, F.M. (ed.): 1986, Research on the Quality of Life (Institute for Social Research, University of Michigan, Ann Arbor).
Andrews, F.M. and S.B. Withey: 1976, Social Indicators of Well-Being: American's Perceptions of Life Quality (Plenum, New York).
Baker, E.: 1962, The Politics of Aristotle (Oxford University Press, New York).
Campbell, A.: 1981, The Sense of Well-Being in America: Recent Patterns and Trends (McGraw-Hill Book Company, New York).
Cantril, H.: 1965, The Patterns of Human Concerns (Rutgers University Press, New Brunswick).
Chey, M., T.W. Kwon and D.S. Kwon: 1989, Ten Years of Social Surveys (Seoul National University Institute of Social Sciences, Seoul) (in Korean).
Cummins, R.A.: 1995, 'On the trail of the gold standard for subjective well-being', Social Indicators Research 35, pp. 170–200.
Csikszentmihalyi, M.: 1990, Flow: the Psychology of Optimal Experience (Harper Perennial, New York).
Cummins, R.A.: 2000, 'Objective and subjective quality of life: an interactive model', Social Indicators Research 52, pp. 55–72.
Cummins, B.: 1998. QOL Definition and Terminology (International Society for Quality-of-Life Studies, Blackburg, VA).
Dannhauser, W. J.: 1976, 'What constitutes "quality" in life?', in The Commission on Critical Choices for Americans (ed.), Qualities of Life (Lexington Books, Lexington, MA, pp. 53–79).
Diener, E., E. Suh, R. Lucas and H. Smith: 1999, 'Subjective well-being: Three decades of progress', Psychological Bulliten 125, pp. 276–302.
Hagerty, M.: 2001, 'Quality of life indexes for national policy: Review and agenda', Social Indicators Research 35, pp. 1–96.
Lane, R.: 2000, The Loss of Happiness in Market Democracies (Yale University Press, New Haven).
McCall, S.: 1975, 'Quality of life', Social Indicators Research 3, pp. 229–248.
Milbrath, L.: 1982, 'A conceptualization and research strategy for the study of ecological aspects of quality of life', Social Indicators Research 10, pp. 135–158.
Mullis, R.J.: 1990: 'Measures of economic well-being as predictor of psychological well-being', Social Indicators Research 26, pp. 119–135.
Naussbaum, C. and A. Sen (eds.): 1993, The Quality of Life (Oxford University Press, New York).
Rescher, N.: 1972, Welfare (University of Pittsburgh Press, Pittsburgh).
Schmuck, P. and K.M. Sheldon (eds.): 2001, Life goals and well-being (Hogrefe and Huber Publishers, Gottingen, Germany).
Shin, D.C.: 1984, 'On the quality of life among the Korean people', Chungkyung Moonhwa, pp. 26–47 (in Korean).

Szalai, A. and F. Andrews (eds.): 1980, The Quality of Life: Comparative Studies (Sage Publications, Beverly Hills, CA).
von Wright: 1972, The Varieties of Goodness (Routledge and Regan Paul, London).

University of Missouri at Columbia
Columbia, MO 65221
USA
E-mail: shind@missouri.edu
Doh Chull Shin

Institute for Applied Phenomenology
Spring Valley, NY 10977
USA
E-mail: abmaphd@aol.com
Conrad P. Rutkowski

INDEX OF AUTHORS
VOLUMES 62 AND 63, 2003

Social Indicators Research Series

1. V. Møller (ed.): *Quality of Life in South Africa.* 1997 ISBN 0-7923-4797-8
2. G. Baechler: *Violence Through Environmental Discrimination.* Causes, Rwanda Arena, and Conflict Model. 1999 ISBN 0-7923-5495-8
3. P. Bowles and L.T. Woods (eds.): *Japan after the Economic Miracle.* In Search of New Directories. 1999 ISBN 0-7923-6031-1
4. E. Diener and D.R. Rahtz (eds.): *Advances in Quality of Life Theory and Research.* Volume I. 1999 ISBN 0-7923-6060-5
5. Kwong-leung Tang (ed.): *Social Development in Asia.* 2000 ISBN 0-7923-6256-X
6. M.M. Beyerlein (ed.): *Work Teams: Past, Present and Future.* 2000 ISBN 0-7923-6699-9
7. A. Ben-Arieh, N.H. Kaufman, A.B. Andrews, R. Goerge, B.J. Lee, J.L. Aber (eds.): *Measuring and Monitoring Children's Well-Being.* 2001 ISBN 0-7923-6789-8
8. M.J. Sirgy: *Handbook of Quality-of-Life Research. An Ethical Marketing Perspective.* 2001 ISBN 1-4020-0172-X
9. G. Preyer and M. Bös (eds.): *Borderlines in a Globalized World.* New Perspectives in a Sociology of the World-System. 2002 ISBN 1-4020-0515-6
10. V. Nikolic-Ristanovic: *Social Change, Gender and Violence: Post-communist and war affected societies.* 2002 ISBN 1-4020-0726-4
11. M.R. Hagerty, J. Vogel and V. Møller: *Assessing Quality of Life and Living Conditions to Guide National Policy.* 2002 ISBN 1-4020-0727-2
12. M.J. Sirgy: *The Psychology of Quality of Life.* 2002 ISBN 1-4020-0800-7
13. S. McBride, L. Dobuzinskis, M. Griffin Cohen and J. Busumtwi-Sam (eds.): *Global Instability.* Uncertainty and new visions in political economy. 2002 ISBN 1-4020-0946-1
14. Doh. Chull Shin, C.P. Rutkowski and Chong-Min Park (eds.): *The Quality of Life in Korea.* Comparative and Dynamic Perspectives. 2003 ISBN 1-4020-0947-X
15. W. Glatzer: *Rich and Poor.* Disparities, Perceptions, Concomitants. 2002 ISBN 1-4020-1012-5

KLUWER ACADEMIC PUBLISHERS – DORDRECHT / LONDON / BOSTON